Judaism and Ecology

**Publications of the Center for the Study of World Religions,
Harvard Divinity School**

General Editor: Lawrence E. Sullivan
Senior Editor: Kathryn Dodgson

Religions of the World and Ecology

Series Editors: Mary Evelyn Tucker and John Grim

Cambridge, Massachusetts

Judaism and Ecology
Created World and Revealed Word

edited by

HAVA TIROSH-SAMUELSON

distributed by
Harvard University Press
for the
Center for the Study of World Religions
Harvard Divinity School

Grateful acknowledgment is made for permission to reprint the following:

Evan Eisenberg, "The Ecology of Eden," from *The Ecology of Eden* by Evan Eisenberg, copyright © 1998 by Evan Eisenberg. Used by permission of Alfred A. Knopf, a division of Random House, Inc.

Arthur Green, "A Kabbalah for the Environmental Age." Reprinted, with permission, from *Tikkun: A Bimonthly Jewish Critique of Politics, Culture and Society* 14, no. 5.

David Novak, *Natural Law in Judaism*, pages 125–37. Copyright © 1998 Cambridge University Press. Reprinted with the permission of Cambridge University Press.

Cover art: Rothschild Miscellany, Northern Italy, 1450–1480. Vellum, pen and ink, tempera and gold leaf; handwritten; 21 x 16 cm. Fol. 84 recto; 180/51. Gift of James A. Rothschild, London. Collection The Israel Museum, Jerusalem.

Cover photo: Copyright © The Israel Museum, Jerusalem/ David Harris.

Cover design: Patrick Santana

Library of Congress Cataloging-in-Publication Data

Judaism and ecology : created world and revealed word / edited by Hava Tirosh-Samuelson.
     p. cm. — (Religions of the world and ecology)
   Includes bibliographical references and index.
   ISBN 0-945454-35-X (alk. paper)
   ISBN 0-945454-36-8 (pbk. : alk. paper)
   1. Human ecology—Religious aspects—Judaism. 2. Nature—Religious aspects—Judaism. I. Tirosh-Samuelson, Hava, date. II. Series.
BM538.H85 J85 2002
296.3'8—dc21

                                                 2002031586

Acknowledgments

The series of conferences on religions of the world and ecology took place from 1996 through 1998, with supervision at the Harvard University Center for the Study of World Religions by Don Kunkel and Malgorzata Radziszewska-Hedderick and with the assistance of Janey Bosch, Naomi Wilshire, and Lilli Leggio. Narges Moshiri, also at the Center, was indispensable in helping to arrange the first two conferences. A series of volumes developing the themes explored at the conferences is being published by the Center and distributed by Harvard University Press under the editorial direction of Kathryn Dodgson and with the skilled assistance of Eric Edstam.

These efforts have been generously supported by major funding from the V. Kann Rasmussen Foundation. The conference organizers appreciate also the support of the following institutions and individuals: Aga Khan Trust for Culture, Association of Shinto Shrines, Nathan Cummings Foundation, Dharam Hinduja Indic Research Center at Columbia University, Germeshausen Foundation, Harvard Buddhist Studies Forum, Harvard Divinity School Center for the Study of Values in Public Life, Jain Academic Foundation of North America, Laurance Rockefeller, Sacharuna Foundation, Theological Education to Meet the Environmental Challenge, and Winslow Foundation. The conferences were originally made possible by the Center for Respect of Life and Environment of the Humane Society of the United States, which continues to be a principal cosponsor. Bucknell University, also a cosponsor, has provided support in the form of leave time from teaching for conference coordinators Mary Evelyn Tucker and John

Grim as well as the invaluable administrative assistance of Stephanie Snyder. Her thoughtful attention to critical details is legendary. Then President William Adams of Bucknell University and then Vice-President for Academic Affairs Daniel Little have also granted travel funds for faculty and students to attend the conferences. Grateful acknowledgment is here made for the advice from key area specialists in shaping each conference and in editing the published volumes. Their generosity in time and talent has been indispensable at every step of the project. Throughout this process, the support, advice, and encouragement from Martin S. Kaplan has been invaluable.

Contents

III. The Doctrine of Creation

IV. Nature and Revealed Morality

V. Nature in Jewish Mysticism

VI. From Speculation to Action

Preface

LAWRENCE E. SULLIVAN

Religion distinguishes the human species from all others, just as human presence on earth distinguishes the ecology of our planet from other places in the known universe. Religious life and the earth's ecology are inextricably linked, organically related.

Human belief and practice mark the earth. One can hardly think of a natural system that has not been considerably altered, for better or worse, by human culture. "Nor is this the work of the industrial centuries," observes Simon Schama. "It is coeval with the entirety of our social existence. And it is this irreversibly modified world, from the polar caps to the equatorial forests, that is all the nature we have" (*Landscape and Memory* [New York: Vintage Books, 1996], 7). In Schama's examination even landscapes that appear to be most free of human culture turn out, on closer inspection, to be its product.

Human beliefs about the nature of ecology are the distinctive contribution of our species to the ecology itself. Religious beliefs—especially those concerning the nature of powers that create and animate—become an effective part of ecological systems. They attract the power of will and channel the forces of labor toward purposive transformations. Religious rituals model relations with material life and transmit habits of practice and attitudes of mind to succeeding generations.

This is not simply to say that religious thoughts occasionally touch the world and leave traces that accumulate over time. The matter is the other way around. From the point of view of environmental studies, religious worldviews propel communities into the world with

fundamental predispositions toward it because such religious worldviews are primordial, all-encompassing, and unique. They are *primordial* because they probe behind secondary appearances and stray
thoughts to rivet human attention on realities of the first order: life at
its source, creativity in its fullest manifestation, death and destruction
at their origin, renewal and salvation in their germ. The revelation of
first things is compelling and moves communities to take creative
action. Primordial ideas are prime movers.

Religious worldviews are *all-encompassing* because they fully absorb the natural world within them. They provide human beings both
a view of the whole and at the same time a penetrating image of their
own ironic position as the beings in the cosmos who possess the
capacity for symbolic thought: the part that contains the whole—or at
least a picture of the whole—within itself. As all-encompassing,
therefore, religious ideas do not just contend with other ideas as
equals; they frame the mind-set within which all sorts of ideas com-
mingle in a cosmology. For this reason, their role in ecology must be
better understood.

Religious worldviews are *unique* because they draw the world of
nature into a wholly other kind of universe, one that appears only in
the religious imagination. From the point of view of environmental
studies, the risk of such religious views, on the one hand, is of dis-
interest in or disregard for the natural world. On the other hand, only
in the religious world can nature be compared and contrasted to other
kinds of being—the supernatural world or forms of power not always
fully manifest in nature. Only then can nature be revealed as distinctive, set in a new light startlingly different from its own. That is to say,
only religious perspectives enable human beings to evaluate the world
of nature in terms distinct from all else. In this same step toward intelligibility, the natural world is evaluated in terms consonant with
human beings' own distinctive (religious and imaginative) nature in
the world, thus grounding a self-conscious relationship and a role
with limits and responsibilities.

In the struggle to sustain the earth's environment as viable for
future generations, environmental studies has thus far left the role of
religion unprobed. This contrasts starkly with the emphasis given, for
example, the role of science and technology in threatening or sustaining the ecology. Ignorance of religion prevents environmental studies
from achieving its goals, however, for though science and technology

share many important features of human culture with religion, they leave unexplored essential wellsprings of human motivation and concern that shape the world as we know it. No understanding of the environment is adequate without a grasp of the religious life that constitutes the human societies which saturate the natural environment.

A great deal of what we know about the religions of the world is new knowledge. As is the case for geology and astronomy, so too for religious studies: many new discoveries about the nature and function of religion are, in fact, clearer understandings of events and processes that began to unfold long ago. Much of what we are learning now about the religions of the world was previously not known outside of a circle of adepts. From the ancient history of traditions and from the ongoing creativity of the world's contemporary religions we are opening a treasury of motives, disciplines, and awarenesses.

A geology of the religious spirit of humankind can well serve our need to relate fruitfully to the earth and its myriad life-forms. Changing our habits of consumption and patterns of distribution, reevaluating modes of production, and reestablishing a strong sense of solidarity with the matrix of material life—these achievements will arrive along with spiritual modulations that unveil attractive new images of well-being and prosperity, respecting the limits of life in a sustainable world while revering life at its sources. Remarkable religious views are presented in this series—from the nature mysticism of Bashō in Japan or Saint Francis in Italy to the ecstatic physiologies and embryologies of shamanic healers, Taoist meditators, and Vedic practitioners; from indigenous people's ritual responses to projects funded by the World Bank, to religiously grounded criticisms of hazardous waste sites, deforestation, and environmental racism.

The power to modify the world is both frightening and fascinating and has been subjected to reflection, particularly religious reflection, from time immemorial to the present day. We will understand ecology better when we understand the religions that form the rich soil of memory and practice, belief and relationships where life on earth is rooted. Knowledge of these views will help us reappraise our ways and reorient ourselves toward the sources and resources of life.

This volume is one in a series that addresses the critical gap in our contemporary understanding of religion and ecology. The series results from research conducted at the Harvard University Center for the Study of World Religions over a three-year period. I wish especially

to acknowledge President Neil L. Rudenstine of Harvard University
for his leadership in instituting the environmental initiative at Harvard
and thank him for his warm encouragement and characteristic support
of our program. Mary Evelyn Tucker and John Grim of Bucknell
University coordinated the research, involving the direct participation
of some six hundred scholars, religious leaders, and environmental
specialists brought to Harvard from around the world during the
period of research and inquiry. Professors Tucker and Grim have
brought great vision and energy to this enormous project, as has their
team of conference convenors. The commitment and advice of Martin
S. Kaplan of Hale and Dorr have been of great value. Our goals have
been achieved for this research and publication program because of
the extraordinary dedication and talents of Center for the Study of
World Religions staff members Don Kunkel, Malgorzata Radziszewska-
Hedderick, Kathryn Dodgson, Janey Bosch, Naomi Wilshire, Lilli
Leggio, and Eric Edstam and with the unstinting help of Stephanie
Snyder of Bucknell. To these individuals, and to all the sponsors and
participants whose efforts made this series possible, go deepest thanks
and appreciation.

Series Foreword

MARY EVELYN TUCKER and JOHN GRIM

The Nature of the Environmental Crisis

Ours is a period when the human community is in search of new and sustaining relationships to the earth amidst an environmental crisis that threatens the very existence of all life-forms on the planet. While the particular causes and solutions of this crisis are being debated by scientists, economists, and policymakers, the facts of widespread destruction are causing alarm in many quarters. Indeed, from some perspectives the future of human life itself appears threatened. As Daniel Maguire has succinctly observed, "If current trends continue, we will not."[1] Thomas Berry, the former director of the Riverdale Center for Religious Research, has also raised the stark question, "Is the human a viable species on an endangered planet?"

From resource depletion and species extinction to pollution overload and toxic surplus, the planet is struggling against unprecedented assaults. This is aggravated by population explosion, industrial growth, technological manipulation, and military proliferation heretofore unknown by the human community. From many accounts the basic elements which sustain life—sufficient water, clean air, and arable land—are at risk. The challenges are formidable and well documented. The solutions, however, are more elusive and complex. Clearly, this crisis has economic, political, and social dimensions which require more detailed analysis than we can provide here. Suffice it to say, however, as did the *Global 2000 Report*: ". . .once such global environmental problems are in motion they are difficult to reverse. In fact few if any of the problems addressed in the *Global 2000*

Report are amenable to quick technological or policy fixes; rather, they are inextricably mixed with the world's most perplexing social and economic problems."[2]

Peter Raven, the director of the Missouri Botanical Garden, wrote in a paper titled "We Are Killing Our World" with a similar sense of urgency regarding the magnitude of the environmental crisis: "The world that provides our evolutionary and ecological context is in serious trouble, trouble of a kind that demands our urgent attention. By formulating adequate plans for dealing with these large-scale problems, we will be laying the foundation for peace and prosperity in the future; by ignoring them, drifting passively while attending to what may seem more urgent, personal priorities, we are courting disaster."

Rethinking Worldviews and Ethics

For many people an environmental crisis of this complexity and scope is not only the result of certain economic, political, and social factors. It is also a moral and spiritual crisis which, in order to be addressed, will require broader philosophical and religious understandings of ourselves as creatures of nature, embedded in life cycles and dependent on ecosystems. Religions, thus, need to be reexamined in light of the current environmental crisis. This is because religions help to shape our attitudes toward nature in both conscious and unconscious ways. Religions provide basic interpretive stories of who we are, what nature is, where we have come from, and where we are going. This comprises a worldview of a society. Religions also suggest how we should treat other humans and how we should relate to nature. These values make up the ethical orientation of a society. Religions thus generate worldviews and ethics which underlie fundamental attitudes and values of different cultures and societies. As the historian Lynn White observed, "What people do about their ecology depends on what they think about themselves in relation to things around them. Human ecology is deeply conditioned by beliefs about our nature and destiny—that is, by religion."[3]

In trying to reorient ourselves in relation to the earth, it has become apparent that we have lost our appreciation for the intricate nature of matter and materiality. Our feeling of alienation in the modern period has extended beyond the human community and its patterns of material exchanges to our interaction with nature itself. Especially in technologically sophisticated urban societies, we have become removed from the recognition of our dependence on nature. We no longer know who we are as earthlings; we no longer see the earth as sacred.

Thomas Berry suggests that we have become autistic in our interactions with the natural world. In other words, we are unable to value the life and beauty of nature because we are locked in our own egocentric perspectives and shortsighted needs. He suggests that we need a new cosmology, cultural coding, and motivating energy to overcome this deprivation.[4] He observes that the magnitude of destructive industrial processes is so great that we must initiate a radical rethinking of the myth of progress and of humanity's role in the evolutionary process. Indeed, he speaks of evolution as a new story of the universe, namely, as a vast cosmological perspective that will resituate human meaning and direction in the context of four and a half billion years of earth history.[5]

For Berry and for many others an important component of the current environmental crisis is spiritual and ethical. It is here that the religions of the world may have a role to play in cooperation with other individuals, institutions, and initiatives that have been engaged with environmental issues for a considerable period of time. Despite their lateness in addressing the crisis, religions are beginning to respond in remarkably creative ways. They are not only rethinking their theologies but are also reorienting their sustainable practices and long-term environmental commitments. In so doing, the very nature of religion and of ethics is being challenged and changed. This is true because the reexamination of other worldviews created by religious beliefs and practices may be critical to our recovery of sufficiently comprehensive cosmologies, broad conceptual frameworks, and effective environmental ethics for the twenty-first century.

While in the past none of the religions of the world have had to face an environmental crisis such as we are now confronting, they remain key instruments in shaping attitudes toward nature. The unintended consequences of the modern industrial drive for unlimited economic growth and resource development have led us to an impasse regarding the survival of many life-forms and appropriate management of varied ecosystems. The religious traditions may indeed be critical in helping to reimagine the viable conditions and long-range strategies for fostering mutually enhancing human-earth relations.[6]

Indeed, as E. N. Anderson has documented with impressive detail, "All traditional societies that have succeeded in managing resources well, over time, have done it in part through religious or ritual representation of resource management."[7]

It is in this context that a series of conferences and publications exploring the various religions of the world and their relation to ecology was initiated by the Center for the Study of World Religions at Harvard. Coordinated by Mary Evelyn Tucker and John Grim, the conferences involved some six hundred scholars, graduate students, religious leaders, and environmental activists over a period of three years. The collaborative nature of the project is intentional. Such collaboration maximizes the opportunity for dialogical reflection on this issue of enormous complexity and accentuates the diversity of local manifestations of ecologically sustainable alternatives.

This series is intended to serve as initial explorations of the emerging field of religion and ecology while pointing toward areas for further research. We are not unaware of the difficulties of engaging in such a task, yet we have been encouraged by the enthusiastic response to the conferences within the academic community, by the larger interest they have generated beyond academia, and by the probing examinations gathered in the volumes. We trust that this series and these volumes will be useful not only for scholars of religion but also for those shaping seminary education and institutional religious practices, as well as for those involved in public policy on environmental issues.

We see such conferences and publications as expanding the growing dialogue regarding the role of the world's religions as moral forces in stemming the environmental crisis. While, clearly, there are major methodological issues involved in utilizing traditional philosophical and religious ideas for contemporary concerns, there are also compelling reasons to support such efforts, however modest they may be. The world's religions in all their complexity and variety remain one of the principal resources for symbolic ideas, spiritual inspiration, and ethical principles. Indeed, despite their limitations, historically they have provided comprehensive cosmologies for interpretive direction, moral foundations for social cohesion, spiritual guidance for cultural expression, and ritual celebrations for meaningful life. In our search for more comprehensive ecological worldviews and more effective environmental ethics, it is inevitable that we will draw from the symbolic and conceptual resources of the religious traditions of the world. The effort to do this is not without precedent or problems, some of which will be signaled below. With this volume and with this series we hope the field of reflection and discussion regarding religion and ecology will begin to broaden, deepen, and complexify.

Qualifications and Goals

The Problems and Promise of Religions

These volumes, then, are built on the premise that the religions of the world may be instrumental in addressing the moral dilemmas created by the environmental crisis. At the same time we recognize the limitations of such efforts on the part of religions. We also acknowledge that the complexity of the problem requires interlocking approaches from such fields as science, economics, politics, health, and public policy. As the human community struggles to formulate different attitudes toward nature and to articulate broader conceptions of ethics embracing species and ecosystems, religions may thus be a necessary, though only contributing, part of this multidisciplinary approach.

It is becoming increasingly evident that abundant scientific knowledge of the crisis is available and numerous political and economic statements have been formulated. Yet we seem to lack the political, economic, and scientific leadership to make necessary changes. Moreover, what is still lacking is the religious commitment, moral imagination, and ethical engagement to transform the environmental crisis from an issue on paper to one of effective policy, from rhetoric in print to realism in action. Why, nearly fifty years after Fairfield Osborne's warning in *Our Plundered Planet* and more than thirty years since Rachel Carson's *Silent Spring,* are we still wondering, is it too late?[8]

It is important to ask where the religions have been on these issues and why they themselves have been so late in their involvement. Have issues of personal salvation superseded all others? Have divine-human relations been primary? Have anthropocentric ethics been all-consuming? Has the material world of nature been devalued by religion? Does the search for otherworldly rewards override commitment to this world? Did the religions simply surrender their natural theologies and concerns with exploring purpose in nature to positivistic scientific cosmologies? In beginning to address these questions, we still have not exhausted all the reasons for religions' lack of attention to the environmental crisis. The reasons may not be readily apparent, but clearly they require further exploration and explanation.

In discussing the involvement of religions in this issue, it is also appropriate to acknowledge the dark side of religion in both its institutional expressions and dogmatic forms. In addition to their oversight with regard to the environment, religions have been the source of enormous manipulation of power in fostering wars, in ignoring racial and social injustice, and in promoting unequal gender relations, to name only a few abuses. One does not want to underplay this shadow side or to claim too much for religions' potential for ethical persuasiveness. The problems are too vast and complex for unqualified optimism. Yet there is a growing consensus that religions may now have a significant role to play, just as in the past they have sustained individuals and cultures in the face of internal and external threats.

A final caveat is the inevitable gap that arises between theories and practices in religions. As has been noted, even societies with religious traditions which appear sympathetic to the environment have in the past often misused resources. While it is clear that religions may have some disjunction between the ideal and the real, this should not lessen our endeavor to identify resources from within the world's religions for a more ecologically sound cosmology and environmentally supportive ethics. This disjunction of theory and practice is present within all philosophies and religions and is frequently the source of disillusionment, skepticism, and cynicism. A more realistic observation might be made, however, that this disjunction should not automatically invalidate the complex worldviews and rich cosmologies embedded in traditional religions. Rather, it is our task to explore these conceptual resources so as to broaden and expand our own perspectives in challenging and fruitful ways.

In summary, we recognize that religions have elements which are both prophetic and transformative as well as conservative and constraining. These elements are continually in tension, a condition which creates the great variety of thought and interpretation within religious traditions. To recognize these various tensions and limits, however, is not to lessen the urgency of the overall goals of this project. Rather, it is to circumscribe our efforts with healthy skepticism, cautious optimism, and modest ambitions. It is to suggest that this is a beginning in a new field of study which will affect both religion and ecology. On the one hand, this process of reflection will inevitably change how religions conceive of their own roles, missions, and identities, for such reflections demand a new sense of the sacred as not divorced from the earth itself. On the other hand, environmental studies can recognize that religions have helped to shape attitudes toward nature. Thus, as religions themselves evolve they may be indispensable in fostering a more expansive appreciation for the complexity and beauty of the natural world. At the same time as religions foster awe and reverence for nature, they may provide the transforming energies for ethical practices to protect endangered ecosystems, threatened species, and diminishing resources.

Methodological Concerns

It is important to acknowledge that there are, inevitably, challenging methodological issues involved in such a project as we are undertaking in this emerging field of religion and ecology.[9] Some of the key interpretive challenges we face in this project concern issues of time, place, space, and positionality. With regard to time, it is necessary to recognize the vast historical complexity of each religious tradition, which cannot be easily condensed in these conferences or volumes. With respect to place, we need to signal the diverse cultural contexts in which these religions have developed. With regard to space, we recognize the varied frameworks of institutions and traditions in which these religions unfold. Finally, with respect to positionality, we acknowledge our own historical situatedness at the end of the twentieth century with distinctive contemporary concerns.

Not only is each religious tradition historically complex and culturally diverse, but its beliefs, scriptures, and institutions have themselves been subject to vast commentaries and revisions over time. Thus, we recognize the radical diversity that exists within and among religious traditions which cannot be encompassed in any single volume. We acknowledge also that distortions may arise as we examine earlier historical traditions in light of contemporary issues.

Nonetheless, the environmental ethics philosopher J. Baird Callicott has suggested that scholars and others "mine the conceptual resources" of the religious traditions as a means of creating a more inclusive global environmental ethics.[10] As Callicott himself notes, however, the notion of "mining" is problematic, for it conjures up images of exploitation which may cause apprehension among certain religious communities, especially those of indigenous peoples. Moreover, we cannot simply expect to borrow or adopt ideas and place them from one tradition directly into another. Even efforts to formulate global environmental ethics need to be sensitive to cultural particularity and diversity. We do not aim at creating a simple bricolage or bland fusion of perspectives. Rather, these conferences and volumes are an attempt to display before us a multiperspectival cross section of the symbolic richness regarding attitudes toward nature within the religions of the world. To do so will help to reveal certain commonalities among traditions, as well as limitations within traditions, as they begin to converge around this challenge presented by the environmental crisis.

We need to identify our concerns, then, as embedded in the constraints of our own perspectival limits at the same time as we seek common ground. In describing various attitudes toward nature historically, we are aiming at *critical understanding* of the complexity, contexts, and frameworks in which these religions articulate such views. In addition, we are striving for *empathetic appreciation* for the traditions without idealizing their ecological potential or ignoring their environmental oversights. Finally, we are aiming at the *creative revisioning* of mutually enhancing human-earth relations. This revisioning may be assisted by highlighting the multiperspectival attitudes toward nature which these traditions disclose. The prismatic effect of examining such attitudes and relationships may provide some necessary clarification and symbolic resources for reimagining our own situation and shared concerns at the end of the twentieth century. It will also be sharpened by identifying the multilayered symbol systems in world religions which have traditionally oriented humans in establishing relational resonances between the microcosm of the self and the macrocosm of the social and natural orders. In short, religious traditions may help to supply both creative resources of symbols, rituals, and texts as well as inspiring visions for reimagining ourselves as part of, not apart from, the natural world.

Aims

The methodological issues outlined above were implied in the overall goals of the conferences, which were described as follows:

1. To identify and evaluate the *distinctive ecological attitudes,* values, and practices of diverse religious traditions, making clear their links to intellectual, political, and other resources associated with these distinctive traditions.

2. To describe and analyze the *commonalities* that exist within and among religious traditions with respect to ecology.

3. To identify the *minimum common ground* on which to base constructive understanding, motivating discussion, and concerted action in diverse locations across the globe; and to highlight the specific religious resources that comprise such fertile ecological ground: within scripture, ritual, myth, symbol, cosmology, sacrament, and so on.

4. To articulate in clear and moving terms *a desirable mode of human presence with the earth;* in short, to highlight means of respecting and valuing nature, to note what has already been actualized, and to indicate how best to achieve what is desirable beyond these examples.

5. To outline the most significant areas, with regard to religion and ecology, in need of *further study;* to enumerate questions of highest priority within those areas and propose possible approaches to use in addressing them.

In this series, then, we do not intend to obliterate difference or ignore diversity. The aim is to celebrate plurality by raising to conscious awareness multiple perspectives regarding nature and human-earth relations as articulated in the religions of the world. The spectrum of cosmologies, myths, symbols, and rituals within the religious traditions will be instructive in resituating us within the rhythms and limits of nature.

We are not looking for a unified worldview or a single global ethic. We are, however, deeply sympathetic with the efforts toward formulating a global ethic made by individuals, such as the theologian Hans Küng or the environmental philosopher J. Baird Callicott, and groups, such as Global Education Associates and United Religions. A minimum content of environmental ethics needs to be seriously considered. We are, then, keenly interested in the contribution this series might make to discussions of environmental policy in national and international arenas. Important intersections may be made with work in the field of development ethics.[11] In addition, the findings of the conferences have bearing on the ethical formulation of the Earth Charter that is to be presented to the United Nations for adoption within the next few years. Thus, we are seeking both the grounds for common concern and the constructive conceptual basis for rethinking our current situation of estrangement from the earth. In so doing we will be able to reconceive a means of creating the basis not just for sustainable development, but also for sustainable life on the planet.

As scientist Brian Swimme has suggested, we are currently making macrophase changes to the life systems of the planet with microphase wisdom. Clearly, we need to expand and deepen the wisdom base for human intervention with nature and other humans. This is particularly true as issues of genetic alteration of natural processes are already available and in use. If religions have traditionally concentrated on divine-human and human-human relations, the challenge is that they now explore more fully divine-human-earth relations. Without such further exploration, adequate environmental ethics may not emerge in a comprehensive context.

Resources: Environmental Ethics Found in the World's Religions

For many people, when challenges such as the environmental crisis are raised in relation to religion in the contemporary world, there frequently arises a sense of loss or a nostalgia for earlier, seemingly less complicated eras when the constant questioning of religious beliefs and practices was not so apparent. This is, no doubt, something of a reified reading of history. There is, however, a decidedly anxious tone to the questioning and soul-searching that appears to haunt many contemporary religious groups as they seek to find their particular role in the midst of rapid technological change and dominant secular values.

One of the greatest challenges, however, to contemporary religions remains how to respond to the environmental crisis, which many believe has been perpetuated because of the enormous inroads made by unrestrained materialism, secularization, and industrialization in contemporary societies, especially those societies arising in or influenced by the modern West. Indeed, some suggest that the very division of religion from secular life may be a major cause of the crisis.

Others, such as the medieval historian Lynn White, have cited religion's negative role in the crisis. White has suggested that the emphasis in Judaism and Christianity on the transcendence of God above nature and the dominion of humans over nature has led to a devaluing of the natural world and a subsequent destruction of its resources for utilitarian ends.[12] While the particulars of this argument have been vehemently debated, it is increasingly clear that the environmental crisis and its perpetuation due to industrialization, secularization, and ethical indifference present a serious challenge to the world's religions. This is especially true because many of these religions have traditionally been concerned with the path of personal salvation, which frequently emphasized otherworldly goals and rejected this world as corrupting. Thus, as we have noted, how to adapt religious teachings to this task of revaluing nature so as to prevent its destruction marks a significant new phase in religious thought. Indeed, as Thomas Berry has so aptly pointed out, what is necessary is a comprehensive re-evaluation of human-earth relations if the human is to continue as a viable species on an increasingly degraded planet. This will require, in addition to major economic and political changes, examining worldviews and ethics among the world's religions that differ from those that have captured the imagination of contemporary industrialized societies which regard nature primarily as a commodity to be utilized. It should be noted that when we are searching for effective resources for formulating environmental ethics, each of the religious traditions have both positive and negative features.

For the most part, the worldviews associated with the Western Abrahamic traditions of Judaism, Christianity, and Islam have created a dominantly human-focused morality. Because these worldviews are largely anthropocentric, nature is viewed as being of secondary importance. This is reinforced by a strong sense of the transcendence of God above nature. On the other hand, there are rich resources for rethinking views of nature in the covenantal tradition of the Hebrew Bible, in sacramental theology, in incarnational Christology, and in the vice-regency (*khalifa Allah*) concept of the Qur'an. The covenantal tradition draws on the legal agreements of biblical thought which are extended to all of creation. Sacramental theology in Christianity underscores the sacred dimension of material reality, especially for ritual purposes.[13] Incarnational Christology proposes that because God became flesh in the person of Christ, the entire natural order can be viewed as sacred. The concept of humans as vice-regents of Allah on earth suggests that humans have particular privileges, responsibilities, and obligations to creation.[14]

In Hinduism, although there is a significant emphasis on performing one's *dharma*, or duty, in the world, there is also a strong pull toward *mokṣa*, or liberation, from the world of suffering, or *saṃsāra*. To heal this kind of suffering and alienation through spiritual discipline and meditation, one turns away from the world (*prakṛti*) to a timeless world of spirit (*puruṣa*). Yet at the same time there are numerous traditions in Hinduism which affirm particular rivers, mountains, or forests as sacred. Moreover, in the concept of *līlā*, the creative play of the gods, Hindu theology engages the world as a creative manifestation of the divine. This same tension between withdrawal from the world and affirmation of it is present in Buddhism. Certain Theravāda schools of Buddhism emphasize withdrawing in meditation from the transient world of suffering (*saṃsāra*) to seek release in *nirvāṇa*. On the other hand, later Mahāyāna schools of Buddhism, such as Hua-yen, underscore the remarkable interconnection of reality in such images as the jeweled net of Indra, where each jewel reflects all the others in the universe. Likewise, the Zen gardens in East Asia express the fullness of the Buddha-nature (*tathāgatagarbha*) in the natural world. In recent years, socially engaged Buddhism has been active in protecting the environment in both Asia and the United States.

The East Asian traditions of Confucianism and Taoism remain, in certain ways, some of the most life-affirming in the spectrum of world religions.[15] The seamless interconnection between the divine, human, and natural worlds that characterizes these traditions has been described as an anthropocosmic worldview.[16] There is no emphasis on radical transcendence as there is in the Western traditions. Rather, there is a cosmology of a continuity of creation stressing the dynamic movements of nature through the seasons and the agricultural cycles. This organic cosmology is grounded in the philosophy of *ch'i* (material force), which provides a basis for appreciating the profound interconnection of matter and spirit. To be in harmony with nature and with other humans while being attentive to the movements of the *Tao* (Way) is the aim of personal cultivation in both Confucianism and Taoism. It should be noted, however, that this positive worldview has not prevented environmental degradation (such as deforestation) in parts of East Asia in both the premodern and modern period.

In a similar vein, indigenous peoples, while having ecological cosmologies have, in some instances, caused damage to local environments through such practices as slash-and-burn agriculture. Nonetheless, most indigenous peoples have environmental ethics embedded in their worldviews. This is evident in the complex reciprocal obligations surrounding life-taking and resource-gathering which mark a community's relations with the local bioregion. The religious views at the basis of indigenous lifeways involve respect for the sources of food, clothing, and shelter that nature provides. Gratitude to the creator and to the spiritual forces in creation is at the heart of most indigenous traditions. The ritual calendars of many indigenous peoples are carefully coordinated with seasonal events such as the sound of returning birds, the blooming of certain plants, the movements of the sun, and the changes of the moon.

The difficulty at present is that for the most part we have developed in the world's religions certain ethical prohibitions regarding homicide and restraints concerning genocide and suicide, but none for biocide or geocide. We are clearly in need of exploring such comprehensive cosmological perspectives and communitarian environmental ethics as the most compelling context for motivating change regarding the destruction of the natural world.

Responses of Religions to the Environmental Crisis

How to chart possible paths toward mutually enhancing human-earth relations remains, thus, one of the greatest challenges to the world's religions. It is with some encouragement, however, that we note the growing calls for the world's religions to participate in these efforts toward a more sustainable planetary future. There have been various appeals from environmental groups and from scientists and parliamentarians for religious leaders to respond to the environmental crisis. For example, in 1990 the Joint Appeal in Religion and Science was released highlighting the urgency of collaboration around the issue of the destruction of the environment. In 1992 the Union of Concerned Scientists issued the statement "Warning to Humanity," signed by over 1,000 scientists from 70 countries, including 105 Nobel laureates, regarding the gravity of the environmental crisis. They specifically cited the need for a new ethic toward the earth.

Numerous national and international conferences have also been held on this subject and collaborative efforts have been established. Environmental groups such as World Wildlife Fund have sponsored interreligious meetings such as the one in Assisi in 1986. The Center for Respect of Life and Environment of the Humane Society of the United States has also held a series of conferences in Assisi on

Spirituality and Sustainability and has helped to organize one at the World Bank. The United Nations Environmental Programme in North America has established an Environmental Sabbath, each year distributing thousands of packets of materials for use in congregations throughout North America. Similarly, the National Religious Partnership on the Environment at the Cathedral of St. John the Divine in New York City has promoted dialogue, distributed materials, and created a remarkable alliance of the various Jewish and Christian denominations in the United States around the issue of the environment. The Parliament of World Religions held in 1993 in Chicago and attended by some 8,000 people from all over the globe issued a statement of Global Ethics of Cooperation of Religions on Human and Environmental Issues. International meetings on the environment have been organized. One example of these, the Global Forum of Spiritual and Parliamentary Leaders held in Oxford in 1988, Moscow in 1990, Rio in 1992, and Kyoto in 1993, included world religious leaders, such as the Dalai Lama, and diplomats and heads of state, such as Mikhail Gorbachev. Indeed, Gorbachev hosted the Moscow conference and attended the Kyoto conference to set up a Green Cross International for environmental emergencies.

Since the United Nations Conference on Environment and Development (the Earth Summit) held in Rio in 1992, there have been concerted efforts intended to lead toward the adoption of an *Earth Charter* by the year 2000. This *Earth Charter* initiative is under way with the leadership of the Earth Council and Green Cross International, with support from the government of the Netherlands. Maurice Strong, Mikhail Gorbachev, Steven Rockefeller, and other members of the Earth Charter Project have been instrumental in this process. At the March 1997 Rio + 5 Conference a benchmark draft of the *Earth Charter* was issued. The time is thus propitious for further investigation of the potential contributions of particular religions toward mitigating the environmental crisis, especially by developing more comprehensive environmental ethics for the earth community.

Expanding the Dialogue of Religion and Ecology

More than two decades ago Thomas Berry anticipated such an exploration when he called for "creating a new consciousness of the multiform religious traditions of humankind" as a means toward renewal of the human spirit in addressing the urgent problems of contemporary society.[17] Tu Weiming has written of the need to go "Beyond the Enlightenment Mentality" in exploring the spiritual resources of the global community to meet the challenge of the ecological crisis.[18] While this exploration has also been the intention of both the conferences and these volumes, other significant efforts have preceded our current endeavor.[19] Our discussion here highlights only the last decade.

In 1986 Eugene Hargrove edited a volume titled *Religion and Environmental Crisis.*[20] In 1991 Charlene Spretnak explored this topic in her book *States of Grace: The Recovery of Meaning in the Post-Modern Age.*[21] Her subtitle states her constructivist project clearly: "Reclaiming the Core Teachings and Practices of the Great Wisdom Traditions for the Well-Being of the Earth Community." In 1992 Steven Rockefeller and John Elder edited a book based on a conference at Middlebury College titled *Spirit and Nature: Why the Environment Is a Religious Issue.*[22] In the same year Peter Marshall published *Nature's Web: Rethinking Our Place on Earth,*[23] drawing on the resources of the world's traditions. An edited volume titled *Worldviews and Ecology,* compiled in 1993, contains articles reflecting on views of nature from the world's religions and from contemporary philosophies, such as process thought and deep ecology.[24] In this same vein, in 1994 J. Baird Callicott published *Earth's Insights,* which examines the intellectual resources of the world's religions for a more comprehensive global environmental ethics.[25] This expands on his 1989 volumes, *Nature in Asian Traditions of Thought* and *In Defense of the Land Ethic.*[26] In 1995 David Kinsley issued a book titled *Ecology and Religion: Ecological Spirituality in a Cross-Cultural Perspective,*[27] which draws on traditional religions and contemporary movements, such as deep ecology and ecospirituality. Seyyed Hossein Nasr wrote his comprehensive study *Religion and the Order of Nature* in 1996.[28] Several volumes of religious responses to a particular topic or theme have also been published. For example, J. Ronald Engel and Joan Gibb Engel compiled a monograph in 1990 titled *Ethics of Environment and Development: Global Challenge, International Response*[29] and in 1995 Harold Coward edited the volume *Population, Consumption and the Environment: Religious and Secular Responses.*[30] Roger Gottlieb edited a useful source book, *This Sacred Earth: Religion, Nature, Environment.*[31] Single volumes on the world's religions and ecology were published by the Worldwide Fund for Nature.[32]

The series Religions of the World and Ecology is thus intended to expand the discussion already under way in certain circles and to invite further collaboration on a topic of common concern—the fate of the earth as a religious responsibility. To broaden and deepen the reflective basis for mutual collaboration was an underlying aim of the conferences themselves. While some might see this as a diversion from pressing scientific or policy issues, it was with a sense of humility and yet conviction that we entered into the arena of reflection and debate on this issue. In the field of the study of world religions, we have seen this as a timely challenge for scholars of religion to respond as engaged intellectuals with deepening creative reflection. We hope that these volumes will be simply a beginning of further study of conceptual and symbolic resources, methodological concerns, and practical directions for meeting this environmental crisis.

Notes

1. He goes on to say, "And that is qualitatively and epochally true. If religion does not speak to [this], it is an obsolete distraction." Daniel Maguire, *The Moral Core of Judaism and Christianity: Reclaiming the Revolution* (Philadelphia: Fortress Press, 1993), 13.

2. Gerald Barney, *Global 2000 Report to the President of the United States* (Washington, D.C.: Supt. of Docs. U.S. Government Printing Office, 1980–1981), 40.

3. Lynn White, Jr., "The Historical Roots of Our Ecologic Crisis," *Science* 155 (March 1967):1204.

4. Thomas Berry, *The Dream of the Earth* (San Francisco: Sierra Club Books, 1988).

5. Brian Swimme and Thomas Berry, *The Universe Story* (San Francisco: Harper San Francisco, 1992).

6. At the same time we recognize the limits to such a project, especially because ideas and action, theory and practice do not always occur in conjunction.

7. E. N. Anderson, Ecologies of the Heart: Emotion, Belief, and the Environment (New York and Oxford: Oxford University Press, 1996), 166. He qualifies this statement by saying, "The key point is not religion per se, but the use of emotionally powerful symbols to sell particular moral codes and management systems" (166). He notes, however, in various case studies how ecological wisdom is embedded in myths, symbols, and cosmologies of traditional societies.

8. *Is It Too Late?* is also the title of a book by John Cobb, first published in 1972 by Bruce and reissued in 1995 by Environmental Ethics Books.

9. Because we cannot identify here all of the methodological issues that need to be addressed, we invite further discussion by other engaged scholars.

10. See J. Baird Callicott, *Earth's Insights: A Survey of Ecological Ethics from the Mediterranean Basin to the Australian Outback* (Berkeley: University of California Press, 1994).

11. See, for example, The Quality of Life, ed. Martha C. Nussbaum and Amartya Sen, WIDER Studies in Development Economics (Oxford: Oxford University Press, 1993).

12. White, "The Historical Roots of Our Ecologic Crisis," 1203–7.

13. Process theology, creation-centered spirituality, and ecotheology have done much to promote these kinds of holistic perspectives within Christianity.

14. These are resources already being explored by theologians and biblical scholars.

15. While this is true theoretically, it should be noted that, like all ideologies, these traditions have at times been used for purposes of political power and social control. Moreover, they have not been able to prevent certain kinds of environmental destruction, such as deforestation in China.

16. The term "anthropocosmic" has been used by Tu Weiming in *Centrality and Commonality* (Albany: State University of New York Press, 1989).

17. Thomas Berry, "Religious Studies and the Global Human Community," unpublished manuscript.

18. Tu Weiming, "Beyond the Enlightenment Mentality," in *Worldviews and Ecology,* ed. Mary Evelyn Tucker and John Grim (Lewisburg, Pa.: Bucknell University Press, 1993; reissued, Maryknoll, N.Y.: Orbis Books, 1994).

19. This history has been described more fully by Roderick Nash in his chapter entitled "The Greening of Religion," in The Rights of Nature: A History of Environmental Ethics (Madison: University of Wisconsin Press, 1989).

20. *Religion and Environmental Crisis,* ed. Eugene Hargrove (Athens: University of Georgia Press, 1986).

21. Charlene Spretnak, *States of Grace: The Recovery of Meaning in the Post-Modern Age* (San Francisco: Harper San Francisco, 1991).

22. *Spirit and Nature: Why the Environment Is a Religious Issue,* ed. Steven Rockefeller and John Elder (Boston: Beacon Press, 1992).

23. Peter Marshall, *Nature's Web: Rethinking Our Place on Earth* (Armonk, N.Y.: M. E. Sharpe, 1992).

24. *Worldviews and Ecology,* ed. Mary Evelyn Tucker and John Grim (Lewisburg, Pa.: Bucknell University Press, 1993; reissued, Maryknoll, N.Y.: Orbis Books, 1994).

25. Callicott, *Earth's Insights.*

26. Both are State University of New York Press publications.

27. David Kinsley, *Ecology and Religion: Ecological Spirituality in a Cross-Cultural Perspective* (Englewood Cliffs, N.J.: Prentice Hall, 1995).

28. Seyyed Hossein Nasr, *Religion and the Order of Nature* (Oxford: Oxford University Press, 1996).

29. *Ethics of Environment and Development: Global Challenge, International Response,* ed. J. Ronald Engel and Joan Gibb Engel (Tucson: University of Arizona Press, 1990).

30. *Population, Consumption, and the Environment: Religious and Secular Responses,* ed. Harold Coward (Albany: State University of New York Press, 1995).

31. This Sacred Earth: Religion, Nature, Environment, ed. Roger S. Gottlieb (New York and London: Routledge, 1996).

32. These include volumes on Hinduism, Buddhism, Judaism, Christianity, and Islam.

Introduction. Judaism and the Natural World

HAVA TIROSH-SAMUELSON

Jews and Nature in Historical Perspective

The Jewish voice has joined the environmental movement relatively recently. Jews are not among the leaders of the environmental movement, and environmental activists who are Jews by birth have not developed their stance on the basis of Judaism.[1] With the marked exception of the Bible, the literary sources of Judaism have remained practically unknown to environmental thinkers, and Jewish values have only marginally inspired environmental thinking or policies. Moreover, since the famous essay of Lynn White, Jr.,[2] many environmentalists have charged that the Bible, the foundation document of Judaism, is the very cause for the contemporary ecological crisis. The biblical command to the first humans "to fill the earth and subdue it" (Gen. 1:28) is repeatedly cited as *the* proof that the Bible, and the Judeo-Christian tradition based on it, is the direct cause of the current environmental crisis.

Jews, too, have not regarded the well-being of the physical environment a Jewish issue.[3] In the post-Holocaust years, the physical and spiritual survival of the Jewish people, rather than the survival of the earth and natural habitats, has dominated Jewish concerns. While environmentalism was gaining momentum in the industrialized West, Jews were preoccupied with other issues, such as the prolonged Israeli-Arab conflict, relations between the State of Israel and the Diaspora, Jewish-Christian dialogue, and pluralism within Judaism. The desired relationship between the earth and the human species has not been at the forefront of the Jewish agenda.

The lack of interest in the natural world among Jews has deep historical and religious causes that go beyond the contemporary Jewish anguish about survival. For most of their history, Jews have been an urban people. In the Greco-Roman world, although Jews dwelled in urban centers, agriculture remained the primary mode of Jewish livelihood in Palestine and Babylonia. After the rise of Islam, heavy taxation on Jews made agriculture unprofitable and accelerated the process of urbanization, leading Jews to concentrate in commerce, trade, finance, and crafts. In medieval Christian Europe the Jewish estrangement from the land was even more pronounced because feudal relations excluded Jews. Although in some parts of Western Europe landed property was granted to Jews as late as the thirteenth century, Jews were increasingly forced to engage in moneylending, an economic activity that was odious to Christians. Frequent expulsions and voluntary migrations further estranged Jews from land cultivation, turning the ancient agrarian past into a distant memory. No longer in practice, the prescribed land-based rituals of Judaism fueled the hope for the ideal Messianic Age in the remote future, when the exiled people will return to the Land of Israel. For two millennia of exilic life, Jews continued to dream about their return to the Holy Land, but they waited for divine intervention to bring it about. Until then, Jewish life was to be shaped by the norms of rabbinic Judaism whose comprehensiveness enabled Jews to remain loyal to their religious tradition, despite the loss of political sovereignty and in the face of hostility and discrimination.

Nature, nonetheless, was not absent from traditional Jewish life. Through prescribed blessings and prayers the traditional Jew acknowledged natural phenomena and expressed thanks for God's benevolent creation. Yet the natural world was not understood to be independent of God's creative power. To venerate the natural world for its own sake or to identify God with nature is precisely the pagan outlook that Judaism rejects as idolatrous.[4] The world created by God is good, but it is not perfect; it requires human action to perfect it in accord with God's will. While nature is not in itself holy, it can be sanctified through performance of prescribed commands from God, the source of holiness.[5] In Judaism, the system of revealed commandments stands in contrast to nature, prescribing what should be done to that which already exists. Steven S. Schwarzschild captured this ethical stance when he coined the phrase "the unnatural Jew."[6]

The prescriptive stance toward nature was compatible with attempts to fathom how the natural world works. During the Middle Ages, Jewish philosophers sought to understand the laws by which God governs the world and availed themselves of contemporary science based on the study of natural phenomena and their causes. Medieval philosophers regarded the study of God's created world a theoretical activity whose reward was the immortality of the rational soul, or the intellect. It was a religious activity that enabled the philosopher-scientist to come closer to God. Moreover, the study of nature was never divorced from the study of the revealed Torah. Even though from the twelfth century onward medieval Jewish philosophers did not use biblical verses as premises of their philosophical reasoning, they all presupposed that in principle there could be no genuine contradiction between the truths of the revealed text and scientific knowledge about the world; both were believed to manifest the Wisdom of God. In premodern Judaism, then, all reflections about the created world, the doctrine of creation, and the doctrine of revelation functioned as the matrix within which Jews speculated about the natural world.

The religious outlook of premodern Judaism reached a crisis in the late eighteenth century. The rise of the centralized, modern nation-state, and, thereafter, the spread of democratic principles, made it impossible for Jews to continue to live in autonomous communities and be governed by their own laws and by special laws imposed by the state. If Jews were to remain in their country of residence, they had to be granted citizenship and civil rights. Many Jews wished to end age-old social and religious segregation and integrate into Western society and culture. For many, especially those who were open to the ideals of the Enlightenment, the sacred myth of Judaism and its traditional lifestyle became untenable. For the first time in their history, Jews evaluated their own tradition by criteria derived from the surrounding society, which they now regarded to be superior to their own. The Emancipation of the Jews during the nineteenth century was accompanied by a rapid process of modernization of Jewish religious practices, beliefs, and social customs. It was helped by more positive attitudes toward finance and commerce in modern mercantile and later capitalist economies. Yet precisely because Jews in Western and Central Europe so successfully and rapidly integrated into modern society, anti-Semitism emerged as a backlash, culminating in the elimination of one-third of world Jewry in the Holocaust. The multiple causes of the Holocaust cannot be discussed here, but it is appropriate to ponder the causal connection between the collective destruction of the Jews and the current environmental crisis.[7]

Zionism was the most radical Jewish response to modern anti-Semitism. A secular, nationalist movement, Zionism called on Jews to leave their country of residence and settle in the Land of Israel where they would rebuild the Jewish homeland and enjoy political sovereignty. For many Zionist ideologues, especially those associated with Labor or Socialist Zionism, the return to the Land of Israel was not merely a political act; it was also a deliberate attempt to create a new kind of a Jew, a person who will be rooted in the soil rather than in the study of sacred texts and the performance of religious rituals.[8] The return of the Jews to nature was supposed to liberate the Jews from the negative character traits they had acquired during their long exilic life and to lead to personal redemption not in the afterlife but in this world, and not through observance of divine commands but through manual labor.[9] The "religion of labor" through land cultivation was the most profound transformation of traditional Jewish values.[10] Along with the return to nature, the Zionists created a new, Hebrew culture that highlighted the agricultural basis of many Jewish festivals and designed new rituals that celebrated the abundance of the land without referring to God or to the sacred sources of Judaism.[11]

Despite the Zionist return to land cultivation and the emotional link to the Land of Israel, the physical environment did not fare well in the State of Israel. Since its establishment, the nascent state has been struggling to survive in a hostile environment, and nature preservation has not been at the top of the national agenda. In fact, the rapid population growth of the Jewish state after 1950, industrialization, and the perpetual state of war with its Arab neighbors dictated overuse of preciously scarce natural resources, especially water.[12] Furthermore, the influx of Jews from the Arab world, which had not been exposed to Western modernization, reintroduced traditional Jewish life and values to the young state, including a certain indifference to the physical environment. The social agenda of these immigrants, as well as of the refugees from Europe after the Holocaust, has had little to do with protection of the land and its limited natural resources.

Environmentalism does exist in Israel,[13] but its forms indicate the complex relationship between Judaism and ecology. On the one hand, intimate familiarity with the landscape, its flora and fauna, and concern for the preservation of the physical environment are popular among secular Israelis. Yet these activities are not legitimated by appeal to the religious sources of Judaism. Even when the Bible is employed to identify plants and animals in the Land of Israel, the Bible is not treated as a revealed text,[14] but as a historical document about the remote, national past. For secular Israelis, attention to environmental issues has more to do with a Western orientation and links to environmental movements in Europe and North America than with the religious sources of Judaism. On the other hand, Jews who are anchored in the Jewish tradition tend to link their love of the Land of Israel to a certain religious nationalist vision. Even though the religious, nationalist parties now promote outdoor activities for their constituents, these activities were not grounded in the values and sensibilities of the environmental movement. Nonetheless, in recent years attempts have been made to include ecological awareness in the religious-nationalist school system.

The creative weaving of Judaism and ecology took place in North America and began in the early 1970s as an apologetic response to the charges that the Judeo-Christian tradition was the cause of the environmental crisis. Defensive responses came first from Orthodox thinkers who showed that the accusations were based either on misunderstanding of the sources or on a lack of familiarity with the richness of the Jewish tradition.[15] Since then, Jews from all branches of modern Judaism—Reform, Conservative, Reconstructionist, and Humanistic Judaism—have contributed to Jewish ecology thinking, giving rise to a distinctive, albeit still small, body of literature.[16]

If reflections about nature from the sources of Judaism began with religiously committed Jews, environmental activism, by contrast, was initiated by Jews who were already involved in the environmental movement and who found their way back to their Jewish roots as part of the Jewish Renewal movement of the late 1960s and 1970s. At the forefront of the Jewish environmental movement was the organization Shomrei Adamah (Keepers of the Earth), whose goal was to raise Jewish awareness about ecological problems, such as pollution of natural resources, deforestation, erosion of top soil, the disappearance of species, climatic changes, and other ecological disasters brought about by the Industrial Revolution and by human greed and unbridled consumerism.[17] Jewish environmentalists have shown how ancient Jewish sacred texts and practices expressed concern for the protection of the earth and its inhabitants and urged Jews to reconnect with the rhythms of nature that are the foundation of many Jewish festivals.[18] In 1993 the Coalition on the Environment and Jewish Life (COEJL) was founded as an umbrella organization of diverse groups in North America to coordinate Jewish educational efforts and influence environmental policies. The final essay in this volume, by Mark X. Jacobs, the current executive director of the organization, documents the political and educational activities of Jewish environmentalists and reflects on the challenges that face them.

Existing Jewish ecological literature has shown that the sacred sources of Judaism are compatible with the sensibilities of the environmental movement, especially the value of stewardship, and that the values of Judaism could be used to formulate viable environmental policies. Contrary to the accusations of secular environmentalists, the Bible itself serves as the point of departure of Jewish environmentalism. Three main areas are commonly cited as evidence of the ecological usefulness of the Bible and rabbinic literature: protection of vegetation, especially fruit-bearing trees; awareness of the distress of animals; and predicating social justice on the well-being of the earth itself.[19] All three areas are framed in the context of covenantal theology, the bond between Israel and God.[20]

The causal relationship between human conduct and the thriving of the natural environment is spelled out in the relationship between the People of Israel and the Land of Israel: when Israel conducts itself according to divine command, the land is abundant and fertile, benefiting its human inhabitants with the basic necessities of life. But when Israel transgresses divine commandments, the blessedness of the land is temporarily removed and the land becomes desolate and inhospitable (Lev. 26:32). When the alienation from God becomes so egregious and injustice fills up God's land, God brings about Israel's removal from the land by allowing Israel's enemies to overcome her. The well-being of the land and the quality of Israel's life are causally linked, and both are predicated on Israel's observance of God's will. In short, the covenant between Israel and God implied specific laws intended to protect God's land and ensure its continued vitality.

Jewish ecological discourse has shown that Judaism harbors deep concern for the well-being of the natural world.[21] To date, however, the movement has not articulated a Jewish theology of nature, nor has it submitted the sources of Judaism to a systematic, philosophical examination. This volume is a first attempt toward that goal. The volume comprises essays presented in February 1998 at a conference at the Center for the Study of World Religions, Harvard Divinity School, as part of the larger study of religion and ecology, spearheaded by Mary Evelyn Tucker and John A. Grim of Bucknell University. Organized by Rabbi Steven Shaw and Moshe Sokol, the conference brought Jewish academics, environmental activists, and educators to reflect about Judaism's attitude toward the natural world. Unlike other gatherings of academics in Jewish studies, this conference intended to bridge the gap between objective scholarship and subjective commitment, between theoretical reflections and recommendations for action. The volume reflects this vision.

Constructive Jewish Theology of Nature

The volume commences with two attempts to construct a Jewish theology of nature in order to address the current ecological crisis. Arthur Green and Michael Fishbane both take their inspiration from kabbalah. Green believes that in kabbalah we can find the correct view of the relationship between God and the universe and that such a view offers useful insights for our environmental predicament inasmuch as it is compatible with the evolutionary model of the life sciences and with the orientation of contemporary physics and cosmology. Green boldly asserts that in order to address the concerns of the "environmental age," it is necessary to formulate "a Judaism unafraid to proclaim the holiness of the natural world, one that sees creation, including both world and human self, as a reflection of divinity and a source of religious inspiration." Adopting the ontological schema of kabbalah, Green maintains that all existents are in some way an expression of God and are to some extent intrinsically related to each other.

Contrary to Michael Wyschogrod, who holds that in Judaism "nature per se is not sacred,"[22] because holiness belongs only to the Creator, Green obliterates the ontological gap between the Creator and the created. Instead he adopts the monistic, emanationist ontology of kabbalah, according to which "multiplicity is the garbing of the One in the coat of many colors of existence, the transformation of Y-H-W-H,

singularity itself—Being—into the infinite variety of H-W-Y-H, being as we know, encounter, and *are* it." Green also endorses the
kabbalistic tendency to blur the distinction between creation and revelation. Both are forms of God's self-disclosure and both should ultimately be understood as linguistic processes. The natural world is ultimately a linguistic structure that requires decoding, an act that only
humans can accomplish because they are created in the image of God.
"Each human mind," says Green in accord with kabbalah, "is a microcosm, a miniature replica of the single Mind that conceives and becomes the universe. To know that oneness and recognize it *in all our
fellow beings* is what life is all about." Thus, Green unambiguously
privileges the human in the order of things, a view that is vehemently
rejected by many environmentalists, especially those associated with
deep ecology.[23] From the privileged position of the human, Green derives an ethics of responsibility toward all creatures that acknowledges the differences between diverse creatures while insisting on the
need to defend the legitimate place in the world of even "the weakest
and most threatened of creatures." For Green, a Jewish ecological ethics must be a *torat hayim*, namely, a set of laws and instructions that
truly "enhances life." He does not specify what these can be, but he
does provide a Jewish way of thinking about environmental ethics and
the policies that could derive from it.

Like Green, Michael Fishbane illustrates how the traditional language of Judaism could be reinterpreted to think about nature in light
of contemporary ecological concerns. But if Green takes his point of
departure from the paradox of unity and multiplicity, Fishbane reflects on the paradox of God's creative act. The Bible depicts the creation of the world as the result of divine speech: God spoke and the
world came into being. If nature is God's speech, nature itself reveals
God. Fishbane's implicit indebtedness to kabbalah is evident when he
regards creation as an act of God's self-revelation. In Fishbane's own
words: "God's speaking is the world's fullness, an infinite revelation
at the heart of creation." The creative/revelatory act, however, has two
aspects: one is the creative energy that brings things into existence,
and the other is the perception of what exists. Fishbane captures these
two aspects by differentiating between "Breath" and "Speech." The
divine Breath is the creative power that vitalizes everything, whereas
Speech is that which articulates things, making them distinct and accessible to human perception. Fishbane then identifies "Speech"

and "Breath" with the two central categories of rabbinic Judaism—
"Written Torah" and "Oral Torah," respectively. He states: "the Oral
Torah is eternally God's breath as it vitalizes being, *ruha be-ruha*
('spirit within spirit'), whereas the Written Torah is this same reality
contracted into the vessels of human cognition, language, and experience."

In Fishbane's poetic theology of nature, the terms "Written Torah"
and "Oral Torah" no longer denote a certain body of Jewish literature,
Scripture and rabbinic deliberations respectively, but two coordinates
that invite Jews to organize their experience vis-à-vis the natural
world. As much as the Written and Oral Torah are interdependent in
traditional Jewish thinking, so are humans interdependent on the
natural world and the divine creative energy that vitalizes it. Fishbane
expresses the duality of the human condition by using yet another set
of terms: "natural eye" and "spiritual eye." As part of nature, human
beings have a physical body and perceive the world through "the natural eye," namely, through their bodily senses. But humans are also
possessed with the ability "to perceive the world with God's Oral Torah in mind." That is to say, humans are aware of being different from
other creatures, but they are also able to see what they have in common with other beings. When we become aware of the "organic coherence" of which we are a part, we are able to exhibit "precious attentiveness to the multiform character of God's Written Torah . . . [while
being] attuned to the Oral Torah speaking in and through it." Becoming aware of the "Godly nature" of everything that exists is precisely
the purpose of Jewish prayers, blessings, and acts of sanctification,
according to Fishbane. These are ways in which Jews acknowledge
the limits of human speech, while using language. At the same time
we also become aware of and attuned to "the rhythms of other persons
and things by adjusting our breathing patterns to them and their way
of being." Fishbane's theology of nature calls people to live as part of
nature and at the same time to seek to transcend the natural.

The ethical conclusions of Fishbane are the same as Green's: we
must be attuned to the rhythm of nature, we must do our best to protect God's nature, and we must recognize that we and everything else
in the natural world are linked to each other. Whether kabbalah and
Hasidism, its modern offshoot, could be legitimately used to anchor
contemporary Jewish ecology, is questioned by other scholars in this
volume.

The Human Condition: Origins, Pollution, and Death

From constructive Jewish theology of nature the volume moves to consider the Bible and rabbinic literature, the foundation documents of Judaism. The essays of the second section advance this conversation in interesting, new directions. Evan Eisenberg presents a comparative reading of the biblical narrative of the Garden of Eden in light of the sacred narratives of other Near Eastern cultures and what is known today about the civilizations of the ancient Near East: the riverbed civilization of Mesopotamia and the terraced-hills civilization of the Canaanites, of which ancient Israel was a part. By establishing the ecological facts behind the Garden of Eden narrative, Eisenberg proposes a rather somber reading of the biblical narrative that carries a moral lesson about the relationship between humans and natural wilderness.

In Eisenberg's comparative study, the Garden of Eden is a mountain that functioned as a "cosmic center," a "world-pole," or the "navel of the world." It is the source of life. Eden, however, was not a place fit for human dwelling, since humans are animals with a unique capacity to make tools and produce farming, writing, and urban dwellings, in short, to create civilizations.[24] In Eisenberg's secular, anthropological reading of the biblical narrative, the Fall of Man was a necessary process of self-expulsion, or self-alienation from nature. Eden belongs to God, and not even gods or angels could remain in it, let alone humans. To develop their potential, humans had to leave Eden and create civilization, which inevitably destroys the very natural resources at human disposal. According to Eisenberg, the tragic human condition cannot be avoided, but its scope can be minimized, if we become aware of it. The biblical Garden of Eden narrative, therefore, should function not as a place to which we aspire to return but as a source of wilderness: "we must revere it, draw sustenance from it, [and] keep it alive." Conversely, we must be cognizant of the fact that our civilizational accomplishments have separated us from the sources of life, and that the quality of our life has been drastically reduced since the dawn of civilization. Eisenberg does not offer a way out of the human conundrum, but he suggests that if we become aware of our tragic ecological situation, we may be able to minimize its scope.

How are humans to negotiate their tragic relationship with the natural world? In traditional Judaism answers to such a question have to be sought, in principle, in rabbinic sources that apply divinely revealed Scripture to concrete human situations. The essays by Eliezer Diamond and David Kraemer treat these sources from two distinct, but complementary perspectives. Whereas Diamond focuses on halakhic (i.e., legal) discourse, Kraemer looks closely at aggadic, that is, the nonlegal, homiletical, and speculative aspect of rabbinic Judaism. From their detailed textual analyses emerge general principles that could be most useful for contemporary thinking about ecological problems.

Humans are social animals and their interaction with each other requires cooperation as well as mechanisms for conflict resolution. Diamond wrestles with one aspect of contemporary ecological problems: pollution. He considers the effects of pollution, not on natural environment, but on humans. More specifically, he is concerned with the problem of environmental justice.[25] Since conflicts about pollution pit the interest of the individual against the interest of the community, Diamond examines how the Mishnah and subsequent medieval and modern legal sources, including rulings by the Supreme Court in Israel, deal with such conflicts. Diamond shows that halakhic sources struggled with the tension between personal and conventional standards, established the parameters of unacceptable pollution, were aware of the difference between inflicting nuisance or discomfort and causing economic deprivation, and that they have evolved over time because they addressed changing life circumstances. While Diamond reasons within the parameters of Jewish legal sources, the ramifications of his essay extend beyond the boundaries of Jewish society, for whom this reasoning is normative. He convincingly argues that halakhic reasoning about notions of conventionality and equity in environmental matters could be applied meaningfully to the problem of global warming. Such application requires a careful analysis of concrete human situations as well as a creative analysis of Jewish legal sources.

The same interpretative creativity can be applied to the nonlegal rabbinic sources that expressed rabbinic theology and shaped religious practices. Kraemer advances our understanding of Jewish views on the relationship between humans and nature by looking at death rituals. On the basis of a comparative analysis with Zoroastrian and Egyptian death rituals, he argues that in all human societies death rituals are rooted in a certain view about the origins of humanity. In rabbinic death rituals the dead body was to be placed in the ground immediately after death. While one can rationalize this ritual by appealing to the hot climate of the Near East and the need to avoid early decomposition of the body, Kraemer cogently argues that the rabbinic rationale for the practice was linked to the biblical narrative of human creation. The Bible, however, has two creation narratives: Genesis 2:7 depicts the creation of the first human from the earth, whereas Genesis 1:26 highlights that the human was created "in the image of God" (*be-tzelem 'elohim*). The two creation narratives have very different consequences concerning the relationship between humans and the natural world. According to the earthbound story, the human (*'adam*) comes from the earth (*'adamah*) and must return to it at death; according to the second narrative, humans are in some sense "above" the earth. Kraemer shows that rabbinic death rituals privileged the earthbound narrative, thereby signifying the essential link to the natural world. From this, Kraemer derives a rabbinically based ecological ethics: the relations between humans and the earth is "a relationship not of subduing or conquest, but of natural partnership. An act of abuse against the natural world is an abuse against humanity, and vice versa." It follows that humans must not "view the natural world as 'other,' something to serve our needs, something to exploit." Rather, "our needs are part of, and must be harmonized with, the needs of the natural world."[26] Kraemer does not tell us how to accomplish the reconciliation between conflicting needs, but it stands to reason that further exploration of halakhic sources could provide an answer.

In his response, Eilon Schwartz clarifies Jewish approaches to the natural world by delineating four models. The first focuses on human rationality and posits an instrumental attitude toward nature. Schwartz admits that this model, in which human rationality manipulates the world to satisfy human needs, makes Judaism susceptible to the accusation of the environmental movement that Judaism endorses human domination of nature. Yet, the Bible offers a second model that affirms human responsibility toward the earth, highlighting the partnership of humans with the earth and its inhabitants. These two models, Schwartz argues, need not be understood as mutually exclusive, as Rabbi Joseph Soloveitchik proposed in his famous essay,[27] because human physicality can be "a source of deep spiritual meaning." While Schwartz agrees that the second model is attractive, he confesses to a certain discomfort with it, given his own environmentalism that is inspired by the wilderness tradition. Therefore, Schwartz finds the teachings of Abraham Joshua Heschel akin to his own sensibility, because Heschel highlighted the "radical amazement model." Whereas this model belittles the human and calls for humility in light of nature's awesomeness, the fourth model, the "holy sparks model" of Lurianic kabbalah and Hasidism, makes the human deeply involved with the transformation of nature. Schwartz insightfully suggests that this religious model was given a secular twist in Zionism, where it cohered with Romantic nationalism, on the one hand, and with Nietzsche's philosophy of life, on the other hand. With a greater awareness to the diverse models within Judaism, Jewish environmental education has more options and can avoid the sense of crisis and despair articulated by Soloveitchik's religious existentialism.

The Doctrine of Creation

All Jewish reflections about the natural world, as Michael Wyschogrod has already noted, take their point of departure from the belief that God created the world and that God is the source of the moral order. The third section of the volume examines more carefully the doctrine of creation in the Bible, rabbinic texts, and Jewish philosophy.

Stephen A. Geller's analysis of the Book of Job captures the core problem in Judaism: the tension between the belief that God created the world and the belief that God revealed His Will to Israel in the form of law, the Torah. The Book of Job is the earliest manifestation of this problem. According to Geller, the book reflected a crisis of faith in Israel during the sixth century B.C.E., after the destruction of the First Temple. The crisis pitted the "Old Wisdom tradition" against a "new militant monotheism" and its covenantal theology, articulated in the Book of Deuteronomy. The ancient Wisdom tradition saw the origin of nature and the origin of the moral order to be the same. Wise is the one who observes nature and knows how to live rightly in accord with it. By contrast, the new Deuteronomic faith posited a covenant law that is discussed in terms of Sinaitic revelation. Geller highlights the tension between the Old Wisdom tradition that proceeded "from God through creation and nature to morality," and the covenant faith that 'deriv[ed] all morality from revelation to humankind, i.e.,

Israel." According to Geller, then, the Book of Job is a hybrid of intellectual piety and covenantal piety, a mixture that is best evident in the speeches of Job's friends. The author of the Book of Job does not resolve the tension logically, but the book ends with an emotional solution to the tension. In chapters 38–42, the climax of the book, the author of Job "wants to rescue a role for nature, but he realizes that this can be achieved only by abandoning the demand for understanding itself." The proper attitude toward nature, according to the Book of Job, is expressed in the category of the "sublime" as understood by the English poets of the eighteenth century. The sublime combines humility, terror, awareness of one's insignificance, and fear with feelings of exaltation, forgetfulness of self, and fascination. The conclusion of the Book of Job is that "Revelation and nature cannot be reconciled by human wisdom."

Although Geller succinctly captures the tension between the doctrines of creation and revelation, the history of Judaism did not follow his conclusion. What is true about the Book of Job, if one accepts Geller's reading, is not true about Jewish philosophy. The Jewish philosophic tradition was grounded in the assumption that human reason can indeed bridge revelation and nature and that the same rational ability to fathom the laws of nature can and should be applied to the interpretation of God's revealed Will and Wisdom in Scripture. For the philosophers, the laws of nature, in principle, could not contradict the truths of revealed Scripture, and it is the task of the Jewish wise man to sort out the relationship between knowledge about the natural world and the true meaning of revealed Scripture.

Focusing on the Jewish philosophical tradition, David Novak explores how the doctrine of creation relates to the idea of nature, and more specifically to the concept of natural law. Writing both as a historian of Jewish thought and as a constructive Jewish theologian, Novak argues that in the classical sources of Judaism—especially in medieval Jewish philosophy—there is an elaborate discussion of natural law. The relationship between the doctrine of creation and the doctrine of revelation has to be configured in the context of a natural law theory. Novak argues that all theories of natural law are necessarily teleological and that they presuppose a hierarchical order of the universe. After elucidating four possible ways to configure the telos of the universe, and critiquing the relationship between creation and revelation in the thought of Saadia Gaon (882–942) and Moses

Maimonides (1135/8–1204), Novak proceeds to articulate his own understanding of the interplay of creation, revelation, and redemption. His views are shaped by the philosophy of Franz Rosenzweig (1886–1929). Properly understood, Novak argues, creation is not in time; it is prior to the experience of every creature; and redemption is "not yet," that is, it is beyond what humans can know or experience in the present. All that humans have is revelation, yet revelation is not a one-time historic event, but is "God's presence in us, with us, and for us." It is the ever-present "Giving of the Torah to Israel," an act which organizes all meaning for Jews. Novak argues, therefore, that nature cannot be grasped as a mere given, or an abstraction of the human mind. Instead, nature is "something that can only be grasped abstractly from within our historical present, a present whose content is continually provided by revelation." On the basis of Rosenzweig's philosophy, Novak proceeds to present what he considers to be the best theory of natural law in Judaism. Novak's theological position can be endorsed by Orthodox, Conservative, and even Reform Jews who accept the primacy of revelation in organizing Jewish life, but it may be difficult for secular Jews for whom the category of revelation is meaningless or who view Judaism as the culture of the Jewish people.

Whereas Novak focused on the philosophical interpretations of the doctrine of creation, Neil Gillman looks at the link between the doctrine of creation and Jewish liturgy and ritual. Gillman's assumption coheres with the claim of Kraemer in the previous section: Jewish rituals express the underlying theology of rabbinic Judaism better than Jewish philosophical theology. Gillman shows how the Jewish marriage ceremony and the prayer of the morning service are organized on the basis of the doctrine of creation that is the linchpin of the sacred narrative of Judaism. Again in agreement with Kraemer, Gillman shows that the rabbis privileged the earthbound creation narrative in Genesis 2:7 and that they ascribed deep spiritual meaning to the physicality of creation. Gillman's interpretation of the doctrine of creation is decidedly critical of the intellectualism of Maimonides as much as it is at odds with Soloveitchik's reading of the creation narrative. In Gillman's exposition of the marriage ceremony, the ritual should be understood as a reenactment of the act of creation that fuses "the two worlds, the transcendent mythic world of the creation story and the actual, real world of the two people who are getting married."

Liturgical acts are not mere ceremonies; they are theology in action. Gillman then looks carefully at three elements from the morning service in which God's creative activity is blessed. He shows how the rabbis intentionally changed the biblical phrase (Isaiah 45:7) to convey their theological views about God, the world, and the origin of Evil. The liturgical language posits God as an omnipotent creator *ex nihilo*, who renews nature daily and whose "power ranges not only over nature but over history as well." The Jewish normative attitude toward the natural world is expressed not through systematic reflections of the philosophers but through the daily liturgy obligatory to observant Jews.

In the response to these three papers, Jon D. Levenson clarifies Geller's reading of the Book of Job while raising questions about Geller's claim that the fusion of intellectual piety and covenantal piety in Job is similar to that found in late Stoicism. Levenson is most critical of Novak's "Judaizing the classical and Roman ideal of natural law" and of Novak's understanding of revelation. Levenson argues that Novak "leaves it unclear about how we are to derive any specific norms from natural law and what we are to do when these norms and those of the revealed law conflict." With a veiled critique of philosophical discourse, Levenson expresses preferences to the study of liturgy as the authentic expression of Jewish views on creation and revelation, in accord with the essay by Gillman.

Nature and Revealed Morality

If it is true, as Novak claims, that verbal revelation is the only context through which Jews can experience the natural world, how does revelation organize Jewish attitude toward nature? In traditional Judaism revelation is understood to be the origin of morality, and so how does morality, the prescriptions and prohibitions of Judaism, relate to the natural world? Does morality, as articulated in the Torah, stand in opposition to nature? Is the human called by God to transform nature? Does Judaism bridge the distinction between nature and morality? The essays in this section wrestle with these questions.

Shalom Rosenberg's essay documents the diverse conceptions of nature in Judaism that flow from different understandings of revelation. In Jewish sources, Rosenberg correctly notes, the term "nature" has a variety of meanings. "Nature" is used generally to denote "the cosmos or . . . the biological world," as well as more specifically to denote the nature of humans, which for some philosophers was identified with the human capacity to reason. Moreover, the meaning of the term "nature" has varied over time in accordance with the function assigned to it. For example, in the modern period "nature" is evoked as a way to criticize existing ethical and legal situations, but it can also be used to justify existing morality presumably anchored in the social order. "Nature" can also refer to the belief in the existence of more basic laws that cut across traditions and create a bond between all people. Or, "nature" and "natural law" can be presented as something that "transcends not only space but also time and allows us to judge different historical cultures." Since morality can be said to relate to nature in different ways, it is incumbent on those who generalize about these issues to be attuned to the rich canvas of Jewish views on the interplay between nature and revealed morality in Judaism.

In the Bible, claims Rosenberg, ethics stands in opposition to the natural world. In rabbinic Judaism a more subtle view emerges in the context of recognizing the stability of nature, on the one hand, and the ability of humans to learn from the ways animals conduct themselves, on the other. In medieval philosophy one finds extensive discussion of the natural world as well as of human nature, which the philosophers identified with rationality. The philosophers articulated a teleological natural morality, where nature is established as a means to reach the unique goals of man. Most instructively, Rosenberg shows that the medieval philosophers regarded the Torah itself as natural law, because it is the Torah that "brings one to perfection." The inherent identity between Torah and nature was challenged by the sixteenth-century Jewish theologian R. Judah Loew of Prague (c. 1525–1609), for whom "morality rises beyond nature" and acts of loving kindness surpass nature. In kabbalah, Rosenberg correctly states, "reality becomes a language. Nature is transformed into a symbol of the divine." The relationship between Torah (and hence morality) and the natural world is ambiguous in kabbalah. For some kabbalists the Torah stands for nature, whereas for others the Torah is the paradigm of nature. Of the modern thinkers who reflected on the relationship between morality and nature, Rosenberg singles out Samson Raphael Hirsch (1808–1888), the founder of Neo-Orthodoxy in Germany, and shows that in Hirsch's analysis of the commandments nature "is not only a model for us in its fulfilling law . . . [I]t places on humans its own demands, its own *mitzvot* [commandments]." Rosenberg concludes that human obligations toward nature include not only respect for nature, but also the specific commandments that are detailed in the Bible. These commandments specify the boundaries within which humans should interact with the natural world.

A different and novel attempt to articulate Jewish ecological philosophy is offered by Lenn E. Goodman within the matrix of "an ontological theory of justice."[28] In such a theory, all things that exist are good and their intrinsic value is the foundation of their deserts. Goodman's point of departure is the intrinsic deserts of animals, plants, and eco-niches that flow from the particular "project" of each thing. Using Spinoza's language, Goodman refers to this project as *"conatus,"*[29] and claims that this is the basis of human respect for "all beings—to the extent possible." Goodman admits that this theory is a form of naturalism, but he denies that it is a form of materialism. Instead, Goodman shows that his hierarchical theory of deserts can be derived from the language of the Bible as elaborated by rabbinic sources. Goodman successfully demonstrates that the Bible and rabbinic sources recognized the inherent deserts of animals or the human obligation to alleviate the suffering of an animal. The command to be compassionate toward animals affirms both human superiority over other animals as well as human responsibility toward nature. Goodman's ecological ethics exemplifies the notion of human stewardship of nature,[30] even though Goodman explicitly rejects vegetarianism, in contrast to Rosenberg who endorses it.[31] Goodman does not explain how the killing of animals for the sake of human consumption is compatible with recognizing the inherent value and desert of the killed animals. Likewise, he does not account for the fact, noted by both Fishbane and Rosenberg, that destruction is integral to nature and that species naturally engage other species in a struggle for survival.

Some of the issues left open by Goodman are addressed by Moshe Sokol. He begins by rejecting Steven Schwarzschild and Michael Wyschogrod, who highlight the opposition between Judaism and nature. Such a claim, Sokol avers, is simply incoherent because "Judaism cannot disapprove of trees and grass." He maintains that it is more accurate to say that "the Bible and rabbinic Judaism objected to certain conceptions of nature but not to nature's constituents." In agreement with Rosenberg, Sokol notes that the category "nature" is a human construct that has changed over time. If one is to explain the presumed conflict between Jews and the natural world, one must turn to the sociology of the Jews as urban people to find the proper explanation. Sokol differentiates between two questions: 1) what are Jewish constructions of nature and how do they relate to each other? and 2) what, if any, are the implications of the varying constructions of nature for developing a useful environmental ethics? The first question is addressed by Shalom Rosenberg in this volume. Sokol attempts to answer the second question.

Sokol's main concern is to explore dominant paradigms about the relationship between God and the world and to ponder whether they can be used as a foundation for a Jewish ecological ethics. He differentiates between the "transcendist position," whose main exponent is Maimonides, and the "immanentist view," represented by kabbalah and Hasidism. Sokol shows that one cannot simplistically equate either of these views with a given ethical implication or recommendation in regard to the natural world. Respect toward the natural world is not a necessary outcome of an immanentist outlook, as is commonly argued, since respect for nature is specifically stated by Maimonides, the advocate of the transcendist position. Conversely, Hasidism, which has served as inspiration for contemporary Jewish environmentalists, cannot be said to be more "green" than its opposition, either in the eighteenth and nineteenth centuries or today. Sokol then examines three models for the relationship between morality and nature— "environmental anthropocentrism," "environmental biocentrism," and "environmental theocentrism"—and shows what is problematic about each of them and why none of them could tell us how to treat the natural world.

Sokol's original contribution to Jewish ecological reflections is the suggestion that we should shift our focus from an ecological ethics of duty toward nature to an ecological ethics of virtue. Environmental virtue ethics will include "a deep sense of humility, not only individually but species-wide; the capacity for gratitude; the capacity to experience awe and sublimity; the virtues of temperance, continence, and respectfulness, among others." The data for the desired character traits of the environmentally virtuous person could come from the very sources of the Jewish tradition, both halakhic and homiletic.

In his response, Barry S. Kogan's exposes Goodman's indebtedness to medieval Neoplatonic ontology and questions Goodman's attempt to ascribe rights of persons to nonhumans, especially after a century that has seen the catastrophic results of the failure to respect human life as such as sacred. Kogan finds Rosenberg's reading of Hirsch more attractive because "the study of ecology, the policy implications that follow from its findings, and the practical intent of the *huqqim*, as explained by Hirsch, would all be religiously mandated." As for Sokol, Kogan challenges his misrepresentation of Schwarzschild and Wyschogrod. While Kogan agrees that theology that emphasizes transcendence does not necessarily desacralize the world and that those that highlight immanence do not necessarily culminate in unqualified reverence and awe toward all things natural, Kogan challenges Sokol's overly schematic classifications of Jewish approaches to nature.

Nature in Jewish Mysticism

The complexity of Jewish approaches to nature is manifested most acutely in the Jewish mystical tradition. The essays in this section problematize any attempt to anchor Jewish theology of nature in kabbalah. Neither kabbalah nor its eighteenth-century offshoot, Hasidism, accepted the natural world as a given that must be preserved and hallowed. In both cases, the corporeality of the natural, especially as manifested in the human body, is viewed either as a veil that hides the truly spiritual, namely, God, or as a negative obstacle that prevents the human from attaining unity with God. To the mystic, who claims to possess knowledge of the linguistic foundation of nature, the world of nature is a symbol of divine reality that has to be decoded and thereby either spiritualized or transcended. Nature is not to be celebrated for its own sake.

Elliot R. Wolfson shows that the key to the kabbalistic approach to nature lies in the claim that nature is a mirror of the divine. This is not a mere metaphor but a metaphysical claim about the very structure of reality. In kabbalah, as Wolfson succinctly states, "the ten resplendent emanations (*sefirot*), which make up the divine pleroma, are the archetypal spiritual beings that function as the formal causes for all that exists in the physical universe." For the kabbalists, there is "one ultimate reality, the divine light, which manifests itself in the garb of the twenty-two letters of the Hebrew alphabet that derive, in turn, from the four-letter name, YHWH, the root word of all language, the mystical secret of the Torah." The corporeal world that we perceive through the senses is by no means ultimate reality. Rather, "the corporeal world reflects the spiritual forms in the manner that a mirror reflects images. Just as the image is not what is real but only its appearance, so nature is naught but the representation of that which is real."

Wolfson argues that kabbalistic ontology cannot be labeled as either "pantheism" or "immanentism," as is commonly done, because kabbalah harbored competing pantheistic and theistic views. Most importantly, Wolfson explains that the kabbalists were not interested in the natural world encountered outdoors, but in the mysterious, esoteric events within the Godhead that are ultimately manifested in the physical environment. What matters to kabbalah is not nature itself—which functions as a veil of divine reality—but the act of penetrating the hidden nature of God. Wolfson then moves on to show that the poetics of nature as the mirror of God is heavily genderized. Nature is identified with the Female, the *Shekhinah*, but "she is no more than the looking glass that reflects what is genuinely real, the masculine image, which is attributed more specifically to the phallic gradation," *Tife'eret*. Wolfson's careful unmasking of the androcentric nature of kabbalistic symbolism undermines any attempt to use kabbalah in order to recover the lost Goddess. Wolfson concludes by showing the connection between the kabbalistic, spiritualist ontology and the ascetic practices and makes it patently clear that the kabbalists were not only de facto remote from the natural world, but that they denied that the natural world as we know it is holy.

Kabbalah, especially as developed in the Land of Israel during the sixteenth century, was the ideational basis of Hasidism. Indeed, it was Hasidism, as popularized by Martin Buber, which brought kabbalah to the knowledge of the Western world and to the attention of the environmental movement.[32] In Buber's representation, Hasidism articulated a positive attitude toward nature, since the I-Thou relationship could be had not only with persons but also with trees and animals. Buber's rendering of Hasidism was vehemently criticized by Gershom Scholem and Rivkah Schatz-Uffenheimer. Jerome (Yehudah) Gellman revisits the critique and further endorses it on the basis of a close reading of those very sources that Buber claimed to have used. Defending himself against his critics, Buber admitted that his reconstruction of Hasidic theology and practice cannot be derived from the teachings of the founder of Hasidism, R. Israel Baal Shem Tov (known as the Besht) (1698–1760), but from the teachings of his disciple, R. Jacob Joseph of Polonnoye, and his disciples. By analyzing the texts that Buber used in his reconstruction of Hasidism, Gellman shows that Buber ascribed to his Hasidic authors views that they did not in fact hold. Gellman concludes that neither Buber's portrayal of Hasidism nor Hasidism itself could serve as a foundation of Jewish ecological theology.

Gellman's skepticism about Hasidism is further corroborated by Shaul Magid, who focuses on the works of the Besht's grandson, R. Nahman of Bratslav (1772–1810). R. Nahman wrote homiletical discourses and symbolic tales. In the former, the attitude of the Hasidic master to the natural world is "exclusively pejorative." Magid explains that for R. Nahman "nature is not identical with the natural world." Instead, "nature" (*teva*) is a human construct on the basis of our perception. Nature is deceptive because it "appears perfect . . . in its stability and predictability." This appearance "is actually the source of its imperfection." In contrast to "nature," R. Nahman posited the "world" (*'olam*), a term that is used to "refer to the natural world in a constant state of renewal" from its divine source. It is "unstable, dynamic, and unpredictable." When we perceive the stability of nature, we actually sever the natural world from its divine creative source. In his homiletical discourses, then, R. Nahman placed nature in "diametrical opposition to miracle and divine providence." The symbolic tales of R. Nahman, however, reveal a more tolerant attitude toward nature, enabling humanity to live simultaneously within and apart from its external environment. On the basis of a close reading of R. Nahman's last tale, "The Seven Beggars," Magid uncovers a view of nature that enables humanity to co-exist with nature but not be part of it.

In her response to the three presenters on the Jewish mystical tradition, Hava Tirosh-Samuelson further problematizes the kabbalistic approach to nature. The notion that nature is a mirror of the divine actually gave rise to two different attitudes toward nature. According to one, the corporeality of nature was to be transcended through kabbalistic sanctifying acts. According to the other, the belief that kabbalah contains the knowledge of the linguistic foundation of the natural world led to a proto-experimental approach to nature, characteristic of so-called practical kabbalah. Tirosh-Samuelson agrees with

Gellman and Magid that eighteenth-century Hasidism could not serve as the basis of environmental theology, since its application of the rabbinic sanctification of nature through observance of divine commandments leads to spiritualization, and hence, annihilation of the empirical world.

From Speculation to Action

The rich Jewish tradition, this volume demonstrates, can support a deep respect toward nature that translates into human stewardship of nature. In the twentieth century the Jewish thinker who reconfigured the relationship between God and natural world most elaborately was Abraham Joshua Heschel (1907–1972). Edward K. Kaplan presents Heschel's "depth theology" of the caring God who "calls for human beings actively to redeem [the world]." Approaching the Bible, not as "human theology but as God's anthropology," Heschel's point of departure was the notion of wonder or radical amazement, which Schwartz has also discussed in this volume in support of his own environmental sensibilities. Kaplan explains how Heschel's writings were designed to enable the reader to shed or question all habitual ways of thinking, and gradually to begin "to perceive the world as 'an allusion' to God, as an object of divine concern." While Heschel's outlook was rooted in kabbalah and Hasidism, he used the kabbalistic notion of "allusion" to reawaken in Jews the reverence toward nature. Reinterpreting the Jewish tradition, Kaplan shows, Heschel instructed twentieth-century Jews to develop the notion of "kinship with the visible cosmos" and to grasp the reciprocal relationship between God and the world. The world is the object of God's concern or love. Heschel presented a vision of interrelatedness of humans, other beings, and God, and emphasized human responsibility to God, "who is both within and beyond nature and civilization." Kaplan, along with Eilon Schwartz, correctly views Heschel as a major ecological Jewish thinker whose theology could inspire sound environmental policies.

Translating Jewish ecological reflection into action is by no means a simple matter. The volume concludes with essays by Tsvi Blanchard and Mark X. Jacobs that reflect on the challenges to Jewish environmental activism. Blanchard notes the tension between the secular nature of the environmental discourse and Jewish religious commitments. Before Jews could join the environmental discourse, it has been important to realize three things. First, even if Jewish sources harbor a certain conception of the natural world, they did not imagine the ecological situation we face today. It is not self-evident that the solution to the environmental crisis could be found in the traditional Jewish sources. Second, Jews were never in a position to formulate policies for the society at large, but only for their own communities. Third, the ecological movement regards the Bible very critically as the source of a negative attitude toward nature that gave rise to destructive policies. Blanchard proposes a way to overcome these difficulties by focusing on select Talmudic sources that blend religious and secular aspects. This model, he claims, would enable Jews to join the general environmental discourse and to speak as committed Jews. Blanchard shows that the rabbis considered human action and were attentive to scientific information, implying that there is room within the religious tradition itself to consider nondivine aspects. He illustrates how the rabbis considered intentional modifications of the environment and the harmful side effects of improper positioning of certain substances. Like Diamond, Blanchard invites Jews and non-Jews to grasp the general principles of Jewish legal sources and to realize how they can be applied to very practical issues that confront the environmental movement. He concludes that "analysis of the Jewish material might help in drafting possible policy strategies as well as in framing the key questions to be asked and answered."

The volume concludes with Mark X. Jacobs's overview of the Jewish environmental movement, its history, accomplishments, and challenges. There is no doubt that the movement has succeeded in raising the awareness of Jews about environmental and ecological matters. The movement has also added a significant Jewish presence to other faith communities in the United States which are deeply concerned about the environmental crisis. However, Jacobs admits that the leadership of the Jewish community lacks passionate commitment to environmentalism and that the very affluence of Jews in North America militates against it. Jacobs voices concern over the tension between the Jewish environmentalists, who are motivated by deep religious insights, and the "relative weak role of Judaism in the lives of American Jews." Thus, contemporary Jews rather than Judaism are the obstacle to a vital Jewish environmentalism.

Conclusion

This volume intends to contribute to the nascent discourse on Judaism and ecology by clarifying diverse conceptions of nature in Jewish sources and by using the insights of Judaism to formulate a constructive Jewish theology of nature. Given the complexity of the Jewish tradition, it is impossible to generalize about Judaism and ecology. Some voices within Judaism are compatible with contemporary environmentalism, and others are either in direct conflict with it or manifest uneasiness about it. Thus, one voice expresses a deep respect for the natural world created by God that is translated into obligations to protect the natural world from human abuse. This voice is rooted in the view that the human is but a steward of God's earth and is totally compatible with conservationist policies. Another voice within Judaism highlights the opposition between the human and the natural. Only humans can receive and respond to divine obligations "to be holy as I the Lord am holy," and only humans can transform the natural world through prescribed acts that sanctify the natural. From this perspective any attempt to identify nature with God is a form of idolatry that Judaism is determined to eradicate. And finally, there is the voice that denies reality to the natural world. The natural world, the world that is accessible to us through the senses, is but a mirror of a divine, noncorporeal reality. Created in the image of God, human beings are most capable of transcending their natural veil, and to fathom or penetrate the ultimate reality beyond the veil. However one interprets this idea, it leads to negative attitudes toward nature, be they indifference, suppression, or manipulation of nature. In short, whatever stance one wishes to highlight results in a different understanding of Judaism vis-à-vis the natural world.

Generalizing about Judaism and ecology is also difficult because Jews today do not agree about the meaning of Judaism. Not only is Judaism defined in both religious and secular terms—and the gulf between religionists and secularists grows ever deeper—religiously committed Jews do not agree about the meaning of the foundational tenets of Judaism or the way of life that should flow from them. Whether one considers the sources of Judaism to be normative, compelling, suggestive, or troubling shapes how one treats what Judaism has to say about environmental matters. This volume respects pluralism in contemporary Judaism and does not seek to impose unanimity and consensus. Yet, precisely because the volume includes thinkers of all branches of contemporary Judaism, it implicitly argues that the current ecological crisis is indeed a Jewish issue. I will go even further and say that because Jews have faced the threat of extinction on account of radically evil, human acts, Jews have a distinctive vantage point from which to speak against the destruction that humans now inflict on God's creation. If Jews stand in covenantal relationship, and are called to mend the world, Jews cannot ignore ecological matters in the name of more pressing social issues. To protect God's world from further abuse by humans is a Jewish moral obligation.

As Jews become more ecologically aware, however, Jewish thinkers will have to become more familiar with the contemporary environmental discourse and its nuances debated among deep ecology, social ecology, political ecology, ecofeminism, and conservationism.[33] Each of these perspectives has a different understanding of the place of the human in the order of things and the attitudes toward nature that flows from it. A future reflection by Jewish thinkers on ecological matters will also require a deeper immersion in contemporary science, especially the sciences of physics, cosmology, the life sciences, and the cognitive sciences. To speak theologically and philosophically about the desired relationship between humans and the natural world requires holding informed views about the natural world. A Jewish discourse on ecology is thus inseparable from the so-called dialogue of science and religion, in which the Jewish voice is still underrepresented. When Jews enter the dialogue of science and religious dialogue in greater number, they will affirm what medieval Jewish philosophers have taken for granted: since God is truth, there can be no conflict between what is true in science and what is true in Judaism.

As Jews become more conversant with this literature and, hopefully, environmentalists become more informed about Judaism, it may become clear not only how Judaism is compatible with conservationism, but also where Judaism conflicts with the radical activism of Earth First! or with the metaphysical claims of deep ecology. Conversely, as the conversation between Judaism and ecology develops, it might question a strict secularist approach to being Jewish. Judaism is a religious civilization and the sources of Judaism are all religious sources. To speak about environmentalism from a Jewish perspective entails a religious outlook. The volume cannot tell Jews how to define the meaning of being Jewish for themselves. It only charts the issues that must concern anyone who takes Judaism and ecology seriously.

Notes

1. The extensive ecological literature cannot be cited here. For readers unfamiliar with it, a good introduction is provided in *Ecology*, ed. Carolyn Merchant, ed., Key Concepts in Critical Theory (Atlantic Highlands, N. J.: Humanities Press, 1994). A quick perusal of this volume bears my point: environmentalism has had little or nothing to do with Judaism.

2. Lynn White, Jr., "The Historical Roots of Our Ecologic Crisis," *Science* 155 (1967): 1203–7.

3. That Arthur Waskow, a Jewish environmental thinker and activist, had to make the case for Jewish involvement in environmentalism in the 1990s attests to the relative limited interest in this topic in the organized Jewish community. See Arthur Waskow, "Is the Earth a Jewish Issue?" *Tikkun* 7, no. 5 (1992): 35–37.

4. For further discussion of this point among contemporary Jewish thinkers, consult Eilon Schwartz, "Judaism and Nature: Theological and Moral Issues to Consider while Renegotiating a Jewish Relationship to the Natural World," in *Judaism and Environmental Ethics*, ed. Martin D. Yaffe (Lanham, Md.: Lexington Books, 2001), 297–308.

5. This position is explained most succinctly by Michael Wyschogrod, "Judaism and the Sanctification of Nature," *Melton Journal* 24 (spring 1991): 5–6; reprinted in *Judaism and Environmental Ethics*, ed. Yaffe, 289–96. Most modern Orthodox thinkers share this viewpoint.

6. See Steven S. Schwarzschild, "The Unnatural Jew," *Environmental Ethics* 6 (1984): 347–62. This essay elicited a serious debate and some serious criticism. See Jeanne Kay, "Comments on the Unnatural Jew," *Environmental Ethics* 7 (1985): 189–91, reprinted in *Judaism and Environmental Ethics*, ed. Yaffe, 286–88; and David Ehrenfeld and Joan G. Ehrenfeld, "Some Thoughts on Nature and Judaism," *Environmental Ethics* 7 (1985): 93–95, reprinted in *Judaism and Environmental Ethics*, ed. Yaffe, 283–85. The debate is discussed in Martin D. Yaffe's introduction to his volume.

7. See Eric Katz, "Nature's Healing Power, the Holocaust and the Environmental Crisis," *Judaism: A Quarterly Journal* 46 (1997): 79–89; reprinted in *Judaism and Environmental Ethics*, ed. Yaffe, 309–20.

8. It is true that Zionism included religious positions as well. For the religious Zionists the return to the land was understood in terms of being able to perform the land-based commandments of Judaism and thus coming closer to God. For an overview of the function of the land in Zionist thought, consult Arnold M. Eisen, "Off Center: The Concept of the Land of Israel in Modern Jewish Thought," in *The Land of Israel: Jewish Perspectives*, ed. Lawrence A. Hoffman (Notre Dame, Ind.: University of Notre Dame Press, 1986), 263–96.

9. The main ideologue of Socialist Zionism who provided the rationale for the Jewish return to nature was Aharon David Gordon (1856–1922). For analysis of Gordon's philosophy, see Eliezer Schweid, *The Land of Israel: National Home or Land of Destiny*, trans. Deborah Greniman (Rutherford, N.J.: Fairleigh Dickinson University Press, 1985); idem, *The Individual: The World of A. D. Gordon* (in Hebrew) (Tel Aviv: Am Oved, 1970).

10. It is instructive to note that Zionism regarded the purchase of land from Arabs as "redemption of land" (*ge'ulat ha-qarqa*), thus framing a secular activity in religious terms. See *Ge'ulat ha-Qarqa be-'Eretz Israel Ra'aion u-Ma'aseh*, ed. Ruth Kark (Jerusalem: Yad Ben Zvi Publication, 1990). I thank Dr. Ada Schein for directing me to this book.

11. The kibbutzim, the agricultural settlements created by Socialist Zionism, were most creative in developing new rituals for the Jewish festivals. While rooted in the Jewish tradition, these innovative rituals all celebrated the seasonal cycle of nature and the fertility of the land, but they did not refer to God and did not seek justification in rabbinic sources.

12. See Susan H. Lees, *The Political Ecology of the Water Crisis in Israel* (Lanham, Md.: University Press of America, 1998); *Water and Peace in the Middle East*, ed. Jad Isaac and Hillel Shuval (Amsterdam: Elsevier, 1994); and Miriam Lowi, *Water and Power: The Politics of a Scarce Resource in the Jordan River Basin* (Cambridge: Cambridge University Press, 1993).

13. For an overview of Israel's environmental perils and the activities of the environmental movement, see Alon Tal, "An Imperiled Promised Land," in *Torah of the Earth: Exploring 4,000 Years of Ecology in Jewish Thought*, ed. Arthur Waskow, 2 vols. (Woodstock, Vt.: Jewish Lights Publishing, 2000), 2:42–71.

14. The works of Nogah Hareuveni, listed in the bibliography of this volume, are typical examples of this trend.

15. For responses by modern Orthodox thinkers to White's charges, see Norman Lamm, "Ecology in Jewish Law and Theology," in his *Faith and Doubt: Studies in Traditional Jewish Thought* (New York: Ktav, 1972), 162–85; Jonathan Helfand, "Ecology and the Jewish Tradition: A Postscript," *Judaism* 20 (1971): 330–35; idem, "'Consider the Work of G-d': Jewish Sources for Conservation Ethics," in *Liturgical Foundations of Social Policy in the Catholic and Jewish Traditions*, ed. Daniel F. Polish and Eugene J. Fisher (Notre Dame, Ind.: University of Notre Dame Press, 1983), 134–48; idem, "The Earth Is the Lord's: Judaism and Environmental Ethics," in *Religion and Environmental Crisis*," ed. Eugene C. Hargrove (Athens, Ga.: University of Georgia Press, 1986), 38–52; Aryeh Carmell, "Judaism and the Quality of the Environment," in *Challenge: Torah Views and Science and Its Problems*, ed. Aryeh Carmell and Cyril Domb (London and Jerusalem: Feldeim Publishers, 1976), 500–25.

16. The rise of Jewish interest in environmental issues reflects in part a growing realization that the ecological crisis is a religious issue and that world religions have been crucial to the shaping of human attitudes toward the physical environment. The emergence of a religious ecological discourse during the 1970s and 1980s was concomitant with the flourishing Religious Studies as an academic discipline committed to the comparative study of world religions. Typical examples of comparative religious ecological discourse in which Judaism is represented are *Spirit and Nature: Why the Environment Is a Religious Issue*, ed. Steven C. Rockefeller and John C. Elder (Boston: Beacon Press, 1992); and *Worldviews and Ecology*, ed. Mary Evelyn Tucker and John A. Grim (Lewisburg, Pa.: Bucknell University Press; London: Associated University Presses, 1993; reprint, Maryknoll, N.Y.: Orbis Books, 1996).

17. The organization was associated with the Reconstructionist Rabbinical College in Wyncote, Pennsylvania, and its main activity was to publish educational material. The materials are available in *Judaism and Ecology, 1970–1986: A Sourcebook of Readings*, ed. Marc Swetlitz (Wyncote: Shomrei Adamah, 1990).

18. A representative sample of Jewish environmental writings in America is *Ecology and the Jewish Spirit*, ed. Ellen Bernstein (Woodstock, Vt.: Jewish Lights Publishing, 1998).

19. For an overview of these themes, consult the essays in *Judaism and Ecology*, ed. Aubrey Rose (London: Cassell, 1992).

20. For a succinct expression of the covenantal model for Jewish ecology, see Bradley Shavit Artson, "Our Covenant with Stones: A Jewish Ecology of Earth," *Conservative Judaism* 44, no. 1 (1991): 25–35; reprinted in *Judaism and Environmental Ethics*, ed. Yaffe, 161–71.

21. For an overview of the relevant sources, consult *Torah of the Earth*, ed. Waskow, 1:212–14, which includes information about Jewish organizations committed to environmentalism.

22. Michael Wyschogrod, "The Sanctification of Nature in Judaism," in *Judaism and Environmental Ethics*, ed. Yaffe, 294.

23. On deep ecology, consult *Deep Ecology for the Twenty-first Century: Readings on the Philosophy and Practice of the New Environmentalism*, ed. George Sessions (Boston and London: Shambhala, 1995). In many respects, however, there is quite an overlap between Green's reflections and the views of deep ecology. The reason for it is historical. Many of the insights of deep ecology, especially as outlined by Arne Naess, are indebted to the philosophy of Spinoza, who was, in turn, familiar with kabbalah.

24. Eisenberg's reading is in accord with the consensus among developmental anthropologists who believe that toolmaking is the determining mark of *homo sapiens*. For a summary of the debates among anthropologists, consult Ian Tattersall, *The Fossil Trail: How We Know What We Think We Know about Human Evolution* (New York: Oxford University, 1995).

25. A main concern of the environmental justice movement is the dumping of toxic wastes in poor neighborhoods that are populated predominantly by African Americans. Environmental justice is thus commonly conflated with the accusation of racism and pertains as well to Mexican Americans and to Native Americans. See Robert Bullard, "Environmental Racism and the Environmental Justice Movement," in *Ecology*, 254–65, and the literature cited there.

26. Kraemer's conclusion, as well as that of other contributors in this volume, accord with ecological thinking that highlights respect for nature. See Paul W. Taylor, "The Ethics of Respect for Nature," in *Environmental Philosophy: From Animal Rights to Radical Ecology*, ed. Michael Zimmerman et al. (Upper Saddle River, N.J.: Prentice Hall, 1993), 71–86.

27. Joseph B. Soloveitchik, "The Lonely Man of Faith," *Tradition* 7 (1965): 5–67.

28. See Lenn E. Goodman, *On Justice: An Essay in Jewish Philosophy* (New Haven: Yale University Press, 1991).

29. For exposition of Spinoza's theory, see Richard Mason, *The God of Spinoza: A Philosophical Study* (Cambridge: Cambridge University Press, 1997), 142–46.

30. See David Ehrenfeld and Philip J. Bentley, "Judaism and the Practice of Stewardship," *Judaism: A Quarterly Journal* 34 (1985): 301–11; reprinted in *Judaism and Environmental Ethics*, ed. Yaffe, 125–35.

31. Whether Jews should be vegetarians is one of the themes of Jewish ecological discourse. For an overview, see Louis A. Berman, *Vegetarianism and the Jewish Tradition* (New York: Ktav, 1982).

32. For an example of Buber's influence on the contemporary ecological discourse, consult Brian J. Walsh, Marianne B. Karsh, and Nik Ansell, "Trees, Forestry, and the Responsiveness of Creation," in *This Sacred Earth: Religion, Nature, Environment*, ed. Roger S. Gottlieb (New York: Routledge, 1996), 423–35. The most influential aspect of Buber's philosophy was his utopian communitarianism that envisioned "a cooperative world culture emerging out of regenerated regional cultures that arise in turn out of a regenerated human spirit"; see John Clark, "A Social Ecology," in *Environmental Philosophy*, ed. Zimmerman et al., 419.

33. An excellent anthology of environmental writings that presents the various schools of environmental thinking is Zimmerman's volume cited above.

Constructive Jewish Theology of Nature

A Kabbalah for the Environmental Age

ARTHUR GREEN

It is an irony of history that kabbalah, jettisoned by generations of modern Jews as so much backward nonsense, is now making a comeback. In an age when modernity itself is being questioned, this renewal of interest in mystical aspects of Judaism is both spiritually exciting and potentially dangerous, even explosive. The danger lies in the deep connection to be found between kabbalah and both the xenophobic and the messianic elements of Jewish tradition. When mystical faith supplants political judgment or when medieval views of the difference between Jewish and gentile souls are reflected in social policy attitudes of Israeli power brokers, the entire Jewish people is endangered. But the promise of the mystical tradition and its potential contribution to a Judaism that could appeal to many seekers is so great that this writer, along with many others in our time, is willing to take the risk.

I am certainly not a kabbalist in the traditional sense, nor do I aspire to to be one. The old system, qua system, does not work for me. The mythic universe of kabbalah, for all its beauty, belongs to another age. Whether we look at its hierarchical structure, at the Jewish exclusivism and spiritual racism implied by its doctrine of the soul, or at the passive–subject role assigned to the feminine, I for one do not believe that a return to the mentality of the ancients is the solution to our current woes. Instead, our age is very much in need of *a post-kabbalistic Jewish mysticism*, one richly nourished, but not dominated, by the old language and structure. That new Jewish mysticism, kabbalah in a universalist and pluralist key, has been slowly emerging over the course of the twentieth century, a process that has more re-

cently moved into high gear. This new pace and high degree of interest is part of a much broader, worldwide reexamination of the great
spiritual traditions, a seeking out of ancient wells of wisdom that
might sustain us in a new and unprecedented period in human history.

Humanity is in urgent need of a new sort of piety, a religious attitude fitting to an environmentally concerned future that is already
upon us. This new mining of ancient religious truth is being applied to
all the traditions. As a Jew who has been studying and teaching
kabbalah and Hasidism for forty years, I believe that our tradition has
much to offer, if we combine deep examination of the sources with a
willingness to choose carefully among them and update their teachings when necessary. Among the elements I seek is *a Judaism unafraid to proclaim the holiness of the natural world,* one that sees creation, including both world and human self, as a reflection of divinity
and a source of religious inspiration. It is in this spirit that I turn to
kabbalah, seeking to learn from, but also to adapt and transform, its
vision. The essential truth of mysticism—that all beings are manifestations of the same one and that the unity of being can be discovered
by a disciplined training of the mind toward insight—is one that our
age both longs and needs to hear. The understanding that God is the
innermost reality of all that is, and that God and universe are related
not primarily as Creator and creature, but as deep structure and surface, is key to the Judaism of the future. But the ways in which we
develop and act upon that insight will have to be appropriate to our
own age.

The magnificent architechtonics of the kabbalists' vision cannot be
articulated here. Their grand picture of the inner universe, in which
the One that encompasses all being opens up to reveal itself as ten, is
the beginning of the kabbalistic system. The ten *sefirot* (literally,
"numbers") are stations in the flow of energy from the One into the
many. The ten-in-one cosmos is a way of responding to the eternal
mystical question "How do the many proceed from the One?" The
kabbalists say: "Very slowly and subtly. Let us show you the process."
As one gets farther into kabbalah, it turns out that each of the ten
sefirot contains all the other nine, and the whole process of ten-fold
manifestation repeats itself four times as one journeys through various upper or inner "worlds." There is thus a basic "grid" of four hundred rungs, each discussed with great finesse in the highly refined
symbolic language of kabbalah. Other versions of the kabbalistic

"map" have the ten *sefirot* open themselves further to reveal more decades, becoming hundreds, thousands, and so forth. Later kabbalists redivide the ten into five configurations of *sefirot* that each exists in six modes or stages, leading to a system of staggering and overwhelming complexity.

For the initiate, the *sefirot* also serve as rungs or marking points of the mystic's inward journey. His goal (it only also can become "hers" in very recent times) is to reverse the journey of God from unity into multiplicity, going back to make the many into one again. The kabbalist who "ascends" those rungs ideally "uplifts" the lower worlds, taking them along on the journey back to oneness. In this way they, along with the mystic's own soul, may be re-included in the one. This is the kabbalistic concept of *tiqqun*, the restoration of the worlds to their original harmony as carried out in this "uplifting" activity of the mystical life. Each person is a microcosm, also built in that same pattern of the *sefirot,* so that cosmology and psychology, our ways of understanding life's origins and our own innermost selves, are quite identical. God's cosmic journey into multiplicity and your inward journey into unity are mirror images of one another.

This "great chain of being" approach to spirituality can be appreciated more than ever by postmoderns, not only for its beauty but for a certain dimly perceived accuracy as well. Each human being contains the entire universe, claims the ancient myth. All the rungs of descent (and potential ascent) are contained in each soul. But that is true, even in demythologized form: all of our ancestors, each stage and ministep in the evolution of life that brought us to where we are today, are present within us. The DNA that constitutes the life-identity of each of us exists indeed *zekher le-ma'aseh bereshit,* "in memory of the act of creation," linking us back to our most remote origins.

Part of our work as self-aware, articulate beings is converting that biological "memory" into consciousness and building a holy structure (i.e., a religion or a civilization) that articulates and *sanctifies* those links between past and future. In this way the actual fact of all our past's presence within us is converted into a basis for meaning, for expression of our deep rootedness in all that is and has come before us. The memory of the entire universe lies within each and every one of us. Hopefully, the values represented by that ongoing project of civilization-building will lead us forward as well, helping us realize that we must be faithful transmitters to all the many future links in the evolutionary chain, just as we are the grateful recipients of the efforts of all those that have fought the ongoing life-struggle to bring us to this moment. All of the upper and lower "worlds" of the kabbalist here become manifest in human terms, as generations that lie before and behind us, but also as multiple layers of human self-awareness that we seek to peel back in search of our deepest and truest selves.

Creation and Revelation, according to esoteric Judaism, are two different but parallel manifestations of the primordial Torah, or the creative wisdom of God. We might think of this as universal Mind, the wisdom that is manifest both in the ways of nature and in the deepest soul of human beings. At the heart of these twin self-revelations of the One, as understood in Jewish language, lies the barely whispered breath of the four semi-consonants *Yod He Waw He*, the verbal noun that tries to express the divine Self. In the hierarchy of language, this is the supreme word. Too holy to be spoken aloud except by the high priest on the Day of Atonement, it is the word that stands closest to the silence that surpasses all language. This name is an impossible conflation of the verb "to be"; hence the God of Exodus, where the name is introduced, says, "I shall be whatever I shall be," meaning that the elusive Self of the universe will ever escape definition. Those four letters are really a term for being—HaWaYaH—itself. But because they are mere breath (for there is no really consonantal "hard" sound in any of them), they also stand for the birth of language itself, the emergence of the word from the universal silence beyond, from what we Jews call the eternal Torah of God, the wordless truth that "was" before creation.

God *is* Being, Y-H-W-H, when existence is seen from a fully unitive, harmonic, and all-embracing point of view—a perspective that ever eludes us mere humans, located as we are in particular identities of time and space. The small self and its limitations keep us from seeing the great Self at work both within and around us. But then the letters, like pieces in a puzzle, are mysteriously rearranged and HaWaYaH, existence itself, reveals itself to be none other than Y-H-W-H, the great name that proclaims so powerful a unity of being that it could be spoken only *there*, in the innermost holy chamber of the holy Temple.

Kabbalah is a tale of origins, an account of how the many come forth from the One and how we may embark on the return journey to oneness. But our beginning point of understanding has to take us beyond kabbalah, back to the biblical tale of origins. The kabbalist's universe depends entirely on the much older biblical creation tale, the ingenious opening chapter of Genesis that for nearly twenty-five hundred years served as chief source for the West's understanding of natural, including human, origins. The account of how God in six days spoke each order of existence into being is now of only antiquarian interest as an actual account of how the world came to be, though it remains alive for us as a liturgical text and a source of religious creativity.

But I would like to lift the veil behind Genesis 1 and ask just what it was that this magnificently penned single chapter managed to accomplish. The old Mesopotamian and Canaanite creation myths, now barely recalled, were well-known to the biblical authors. They include the rising up of the primal forces of chaos, represented chiefly by Yam or Tiamat, gods of the sea, against the order being imposed by the sky-gods. The defeat of that primordial rebellion and its bloody end is well-documented, as scholars have shown, in a number of passages within the Bible: in the Prophets, Psalms, Job, and by subtle implication even in the Genesis text itself. That tale of origins was a part of the cultural legacy of ancient Israel. The fact that it is reflected even in postbiblical midrashic sources shows that it had a long life, continuing even into the Zohar of the thirteenth century. The original readers and hearers of Genesis 1, in other words, knew of another account of creation, one of conflict, slaughter, and victory: "the survival of the fittest" among the gods. What is striking about this account is precisely the *absence* of those elements of conflict: Genesis 1 offers a purely harmonistic version of the origin of creatures, one where everything has its place as the willed creation of the single Deity and all conflict has mysteriously been forgotten.

Our civilization has been transformed over the past century and a half in no small part by our acceptance of a new tale of origins, one that began with Darwin and is refined daily by the work of life-scientists and physicists, the new kabbalists of our age who claim even to know the black hole out of which being itself came to be, speculating on the first few seconds of existence as our ancestors once did on the highest triad of the ten *sefirot*, or rungs of divine being. The history of living creatures is again depicted as a bloody and violent struggle, the implications of which for human behavior—even for the possibilities of human ethics—have hardly gone unnoticed. We, too, are urgently in need of a new and powerfully harmonious vision, one that will allow even the weakest and most threatened of creatures a legitimate place in this world and protection from being wiped out at the careless whim of the creature who stands, at least for now, at the top of the evolutionary mound of corpses. A beautiful attempt at articulating such a vision was made by Brian Swimme and Thomas Berry a few years ago in their *Universe Story.* Such a vision more willing to base itself on the biblical-Judaic legacy would also be a welcome contribution.

But let us return for a moment to the old creation tale. While I no longer believe it in any literal sense and do not look to it, even through reinterpretation (each "day" is a geologic era, etc. . . .) as a source of information about geo-history, I claim it still as a *religious* text for me as a Jew and for us as a people. We still read it in the synagogue, and its closing section is the introductory rubric for our most precious and best-beloved sacred form—the observance of the Sabbath: "Heaven and earth were finished, and all their hosts. . . ." What then does the text mean to me? What underlies the myth, or to what truth or value am I pointing by so privileging this ancient text?

The text says that before there were many, there was only the one. Before the incredible variety and richness of life as we know it could come to be, there had to exist a simple self, a source from which all the many proceeded. I refer not to some single-celled amoeba that existed in the ocean hundreds of millions of years ago. I read the text on a different level by asserting that *the primacy of the one to the many is not necessarily temporal in meaning.* Sacred myth describes a deep and ineffable reality, one so profound that it is not given to expression except through the veil of narration, through encapsulation in a story. And stories, given the need for a sequential plot, require time. So the precedence of the One over the many, placed into story form, comes out sounding like, "In the beginning God created. . . ." Its meaning, however, is that the One underlies the many then, now, and forever. A dimly perceived but awesome deep structure links all things and ties them to the root out of which they all emerge. Multiplicity is the garbing of the One in the coat-of-many-colors of existence, the transformation of Y-H-W-H, singularity itself—Being—into the infinite varieties of H-W-Y-H, being as we know, encounter, and *are* it.

The Genesis "Creation" story is really a tale of the origins of multiplicity, a biblical attempt to answer that eternal question of mystics to which the later account of the *sefirot* was also addressed: "How do the many proceed from the One?" This reality is symbolized by the beginning of the Torah with the letter *bet,* long a subject of speculation within Jewish tradition. *Bet* is numerically "two"; its positioning at the beginning of the Torah indicates that here is the beginning of *duality.* From now on there is not just "God" but "God and. . . ." This meaning is dramatically reinforced by the emergence of creation in what are repeatedly described as pairs: light and darkness, day and night, heaven and earth, upper and lower waters, sun and moon, male and female, and all the rest. Behind all these twos, however, behind the *bet* of *bereshit bara* ("In the beginning God created") lies the hidden, singular, silent *aleph.* This One, representing the absolute oneness of being, the one after which there is no "two," is to be proclaimed at Sinai in the opening letter of *'anokhi,* "I am," the very heart of revelation. So there are two ways in which the One is revealed. One leads through the path of infinite multiplicity and diversity, the One as manifest within the many, God in creation. The other is the invitation to the return journey, revealing to us the *aleph* that underlies all being, the One to which we all return, both in the ecstatic silence of mystical journey and in the ultimate ego-transcendence of death.

This One, I believe, is the only Being that ever was, is, or will be. It is the One that undergoes the only sacred drama that really matters: the bio-history of the universe. *I believe that it does so as a conscious and willful Self.* From those first seconds of existence, through the emergence of life in its earliest manifestations, and along every step, including the seeming stumblings, missteps, and blind alleys along the way of evolution, it is this single Being that is evolving, entering into each new life-form, ever carrying within itself the memory of all its past. I thus seek to re-vision the evolutionary process, not as the struggle of creature against creature and species against species, but as the emergence of a single life-energy, a single cosmic Mind that *uses* the comparative adaptabilities of all the forms it enters as a means of ongoing striving, ever forward, into richer and more diverse forms of life. The formless Self searches out endless forms, delighting to rediscover its own identity anew in each of them. That constant movement of the One, expansive in all directions at once, is at the same time a directed movement, pointing toward the eventual emergence of a life-form that can fully know and realize the One that lives in all beings. This creature, the one in whom the self-knowledge of

Being can be ultimately fulfilled, is thus the telos of existence.

In this process, the emergence of humanity with its gifts of intellect, self-awareness, and language, is indeed a major step forward.
Judaism has always taught a distinction between humans and other
forms of life, a sense in which the human stands beyond the vegetative
and animal realms out of which we emerged. Each creature embodies
the life-energy and hence the presence of the One, but only humans
are called "God's image" in our tradition. This means that we are the
first to have the mental capacity to recapitulate the process, to be self-
conscious about our roots within the One. The implications of that
potential are tremendous if we understand the mystical journey back
to oneness as a central value within human existence, the "opposite"
that complements our drive toward progress, growth, and forward
movement. But surely our being "in the divine image" is not meant to
give us license for the rapacious destruction of all so-called lower
forms. God forbid! That would be the model of the "species eat species" view of evolution. Although we are indeed by design and necessity eaters of the "lower" species, we still seek a life of harmony and
balance with them. The Bible provides two models for defining humanity's role in relation to the natural world. One is that of Genesis 1:
humans as stewards, the viceroy who is to "rule over the fish of the
sea, the birds of the sky, and all the beasts who roam the earth." But if
we look into the Psalms, the concluding chapters of Job, and other
scriptural sources, we find another option. I quote from Psalm 148
(using a recent contemporary adaptation by Stephen Mitchell):[1]

> Praise God upon the earth,
>   whales and all creatures of the sea,
> fire, hail, snow, and frost,
>   hurricanes fulfilling his command,
> mountains and barren hills,
>   fruit trees and cedar forests,
> wild animals and tame,
>   reptiles, insects, birds,
> creatures invisible to the eye
>   and tiniest one-celled beings,
> rich and poor, powerful
>   and oppressed, dark-skinned and light-skinned,
> men and women alike,
>   old and young together.

Here the Psalmist envisions us as *part* of the universal chorus of praise, rather than isolating us as the final creation of Friday afternoon, with the message of "stewardship" that accompanies it. A true understanding of the unitive vision being proclaimed here would lead us beyond the demands of "stewardship," the ethic usually derived from the biblical tale. Life's meaning is to be found in discovering the One, and that means realizing the ultimate unity of all being. It is in *yihud*, discovering and proclaiming the underlying oneness of all existence, that our humanity is fulfilled.

We are of the One; each human mind is a microcosm, a miniature replica of the single Mind that conceives and becomes the universe. To know that oneness and recognize it *in all our fellow beings* is what life is all about. But that recognition leads us to another level of awareness. The One *delights* in each of the infinite forms in which it is manifest. To play on that lovely English verb, this means that the One sends its *light* into each of these forms. Vegetative forms indeed experience this gift most in sunlight, stretching toward it as they grow. We humans are privileged to experience that same radiating light-energy as delight or love.

The One *loves* the many. The coat-of-many-colors in which Being comes to be garbed is a garment of delight. We, as the self-conscious expression of Being, are called upon to love as well, to partake in and give human expression to the *delightfulness* of existence. This is expressed in Jewish liturgy by the order of our daily prayers. The blessing of God as the source of nature's light is directly followed by a blessing for God's love. The One does nothing different in the interim between these blessings. God does nothing different in giving light to all creatures, plant and animal, and in giving love to human beings and holy communities, assemblies of God-seekers wherever they are. As humans who are creatures of love, we receive the divine life-flow in the form of love, turning toward it and being fulfilled by it just as naturally as plants stretch toward the light. Nature experiences this shining as light; we humans receive it as love. But as recipients of love we are called upon (Dare I say "commanded?") to love as well.

I am also fully willing to admit that we may be but an early stage in an ongoing evolution of aware beings. Perhaps our period will be looked upon in the distant future, by creatures no more willing to demean themselves by the word "human" than we are comfortable being called "ape," as a primitive life-stage. Surely they will not be wrong, those wise beings of the future, in seeing our age as characterized by nothing so much as pretentiousness and self-glorification, on the one hand, and wanton consumption and pillage of earth's resources, on the other. Let us hope we leave room for that wise future to emerge.

Discovering the presence of the One within the natural order, and therefore the sacred quality of existence itself, is exactly what our father Abraham did, according to Philo of Alexandria, the hidden grandfather of all Jewish philosophy. This One manifested itself to him in terms of law: Abraham felt that he was being taught how to live in harmony with the forces of nature. Moses' Torah, according to Philo, is the lawgiver's attempt to legislate for a whole human community the life of harmonic insight with the God of nature that Abraham had already found for himself. I have tried to show elsewhere that certain writings of the Hasidic masters, unaware of the ancient precedent, continue this trend. Rabbi Levi Yitzhak of Berdichev, the eighteenth-century Hasidic master, introduces his treatise on hidden miracles, or the miraculous within nature, with precisely this claim: Sinai allows the entire people to apprehend that which wise old Abraham had already long earlier discerned on his own.

The law that teaches us how to live in harmony with the natural world should be one of eternal principles and countless new applications. Its most basic teachings should demand of us that we live ever at the cutting edge of sensitivity toward the suffering we cause God's creatures. We need be aware of the rest and reinvigoration that we give to the soil, the waste of living resources, for each is the embodiment of divine presence. We may not take the endless material gifts with which we are blessed any more casually than we would take God's *name* in vain. We may not take the One's great gift of holy *water* in vain—or *air*, source of *nishmat kol hai*, the sacred breath of life. To rest on the laurels of forms our ancestors created long ago or to boast of their progressivism in the tenth or sixth century B.C.E. is very much not to the point. What is the point of observing *shemitah*, the sabbatical year, but using earth-destroying pesticides? Of insisting on the humanity of *shehitah*, kosher slaughter, but hoisting and shackling and refusing to stun animals to lessen their awareness before they die? Of washing the bugs out of our lettuce while investing that other green stuff in multinational corporations that daily destroy entire forests? How can we *today* create a civilization and a law that will be such a *torat hayyim*, a teaching that enhances life? And what will it demand of us? Surely a return to the reverence for air, water, soil, and fire (by limiting the amount that we, including our automobiles, burn!), would be a good place to start.

Another potentially useful rubric within tradition for proclaiming this insight is the parallel between the ten divine utterances (of "let there be . . .") in creation and the ten "commandments" (the Hebrew might be better rendered as "speech-acts") of Sinai. This is another way of expressing the unity between the revelation that lies within creation and that which is manifest in Torah. The presence of the One that underlies all being is depicted as pure verbal energy: God is the One who ever, unceasingly, says *"Yehi!"* ("Let there be!"), speaking the world into being. But at Sinai, those ten *yehi*'s are translated into imperatives for us; the inner "law" of God's presence in nature is now manifest in the form of imperatives that can govern human existence, bringing us into harmony with the ten words within ourselves as well as within all creatures. And since the ten "commandments" are the basis of all the six hundred thirteen yeas and nays that comprise Torah, all of it is tied through them to the ten cosmo-generative utterances of the One. This parallel is a great favorite of certain mystical teachers. Creation and revelation are two deeply interrelated manifestations of the same divine Self, one showing us that all existence is fraught with holiness, the other instructing us on how to live in the face of that awareness.

Here the language of kabbalah may be useful again. These two tens, the utterances and the commandments, are both versions of the ten *sefirot*, those primal numbers that allow us deeper entrée into the "secret" of existence. We manifest that secret by turning outward and inward toward the world around us, seeing it in all its awesome beauty and recognizing how deeply we are a part of all that is. We then ask (in good Jewish fashion): "What does this awareness *demand* of us?" Here we have the beginning point of a new kabbalah and a new halakhah ("path" of religious practice) as well. This praxis, one using and adapting the rich forms of Jewish tradition, should be one that leads us to a life of harmony with the natural world and maximum concern for its preservation.

All this talk must seem terribly mythical to readers of a more scientific bent of mind. Perhaps it also seems obscure and irrelevant to some of those most keenly aware of the several immediate threats to global existence. Let me assure you that I share that sense of urgency.

Life has so evolved that the fate of the biosphere itself is now determined by human actions. We are masters not only over our own species and over those we consume, as so many others have been. The
very existence of our planet as a fit habitat for *any* living thing has
now fallen into human hands.

With this increase in human power comes a manifold increase of
responsibility. Each day, we threaten the future, not only of our own
offspring, with a million decisions weighted with political, economic,
and competitive baggage. The land itself, the *'adamah* from which we
humans derive our name—the earth and all that is upon it— is threatened by us. The changes needed in collective human behavior in order
to save us from self-destruction are stupendous. Belief in their possibility stretches our credulity as much as it is demanded by our need
for hope. Our economic system, including the value we place on constant expansion and growth, will have to change. The standards of
consumption, created by our wealthiest economies and now the goal
of all others, will have to be diminished. Effective world government,
perhaps even at the cost of some of our precious freedoms, will have
to triumph over the childish bickering and threats that currently characterize world affairs.

Such a transformation is hardly believable, indeed. But consider
the alternative. If any of this deep-seated change is to come about,
religious leaders and thinkers need to take an early lead. A seismic
shift in the mythical underpinnings of our consciousness is required:
nothing less will do the trick. That shift will have to come about
within the framework of the religious languages now spoken by large
sections of the human race. Experience tells us that newly created
myths do not readily take hold; they usually lack the power to with-
stand great challenge. But a rerouting of ancient symbols, along channels already half-cleared by the most open-eyed thinkers of earlier
centuries, might indeed enable this conversion of the human heart.

In the emergence of a new tale of origins, we Jews, who have for so
long been bearers of the old tale, have a special interest. The new tale
will need to achieve its own harmony, summarized with no less genius
than was possessed by the author of Genesis 1. It will need to tell of
the unity of all beings and help us to feel that fellow-creaturehood
with trees and rivers as well as with animals and humans. As it brings
us to awareness of our common source, ever-present in each of us, so
must it value the distinctiveness and sacred integrity of each creature

on its own, even the animals, or fish, or plants we eat, even the trees
we cut down. If we Jews are allowed to have a hand in it, it will also
speak of a human dignity that still needs to be shared with most of our
species and of a time of rest, periodic liberation from the treadmill of
our struggle for existence, in which we can contemplate and enjoy our
fellow-feeling with all that is. This sacred time also serves as a model
for the world that we believe "with perfect faith" is still to come, a
world of which we have never ceased to dream.

Note

1. Stephen Mitchell, *A Book of Psalms, Selected and Adapted from the Hebrew*
(New York: Harper Collins, 1993).

Toward a Jewish Theology of Nature

MICHAEL FISHBANE

Jewish theology has lost its voice—its ability to direct our attention to God as a real presence in our life and experience. More precisely, it has lost the ability to speak of God as the source and sustainer of this world, so that the manifold of this reality might be understood and experienced theologically. This impoverishment of speech results in an impoverishment of hearing. The clatter and din of things, with their echoes and buzz, have become the everyday sound of the world. What is lost is the ability to attune one's ear to the undertones of this noise, as to some deep divine grammar flowing into worldly being. Reconstructed, or reconceived, theology may provide an opportunity to catch these reverberations—and thus restore us to a precious attentiveness, which is the sacred ground of living religion.

The proclamation that calls all creatures to hear and know that the Lord is One is the first task of a monotheistic theology; its ultimate goal is to justify the call for the faithful to all dimensions of their lives—natural and spiritual, personal and cultural. Such a justification is the fruit of experience and tradition as they combine to formulate a theological language in each generation. It is here that the challenge lies. How may the subjective sensibilities of this historical time join with the treasure of collective culture in a creative synthesis? Certainly, reflections on the past will provide important resources toward this task. This involves the clarification and retrieval of earlier Jewish perspectives through study and scholarship. The full range of such expressions will reveal the many historical theologies of Judaism, and their multiple trajectories of thought and textual interpretation. Thus, when it comes to the matter of nature and Jewish theology, a vast panoply of possibilities emerges—possibilities all derived (in whole or in part) from different readings of Genesis 1 in the light of diverse exegetical and philosophical presuppositions, and also from different applications of one's duties as a creature, resulting in distinct halakhic perspectives on the population or subjugation of the earth and the care for its resources. These views provide models of thought and attitude, as well as task and responsibility, that have existed in the past and that continue to nurture Jewish tradition in the present.

But can we go further? Can we go beyond these cultural catalogs and continuities and ask ourselves if they derive from a theology of creation that compels our most subjective assent—now, at this historical hour? In asking this question, the issue is not to ignore the resources and obligations of tradition but to renew its theological ground. Those of us for whom theology is no mere historical or abstract matter, but a personal and living necessity, have no choice. We must go further because we must live in relation to God as a living presence—not as a historical or exegetical rumor. But for all the reasons you know so well, our contemporary sensibilities do not fit into the minds and words of past masters of Jewish thought without remainder. And even were this possible, even if we could identify with a prior world of faith and its formulations, I would stress that the modern theologian does not have the luxury or obligation to serve as a mere ventriloquist for older voices. Our language must be our own, however much it has been influenced by the images or ideas of the past.

And so let me try to articulate something of my own theology of nature and speak in my own voice. As you will hear, it is formulated as a narrative that tries to speak theologically in the way one might write poetically—within a stream of language and imagery that formulates an attitude and orientation to the world. The endeavor is specifically Jewish because my world and language and the core of my commitments are all Jewish. The classics of the tradition condition my sensibilities, inspiring exegetical possibilities that ring true in my soul. Thus, my subjectivity is at once shaped by the past and by the present, and the interpretative entanglements that emerge are the mixed weave of traditional and contemporary concerns. I cannot ignore either—and they spring to mind as the complex literary canon of my inner world.

But this meditation is no exercise in theological exegesis for its own sake. Nor do I care to provide a contribution to historical theology by connecting my thoughts to earlier opinions through argument or justification. Many voices have enriched my own, but the hour does not demand sorting out the strains. The task is rather to recover a voice for theology—and that means speaking directly. The need is not for footnotes to earlier speakers, but to speak in such a way that my words are a proof to the texture of my own thoughts about God and what we commonly call the natural world. Just this is in fact the larger framework of my discourse, because I am convinced that theologizing on this subject must take in more than trees and animals or their ecological balance. A modern Jewish theology of nature must, I believe, include the creation as a whole, and the place of our being within the divine scheme of things—as we may imagine it through thought, through tradition, and through experience. In what follows I shall briefly try to talk my way into such a framework.

As I understand and experience it, the world is the pulsing, indivisible expression of God's breath as it takes shape and form. This is its fullness and foundation. As an extension and as a vitalization of divine Being, such a primordial articulation is an Oral Torah.[1] Call this creative dimension spirit, if you wish, or perhaps even a hovering, brooding breath that is as it is and shall be through its own godly nature. All that we know and experience in the world thus comes from God and is the realization of this *Torah She-be'al Peh*, or Oral Torah, through infinite condensations and configurations, at all levels of organic coherence—be these sensate or otherwise, whether vegetable or mineral, and in all their parasitic and interdependent forms. Were it not for God's breath and its phonetic displacements, so to speak, all this being that we call the natural world would not be. Put differently, God's speaking is the world's fullness, an infinite revelation at the heart of creation. God says of Himself, *'eheyeh 'asher 'eheyeh*: "I shall be as I shall be"—evermore. And in response the creature can only say, *ve-'attah mehayeh 'et kullam*: "Surely You [God] are the enlivener of all Being" (Nehemiah 9:6)—and thereby confesses an entailment in this whole. Thus, on this view, God and the deep Torah of creation (what I have called here the primordial Oral Torah) are one and inseparable, a vast syntax of divine wisdom and vitality embodied in all the structures of existence. There is no gap here between spirit and nature. To the contrary, all that we call nature is but the sensate correlate of God's living breath, his inspiring spirit.

Our human consciousness, however, naturally distorts this divine truth and perceives God's Oral Torah through the forms imprinted on our human senses. In this way the preternatural *Torah She-be'al Peh* (or Oral Torah) is converted by practical reason into a Written Torah, a *Torah She-bi-Khtav*, whose alphabet is constituted by the shapes of earthly existence from the human point of view. It is this Torah that we attempt to read as we parse, name, and interpret the world of experience again and again.

The Written Torah, then, as I understand it here, is the natural world of human perception, thought, and imagination; it is the sensate stuff whose structures scientific rationality seeks to penetrate through experiment and abstraction. This leads to a perceptual paradox; for, on this view the Written Torah is nothing other than the humanly cognizable Oral Torah of God—it is the divine reality as understood and explained by human language. Put more directly, the Oral and Written Torah (of divine being and human cognition) are in truth one and the same Torah; they are two levels of God's truth and worldly reality as we try to formulate this matter theologically. Returning to my earlier metaphor of the brooding breath of God that hovers over the deep, we may say that the Oral Torah is eternally God's breath as it vitalizes being, *ruha be-ruha* ("spirit within spirit"), whereas the Written Torah is this same reality contracted into the vessels of human cognition, language, and experience.

These vessels are thus godly embodiments, or *gufei torah*. They are analytical structures and constructions to be sure; but they are, for all that, true expressions of God's Truth to the extent that we (in however limited and refracted ways) mediate this truth through our human consciousness—which is itself an expression of God's creative Being. God is thus known through His own image in us, by the way we bring this reality to consciousness through our human forms. Tradition has always known this—*mi-besari 'ehezeh 'eloah*, "I shall behold God from my body" (Job 19:26): my natural body and yours is a template for divine reflection. The structures of the human mind constitute the knowable grammar of the world; through the (embodied) human imagination God's eternal Name ("I shall be") is named by the vast lexicon of language.

Let me take this a bit further. Because the Written Torah is God's Truth as revealed to our everyday consciousness, the spirit-breath of divinity that structures all Being is concealed from view—whether this be reality in its gross or its subtle form, a water buffalo or a genetic code. This being so, mind and matter as we know them are both *gufei torah*; they are both part of the Written Torah whose revelation we interpret and whose divinity is hidden. All this is reality dominated by the natural eye, and it is this eye that fosters all the positive perceptions that we know and understand as the natural world. Looking at the world with this eye may evoke wonder, reverence, or even reverie—all the states of the sublime that raise our consciousness to transcendent heights—or it may simply serve as a sensory device useful for driving a car, perceiving puddles, and being able to recognize a friend. The natural eye is thus dominated by subject-object distinctions, by object-object differentiation, and by subject-subject acknowledgments. As a filter for self-identity, the natural eye of a human being also signals the helpful knowledge that the self is neither a turtle nor a tree—however much we may love the fruit of a tree and metabolize it into our very being, or however much we may identify with turtles and work politically to make sure that their mud is up to the highest standards of ecological ooze.

The spiritual eye is different and tries to perceive the world with God's Oral Torah in mind. I shall try not to get too mystagogic here but still make my point. What I mean to indicate is that the spiritual eye tries to transcend the naturally apparent distinctions of our common world and to cultivate a level of consciousness that attends to the unitive divine vitality that informs all Being. This orientation or attitude is of course no denial of the tactile quality of reality that we call nature, but rather an affirmation of the divine quality (called spirit) that shapes and sustains existence along with the perceiving self.

From this theological perspective the world is experienced as the creative spirit of God, realized and perceived in different modes of coherence and form and conceptual embodiments—and is related with this in mind. The implication is that our relations with what is conventionally called the world and nature are transformed. In its attentiveness to the Oral Torah, the theological self tries to be resonant with the divine vitality that gives organization and uniqueness to every person or thing in one's field of consciousness, and the self adjusts its spiritual center to the vitality of its rhythms, in order to enhance the effectiveness of that being (if it is a person) or respect its ecological balance (if it is otherwise, animal, vegetable, or mineral). In this way living unities may be experienced within the living unity God, as the manifestations of God's real presence.

The kind of action I am advocating, then, is one that lives in a precious attentiveness to the multiform character of God's Written Torah (which we commonly designate as the outer physical world) and tries simultaneously to be attuned to the Oral Torah speaking in and through it (what we theologically designate as the inner world of the spirit). This is done at various levels of reflective consciousness, depending upon circumstances and one's spiritual level. The ideal here is a bi-leveled consciousness, a doubling of awareness that is variously poised (as we live our lives) between a sense of the multiplicity of things (as conventionally named and experienced) and the oneness of Being. To eliminate the tension in either direction would numb our sensitivity to God's two-fold Torah—leading to the mindlessness of natural routine, on the one side, or to the mindlessness of nature reveries, on the other.

How then might we establish this rhythm and balance, so that it may do justice to the multiform (and always changing) reality of God's presence in our world? Where is the moral point of balance, which does not dissolve experience into mystical ecstasy but consecrates it as a shape of divine truth? My concern is therefore to find some way of moving from the largely epistemological dimensions of the foregoing discussion to theological reflections that carry the seeds of moral action. Such a moral grounding must lie in our natures as creatures of God in symbiotic relationship with other creatures of the divine Being.

Let me offer the following suggestions, by means of the metaphors of speech and breath evoked earlier as ways of imagining divine creativity. I begin with the role of human speech as a theological act. As persons who receive the images of God's Written Torah—our world—to read, we name its many features and their relations with other things. To the extent that we name things for self-referential and utilitarian purposes only, we ignore the many ways that they exist for their own sake or for integrated perspectives that have nothing to do with us and our consciousness. In order to avoid this danger of moral solipsism, it is necessary to slow down our engagements with the world so that they might be perceived in their godly nature, as *gufei torah*, or worldly configurations originating through divine speech. Halakhic attentiveness is paradigmatic in this regard, for it keeps the world of nature and experience at a human pace for the sake of sanctification or blessing. By such focus we direct our speech to the divine origin of things, and thereby allow our consciousness (or spiritual eye) to be elevated beyond the diversity of natural phenomena to their divine ground. Moreover, inasmuch as God's life-giving speech always transcends a naming in our natural sense, human speech in the context of prayer and sanctification may equally recognize the limits of its own assertions. Natural language is thus humbled through awareness of God's preternatural speech. The psalmist cryptically captures this point when he says, *'ein 'omer ve-'ein devarim beli nishma qolam* (Psalm 19:4). For present purposes I interpret this paradox to mean that there is no expression of reality that does not also reveal the speech of God to those who are attentive.

Breath is another God-given way to attend to the Oral Torah concealed within its Written expressions. What I have in mind here is the added challenge of attuning ourselves to the rhythms of other persons and things by adjusting our breathing patterns to them and their way of being. In this way we may help make the hidden Oral Torah more manifest. For example, through diverse physiological and emotional alignments we may hope to establish some connection with the seasonal patterns, ecosystems, or human beings on their own terms. Respect for the phenomena at the natural level is an opening to their hidden divine truth. Put differently, the spiritual goal is to adjust our breath to the divine nature of things in order to sense the reality of the Oral Torah within the Written Torah of the world. Such an orientation may remind us that God's Oral Torah exceeds and informs the natural world that we read and name and manipulate every day.

I had thought to end my theological reflections on this point, or even to conclude with a final statement about trying to keep the Oral and Written Torahs simultaneously in mind—to the degree possible. But a disturbing memoir that I recently read has chastened me and the easy intimacy with nature that might be inferred from my remarks. To be sure, I tried not to overlook the otherness of nature in my earlier comments when I spoke allusively of its different levels of coherence and complexity. But I did not look this otherness squarely in the eye; and so, lest we think only about the marvels and mysteries of nature, let me correct the balance and say it out plainly. Nature is not all redwoods and salmon streams, and its dangers come not only from spray cans and cigarette butts. Nature is also red in tooth and claw—including animals and people and genetic diseases; and it is also full of gaping horrors—causing its species to die of hunger and cold and warfare. Make no mistake: this too is God's Written Torah, which we try to affirm and change at the same time. Moral and medical action are also attempts to align our consciousness to the reality before us and, in the interests of love and life, to repair the broken vessels of the world. This impulse leads to all the ameliorative acts of science, but also to its Faustian drive. I need not remind any of us at the beginning of this century about the dangers and turmoil that lie ahead, as we try to assess just when ameliorative acts serve God's redemption and when they may lead to damnation.

It is to be hoped that some sense of the Oral Torah (as I have portrayed it) can check our drives, through the realization that God's truth can never be comprehended from the outside. And where this restraint does not work (and even where it does), perhaps law is the best or last handmaiden of theology and prudence.

Note

1. In this essay I employ the rabbinic categories of Written and Oral Torah (meaning Scripture and Tradition) and adapt them for new ends—even inverting their historical relationship.

The Human Condition: Origins, Pollution, and Death

The Ecology of Eden

EVAN EISENBERG

Two ways of looking at the world arose in the ancient Near East and are with us yet. For one, the heart of the world is wilderness. For the other, the world revolves around the city, the work of human hands.

A cartographer's quibble? Hardly. It is a fundamental dispute about the way the world works and what our role in it should be. From the point of view of ecology, there is no more important question one can ask about a civilization than which of these views it adopts and acts on. Indeed, the prospects of our own civilization may hinge on whether we can, at this late date, change our minds.

The two great worldviews I am speaking of belonged to two kinds of civilization: those of the hilly uplands and those of the great river valleys.[1] The first kind is typified by the Canaanites, the second by the Mesopotamians. The peoples of the hills, narrow valleys, and narrow coastal plains made their living from small-scale mixed husbandry. This was a much refined but still modest descendent of the earliest farming known, which had arisen in those same hills. The peoples of the great river valleys were more ambitious. They practiced large-scale, irrigated agriculture that was not so different, at heart, from what large corporations do in California today.

Tied to these different ways of living on the land were different economies, different social structures, different political forms, and different ways of looking at the world. Above all, the hill peoples and the valley peoples had different world-poles.[2]

The world-pole is the axis on which the world turns. It is the heart of the world, the source of all life. Nearly every people has a world-pole, but they do not all agree on its shape. For the Canaanites, the world-pole was the Mountain: the wild place sacred to the gods, the font of life-giving water. For the Mesopotamians, it was the Tower: the ziggurat that rose in the midst of the city.

The World-Pole

If there is one thing all cosmogonies agree on, it is the need for division. Pine as they may for a time of perfect oneness, all peoples know that a world undivided cannot stand. For life to feed and reproduce itself, there must be division: between heaven and earth, male and female, man and beast and god. But for life to flourish—and on this point, too, all cosmogonies agree—there must be some place where all these things are reconnected. That is the world-pole.

On the exact shape the world-pole must take there is less agreement, yet more than one might expect. Hindu texts tell of a mountain at the center of the earth called Meru, on which stands a tree called Jambu. Its fruits are as big as elephants. When they fall and splatter, their juice becomes the stream Jambunadi, drinking from which makes one proof against old age, vice, and body odor. Among the Buddhist Kalmucks of Siberia, Meru becomes Sumeru, a vast pyramidal mountain rising from the cosmic ocean. It sits on a sunken cushion of gold, which in turn sits on a tortoise. The cannibals of West Ceram, an island near New Guinea, say that the nine families of humankind emerged from the banana trees of Mount Nunusaku. The Norse Eddas sing of the great ash tree Yggdrasil on whose trunk the heavens spin and whose roots clutch the netherworld. The tree is a hive of activity: a great eagle perches on its crown, four stags romp and browse in its branches, a great serpent gnaws on its roots, and honeydew trickles from its bark. In the Zoroastrian Avesta, a mountain called Hara stands at the center of the world. From its peak flow all the world's waters, which course through the sea Vourukasha and water the seven regions of the world. Purified by the earth, they rise to the peak of Hara and start the cycle again.[3]

What do all these places have in common?

As a rule, the world-pole is the source of life. Although I have used "world-pole" because it is plainer than Eliade's *axis mundi*, I would almost rather say "world-pipe," for the act of connecting heaven and earth would be meaningless if stuff could not move from one to the other. Like the trunk of a tree, the world-pole is something through which life flows. It is at once phallus and vulva, ram's horn and cornucopia. It is the uterus from which all creatures crawled and the teat from which they continue to suck. If a man or woman—a shaman, a hero, a prophet—would ascend to the heavens or descend to the underworld, here is the stairwell. Here the adept can powwow with gods and animals, even merge with them, as all of us used to do at the beginning of time.

The Canaanites

The fact that Canaan—the region now occupied by Israel, Lebanon, and Syria—contains the lowest dry land on the planet (the shore of the Dead Sea), as well as deserts, coastal plains, and steppe, only makes its great mountains the more imposing.[4] The ranges of Persia and Anatolia sprawl for so many hundreds of miles that it is hard for any one peak to seem a World Mountain; but the Lebanon, Anti-Lebanon, and Amanus ranges are so compact that they were spoken of in ancient times almost as if they were monadnocks.[5] The Lebanon and Anti-Lebanon ranges reach heights of 10,131 and 9,232 feet, respectively, the Amanus of 7,418 feet. Their splendor was a byword throughout the Near East, as was the price their timber could bring: in particular, the huge ancient cedars that grew on the upper western slope of the Lebanon.

It is no surprise, then, that in Canaanite poetry both the elder god El and the younger god Baal have their houses or tents on mountaintops. For that matter, so does Baal's sister and bride, the goddess Anat. The Mountain of El is preeminent, being the place where the gods meet in council, to dine and haggle, and the fate of the universe is decreed. El lives at "the source of the Two Rivers, in the midst of the Pools of the Double-Deep."[6] (The last phrase can also be rendered "headwaters of the Two Oceans" and may refer to the male ocean of the heavens and the female ocean that undergirds the earth.) From El's mountain flow the waters that bring life to the world. It is proof of his power that he has broken and yoked the primal waters and that, instead of breaking out and swamping the world, they run dutifully in two rivers that give the world life. El does not merely sit by the waters like a poet; he sits on them, keeps a lid on them, and ladles them out.

Nevertheless, by the time of the great Ugaritic epics the waterworks
are being handed over in part to a younger and abler god, El's son
Baal. Baal's mountain is called Mount Zaphon (or Sapanu), from a
root meaning "to look out" or "spy out."[7] That it is a place where heaven
and earth fruitfully meet is hinted at in a message he sends to Anat:

> Pour out peace in the depths of the earth,
> Make love increase in the depths of the fields. . . .
> The speech of wood and the whisper of stone,
> The converse of heaven with the earth,
> Of the deeps with the stars . . .
> Come, and I will seek it,
> In the midst of my mountain, divine Zaphon. . . .[8]

Whether the "speech of wood and the whisper of stone" refers, as
some think, to the palace or temple which Baal plans to build on his
mountain, or rather to the wooded mass of the mountain itself, the role
of Zaphon as world-pole is clear. In his message, Baal calls Anat to his
side. The flow of love and fertility will be clinched, it seems, by a
sacred marriage between Baal and Anat—icing on the cake of his victory and enthronement on Zaphon.[9]

The World-Pole as Ecological Fact

To say that the world-pole is a mountain is to state, in mythic shorthand, an ecological fact.[10] There are certain places on earth that play a
central role in the flow of energy and the cycling of water and nutrients, as well as the maintenance of genetic diversity and its spread by
means of gene flow. Such places provide many of the services that
keep the ecosystems around them (and the biosphere as a whole) more
or less healthy for humans and other life-forms. They help control
flooding and soil erosion. They regulate the mix of oxygen, carbon
dioxide, water vapor, and other ingredients in the air and keep its temperature within bounds. They are spigots for the circulation of wildness through regions made hard and almost impermeable by long human use. All such places are more or less wild; many are forested;
many are mountainous, and from them great rivers flow.

The mountains of Lebanon, Syria, and Armenia are the source of
water for much of the Near East. From their slopes flow the headwa-

ters of the Jordan, the Orontes, the Tigris, and the Euphrates. The pattern is copied on smaller scales as well, in the brooks, wadis, and underground aquifers that slide from the Judean hills to the coast.

Canaan as a whole, situated at the junction of three continents, has always been a maelstrom of gene flow. Even today, its genetic diversity is dazzling, with flora and fauna of Europe, Africa, and Asia mingling in sometimes unsettling ways. A few thousand years ago, when the region was less bruised by human use, the mix was more dazzling still.[11]

In this matter, too, the uplands have played a special role. During the Pleistocene Ice Age, when the locking up of water in glaciers made the earth as a whole drier and much of the Near East was arid steppe, the mountains gave refuge to species in flight from drought.[12] Among these species were humans, as well as some of the trees, grasses, and quadrupeds they would later tame. It was the expansion of these species, at the end of the last ice age, from their mountain hideouts to the lower foothills of the Levant that set the stage for domestication.

It was also the slopes themselves. For the play of farming to get started, it was helpful that the stage be slanted. On hillsides, a wide range of climates can be collapsed accordion-like within the space of a few acres. This produces a menu of variation in wild plants that fairly begs humans to pick and choose: that is, to select. It also encourages transhumance.

Transhumance, the practice of herding livestock to summer pasture in the hills, then back to the valley for the winter—or the other way around in some dry regions—can be seen as a telescoped form of nomadism. (That is not to say it arose later than nomadism; more likely it came first.) It is made possible by Humboldt's Law, which states that climbing a one-hundred-meter hill yields roughly the same drop in temperature as trekking 110 kilometers (one degree of latitude) away from the equator.

Giving hard-earned grain to animals is a late and luxurious practice. The first domestic animals had to fend for themselves. Their wild forebears had followed the grass, the brush, and the seasons. If more or less settled farmers were able to keep them, it was only because those farmers lived in the hills, where the seasons crept up and down the slopes instead of (or as well as) gliding hundreds of miles north and south.

The same piece of legislation made the hilly flanks of the Fertile Crescent the ideal place for the domestication of grains. Variations in elevation produce variations in climate, which produce variations in plants; these in turn provide the raw material for breeding. Emmer, einkorn, and six-row barley were lining up along isotherms (lines of equal temperature) long before they were lined up by farmers. In effect, natural selection had set out upon the tablelands and in the bowl-like valleys of the Near East a smorgasbord from which human selection could take its pick. So the uplands of the Levant were the ideal setting for the domestication of plants and animals alike.

Myths of the world-pole say that the source of the first human life will be the source that sustains human life. It is a paradox that a wild or sparsely settled place should seem to be the point of origin of humankind, that is, Eden. But, in fact, Holocene humans do seem to have come out of the uplands of the Near East, descended into the valleys to build civilization, then edged up the hills again as their numbers swelled. Outside Africa, anatomically modern humans make their first clear appearance in the archaeological record in the uplands of the Levant, in roughly the same place as the first protofarmers. Some ninety thousand years ago, while Neanderthals had the run of Europe, *Homo sapiens* dwelt in the caves of Mount Carmel.[13]

The Mountain was thus the source of one great wave of human advance—farming—and at least the proximate source of an earlier wave, made up of the first creatures whom, if they sat down next to us at a luncheon counter in modern dress, we would not hesitate to ask to pass the ketchup.

The real lesson of the Mountain, though, has nothing to do with any particular mountains, or even with mountains as such. It has to do with wilderness.

The point is that man-made landscapes, from the wheat fields and vineyards of ancient Canaan to the strip malls of New Jersey, survive only by the courtesy of the wilderness around them, and the wildness that remains in them. Energy flows, water and nutrients circulate, climate is kept within bounds, the ingredients of the air are kept in balance, the soil is made fertile. All these things are matters of life and death for us. All are done for us free of charge, in ways we do not fully grasp. Even if we knew how these jobs are done, we would be unwise to try and take them over. For we would then spend most of our time trying desperately to manage what used to be managed for us.

As the postmodernists never tire of telling us, wilderness is a myth. What they fail to tell us, because they do not comprehend it, is that it is a necessary myth—necessary because, on a biological level that mutely resists deconstruction, it is deeply and urgently real.

True: few wildernesses are certifiably pure. True: all wilderness has a history, in which humans have generally played a part. True: the idea of wilderness has been used as an excuse for elitism, imperialism, and sheer complacency. But the trendy debunking of wilderness may breed even greater mischief. Advanced in the name of the people, it has been seized upon by corporate and political elements whose only interest in people or nature is to squeeze them dry. Even in the best hands, it leads us toward a slippery slope whose final declension we cannot measure.

Wilderness is a social construction. So is the guardrail at the edge of a precipice: and I would not gladly see either dismantled.

The Mesopotamians

When farmers first wandered down from the hills of Iran or the Syrian steppe, or wandered up the shore of the Persian Gulf, and gazed on the vast floodplain of the two rivers, they must have been intrigued but not altogether pleased.[14] They knew that rivers were arteries of life, and here were the two biggest rivers they had ever seen. Yet the land before them was no well-watered paradise, but a patchwork of swamp and desert. Swept in summer by a wind like the blowback of a kiln, the dunes shifted irritably under a sparse cover of artemisia (a cousin of sagebrush) and other shrubs, while the remnants of the spring annuals dried up and blew away. What was a farmer to make of this? His wheat and barley would not tolerate either the wet or the dry. His livestock would founder in the marshes or go thirsty among the dunes.

The first signs of permanent settlement on the floodplain date to the sixth millennium B.C.E. Two thousand years later—the length of an afternoon nap in prehistory—Mesopotamia was a paradise. It was a man-made paradise, a thing without precedent on earth. Although there were still marshes in the south, and plenty of semidesert in which seminomads as well as villagers and cityfolk grazed their herds, a wide tract of land on either side of the Euphrates was generously spangled with grain fields, date plantations, fish ponds, and gardens of lettuce, onions, lentils, garlic, and cress.[15] Cities of sun-baked or kiln-baked mud brick sprawled like lions amid these spoils, outwardly reposeful but inwardly (like the lion of Samson's riddle) buzzing.

The magnitude of this achievement can stun us even now if we stop to think about it. These people—the Sumerians and their predecessors in the region, the Ubaidians—gave us wheeled vehicles, yokes and harnesses so that animals could pull them, animal-drawn plows, sailboats, metalworking (casting, riveting, brazing, soldering, inlay, and engraving in copper and bronze), the potter's wheel, the arch, the vault, the dome, surveying, mapping, and a rough-and-ready mathematics. Above all, they gave us the process in which you and I are now engaged, even if we no longer use hen's-foot marks on soft clay. On the debit side of the ledger (another Sumerian invention), we might place large professional armies, siege engines, war chariots, a rigid division of labor and status, imperialism, and bureaucracy.[16]

All this is the more remarkable in that hardly any of the raw materials of civilization, apart from the clay to make bricks and tablets, was to be found in the place where civilization began. Metal, wood, stone, and other things needful the Mesopotamians got in exchange for their agricultural surplus and the finished products of their craftsmanship. (By "Mesopotamians" I mean all the civilized peoples who lived in the valley of the Tigris and Euphrates in ancient times: in chronological order, the Sumerians, the Akkadians, and the Babylonians. For the most part they were the same people under different rulers.)

What made it all possible was a series of trenches running alongside the rivers in a pattern like a chain, or like the braids of a young girl.[17] (Later the pattern would be dendritic, sharing the efficient layout of a tree's branching or a leaf's veins.) The sandy soil, with its patchy drainage, had made a mess of the job of distributing the groundwater that seeped from the riverbeds. The canals took over that job. What had looked like desert now proved to be soil far richer than anything wheat or barley had known in their native hills.

In a sense, though, this *was* the soil they had known in their native hills. Each winter for millennia, the rains had gouged the hillsides of Syria and Anatolia. In recent millennia the gouging had been especially cruel, egged on by axes and hoes. Periodic floods had spread the deducted soil over the Mesopotamian plain. Wheat, barley, and humans followed the soil downstream.

But the floods had not spread the soil evenly. When the rivers over-flowed their banks, they dropped coarse particles first, fine particles last. As the rivers wound, unwound, and changed their courses, they laid down a patchwork of coarse and fine soils: the former draining too quickly, the latter too slowly. So the humans who now showed up to claim the humus they had lost found it less immediately usable than they might have hoped. The answer was irrigation.

In Sumerian a single word denotes both rivers and canals. Both were supposed to be the work of the gods, which humans merely maintained. Many ostensible canals were in fact natural channels in which the Euphrates had sometimes run. Unlike the Tigris, whose short course and swift current let it cut a deeper and straighter path, the Euphrates—sluggish as a pasha, and luxuriously indecisive—would flow now here, now there, now both ways at once. As it dropped sediment it made its bed ever higher, like a princess piling up mattresses. In fact, it flowed above the surface of the plain and was kept from overflowing only by the natural levee it built up on either side. But then at some point it would break through the levee and find a new channel. So the river took on a braided look. Although the first settlers on the plain had some experience of small-scale irrigation, by and large they took their cue from the river itself. Some canals were made by adapting the existing side channels, others by mimicking the process by which they were formed.

The Tower of Babel

At the heart of every Mesopotamian city was a sacred precinct, and at the heart of every sacred precinct was a ziggurat, a stepped pyramid of mud brick.[18] Unimposing by our standards—the great ziggurat of Ur was about seventy feet high—they were by far the tallest objects, natural or man-made, to be found on the Mesopotamian plain. Oddly, some ziggurats seem to have imitated mountains in a fairly literal way. One of the first, in Uruk, stood on an artificial hill about forty feet high. Although in most later temples the hill was replaced by a platform, the tower itself was often called a "cedar-scented moun-tain." It is not clear whether this was a bare-faced metaphor or whether some planting was done to buttress the claim. Most likely cedar and cypress oils were used as air fresheners within the temple.

In the reborn Babylon of the sixth century B.C.E., the fabled Hanging Gardens were planted in the steps or terraces of a ziggurat. Legend has it that Nebuchadnezzar planted them for his Persian bride, who pined for the hills of Ecbatana.[19]

Every great temple claimed to stand on the *axis mundi*, or elevator shaft of the cosmos, offering the gods a way station between the upper and lower worlds. The creation epic *Enuma Elish* assigns to Babylon the role of divine motel and convention center, a role that seems to have been competed for and claimed by other cities at other times.[20] For the Mesopotamian gods are city slickers. If one or another has his or her "throne-seat" or "abode" on the Cedar Mountain, it is evidently used for ceremonial purposes, or as a summer place. Compared to the city the countryside is godforsaken.

It is a sign of the Mesopotamians' pride that they drew the gods—and paradise itself—down from the mountains and into their own cities. If the source of life is upstream, downstream is where the fat collects: the rich bottomlands, the canals, the cities, the good life. While the mountains may give life, in these matters it is better to receive.

In preferring the plain to the hills, the river valley to the headwaters as a place to lay out fields and build cities—in noting that the fat collects downstream—the Mesopotamians had a point. They were in fact recipients of the hills' largesse. Their mistake was to forget that fact.

Giddy with prosperity and progress, they came to think they had done it all themselves. Instead of recipients, they came to think of themselves as the source of life and plenty. They controlled the waters, tapped the great rivers like kegs of beer. It was easy to forget that the water came from somewhere. They had agriculture down to a science. It was easy to forget that it had arisen among the savages of the hills. The storehouses spat out grain; the markets were littered with dates and slippery with oil. Surely the city was the source of all life.[21]

One can hardly blame the Mesopotamians for wanting a world-pole closer to home than the distant and (to most of them) invisible mountains. They might have chosen some flatter, but still natural, world-pole to match the world they knew. They might have embedded the gods in the rivers, or in the salt marshes at the rivers' mouths, which were great dispensaries of wildness and of natural wealth. Maybe they did, at first: Enki, for instance, seems to have spent a lot of time among the canebrakes. But by historical times Enki, like the other great gods, is safely installed in a city.

For some peoples, religious feeling is the feeling that some things are beyond society's control, that the sources of good and bad are unplumbable and can easily drown the flimsy channels we make to contain them. For others, the man-made order is so firmly established that it seems god-made. Awe is stripped from nature and affixed to the social and technical order. On the whole, the Canaanites were a culture of the first type, the Mesopotamians of the second.[22]

Today, southern Mesopotamia is once again the patchwork of swamp and desert it was when the first settlers arrived. The main difference (apart from the fact that the wildlife is gone) is that much of the soil is no longer even potentially fertile.

In arid climates, the groundwater is often brackish. As long as it stays below the level to which the roots of crops penetrate, it is no problem; but when a field has been used for a while, irrigation without proper drainage can raise the water table. Crops can filter out some of the salt when they drink, but in so doing they make the remaining water that much saltier. Eventually it catches up with them. Falling yields are the first sign of trouble. Then, when the saline groundwater has nudged within a few feet of the surface, capillary action starts to lift it the rest of the way. At the surface the water evaporates while the salt "blossoms out in mockingly beautiful floral patterns."[23] The Mesopotamian idea that a spiteful Tiamat was rising up was not far wrong.

Having a general sense of what the problem was, farmers would fallow a field or else try to flush out the salts with more water. Fallowing might work for a while, because salt-tolerant weeds would move in, suck up some water, and lower the water table. Flushing would work very briefly and then backfire, by raising the water table and with it the salt.

Among the many favors that pots do for archaeologists is to retain, under certain conditions, marks of the kernels of grain that were stored in them. Pots dug up in southern Mesopotamia suggest that from 3500 B.C.E. onward the ratio of wheat to barley in the harvest steadily shrank.[24] By 1700, no wheat was grown at all. In an age before advertising, tastes in food were very stable, so, barring a major rise in beer consumption, it seems likely that the shift to barley was a matter of necessity rather than choice. One factor may have been the growing importance of wool textiles for export, which meant that more barley had to be grown for fodder. But the evidence points to a necessity a good deal more dire.

As befits a poor cousin, barley is on the whole less finicky than wheat about where and how it grows. In particular, it is far more tolerant of salt. Given the crust of salt that covers so much of Mesopotamia today, and the half-comprehending references to the problem that can be found in ancient texts, it has been suggested that salt must have caused failures of the wheat crop, forcing a shift to barley.[25] Estate records from the period show a steady decline in yields of wheat and a lesser but vexing drop in yields of barley. As the soil turned to salt, the economic base of Sumer fissured and slowly crumbled. This helped make it vulnerable to the growing power of its northern neighbor, Akkad.

In modern times, farmers north of Baghdad grow nine times as much wheat as barley, while farmers near the Gulf grow nine times as much barley as wheat. For both crops, yields are far lower than they were in ancient times.

No one can say "I told you so" to the Mesopotamians. No one told them so. What they did was done for the first time on earth. It seemed a good idea at the time, and in many ways it was. Then the edge of civilization moved on, leaving a desert behind it.[26]

The Hill Farmers

There were, I said, two broad types of culture in the ancient Near East, broadly matched to two types of agriculture: that of the irrigated river valleys and that of the hills. The first is typified by the Mesopotamians, the second by the Canaanites, *including the Israelites.*

Let us not be deceived by the Bible's polemics against the Canaanites. As anyone who follows radical politics knows, the sharpest barbs are always reserved for those closest to one's own position: the group one schism away. In ecological terms, it's the species one has just split off from that one must compete with for a niche.

The more we know about the Israelites, the clearer it is that they were Canaanite hill farmers who practiced a sophisticated and fairly sustainable mixed husbandry of grains, vines, livestock, and trees yielding fruit, nuts, and oil.[27] They were neither desert nomads mistrustful of nature, nor proud hydraulic despots lording it over nature. They were good farmers living frugally on the margins and using the best stewardship they knew. They were dependent on rain and groundwater, neither of which was overabundant, and on thin and rock-strewn soil, and had to use their wits to conserve both. They were not so different from present-day farmers of the Andes or of Szechwan. They were not so different, perhaps, from other peasants of the Mediterranean basin, past and present.

When archaeology first finds the Israelites—about 1100 B.C.E.—they are pioneers in the hills of Judea and Samaria, part of the central range that runs like a spine down the length of Canaan (its Apennines, one might say). There is no evidence that this pioneering was prelude to a "conquest" of the valleys and the coastal plain ("destruction layers" of ash and debris are mostly absent from the relevant strata of the Canaanite sites mentioned in the Bible). Nor is there much evidence of a flight from Egypt. Yet it is true that these settlers had just escaped the pharaoh's yoke. They were not so much settling as resettling the uplands, which had been depopulated during the four centuries when Egyptian rule ravaged Canaan.

Having known both the axe and the torch in earlier times, and getting at the best of times only modest rainfall, the hills of Judea and Samaria were not clothed in what we would call "forest primeval." Where least disturbed, the landscape was the sort of open Mediterranean woodland known as high maquis, with evergreen oak, Aleppo pine, and pistachio (known in the Bible as terebinth) the most common trees. Elsewhere this would dwindle to low maquis, a mix of shrubs and herbs such as rosemary, sage, summer savory, rock rose, and thorny burnet. The settlers cleared a good deal of this forest for pasture and cropland, knowing that beneath lay the red soil now called *terra rossa*, the richest of all mountain soils. (In Hebrew the words for "earth," "human," "red," and "blood" sound alike and may have a common derivation.) Of this process the Book of Joshua (17:14–15) preserves a hint:

> And the children of Joseph spoke unto Joshua, saying: "Why has thou given me but one lot and one part for an inheritance, seeing I am a great people, forasmuch as the Lord hath blessed me thus?" And Joshua said unto them, "If thou be a great people, get thee up to the forest, and cut down for thyself there in the land of the Perizzites and of the Rephaim; since the hill-country of Ephraim is too narrow for thee."

This new round of deforestation promised to be the worst yet. Besides the usual sheep and shoot-nibbling goats, these settlers had big animal-drawn plows with bronze shares, a loan from Mesopotamia.[28] Although still only scratch plows, which did not turn the soil upside-down as mold-board plows do, these could still be lethal to the soil of any slope steeper than a wheelchair-accessible entrance ramp. The red soil was rich but rarely more than a foot deep.

As the slopes began to lose their thin layer of rich red soil—and as population growth made land dearer and labor somewhat more plentiful—the Israelites began to build terraces. Whether this was their own invention is unclear; a word appearing in the Ugaritic epics may refer to the same device. Either way, there is a good chance that some group or other of Canaanites came up with the idea. As the first farmers of the Mediterranean basin, they devised many of the methods that its peasants use to this day.

To make a terrace was no small matter. Remaking a ramp as a series of steps meant moving a lot of earth and rock, though the naturally blocky karst limestone of some regions helped somewhat. (Today, in the vicinity of Jerusalem it is hard to tell offhand whether a particular hill got its staircase shape from ancient man or ancient nature.) Pillars made of large boulders would be erected and the gaps between filled in with smaller stones. Behind these walls, it would not do just to pile up dirt any which way. Above the bedrock would be a layer of soil, on top of that a layer of gravel, and on top of the gravel another layer of soil. In this way water would percolate from one terrace to the next one down. Some of the soil in the terraces seems to have been hauled up from the valley floor, perhaps because erosion was already well along.

For all this effort the farmer got a number of benefits. He got a nice, nearly level surface to plow with his ox and his ard. He got the soil to stay put, at least for a while. And he got rainwater to tarry far longer than it would usually care to do on a denuded slope. (The same could be done with spring water: in Roman times, if not earlier, a system of channels might distribute the water of a spring near the top of a hill among the terraces below.)

This last was the main reason he took the trouble, for water is the limiting factor in almost all farming in the Near East. Another way he tried to control this variable was by catching runoff from the rains in cisterns dug in the bedrock. To make the limestone watertight, he cemented the pits with lime: another technique that the Israelites or Canaanites may have pioneered. Evidently it worked, for the Mishnah

(Avot 2.11) compares the prodigious memory of Rabbi Eliezer ben Hyrcanus to "a cemented cistern, which loses not a drop."[29]

In general, the way the hill farmers dealt with the whims and capers of nature was by hedging their bets. While they did not exactly have hedges they did have plenty of borders between plots of different crops. The hills were full of nooks and crannies, of microclimates and microenvironments. As their natural flora and fauna were diverse, so (up to a point) were the flora and fauna the settlers put in their place. A single household might have fields of wheat and barley as well as lentils, peas, and other legumes; a vineyard enclosed by a wall of thorns or of stone, with the vines trailing on the ground or trained to form arbors; and orchards of fig, apricot, almond, and pomegranate. Any patch of hillside that was left would be planted with olive trees, whose fruit was not eaten (the art of curing being unknown) but pressed for the oil used in cooking, lighting, and grooming. A household would also have herds of sheep, goats, and cattle that would winter in dry areas, grazing on rain-primed seasonal growth, or in the upper hills, where they would help to degrade the maquis to the lower and sparser mix of shrubs and herbs known as garigue. In summer the livestock would stay closer to the village, nibbling on stubble and fallow weeds and paying the check with manure.

Nor was husbandry the only source of food. The women might forage for pistachios, acorns, herbs, and other wild foods, the men hunt the gazelles and wild goats that still roamed the hills. To the hearers of the legends from this period collected in the Book of Judges, it apparently did not seem odd that Samson should run into a lion among the vineyards (14:5). Even the poet of Canticles, who lived some centuries later, knew a world in which wild and man-made mingled, not least in the imagery of the human body itself.

When I say that a single household might do all these things, I mean a *bet av*, an extended family of perhaps ten to thirty persons led by a patriarch and living in a cluster of stone or mud-brick dwellings.[30] Such a household shielded itself from nature's whims by sharing labor (at harvest, for instance) and food (at times of scarcity) with an even more extended family called a *mishpahah*, a kind of clan or tribe that might take the form of a village. (What is called a tribe in the Bible was a still more fluid grouping in which political allegiance was thicker than blood.) The command to "be fruitful and multiply" (Genesis 1:28), while common to most farming peoples, must have had double force in this frontier setting, where two new hands added far more food than one new mouth subtracted.

Land seems to have been held communally within the *mishpahah*, at least in the sense that a piece of land, even if "sold" to an outsider, would eventually revert to the clan. In contrast to the plantations that sprawled across the great river valleys of the Near East, the hills nurtured a world of small holdings, painstakingly husbanded. When in a larger Israel the royal houses and others began to amass great estates, the prophets were outraged: "Woe unto them that join house to house, that lay field to field . . ." (Isaiah 5:8).

In this respect the Israelites out-Canaanized the Canaanites, who were somewhat more prone to plantation farming and cash-cropping. The Phoenicians (as the Canaanites came to be called when, squeezed by Israelites on one flank and Philistines on the other, they bunched up in the cities of the Syrian coast and increasingly took to the sea) were both crackerjack farmers and peerless merchants. Though it is hard to know which role came first, farm produce—in particular, olive oil and wine—was among their primary wares. (This became true of the Israelites during the monarchy, when the kings wanted cash crops for export.)

To the Canaanites the ancient world owed not only the alphabet and the art of seafaring, but much of its agricultural science as well. The bible of ancient farming was the work of a descendent of Canaanites, Mago of Carthage. Even the Romans, who were not likely to overpraise a Carthaginian, acknowledged Mago as the father of agricultural knowledge. The twenty-eight books of his treatise were translated from Punic into Latin by order of the Roman senate; though lost, they left their traces in passages cribbed by Pliny, Varro, and Columella. The farm belt of North Africa remained fertile as long as the Carthaginians were in charge. It was the Romans who ran it into the ground.

Mount Eden

Being Canaanites—if Canaanites of a rather peculiar sort—the children of Israel might be expected to have some notion of a World Mountain. So they did. It took several forms, some of which we will deal with later; but foremost among them was Eden.[31]

Today, it is not common to think of Eden as a mountain. But in earlier times—from at least the sixth century B.C.E., when Ezekiel prophesied, to the seventeenth century C.E., when Milton wrote *Paradise Lost*—it was very common.

Although the Bible never specifies Eden's elevation, the fact that it is the source of four great rivers speaks for itself. Armed with the knowledge that water does not flow uphill, scholars from Philo's time to the present have placed Eden in the mountains of Armenia, or in other mountains vaguely north of Mesopotamia.[32]

These same mountains are vaguely north of Canaan, too. The Tigris and Euphrates arise in the mountains of Turkish Armenia. While the Tigris runs straight into Mesopotamia, the lordly Euphrates adopts a more leisured route, taking in the sights and waters of eastern Syria. Some affluents of the Upper Euphrates start within seventy kilometers—a god's spitting range—of the Amanus mountains. The closest thing in Canaan to what we would call a river, the Jordan, has its ultimate source in the mountains of Syria.

No wonder, then, that the peoples of the Fertile Crescent shared a firm if somewhat cloudy feeling that life flowed from the north. (As great dams go up, that feeling gets less cloudy and more anxious. An open secret of Near Eastern politics—closed until recently to the publics of the West—is the fact that many struggles in the region, from the fight over the Golan Heights and West Bank to the tussles between Syria, Iraq, and Turkey, have less to do with oil or blood than with water.)[33]

To be the Mountain, it is not enough to be a mountain. But Eden has other qualifications. It is the source of life, in several ways. First, it is the source of water not only for the Near East, but for the known world. That is the import of the four rivers, two real and two mythic (or semimythic), whose hydrologically improbable courses extend to the ends of the earth. Two of these are labeled clearly as the Tigris and the Euphrates; the other two are identified by the rabbis with the Nile and the Ganges.[34] The two rivers that run from El's mountain have been doubled—perhaps under Mesopotamian influence, perhaps in sheer one-upsmanship—so that they may reach and refresh the very corners of the world, dividing it neatly in four quarters.

Like many world-poles, Eden crowns its mountain with a Tree of Life. According to the Midrash (*Bereshit Rabbah* 15.6), this means "a tree that spread its canopy over all living things. . . . All the primeval waters branched out beneath it." To walk around its trunk would take a man five hundred years.[35]

Eden is the source of life in another sense, too. It is the navel of the world—the first home of all creatures, both human and nonhuman. It is even a home of sorts for God, who walks in the garden in the cool of the day. But while God and plants and animals get to stay in Eden, humans get the boot. And this, too, is a hint that what we are dealing with is nothing less than the Mountain of God.

The Fiery Sword

The failure of the author of the Eden story to mention that the garden was on a mountain makes one wonder what else got left on the cutting-room floor. Two passages from Ezekiel give some bright if jagged clues. One is a parable against the king of Tyre:

> Thus saith the Lord God: Thou seal most accurate, full of wisdom, and perfect in beauty, thou wast in Eden the garden of God; every precious stone was thy covering, the carnelian, the topaz, and the emerald, the beryl, the onyx, and the jasper. . . . I put by thee a towering cherub for protection; and I set thee, so that thou wast upon the holy mountain of God; thou hast walked up and down amidst fiery jewels. Thou wast perfect in thy ways from the day that thou wast created, till unrighteousness was found in thee. By the multitude of thy traffic they filled thee with violence, and thou has sinned; and I have destroyed thee, O covering cherub, from the midst of the stones of fire. (28:12–16)

In the second passage (Ezekiel 31), the king of Egypt is compared to Assyria, which is compared to a cedar in Lebanon, which is compared to the trees of Eden. "All the trees of Eden were jealous, in the Garden of God." Yet this great tree is cast down into the netherworld.

Apart from the clear identification of Eden with the Mountain of God, some scholars have glimpsed here the glittering shards of a lost Hebrew epic of Eden.[36] The Eden story in Genesis gives reason to think such an epic may have existed. Several terms in the narrative carry the definite article at first use—"the tree of life," "the tree of the knowledge of good and bad," "the cherubim and the sword of flame which turned every way"—which in Hebrew is done only if the reader is assumed to be familiar with the thing mentioned.

What that epic might have looked like is anybody's guess. Combining the passages above with the lines from Isaiah (14:9–15) about Halal ben Shahar, "the son of morning," we can assume the action had to do with an angel or god who rebelled against YHWH and was cast down to earth, or into the pit (an easy thing to do from Eden, since the world-pole is the shortest distance between the top and bottom of the world). It is a familiar plot, alluded to in the story (Genesis 6) of the sons of God who descended to earth and married with the daughters of men, and elaborated in the legend of Lucifer. The drama would be played out in a garden of God or of the gods, a divine country club to which earthlings (if they exist yet) need not apply. Some of its trees would be gigantic mountain trees, such as cedars, while others would bear jewels for fruit—both being found in the garden of Siduri, the "barmaid of the gods" who entertained Gilgamesh.[37]

In any case, the moral I want to draw from the lost epic is this: If even gods and angels were cast out of Eden, what chance did humans have of lasting out their term?[38]

Modern scholars tend to picture Eden as a formal garden in the Mesopotamian style, irrigated to a fare-thee-well. While some of the sources of the Eden story may have had that squared-off and strait-laced shape, others were a good deal wilder and woollier. In the Mountain of God, even the Garden of God, we have a vision of paradise as a forested peak—the summa and last resort of wildness in a region chockablock with cities, fields, canals, herds, and armies.[39] While the Hebrew word *gan* usually means an enclosed vegetable garden or fruit orchard, the phrase *gan 'elohim*, "garden of God," seems to be meant as a kind of analogy: just as we might call the prairie "God's lawn," so the ancients saw the wooded mountain as God's private garden.

Such wild places were not paradises for humans, but for gods. They were not meant for humans at all.[40]

The cosmic center is not always thought of as a nice place for humans to live or even to visit. Nevertheless, it is the source of life. "All the world is watered with the dregs of Eden," the Talmud says (*Ta'anit* 10a); and the dregs are as much as it can take. Humans cannot see God's face and live.[41]

If God is the heart of nature, then to say that we cannot stand pure godhead is to say that we cannot stand pure wildness, except in small doses. We can stand (if sometimes just barely) the electric blue of the sky, the buzz of bees, the jolt of sex. Uncut, nature is too much for us. The main lines of wildness make us jumpy—and rightly, for an instantaneous surge can kill.

To think of living in Eden is to deny the primal sundering of heaven and earth, of god and animal and human. The world-pole is the one place where the sundering has not happened, or has been repaired. We must revere it, draw sustenance from it, keep it alive, keep the channels of wildness open. But to think of living in it—why, it's like wanting to live in the sun.

In a Bushman story of beginnings, the sun was on earth and hid its light in its armpit. It was so close, it was useless—darkening with excessive light.[42] Hunter-gatherers agree that division is necessary, that you can't have heaven smothering earth. It follows that you can't live on the world-pole. In fact, even shamans can only climb it once in a while, and soon slip off. It is slippery—wet with the water of life, greasy with the fat of offerings, alive with energy of all kinds.

The peak of the World Mountain is like the head of a pin on which only angels and animals can dance. It is the vanishing point of the trophic pyramid. There is room at the top, but not for us.

Nowadays most people (as opposed to scholars) like to imagine Eden as a wild place: a rain forest rife with orchids and lianas, a savanna rumbling with game. Conversely, they like to stick the words "Eden" and "garden," like Sierra Club stamps, on any wilderness that is not unlivably frigid or arid, especially if they have never been in it themselves. And while they are right to imagine Eden as a wild place, they are wrong to think that such places are still paradises *for us*. A brief backpacking trip is about as much of real wilderness as most of us can stand, and even that will seem like paradise only if nothing goes wrong: no rain, no grizzlies, no marmots eating our boots. After a week or two, we are glad to be expelled. And if we were to stay—to become settlers, pioneers—we would soon transform the place, or at least our immediate patch of it, into something wildly different.

The World Mountain is a paradise only when seen from a distance, or with the moist eye of memory. Once, wilderness was our home. Looking back, we endow it with all the longed-for comforts of home. We see a garden: a place wholly benign, a place of harmony and plenty. We forget that the harmony, such as it was, was possible only because we were still animals, and the plenty only because we were scarce. As soon as we become fully human, we begin to "fill the earth and subdue it." We begin to destroy Eden, and thereby expel ourselves.[43]

Wheat and the Fall of Man

The myth of the Fall, like that of the World Mountain itself, is based on ecological fact.[44] In fact, of course, the Fall was not a single event. It was a gradual slipping that, by degrees, snowballed into a full-speed charge downhill. Humans began to change their surroundings in a drastic way as soon as they mastered fire, but it was the second great wave of human expansion—based on the alliance with annual grasses, which came to be known as grains—that sealed our self-expulsion. We and our allies moved outward, driving Eden before us. We stripped forests, troubled the soil, uprooted whole ecosystems.

On this point the Bible is clear. "Cursed is the ground for thy sake; in sorrow shalt thou eat of it all the days of thy life. Thorns also and thistles shall it bring forth to thee; and thou shalt eat the herb [grass] of the field. In the sweat of thy brow shalt thou eat bread, till thou return unto the ground; for out of it wast thou taken: for dust thou art, and unto dust shalt thou return" (Genesis 3:17–19). Agriculture as we know it: the earth is tilled, grain (a kind of grass) is planted, weeds interfere.[45] The Hebrew word *lehem* means food in general, bread in particular. In place of the herbs and fruits of paradise, man will eat bread. As we have said, the culture of barley and wheat—first for beer and toasted seedheads, then for bread—did apparently begin in the uplands of the Near East, some ten thousand years ago. That it was woman, not man, who surely began it—being the foremost gatherer, she must have been the first farmer—may be dimly recalled in the story that it was Eve who first tasted the forbidden fruit, then handed it on to Adam.

What was the forbidden fruit? In the Midrash (*Bereshit Rabbah* 15.7), a rabbi of the second century C.E. gives a remarkable answer:

Rabbi Meir said: It was wheat, for when a person lacks knowledge people say, "That creature has never eaten bread of wheat." Rabbi Samuel ben Isaac came to Rabbi Ze'ira and asked: "Is it possible that it was wheat?" "Yes," he said. "But is not 'tree' written?" he asked. "It rose high as the cedars of Lebanon," he replied.

If Rabbi Meir is half joking—for this is a typical midrashic game of competitive whimsy, with other rabbis one-upping him by proving that the forbidden fruit was the grape or the fig—his half-joke has deep roots in the Near Eastern mind. Wheat is the premise of civilized life. Whoever has not eaten bread made of wheat is a savage, at best a Bedouin. The Sumerians had a similar gibe for the nomads at the fringe of their world: "The Martu eat bread, but they don't know what it's made of."[46]

Rabbi Meir's notion sounds less odd in Hebrew than in English, for the word translated "fruit" can mean any kind of produce. And if the forbidden fruit is indeed wheat, the role of the snake becomes clear: in ancient times, snakes were used to protect granaries from rodents.[47]

If grains meant knowledge, they also meant hard work, and it was work man had not previously evolved to do. Man was born to labor, as the Book of Proverbs says, but not to labor like this. For five million years we had foraged, scavenged, hunted, gardened a little, which was hard work at times, but desultory, even leisurely. Adam's punishment, like Eve's, was a wrenching departure from the path of primate evolution. Eve was sentenced to pain in childbirth—outrageous pain by any reasonable mammalian standard—because infants were being selected for bigger brains than the pelvis of a bipedal female could accommodate. To be sure, Eve's penance began long before Adam's, millions of years before the start of farming. But farming, by raising the birthrate, made it necessary for her to bear that penance more often. Farming meant more children; children meant more farming. Adam's and Eve's punishments fed each other.

They fed other things, too. With time, with irrigation, mountains of grain became the foundations of cities. To protect the grain from marauding nomads, armies arose and enslaved those whose grain they protected. To dig the great irrigation canals and keep them clear, slaves were called for, and bureaucrats, and despots. (The first great emperor in history, Sargon the Great of Akkad, began his career as a gardener, so it is fitting that the last great emperor, Pu Yi of China, ended his career that way.) Humans were winnowed like grain, separated by function, wealth, power. Civilization arose, and writing, and real estate. All this happened just a few miles downriver from Eden.

Adam's fate was to outrun his own nature: to be dragged by his big brain, by his snowballing technology, into regions his body had never known. Like Eve, he was the victim of an overgrown head.

Of course, our big brain is our nature, too. But the fact remains that in eating the forbidden fruit, though we failed to become gods, we ceased to be animals. At that point, Eden could no longer be our home. For whatever place we made our home ceased to be Eden.

The Hebrew phrase usually translated "Cursed is the ground for thy sake" can, with a bit of license, be read to mean "Cursed is the ground by thy passing over."[48] As the waves of human expansion move across the earth, Eden is trampled underfoot.

Adam was put in the garden "to work it and protect it" (Genesis 2:15).[49] The two jobs are complementary, but they are also contradictory. From what are we to protect Eden, if not from our own work? The more we work the earth—by which I mean not only tilling but the whole spectrum of human meddling, from setting grass fires to splitting the atom—the more we are obliged to protect it. If we fail to do either, we fail to be fully human.

These tasks were set us not just for our brief tenure in Eden, but for the whole span of our stay on earth. Indeed, by setting us the first task God set us up for expulsion. For when we work the earth we work her hard, and the place we work ceases to be Eden. We move outward in waves of work—waves of improvement and devastation, of fruitfulness and waste. By setting us the second task, God set (or tried to set) a limit to the height and reach of those waves.

Humankind's Zigzag

"So he drove out the man; and he placed at the east of the Garden of Eden cherubim, and a flaming sword which turned every way, to keep the way of the tree of life" (Genesis 3:24). The tree of life is the inner core of the world-pole: the heart of the heart of the world. Man must be prevented from reaching—and ruining—the source of life.

What exactly is the fiery sword? Is it our awe of wilderness? Our fear of its rigors and dangers? Our discomfiture in the face of its unearthly beauty? Whatever it is, it is the best friend we have. For only by keeping our distance from wilderness—some wilderness, at least—can we keep from fouling the wellspring of our own life.

It is paradoxical that wilderness seems to be at once the center of the circle of human expansion, and the region outside the circle. The paradox vanishes when we look back to the instant of origin when there was no circle. But there is another, more matter-of-fact way of looking at this problem.

Is the Mountain our point of origin, or is it our destination? Is it where we come from or where we are inexorably and ill-advisedly going? It is both. Our past has been a zigzag. Humans and their allied species come from the World Mountain, descend into the valley and fill it—becoming more or less domesticated in the process—then turn and edge their way up the slopes of the World Mountain, crushing its wildness as they go. Grasses edge out trees, domesticated grasses edge out wild ones, hybrid crops edge out hoary and varied domesticates. The beginnings of this reflux can be seen clearly in the ancient Near East, for instance in the various resettlements of the Judean and Samarian hills. It is still going on. But as the hour gets later and space gets dearer, we find ourselves assaulting earlier and earlier world-poles: wild places in which were born not our species, but the families from which we descend: even the family of life itself.

In recent years, we have set about dismantling our primate home, the rain forest, which is perhaps the greatest of terrestrial world-poles. As the uplands of the Near East are vital to the ecology of the Near East, so the rain forest of South and Central America, Africa, and Asia is vital to the ecology of the entire planet. Its role in regulating climate and maintaining biodiversity is well known, and yet we do not know the half of it. It is also the only home of most of our primate relatives. That home was already shrunken by the drying trend of the Pliocene, at which point we moved out. Now we have returned and are hacking away at what is left, pushing our own cousins into destitution and death. Their only consolation is that, if we keep it up, we may be next.

What will be left after the rain forest is gone? Our oldest home, the sea? The continental shelf, with its host of atmosphere-regulating microbes, may prove to be the most vital wild place of all—the ultimate world-pole. Yet densely settled seaboards ooze sewage into coastal waters, and rivers spew out the runoff of farms. Offshore drilling and aquaculture threaten to change the continental shelf as thoroughly as we have changed the continents. As usual, we do not know what we are doing.

Humans fail to grasp the fact that the world-pole cannot be grasped without choking off its flow of blessing. "I will not let thee go except thou bless me," they say, as Jacob said to the angel (Genesis 32:27); but they grip the angel's throat and throttle him speechless.

By definition, humankind was born in wilderness. To destroy wilderness is therefore to cut off the source of human life. Yet it is likewise true by definition that to destroy wilderness—at least, to make it something other than wilderness—is something humans must do.

These elementary truths stand behind many myths of paradise and the Fall. As soon as man becomes man he must leave the place where he was born, namely, wilderness. But the expulsion takes a subtle form. For he leaves wilderness by entering wilderness. Each place he enters ceases to be itself, and so he is expelled from its true self: he is left with the husk of a place. The only way to avoid expulsion is not to enter at all. (Or to enter only briefly, treading lightly, breath held.) The fiery sword is a necessity that our own wiser selves acknowledge.

The lease on the World Mountain forbids major alterations of the premises. It forbids not only cats and dogs but all domesticated species, including humans. If we return to Eden, we destroy either Eden or our own humanity.

Notes

This paper is adapted from several chapters of my book, *The Ecology of Eden* (New York: Knopf, 1998), in which interested readers will find my argument refined and expanded. I thank Yochanan Muffs, Joel Kaminsky, Daniel Hillel, Ellen Bernstein, and Paul Sanford, as well as my editors Daniel Frank and Jon Beckmann, for reading this material in various forms. The errors that remain are my own. My thanks go as well to Eilon Schwartz, Tikva Frymer-Kensky, David Kraemer, Eliezer Diamond, and others for their comments on the paper at the Harvard conference, and to Steve Shaw and Moshe Sokol for giving me the chance to present it.

1. On the geography and ecology of the ancient Mediterranean and Near East, see Ellen Churchill Semple, *The Geography of the Mediterranean Region: Its Relation to Ancient History* (New York: Holt, 1931); Yohanan Aharoni, *The Land of the Bible: A Historical Geography*, trans. and ed. A. F. Rainey, 2d ed. (Philadelphia: Westminster, 1979); Adolf Reifenberg, *The Struggle between the Desert and the Sown: The Rise and Fall of Agriculture in the Levant* (Jerusalem: The Jewish Agency, 1955); Daniel Hillel, *Out of the Earth Civilization and the Life of the Soil* (New York: Free Press, 1991); and the well-illustrated book by David Attenborough, *The First Eden: The Mediterranean World and Man* (Boston: Little, Brown, 1987).

2. Though I have borrowed the concept from Mircea Eliade, *Cosmos and History: The Myth of the Eternal Return*, trans. Willard R. Trask (New York: Harper and Row, 1959), 12ff., I have chosen a cruder term than his *axis mundi*. Eliade, by the way, makes no distinction between "cosmic mountains" that are real mountains and "cosmic mountains" that are fakes. "The names of the Babylonian temples and sacred towers themselves testify to their assimilation to the cosmic mountain," he writes, which is true enough as far as it goes.

For examples of World Mountains and other world-poles, see ibid.; E. A. S. Butterworth, *The Tree at the Navel of the Earth* (Berlin: de Gruyter, 1970); Joseph Campbell, *The Masks of God*, vol. 1 (New York: The Viking Press, 1959); as well as the splendidly illustrated book by Edwin Bernbaum, *Sacred Mountains of the World* (San Francisco: Sierra Club, 1990).

3. *Textual Sources for the Study of Zoroastrianism*, ed. and trans. Mary Boyce (Totowa, N.J.: Barnes and Noble Books, 1984).

4. To avoid the political freight, as well as the imprecision in an ancient context, of such terms as Israel, Palestine, Syria, and Syro-Palestine, I use the most ancient name for the region that still means something to modern ears. Several thousand years of bad press in Hebrew and Latin sources have helped keep the Canaanites, and their cousins the Phoenicians and Carthaginians, from getting the serious study they deserve. For general treatments, see Donald B. Harden, *The Phoenicians*, rev. ed. (Harmondsworth: Penguin, 1980); John Gray, *The Canaanites* (London: Thames and Hudson, 1964); Emmanuel Anati, *Palestine before the Hebrews* (New York: Knopf, 1963); and Sabatino Moscati, *The World of the Phoenicians*, trans. Alastair Hamilton (London: Weidenfeld and Nicolson, 1968). Canaanite texts are translated by H. L. Ginsburg in *Ancient Near Eastern Texts Relating to the Old Testament*, ed. James B. Pritchard, 3d ed. with supplement (Princeton: Princeton University Press, 1969); short selections are translated and discussed by Frank Moore Cross, *Canaanite Myth*

and Hebrew Epic: Essays in the History of the Religion of Israel (Cambridge, Mass.: Harvard University Press, 1973); and Richard J. Clifford, *The Cosmic Mountain in the Old Testament* (Cambridge, Mass.: Harvard University Press, 1972).

5. Amanus is the ancient name; modern names include Alma Dag, Nur, and Hatay.

6. This may be the site in the Lebanon range now called Khirbet Afqa, where the river called Nahr Ibrahim appears to rise dramatically from a great cave, or it may be some vaguely defined part of the Amanus range. See Clifford, *The Cosmic Mountain*, 49. The alternative rendering is Ginsburg's.

7. It is usually identified with Jebel 'el-Aqra', at the mouth of the Orontes in Syria. (The Hebrew word *tzafon*, "north," is derived from the name of the mountain, not the other way around.)

8. Clifford, *The Cosmic Mountain*, 68. Most extant Canaanite poems are found on clay tablets from Ugarit in northern Syria (the modern Ras Shamra) that date from about 1400 B.C.E. But the myths they relate may be far older. It now seems likely that the Canaanites were autochthonous—that they grew from the soil of Canaan. They were offspring of the first farmers in the region (the first in the world, as far as we know), probably of the first proto-farmers (the Natufians, whose villages were supported by the harvesting of wild grains), and possibly of the first modern humans. The seeds of the myths that bloomed so profusely in late Bronze Age Ugarit may have been planted by farmers of the late Stone Age. While the myths of Mesopotamia are far older in their written forms than those of Canaan, it seems likely that those of Canaan represent an older way of life.

The growth of the cult of Baal in Syria around the fourteenth century B.C.E. has been linked (by Cross, *Canaanite Myth and Hebrew Epic*, 48) to the appeal of the seasonal myths associated with him, which agreed so well with the needs of settled farmers. It is often assumed that earlier Canaanites were seminomadic herdsmen, but of this there is scant proof. It is true that El is called "Bull," but such gods are common among mixed farmers. That he lives in a tent is a stronger piece of evidence, but may tend to show only that his origins were not Canaanite at all.

9. For a more detailed consideration of Canaanite myth, see Eisenberg, *The Ecology of Eden*, chap. 7.

10. Carl Gustav Jung, *Memories, Dreams, Reflections*, ed. Aniela Jaffe, trans. Richard and Clara Winston (New York: Pantheon, 1963), 251. Jung says that on a visit to the pueblos of New Mexico, he "stood by the river and looked up at the mountains, which rise almost another six thousand feet above the plateau. . . . Suddenly a deep voice, vibrant with suppressed emotion, spoke from behind me into my left ear: 'Do you not think that all life comes from the mountain?' An elderly Indian had come up to me, inaudible in his moccasins, and had asked me this heaven knows how far-reaching question. A glance at the river pouring down from the mountain showed me the outward image that had engendered this conclusion."

For a more scientific assessment of the services rendered by wilderness, see *Nature's Services: Societal Dependence on Natural Ecosystems*, ed. Gretchen C. Daily (Washington, D.C.: Island Press, 1997).

11. In a series of reliefs in the temple of Amon at Karnak publicizing the triumphs of Thutmose III (reigned 1504–1450 B.C.E.) in Canaan, several panels display specimens of flora and fauna that the pharaoh carried back to Egypt from his third cam-

paign. (The Egyptians were avid gardeners and the first collectors of exotic plants and animals.) The caption reads in part, "All plants that [grow], all flowers that are in God's land [which were found by] his majesty when he proceeded to Upper Retenu." Oded Borowski, *Agriculture in Iron Age Israel* (Winona Lake, Ind.: Eisenbrauns, 1987), 4.

12. Donald O. Henry, *From Foraging to Agriculture: The Levant at the End of the Ice Age* (Philadelphia: University of Pennsylvania Press, 1989); and *The Environmental History of the Near and Middle East since the Last Ice Age*, ed. William C. Brice (New York: Academic Press, 1978).

13. Ofer Bar-Yosef and Bernard Vandermeersch, "Modern Humans in the Levant," *Scientific American* 268, no. 4 (1993): 94–100. Creatures once dignified (if that is the word) with membership in the human race, and classified as archaic *H. sapiens* and *H. sapiens Neanderthalensis*, are now generally placed in separate species.

14. On the unpromising natural endowments of ancient Mesopotamia, see Hillel, *Out of the Earth*, chap. 11; and Samuel Noah Kramer, *The Sumerians* (Chicago: University of Chicago Press, 1963). On ancient Mesopotamia generally, see Kramer, *The Sumerians*; Samuel Noah Kramer, *History Begins at Sumer* (New York: Doubleday, 1959); A. Leo Oppenheim, *Ancient Mesopotamia: Portrait of a Dead Civilization*, rev. ed., comp. Erica Reiner (Chicago: University of Chicago Press, 1977); and Harriet E. W. Crawford, *Sumer and the Sumerians* (Cambridge: Cambridge University Press, 1991). Sumerian, Akkadian, and Babylonian texts are translated in *Ancient Near Eastern Texts*, ed. Pritchard, as well as in the cited books by Kramer; Thorkild Jacobsen, *The Treasures of Darkness* (New Haven: Yale University Press, 1976); Clifford, *The Cosmic Mountain*; Helmer Ringgren, *Religions of the Ancient Near East*, trans. John Sturdy (London: S.P.C.K., 1973); Alexander Heidel, *The Babylonian Genesis*, 2d ed. (Chicago: University of Chicago Press, 1951), and *The Gilgamesh Epic and Old Testament Parallels*, 2d ed. (Chicago: University of Chicago Press, 1949).

15. Kramer, *The Sumerians*, 109; but for caveats as to when some of the items on this list may first have been introduced, see Gerlinde Mauer, "Agriculture of the Old Babylonian Period," *Journal of the Ancient Near Eastern Society* 15 (1983): 63–78.

16. Kramer, *The Sumerians*, chap. 8.

17. The best account of ancient Mesopotamian irrigation is in Hillel, *Out of the Earth,* chap. 11. See also Robert McCormick Adams and Hans J. Nissen, *The Uruk Countryside: The Natural Setting of Urban Societies* (Chicago: University of Chicago Press, 1972).

18. See Ringgren, *Religions of the Ancient Near East*; Kramer, *The Sumerians*, chap. 4; and Jacobsen, *The Treasures of Darkness*.

19. Elizabeth B. Moynihan, *Paradise as a Garden: In Persia and Mughal India* (New York: Braziller, 1979), 23ff.

20. In the fifth tablet (*Ancient Near Eastern Texts*, ed. Pritchard, suppl., p. 502), the victorious Marduk tells the other gods of his plan to build a temple and a "luxurious abode" for himself and his cronies:

When you come up from the Apsu for assembly,
You will spend the night therein, (it is there) to receive
all of you.

When you des[cend] from heaven [for assem]bly,
You will spend the night there[in], (it is there) to receive
all of you.
I will call [its] name ['Babylon'] (which means) 'the houses
of the great gods'. . . .

In the same way a city might claim—what amounted to the same thing—that it was the navel of the world. This was no figure of speech, for Sumerian priests held that in the temple of Inanna in Nippur lay the scar that was left when the great god Enlil parted heaven and earth. Although the birth cord had been cut, the temple remained a kind of cable between the worlds. The precinct was called Dur-an-ki, "the bond of heaven and earth." Its center was called "flesh producer" or "the place where flesh sprouted forth"—for it was here that human beings first sprang like seedlings from the earth ("The Creation of the Pickaxe," in Clifford, *The Cosmic Mountain*, 14).

21. "And, by the way, who estimates the value of the crop which Nature yields in the still wilder fields unimproved by man?" To the question posed by Henry David Thoreau in *Walden* ("The Bean-Field"), a first effort at an answer was recently made: a systematic attempt to estimate the annual economic value of the earth's (more or less) natural ecosystems. Though the researchers cast their net wide—taking in such varied things as recreation value, pollination services, forest timber, the effect of wetlands on shrimp harvests, and the role of the oceans in regulating atmospheric carbon dioxide—plenty of things slipped through, among them nonrenewable fuels and minerals and the merits of such relatively unstudied ecosystems as deserts, tundra, and urban parks. Despite its conservative assumptions, the study came up with an annual value of $33 trillion. By contrast, the GNPs of all nations on earth total about $18 trillion. In short, the Mountain has challenged the Tower on its home turf, economics, and bested it nearly two to one. See Robert Costanza et al., "The Value of the World's Ecosystem Services and Natural Capital," *Nature* 387 (1997): 253–60, as well as Stuart Pimm, "The Value of Everything," in the same issue, pp. 231–32. See also Daily, *Nature's Services*.

22. The Canaanites, too, had their artificial world-poles, the stone pillars which the Bible calls *matsevot*. Artificial world-poles were common in the ancient world, as they are in surviving shamanic cultures. But there is a difference between these jury-rigged world-poles and the monstrosities heaped up in Mesopotamia. The former may be seen as signs of rugged individualism, or of a god's ubiquity, or of his whimsy— his love of sudden cameo appearances, of leaping out from behind a rock or setting a bush on fire, of dropping a ladder from the sky a pillow's length from your head. ("Surely the Lord is in this place, and I knew it not": Genesis 28:16). The latter show only the self-importance of city, priest, and king.

23. Hillel, *Out of the Earth*, 83. His account (chap. 11) of salinization in ancient Mesopotamia is both expert and readable.

24. Thorkild Jacobsen and Robert M. Adams, "Salt and Silt in Ancient Mesopotamian Agriculture," *Science*, n.s., 128, no. 3334 (1958): 1251–58.

25. First proposed by Jacobsen and Adams in 1958, the theory has intermittently been attacked , e.g., by M. A. Powell, "Salt, Seed and Yields in Sumerian Agriculture: A Critique of the Theory of Progressive Salinization," *Zeitschrift der Assyrologie* 75

(1985): 7–38; and defended, e.g., by Michal Artzy and Daniel Hillel, "A Defense of the Theory of Progressive Soil Salinization in Ancient Southern Mesopotamia," *Geoarchaeology* 3, no. 3 (1988): 235–38, in the years since. What is in question is not the fact that salinization occurred, but whether Mesopotamian farmers had effective methods to arrest, reverse, or soften its effects. Most recently, the trend has been to explain the vicissitudes of farming in various parts of Mesopotamia and the attendant fates of cities and empires in terms of climate change; see, for example, H. Weiss et al., "The Genesis and Collapse of Third Millennium North Mesopotamian Civilization," *Science* 261 (1993): 995–1004. While no single factor can explain the whole course of Mesopotamian history, my own (lay) hunch is that salinization played a major role.

26. For a reading of various Mesopotamian myths and epics that brings out their ecological significance—linking, for example, the Sumerian poem "Enki and Ninhursag" to the problem of soil salinization—see Eisenberg, *The Ecology of Eden*, chap. 11. And see chap. 27 of that book to correct the impression I may have given here that I am somehow opposed to cities. To summarize my later conclusions:

It is easy to chide the Mesopotamians for making the city the world-pole, yet it was a necessary step. They would not have been able to do the remarkable things they did if they had not been able to abstract human culture from nature to some degree. The same can be said of the Western civilization they helped shape. To view human culture as having its own logic, its own map, its own font, and its own channels is both useful and true—up to a point. If a child does not assert its independence from its mother, it does not grow up. True independence may be an illusion, but it is a useful one.

Despite Arcadian cant, the city is not a place you must escape from if you want to live a fully human life. Cities are natural. Even their unnaturalness is natural, for it springs from our nature and (if kept within bounds) can meet our quirky needs without doing nature too much harm. And it turns out that the Tower, which figures in this essay as a bastard pretender and enemy of the Mountain, can be its best friend and staunchest defender. Ideally, it concentrates both the warm bodies of humans and their steamy cultural energies in a small, bounded, insulated place, so that wild nature need not take the heat. A final note: Since September 11, 2001, the word "tower" has born an emotional weight it did not carry when these pages were written. Some readers have told me my work helped them make some sense of that senseless event, but I leave that to each reader to decide.

27. In the first half of the twentieth century the German school of Alt and Noth predominated: this school denied the historicity of the Bible and spoke of gradual infiltration of Canaan by seminomadic tribes, which in time formed a loose confederation. About mid-century, a counterattack was led by William Foxwell Albright and the more radical Yehezkel Kaufmann, who propped up the patriarchal stories, and those of the conquest of Canaan, with shards and other evidence newly unearthed. In the last couple of decades the winds have shifted yet again, with William G. Dever, John van Seters, Norman K. Gottwald, and George E. Mendenhall, among others, placing the Israelites more firmly in a Canaanite context. (Mendenhall goes farthest, making the Israelites out to be downtrodden peasants of wholly native origin.) For a

clear presentation of this general approach, see Robert B. Coote, *Early Israel: A New Horizon* (Minneapolis: Fortress Press, 1990).

When I had finished my text and was revising these notes, I came across Theodore Hiebert, *The Yahwist's Landscape: Nature and Religion in Early Israel* (Oxford: Oxford University Press, 1996), which, drawing on many of the same sources, appears to have reached some of the same conclusions as the present work about the role of nature in the Hebrew Bible. Although it is reassuring to have my solitary, lay speculations confirmed by a biblical scholar working at Harvard, it is also a blow to my vanity—which, outweighing shame for my tardiness, compels me to point out that this part of my book, in substantially the present form, was circulated in manuscript as early as 1992. It is obvious to me that Hiebert was as oblivious of my work as I was of his.

On the ecology and husbandry of ancient Israel, see Aharoni, *The Land of the Bible*; David C. Hopkins *The Highlands of Canaan: Agricultural Life in the Early Iron Age* (Sheffield, England: Almond, 1985); Borowski, *Agriculture in Iron Age Israel*; Reifenberg, *The Struggle between the Desert and the Sown*; Hillel, *Out of the Earth*; and the eccentric but interesting works of Nogah Hareuveni, founder of the biblical landscape garden Ne'ot Kedumim.

28. In the early part of the so-called Iron Age, bronze was still the metal of choice because the techniques of steeling, quenching, and tempering were as yet unknown, and without them iron is more brittle than bronze.

29. A century or two later, Israelites would use the same principle to make farming possible in the Negev Desert. Runoff from the rare and violent rainstorms would be channeled into sunken fields and orchards, so that the rain falling on an acre of ground might sustain a single tree. Mastery of this technique by the Nabateans of the Hellenistic period allowed them to plunk cities down in the heart of the desert, and so to inhale the wealth of the spice trade. See Daniel Hillel, *Negev: Land, Water, and Life in a Desert Environment* (New York: Praeger, 1982).

30. See Hopkins, *The Highlands of Canaan*, 252ff.

31. On Eden as the Mountain of God, see Jon D. Levenson, *Theology of the Program of Restoration of Ezekiel 40–48* (Cambridge, Mass.: Harvard Semitic Museum, 1976), and *Sinai and Zion: An Entry into the Jewish Bible* (San Francisco: Harper and Row, 1987).

32. This was the received opinion in Philo's day, though Philo himself was unconvinced; *Questions and Answers on Genesis*, cited by Frank E. Manuel and Fritzie P. Manuel, *Utopian Thought in the Western World* (Cambridge, Mass.: Harvard University Press, 1979), 43. Those modern scholars, such as Speiser and Zarins, who take the four rivers to be tributaries, and situate the Garden at the point where their joined waters debouch—that is, at the head of the Persian Gulf—have the weight of ancient tradition against them.

33. See Daniel Hillel, *Rivers of Eden: The Struggle for Water and the Quest for Peace in the Middle East* (New York: Oxford University Press, 1994).

34. Louis Ginzburg, *The Legends of the Jews*, trans. Henrietta Szold and Paul Radin, vol. 1 (Philadelphia: Jewish Publication Society, 1909), 70; Josephus *Antiquitates Judaicae* 1.39; Rashi ad loc.

35. Others render, "to walk a distance equal to the diameter of its trunk."

36. See Umberto Cassuto, *A Commentary on the Book of Genesis*, trans. Israel Abrahams, 2 vols. (Jerusalem: Magnes Press, 1961).

37. The *avnei esh* (literally, "stones of fire") of Ezekiel 28:14–16 may refer to "stones of lightning" or "stars of El" mentioned in various Ugaritic and Akkadian texts; they may be the lightning that flashes from the Mountain of God, or they may simply be "fiery jewels." Jewels, especially sapphire or lapis lazuli, are found in Baal's temple on Mount Zaphon, as well as downstream of Eden in the Yahwist's (J's) account. Lapis even makes its way into accounts of God's appearance on his other great mountain, Sinai.

38. According to one legend—*Pirke de-Rabbi Eliezer*, chap. 20, cited in *Safed Spirituality: Rules of Mystical Piety, the Beginning of Wisdom*, trans. and ed. Lawrence Fine (New York: Paulist Press, 1984), 99—Adam was not just expelled from Eden but was, in effect, cast into the netherworld, like Lucifer. Begging forgiveness, he stood in the waters of upper Gehenna for seven weeks "until his body became like a species of seaweed." Of course, you might say he was trying to merge with nature—with the primeval ooze—as a penance for parting from nature.

39. True, the word *midbar*, or wilderness in the sense of desert—an arid or desolated place—is sometimes used in opposition to Eden; but to conclude from this (as, for example, does Roderick Nash, *Wilderness and the American Mind*, 3d ed. [New Haven: Yale University Press, 1982]), that Eden and wilderness in the more general sense are opposites in Hebrew thought is a misunderstanding.

40. Cf. Thoreau: "The tops of mountains are among the unfinished parts of the globe, whither it is a slight insult to the gods to climb and pry into their secrets, and try their effect on our humanity. Only daring and insolent men, perchance, go there. Simple races, as savages, do not climb mountains,—their tops are sacred and mysterious tracts never visited by them. Pomola is always angry with those who climb to the summit of Ktaadn." "Ktaadn," in *The Maine Woods*.

41. The voltage of pure godhead would cinder us like Semele, like Nadab and Abihu. To prevent this, the *sefirot*, or divine spheres of kabbalah, serve, one might say, as step-down transformers. For a general theory of "the holy" along these lines, see Rudolf Otto, *The Idea of the Holy*, trans. John W. Harvey, 2d ed. (London: Oxford University Press, 1957).

42. W. H. I. Bleek and L. C. Lloyd, *Specimens of Bushman Folklore* (London: George Allen, 1911), 54ff.

43. In chapter 12 of *The Ecology of Eden*, I refine somewhat the picture I have painted here in such broad strokes, noting Egyptian and Mesopotamian influences on the Hebrew Bible; varying attitudes to nature in various sources of the Pentateuch; the hybrid of Mountain and Tower that is Zion, and its rabbinical links to Eden; the role of Sinai as wild World Mountain; and the role of wildness in Sabbath, sabbatical, and jubilee. I also respond more explicitly to various forms of ecological anti-Semitism.

44. By "the Fall of Man" I mean the expulsion from Eden; there is no reference to the concept of original sin.

45. Other peoples, too, have identified farming with the Fall. The Bobo of Burkina Faso believe that the primal harmony of the world was destroyed when humans began farming. Similarly, the Khasi of Assam say humans were once able to reach heaven

by climbing a great tree—until they cut the tree down to clear space for a garden. In a Dogon myth from Mali, heaven and earth were once adjacent, but God parted them (and made humans mortal) after being annoyed by the din of women crushing millet. Julien Ries, "The Fall," in *The Encyclopedia of Religion*, ed. Mircea Eliade, 16 vols. (New York: Macmillan, 1987).

46. Adapted from Kramer, *The Sumerians*, 287.

47. They are still used that way. In Iowa, farmers keep bull snakes to rid their barns of rats and mice. E. Laurence Palmer, *Fieldbook of Natural History*, 2d ed., rev. by H. Seymour Fowler (New York: McGraw-Hill, 1975), 543.

48. Gesenius, the great nineteenth-century Hebraist, notes that *'avur* can also mean "produce" or "yield" (cf. Joshua 5:11f.). Thus, the phrase might be read, "Cursed is the ground in (i.e., with respect to) thy produce"; or, more intriguing for our purposes, "Cursed is the ground by thy produce."

49. My translation. There are, of course, many other licit interpretations of the two Hebrew words. Among the more interesting is Cassuto's: he makes *le-'ovdah* refer to "divine service" (following *Bereshit Rabbah* 16.5: "These denote sacrifices"). And he makes *le-shomrah* refer to the task of guarding which was formerly (in Babylonian tradition and the lost epic tradition to which Ezekiel alludes) that of the cherubim—to whom it reverts when Adam is expelled.

How Much Is Too Much?
Conventional versus Personal Definitions of Pollutions in Rabbinic Sources

ELIEZER DIAMOND

Normally one thinks of pollution as an act that degrades the natural environment. Acid rain kills off trees and fish; CFCs thin the ozone layer; an excess of CO_2 causes, or may cause, global warming, which in turn causes, or may cause, the polar ice cap to melt. We all know, however, that pollution affects not only the environment. It also harms the individual and society. Thus, pollution is not only an assault on nature; it is also an attack on humankind. This is true both in that pollution presents a threat to health and because of its negative impact on the quality of human life.

The problem of pollution is further complicated by its ubiquity. When speaking of pollution we often focus on factories spewing chemicals into the air and water or oil companies drilling in the pristine tundras of the north. However, the average resident of a developed country pollutes every day, albeit in far less spectacular fashion. Whether using carbon monoxide-producing vehicles or electric appliances dependant on fossil fuels to produce the electricity they use, whether tossing out refuse that will be buried or burned or buying food in portion-size rather than bulk packaging, the typical First World consumer does his or her share to spread more pollutants throughout the environment.

Moreover, pollution can take forms that are more difficult to quantify than temperatures or CO_2 levels. Daily human activity produces smoke, odor, noise. Even the appearance of one's property may cause discomfort to one's neighbor. In these and the cases mentioned above, pollution is not gratuitous but rather the by-product of a commercial, industrial, or domestic activity deemed necessary or desirable by its performer. How are we to adjudicate between the needs of everyday life and the right of others to be protected from pollution?

The foundational works of halakhah, or Jewish law, were compiled between the first and seventh centuries, well before the discipline of science had advanced to the point enabling us to understand the global consequences of pollution. Nonetheless, the rabbinic authors of these works, and the biblical writers before them, considered the question of the proper relationship between humankind and nature. Some degree of human manipulation and pollution of the environment is necessary for human habitation, production, and commerce. The thirteenth-century Spanish sage R. Moses ben Nahman (Nahmanides) encapsulates this notion succinctly when in his definition of God's blessing and charge to humanity, "[fill the earth] and subdue it" (Gen. 1:28), he states that "God gave them power and authority . . . to uproot that which is planted and to mine copper from [the earth's] hills." Subduing inevitably entails destroying.

Of course, the rhetoric of some environmentalists notwithstanding,[1] Genesis 1:28 is neither an invitation nor a command to pillage nature indiscriminately. Genesis 1 describes the role of humanity relative to the rest of creation, and the role described is that of priority and therefore mastery. Genesis 2 describes human responsibility relative to God the Creator, and there we are told that Adam was placed in the garden "to till and tend it." Moreover, the first explicit commandment that Adam and Eve are given is, among other things, an environmental restriction; they are denied unlimited access to nature's bounty.

As noted above, balancing human need and desire with protecting the beauty, integrity, and viability of the earth is only part of the environmental agenda. Another is the impact that manipulation of the environment by one or more individuals has on their fellow human beings. In contemporary terms this issue is often referred to as "environmental justice." While the halakhic corpus has, for a variety of reasons, relatively little to say about the first set of issues, there is a copious body of halakhic literature devoted to the problems of competing use of space and resources, generally referred to as *hilkhot shekhenim*, "the laws of neighbors."

One of the most difficult problems in this area of law—and life—is the conflict that arises frequently between the needs of the community and those of the individual. This is often complicated by the fact that the individual is, for the purposes of many of the conflicts that arise, an interested member of the community as well. As an individual I may object to the smoke and odor emitted by a nearby incineration plant; as a resident of the township, I depend on that facility to burn my trash. This is not to say that my dependence invalidates my objection, only that it complicates it.

This conflict is further complicated when the pollution in question is more in the nature of nuisance than of hazard. When faced with evidence that second-hand smoke is demonstrably hazardous to the health of bystanders, many halakhists, even those unwilling to forbid smoking outright as a danger to oneself, unhesitatingly forbade smoking in the presence of others, particularly if those others objected.[2] What, however, of loud noises and unpleasant odors? Absent actual detriment to physical well-being, do we allow those affected to establish what is intolerable, or is some form of communal standard followed? If the latter, how is it determined?

It should be clear that these two issues are related. In both cases an underlying question is how to balance our concern for the individual with the need for halakhah to be communally responsive for reasons of manageability and social policy. The remainder of this paper will present, classify, and analyze the approaches of halakhists to these issues and will suggest how they might bear on constructing a contemporary environmental policy in this area.

Let us turn first to a mishnah[3] which touches on both of the questions raised above:[4]

> A store in a courtyard:[5] Another may protest against him and say, "I cannot sleep because of the noise made by those who come and go [i.e., the customers]."
>
> One who manufactures utensils [in his home] must go and sell them in the marketplace; however, one may not object and say, "I cannot sleep because of the noise of the hammer, or because of the noise of the mill, or because of the noise of the children."[6]

Although the Mishnah presents the case as involving a conflict between two individuals, more often than not such instances pit the individual who is the source of the disturbance against the neighborhood—represented in modern times by a tenants' or homeowners' association—as a whole.[7] This can be seen in the language of a related baraita cited in the Babylonian Talmud:[8]

> If one of the residents of a courtyard wished to become a doctor, a bloodletter, a weaver or a teacher of young children, the other residents of the courtyard may prevent him from doing do.

All of these occupations would result in increased traffic and consequent inconvenience, in the form of noise and/or congestion,[9] for the other residents; therefore, they may prevent the establishment of such an enterprise in their courtyard. In short, we are dealing with zoning laws designed to protect the quality of life of the neighborhood's residents.

Note, however, that the Mishnah protects neighbors from some, but not all, annoyances. Moreover, the distinction between tolerated and prohibited noise does not seem to be based on decibel level, because the sound of the hammer is undoubtedly at least as loud as that of milling shoppers.[10] This problem is already addressed by the fourth-century Babylonian amora Abbaye. He argues that the first instance in the Mishnah speaks of the rights of courtyard residents to object to a fellow resident setting up shop, while the second half of the Mishnah addresses the residents of one courtyard objecting to sounds coming from another. In the second instance, the neighbors' right to object is dismissed not because the noise level is negligible, but because the residents of one courtyard cannot restrict noise level emanating from another.

A different but related explanation is offered by the medieval Provençal commentator Meiri[11] and the sixteenth-century halakhist R. Levi ibn Habib.[12] Both claim that courtyard neighbors may not object to the noises of hammer and mill because these are the result of normal household activities to which each householder is entitled. It is only when one occupant attempts to conduct business that may be conducted elsewhere (ibn Habib) and/or is normally conducted there (Meiri)—as in the case of opening a shop—that neighbors may object.

Of course, a difficulty remains for both of the above interpretations. If noise is a form of actionable injury, as one might conclude from the beginning of the Mishnah, why should the economic needs of the individual producing noise or his being in another courtyard make such injury permissible? Both Meiri and ibn Habib address this problem. Meiri states that one may use one's own property to practice one's craft "and one may not be restrained from doing so because of the damage caused [thereby] to [the neighbors'] sleep." His concluding words imply that while loss of sleep is indeed a form of harm suffered, it is outweighed by the need of one's neighbor to earn his daily bread. The corollary of this statement is that not all resultant damage from the professional use of one's home is exempt from legal action by one's neighbors. Interfering with one's neighbor's sleep is tolerated in order to enable one to earn a livelihood; injuring their health or property presumably is not.

Meiri's stance can be seen as complementing a position espoused by the twentieth-century Talmudist R. Yehezkel Abramski.[13] He suggests that the right of neighbors to prevent the opening of a shop cannot be rooted in the right not to be injured by one's neighbor, because the noise and congestion are not being produced by the shop owner and are not an inevitable outcome of his actions; people may patronize his shop or not as they wish. Rather, the right to object to the opening of a shop is part of an implicit compact among the occupants of a courtyard. This social contract can be formulated to prohibit even those activities not actionable as torts. Meiri is suggesting that, conversely, the social contract can—and must, for practical reasons—be designed to exempt neighbors from liability from "low-level" damage that is the inevitable result of pursuing one's profession.

Ibn Habib speaks of the injury resulting from noise as being "uncertain." Presumably, he is alluding to the Babylonian Talmud's[14] explanation of a baraita exempting someone who shouts into someone's ear, thereby deafening him, in contrast to one being obligated for earthenware shattered by the crow of one's rooster. The difference, says the Bavli, is that, unlike earthenware, humans are sapient beings, capable of intended and independent action; we therefore assume that the person "frightened himself" into deafness in response to the shout. Were we to transpose both the Bavli and ibn Habib into modern parlance, we could say that they view the damage in each case as resulting from internal psychological forces rather than from external physical ones. This is seen as giving power to the injured party to avoid injury by exerting psychological counterforce. In this view,

Judaism and Ecology

noise is only as damaging to the individual as the individual allows it to be. Therefore, it includes a subjective element stemming from the damaged party for which we do not hold the damager responsible. Nonetheless, continues ibn Habib, "we provide a remedy whenever possible."[15] That is, if one can pursue a livelihood outside of the court-yard and not create noise there, one can be required to do so. In the case of opening a shop, argues ibn Habib, one has the alternative of selling one's wares in the marketplace. Not so for one who is engaged in manufacture or milling; therefore, one may engage in these activi-ties in one's home despite the inconvenience to one's neighbors.

Were we to cast the arguments of Meiri and ibn Habib in modern legal terminology, we might represent them as saying that the noise in question is not actionable as a tort but only as a nuisance. That is, no quantifiable monetary damage or personal harm results from the noise of the mill and hammer; rather there is "interference . . . with [one's neighbor's] comfort and convenience."[16] It is its being an inconve-nience rather than damage that allows (certain types of) noise pollu-tion to be inflicted on one's neighbors in the pursuit of one's liveli-hood.

On the surface it appears that, in the instances of the hammer and the mill, the rights of the individual are apparently being favored over those of the community. In fact, however, the individual is exercising a right reserved by each of his neighbors. To put it differently, a per-son hammering away in the confines of his home is relying on a pre-rogative deemed essential by his community for each of its constitu-ents and for the community as a whole. I may not like it when my neighbor claims his right to make noise, but I recognize that in grant-ing it to him I am protecting my own right to do the same and thereby protecting my own domestic and economic interests.

All of the above assumes that the Mishnah is speaking *ab initio*; a courtyard resident has not yet set up a mill or opened a shop and the question is whether or not he is permitted to do so. However, from Maimonides' formulation of the Mishnah's ruling, it appears that he understands the Mishnah to be addressing an *ex post facto* situation. That is, only if one had already begun operating a mill in one's home and no neighbor had objected may one deflect future complaints based on a *hazaqah*, that is, a presumption of right based on his neigh-bors' earlier silence. In all cases, however, a neighbor may prevent *ab initio* the establishment of a noise-producing enterprise of any kind.[17]

This opinion presents us with a significantly different approach from that described above to the problem of balancing communal and individual needs. In this view the amount of permitted noise pollution, at least if it is work-related, is limited to what the most noise-sensitive individual is willing to accept. Noise levels are not the result of social contract, then, but rather of the perceived needs of each individual. Standards are personal, not conventional.

Thus far we have dealt only with work-related noise pollution.[18] Let us consider another text, a story involving the Babylonian amora R. Joseph,[19] that deals with other forms of pollution, some of which are the result of domestic rather than economic activity.

> R. Joseph had *talei* [a species of palm trees or, according to some, saplings]. Bloodletters would come and sit under them.[20]
> Ravens came to eat the blood. They perched on the palm trees and spoiled the dates.
> R. Joseph said to the bloodletters, "Remove the 'korkor' [i.e., the ravens whose cry sounds something like 'korkor'] from here for my sake [in other words, move your base of operations so that the ravens will not gather on my trees]."
> Abbaye objected, "They are only causing damage to you indirectly." R. Joseph replied, "Thus stated R. Tuvi bar Matna [in another context, commenting upon a mishnah]: 'This is to say, It is forbidden to cause indirect damage.'"
> Abbaye objected further, "Have they not already established a presumption of right [through their previous activity to which you did not object]?" R. Joseph replied, "Behold, R. Nahman said in the name of Rabbah bar Abuha, 'There is no presumption of right regarding damages.'"
> [Abbaye objected further], "Was it not stated concerning this dictum, 'R. Mari limits it to smoke damage; R. Zebid limits it to the digging of a privy'?" He said to him, "For me, who is sensitive, these birds are like [the cases of] smoke and the privy."

Although the nuisance—whose exact nature is not clear[21]—to which R. Joseph objects is work-related, the mention of smoke, and especially of the privy, makes it clear that domestic sources of pollution and annoyance are being considered as well.

Two points in this passage must be defined to determine its implications for the adjudication of pollution-related disputes between

neighbors. The first is to establish the parameters of unacceptable pollution exemplified by smoke and the privy. In offering such examples,
the sages are limiting the types of pollution to which one's neighbor
can object at any time. In the medieval period we find halakhists defining more precisely the categories implied by these examples,
thereby limiting them even further. The tenth-century North African
scholar Rabbenu Hananel already limits the case of smoke to "frequent smoke." Actually, this view is already found in the Jerusalem
Talmud,[22] which may indeed be the source for Rabbenu Hananel's ruling. This qualification results later on in a number of rulings favorable
to defendants in nuisance cases. Thus, for example, the thirteenth- and
fourteenth-century Spanish authority R. Solomon b. Abraham Adret
(Rashba) affirms the right of a homeowner to leave his chimney intact
despite the fact that the smoke it emits is entering his neighbor's home
through an upper-story window which the neighbor had installed recently.[23] The thirteenth-century German halakhist R. Meir of Rothen-
berg allows a Jewish bathhouse owner to continue operating his bathhouse next to a synagogue despite congregants' complaints about
smoke and odor. His ruling is based in part on the fact that the bathhouse is in use only once a week.[24] The most far-reaching ruling regarding smoke pollution is that of the fifteenth-century German
halakhist R. Israel Isserlein. He concludes that not only may one who
is producing periodic smoke already ignore his neighbors' objections,
but he may even install *ab initio* an oven that produces occasional
smoke, and this despite his neighbor's protests.[25] R. Moses Isserles
later codifies this as the authoritative view.[26]

A similar distinction is made by medieval legal authorities with regard to privies. Rashi[27] (implicitly) and the Tosafists[28] (explicitly) distinguish between the open air privies of talmudic times and the covered privies of their own period. The latter, they say, are protected by
established use from a neighbor's objections. The impetus behind
these limitations seems to be that expressed by Rashba in connection
with allowing household smoke emission: "If we do not allow [such
periodic smoke emission] no one will build a house or light a fire
under one's food lest smoke escape from the house."[29] Once again, the
argument seems to be that the individual must bear with the nuisance
caused by his neighbor for the sake of a right which he himself would
not want to relinquish.

The second point of importance is to gauge the significance of
R. Joseph's confident assertion that, because he finds the presence of

the birds intolerable, he has a right to force the bloodletters to move—this despite their already having an established right of usage. Does this mean that anyone finding offensive any odor or noise originating in his neighbor's domain is entitled to have it stopped? Talmud commentators, and halakhists who invoke R. Joseph as a precedent, shy away from this conclusion. Thus, the medieval Spanish commentator R. Jonah limits the applicability of R. Joseph's dictum to one who is known to be hypersensitive to the form of nuisance in question.[30] Most commentators and halakhists concur with this view.[31] When the fifteenth-century Spanish and Algerian halakhist R. Isaac ben Sheshet Perfet, relying in part on R. Joseph's ruling, requires a weaver to cease operating his loom because of his neighbor's complaints that it is aggravating his wife's illness, he is careful to say that it is established that the woman is ill.[32] On the other hand, when someone applied for relief to the present-day rabbinic court of Jerusalem, claiming that he could not sleep because his upstairs neighbor was moving chairs and beds around at midnight and one in the morning,[33] the court was sympathetic, but it ruled that "while there is an obligation of neighbors to insure that they do not injure one another, the obligation of refraining from causing injury does not include one's remaining totally idle, that is, that one should straitjacket one's self."[34]

The consensus of halakhists, then, is to minimize the degree to which R. Joseph's ruling can be used as a precedent for objecting to "routine" smoke and odor pollution absent a verifiable claim of danger to one's health;[35] in other words, conventional standards prevail over personal ones. Interestingly, we find the converse corollary of this question considered as well. That is, to what degree can personal standards prevail in allowing permanently more pollution than is considered acceptable conventionally? This question first arises in the Tosefta[36] and Yerushalmi.[37] There is a tannaitic dispute as to whether someone who has granted someone living in his building or in his courtyard the right to open a store may subsequently void this arrangement unilaterally. The anonymous first tanna regards such an agreement as irrevocable, whereas R. Simeon b. Gamaliel allows for cancellation. The Yerushalmi compares his view to that of R. Meir, who allows a woman who has married a man with a repugnant blemish or odor to sue subsequently for divorce, saying, "I thought I could accept him but I cannot."[38] One can understand the anonymous tanna and R. Simeon b. Gamaliel to be arguing about whether or not one's personal acceptance of a relatively high level of pollution overrides

the conventional standard. For the anonymous tanna, one's acceptance of a different standard establishes that new standard uncondi-
tionally for the case at hand unless both parties agree to void it. R.
Simeon b. Gamaliel, on the other hand, sees the conventional standard
as still being in place for the present situation; therefore, one may
unilaterally withdraw one's granting of "excessive" pollution rights at
any time.

A corollary discussion takes place in the medieval period as follows: If one actually sells to his neighbor the right to set up a privy or
produce smoke, may that sale be revoked subsequently if the seller
finds the degree of pollution unbearable? In effect, we are speaking
here of an early form of selling pollution rights or credits. Most
halakhists view such a sale as valid; this is the view codified in the
sixteenth-century *Shulhan Arukh* of R. Joseph Karo.[39] The twelfth-
century French Tosafist R. Jacob Tam, however, allows one to renege
on such a sale by stating, "I thought I could accept this level of pollution but in fact I cannot."[40] While Rabbenu Tam is not invalidating
such a sale outright, he is reserving the right for the seller to revert to
the conventional standard of acceptable pollution.

Because pollution standards are conventional, not objective, they
may and do change over time. A classic instance of this is the response
of the nineteenth-century rabbinic scholar R. Moses Schreiber[41] to the
following question: May someone prevent his neighbor from selling
liquor by the glass—in effect, opening a pub—in one's home?
R. Schreiber replies that on the face of it this case is like that of opening a store in the courtyard, which can be prevented by one's neighbors. However, he goes on to cite R. Levi ibn Habib's explanation that
opening a store may be vetoed by neighbors because it can be opened
elsewhere, while practicing a craft may not because craftsmen generally have nowhere else to ply their trade. In his time and place, argues
R. Schreiber, people interested in sitting over a drink do not want to
do so in a town's commercial area; they prefer coming to a residential
section. Therefore, anyone planning to operate a pub has no choice
but to do so in a residential area, and should be allowed to do so over
his neighbor's objections.

Part of what is instructive about R. Schreiber's responsum is his
awareness of the broader social implications of each particular ruling.
On the one hand, part of the impetus for seeking relief for the liquor
vendors is "this [i.e., barring the liquor vendor in question from oper-

ating out of his home because of his neighbor's objections] will encourage the filing of suits by those who until now have said nothing; and when others hear that these individuals are successful in their suits they will bring action against their many neighbors who sell wine [by the glass] who will then be left without a livelihood." The implication here, more explicit in his later remarks, is that he would not be particularly sorry to see the liquor establishments, which were patronized heavily by non-Jews, closed down, but he is concerned about the wine bars, which he apparently considers more respectable because their clientele is almost entirely Jewish, being tarred with the same brush. On the other hand, at the end of his responsum he suggests a way of distinguishing between the two so that the law can be employed to shut down one without affecting the other. In any case, R. Schreiber realizes that in protecting the rights of one vendor, he is protecting the rights of his business colleagues as well.

The consideration of personal and conventional standards of pollution takes an interesting turn with the introduction of two notions to the discussion. The first is that of relying on the judgment of experts to determine whether or not a state of intolerable pollution exists. Originally, this concept appears simply to fill a lacuna in the halakhic framework. Whereas the Mishnah specifies the distance that certain causes of damage and/or nuisance must be kept from one's neighbor's property, there is no discussion of the distances to be required in other such cases. Therefore, the late thirteenth- and early fourteenth-century German halakhist R. Asher b. Yehiel rules[42] that, for all cases where distances have not been established by the Talmud, they are to be established by experts. These experts, he adds, are empowered to dictate distances greater than the ones required by the Talmud itself. In the twentieth century, however, this notion is used by R. Hosea Rabbinowitz[43] to shift the power to define what constitutes unacceptable pollution away from the plaintiff. Responding to a suit by a town in Israel complaining of odor coming from a nearby agricultural settlement that is using a mixture of fresh water and sewage water for irrigation, he rules that if experts determine that the town in question is a sufficient distance from the agricultural settlement to render the odor pollution negligible, we accept their evaluation in the face of plaintiff claims to the contrary. Presumably, R. Rabbinowitz is motivated both by a desire to remove this determination from the hands of an interested party and by a wish to objectify to the degree possible an admittedly amorphous point of law.

The second concept, the talmudic principle *dina de-malkhuta dina,* "the law of the land is law," is introduced into the discussion by R. Joel Sirkes, a seventeenth-century halakhist who lived in Poland. He comments on an observation of R. Joseph Karo's that, although one may claim presumption of right for contemporary privies, unlike those of talmudic times, a neighbor may still object to one's establishing a privy *ab initio.* (R. Karo codifies this view in his *Shulhan Arukh*;[44] it is not shared by his Ashkenazic counterpart R. Moses Isserles,[45] who allows the digging of a covered privy despite a neighbor's objections.) R. Sirkes glosses R. Karo's comment, saying, "In the present era it is the law of the land [to have a privy next to one's house] and no one may object to it."[46] Here, personal standards of acceptable pollution give way to governmentally established ones.

In the twentieth century R. Abraham Isaiah Karelitz, known as the Hazon Ish, takes R. Sirkes's point a step further: "Moreover, today that there are no privies outside the city and each house contains a privy in the style of the Persian privies [that is, it is enclosed], the custom has been established that one may not object to a neighbor's [privy] *even if one is ill* [emphasis added—ED]."[47] R. Karelitz then cites R. Sirkes's aforementioned ruling as a precedent. That is, the social contract as it is concretized in law or usage supersedes, in this view, not only the perceived but also the actual, health-based concerns of the individual.

The tension between personal and conventional standards is also the subtext of a pollution-related decision rendered by the Israeli Supreme Court in 1966.[48] In 1961 the Knesset passed a pollution control statute, forbidding excessive noise, odor, and smoke pollution. Rather than defining what constitutes "excessive," however, the law, in somewhat confusing language, requires the ministers of health and the interior to formulate regulations that would flesh out the actual contours of the law, including—it is not clear if this is mandatory or optional[49]—setting definite standards for what constitutes unacceptable levels of noise, odor, and smoke pollution. After close to five years these regulations were still not in place. Consequently, a number of individuals who were suffering from noise, odor, and/or smoke pollution caused by their neighbors—these included a bakery, a cement plant, and a fertilizer factory—appealed to the Supreme Court asking for an injunction requiring the ministers of health and the interior to show cause why they should not immediately formulate such regulations.

There were several issues considered by the court (which, incidentally, ruled two to one in favor of the plaintiffs). I wish to consider only one of them here, namely, the contention of the respondents (the ministers of health and the interior) that such regulations were not essential to the plaintiffs bringing their cases to court and having them heard. Justice Haim Kohn was inclined to agree with this argument:

> It is certainly true that established, objective guidelines for what constitutes "intense" or "unreasonable" [pollution] would simplify greatly the court's judicial task. . . . Nonetheless, the fact that rendering judgment without *a priori* standards and measurements is likely to be more difficult and complex, this does not mean that it is impossible. . . . I see nothing preventing the court from establishing, whether by means of witnesses who saw the nuisance or heard the noise or inhaled the odor, or through personal impression from having seen the place or heard the noise or inhaled the odor, whether the nuisance which is the basis for the complaint is "intense" or "unreasonable" or not.[50]

Thus, while not necessarily favoring case-by-case standards for establishing levels of acceptable pollution, Justice Kohn sees such a system as workable.

In contrast, his colleague Moshe Zilberg is dismissive toward such a modus operandi. Among his reasons for extreme skepticism is the following:

> If no precise definitions are formulated [for the unacceptable forms of pollution enumerated in the statue] than the reasonability of the noise level will be determined in each case, and for that case only, by the presiding judge. People's sensitivity toward noise is quite subjective. . . . There are those who are bothered by sudden, loud noise that comes, for example, from nearby thunder, and there are people who can be driven to the brink of insanity by a faucet dripping once every ten seconds. . . . I imagine that a married man with ten children between the ages of one and twelve is much less sensitive to noise than an elderly bachelor who spends his days in his silent library. We may conclude, therefore, that, absent rules and guidelines . . . the fate of the defendant will depend on how many children the judge has."[51]

Justice Zilberg is opposed to case-by-case rulings, not only because
they are unwieldy, but because they are highly subjective and therefore unjust. Established standards make it possible for everyone to
know what the law expects of him and to abide by it—or to choose not
to and risk suffering the consequences.

We have seen that there is a general, though not universal, inclination
among halakhists to move away from personal definitions of pollution
and toward conventional or even externally imposed ones. In part, this
may reflect the tendency of halakhah, like all legal systems, to prefer
conformity and simplicity over relativity and complexity. In large
part, however—and we have seen only a few of the dozens of expressions of this concern in halakhic literature—halakhists are acutely
aware that limiting pollution may have adverse economic consequences for the one so limited and therefore, ultimately, for the
economy as a whole. Where possible, halakhah tries to satisfy both
the economic and environmental needs of the community. Thus, the
Mishnah allows the establishment of a tannery near a town only if it is
at least fifty cubits away and to the town's east[52]—which meant, given
that the prevailing winds in Israel come in from the Mediterranean in
the west, that the tannery and its noxious odors were generally down-
wind. But such solutions are not always possible, and halakhah, faced
with the prospect of nuisance or pollution on the one hand or economic deprivation on the other, accepts the former to avoid the latter.

This may seem a depressing conclusion to reach at a conference
devoted to exploring Jewish concern for nature and the environment.
However, two important qualifiers must be added, one of which distinguishes us from the societies addressed by premodern halakhists,
the other of which unites us with them. The first, distinguishing, observation is that the economic condition of Jews, indeed of humanity,
in late antiquity and the medieval period was radically different from
our own. Many more people were living at or near the subsistence
level. Closing down someone's mill or shop could have resulted in
starvation for the owner or for members of his family. Before evaluating the rabbinic rulings reviewed here, we must understand the stakes
involved.

Second, these rulings are an important reminder that there are costs
associated with pollution control, and halakhah's preference for conventional standards of acceptable pollution levels makes it more

likely that the cost of such control will be shared by all the beneficiaries in an equitable fashion. Otherwise, what we have is the NIMBY ("not in my backyard") syndrome in which the politically powerful prevail and the politically weak get an incinerator or a toxic waste dump next door. Perhaps if we all knew that we, too, might be neighbors to an ecological eyesore, we would be more willing to spend time and money finding ways to prevent such eyesores from being necessary in the first place.

This last point was nicely summarized by the Federal District Court for the District of Vermont in *International Paper Co. vs. Oulette* (107 S. Ct. 805 [1987]). Residents of Vermont living on the shore of Lake Champlain applied to the Vermont courts to sue the International Paper Company, which was releasing effluents into the lake from the New York side. The paper company claimed that the Vermont court's authority was superseded by that of the federal government under the Clean Water Act, and therefore moved for summary judgment. The court eventually determined that while the residents could undertake to sue the paper company in a New York court, to subject a New York firm to Vermont statues would be an infringement on federal authority. Part of the court's judgment follows:

> By establishing a permit system for effluent discharges, Congress implicitly has recognized that the goal of the Clean Water Act—elimination of water pollution—cannot be achieved immediately, and that it cannot be realized without incurring costs. The EPA Administrator issues permits according to established effluent standards and water quality standards that in turn are based on available technology . . . and competing public and industrial uses. . . . If a State elects to impose its own standards it must consider the technological feasibility of more stringent controls. Given the nature of these complex decisions, it is not surprising that the Act limits the right to administer the permit system to the EPA and the source states. . . .
>
> An interpretation [of the Clean Water Act] that preserved actions brought under an affected State's law would disrupt this balance of interests. If a New York source were liable for violations of Vermont law, that law could effectively override both the permit requirements of and the policy choices made by the source State. The affected State's nuisance laws would subject the point source to the threat of legal and equitable penalties if the permit standards were less strict than those imposed by the affected State. Such penalties would compel the source to adopt different control standards and a different compliance sched-

ule from those approved by the EPA, *even though the affected State had not engaged in the same weighing of costs and benefits* [emphasis added—ED].

The court is arguing that one state cannot impose its own, "personal," environmental standards on another state without having taken into account all the factors involved in the formulation of the federal, "conventional," standard. To do otherwise is to allow one party to impose exacting environmental standards on the other without sharing the cost and responsibility for maintaining those standards.

The application of notions of conventionality and equity in environmental matters is far from simple, especially at the global level. These difficulties notwithstanding, I will conclude with some thoughts about how these concepts might be usefully applied to the problem of global warming. Although there is some debate about the degree of the danger and its causes, it is generally acknowledged that the planet's temperature is rising gradually, that this is due in part to our constant production of carbon dioxide, and that the potential results of continued warming could be catastrophic, including the inundation of coastal areas and the submersion of the Japanese islands.

Now comes the hard part. In order to avoid this scenario we need to reduce fossil fuel emissions significantly. The problem is: Who is going to do the reducing and by how much? The developing countries argue that the Western countries are producing much more carbon dioxide than they are and are much more able to absorb the financial costs of reducing emissions. The Western countries argue that the burden must be borne by all. If one were to adopt halakhah's preference for conventionality, which position would one support?

Although on its face the Western position of shared burdens may seem to be the more conventionally oriented one, we must recall the economic basis for halakhah's stance. A halakhist might turn to Western leaders and say, "Would you be willing to accept for yourselves the level of economic hardship that will be imposed on the developing nations if they accept the levels of emissions control you are demanding? If not, you ought to be ready to compensate them for economic losses sustained as a result or to agree to shift more of the reductions to yourselves, given that you are more able to sustain such reductions financially." It is always dangerous to speak in the name of others;

nonetheless, I believe that such a response is a reasonable if not compelling extrapolation from halakhic sources.

Halakhah and the modern world have much to say to each other. Halakhah, if approached with care, on the one hand, and with creativity, on the other, can yield important insights for wrestling with the burning issues of our day, the environmental crisis among them. On the other hand, modernity challenges halakhists, and the larger Jewish community, to break out of the narrow view that "Jewish" issues are limited to reliable kosher supervision, the use of modern technology on the Sabbath, and the problem of obtaining Jewish divorces for women whose husbands refuse to grant them. We live in the world, and its problems are ours. The environment is a Jewish problem; let us look to our age-old tradition for responses that are often as timely now as they were centuries ago.

Notes

1. For the classic statement of the view associating rapacious environmental policies with the "Judeo-Christian tradition," see Lynn White, Jr., "The Historical Roots of Our Ecologic Crisis," *Science* 155 (1967): 1203–7.

2. See, for example, R. Moshe Feinstein (20th cen., Poland and the United States), *Responsa Igrot Moshe*, Hoshen Mishpat 2, responsa 18 and 76. For a summary of the halakhic literature on smoking, see Menachem Slae, *Smoking and Damage to Health in the Halachah* (Jerusalem: Acharai Publications, 1990).

3. The following terms are used in this article: Mishnah, baraita, Tosefta, Yerushalmi, Bavli, and tanna. The Mishnah is a collection of rabbinic teachings from roughly 50–200 C.E. compiled and edited by Rabbi Judah the Patriarch in Palestine at the beginning of the second century. A sage from the period 50–200 is referred to as a tanna—literally, a repeater of teachings. A teaching from this period that was not incorporated into Rabbi Judah's Mishnah came to be known as a *baraita*—an "outside" text. For the most part, these texts are no longer extant in an organized form. An exception is the Tosefta, a collection of uncertain date of tannaitic traditions different, for the most part, in style and content from the Mishnah's teachings. Beginning in the third century the continuators of the tannaim, who came to be known as the amoraim, wrote commentaries to the Mishnah and the baraita texts known to them and continued to discuss issues related to or generated by the previous tannaitic teaching. This occurred both in Palestine and in Babylonia (present-day Iraq). The document containing the Palestinian traditions, completed sometime between 360 and the end of the first quarter of the fifth century, became known as the Yerushalmi, or the Jerusalem Talmud. In Babylonia, probably sometime in the seventh or eighth century, the document known as the Bavli, or the Babylonian Talmud, was completed.

4. Mishnah Bava Batra 2.3.

5. I am intentionally translating the original literally to show its ambiguity. The Mishnah could be referring either to one who wishes to open a store or to a store that already has been opened.

6. The meaning of this last phrase is unclear. The Bavli interprets it as the right to teach Torah to young children in one's home despite the resulting additional noise in the courtyard. More convincing is the suggestion of Z. M. Pineles, *Darkah shel Torah* (Vienna, 1861), 125–26, that the children in question are apprentices who help the craftsman in his labors. The neighbors must bear with the noise and disturbance created by their presence.

7. Cf. Meiri's paraphrase of the Mishnah: ". . . the neighbors, or one of them, can restrain him. . . ." And see Rashi to Bava Batra, 20b s.v. *ve-'im hiziq*, and R. Jonah to Bava Batra 21a, s.v. *u-veraita*.

8. Bavli Bava Batra 21a.

9. See the following note.

10. In fact, this seeming anomaly leads some commentators (Ramban, Bava Batra 20b, s.v. *ha de-tenan*, and Rashba, loc. cit., s.v. *hanut*), based on Tosefta Bava Batra 1.4 and Yerushalmi Bava Batra 2.3 (13b), to understand the objection in the case of the shop as having to do primarily with increased foot traffic in the courtyard rather

than with noise. See also A. Sofer's comment in his edition of Meiri's *Beit ha-Behirah*, Bava Batra 20b, s.v. *hanut* n. 4.

11. *Beit ha-Behirah* Bava Batra 20b, s.v. *hanut shebe-hazer.*

12. Responsa Maharalbah, no. 97.

13. *Hazon Yehezkel*, Neziqin: vol. 2, Bava Batra 2.6 (novellae).

14. Bavli Qiddushin 24b. For the actual terminology used by ibn Habib, see Bavli Bava Qamma 9b.

15. Ibn Habib's language echoes Bavli Yoma 83a.

16. William M. Prosser, John W. Wade, and Victor E. Schwartz, *Torts: Cases and Materials*, 8th ed. (Westbury, N.Y.: The Foundation Press, 1988), 811.

17. Maimonides, Laws of Neighbors 6.12.

18. In the Tosefta's version of the Mishnah's teaching (Tosefta Bava Batra 1.4), foul odors are also mentioned.

19. Bavli Bava Batra 22b–23a.

20. Apparently R. Joseph's trees overhung property belonging to the bloodletters (Tosafot Bava Batra 23a, s.v. *atu*) or the public domain (Meiri, *Bet ha-Behirah*, Bava Batra 23a, s.v. *me-ahar*). R. Jonah of Gerona, *Aliyot de-Rabbenu Yonah*, Bava Batra 23a, s.v. *Rav Yosef*, suggests that R. Joseph owned trees in the middle of a field belonging to someone else.

21. From the Bavli's comment about the birds spoiling the dates, and from the later implication that the damage caused would not be viewed as such by everyone, it would appear that the birds, initially attracted by the blood, subsequently fouled the fruit on R. Joseph's trees by tracking blood on them. R. Joseph's remark about "removing the 'korkor'" suggests to some commentators that R. Joseph was disturbed by the noise of the birds as well; see, for example, Maimonides, Laws of Neighbors 11.5.

22. Yerushalmi Bava Batra 2.2 (13b).

23. *Responsa Rashba*, 2.45.

24. *Responsa Maharam mi-Ruttenburg*, Prague ed., no. 233.

25. *Terumat ha-Deshen, Pesaqim u-Khetavim*, no. 137.

26. *Rema* to *Shulhan Arukh* Hoshen Mishpat 155.37.

27. Rashi to Bava Batra 23a, s.v. *beveit.*

28. Tosafot Bava Batra 23a, s.v. *bequtra.*

29. *Responsa Rashba*, loc. cit.

30. *Aliyot de-Rabbenu Yona*, Bava Batra 23a, s.v. *hani.* See also *Hiddushei ha-Rashba* Bava Batra 23a, s.v. *amar lei.*

31. See *Shulhan Arukh* Hoshen Mishpat 155.41 and *Be'er ha-Golah* ad loc., no. 50. A similar ruling can be found in a different but related context, defining the individual of delicate constitution who may bathe during the initial week of mourning; see *Shulhan Arukh Y.D.* 381.3.

32. *Responsa Ribash*, no. 196.

33. *Pisqei Din Yerushalayim: Dinei Memonot u-Verurei Yahadut*, 2.167.

34. Ibid.

35. It should be noted that Nahmanides, in his novellae to Bava Batra 59a, s.v. *ha de-tenan*, argues that the reason no presumption of right can be established for the

pollution caused by smoke and the privy is that, unlike other forms of nuisance, they do not damage one's property but cause actual physical harm.

36. Tosefta Bava Batra 1.4.

37. Yerushalmi Bava Batra 2.3 (13b).

38. Mishnah Ketubot 7.10.

39. *Shulhan Arukh* Hoshen Mishpat 155.44.

40. Tosafot Bava Batra 23a, s.v. *ein hazaqa.*

41. *Responsa Hatam Sofer* Hoshen Mishpat, no. 92.

42. *Responsa Rosh,* 108.10.

43. Hosea Rabbinowitz, "The Degree of Liability for Ecological Damage Caused by Irrigation" (in Hebrew), *Tehumin* 7 (1986): 405.

44. *Shulhan Arukh* Hoshen Mishpat 155.38.

45. Glosses of the *Rema* to *Shulhan Arukh* Hoshen Mishpat 155.37. However, R. Karo's view is shared by the authoritative seventeenth-century halakhist R. Shabbetai Cohen (*Siftei Kohen* to *Shulhan Arukh* Hoshen Mishpat 155.19).

46. *Bayit Hadash* Hoshen Mishpat 155, s.v. *u-veit ha-kissei.*

47. *Hazon Ish* Hoshen Mishpat, Bava Batra 13.12.

48. *Pisqei Din shel Bet ha-Mishpat ha-Elyon le-Yisrael* 20 (1966), part 1, 309–38.

49. This question is debated by the judges in the case; see ibid., 321–22, 327, 333.

50. Ibid., 322.

51. Ibid., 324–25.

52. Mishnah Bava Batra 2.9.

Jewish Death Practices:
A Commentary on the Relationship of
Humans to the Natural World

DAVID KRAEMER

Writing about death practices of the Mambai people of the island of Timor, Peter Metcalf and Richard Huntington remark on "the constant reiteration in ritual language of the motif of the decaying corpse. . . ." Commenting on the centrality of this motif, the authors suggest:

> The significance of this motif relates directly to fundamental ideas of Mambai religion and cosmology. These ideas are expressed in the most sacred and esoteric of their myths. . . . It is a creation myth. Impregnated by Father Heaven, Earth Mother gives birth to the mountains, the trees, and the first people. Having instructed her children about mortuary rituals, she dies. But her body does not entirely decompose. An outer layer forms the "black earth," but beneath this topsoil formed out of her own body the Mother remains whole and pure, her white milk undiminished by death and decay. From this milk plants draw life, and in turn men and animals feed on the plants.[1]
>   The debt that humans owe to the Mother for the gift of life is the underlying motivation behind Mambai death rituals. That debt must be paid back with their bodies, which return to black earth again. Failure to return the debt would throw the entire cosmos out of kilter; plants would not grow to nourish humans, and children would not be born.[2]

Death ritual is here an expression of the relationship of humans to the earth. The relationship established at creation is recapitulated in the ritual of returning-to-the-earth for the Mambai dead.

This example, meant by Metcalf and Huntington to represent one possible interpretive paradigm, suggests that death rituals might be one of a society's most significant expressions of their perceptions of the relationship of humans and the natural world. The foundation of such an interpretive paradigm is the recognition 1) that the relationship between humans and the earth is likely to be established in a people's creation myths (though it might, in theory, originate in myths concerning a subsequent age); 2) that the relationship might be re-lived in a variety of a people's rituals; but 3) that death rituals are likely to be first among them. This recognition demands that serious consideration always be given to the possibility that death rituals might serve as a lens through which to view and interpret a people's conceptions of this relationship.

Other examples, which I take from the ancient world, will buttress the plausibility of this interpretive approach. Ancient Egyptian religion assumed an essentially static world, in which nothing significant ever changes. In such a world, "creation is the only event that really matters supremely, since it alone can be said to have made a change." Because everything that is was established at creation, it is the story of creation uniquely that holds the key to understanding the present.[3]

Ancient Egyptian death practices express complete fidelity to this belief in the unchanging quality of the created world. On the surface, death would appear to be the ultimate change in status—a radical challenge to the beliefs described above. But, as is well known, Egyptians fought this challenge by rendering death an "unchanged" state. In preparing their deceased for entombment, they sought, to the extent possible, to preserve the body from physical change (decay). This might have been accomplished through mummification. Alternatively, a stone effigy could serve as a "replacement" for the body of the deceased, creating a permanent body that was immune to decay. The liturgy of burial, as well, was directed toward this end. Mortuary priests addressed the deceased by declaring (for example): "Thy bones perish not, thy flesh sickens not, thy members are not distant from thee."[4] In addition to these steps, each person was entombed along with his or her personal ornaments, toiletry needs, pots and dishes containing food and drink, and sometimes with weapons and tools. All of this was evidence, of course, of the belief that nothing substantial had changed, for the needs of death were essentially identical to the needs of life. The body, without which the individual could not survive, continued to demand the same sustenance.[5]

In this system, death practices clearly served as a reflection of and commentary on the created world. In this static world, humans, like the rest of creation, were in their essence static, unchanging even in the face of death. An Egyptian who witnessed these rituals and experienced death in this way could have little doubt of this "fact."

Zoroastrianism, the ancient Persian religion, provides an equally powerful example. The *Vendidad*, a part of the Avesta, opens with the following words:

> Ahura Mazda spake unto Spitama Zarathustra, saying:
> I have made every land dear (to its people). . . .
> The first of the good lands and countries which I, Ahura Mazda, created, was Airyana Vaego, by the Vanguhi Daitya.
> Thereupon came Angra Mainyu, *who is all death*, and he counter-created the serpent in the river and Winter, a work of the Daevas. . . .
> The second of the good lands and countries which I, Ahura Mazda, created, was the plains. . . .
> Thereupon came Angra Mainyu, *who is all death*, and he counter-created the locust, *which brings death* unto cattle and plants.
> The third of the good lands and countries which I, Ahura Mazda, created, was the strong, holy Mouru.
> Thereupon came Angra Mainyu, *who is all death*, and he counter-created plunder and sin. [emphasis added][6]

And so forth. The creation of the world is enacted in a series of steps and countersteps, the benevolent god, Ahura Mazda (or Ohrmazd; see below), creating good land and his evil counterpart, Angra Mainyu, creating suffering and death. The text is emphatic in its insistence that Angra Mainyu, who creates death, is all death.[7]

The creation of humanity itself proceeds in the following steps: The Just Man was created sixth in the order of creation (followed only by Fire). Man was created in five parts—"body, breath, soul, form and fravahr" (that part of man "which is in the presence of Ohrmazd the Lord"). The tradition explains the reason for creation in these parts: "so that when during the Assault men die, the body rejoins the earth, the breath the wind, the form the sun, and the soul the fravahr, so that the devs should not be able to destroy the soul." The first man, Gayomard, met death because of the Evil Spirit, but, upon death, he

emitted seed which was purified by the light of the sun. This seed led
to the growth of special plants, from which all of humanity ultimately
emerged.[8]

According to the system outlined above, there is a primeval enmity
built into the very fabric of creation. Good and evil, products of different and antagonistic creating gods, are and will ever be in opposition
to one another (until, that is, the end of history and the final defeat of
the force of evil). Since, in this belief, evil and death are essentially
equated, death must be seen as the greatest of mundane evils, to be
hated and shunned. Indeed, Zoroastrian religious practice, as codified
in the *Vendidad*, was as much as anything else a system for dealing
with the danger of death.

The deceased, whose soul had departed and whose body had been
possessed by the demon of death, the Drug Nasu, was to be disposed
of as immediately as possible. But there were practical limitations on
the disposal of the dead. As is well known, ideally, corpses were to be
placed on *dakhma*s, towers for the dead, where their bodies would be
consumed by dogs and birds. In a territory where there were no
*dakhma*s, corpses were instead to be placed "on the highest summits,
where they know there are always corpse-eating dogs and corpse-eating birds" (*Vendidad*, Fargard 6, 6:45). If the season or weather made
proper disposal impossible (in the winter, for example, there may be
no dogs and birds about to consume the corpse), the dead were to be
buried in the house until conditions changed, at which time they could
be exhumed and properly exposed (Fargard 8, 2:4–10).

From even these few details, it is clear that Zoroastrian death practices recapitulate the enmity built into creation at its origins. Evil and
impure death, brought into the world by the Evil God of creation and
the demons who do the work of that God, must be kept separate from
the pure earth. Humans must similarly maintain their distance from
death impurity. Thus, death must literally be carried away; permanent
interment of the corpse is a sin, bringing together, as it does, opposing
forces. But to say that impure death and pure earth must be separated
is not to say that humans, purified of death long after death, remain
separated from the earth. Rather, the dust of the person, consumed and
then scattered, will rejoin the earth, later to be reassembled for resurrection.[9] Earth and death cannot be united, Earth and humans ultimately must be. In practice, the purity of the earth must always be

protected. To fail to do so is, in Zoroastrianism, a sin of the highest degree.

We could multiply examples to demonstrate the claim made earlier, but these should already suffice. Death and creation are inextricably linked. Death practice, therefore, will serve as a commentary on the meaning of creation and the place of humans within it.

We may now turn to classical Jewish death practices, as described in rabbinic literature,[10] to consider the nature of their commentary on the relationship between humans and the natural world.

According to Mishnah[11] Shabbat 23.5, immediately following death, the "needs of the dead" must be attended to. These "needs" (nearly identical to contemporary Roman practice)[12] include closing the eyes of the dead, anointing and washing the body, removing the pillow (or mattress), placing the dead on the sand (i.e., the ground), and tying the jaw in place. For present purposes, the most interesting of these practices is the removal of the body to the ground. What is the purpose, practically and symbolically, of this long forgotten practice?

The Mishnah explains that the purpose of this requirement is "so that he may remain" or, according to another version, "be cooled." Reasonably enough, in a warm climate where the dead might quickly begin to decompose, steps must be taken to delay the process, particularly if we interpret this requirement as pertaining only on Shabbat (when delay of burial until the next day is necessary). But the other practices described by the Mishnah are not restricted to the Sabbath, so such a limited interpretation is at least problematic. Moreover, as noted parenthetically above, the rabbinic customs closely mimic prevalent Roman customs, which include the laying of the deceased on the ground. Obviously the Roman custom was not motivated by Sabbath restrictions. It seems to me likely, therefore, that laying on the ground is a more popular Jewish custom, one which the rabbis behind the Mishnah endorse. The Mishnah's explanation of this practice may simply be a "rationalization" intended to deny popular explanations of the same practice. But, be that as it may, this doesn't change the fact that the placing-on-the-ground is the first step in a process which ultimately leads to the laying of the deceased in a cave under the ground. It is in this context that the practice must be interpreted.

Also crucial to interpretation is the more immediate mishnaic context. The Mishnah's discussion of the "needs of the dead" is part of a larger discussion of stringencies and leniencies pertaining to acts which are technically permitted on the Sabbath but are still problematic. For example, immediately preceding its discussion of preparations for burial, the Mishnah prohibits a person from waiting at the boundary of Sabbath-settlement in order to be closer to his fields at the Sabbath's end. In fact, merely standing by the boundary is technically permissible. The Mishnah's prohibition is motivated by the problematic intent of the person who would perform this act. By contrast, in the next ruling, "the business of the bride" and "the business of the dead" (bringing the casket and shroud) are permitted—though one who does these things runs the risk of actually transgressing the Sabbath—apparently because of the perceived importance of marriage and burial.

Which brings us to "the needs of the dead." These "needs of the dead" are distinct, in this mishnah, from the "business of the dead"— the latter involving preparations for the funeral and the former acts directly relating to the deceased. The needs of the dead are apparently considered sufficiently important to warrant some flexibility with respect to acts that would under other circumstances be prohibited on the Sabbath. Why so? If we admit (as the rabbinic record broadly suggests) that the deceased person was considered sentient, then he or she would have bona fide needs—needs relating to what he or she was actually *feeling*. What the deceased "needs," in other words, are steps to diminish the discomfort of death. So "oiling" (anointing) would be called for even on the Sabbath, because it would help eliminate the discomfort that stiffness brings the deceased. Similarly, if the body is sentient, decomposition would hurt, and slowing the process—as this mishnah suggests—would postpone discomfort. In this context, the question becomes whether separation of the body from the earth was also believed to be the source of discomfort. Evidence available elsewhere leads me to answer a tentative "yes."

Saul Lieberman documents the ancient Jewish belief (held by other peoples as well) that no fate was worse than lack of burial—lack of return to the soil.[13] If the dead would suffer by distance from the soil, then this practice may properly be construed as a "need of the dead," intended to avoid discomfort. This act, like others listed in the Mishnah, addressed or responded to genuine needs of the deceased, literally conceived. For this reason these practices were permitted on the Sabbath.

As mentioned, this placing on the ground was the first step in a long process of returning the body of the deceased to the soil. Of course, part of the process—a significant part—was the entombment of the deceased under the ground. But this was not identical to burial, and the difference is important. The Mishnah assumes, and archaeology has confirmed, that Jews would be buried in caves (see Mishnah Bava Batra 6.8). The bodies would be placed in spaces carved in the walls of the caves, and these niches (or ditches carved in shelves) would be closed with stones (or covered with stone slabs). But, crucially, the stones could be removed, and those who visited the deceased could therefore know—because they would witness—the progress of the decay of the flesh and its return to "dust." It was important to know when the flesh had decayed fully because, when the bones alone were left, they would be gathered and reburied—an occasion for both sadness (because it recalled the death itself) and celebration (because the deceased was finally "gathered unto his ancestors") (see Mishnah Mo'ed Qatan 1.5). Only at this final point was death fully realized—atonement complete and peace in the world of the dead assured.

The centrality of the return-to-the-earth in rabbinic death ritual is reinforced in a long-forgotten mourning ritual. Among the various obligations and prohibitions which apply to the mourner is the obligation to overturn all of the couches and beds in his home (see Mishnah Ta'anit 4.7 and Tosefta Mo'ed Qatan 2.9). Of course, if couches and beds (i.e., places to sit and recline) are unavailable, the mourner will be forced to sit on the ground—close to and in striking imitation of the deceased. It is crucial that we be mindful of this latter factor: that is, the partial participation of the mourner, through ritual enactment, in the experience of the deceased. The parallel of the experience of mourner and deceased takes many shapes: the special quality, for each, of the first three days following death, the inability of each to participate in "the settlement of the world" (through work and sex), *both* mourning the death for seven days (see Talmud Bavli, tractate Shabbat, p. 152a, bottom), and so forth. The requirement that the mourner be on or close to the ground is another of these parallels, one which ritually emphasizes the importance of such terrestrial proximity. As we saw above, death is about returning to the ground, the flesh returning to dust. But life, too, is never far from the earth.

The relationship between the rituals just recounted and Judaism's creation myth will be obvious. In its brief description of the creation of the first human, Genesis 2:7 relates that "the Lord God formed the person of dirt from the ground and blew into his nostrils the breath of life, and the human became a living soul." Humans (this first human, later separated into male and female) are earth, and therefore, as the author of Ecclesiastes much later states, just as all life comes from dirt, so must all life return to dirt (3:20). At first reading, the association between creation myth and death ritual is straightforward and the lesson of this association matter-of-fact. We are, in our essence, one with the earth, as our ritual of return-to-the-earth will ever remind us.

But the associations and ritual choices are not as simple as they initially seem. To begin with, as has often been noted, the Torah commences with not one creation story but two, and the accounts of the creation of humans differ significantly. In contrast with the story of Genesis 2, which we just considered, Genesis 1 emphasizes that God created humans by God's word, created them "in the image of God." This account allows for no essential connection between humans and the earth, for God did not create humans out of a preexistent substance. Moreover, the claim that humans are "in the image of God" seems to suggest that humans are "above" the earth, and certainly essentially different from it. So, by a critical reading, the Torah offers a choice of creation stories, a choice that will lead to drastically different conclusions concerning the relationship of humans and the natural world.

I am sensitive to the fact that traditional readers, reading stories that are canonically juxtaposed, are unlikely to have read these two stories as opposing one another. Instead, apparent tensions or contradictions would surely have been smoothed over, somehow reconciled. Still, such readings will inevitably demand differences of emphasis or priority, that is, the reading of one of these two stories in light of the other. So, for example, the second, earth-bound story, might be viewed as a specification and elaboration of the first, God-directed story. But choices of emphasis are significant too, and the fact that living (and dying) Jewish culture, as portrayed by the rabbis, emphasized, in its death rituals, the second story instead of the first, is a matter of considerable note.

Imagine the alternative: If a Jewish society viewed as centrally important the belief that humans were created by God's word in God's image, then they might distance their dead from the earth—like Zoroastrians but for different reasons—or they might struggle to preserve the image of God, the human form, against deterioration—such as the ancient Egyptians did, but again for different reasons. The first version of the creation, like the second, could have been recapitulated in death ritual, and that ritual choice would have made an equally important point. The fact that this way was not taken, that the ritual draws our attentions to the primacy of the version of chapter two, shapes considerably our appreciation of the essential relationship between humans and the earth.

Moreover, the second creation story is not just about the creation of humans from the earth, as Ecclesiastes already appreciates. According to this same story, not only did God form humans out of the earth, but God also "formed out of the earth all the wild beasts and all the birds of the sky . . ." (Gen. 2:19). All life emerges from the earth, all life (as Ecclesiastes teaches) must return to the earth—all life is one with the earth and with each other.

The essential relationship between humans and all life, therefore, is enacted in the rabbinic death rituals described above. This too, of course, was not necessary. Again, imagine the alternative: The first creation story describes animals and humans in a strictly hierarchical relationship—the former were created by way of preparation for the latter, the latter were created to "rule over" the former. There is no obvious or necessary relationship between the two (that is, in their essence). To symbolize this hierarchical division, humans might have been distanced from the earth upon death, because there, in the earth, is the final resting place of animals. If animals become one with the earth, humans might be imagined to flee terrestrial life to the heavens (by "mysteriously" disappearing from high mountains, for example). This is a way that might have been. It is a way not taken.

To reiterate, the death rituals teach a lesson. In their recapitulation of the second creation story, they declare that humans are one with the animal kingdom and with the earth—one with the natural world. This is a relationship not of subduing or conquest, but of natural partnership. An act of abuse against the natural world is an abuse against humanity, and vice versa. In fact, the dichotomy of "human" and "natural world" is undermined in the view of this ritual mythology, because humans and the natural world are one—originating in the same substance, temporarily taking different forms, but returning, in their end, to the same form.

What are the normative implications of this conclusion? If we understand, with Robert Cover, that law (*nomos*) is the other side of narrative,[14] then the narrative and ritual telling of this story of the origins of humanity in-and-of-the-earth will have concrete ethical and normative consequences: The ancient Jewish ritual narrative demands that we not view the natural world as "other," something to serve our needs, something to exploit. Instead, it requires us to relate to the natural world—that is, to ourselves and the nonhuman world around us—as parts of an organic whole. Moreover, the death ritual narrative stands in tension with the basic premise of the (rabbinically construed) law of *bal tashhit* ("do not destroy")—that is, that any use of resources which serves human needs is not viewed as wasteful. Only if we recognize that no human need stands independent of the needs of the earth as a whole can we eliminate this tension. Indeed, though rabbinic teachings and practices might conflict with one another, in this case the reconciliation of the apparent conflict might yield the simplest translation of rabbinic values: our needs are part of, and must be harmonized with, the needs of the natural world.

Notes

1. Citing Elizabeth G. Traube, *Cosmology and Social Life: Ritual Exchange and the Mambai of East Timor* (Chicago: University of Chicago Press, 1986), 38–40, 215–16

2. Peter Metcalf and Richard Huntington, *Celebrations of Death: The Anthropology of Mortuary* Ritual, 2d ed., rev. (Cambridge: Cambridge University Press, 1991), 106–7.

3. Henri Frankfort, *Ancient Egyptian Religion* (New York: Columbia University Press, 1948; reprint, New York: Harper, 1961), 50–51.

4. Quoted in James Henry Breasted, *Development of Religion and Thought in Ancient Egypt* (New York: Scribner's, 1912), 57.

5. Frankfort, *Ancient Egyptian Religion*, 90, 93.

6. *The Sacred Books of the East*, vol. 3, *The Zend-Avesta*, trans. James Darmesteter (New York: The Christian Literature Company, 1898), 2–5.

7. Yasna 30.3–4, expresses the same belief in this language: "Truly there are two primal Spirits, twins renowned to be in conflict. . . . And when these two Spirits first came together they created life and not-life, and how at the end Worst Existence shall be for the wicked, but (the House of) Best Purpose for the just man." Translation by Mary Boyce, in *Textual Sources for the Study of Zoroastrianism* (Chicago: University of Chicago Press, 1984), 35.

8. For this record of creation, see Boyce, *Textual Sources* 48–52. Though these traditions are included in a later record of the Zoroastrian Zand, Boyce's judgment is that they are earlier Zoroastrian beliefs: see p. 45.

9. See ibid., 52.

10. Though the practices of non-rabbinized Jews, and even of the rabbis themselves, may often have diverged from the rabbinic record, as the evidence of Beth Shearim testifies.

11. The Mishnah is the first of the classical rabbinic compositions, completed in ca. 200 C.E. It is, by appearance, a law code, though some have argued for alternative interpretations of its intended or primary purpose.

12. J. M. C. Toynbee, *Death and Burial in the Roman World* (Ithaca, N.Y.: Cornell University Press, 1971), 44.

13. Saul Lieberman, "Some Aspects of After Life in Early Rabbinic Literature," in *Harry Austryn Wolfson: Jubilee Volume on the Occasion of His Seventy-Fifth Birthday* (Jerusalem: American Academy for Jewish Research, 1965), 515–22.

14. Robert M. Cover, "The Supreme Court, 1982 Term—Foreword: Nomos and Narrative," *Harvard Law Review* 97, no. 4 (1983).

Response.
Mastery and Stewardship, Wonder and Connectedness: A Typology of Relations to Nature in Jewish Text and Tradition

EILON SCHWARTZ

My academic home is in the School of Education at the Hebrew University. Every year for the past five years I have traveled to the United States and visited Jewish day schools on the eastern seaboard. I have probably visited forty schools from all denominations. I imagine that on this coming trip, like others, a principal who knows that my particular field of research is "something about the environment" will proudly escort me into an elementary school classroom—Reform, Conservative, Orthodox, community—that has been turned into a rain forest. It would do E. O. Wilson proud. Often papier-mâché ants are on the floor and on newspaper-constructed plant leaves—several species. Epiphyte vines climb on trees. Names of bird species are pinned to the branches. In one school, at the entrance to the enchanted forest stood a sign: "Welcome to the Garden of Eden." The identification of Eden as "the world-pole of wilderness," to use Evan Eisenberg's phrase from *The Ecology of Eden,* is an active metaphor among teachers and students.[1] I might add that the language of discourse used in the schools is clearly not secular in tone. Like John Muir's cathedral of Yosemite, language of nature in the Western world is infused with religious language.

But what nature are we talking about? And what kind of religiosity? While I invariably smile at these demonstrations of environmental awareness in the schools, I have learned to see such demonstrations more as part of the problem than the solution. It is a problem philosophically, in that, as the environmental historian William Cronin has pointed out, wilderness is by definition a landscape without people. Nature is removed from history. In the Americas, it has often meant ignoring the natives, or dehumanizing them by romanticizing them as part of nature in the great culture/nature divide. Culture is civilized. Nature is primitive. Dealing with the Yanomami tribes in this manner has been well documented in Candice Slater's "Amazonia as Edenic Narrative."[2] In Israel, I have taken many hikes with guides through "pristine nature"—an absurd notion in the most settled landscape in human history, and politically troubling when one realizes that pristine nature more often than not masks the Arab historical narrative in the landscape, as Yael Zerubavel has alluded to in her work on trees and Zionism.[3] All too often, nature preservation has been enlisted in the cause of erasing or confining the Arab presence in the Jewish homeland.[4] Nature becomes an escape from history.

It is an escape in space, as well as in time. Wilderness is about places far from our lives, where no humans live. Wilderness teaches us nothing about how to live our lives since wilderness, by definition, is a place without (cultured) people. Cities, then, are not an alternative landscape, but rather are understood as the flip side of the same coin. Nature is nature and culture is culture, and never the twain shall meet. By dealing exclusively with wilderness, we are liable to ignore the fact that our lives are embedded in the natural world, no matter where we live. Focusing only on wilderness allows us to ignore the social, environmental, and political implications of our civilized lives. Wilderness teaches us to leave parts of nature untouched; it does not teach us how to touch nature, which is the central environmental issue facing humanity.

This philosophical deconstruction of wilderness might be seen as good news for those of us who seek to reunite Judaism with the natural world. Judaism's reported lack of a wilderness idea has often been seen by environmental philosophers as part of its shortcomings, further evidence of its radically anthropocentric assumptions, symbolized for environmentalists in the biblical command "to fill the earth and master it."[5] The contradictory, or complementary command of Genesis 2, "to till and to tend," which became the major prooftext for a stewardship model of environmentalism, has been perceived, nevertheless, from the wilderness perspective of environmentalism to maintain an exalted role for humans in the Creation. Tikva Frymer-Kensky concurs. According to her reading of the Bible, nature without humanity (wilderness) is seen as the demise of the divine plan.[6] Therefore, the postmodern attack on the wilderness idea from within environmental ethics suggests the possibility of a more sympathetic appraisal of Jewish environmental intuitions by a post-wilderness environmentalism. Conversely, for Jewish traditional views, it creates a safer place to unite with environmentalism, as wilderness perspectives were often deemed to deify nature, and thus to advocate a neo-pagan theology. Judaism and environmentalism were often seen at odds from both sides when environmentalism was framed through a wilderness perspective. Judaism and environmentalism seem to have a safer starting point when humans are reunited with nature.

The linking of humans and nature is becoming an increasingly attractive place to sit, from an ecological point of view as well. Witness Daniel Botkin's *Discordant Harmonies*, which points out the failure of the wilderness myth for scientific policy in the environmental movement.[7] The abandonment of the static view of the natural world for a natural world with an unfolding history places human beings into the story. As landscape ecologists contend, humans are part of the natural world.[8] Such a constructivist view of nature, one which returns humans to their place in the world, is a more obvious place for biblical Judaism, as described by Tikva Frymer-Kensky. It is a more obvious place for rabbinic Judaism as described by David Kraemer, as well, in which the Genesis 2 version of the human-nature relationship is literally memorialized.[9] Ecological science no longer suggests only Lynn White's St. Francis as the proper environmentalist. Rene Dubos's St. Benedictine, and a view of Eden as human-tended garden, becomes a validated environmental role model.[10]

So, if wilderness is such a problematic idea, and stewardship is both environmentally and Jewishly attractive, why do I feel so uncomfortable at the shift in focus? Partly, I am sure, it is because my own environmentalism is the product of a wilderness tradition. John Muir sits deep in my bones. And another part of my discomfort is my recognition of shortcomings in the stewardship model. While the stewardship model is perhaps a corrective to the wilderness idea, can we celebrate religiously and ecologically the replacement of one with the other? The dangers are no less serious, environmentally and religiously, with a stewardship model. Is nature something to be managed? And is our religious ideal one of improving on God's Creation? There is the danger of a technocratic model as our environmental and religious ideal, a danger often seen in the popular literature. A few years back, *Scientific American* put out an issue called "Managing Planet Earth," one which made spiritually-leaning environmentalists quite uneasy. The wilderness model, after all, has a strong humbling dimension. Such a religious ideal might get lost in the stewardship model.

However, while mourning the loss of wilderness values in an environmental worldview, and wary of stewardship values, my discomfort is generated primarily from a third place. The hegemonic notion of a proper attitude toward the natural world, the search for an unambiguous cultural metaphor, strikes me as philosophically dangerous and spiritually and environmentally shallow. Monocultures are problematic, culturally and ecologically, and the loss of dialectical tension in our worldviews—the flattening of our cultural metaphors into one overarching metaphor—inevitably reduces the depth and range of our cultural vision.

Genesis 1 and 2, according to Joseph Dov Soloveitchik, offers us a dialectical model of the human situation. Adam I, a "little lower than the angels," was for Soloveitchik "majestic man." Majestic man was indeed an ideal, celebrating the unique position of humans in the Creation. Its danger, according to Soloveitchik, was when it was removed from dialectical tension with Adam II who "tills and tends"—Adam I's alter ego in a dual personality. It was then that Adam I was in danger of becoming what the environmental critique of the Judeo-Christian tradition claimed was the tradition's ideal: a human who viewed the world as being created for his or her use. For Soloveitchik, that was the modern situation.[11] Modernity celebrates Adam I at the same time that it delegitimizes the deep religious existentialism of Adam II.

I believe that an environmental reading of Genesis 2 leads in different directions from that which Soloveitchik maintains. Far from the existential loneliness which is at the heart of Soloveitchik's reading, I would hold that there is a very deep sense of belonging to the world, and that physicality, rather than being a problem, is a source of deep spiritual meaning. But the educational insight—that there are different views of the human which need to interact, and that the loss of any of these ideals leads to a life, and world, out of balance—is an important one. The wilderness ideal became problematic, perhaps, when it became the only environmental metaphor, or primary metaphor, for human relations with the natural world. One-dimensional ideals are flat and have no anchor to prevent their misinterpretation. Rather than Adam I and II, an environmental Genesis might have preferred a wilderness-stewardship dialectic. It is tempting to wonder how Western civilization would have played itself out if these had been the root metaphors of the Judeo-Christian tradition.

They are not, however, and Evan Eisenberg's courageous effort to reconstruct the root metaphor with the wilderness idea does not strike me as having enough of a base or cultural resonance to work. As Simon Schama has so eloquently argued in his *Landscape and Memory*, a culture should not, and indeed cannot, turn to a supermarket of cultures, rationally picking and choosing cultural preferences. The work of culture is long and arduous but, once engaged, is deep and rich.[12] This is not to suggest that culture is fixed, or reified. Jews are products of a host of cultural influences, and Judaism is understood and expressed in different ways historically and sociologically as a consequence of these influences. I do mean to suggest, however, that themes and perspectives which have been present historically in Jewish cultures are most probably present in contemporary Jewish cultures and can be reclaimed. Our views of the human have become one-dimensional, as, by the way, have our views of the divine. Substituting a stewardship perspective for a wilderness perspective, or a wilderness perspective for a "majestic man" perspective might be an important corrective but will still leave our view of human life and the natural world flat, and ultimately vulnerable. Our culture suffers from a lack of metaphoric diversity, just as our world suffers from a lack of biological diversity. There is a connection.

I would like to present four metaphors of human-nature relations which can be found in the tradition, two of which have already been initially represented in the alternative/complementary stories of Genesis 1 and 2. After presenting the four models, I would like to propose ways in which the four might interact and serve as a means of repairing the balance which has been lost between the human, the natural, and the divine.

The first model, what Soloveitchik called "majestic man," I call the "little lower than the angels" model. The controversial text of Genesis 1:28 is clearly part of such a model, but it is articulated most clearly in a rabbinic commentary, in which the human being is presented as the telos of creation. Why was the human being created last, the rabbis ask? One answer is so that the human being can enter straight into the banquet which God has prepared for him. The natural world is "served" to the human being, who is the guest for which everything has been created.[13] Such a view appears in commentary on the story of Noah, as well, when the medieval commentators attempt to explain why the earth was punished for human sins. Nature, so Nahmanides claims, has no worth without human existence. The world is a background for the human experience.[14] Even here, however, where nature is truly a resource for human use, it must be emphasized that in the great chain of being God, and not humans, is at the top. However, the human being is firmly situated a little lower than the angels and the rest of nature has no articulated worth independent of the human being. As stated in Psalms:

> What is man that You have been mindful of him,
> mortal man that You have taken note of him,
> that You have made him little less than divine,
> and adorned him with glory and majesty;
> You have made him master over Your handiwork,
> laying the world at his feet,
> sheep and oxen, all of them,
> and wild beasts, too;
> the birds of the heavens, the fish of the sea,
> whatever travels the paths of the seas. (8:5–9)

Human worth, granted through being created in the image of God, was associated with human rationality. Thought, reasoning, consciousness were relatives of the soul. Physicality, on the other hand, was something utterly different, connected to the animals:

> Six things are said of human beings: in regard to three, they are like the ministering angels, and in regard to three, they are like the beasts. 'In regard to three, they are like the ministering angels': they have understanding like the ministering angels; and they walk erect like the ministering angels; and they can talk in the holy tongue like the ministering angels. 'In regard to three, they are like beasts': they eat and drink like beasts; and they propagate like beasts, and they relieve themselves like beasts.[15]

The secularization of society during the Enlightenment, as Arthur O. Lovejoy has pointed out, removed God and the angels from the chain and placed the human being firmly on top, with no constraints from above.[16]

The second model, what we have defined as the stewardship model, presents a very different version of anthropocentrism. I believe it was first articulated by Rene Dubos with regard to the Benedictine tradition in Christianity. In the Jewish tradition, one might see hints of it in Rabbi Akiva's rejoinder to the Roman ruler Turnisrufus in their argument about circumcision. When asked by Turnisrufus whether human or divine acts were finer, Akiva replies that human are, anticipating a pagan critique of circumcision. Like loaves of bread to grains of wheat, circumcision completes the work of Creation with the raw materials given by God.[17] The human being is God's partner, completing the creative process. The stewardship model maintains human uniqueness, but it then understands the uniqueness in terms of human responsibility for maintaining and improving on the rest of the creation. Rooted in Genesis 2, perhaps the most famous of passages of the stewardship model is from the rabbinic tract of Midrash, Ecclesiastes Rabba:

> When God created the first human beings, God led them around the Garden of Eden and said, "Look at my works! See how beautiful they are! For your sake I created them. Do not spoil and destroy My world; for if you do, there will be no one to repair it."[18]

The third model I shall call "the radical amazement model," after Abraham Joshua Heschel and his theology, in which the human being is left awed and subsequently humbled when truly confronting the wonders of nature.[19] It is articulated clearly in Ecclesiastes, and most famously in Job. Historically, one could argue that it is the Wisdom literature's contribution to environmental perspectives. When Job despairs of his suffering, lost as to how God could possibly dictate such punishment on such a seemingly righteous individual as he, God answers out of the whirlwind. A few verses will suffice:

> Do you know the time when the wild goats
> of the rock bring forth?
> Or can you mark when the hinds do calve?

> Can you number the months that they fulfill?
> Or do you know the time when they bring forth? . . .
> Does the hawk soar by your wisdom,
> And stretch her wings toward the south?
> Does the vulture mount up at your command,
> And make her nest on high?
> She dwells and abides on the rock,
> Upon the crag of the rock, and the stronghold.
> From there she spies out the prey;
> Her eyes behold it from afar.
> Her young ones also suck up blood;
> And where the slain are, there is she. (39:1–2, 26–30)

Job's response is brief:

> Then Job answered the Lord, and said:
> I know that Thou can do everything,
> And that no purpose can be withheld from thee.
> Who is this that hides counsel without knowledge?
> Therefore have I uttered that which I understood not,
> Things too wonderful for me, which I knew not. (42:1–3)

The mystery of nature stands as a humbling experience. The vastness and complexity of the world removes human action from the center of its structure and places the meaning of human life in the context of the world around. Maimonides understood Job exactly this way, and much of Maimonides' intellectual enterprise was in rejecting the anthropocentric model of the world, which also projects human conceptions onto God, instead of seeing God as something wholly other from human understanding and action.[20] The theme of radical amazement, both in its phenomenological and rationalist traditions, is the closest that classical Jewish texts come to a wilderness tradition. The otherness of the natural world, a world apart from the human experience, puts human life into its proper perspective.[21]

Finally, the fourth model, most visibly present in the Jewish mystical tradition, and especially in Hasidut, sees the entire natural world as an extension of God and, as such, as holy. I shall call this "the holy sparks model." Such a view sees mystical significance in a relationship with the natural world, in which communion with nature is a form of communion with God. Paradoxically, the model sees value both in a relationship with the material world, which is part of God, and a relationship with the spiritual world, which hides beneath the mask of the material.

> It seems and appears to us, that the earth and the heaven and all the created things, are like existent things. But in truth, "I the Lord have not changed," it is written . . . and everything before Him is as nothing, verily as null and void, only the world seems and appears to the eyes of the flesh as an existent thing in itself. (Rabbi Shneur Zalman, Liqqutei Torah, Ba-Midbar)[22]

In this paradoxical relationship, in which the natural world has value as a physical manifestation of the extension of the Holy into the world, while simultaneously being an illusion which separates the unity of God's reality into seemingly disparate matter, the Hasidim placed increased emphasis on the material value of the world as an integrated and essential part of the spiritual essence. In a tale attributed to the Baal Shem Tov, the founder of the Hasidic movement, the Baal Shem Tov seeks to protect the material from being divorced from the spiritual:

> The Baal Shem once asked an outstanding scholar about his relation to prayer: "What do you do and where do you direct your thoughts when you pray?" He answered: "I bind myself to everything of individual vitality which is present in all created things. For in each and every created thing there must be a vitality which it derives from the divine effluence. I unite with them when I direct my words to God in order by my prayer to penetrate the highest regions." Then the Baal Shem said to him: "If that is what you do, you destroy the world, for in extracting its vitality and raising it to a higher level, you leave the individual created things without their vitality."[23]

And so, the Baal Shem would go to the woods to pray, not to find the prayer lying dormant behind the mask of the material, but to celebrate the prayer which is a part of, or perhaps synonymous with, the material. The environmental voice within the kabbalah suggests an immanental, or panentheistic, theological position.

This is not to say that the kabbalistic-Hasidic tradition is, as a whole, sympathetic to environmental positions. There is a strong voice in that tradition which sees the sensual world of nature as evil. The evils of the material world need to be transformed and transcended into the world of the spirit.[24] The interpretation of the norma-

tive kabbalistic voice from an environmental perspective is inconclu-
sive, at best. Yet, in modern Jewish thought, all four of the major
thinkers that I associate with an environmental perspective—Rav
Kook, A. D. Gordon, Martin Buber, and Abraham Joshua Heschel—
are deeply influenced by the kabbalistic and Hasidic traditions, and at
least three of the four strongly emphasize immanental theological
themes.[25] Arguing that they misinterpret that tradition is beside the
point.[26]

Such an immanental theological voice found its clearest expression
in modern Judaism through the Zionist movement. The return to the
land, after two thousand years of disjunction between land and culture, can be viewed in retrospect as an environmental statement. Jewish culture, nurtured in a particular landscape, lost its context in the
Diaspora. The return of the Jewish people to the Land of Israel is not
simply a return to the historical landscape, but to nature, as a whole.
As Berdichevski states in his rejoinder to the other infamous "anti-
nature" quote of the Jewish tradition (second only to Genesis 1:28):[27]

> Is it any wonder that men like Rabbi Isaac in our academies who
> said: The Bible should not have begun with Genesis, but with the
> Law? . . .
> Is it any wonder that there arose among us generation after genera-
> tion despising Nature, who thought of all God's marvels as superfluous
> trivialities? Is it surprising that we became a non-people, a non-na-
> tion—non-men, indeed?
> I recall from the teaching of the sages: Whoever walks by the way
> and interrupts his study to remark, How fine is that tree, how fine is that
> field, forfeits his life. (Ethics of the Fathers 3:8)
> But I assert that then alone will Judah and Israel be saved, when
> another teaching is given unto us, namely: Whoever walks by the way
> and sees a fine tree and a fine field and a fine sky and leaves them to
> think on other thoughts—that man is like one who forfeits his life!
> Give us back our fine trees and fine fields! Give us back the Uni-
> verse.[28]

The return to nature in Zionist culture was, and remains, a central
theme. Romantic nationalism, Nietzschean philosophy, and immanental theologies intertwined to create the intellectual foundation for
a renewed relationship with the holy land. The secular Zionist movement, as well as its religious partner, can certainly be understood as

having deep religious underpinnings, connected to a return not only to history, but to the natural world.[29]

The cultural dialectic of these four models has been eclipsed in Jewish and Western traditions into one overriding image, consonant with modernity: the majestic man, "a little lower than the angels." It is not, as Soloveitchik rightly suggests, that there is something inherently wrong with the metaphor. It is problematic when it becomes the overarching metaphor, snuffing out alternative voices. We do not need one cultural metaphor to express our relationship with the natural world; we need metaphors that live in dynamic tension with one another, that force us as individuals and as a society to enrich our views and to deepen our relationships with the world around us and with our notions of the Divine. The world is too complex to be viewed through one "true" prism; it is not two-dimensional, and therefore must be seen from many vantage points.

The Midrash often understood that. Rather than presenting only one voice, the compilations of Midrash contrasted one interpretation with another, always suggesting that reality is far more elusive than any one interpretation can claim. In the midrashic rendering as to why the human was created on the sixth day, not only the exalted version of "a little lower than the angels" is presented. As an alternative to the view that the human is the guest of honor in the banquet of Creation, the Midrash offers a contrasting image: even the gnat can say that it was created first! A Job-inspired humility rivals the otherwise unbridled vision of human self-worth and suggests a third position, negotiated between these two. Educationally, such an approach opens up the debate on the human place in the world. Rather than giving an unambiguous answer, it at least offers its student the possibility of becoming a participant in exploring the complexity of human existence.

Going back to Jewish day schools constructing papier-mâché rain forests, I might suggest that next time, if we truly want our children to experience the wonder of the world, they need to open the door and explore the anthill, the bird migrations, and the trees around them. If we want them to be stewards, they should learn the ecological, social, and political implications of their actions in the world, and learn to walk softly and responsibly. And if we want them to feel truly part of the world, with an identity rooted in the only place in the universe where we have been created to live, than they should "contemplate a tree," to use Buber's phrase, and feel the unity of all living things, of which they are a part, physically and spiritually. Perhaps returning these actions to our cultural lives can help us to reach a richer, more meaningful, more complex, and ultimately more responsible understanding of what it might mean to be "a little lower than the angels."

Notes

1. This article was written as a response to several papers presented at the Harvard conference, among them Evan Eisenberg's article, adapted from his then forthcoming book. His book, as well as his revisions of his article for this volume, in fact answer my most serious criticism about his continuing the wilderness/urban dichotomy. See also Evan Eisenberg, *The Ecology of Eden* (New York: Alfred A. Knopf, 1998).

2. Candice Slater, "Amazonia as Edenic Narrative," in William Cronin, ed., *Uncommon Ground: Rethinking the Human Place in Nature* (New York: W. W. Norton and Company, 1996), 114–31.

3. Yael Zerubavel, "The Forest as National Icon: Literature, Politics, and the Archeology of Memory," *Israel Studies* 1, no. 1 (spring 1996): 60–99.

4. The various Arab minorities in Israel have had a rather antagonistic relationship with representative organizations of environmental concerns. In the Negev, for example, traditional Beduin seminomadic life has historically been in conflict with representatives of nature protection. In the Galilee, Arab towns and villages often perceive restrictions on their growth in order to protect "nature" as an excuse to prevent Arab parity with the Jewish sector. See Eilon Schwartz, "Israeli Arabs and Environmentalists at Odds: Nature Protection and Its Context" (paper presented at the Conference on Moral and Political Reasoning in Environmental Practice, Society for Applied Philosophy, Mansfield College, Oxford University, 27–29 June 1999).

5. What is considered by many to be the first work in environmental ethics was a direct attack on the Judeo-Chrstian lack of an environmental ethic, as symbolized in Genesis 1:28. Lynn White, Jr., "The Historical Roots of Our Ecologic Crisis," *Science* 155 (10 March 1967): 1203–7. The stereotyping of both traditions that was thus launched motivated one Jewish medieval historian to write a full book, proving that such an anti-environmental interpretation of the verse had no basis in the history of the verse's exegesis by both Jews and Christians; Jeremy Cohen, *Be Fertile and Increase, Fill the Earth and Master It: The Ancient and Medieval Career of a Biblical Text* (Ithaca, N.Y.: Cornell University Press, 1989).

6. Tikva Frymer-Kensky, "'Leshev' and Gaia: The Limits of Biblical Ecology," (paper presented at the conference Judaism and the Natural World, Center for the Study of World Religions, Harvard Divinity School, February 1998). Regrettably, Professor Frymer-Kensky did not submit her conference presentation to the volume.

7. Daniel B. Botkin, *Discordant Harmonies: A New Ecology for the Twenty-first Century* (New York: Oxford University Press, 1990).

8. Zev Naveh and Arthur Lieberman, *Landscape Ecology: Theory and Application* (New York: Springer-Verlag, 1994).

9. David Kraemer, "Jewish Death Practices: A Commentary on the Relationship of Humans to the Natural World" (in this volume).

10. Rene J. Dubos, "Franciscan Conservation versus Benedictine Stewardship," in *A God Within* (New York: Scribner, 1972).

11. Joseph Dov Soloveitchik, *The Lonely Man of Faith* (New York: Doubleday, 1992).

12. Simon Schama, *Landscape and Memory* (New York: Alfred A. Knopf, 1995), 17–19.

13. Sanhedrin 38a, Babylonian Talmud. Note even here that the human is the guest

of honor in the home, but not the owner of the home. The chain of being maintains God, and not man, as the owner.

14. Nahmanides commentary on Genesis 6:11–13.

15. Hagiga 16a, Babylonian Talmud; See also Genesis Raba 12:8.

16. Arthur O. Lovejoy, *The Great Chain of Being* (Cambridge, Mass.: Harvard University Press, 1964).

17. Midrash Tanhuma on Parshat Tazri'a, 5.

18. Ecclesiastes Rabbah 7:28

19. Abraham Joshua Heschel, *God in Search of Man: A Philosophy of Judaism* (Philadelphia: Jewish Publication Society of America, 1956), 43–51.

20. Moses Maimonides, *The Guide of the Perplexed*, trans. Shlomo Pines (Chicago: University of Chicago Press, 1963), 496–97.

21. It is interesting to compare the uses of nature in Ecclesiastes and Job. While in Job nature humbles humans and gives a perspective to life which also, at least for some commentators, provides meaning and suggests celebration for the vitality and diversity of the natural world, in Ecclesiastes nature's message, while also teaching perspective, suggests the ultimate meaninglessness of human life.

22. Quoted in Rachel Elior, *The Paradoxical Ascent to God: The Kabbalistic Theosophy of Habad Hasidism* (Albany: State University of New York Press, 1993), 52.

23. See Baal Shem Tov, *Sefer Or HaMeir* (in Hebrew), Drush Shabbat Teshuva.

24. For a discussion on the seemingly paradoxical relationship of the *Zohar*, the primary Jewish mystical text, to the natural world, See Isaiah Tishby, *The Wisdom of the Zohar* (Oxford: Oxford University Press, 1989), 653–55.

25. The influence of the kabbalah and Hasidism on Kook, Buber, and Heschel is well known. In a recent work, their decisive influence on Gordon's thought is also demonstrated. See Abraham Shapira, *The Kabbalistic and Hasidic Sources of A. D. Gordon's Thought* (in Hebrew) (Tel Aviv: Am Oved Publishers, 1996). Kook, Buber, and Gordon all emphasize immanental themes in their work. Heschel's declarations of an unambiguous transcendental theology seems inexplicable, given the immanental sympathies of his theology, although there might be a historical explanation for the seeming dissonance. Edward Kaplan, personal discussion.

26. Jerome (Yehuda) Gellman, "The Attitude of Early Hasidism to the Natural World" (in this volume). For example, Gellman argues that Buber paints a misconstrued picture of Hasidic sympathies to the natural world. Yet, the fact that all four of the environmental Jewish philosophers' are deeply influenced by the kabbalistic and Hasidic traditions seems to suggest that such a misinterpretation is nevertheless strongly suggested.

27. For a full history of the interpretations of the quote from Ethics of the Fathers, see Jeremy Bernstein, "'One, Walking and Studying . . .': Nature versus Torah," *Judaism* 44, no. 2 (spring 1995): 146–68.

28. Micah Joseph Berdichevski, "In Two Directions," in *The Zionist Idea*, ed. Arthur Hertzberg (New York: Atheneum, 1973), 297.

29. Using the typology of William James's classic account of religious experience, the secular Zionist tradition has manifestations similar to James's model of "healthy-mindedness," associated with Walt Whitman. See William James, *The Varieties of Religious Experience: A Study in Human Nature* (New York: Collier Books, 1961), 78–113.

The Doctrine of Creation

Nature's Answer: The Meaning of the Book of Job in Its Intellectual Context

STEPHEN A. GELLER

I

The Book of Job has universal appeal because it deals with a universal problem: why do good people often suffer and, worse, bad people frequently prosper?[1] Part of the book's appeal stems from the fact that it deals with these issues not in terms of standard Judeo-Christian religious dogma, which definitively solved the problem of suffering in this world by positing a next one where all inequities would be made good, but on a broadly human, one might even say humanistic, level. Job knows of no blissful, or tortured, afterlife and will accept no answer not of this world.

But for all its universality, the Book of Job must not be viewed as a work detached from all historical and cultural context. It is, of course, quite legitimate to read the book in universal human terms, as one may with any work of literature, provided one respects the text. But Job represents a particular tradition at a particular moment of crisis. Moreover, it was never aimed at the masses, who could scarcely have followed its complicated arguments or understood its learned and dense poetic diction. It was aimed at a small group of intellectuals with a common heritage of discourse and ideas. It also represents the internal religious struggle of that group at a particular historical moment of crisis. A key issue in that struggle was differing views of the role of nature in religion—more exactly, the relationship between nature and morality, with the sharpest focus on the issue of theodicy, the justification of God's providential rule over the cosmos. My discussion aims at an interpretation of the book true to these specific intellectual and historical circumstances.

The Book of Job is composed of two radically different types of literary materials: a short, traditional folktale, in prose, and a long didactic, dramatic poem, a disputation among savants. The author has divided the old tale into two sections, which he uses as the prologue and epilogue of the poem. The effect is ironic, intentionally so, I believe. For the folktale, probably much older than the Book of Job, related the adherence to absolute piety of a famous wise man of the past when confronted by suffering brought on by a rather nasty bet between God and His chief prosecutor, Satan. Urged by his wife to curse God and die, he refuses: "the Lord gave and then took away, Blessed be the Lord's name!" At the end, this pious man, the "patient Job" of Judeo-Christian tradition, is rewarded doubly for his loyalty. Problematic is only one aspect. In the epilogue the friends who come to comfort Job are rebuked by God for not having spoken the "truth about me like my servant Job." This seems to imply that in the original tale the friends came to shake Job's faith, like his wife. But the author has excised this aspect entirely and instead composed a long poem in which the roles of the folktale are reversed: it is the friends who mouth piety, and Job who utters blasphemies. Thus, God's divine praise of Job's "truth" in the epilogue seems to state that God welcomes blasphemy and rejects confident piety! (excluded from discussion are later additions, like the bombastic Elihu speeches of chapters 32–37).

It is clear that the author has some polemic in mind. In fact, he has cleverly used the old tale to present a radical attack on the kind of religion he, reversing the roles of the old tale, has himself put into the mouths of the friends. In its place he seems to recommend a quite different type of religion. To understand the real issues in the polemic, one must know the particular intellectual tradition it reflects.

II

Job is a work of the ancient Near Eastern Wisdom tradition. Wisdom is here a proper noun and refers to the tradition carried by teachers and schools, and, in a broader sense, by all educated persons, a small group in antiquity. Wisdom dealt with two main areas. Practical Wisdom attempted to inculcate the rules of successful living, leading to prosperity and inner contentment. The maxims of the biblical Book of Proverbs are an example. What scholars term Speculative Wisdom dealt with a grander issue: the origin of nature, which in biblical terms means creation, and of the moral order, which is the same, according to Wisdom teachers.[2] Above all, Wisdom wrestled with the problem of theodicy, the justification of the divine management of the cosmos. As an attempt to find order in all things, Wisdom's ruling principle was cause and effect.

Wisdom was an international tradition, common to all ancient peoples. It drew its answers from observation of nature, both cosmic and human, not from the particular religious traditions of any people. This was true even in Israel. Solomon wrote proverbs that spoke of "trees, birds, beasts, and reptiles" (1 Kings 4:33–34) and drew universal admiration, even of pagans, like the Queen of distant Sheba, for his wisdom. Job is presented as someone from the land of Uz, not a Hebrew at all. The main portion of the book even avoids the name of the specific Israelite deity, Yahweh, in favor of the universal apellation "deity" ('*eloah*). Ecclesiastes, a late representative of the Wisdom tradition in the Bible, is notoriously outside the thought realm of biblical covenant religion, except for the pietistic ending tacked on by nervous editors. What might be termed Old Wisdom represents this type of nature-rooted speculation, which sought to establish the essential unity of natural and moral orders.

From the late seventh century B.C.E. the Israelite branch of Old Wisdom was in a state of crisis. By this time, monotheistic Deuteronomic covenant faith had established its dominance. It demanded total, single-minded submission to One Deity, the national God Yahweh. Loyalty to God required faithful performance of His laws and radical exclusion of anything foreign. The source of all authority was sacred canon, not observation of nature and humanity. Old Wisdom, and especially its view of the importance of nature, had to go. The new Deuteronomic system, the new Torah piety, redefined Wisdom as the study of holy texts and the observance of covenantal commandments. Much of the Book of Proverbs submitted to this demand. It opens by declaring that the "beginning of wisdom is the fear of the Lord," i.e., piety. Nature was ousted from this new, pietistic wisdom. Observation of nature and society was replaced, as Psalm 119:18 states, by espying "the wonders" of God's law.

As Wisdom teachers scrambled to accommodate Old Wisdom to the new dispensation, a subtle melding of both occurred, leading to a kind of hybrid, pietistic, Wisdom faith that focused on obedience to covenant law, but still used the universalistic language of the Old Wisdom tradition. It still spoke of man and of nature, but only in terms of the relationship of both to the absolute demands of the radical new monotheism. Covenant law was discussed not in terms of Sinaitic revelation, as in the standard Deuteronomistic faith, but as if it were, in the manner of the Old Wisdom, the result of observation of nature and of society. Cause and effect were deified, or, better, the reverse: God was discussed as if He were merely the embodiment of the cause-and-effect relationship. Simply put, these pious sophists taught that good action inevitably, automatically leads to well-being and that, conversely, bad action leads, not necessarily immediately, but soon, and permanently, to disaster and ruin. The good are always rewarded, the wicked punished, because that is the order of things (though they talked openly of the will of God and, by "order," seemed to imply "command," in outward conformity to covenant faith and not what they really meant, "system").[3]

In the Book of Job, the friends who come to comfort him represent this hybrid of covenantal and intellectual piety. It must not be viewed as negatively as the author of Job does. He opposes it vigorously and presents its viewpoints unsympathetically, perhaps unfairly, certainly polemically. It may have been a pious sophistry, but it also had some of the elements of a true faith. One of its other documents is Psalm 37, in which the psalmist-sage declares, amazingly, that from youth to old age he has never seen "a just man abandoned or his seed begging bread" (v. 25). Such an absurd statement, so opposed to universal experience, can only reflect, not observable reality, but religious dogma. It immediately raises the question of what one means by a truly "just man," and so opens the door to the kind of speculation and inward examination that was the delight of the wise.

The clearest exposition of the hybrid Wisdom-covenantal faith is in the opening speech of Eliphaz, Job's chief "comforter" and accuser, in chapters 4 and 5 of the Book of Job. Despite the author's clear disapproval, he nevertheless presents a kind of grudging manifesto of the hybrid piety. The speech contains some famous difficulties of interpretation, some of them so grievous as to have led some scholars to assign large parts of his speech to Job! Such amputations are quite unnecessary if one recognizes the subtlety of the argument and Eliphaz's indirect, allusive mode of expression. It is a masterpiece of the expression of two simultaneous levels of meaning.

The speech may be divided into two sections: chapter 4, verse 1, through chapter 5, verse 8, Eliphaz's negative argument to Job; and chapter 5, verses 8–27, his positive argument. The further breakdown is as follows:

PART ONE: 4:1–5:8—The Negative Argument
4:1–5:   introduction: reaction to Job's vexation in chapter 3
4:6–10:   statement of the dogma of cause-and-effect retribution
4:11–5:1: argument proper, first stage: the dream vision:
           overt level: God's suspicion of immortals and mortals
           allusory level: the inevitability of punishment for sin
              and uselessness of expecting angelic intercession
5:2–7:   argument proper, second stage: Eliphaz's curse of the
           wicked:
           overt level: the uselessness of vexation
           allusory level: resignation to the inevitability of sin
              and punishment (*'amal, 'awen*)

PART TWO: 5:8–27—The Positive Argument
5:8–15: the retribution dogma restated: God as creator and
           provider of justice
5:17–18: argument proper: suffering as "correction"
           overt level: the "benefits" of suffering
           allusory level: the necessity of Job's repenting for his
              sin
5:19–27: the rewards of submission.

Eliphaz first reacts to Job's loss of composure, reflected in his cursing of the day of his birth. "You, Job, used to comfort others, buck them up. Now that you yourself are in distress, you are confused and confounded. Instead, your very piety should be a source of confidence to you because"—and here Eliphaz states the dogma—"what innocent person was ever lost, when have the upright ever been deprived?" (4:7–10).

Verse 8 contains an important double entendre. Many Hebrew words for "sin" and "crime" also mean "punishment." For example, Cain protests, when he hears the curse placed on him by God for hav-

ing killed his brother Abel, "My *'awon* is too great to bear," that is,
"my crime" and also the punishment for it. In Job 4:8 the words *'amal*
and *'awen* have a similar duality of meaning, which encapsulates the
cause-and-effect relationship perfectly. To catch the effect, I would
translate the terms with English ones that bear the same duality: "I
have seen that those who plow disaster and sow trouble reap it." Those
who sin by planning crimes against others will themselves suffer, "fall
into the pit they have dug," as Wisdom texts are fond of putting it. In
the manner of Wisdom teachers, Eliphaz supports and illustrates his
point by a reference to nature. Lions in this context stand for the
wicked who are often said to lie in wait for the innocent like a lion for
its prey.

Having stated the doctrine of cause-and-effect retribution, Eliphaz
then begins what looks like a digression. He recounts a terrifying
dream-vision he had, a source of special knowledge of the divine
sphere, revealed to him by a spirit. Dream interpretation was always
the province of Wisdom. The message of the spirit seems to be a statement of a stock Wisdom theme: the frailty of humanity. "Can a human
ever be innocent before God? He doesn't trust His angels! How much
less mortal man, a work of clay!" Eliphaz seems to be offering a kind
of consolation to Job: "Look, I have a bit of secret information about
God relevant to your situation. He is very, very suspicious and strict,
even with members of His own court, the angels." The implication is
that he may punish a mortal, like Job, even for a tiny transgression. So
Eliphaz manages to insinuate the idea that Job may actually have
sinned, however insignificantly, while at the same time implying Job's
general, almost angelic, uprightness. This is an example of Eliphaz's
great, cruel, delicacy.

But if one examines Eliphaz's vision in terms of biblical tradition,
the point shifts from a general commiseration about the strictness of
God and human weakness to a covert recapitulation of the dogma of
cause-and-effect retribution, with, again, a strong implication of Job's
sinfulness. It is therefore not a digression at all, but supports the preceding lines directly. Reference in verse 18 is probably not to an unreasonable divine suspicion of the angels, a generalized irascibility,
but to an ancient myth, still palpable in a few biblical passages and
revived in later apocalyptic literature, of an angelic revolt against
God's rule, similar to the rebellion of the Olympian gods against Zeus
(Psalm 82, Isaiah 14). The point is this: God has to keep His eye on

the angels, beings of ethereal light, lest they rebel again; how much more on earthly humans, creatures of clay, *if they sin*! The statements about mortals in verses 19–21 are then not only, on one level, a statement of universal human frailty, but also, on another level, a reaffirmation of the law of retribution: if angels do not escape punishment, how much less mortals!

The first stage of the negative argument ends in 5:1, which reveals another reason Eliphaz recounted his dream-vision. This statement forms a contrast with 5:8, which enjoins Job to turn directly to God for help rather than to an angel. This alludes to an apparent older belief, also mentioned in the Elihu speeches (33:23), that humans in trouble might turn to intercessory angels, *mal'akhei melitz*, to make their case before God. But Eliphaz's vision has shown that God does not even trust the angels.

Eliphaz now returns, in 5:2, to the issue of Job's inner turmoil. In Wisdom tradition such vexation itself was held to be a sign of evildoing. No matter what happens, the wise are expected to maintain their equilibrium. Specifically, they must exhibit a calm, steady confidence in the law of cause-and-effect retribution, however tardy it might prove to be in manifesting itself in a specific case. Wisdom taught that when confronted by the prosperity of the wicked, one must not fly into a rage or, especially, envy their prosperity. One must keep calm with the assurance that the law of cause-and-effect retribution would eventually bring the sinners' downfall. So Eliphaz now says to Job: "Look, your violent cursing of your life, and by implication of God, not only cuts you off from the only source of help, but is also most unseemly for a wise man like you, for only a fool is killed by vexation, only a simpleton by jealousy."

Eliphaz then offers, in verses 3–7, his second two-leveled argument, another seeming consolation to Job that is actually a warning. "I, too, once allowed myself to get angry and produce a curse, when I saw a wicked person (the same word for "fool" used in the previous verse!) seemingly firmly rooted in prosperity, and I cursed him impulsively, saying, 'May his children be far from help. . . .'"

The climax of this section relies on the dual meaning of the terms for evildoing and punishment mentioned above. Like the dream-vision, Eliphaz seems to be making a traditional statement about human frailty: "Humanity is born to trouble as sparks[4] fly upward." Two comforts emerge: Job is not the first sage to loose his composure—but he must regain it! And, after all, are we not all born to suffer?—a truism that people often find vaguely consolatory, the pessimism of which has a long history in Israelite and pagan wisdom.[5]

But closer examination, in terms of Israelite traditions, shows that, like the reference to the angels above, a specific context is meant, implying sin. The statements are, therefore, also like those in the dream-vision, meant as a restatement of the cause-and-effect law. "It is not from the dust that disaster comes, trouble does not grow from the ground. . . ." An Israelite hearing these words would not fail to hear in them an allusion to the sin and punishment of Adam. Adam was created from the earth, but his sinfulness and the resulting curse placed on the earth by God were not the fault of the soil itself, but of humanity's rebellion. In short, just as earlier Eliphaz alluded to the angelic rebellion in heaven, here he uses language that evokes rebellion on earth of humankind's first ancestor. It is in this implied, allusive, context that one must understand the rest of the statement: "Rather, humanity (*'adam* = Adam) is born to trouble as sparks fly upward." Humans have an innate tendency to sin, an evil *yetzer*, as Genesis 8 puts it, which, by the law of retribution, must inevitably bring disaster. On the covert level, Eliphaz is restating the retribution dogma, a point made more forceful by the recapitulation of the words *'awen* and *'amal* used in 4:6, where an agricultural image is also employed, as here, and specifically one involving the dual nuance of the terms in question to strengthen the idea of inevitable retribution. So, on one level, Eliphaz may be commiserating with Job, but on a deeper one he is saying, "All humans are sinners. How can you claim to be an exception? You must accept your miserable sinfulness, not repeat Adam's rebelliousness, but repent" and, in the words of the following verse, 5:8, the transition to Eliphaz's positive argument, "direct words (of contriteness, not blasphemy) to God, who alone can help you."

Eliphaz's aim in the first part of the speech has been gently to calm Job and get him to admit that his sufferings must be the result of some sin, even if a slight one. To be sure, such extreme punishment as Job is experiencing would normally be taken as sign of a grave crime; but, after all, as the vision informed him, is not God strict even with the angels? Eliphaz endeavors, in the second, positive, part of the speech, to direct Job toward the path of repentance. Once again, the approach is allusive. Eliphaz once again makes his points without ever mentioning overtly either Job's sinfulness or the need for repentance, a masterpiece of subtle argumentation.

The most important point in the rest of the speech is verse 17, Eliphaz's positive solution to Job's dilemma: "Fortunate the man God reproves; don't reject Shaddai's correction." Wisdom maintained that the sufferings of those who were basically righteous should be viewed in the light of the father-son or teacher-pupil relationship. Just as a father, or teacher, may have to "instruct," i.e., beat, a child to punish an action that might lead to a self-destructive pattern of behavior, so God may occasionally have to "chastise" those He loves, for their own good. It hurts God more than it does them. This notion, found in the Book of Proverbs (3:11–12), was also taken over into covenant Wisdom, in Deuteronomy (8:5). Job must abandon insolence and vexation, regain his composure, and regard his predicament as God's beneficent, providential "instruction." Again, Eliphaz never mentions openly the fact that Job must have sinned, nor does he openly call upon him to repent; but his meaning is clear.

If Job does repent, he will encounter the positive side of the retribution doctrine. A new cause, repentance, will engender a new effect, reward and restoration: "He gives pain, but binds up; he wounds, but his hand brings healing." The rest of the speech presents a luminous picture of the renewed prosperity, salavation, and bodily vigor that await a repentant Job. Such is the accumulated wisdom of the sages, which they have investigated and found true (5:27).

Job reacts violently to Eliphaz's speech. Far from soothing his vexation, the speech increases it. What seems especially to enrage Job is that Eliphaz will not allow him to be enraged. The very soothing delicacy of Eliphaz's speech vexes him even more. His friends have failed him, offering pap for wisdom. His pain is unbearable; he wishes God would just kill him and make an end of it. But what is actually wrong with what Eliphaz has said? As we have seen, he sought to spare Job's feelings in the most delicate, considerate way. First, with the other friends, he remained silent for several days, while Job was sunk into himself. They followed the procedure recommended by the rabbis, of not attempting to comfort a mourner "while his dead lie before him." Their silent presence bespoke their sympathy and commiseration. Eliphaz speaks only when Job has suddenly produced an outburst that betokens a mental attitude that will, he is sure, lead to

Job's destruction. He then gently reminds Job of the dogmas of the Wisdom faith that Job also shared, before his calamities overtook him. Only indirectly does he allude to Job's sin and the necessity of repentance. Never does he speak of punishment, only of testing and trial. Why does Job react so furiously? What is wrong with Eliphaz's speech?

III

It is often said that the friends have a totally mechanistic view of the workings of cosmic and moral order, that in their system God has lost His freedom. They believe there is a science of piety in which the deity itself is bound by iron casuistries. I think that the reverse may be true, that the trouble with their worldview is that it is too pious, leaves too much room for God's intervention. A truly mechanistic worldview opens the possibility of a final answer to the problem of suffering: complete and total resignation, in the manner of Qoheleth: "all is nothingness, futile!" If Eliphaz said to Job,"This is the way the world is. You must accept it or be destroyed," Job would at least have had a clear course laid out for him. But the mechanistic moral system of the friends is muddled by constant reference, directly and by inference, to the possibility of direct divine intervention. They say that God is personally interested in what Job does; God takes notice of it Himself. The reference in Eliphaz's speech in chapters 4 and 5 to God's "wonders" of creation, and the reversal of fortunes, "lifting the lowly on high," implies that a similar "wonder" can be performed for a repentant Job, and his fortune reversed.

What is wrong with the friends' philosophy is that it contains a grave internal inconsistency. In historical terms, it has blended the mechanistic views of Old Wisdom, which subsumed God under the cosmic order, with the new piety of a covenant religion that viewed God as a totally free agent. This inner confusion in their doctrine is what leads Job to fume at his friends as "useless comforters." It stems from the religious-historical situation.

The victory of radical and absolute monotheism swept away the hierarchy of intermediate supernatural beings, like the intercessory angels, that earlier monolatrous Israelite religion had allowed to exist alongside the deity. The divine will now stood alone and supreme: the Lord is One. The new militant monotheism also insisted on individual reponsibility for sin. Gone also was the earlier view of corporate culpability that would allow the Decalogue to state that God would punish the children of sinners down to the third, even the fourth, generation. Now, "each person dies only for his own sin," in the words of the prophet Ezekiel.

The victory of absolute monotheism and individualism meant that God could no longer escape responsibility for all glitches in justice. Earlier, one might blame an incompetent angel, as in paganism one might blame a hostile divinity or malicious demon. Now God Himself was on the spot. And the new doctrine of individualism demanded that God punish sinners immediately as well as directly, "to their face, without delay," as Deuteronomy says. The issue of theodicy became critical just as the nation entered the crisis of the Exile, when many people must have asked themselves the cause of their suffering. To be sure, the prophets told them it was for their sins; but were all the people equally guilty? Surely not the prophets themselves and their followers, who also suffered with the rest of the populace.

In the struggle for understanding, in this heightened crisis of the problem of theodicy, people naturally looked to the wise men for counsel. After all, Wisdom had always been the tradition that concerned itself most with the issue of theodicy and suffering. But, as described above, the Wisdom tradition was also in crisis. It had to accommodate the nature-focused worldview of Old Wisdom with the new demands of victorious covenant faith, with its exclusive emphasis on divine revelation as the source of all truth, including morality. Their dilemma may be presented schematically:

God

Revelation   Creation

Man   Nature

Morality

If Old Wisdom had proceeded clockwise, from God through creation and nature to morality, covenant faith ran counterclockwise, deriving all morality from revelation to humankind, i.e., Israel. Covenant religion did not deal with the problem of theodicy as such. It merely asserted that sin would result in punishment, obedience in blessing, in faith. It was left for Wisdom to cope with the demand that God's justice be explained—a demand that covenant faith regarded as inherently impious.

The inner inconsistency of the friends' position stems from an inability, quite understandable, to proceed both clockwise and simultaneously counterclockwise around the above schema. They accepted from the radical new covenant faith the piety, the sense of direct personal connection to God, and the consequent primacy of revelation; but, as wise men, they felt they must also retain the idea of underlying mechanism of the Old Wisdom, its rootedness in nature.[6] Instead of saying, "resign yourself to the mechanism," as Old Wisdom would have done, or "have faith in God's justice," as the new piety of covenant said, they combined them and said, in effect: "have faith in the mechanism." The result is the kind of absurd statement in Psalm 37, with which we began, "I have never seen a just man abandoned . . . ," and Eliphaz's assertion that "no just man has ever been lost." Such statements are obviously not facts—even though, in the manner of Old Wisdom, they are put in terms of experience—but statements of faith, a hybrid quasi-scientific piety. Behind the faith is a dread of chaos, a fear that their concept of world order will be shattered unless their dogma is upheld. They are like interrogators in a totalitarian system urging a prisoner to confess. It matters not whether or not he has committed a crime; the important thing is that he submit and so confirm the interrogators in their worldview. So Job's friends do not really care what his sin is, or even if he has one, so long as he confesses that he does, so that they can be confirmed in their view of the iron law of retribution. As one of them says (18:4), "Will the rock [=cosmic order] be pulled from its place for you?"

The friends' views are logically inconsistent, but in religion and even in philosophy strict logic is not everything. I believe one may find a typological analogy to their blend of faith and intellect, within the general patterns of human spirituality, in Stoicism, especially the later Stoicism of the Roman era. The latter also made the claim that no one ever really suffers, certainly not the wise man. What is termed suffering is illusory, a matter of mental opinion, because no one can ever really be harmed, in his inner being, by illness or evildoers. Of course, Stoicism had an elaborate rationale of Greek logic and physics that is much more complex than anything available to earlier Israelite sages like Job's friends. The inner inconsistency of the friends' views would have been intolerable to later Stoics. But in its ethics, the real heart of Stoicism, there is a striking resemblance to their position. There is a similar, if much more developed, appeal to the link between the order of nature and human morality. The real deity of the Stoics, the "ruling principle," is much more abstract than the God of the sages, but is really a working out of the mechanistic aspects of the latter as administrator of the eternal cosmic order of things. The typological similarity can be seen especially in the horror of vexation in each system. Eliphaz, urging Job to calm down and take a more philosophical, as it were, view of his situation, says (Job 5:2), "Only the fool is killed by vexation, passion slays the simple." The later Stoics preached imperturbability (*ataraxia, apatheia*) as the chief emotional characteristic of the enlightened, who understood how everything fits into the world order (hence, the common sense of "stoic" as one who accepts suffering staunchly and without complaining). In such a context, suffering is eliminated, except as something to be overcome in one's mind by focusing on eternal principles. The human soul, which the Stoics associated with the physical principle they termed "God," can never be harmed. Nothing essential to one's self can ever be changed by any vicissitude of life, or death. The Stoics often use the language of traditional Hellenistic piety, even referring to the Olympian gods as personalities, but they mean something quite different from popular religion.

Of course, the religion of Job's friends lacked the theoretical rigor of the later movement, but the comparison is not, I believe, forced.[7] As did some Stoics, the friends of Job talk the language of traditional theism, still speak of "God" as a person. But they really mean by it a Ruling Principle of retribution which also incorporates the underlying order of the cosmos. This is the way things are and the wise man will recognize the system and conform to it. He will not be shaken by the spectacle of the seemingly happy wicked. Above all, he will maintain composure because he knows the true nature of the moral realm as an expression of cosmic cause and effect. For the truly righteous, suffering is not, to be sure, illusory—the friends do not have the developed Greek physics of the Stoics to support such an assertion—but it is temporary. Suffering is the momentary result of a sin and as such may even be viewed as a divine blessing, in that it is a test that refines the souls of the righteous and brings them even closer to God. Repentance brings restoration. Job must work his way through to peace of mind. Like Stoicism, this is a religion for the enlightened few. If this faith is mechanistic, and not logically satisfactory, it also possesses a certain stoic nobility in suffering, the kind of behavior the friends recommend to Job, and which he rejects.

IV

Job is most unstoic. He rails against God. The bitterness of Job's accusations are unparalleled in ancient literature. By chapter 17 he is describing God in terms used in the ancient world for the utterly demonic. In fact, Job is, in ancient terms, an atheist, because he denies providence: not that God exists, but that God cares. Instead, God treats good and wicked exactly alike, with total indifference to the moral standing of each. He is a brutal bully, using cosmic power to browbeat the just. Job fully expects such a God to crush him forever. He has no hope. Since the concept of a blissful afterlife, of judgment and reward in the next world, had not yet developed in biblical religion at the time of Job, he states that, unlike a tree, which, even if cut down may sprout again, he has no hope whatsoever of personal survival.

Yet, paradoxically, with the inconsistency of great art if not philosophy, Job still calls upon God Himself to appear and justify His ways. The image is forensic: God must be called to court, even if, as judge as well as defendant, He will inevitably condemn the human plaintiff. The bitter accusations of God's justice are interspersed with statements of implicit confidence in God's uprightness, like "no flatterer can appear before Him" (Job 13:16).

This pattern of despair and, in the case of Job, limited hope must be viewed against the background of the literary-religious figure Job both represents and transcends. This is what scholars term the "righteous sufferer," a stock figure of Wisdom theodicy literature from early times in Egypt and Mesopotamia, as well as Israel—for there are pagan analogues to Job also in those cultures. The righteous sufferer knows that his misfortune is unjustified. He has done no wrong, why are the gods punishing him? The list of complaints is long and varied, all sorts of physical, psychic, and social troubles: disease, aches, and pains in general, leprosy in particular, abandonment by family and friends, persecution by enemies, feelings of dread, and so on. Such inventories also fill many of the biblical and ancient Near Eastern psalms. The typical "answer" ranges from a despairing cry that one cannot know the way of the gods to expressions of confidence in ultimate redemption.

But Job goes beyond the stock figure. Not only does he suffer totally from all possible ailments, plus loss of family and property, but his accusations against God are, as noted, much more radical than those found in the standard Wisdom and psalmodic texts; and his expressions of hope and vindication are, as also noted, much briefer and more veiled. He is a super, a radical, indeed, a sublime, righteous sufferer. The author is striving to bring the underlying issue to a point because he alone of biblical authors fully apprehends that the ancient problem of theodicy has reached a new level in the religious crisis described above.

He is aware not only that the victory of monotheism has put God on the spot, so to speak, in regard to the problem of undeserved suffering, but also that the strategy of the kind of hybrid pietistic wisdom, like that of the friends, is inherently flawed because, simply put, one cannot run in two opposite directions at the same time. Its inner tensions tear it apart. Is nature or revelation the source of morality? Even if one asserts the general validity of both, one of the two must dominate. Which? Covenant faith answered simply, "revelation." But the wise could not bring themselves to abandon the role of nature, because it really meant abandoning the attempt to understand the relationship between things, i.e., wisdom itself. The insight of the author of Job is that the internal rift can be overcome only by stepping completely outside the framework of comprehension. He, too, wants to rescue a role for nature, but he realizes that this can be achieved only by abandoning the demand for understanding itself; not, however, in favor of mere dull, sullen incomprehension or resignation. Rather, the true "answer" offered by the author of Job to the problem of suffering lies in a quite different realm, that of emotion.

V

Job's answer, if such it is, ought to come from the climax of the dialogue, the divine speeches of chapters 38–42 and Job's reaction to them. Unfortunately for those who like simple solutions to cosmic problems, the author has clothed his meaning in the poetic ambiguity of art, not the exposition of logical argument. God appears in a whirlwind and, like any talmudically trained Jew, answers the questions

Job had put to him with questions of his own. These are rhetorical, because they deal with something no human can know, God's creation of the cosmos. The verse is among the greatest in the Bible and is captured in Raymond Scheindlin's masterful poetic translation:[8]

> "Where were you when I founded the earth?
> Speak, if you have any wisdom:
> Who set its measurements, if you know,
>   laid out the building lot, stretching the plumb line?
> Where was the ground where He sank its foundations?
> Who was setting the cornerstone
> when the morning stars were all singing,
>   when the gods were all shouting, triumphant?
> Who barred the sea behind double gates
> as it was gushing out of the womb?
> When I made the clouds its covering, fog its swaddling,
> broke its will with my decree,
> set bar and double gate,
> and said, 'This far, no farther!
> Here stops your breakers' surge.'" (Job 38:4–11)

God then delivers a second speech from the whirlwind (chapters 40–41), which challenges Job to create or explain two great beasts, the hippopotamus- or water buffalo–like Behemoth and the serpentine, crocodile-like Leviathan.

What is going on? What is the point? God has not answered Job's challenge that he "inform me of why you are contending with me" (Job 10:2). What kind of "answer" is this?

We must examine Job's responses to God's two speeches more closely, starting with the second of them, Job's final words in the book (42:2–6), and so, one presumes, his final position as regards the issue of suffering. (The translations I offer are loose and fuller than the original to catch certain key nuances).

Job says, after the second divine speech:

> "I know that you can do anything, and that no undertaking is
> beyond you. (You said): "Who is this one who would
> obscure my plan without any understanding of it"—truly
> I declared what I didn't comprehend, things too
> wonderful and difficult. (You challenged me:) "Hear now
> while I speak, I shall ask you the questions and you

> inform me!" Only by hearing had I experienced you before,
> but now that my own eye sees you, I. . . ."

There follow, as Job's very last utterances, words of such complete ambiguity that it must be intentional. The chief uncertainties are two: the first word, *'em'as*, is the common Hebrew word for "reject" (although some say it is here a related root meaning "melt away"). But the object of the rejection is unstated. The next term, *ve-nihamti*, means both "to change one's mind, recant," and "to take comfort, become reconciled to something." At least three major possibilities of translation and interpretation emerge:

1. "I reject (melt away) and recant, on the dust heap."

This a statement of humility. Intimidated by God's challenge, Job admits the truth of the friends' viewpoint, that God is all powerful, his ways beyond human comprehension. He is again the "pious Job" of tradition. The only problem is that in the next chapter God himself says it was Job who was telling the truth about him, the friends who were mistaken. Does God also recant?

2. "I reject recanting, even on the dust heap," or "I reject taking comfort for the dust heap."

In this, the opposite interpretation, Job recognizes God's power but refuses to be intimidated. He remains defiant, though subdued. One could even translate: " I reject recanting concerning the dust heap." Even after hearing God's recitation of the wonder of creation, this world still seems to Job to be a dust heap. This nihilistic interpretation is appealing to some modern sensibilities. Some take the further step of reading into the words an existentialist rejection of God's relevance to morality. He is "beyond good and evil," and so is Job himself.

3. "I reject but take comfort for the dust heap."

Job is humbled but also, as a result of God's appearance and defense of His own ways, paradoxically reconciled to his condition. The implied object of "reject" may be his own accusations against God; or, it may be God's arguments. In other words, he may have given up his defiance or redoubled it. Or perhaps he is implying that in light of the "comfort" he feels, his defiance,

while upheld, is now irrelevant. While unresolved, the issue of
Job's suffering must be put aside, not because the opponents are
worn out, but because there is some third factor in play.

To sum up, Job may be humbled, defiant, or both humble and defiant, taking "comfort" for something that remains unstated. As a pro-
ponent of the "literary approach" to the Bible, and a lover of paradox,
I will always opt for the approach that best utilizes the ambiguities
inherent in the text, in this case, the third interpretation. But this can
make sense only if I can explain what is the source of Job's new "comfort," which has neutralized his still unrecanted defiance of God's justice.

For an answer we must turn to 40:4–5, Job's response to the first
divine speech, to establish the true emotion of his reaction.

"Since I am so insignificant, How can I answer you? I put my hand to
my mouth. I had spoken one or two things before, but have no response
now."

Clearly Job is silenced and humbled by the revelation of the immensity of creation and God's wisdom in performing it. But is that all?
When one looks up at a starry sky (if one can find one today), is one's
typical reaction depression, a feeling of being crushed?

The final stage in this search for Job's answer to the problem of
human suffering lies, I believe, in the gesture Job makes. Again, we
are dealing with a perfect ambiguity. Putting hand to mouth means
being silenced, having no answer to the accusations of one's foes, being weak and powerless (cf. Job 21:5). But the same gesture is performed when one is astonished by something grander than oneself,
when all attempt at description is impossible (Job 29:10).

In fact, placing the hand to the mouth was the universal gesture of
adoration in the ancient world. A significant passage in this regard is
Job 31:26–27. In a long oath, his final extended speech, Job protests
that his piety was always unblemished. One of his statements is:

I never looked at the radiant light [=the sun],
Or at the moon when it went in splendor
And my heart never was seduced in secret,
And my hand kissed my mouth.

The sight of heavenly light as inciter to idolatry is a common theme of covenantal religion (cf. especially Deuteronomy 4:19). The poet here strikingly reverses the gesture of adoration: it was the mouth that kissed the hand, not the reverse.[9]

I believe that Job is both silenced and humbled and yet also inwardly exalted by what he has seen, the theophany, and by what God has told him about the acts of cosmic creation. Job is, in fact, filled by that emotion that uniquely combines opposites: terror, awareness of one's insignificance, and fear of extinction, on the one hand, and, on the other, feelings of exaltation, forgetfulness of self, and fascination. The emotion in question is a sophisticated one: astonishment or, better, awe at the sublime. Further evidence comes from the fact that the divine speeches, while phrased as challenging questions, in fact serve to reveal to Job the immensity and scope of creation. Their form may be that of the question, but their tone is exalted and hymnic. The Book of Job is not a philosophical treatise but a great poem, and the message of its poetry must be taken into account, quite apart from the logic of the arguments. That message is one of awe at the sublime.

My understanding of the sublime comes not from reading the original works of (Pseudo-) Longinus, Boileau, Burke, and others, but from Samuel Monk's work on the concept of the sublime in eighteenth-century English thought.[10] The following is a short pastiche of statements about the sublime by the thinkers just mentioned, interspersed with Monk's, and my own, comments.

The sublime applies properly, of course, to a high literary style. But from its Longinian beginnings it was associated with deep emotional reaction both to language and to nature. Longinus: "The sublime is a certain eminence or perfection of language that not only persuades but even throws an audience into transport. . . . In most cases it is wholly in our power either to resist or yield to persuasion. But the sublime, endued with strength irresistible, strikes home and triumphs over every hearer."[11] In contact with the sublime, "the mind . . . swells in transport and an inward pride. . . ."[12] The sublime is therefore a literary style that not only reflects certain emotions but is also capable of inducing them in an audience. The chief aspect of the style is greatness of thought combined with simplicity of expression. The emotion it arouses is described by Burke as "astonishment,"[13] i.e., awe.

In regard to nature, already Longinus had declared that "whatever exceeds the common size is always great and amazing. The Nile or the Rhine, not the common rivulet, excites the emotion of awe. . . . Mountains and the ocean were especially apt symbols in the physical world of the moral greatness to which Longinus attributed the sublime in art."[14] The sublime arises from the grand and terrible, from whatever is obscure, dark, powerful, vast, and infinite.[15] But the emotion it arouses is not naked fear. In the case of a storm, "to the man who sees danger [in it] and who does not fear, the phenomenon is sublime; but the moment that it becomes terrible . . . all relish for the sublimity in it is at an end."[16] Put in another way, fear involves extreme concern for extinction of self; awe, however, involves forgetfulness of self, including the danger to it, through a transporting emotion.

Job's reaction to God's speeches is similar to what the eighteenth century viewed as the reaction to encounters with the sublime, both in regard to the beauty of the poetry and the attitude it induces in Job. He is humbled, filled with terror at the theophany, which, as usual in covenant religion in the Bible, takes the form of a storm, presumably accompanied by the full theophanic panoply of wind, thunder and lightning, earthquake. But the voice that comes from the churning cloud reveals to Job something of the scope and intricacy of God's creation, and also the extent of His providence in governing it. Therefore, Job is also filled with awe. His contradictory emotions are analogous to those that people began to feel in the eighteenth century when confronted by any gigantic natural phenomenon, such as mountains or storms: "The sense of all this danger and beauty produced different emotions in me: a delightful horror, a terrible joy, and at the same time that I was infinitely pleased, I trembled."[17]

Now, it must seem absurdly anachronistic to read Job in light of an emotion first discussed openly by a first-century Greek and taken up only in the late seventeenth century as an active concept in Western culture, reaching its height in the eighteenth. Absurd, that is, until one remembers that the example that Longinus cited as the epitome of the sublime as a combination of simple language and grandness of thought came from the Hebrew Bible: "And God said, 'Let there be light,' and there was light." Absurd also, until one realizes that the issue involved with the sublime, especially as understood in the eighteenth century, was a changed reaction to nature itself.

VI

Above, I listed three possibilities of interpretation of Job's final words, all equally allowed by the language. The first, that Job is merely humbled, comports to the covenantal Torah piety, which demands absolute faith. This reading is probably why Job is in the canon, as the patient, pious Job of the folktale, his blasphemy recanted. It may have been intended by the author as the meaning the conventionally pious should take from the book, backed up by the "happy ending" of the epilogue, where Job is restored to his former state. The second, nihilistic, reading, while attractive to some moderns, and even more postmoderns, is quite impossible in the context of ancient Wisdom circles. A scholar must resist its seduction.[18] But the essential message, I believe, lies in the third reading, awe at the sublime in nature, which fits the intellectual context of the book and is, I believe, the answer to suffering the author directs at his true intended audience, the wise, and their new hybrid Wisdom piety.

The author of Job presents his own solution to the dilemma of Wisdom confronted by covenant faith. From the latter he accepts, no doubt ironically, only the idea of revelation though a storm theophany, like that at Sinai. God also appears to Job, the new Moses, from a storm wind, *deus ex turbine*. But the content of the revelation has both the form and substance of the pure Old Wisdom tradition. Lists of rhetorical questions, often presenting inventories of natural and social phenomena, were a favorite device of challenge by one wise man to an inferior one already in Egyptian and Mesopotamian traditions.[19] By putting the answer in the form of a series of unanswerable questions, the author concedes that the order of the cosmos will always be beyond penetration by the intellect. However, the content of the divine speeches in chapters 38–42, dealing not with covenant law as at Sinai, but with the wonders of nature, transmutes the argument from logic to emotion. The hymnic passion inspires in the reader, as well as in Job, the emotion of awe at the sublime in nature.

Of course, the core issue has not yet been attacked: how is awe at the sublime an answer to the problem of suffering? That answer is not logical. The issues remain unresolved intellectually (although they may be alleviated by having been aired and vented). Rather, through awe at the sublime in nature, one may forget enough of one's self to neutralize one's pain. Intellect must give way to emotion. Revelation and nature cannot be reconciled by human wisdom. Only through transfiguring emotion can even the demand for reconciliation be made sublimely irrelevant.

The author of Job is perhaps more interested in protesting the victory of covenant faith, especially in the mechanistic, hybrid Wisdom form it took in the kind of religion represented by Job's friends, than in presenting the groundwork of a true nature-centered religion that would attempt to solve the problem of suffering. Intimations of such an answer suffice for him, or, probably more accurately, are all that could be achieved in his era. In any case, he was a poet, not a true philosopher, and poets are not required to solve anything. And it is perhaps his poetry itself that represents, paradoxically, his most practical "solution" to the problem of suffering.

After all, not everyone can be Job, either in the degree of one's suffering or in achieving the victory of wresting a personal revelation from God. But I believe that the ultimate answer to suffering offered by the author lies in his own poetry, especially in the magnificent nature poems of chapters 38 and 39. Through the sublime in poetry he hopes to arouse the feeling of awe one should experience when confronted by the topic of that poetry, nature. The emotion is to sweep us up and along, away from all petty concern with our pain: a catharsis effected by poetry.

Theologically and intellectually, the Book of Job will always remain unfulfilling to those who demand logical answers to suffering and insist on finding comprehensible meaning in the cosmos. To them the author would give the dual reply: it is within your *rights* to do so, but who are *you* to demand it? The Book of Job is a grand torso, a work of uneven genius, quite of the sort that already Longinus regarded as the hallmark of the truly sublime in literature.[20]

Indeed, there is something heroic, sublime in itself, in the author's struggle to save Old Wisdom's fascination with nature by employing his great art, at a time when nature was being ousted from biblical religion, exiled to a peripheral testament to God as creator. It has kept this lowly position in Western religion to this day, and in Western culture in general, so long as it remained tied exclusively to religion. Nature was not restored to prominence until the Renaissance, and to centrality until the revival of the concept of the sublime and the nature worship of the Romantic movement, a couple of centuries ago. Indeed, Job, with his extremism, the *Sturm und Drang* of his language and emotions, deserves to be viewed at least as a biblical prefiguration of a romantic.

Notes

1. This essay is an expansion and development of a thesis presented in my *Sacred Enigmas: Literary Religion in the Hebrew Bible* (New York: Routledge, 1996), chap. 5, esp. pp. 101–7.

2. The discussion presented here is substantially like that of Gerhard von Rad, *Old Testament Theology*, vol. 1, trans. D. M. G. Stalker (New York and Evanston, Ill.: Harper and Row, 1962), 418ff., esp. 424ff. That ancient Wisdom posited a cosmological dimension to the moral order, implied by such terms as *ma'at*, "truth," in Egypt, or *mesarum*, "right," in Mesopotamia, has been questioned; see especially J. Assmann, *Ma'at: Gerechtigkeit und Unsterblichkeit im Alten Ägypten* (Munich: C. H. Beck, 1990); and for biblical Wisdom, Roland E. Murphy, "Wisdom Literature and Theology," in *The Tree of Life: An Exploration of Biblical Wisdom Literature* (New York: Doubleday, 1990), chap. 8. See also M. V. Fox, *Qoheleth and His Contradictions* (Sheffield: Almond Press, 1989). But see the critique of Murphy and defense of the viewpoint shared by this essay in James L. Crenshaw, *Urgent Advice and Probing Questions: Collected Writings on Old Testament Wisdom* (Macon, Ga.: Mercer, 1995), esp. chap. 20. The interpretation offered by standard works on ancient Wisdom seems to me to be still justified, provided one does not present the ancient views as more systematic and coherent than they actually were.

3. The important point, then, is not that much of the language of Wisdom books like Proverbs and Qoheleth is theistic, but that such works generally eschew reference to covenant in favor of a universal human frame of reference. There is no point in speculating whether the wise would have admitted that God could work against the principle of cause and effect, if he chose. Probably, such a notion would not even have occurred to them.

4. Or "demons."

5. Even the rabbis shared the view that it would have been better for man had he had never been created, although they do not recommend that he forthwith do away with himself, as Silenus did, but rather that he examine his actions.

6. In fairness, it must be admitted that already ancient Near Eastern Wisdom contained a strong pietistic element, especially in Egypt. The inconsistency between the older view of the gods as natural forces and the later tendency to view them anthropomorphically, with a consequent focus on personal piety, is much older than Job. But it is only in that book that the tension becomes the focus of a polemic.

7. There may even be a historical link. The founder of Stoicism, Zeno, was a Phoenician from Cyprus, and many have noted the oriental aspect of some features of Stoicism. It may be that Zeno continued the ancient Near Eastern Wisdom tradition in a rigorous Greek intellectual framework.

8. *Book of Job*, trans. Raymond Scheindlin (New York: W. W. Norton, 1998).

9. On the gesture, see the commentaries of Dhorme and Pope, *ad locum*.

10. Samuel H. Monk, *The Sublime: A Study of Critical Theories in Eighteenth-Century England* (Ann Arbor: University of Michigan Press, 1960).

11. Ibid., 12.

12. Ibid.

13. Ibid., 92.

14. Ibid., 204.

15. Ibid., 93.

16. Ibid., 162.

17. John Dennis as quoted in Monk, *The Sublime*, 207.

18. I cannot agree with the very popular reading of Job which holds that the meaning of the book is that there is no moral order comprehensible to man, that God's power as creator has no relationship to right and wrong. While it must be admitted that this would be a powerful meaning, it seems to me to be grossly anachronistic in its modern separation of nature and morality, creation and piety. Such a reading is simply beyond the bounds of the thought realm of the ancient world. The ancients may rail against and bemoan the dissonance of natural and moral orders, as Job does, but even he, the most extreme sufferer in ancient literature, still has hope that God will appear and justify His ways. To hold that the actual revelation comes, then, only to completely and utterly crush Job, with no further meaning, reflects a superficial understanding of Job's final words and an eggregiously postmodern sensibility. Nor should one make the mistake of taking the lesson of the divine speeches to be simply that man cannot know God's ways. Such a reading is quite otiose in the context of the book, since God would be merely repeating, anticlimactically, the viewpoint of the friends, and recapitulating the famous poem on hidden wisdom in chapter 28, which already makes the same point. Of course, one might counter that the logical content of great poetry is often banal, since in poetry the medium itself is the message. But why not opt for a reading that does justice both to art and sense?

19. See von Rad, *Old Testament Theology*, 425.

20. Monk, *The Sublime*, 15.

Creation in the Bible and in the Liturgy

NEIL GILLMAN

The major methodological assumption of this paper is that in Judaism those portions of the liturgy that originate in the literature of the talmudic period (ca. 100–600 C.E.) should be viewed as the extension, frequently the transformation, and, at times, even the subversion of biblical doctrines. We are fully aware that the Bible does not always speak in one voice on significant doctrinal issues. Yet, if the Bible represents the initial canonization of at least the core of the Jewish religious myth, then in postbiblical Judaism the extension of that process of canonization can be found most explicitly in the liturgy.

The liturgy uses biblical texts in many different ways. Over seventy psalms, almost half of the Book of Psalms, appear in their entirety somewhere in the liturgy.[1] Countless individual verses from the psalms were introduced into later liturgical texts. Specific prophetic texts were used as *haftarot* accompanying the yearly Torah reading cycle on Sabbaths and festivals. But what interests us more are those liturgical passages, formulated by the talmudic rabbis, which appropriate biblical themes by using distinctively biblical code words or phrases, or which in some other way echo biblical texts, thereby identifying themselves as biblically based.

The large majority of worshiping Jews, from the end of the talmudic era to our own day, are much more familiar with these liturgical passages than with their original formulation in the Bible itself, certainly more familiar than with the contents of the Prophets and the Writings. (Of course, the yearly cycle of Torah readings on the Sabbath enables them to be totally familiar with the Pentateuch.) Without necessarily being aware of it, Jews encounter much of the Bible through the liturgy. These liturgical texts have played a decisive role in shaping the belief system of postbiblical Jews, a much greater role than the more scattered and unfamiliar talmudic homilies which also frequently transform a biblical doctrine in ways that echo or anticipate their transformations in the liturgy.

The difference between these two forms of expression is that the talmudic homily is the individual statement of one rabbi in a specific historical context which can only rarely be recaptured today. In contrast, the liturgical formulation is much more of a consensual statement. Because it frequently uses the original, unpronounceable four-letter name of God, the precise wording of the statement acquired a halakhic, or legal, standing, and therefore, had to win consensual rabbinic approval.

These liturgical texts should be studied not as a text to be read, but rather as an activity to be performed.[2] The specific activity being performed here is what can be called "doing theology." Though we conventionally use the all-purpose English term "prayer" to designate all forms of worship, in Judaism, worship is fine-tuned and subdivided into a number of different models. One familiar model, embodied in the daily Amidah, is petitionary prayer; we petition God for forgiveness, healing, and the rest. But another model, the one that interests us here, is the one in which the liturgy articulates a series of theological claims, much like in the Credo portion of the Roman Catholic Mass. Frequently, however, in its liturgical guise, a biblical doctrine undergoes a subtle transformation which lends it a new meaning. It is precisely this transformation that takes place within the liturgical passage that we refer to as "doing theology."

Of these texts, we can ask a series of questions: Why do the rabbis choose specific biblical phrases, verses, or passages for liturgical purposes? Why in this specific liturgical context? What happens to these terms in their new formulation? How do these transformations reveal the way the rabbis read and understood the biblical text? Finally, how do these texts work for us, the worshipers? In this paper, we will concentrate on texts that deal with the doctrine of creation. We will also compare the biblical/liturgical understandings of creation with a very different model in Jewish mystical literature, and suggest some methodological issues for further investigation.

On the question as to how these texts work for the worshiper, I will use a conceptualization suggested by Clifford Geertz in his seminal

"Religion as a Cultural System."[3] We sense, intuitively, that there is a tight relationship between liturgy and ritual, on the one hand, and the feelings and behaviors of those who worship and perform the ritual, on the other. But it is not intuitively clear just how that relationship is established and how it works. Geertz provides us with a conceptualization that enables us to deal with this question. Geertz's definition of religion is

> . . . a system of symbols which acts to establish powerful, pervasive and longlasting moods and motivations in men by formulating conceptions of a general order of existence, and clothing these conceptions with such an aura of factuality that the moods and motivations seem uniquely realistic.[4]

My own preferred terminology is to refer to this "system of symbols" as "myth." A myth is a set of symbols extended and systematized into one coherent structure of meaning. A myth can articulate or describe that structure (a structural myth), and/or narrate how that structure came into being (a narrative myth).[5]

It is a device through which an individual or a community organizes its experience of the world, or of one part of the world (as in the Freudian psychoanalytic myth that attempts to make sense of human behavior), so that it forms a coherent whole. Following Geertz, myths are ordering devices. Rollo May provides an alternative definition:

> A myth is a way of making sense in a senseless world . . . myths are like the beams in a house: not exposed to outside view, they are the structure which holds the house together so people can live in it.[6]

Or, to use still another metaphor, myths are the lines that connect the dots on the page of our experience of the world, so that we can "see" a tiger or an igloo.

Two points about these definitions: first, a myth is a selective, interpretive reading of "the real," designed to introduce or reveal an underlying, hidden structure or order that we can now see. And second, no myth is a photograph of the real. We cannot photograph, or even observe, the real without some preexistent structuring device. So much for the common distinction between a myth and "the facts"; without a myth, we are not even aware of what the significant facts are in the first place.

In the course of unpacking his definition, Geertz addresses the question of how precisely this "system of symbols" acquires that "aura of factuality" that makes "the moods and motivations seem uniquely realistic." His answer is that it is through ritual. He writes:

> In a ritual, the world as lived and the world as imagined, fused under the agency of a single set of symbolic forms, turn out to be the same world.[7]

In ritual, which Geertz defines concisely as "consecrated behavior," the moods and motivations, the feelings and behaviors induced by the sacred symbols (or religious myths) and the general conceptions of an ordered world that the myths formulate, meet and reinforce one another.

I understand the liturgy that accompanies the ritual to be an integral part of that complex ritual activity. Ritual and liturgy differ in that they use two different languages, one behavioral and the other verbal. But in significant ritual moments, such as the Passover Seder, the rites of passage, or the Christian Eucharist, these two languages are woven together to convey one set of meanings. At these moments, the mythic world and the real world of real people fuse and become one. It is ritual, then, that brings the mythic system into the life of the believer so that it can accomplish its function of ordering the world.

One addendum is necessary to our previous discussion of the relationship between liturgy and the Bible. Myths exist in time. They live and they die but, more frequently—because myths are singularly tenacious—they evolve and change. Portions of a myth can be discarded and new elements can be introduced. This is what we mean when we say that myths enjoy a certain "plasticity." This is precisely what happens to some biblical versions of the myth as it enters into the later liturgy.

My specific interest here is to study some liturgical passages that deal with the biblical accounts of creation. These creation narratives form an integral part of the canonical Jewish religious myth. They both portray the structure of the ordered, transcendent world that explains how the world we live in coheres and describe how that structure came to be. Our purpose is to understand how some liturgical passages reflect and transform the biblical texts that they invoke, and thereby extend and transform the body of the Jewish myth. We will use four such specific liturgical texts, all of which refer to biblical doctrines of creation.

The Sheva Berakhot

These seven benedictions of the Sheva Berakhot, which originate in the Talmud,[8] form the major part of the liturgy that accompanies the Jewish marriage ceremony. The most difficult of these seven benedictions is the fourth in the order in which they are recited under the *huppah* (wedding canopy).[9] Its concluding words, in which we praise God as *yotzer ha-'adam*, are identical to the concluding words of the benediction that immediately precedes it. The precise meaning of these concluding words is obscure. They could be translated literally as "creator of the man" or as "creator of mortals" (echoing Genesis 1:26 where God creates *ha-'adam* both male and female). But in its broader context, this fourth benediction clearly refers to the creation of the first woman (as in Numbers 31:35 where the word *'adam* is used to refer to women), while the preceding benediction lacks any specific gender connotation.

This benediction then represents a further narrowing of God's creative activity. In the second, God creates all things; in the third, God creates the human person(s). Now, in the fourth, God creates the woman, and through the woman, *binyan 'ade 'ad*, or eternal human posterity. That this text refers to the creation of woman is explicitly conveyed by the term *binyan* (literally, "building" or "edifice"), which alludes to Genesis 2:22 where the verb *va-yiven* is used to describe God's fashioning (or building) of the woman from the rib taken from the man. Through the children born by the woman, the man achieves posterity or eternity.

The problem is with the three words *tzelem demut tavnito*, on which much scholarly effort has been expended.[10] The three terms all convey the general sense of "image" or "likeness." The human person was created in someone's image. But whose "image" is being invoked here? The first two terms surely do refer to God's image; they are used in Genesis 1:26 and 27 to indicate that the first human person or persons, depending on how we read 1:27, was or were created in God's image.

But *tavnito* should not refer to God; it is much too physicalistic. Maimonides, in the *Guide of the Perplexed* (1.3) suggests that *tavnit* means an object's (physical) shape, as in Exodus 25:8, where the phrase *tavnit ha-mishkan* refers to the shape of the desert sanctuary, or in Isaiah 44:13, which refers to an idol as having a *tavnit 'ish*, or "human (clearly physical) form." On this basis, Maimonides insists that it can never be used to apply to God, because God has no physical form. However, in 2 Kings 16:10, *tavnit* is used as a synonym for *demut*, and both refer to a sketch, plan, or blueprint.

The conventional interpretation of the passage follows Saadia's reading, which either transposes the *vav* from before the word *ve-hitqin* earlier in the passage, to a point immediately prior to the word *be-tzelem*, so that our phrase now reads *u-vetzelem demut tavnito hitqin lo mi-menu binyan ʿade ʿad.*[11] Now, the three synonyms, *tzelem, demut,* and *tavnito,* refer to Adam, not to God. Or, without actually moving the *vav,* we simply read the text as if it were transposed. The text now begins by claiming that Adam was created in God's *tzelem,* or image, and then concludes that the woman was created in Adam's image; the three synonyms now refer to Adam. Since Adam was created in God's image, so was the woman.

Note also that the word *tavnit* foreshadows the word *binyan,* both stemming from the biblical (Gen. 2:22) *va-yiven,* which refers to the creation of the woman. But what is unusual about the term *tavnit* is precisely its physicality. As David Flusser and Shmuel Safrai emphasize, this formulation constitutes a rejection of any dualistic anthropology.[12] There is no reference here to a soul, to a *nefesh* or a *neshamah,* as these terms are understood in the later literature.[13] In the medieval philosophical tradition, the *tzelem* in which the human person was created was the faculty of intellectual apprehension.[14] But our text reflects a thoroughly biblical anthropology following Genesis 2:7, where God creates the human person by vivifying a clod of earth. The human person is composed of some physical matter that has been given a breath or spark of life. The anthropology is thoroughly monolithic.

This liturgical text then extends the biblical narrative in three ways. It teaches us that the first woman was created in the image of the first man; that it is through the woman that the man achieves eternal posterity; and that, in both cases, the image of God in both man and woman is not exclusively spiritual, but also denotes the body. Leaving aside the much broader question of what, in the first place, the Bible means by claiming that the man was created in God's image, here at least it means some form of vivified matter.

The liturgical text also reflects a rabbinic dispute which stems from an ambiguity in Genesis 1:26. Here, "God creates *ha-ʾadam* in his image, in the image of God he created him . . . ," and then, "male and female he created them." Does this text refer, then, to one act of creation, or to two? Did God create *ha-'adam*, and then the woman? Or did God create both man and woman in one act of creation, with the subsequent (Gen. 2:22) reference to the creation of the woman, simply indicating that God separated the original woman from the original man?

The rabbinic dispute[15] revolves around the two separate benedictions, the third and the fourth, dealing with the creation of the original human persons. That there are two such separate benedictions suggests that the rabbis understood that there were two separate creation acts here, one relating to the first man and the other to the first woman.

Using Geertz's conceptualization, how does this ritual work? Precisely by fusing the two worlds, the transcendent mythic world of the creation story and the actual, real world of the two people who are getting married. This is explicit in the sixth benediction, where the two people being married are identified with the first two human beings. In effect, then, two weddings are taking place simultaneously. The *huppah* becomes Eden, the couple becomes Adam and Eve, and the presiding rabbi becomes God. The rabbis here echo the familiar Midrash in which God prepares Adam and Eve for their wedding and pronounces the wedding blessings.[16]

Actually, three weddings are taking place simultaneously because the fifth benediction portrays the "wedding" of Zion and her children. Here, the *huppah* becomes Jerusalem, the couple becomes Zion and her children, and again, the rabbi becomes God who unites Zion and the people Israel. Two significant dimensions of the classic Jewish mythic structure enter our consciousness: the universal creation myth and the national Zion myth.

Finally, why did the rabbis incorporate references to creation in the wedding liturgy? There are three possible reasons: First, to echo the Mishnah where the rabbis note that God created only one person from whom the entire world was populated; thus, every single human being (and now, this couple who will procreate) is potentially the source of an entire world.[17] Second, because they understood marriage in sexual terms. The wedding canopy symbolizes the marital bed, and for the rabbis, sexuality means posterity, posterity means Jewish continuity, and continuity is important.

Third, the rabbis include the creation references because the last of the seven benedictions is explicitly eschatological. The liturgy locates this marriage within the broadest possible temporal canvas of the myth, between creation and redemption. The rabbis incorporate the very words of Jeremiah 33:10–11 with their reference to marriage. Jeremiah 32:2 enables us to date this entire passage within weeks prior to the destruction of the Temple. In this context, marriage is a metaphor for the eventual restoration of Israel to its land. Its thrust is eschatological. The liturgical use of this passage makes every marriage a redemptive act, effectively a statement of hope in the future at the moment of utmost despair. To establish that broad canvas, the rabbis open the seven benedictions with creation and close with eschatology. Echoing Geertz, this is a striking example of ordering.

Finally, I believe that the breaking of the glass, the ritual that concludes the marriage service as a whole, is not at all as it is conventionally understood—a recollection of the destruction that was—but rather, is an anticipation of the chaos that remains, a return to history, a breaking of the messianic spell.[18] Again echoing Geertz, it separates the two worlds, the mythic and the real, that had been momentarily fused. For just a moment, redemption was in the air; but we know that the world has not been totally redeemed, that chaos still rules "out there," and that this couple must now return to the unredeemed real world.[19]

My next three examples are drawn form the Yotzer (creation) benediction of the *shaharit* (morning) service.

Yotzer 'Or U-vore Hoshekh

These words form the opening core of the Yotzer benediction for the morning service.[20] We praise God ". . . who fashions light and creates darkness, who makes *shalom* [which we leave untranslated for the present] and creates all things."

In Genesis 1:2, God begins by creating light. Darkness, together with deep waters, a mighty wind, and the earth in its state of *tohu vavohu* (which the Jewish Publication Society's 1985 *TaNaKH* translates as "unformed and void"), exists before the creation of light. The liturgy, however, incorporates a different version of creation, one based on Isaiah 45:7: "I fashion light and create darkness, I make *shalom* and create evil—I the Lord do all these things."

First, then, in deliberate contravention of Genesis, the Isaiah text

has God also creating darkness. God creates all things, light and darkness, good and evil, and not only these polarities but also probably
everything in between. In other words, God really creates *kol 'eleh*, or
"all these things." But though the liturgy has God creating darkness,
Isaiah's word for "evil," *ra*, is dropped and replaced with the words *'et
ha-kol*, or "all things," taken from that concluding phrase of the verse,
from *kol 'eleh*.

In formulating the opening benediction for the Yotzer, the rabbis
decided to use the Isaiah text to the effect that God creates light as an
appropriate phrase for the beginning of the formal service at dawn.
But the benediction could simply have read, *Yotzer 'or u-vore 'et ha-
kol*, God "creates light and forms all things," omitting the reference to
darkness.

Why, then, did they include the claim that God also creates darkness, in explicit contravention of Genesis 1? I believe for three reasons: First, they did not want worshipers to puzzle over who created
darkness; of course, God created darkness too. Genesis may not have
said this, but they wanted to. Second, they were uncomfortable with
the dualistic implications that anything coexisted with God before
God's creation of the world.[21] Third, they also did want to make a
statement about the source of evil, though they were more ambivalent
about the issue than the author of Isaiah 45. In Isaiah, darkness is
parallel to *ra*. This enables us to translate *shalom* not as the conventional "peace," but rather as "completeness," "harmony," or simply
"cosmos," and *ra* as its opposite, "chaos." Since they assumed that the
worshiper might hear the echo of Isaiah, and since *ha-kol* also includes evil, they were able to make that point as well.

The biblical understanding of creation does not teach *creatio ex
nihilo*. That may have been a burning issue for medieval philosophers,[22] but in Genesis at least, creation is not something out of nothing, but rather cosmos out of chaos, with the chaotic or anarchic nature of the preexisting stuff captured in the theme of the "deep waters"
and more particularly in the phrase *tohu va-vohu*. Rashi (on Gen. 1:2)
accurately captures the sense of that phrase through his use of the
early French, *étourdir*, which means "to swirl," or "to make dizzy."
The Genesis narrative portrays God's creative work, not as creating
"all things," but rather as controlling, disciplining, ordering, or structuring the preexisting chaotic forces in the world.

The liturgical passage thus forms a way station between the Bible and the medievals. It does not invoke *tohu va-vohu*, but it does include darkness within God's creation, and darkness can also be understood as part of that preexisting chaos, now part of God's creation.

We should not underestimate the theological power of this statement. Genesis 1 claims that God did not create darkness; it was there at the outset. What Genesis does claim (in 1:4) was that God separated the darkness from the light, or, in other words, placed boundaries about the darkness, as God does with the waters (in 1:9). In contrast, the Isaiah text has God creating darkness (and presumably the waters as well) and then proceeds to identify this darkness with evil, with the opposite of cosmos, with chaos. God then creates evil as well. In Genesis, God controls chaos; in Isaiah, God creates it. One can understand why the liturgy wished to dilute that claim. In fact, the substitution is discussed in the Talmud (B. Berakhot 11b) and is explained by the rabbinic preference for what may be loosely translated "more exalted language" (*lishna me'alya*).

Here is a classic example of liturgy as "doing theology." The worshiper is led through a complex theological exercise consisting of: first, Isaiah's departure from Genesis to the effect that God created darkness as well as light; second, the change from *ra* to *ha-kol*; third, the claim that God, too, is responsible for evil; and finally, that creation was, in a way, *ex nihilo*.

U-vetuvo Mehadesh Bekhol Yom Tamid Ma'aseh Vereshit

The claim, here, is that God, ". . . in [God's] goodness, daily renews the work of creation." This phrase appears originally in B. Hagigah 12b, which quotes Isaiah 40:22b as a proof text (reading the two verbs in that passage in the present tense). In our version of the Yotzer benediction the phrase appears twice, once near the beginning and again, in a very slightly altered form, near the end. The effect of this second appearance is to restore the thematic unity of the benediction by picking up the thread of the opening words of the Yotzer benediction. Apparently, the later insertion of the extended angelology liturgy, which in our texts makes up the bulk of the benediction, required this second appearance of the phrase.[23]

The claim here is that God's work of creation was not a one-time event in the distant past, but rather an ongoing activity that continues daily, every day. This constitutes another transformation of the Genesis version. Genesis suggests that God created the world in one series of acts at the outset. Now, creation is not only a statement about how the world came into being at the outset, but also a statement of the created world's ongoing dependence on God's daily intervention.

How does the liturgy reach that conclusion? It does so, first, from the liturgical proof text, Psalm 136:7, "Who makes [*le-'oseh*] the great lights, God's steadfast love is eternal." The emphasis is on the present tense of the verb, *'oseh* ("God makes"), and on the "eternal" quality of God's steadfast love. God then continues to create today, every day. And second, this conclusion is drawn from the daily experience of sunrise. The rabbis understood that daily experience is a new act of creation all over again.

In this context, compare the Yotzer benediction with its parallel in *ma'ariv,* the evening service, which also celebrates God's creative work. First, it is intriguing to note that, though the rabbis chose to characterize God as *yotzer 'or* ("creates light") at dawn, they did not characterize God as *yotzer hoshekh* ("creates darkness") at evening. Even more, though in the morning they portray God as creating both light and darkness, none of this is echoed in the evening service. In its place, the emphasis is on God's daily maintenance of creation. Daily, God brings on evenings, changes seasons, creates day and night, removes light before darkness and darkness before light, causes day to pass and brings night, and separates day and night.[24] Creation is not a single event in the distant past, but a daily manifestation of God's power.

Finally, the single theme of the entire evening text is God as creator of distinctions. It then echoes forcefully the creation account of Genesis 1 where God is portrayed again and again as distinguishing between light and darkness, day and night, waters above and waters below, the Sabbath and the common days of the week. The emphasis is on creation as a process of bringing cosmos out of chaos. Distinctions or boundaries are intrinsic to the process of creating an ordered world out of a preexistent anarchy.

Though the opening of the Yotzer benediction is closer to the Isaiah 45 version of creation, the theme that God daily renews the work of creation coheres more closely with the Genesis version. If, as in Genesis, God does not create darkness but rather confines it within boundaries, then God must continue daily to control the chaotic forces in the

world. That is why God must renew creation every day. But, if following Isaiah, where God creates the chaos, why the theme of daily renewal?

The key to this lies in the single word *u-vetuvo*. It is God's "goodness" that leads to God's daily renewal of creation. The original Hebrew for what we have interpreted as chaos is *ra*. God creates evil. But
once God has created evil, then the contrary or balancing impulse in
God, God's goodness, requires that God work constantly, daily, to insure that the chaotic be kept under a measure of control. Hence, creation demands God's daily attention.

'Or Hadash 'Al Tzion Ta'ir

The Yotzer benediction concludes with this supplication that God
"cause a new light to shine on Zion." The thrust of the petition is
clearly eschatological; this is precisely why it was so controversial.
Saadia Gaon opposed its use, first, because it is a petition which he
felt was out of place in this part of the liturgy, and mainly, because he
felt it represents a confusion of categories. The theme of the Yotzer as
a whole is God's creative work in nature. Hence its reference to God's
creation of natural light in the opening and concluding words of the
benediction. But the petition extends and transforms that theme by
using God's creation of light as a metaphor for God's redemptive
work. Its inclusion dilutes the integrity of the larger passage. To use
another idiom, it confuses God's work in nature with God's work in
history. That God also works in history is the theme of the next benediction in the sequence, the Birkat Ha-Torah, which praises God for
choosing Israel and for the revelation of the Torah.[25]

But if we understand this liturgy as a case of "doing theology," and
if we agree that it is not infrequent for rabbinic liturgy to transform a
biblical doctrine, then this passage belongs perfectly. What it says in
effect is that God's power ranges not only over nature but over history
as well; that if God recreates nature daily, then God can recreate the
fate of God's people on any day. In praising God for creating nature,
we can also praise God for working in history. In fact, only a God who
is sovereign over nature can be sovereign over history. The distinction
between nature and history fades in the face of God's transcendent
power over everything.

And, this passage accomplishes all of this through the use of a singularly powerful literary device, whereby the light of nature becomes a metaphor for the light of God's favor.

Creationism as Myth

My first encounter with the notion that religion has something to do with myth was in the magisterial, multivolume *Toledot Ha-Emunah Ha-Yisra'elit* (*History of Israelite Religion*), published between 1937 and 1956, by the Israeli scholar Yehezkel Kaufmann. The opening chapters of this study are devoted to a comparative phenomenology of pagan and Israelite religions, designed to document the author's thesis that monotheism could not have evolved out of paganism but, rather, constitutes a radical, revolutionary break with the pagan culture of the age. One of the differences between the two, Kaufmann maintains, is that whereas pagan religions are replete with myths, biblical monotheism is not.

Kaufmann can make this distinction because he defines myth as ". . . the tale of the life of the gods."[26] The pagan god has a biography: he is born, he dies, he loves, he wars with other gods, and his destiny is shaped by his interaction with these other gods and by their mutual dependency on a force that is superior to them all. In contrast, Kaufmann claims, the God of Israel has no biography: God is not born and does not die. God does not mate, and God is not challenged (except by human beings). God's will and God's power are sovereign and absolute over all of nature and history, not dependent on any prior force or power.

In retrospect, Kaufmann's definition of myth, though possibly in line with the state of scholarship on that subject decades ago, appears to us now as excessively narrow. Though we do continue to refer to narrative myths, our definition of myth now includes the notion of what we have called a structural myth, a phenomenological description in symbolic terms of an ordered world, as it is, not only how it came to be. We have also expanded the definition of narrative myth to include stories of major, transformatory events that portray gods, or God, interacting with human beings, in space and time. The biblical account of the revelation at Sinai in Exodus 19 is an example of that use.

The biblical accounts of creation are, explicitly, narrative myths

and, implicitly, structural myths. They describe how the ordered
world came to be, and they imply a portrait of what that world looks
like. The most accurate description of that ordered world lies precisely in the benedictions that surround the daily recitation of the
Shema: the Yotzer blessing and the Birkat Ha-Torah before, and the
Ge'ulah (or redemption) blessing after. God reigns over all of creation, nature and history, and maintains, daily, the created world; God
is covenanted with Israel, having redeemed Israel from slavery and
revealed a Teaching (*Torah*) that instructs that community on how it is
to conduct its communal and personal life in order to please God; God
rewards obedience and punishes transgression; God will again, in
time, redeem that community and restore the original order of creation. The core of the structural version of the myth is the image of a
transcendent, sovereign God who cares deeply about what transpires
in nature and history.

   One implication of this myth is that God abides "outside" the created world. At the beginning (in this liturgical version), there was only
God. After creation, there was God and the world, and these two are
distinct. That chasm is bridged in various ways: first, by God's constant concern for what goes on in the world; second, by the concrete
expression of that concern in God's revelation of Torah; third, by
God's interventions in history in the light of God's ongoing designs
for humanity; and fourth, by human prayer.

   That mythic model of creation is not the only one in Judaism. The
sixteenth-century Safed mystics, disciples of Rabbi Isaac Luria, proposed a very different model: God creates by emanation, an explosion
of God's own essential nature into a preexistent void. That emanated
"God-matter" becomes the created world. This emanationist understanding of creation skirts two potential classic Jewish heresies, pantheism and dualism. It skirts pantheism by insisting that one facet of
God's nature, *Ein Sof* (literally, "Infinity," not, as conventionally understood, "The Infinite One"), remains distinct from the world. It
skirts dualism by insisting that ultimately these are simply two faces
of the single God.

   In this model, God is identified with the created world. The split
between God and the world vanishes. The result is that what happens
in the world also happens "in" or "to" God, not, as in the Bible, in the
presence of God. If, as this mystical model teaches, the created world

is "broken" through some primordial catastrophe that accompanied creation, then God too is "broken." The most imaginative metaphor for this state of God's brokenness is the "exile of the *Shekhinah*." In mystical literature, this suggests that the two aspects of God—God in Godself or God as Infinity, and God's presence in the created world— are split apart, only to be rejoined eschatologically. And if the world demands redemption, so does God, with the impetus for that redemptive process being Israel's performance of God's commandments. To put it somewhat concisely, in this model God is responsible for the state of brokenness in the world, and Israel, for its repair.[27]

These alternative creation myths convey alternative images of the natural world and its relationship to God. In the mystical, emanationist model, the world is infused with the presence of God. God permeates creation, metaphysically. The created world becomes sacralized. We experience God by simply looking at the created world through the spectacles of this mystical model. To experience nature is to experience God.

In the biblical and liturgical model, God remains distant from what transpires in the world. God may care about the natural order, and God may command humans to care for it, but ultimately, God is not intrinsically or metaphysically affected by what transpires on earth. That is not to suggest that our behavior may please or anger God, but God remains apart from the scene of human activity.

These two creationist myths imply two different models for human activity. In the biblical/liturgical model, we are commanded to obey God's instructions on how to deal with the natural order, and hence to please God, for which we will be rewarded by bountiful crops, freedom from oppression by other nations, and a long and fruitful life. In the mystical model, our behavior has a sacramental quality. Every single divine command, even the most "humanistic" or interpersonal act, such as giving charity to the poor, accompanied by an awareness of mystical cosmology and its understanding of redemption, not only redeems the world but also redeems God. To put it concisely, the first model recognizes the distinction between God's interpersonal commands, what may be called the realm of the ethical, and those commands that affect our relationship with God, the realm of ritual. In the mystical model, everything we do is ritual.

The mystical model is extraordinarily suggestive, but it is vulnerable on one significant issue. In effect, it denies the reality of the natural world. Nature becomes a shell that conceals (or reveals) God. For the mystic, enlightenment comes with the ability to "see through" the shells of our common experience and perceive God's presence in the world, which is the "really real," the ultimate reality. The mystic's relation to nature is intrinsically ambiguous. On the one hand, he venerates nature, but on the other hand, it is ultimately not nature itself that he venerates.[28]

Both of these models are mythic—as mythic as Darwin's evolutionary model with which all creationist models are conventionally contrasted. They are all attempts to disclose hidden or elusive patterns in our experience of the world in order to make that experience cohere and acquire meaning. It is precisely that mythic standing that makes it possible for proponents of the alternative models to speak to each other. None of them claims to be objectively true; each is a selective and interpretive version of "the facts." But without such interpretive visions, what we call "the facts" are simply a blooming confusion. Without them, we don't really know what "the facts" are in the first place. The covert message of the myths is not only a description of what happened eons ago, but also a prescription as to where we are to locate ourselves within the created world, and how we are to live in accord with this vision.

Finally, though Jewish mysticism contributed much to Jewish liturgy, it did not substantially affect the liturgical tradition of creation, possibly because this liturgical version was firmly canonized centuries before the mystical model became popular, or possibly because of the pantheistic and/or dualistic implications of that model. With some relatively minor changes, that liturgical version remained securely anchored to the biblical version.

As Daniel Breslauer suggests in the title of his anthology *The Seductiveness of Jewish Myth*,[29] powerful, longstanding religious myths are extremely seductive. They are properly indispensable, but they also contain within themselves the possibility of betrayal. Myths are betrayed when they are no longer understood as myths but as objective and factual. They then become idolatrous. The precarious stance of the modern believer requires that he accept the myth precisely as myth or, to use Tillich's language, as a "broken" and "living" myth, and therefore to mistrust it.[30]

Conclusions

We return to our central methodological issue. In order to understand what happens to classical biblical doctrines in the course of their post-biblical development, the place to look is in the rabbinic liturgy. The words of the liturgy are codified. The recitation of these specific texts is mandatory for the observant Jew. Their wording is the result of submitting a theological claim to a process of legal decision-making so that what emerges at the end acquires canonical standing.

What we gain by looking at these liturgical passages is a glimpse of the rabbis doing constructive theology, a theology in process. We catch the way in which these biblical doctrines are extended, transformed, and sometimes even undermined in the course of their later development.

Second, on substantive issues regarding creation, we have learned a great deal. In reverse order, beginning with our three texts from the Yotzer benediction, we have learned: that *contra* Genesis 1 but in accord with Isaiah 45, the rabbis insisted that God created darkness as well, and also that God created evil, a striking theological claim; and that the rabbis are moving away from creation as cosmos out of chaos in the direction of the doctrine of *creatio ex nihilo*.

Third, the rabbis also understood creation as an ongoing process continuing daily, an original view of the nature of God's creational activity. It becomes a statement of the world's continuing dependence on God's power. Fourth, the conventional distinction between the two benedictions preceding the Shema—which maintains that the first benediction deals with God's power in nature, and the second with God's power in history—is no longer as obvious as it might be. Whoever inserted the *'or hadash* phrase into the Yotzer believed that there was no such distinction. Instead, what we proclaim is that a God who controls the natural order must, by definition, also control history. Even more, God's control over nature becomes a quasi-guarantee that God also controls history.

In regard to the wedding liturgy, we note, first, that the woman was created through a separate act of creation and in the first man's physical image, and second, that at least here, rabbinic anthropology was thoroughly monolithic. But the more important point in this instance deals less with the specific contents of the benedictions and more with the very fact that the rabbis understood marriage within the context of creation in the first place. To the rabbis, every marriage is a reenactment of creation. Every couple is Adam and Eve from whom all of humanity can emerge. At every wedding, the world begins anew. And if God created Adam and Eve and performed their marriage, then God continues to perform every marriage and begins the propagation of humanity anew. In Geertz's terms, the transcendent mythical world and the real world of real people fuse and become one. The mythic world of Eden enters our lives and, for a brief moment, we reexperience the moods and motivations appropriate to living in Eden.

The same process applies during the Yotzer benediction. That God created the world is one of the linchpins of the Jewish myth, as are the further claims that the world demands God's constant surveillance and that God's power extends over both nature and history. For a brief moment, the world is ordered.

Implications for Practice

Finally, some thoughts on the implications of this discussion for the issue of liturgical change. The basic assumption of this inquiry is that in Judaism, the liturgy represents a primary locus for theological expression; here, Jews encounter Judaism's belief system. But this belief system was hardly static; as we have seen, it was transformed between the biblical and the rabbinic periods. Nor did this process end with the close of the talmudic era. The image of an original, normative, enduring system of this kind persisting over generations is simply a fiction. To use our earlier terminology, the myth enjoys a certain plasticity.

This conclusion would seem to support the efforts of modern, post-Enlightenment Jews to continue to change the liturgy in the light of their own reformulations of Jewish beliefs. It would seem to justify, for example, the elimination, by the early Reform Jews, of references to Israel's chosenness, the resurrection of the dead, the return to Zion, and the restoration of sacrifices from the liturgy.[31]

On the other hand, a convincing argument can be adduced in favor of a more conservative stance toward liturgical change. It is not unreasonable to attribute some "normative" authority to the biblical/rabbinical belief system and its liturgy. Jewish doctrines did continue to evolve in post-talmudic times, but the liturgical impact of these further changes was relatively peripheral in comparison with those of the premedieval period. The structure of the core, daily, Sabbath, and festival liturgies and the rites of passage was basically canonized by that time. Further liturgical creativity, such as medieval liturgical poetry (the *piyyut)* or Kabbalat Shabbat, the service that welcomes the Sabbath at sunset on Friday, took the form of additions to the basic structure, not changes within that structure.

Further, whether or not moderns believe as the authors of the biblical and rabbinic texts believed, there is at least a pedagogical value in exposing the worshiper to those original formulations. There should be one place in the worshiper's experience where that original version of the myth is articulated. The ensuing tension can be handled either outside the liturgical service, in the classroom, or by introducing explanatory comments that deal with the tension and justify the change "below the line," at the bottom of the page of the prayer book, or by providing the worshiper with various alternative versions of a specific prayer "above the line" in the service itself, with the original version included as one of these options.

Whatever position we take on this issue, what remains clear is that the liturgy represents the cutting edge of ideological or theological expression in Judaism. It is when the worshiper is confronted with a specific prayer book and the wording of a specific prayer that he must confront firsthand just what he believes and, therefore, where he belongs in the range of contemporary models of Jewish religious identity. That fact alone confirms our thesis that a primary resource for any authentic exploration of Jewish thought must include a close study of the liturgy.

Notes

1. An index of the Psalms that appear in their entirety in the liturgy is in Joseph H. Hertz, *The Authorized Daily Prayer Book*, rev. ed. (New York: Bloch Publishing Company, 1948), 1120.

2. For this understanding of worship as a form of human activity, I am indebted to Lawrence A. Hoffman, *Beyond the Text: A Holistic Approach to Liturgy* (Bloomington and Indianapolis: Indiana University Press, 1987), 6ff.

3. In Clifford Geertz, *The Interpretation of Cultures: Selected Essays* (New York: Basic Books, 1973): 87–125.

4. Ibid., 90. Geertz's paper is a systematic unpacking of that definition.

5. There is no end to the literature on the nature and definition of myth and on the relation of myth and symbol. My own preferred studies are Paul Tillich, *Dynamics of Faith* (New York: Harper and Row, 1957), part 3; and Ian G. Barbour, *Myths, Models, and Paradigms: A Comparative Study in Science and Religion* (Harper: San Francisco, 1974), chap. 2. On the role of myth in Judaism, see the collection of papers in *The Seductiveness of Jewish Myth: Challenge or Response?* ed. S. Daniel Breslauer (Albany: State University of New York Press, 1997).

6. Rollo May, *The Cry for Myth* (New York: A Delta Book, 1991), 6.

7. Geertz, *Interpretation of Cultures*, 112ff. Whether a ritual preceded the myth or developed out of the myth remains an open question which does not bear upon this discussion. See Barbour, *Myths, Models, and Paradigms*, 22.

8. B. Ketubot 8a.

9. The seven benedictions are recited both at the wedding ceremony itself and again in conjunction with the blessings following the wedding meal (and again when the bride and groom partake of a festive meal with friends and family during the seven days of celebration following the wedding). In the latter recitations, the blessing over wine that is the first in the series at the wedding becomes the last.

10. For a partial bibliographical listing, see Joseph Tabory, "Jewish Prayer and the Yearly Cycle: A List of Articles," *Kirjat Sepher* (Jerusalem: The Jewish National and University Library), supplement to vol. 64 (1992–1993): 130–31.

11. See the note on this text in Yitzchak Baer, *Seder Avodat Yisrael* (Tel Aviv, 1957), 563.

12. David Flusser and Shmuel Safrai, "*Betzelem D'mut Tavnito*," *Sefer Yitzchak Arye Zeligman*, ed. Yair Zakowitz and Alexander Rofe (Jerusalem: Elchanan Rubenstein, 1983), 1:461.

13. The postbiblical understanding of these two terms reflects a Platonic influence. In the Bible, they signify simply "a living person" as in Exod. 1:5 and Ps. 150:6. The two terms appear in the Gen. 2:7 account of the creation of the human being: God formed man from the dust of the earth and blew into his nostrils the "breath of life" (*nishmat hayyim*), and man became "a living being" (*nefesh hayyah*). God created man by vivifying a clod of earth, not by implanting within the body a preexisting entity of any kind. See the extended discussion of these terms in biblical and postbiblical tradition in my *The Death of Death: Resurrection and Immortality in Jewish Thought* (Woodstock, Vt.: Jewish Lights Publishing, 1997), 75ff. and 106ff.

14. See, e.g., Maimonides, *Guide of the Perplexed*, 1.1.

15. B. Ketubot 8a.

16. See the paraphrase of the rabbinic traditions on Adam and Eve's wedding in Louis Ginzberg's *The Legends of the Jews* (Philadelphia: The Jewish Publication Society of America, 1968), 1:68, and the listing of his sources, 5:90, n. 48.

17. M. Sanhedrin 4:5. In the Mishnah, this is part of the judges' admonition to witnesses regarding their responsibilities in a capital case.

18. This conventional interpretation uses Ps. 137:5–6 as the basis for recalling the destruction of Jerusalem at our happiest moments.

19. I find a parallel "return to history" in the custom of opening the door while Elijah is present in our homes at the climax of the Passover Seder. Elijah's presence is a totally appropriate (for the climax of the festival of redemption) eschatological symbol, following Malachi 3:23.

20. The formal, communal (as distinct from the personal) morning worship service is centered about "The Recitation of the Shema," composed of three biblical portions (Deut. 6:4–9, Deut. 11:13–21, and Num. 15:37–41). This is preceded by two liturgical units or extended benedictions and followed by one. The two opening benedictions are, first, the Yotzer that praises God for creation, and then the Birkat Ha-Torah, which praises God for revealing the Torah. The benediction following the Shema is the Ge'ulah, which praises God's redemptive work. The service as a whole may be found in any traditional prayerbook, e.g., *The Complete ArtScroll Siddur: Weekday, Sabbath, Festival* (Brooklyn, N.Y.: Mesorah Publications, 1986), 85–96.

21. Isaiah 45:7 is conventionally understood as a rejection of Persian dualism. But see the qualifying comment in *Second Isaiah*, intro., trans., and notes by John L. McKenzie, *The Anchor Bible*, vol. 20 (Garden City, N.Y.: Doubleday and Company, 1968), 77.

22. On the controversy regarding *creatio ex nihilo* in medieval Jewish philosophy, see, e.g., Colette Sirat, *A History of Jewish Philosophy in the Middle Ages* (Cambridge: Cambridge University Press, 1985), 22–24 (on Saadia), 188–92 (on Maimonides), 304–8 (on Gersonides), and 305 (on Abrabanel).

23. On the place of the angelology in the liturgy, see the extended discussion in Ismar Elbogen, *Jewish Liturgy: A Comprehensive History* (Philadelphia: The Jewish Publication Society, 1993), 59–62.

24. See the full text in *ArtScroll*, 256–59.

25. On the controversy surrounding the use of this passage, see Elbogen, *Jewish Liturgy*, 18–19, and more extensively, Lawrence A. Hoffman, *The Canonization of the Synagogue Service* (Notre Dame, Ind.: University of Notre Dame Press, 1979), 24–30.

26. In the translation and abridgement of Kaufmann's work by Moshe Greenberg, *The Religion of Israel: From Its Beginnings to the Babylonian Exile* (Chicago: The University of Chicago Press, 1960), 22.

27. The classic summary of Lurianic thought is in Gershom G. Scholem, *Major Trends in Jewish Mysticism* (New York: Schocken Books, 1941), seventh lecture. On the exile of the *Shekhina*, see pp. 232, 275.

28. I am indebted to my colleague Rabbi Lawrence Troster for this point.

29. See note 5 above.

30. In Tillich, *Dynamics of Faith*, 50–54.

31. On the liturgical changes introduced by the early Reform Movement, see Jacob J. Petuchowski, *Prayerbook Reform in Europe: The Liturgy of European Liberal and Reform Judaism* (New York: World Union for Progressive Judaism, 1968).

The Doctrine of Creation and the Idea of Nature

DAVID NOVAK

> If My covenant does not endure by day and by night, then I
> will not have established the laws of heaven and earth.
> —Jeremiah 33:25

Creation and Nature

Those who posit the basic character of Western thought as a dialectic
between the poles of Athens and Jerusalem usually see the doctrine of
creation as what has come to us from Jerusalem, which is the Hebraic
pole of the relation, and the idea of nature as what has come to us from
Athens, which is its Hellenic pole. Some have seen the Hebraic doctrine (*torah*) and the Hellenic idea (*eidos*) as being at odds, at least
prima facie. For the Hebraic doctrine seems to be concerned with an
event that has taken place within time, one that is the direct result of
the inscrutable will of the transcendent God. That will of God is what
God's creation is to obey, especially His human creatures, who seem
to be unique in having a choice whether or not to obey God's will. The
Hellenic idea, conversely, seems to be concerned with an order that is
eternal, within which even God (or the gods) must function. Since
God functions within that order as a person who can know its structure and purposes, humans can also know that same order, but often
needing the help of God, who is wiser than they are. Thus, obedience
characterizes those who see themselves situated within creation;

knowledge characterizes those who see themselves situated within nature.[1] The will of God is revealed; the order of nature is discovered.

However, the opposition between the doctrine and the idea should not be left at such a final impasse. Historically, they have been brought together, and one has transformed the other. They have been brought together by the fact that Jerusalem conquered Athens when the West became Christian. For the basic political and intellectual character of Western (that is, European) thought now derived its primary legitimacy from Jerusalem's document: the Hebrew Bible. Greek philosophy, including its idea of nature, became the "handmaiden of theology" (*ancilla theologiae*) in the same way that admission to the Western literary canon was ultimately determined by whether a written work could—with great leeway to be sure—be justified as a commentary on the Bible.[2] Moreover, since the connection of the Greek idea to the Hebraic doctrine was made at the level of the theology of creation rather than the theology of revelation or redemption meant, for the most part, that earlier Jewish thinkers could very easily be used as resources in this thought process, and later Jewish thinkers could even learn from Christians thinkers who themselves had learned from their ancestors.

After Spinoza, when Western thought no longer derived its primary legitimacy from the Bible, it did not return to the Greek thought that it knew from the time before Athens met Jerusalem, that is, it did not return to the thought of Plato and Aristotle. Instead, Western thought attempted to transcend both of its ancient poles. Those few modern thinkers who have tried to retrieve the ancient connection, however, seem to have wanted to begin in Athens and then attach Jerusalem to it as much as possible. How successful they have been in terms of intellectual cogency is a point of great debate. But is the reverse possible? That is, can the doctrine of creation be retrieved in such a way that the idea of nature can be successfully connected to it?

In this paper, I propose that this can be done by a retrieval of the notion of natural law, which, despite some protests to the contrary, is very much present in classical Jewish thought, especially in that form of classical Jewish thought moderns have termed "Jewish rationalism." For the notion of natural law sees nature as lawful, that is, it sees the order of the universe itself as obedience to the commandment of its creator—*ex nihilo*. And that obedience in the case of intelligent human creatures is an obedience based on knowledge of nature, first and foremost human nature as social in essence.

As Helmut Koester of Harvard University has shown in a brilliant, but sadly ignored study, Greek philosophy only knew nature *and* law. Its notion of "law according to nature" (*kata physin*) is not the same as natural law (*lex naturalis*), that is *obedient nature*.[3] In other words, contrary to the view presented in virtually all historical studies of natural law, namely, that it is an idea taken up by biblically based theology intact from Greek philosophy (especially via the Stoics), it is only the idea of nature itself that was taken up—and by no means intact.[4] Natural law itself, *nomos physeos*—which would have been an oxymoron in classical Greek philosophy—is the result of that appropriation, not what was originally appropriated by biblically based theology.

To be sure, this retrieval is not a simple matter of picking up where we left off, so to speak. It requires the intelligent appropriation of new paradigms in natural science and in politics. In natural science, it means first and foremost accepting the notion that human beings are the only teleological intelligences in the universe of whom we have any experience. As we shall see, this means that teleology, which used to be constituted through philosophy, is now going to have to be constituted through theology. In other words, any ethics that presupposes a teleological natural science will have to be abandoned. In politics, it means that the notion of human rights, which has been the hallmark of the only rationally defensible form of human government today—constitutional democracy—is going to have to be seen as compatible with the older idea of natural law.

Law and Nature

A cogent natural law theory must correlate the concept of law and the concept of nature. For law without nature becomes the expression of the will of someone powerful enough to utter it effectively, be it God or a human being—the only two wills of which we have experience hearing. Law without nature is law without a discernable reason. And nature without law becomes the experience of impersonal forces, which themselves are incapable of making any demands on rational beings. (That is why the term "law of nature"—*lex naturae*—is an

anthropomorphic metaphor.)[5] Nature without law is mute; law without nature is blind.[6] Indeed, human beings are the only beings we experience who are addressed by law. Law presupposes addressees who
are intelligent enough to hear it and free enough to either accept it or
reject it. Thus, law presupposes addressees who hear before they
speak. Conversely, God speaks before He hears, and that is why He
makes laws but laws are not addressed to Him.[7] And, conversely, nature neither speaks nor hears; therefore, it is neither the source of law
nor its addressee.[8] God is too free to be addressed by law; nature is not
free enough to be addressed by law.

Joseph Albo, the fifteenth-century Spanish Jewish theologian who
introduced the term—but not the concept—"natural law" into Jewish
theology, divided law into three categories: one, natural law (*dat
tiv'it*); two, conventional law (*dat nimusit*); three, divine law (*dat
'elohit*).[9] Although he may very well have been influenced by Thomas
Aquinas's distinction between *lex naturalis*, *lex humana*, and *lex
divina*, the distinction is extremely helpful in understanding the role
of law in Judaism, nevertheless.[10] As I shall try to show, the introduction of the term *nature*, hence *natural law*, into a Jewish theology of
law is an improvement over the more vague term "rational commandments" (*mitzvot sikhliyot*) used earlier. Following Albo's lead, I think
the relation of *nature* and *law* contained in the term *natural law* must
be seen in the context of the interrelation of the three types of law he
so insightfully outlined. That is, natural law must be understood in
relation to divine law above it and human law beneath it.

In terms of law and nature, the question of ends is essential to any
theory of their interrelation. Any such theory involves *teleology*. Thus,
in a philosophically developed Jewish theory of natural law, the theological concept of the "reasons of the commandments" (*ta'amei ha-
mitzvot*), of which it must be seen as part, now becomes a Jewish perspective on the true end or *telos* of human active existence in the
world.

All teleologies assume that there is a hierarchal order in the world,
one whose recognition enables us to call the world *cosmos*, not *chaos*.
After this fundamental apprehension, only four options are possible,
it seems to me.

First, it can be assumed that this order of the world is itself ultimate
reality and that the highest human task is to reverently perceive it.
That approach is essentially one of *theōria*, which comes from the

Greek word *theōrein*, "to gaze." This view has long been called "metaphysical" because it is our ultimate concern with what is beyond (*meta*) the physical, the ordinary world in which embodied humans live and work.[11] All other human activity, confined as it is to mundane, finite tasks in the world, that is, *praxis*, must be subordinated to the higher supermundane task of *theōria*. Maimonides is the most prominent example of one who appropriated for Judaism, largely from Plato and Aristotle.

Second, it can be assumed that the order we perceive in the world only has meaning when placed in the context of what we ourselves make *of* the world. The world's meaning lies within us, not in or above the world itself. The highest human task, then, is to properly incorporate that order into the higher order of our own making. It is the assertion of the primacy of human inventiveness, that of *homo faber*, which Kant's notion of autonomy gave its most impressive philosophical grounding. It is the approach of *praxis*, which comes from the Greek word *prattein*, "to make."[12] This is what Hermann Cohen, most prominently, appropriated for Judaism, largely from Kant.

Third, one can combine the theoretical and practical approaches to the world as follows. On the one hand, we recognize the priority of a maker over any material that maker can use. As such, we see our own *praxis* as giving us a priority over that which we use or can use. It is the priority of subject over object, of intelligence over intelligibility. But, on the other hand, we recognize that we ourselves are part of an order greater than anything we ourselves could possibly make. Therefore, we conclude that the world itself is the product of a mind far greater in power than our own. And since our highest principle of order is purpose, we conclude that the orderer of the order of which we are part is a purposeful intelligence.[13] To assume anything less would involve the absurdity of concluding that there is an unintelligent cause of our own intelligence, and the absurdity of concluding that there is a nonpurposeful cause of our own purposefulness.[14] "Could it be that he who planted the ear himself does not hear; that he who formed the eye himself does not see?" (Psalms 94:9).

So far, though, we have only asserted that there is a purposeful order of the cosmos and that our own purposefulness somehow fits into it. But *what* is the end of that cosmic purposefulness, and *how* does our own purposefulness fit into it? That is the question addressed by Saadia Gaon.

Saadia's Teleology

For Saadia, the fundamental question is this: *For whom* is that order so created? What is its end? His answer is that man is the end of this purposeful, orderly creation.[15] Saadia well appropriated a teaching of the Mishnah: " Everyone should say that for my sake (*bishevili*) was the world created (*nivra*)."[16] What this means, at least in his theology, is that the world in general is beneficent, and this is especially and supremely so in and for the creation of humans.

Natural law, for Saadia, is an aspect of the creation of multiple goods by the one God.[17] Natural law is the recognition of those goods that humans can actively pursue and which are readily discernable by them. The imperative comes from the very attractiveness of these goods. That is a matter of what some have called "general revelation." Other goods that are less readily discernable require what some have called "special revelation."[18] Such special revelation is itself an act of divine beneficence. It enables most people of ordinary intelligence to actively attain many goods which they could never discern for themselves, and it enables even people of extraordinary intelligence to actively attain some goods far sooner than would be the case if they were simply left to their own pursuits.[19] Thus, the difference between divine law (what Saadia called *mitzvot shim'iyot*, "revealed commandments") and natural law is one of degree rather than one of kind.[20] For even revelation is from within creation itself, which is the origin of both types of law. As for human law, it is a further specification of the law of creation, whether divine or natural. One could say that Saadia's constitution of the relation of nature and law—the relation that a theory of natural law requires—is that *nature is for law*, that is, our lawfulness is intended by the beneficent order revealed to us by nature in its various workings on our behalf. Ultimately, the theoretical is for the sake of the practical.

Saadia's teleology has had a recurring attractiveness to many Jews. It has sufficient support in the primary scriptural and rabbinic sources of the tradition, especially because of how seriously it takes the scriptural doctrine of creation. And it is not wedded to any specific scientific paradigm of the physical world that is incommensurable with the current scientific paradigm (a problem with Maimonides' teleology, as we shall soon see). Yet there is a fundamental theological problem with what might be termed its "naturalism." That problem is connected with its conflation of revelation into creation. Because of that, it seems to me, Saadia could not very well constitute the key scriptural doctrine of covenant (*berit*).

It can be maintained, I think, that in Saadia's theology everything is for the sake of the world, especially for the sake of humans, namely, as they are already situated within the world. This even includes the human relationship with God. Humans receive everything from God by means of the world (with effort appropriate to authentic human dignity, to be sure).[21] Thus, the human relationship with God is not only *in* the world, a point common to any theology of creation, but it is always *through* the world as well.

But here it seems a fundamental element from the tradition has been lost. For the doctrine of the covenant teaches that there is a relationship with God, indeed *the* relationship with God, which although *in* the world is clearly not *of* it or *through* it. That relationship, as Franz Rosenzweig best taught us earlier in this century, is not *about* the world either.[22] It does not simply supply us more truth about the world than our unaided intelligence could learn, or could very readily learn. Instead, it enables our relation *to* the world to be ontologically (even if not usually chronologically) subsequent to our direct relationship *with* God. It places the world in its true place ultimately. The subject of revelation is *God-with-us*, not *we-with-the-world-because-of-God*. So when the Psalmist says, "the nearness of God, that is what is good for me (*tov li*)" (Psalms 73:28), that means that God is nearer than anything else in the world possibly could be *for* me. And soon before that, when he says "who is there for me in heaven, and along with you (*'imekha*) I desire none on earth" (73:25), that means that there is nothing that could come between God and me in the covenant, that everything else must wait, so to speak.[23] For at this level of covenantal exultation (which, being precious, is rare), "all who are far away from it (*reheqekha*) are lost" (73:27). That is what it means to declare "my flesh and my heart, my steadfast heart, fail me since God is my portion (*helqi*) throughout all worldly time (*le'olam*)" (73:26).[24] In rabbinic teaching the more direct relationship with God intended by the commandments that pertain to what is "between (*bein*) humans and God" has a priority over the less direct relationship with God intended by the commandments that pertain to what is "between (*bein*) humans themselves." The latter must fit into the former, not the former into the latter. A theory of natural law must fit into the context of the covenant.

This aspect of the tradition, which Saadia could not constitute in his theology, is especially significant for modern Jews for whom modernity has emphasized the phenomenal aspects of history as being distinct from that of nature. As Wilhelm Dilthey clearly saw, the way we constitute the realm of freedom and purpose (what he called *Geisteswissenschaften*) is essentially different from the way we constitute the realm of necessity and causality (what he called *Naturwissenschaften*).[25] The greatest modern Jewish theologian to my mind, Franz Rosenzweig, whatever his critique of other aspects of modernity might have been, built on modernity's insistence on the independence of history from nature. He did that because the very centrality of temporality (*Zeitlichkeit*) to Jewish revelation and its tradition has some essential commonality with that modern insistence.[26] History, not nature, is the integral realm of persons and their interrelationships. It is only when creation is seen as being *within* time rather than time being a result of creation that we can then see nature as subordinate to creation rather than creation being subordinate to nature.

Maimonides' Teleology

From our present philosophical perspective, Saadia's teleology has both a strength and a weakness. Its strength is that it is general enough not to be wedded to any specific scientific paradigm. Thus, one can be convinced by the argument from design, which forms the basis of Saadia's cosmology, and still operate within any of the subsequent scientific paradigms that have been operative since his own time. But its generality, which keeps it out of trouble on the scientific front, is also its weakness. For his teleology, which we might term pluralistic, lacks the univocal universal hierarchy that the teleological quest is itself searching for.

This designation of the weakness of Saadia's teleology on the ontological front is where we might well locate Maimonides' criticism of it and his own determination to think out a more systematically satisfying teleology. This is especially so in Maimonides' teleological constitution of the "reasons of the commandments" (*ta'amei ha-mitzvot*), which is the traditional matrix for the development of a Jewish natural law theory.

Maimonides' criticism of Saadia's concept of "rational command-ments" has often been misinterpreted to mean that he rejects the no-tion of rational commandments altogether.[27] If that is so, then it is concluded, especially as a point within the current debate about natu-ral law in Judaism, that Maimonides is opposed to the very idea of natural law, certainly within the Jewish tradition. That, however, as I have shown elsewhere, is an erroneous interpretation of Maimonides' critique.[28] When that critique is properly understood, it is not only not a rejection of the idea of natural law in Judaism, it is actually a consid-erable development of it from the legacy of Saadia.

One could characterize Maimonides' critique of Saadia's teleology of the commandments as being a critique of a theory that is not teleo-logical enough. What Saadia's teleology lacks is an overall hierarchy, namely, a teleology having one supreme end that orders everything beneath it according to each respective entity's capacity to approxi-mate it. Thus, what Saadia's teleology, and hence his natural law theory, lacks for Maimonides is a properly constituted metaphysics. The authentic relationship with God, especially for humans whose in-telligence is below that of the angels but above that of the beasts, is not primarily with God as the efficient cause of the universe. For the latter type of relationship would always have to be mediated by some sort of cosmic nexus. Instead, the authentic relationship with God is with God as the supreme *telos*, the intelligible and intelligent apex of the entire cosmos.[29] That apex can be reached by human intelligence, beginning in philosophy and ultimately graced by prophecy.[30] The very operation of that intelligence in its fullest and highest sense in-tends a vision of God not mediated by the world or anything in it, a vision of God beyond God's envelopment in any concealing mist. It is a vision for which Moses, the prophet of all prophets, must remove the veil that separates him from all other people.[31] Therefore, in the theory of natural law that emerges from this philosophical stance, *law is for nature*, that is, our lawfulness is for the sake of affirming and approximating the highest order of nature: God. *Praxis* is ultimately for the sake of *theōria*.

To know God as the End of all ends, however imperfectly in a world where one's soul is incarnate in a finite, mortal body, is the summit of intellectual excellence, what Maimonides called the "or-dering of the soul" (*tiqqun ha-nefesh*).[32] Furthermore, following Plato, he saw the ordering of the moral life, which is the ordering of the society of an essentially political creature, as the necessary step before the ordering of the soul.[33] This secondary ordering he called the "ordering of the body" (*tiqqun ha-guf*). By "body" he meant what later philosophers called the "body politic."[34]

Yet, for Aristotle, true intellectual excellence leads one away from the life of the political body never to return.[35] Maimonides, being a theologian in a tradition where the law as the structure of the polity is never to be transcended by anyone (at least in this world), had to think in a way closer to Plato than to Aristotle, therefore, in constituting the relation between moral excellence and intellectual excellence as reciprocal. That is, one moves up from the life of the body to the life of the soul, and then one brings the enlightenment of the soul back down to properly rule the life of the body. The excellence of the soul entails the excellence of the body. And the excellence of the soul presupposes an ordered bodily life.[36] For Maimonides and others thinking along these same lines, this is because the ordering of the body is an ordering that does not allow any of the body's appetites, or even all of them together, to claim ultimacy. Anyone who was that attached to bodily ends would not only not be leading a truly ordered moral life, but such a person would also not have the proper desire for the ends of the soul, which are the locus of true human fulfillment.

Maimonides saw all of the commandments of the Torah in the context of this reciprocal relation of body and soul, a relation that participates in the cosmic relation of matter and form. In this sense, all of the commandments of the Torah are natural law. They all contribute either to spiritual betterment or to political betterment. That does not mean, though, that one can give a rational explanation for every one of the details of every law.[37] But that usually means not all of the details of the ritual law, especially the many details of the sacrificial system, a system that even by Maimonides' time had become totally detached from anyone's experience. Yet, when it comes to the moral law, what for us is the locus of natural law, Maimonides seems to have been able to explain just about every detail quite rationally. For moral law and its details are all either part of our own experience or are quite close to it. In fact, Maimonides probably had the most rationally developed theory of explanation of the reasons of the commandments of anyone in Judaism. To this day, many of his rationales are invaluable when presenting Jewish views on many questions of general normative concern. Intelligent participation in such generally normative discussions involves the development of a theory of natural law out of the sources of the Jewish tradition. Maimonides certainly did that with great brilliance.

Whereas Maimonides was better able than was Saadia to constitute a direct divine-human relationship unmediated by the world, one cannot describe that constitution as truly covenantal either. The relationship Maimonides constitutes is more than anything else a relation *to* a God who seems to closely resemble the God of Aristotle. It is a relation where only God and not man is the object of love. All concern is in one direction: from man to God.[38] Maimonides in no way ever attempts to constitute a truly responsive role for God. There is no real reciprocity here. But the covenant is surely characterized by what is actively between God and Israel, with that activity being mutual. Even when God is actively saving Israel, Israel's participation in her salvation is not wholly passive. She is required to do something *with* God in response to what God is doing *for* her. In fact, there is a trend in rabbinic teaching, which is considerably developed in kabbalistic theology, that sees what Israel does *with* God as also being *for* God.[39] That is the theological problem with Maimonides' natural law theory. Minimally, it is noncovenantal; maximally, it is countercovenantal.

The philosophical problem with Maimonides' natural law theory is one that a number of modern philosophers have noted about all Aristotelian and neo-Aristotelian ethical theories. That problem is that teleological ethics, where real and not projected ends are intended, seems to presuppose a teleological natural science.[40] Teleology is only real, that is, prior to the human intention of the ends it proclaims, when these ends are not confined to human intelligence, but are part of a larger order than that populated by humans alone and constructed by them. Only when man is seen as acting within a cosmic teleology can the purposeful action of humans be presented as more than the projections of human will. That is what fundamentally distinguishes a *telos* from an ideal in the modern sense.[41] That is especially so for someone like Maimonides, who so heavily invested in the importance of natural science for theology. In his view, one truth encompasses both the Torah and the world.

The strength of Maimonides' more highly developed teleology as compared to that of Saadia worked to its persuasive advantage when the reigning scientific paradigm was Aristotelian-Ptolemaic. But with the shift in scientific paradigms after Galileo and Newton, the earlier paradigm seems to be irretrievable. That is certainly so in astrophysics, where all Aristotelians have located the teleology *toward* which human intelligences aspire. It is the teleology of the heavenly bodies, which before Galileo were assumed to be separate intelligences higher than that of earthbound humans. These higher intelligences inspire human intelligences to aspire to be like them in their knowledge of the unmoved mover, the God who is End of all ends.[42] Biological teleology, which some forms of natural law theory still seem to regard as normative, was never normative for humans in the view of Aristotle and his authentic disciples. Any order less intelligent than our own is more often than not something to be manipulated *by* us, not something for us to respect and aspire *to*. The only order having an inherent normative pull on us is one that is more intelligent than our own.

Hence, despite the many specific things we can learn from Maimonides in connection with our search for natural law materials, I think his overall theory has insurmountable difficulties for us.

Creation and Revelation

As Franz Rosenzweig taught modern Jewish theology quite well, any aspect of Judaism is best understood when seen within the interrelation of three events: creation, revelation, and redemption.[43] However, if an event is something which one experiences, that is, something with which one can be cotemporaneous, then the only one of these "events" that so qualifies as a literal *event* is revelation. Creation as primal origin is necessarily prior to the experience of any creature. It is an experience only God could have. And redemption as the ultimate end of history is neither the experience of man nor even of God because it has not happened at all to anyone yet. It is only within the reach of God's action.[44] No one is or has ever been cotemporaneous with it. Creation is humanly irretrievable past; redemption is humanly unattainable future.[45]

Revelation is God's presence to us, with us, and for us. It is the ever-present giving of the Torah (*mattan torah*) to Israel.[46] As such, it must always be our fundamental standpoint in the present when looking at either the past or the future. Initially, Torah is the point from which we look for our retrievable past, that is, what we have from tradition (*masoret*).[47] And it is the point from which we look for our attainable future, that is, what we can reasonably anticipate in this world.[48] But, more profoundly, Torah is the point from which we look for our irretrievable past, which is creation, and for our unattainable future, which is redemption.[49]

Any Jewish universalism must be constituted by reference to a primordial origin or to an eschatological consummation. The idea of natural law does figure into the interrelation of revelation and redemption, namely, when the universality of nature and the substance of history finally become one.[50] But its main function comes out of the interrelation of revelation and creation, when nature and history are still separate and distinct. For only this interrelation is connected to our present experience.

The great mistake of what I have called ethocentric (usually liberal) modern Jewish thought has been its grounding of revelation in the world. This modern world is taken to be what human reason (or consciousness, for those thinkers less rationalistic) can readily bring to presence. Revelation, then, becomes the epitome of human effort itself. But that is fundamentally what we can learn for ourselves with what God alone can teach us. Furthermore, liberal Jewish thought has conflated revelation into redemption by constituting it as potential for human progress.[51] That conflation has confused what we can do for ourselves with what only God can do for us. Authentic Jewish eschatology is not to be confused with Utopianism.[52] Thus, by identifying revelation essentially with natural law instead of seeing natural law functioning at the juncture of revelation and creation, liberal Jewish theology has confused the necessary distinctions and interrelations between all three prime events Judaism affirms.

Because the nature from which we learn natural law is rooted in irretrievable creation, it is not simply what we ourselves can bring to presence. Nature is not an object right before us about which we can argue using the truth criteria of correspondence. It is something that can only be grasped abstractly from within our historical present, a present whose content is continually provided by revelation. The truth criterion here is much more one of coherence.[53] This is especially so when we speak of nature in the context of human action, inasmuch as the truth of practical reason is characterized much more by coherence than by correspondence.[54]

Nature is not the ground of history anymore than revelation is derived from creation. Yet, created nature is vital, and to eliminate concern with it is to lose something essential in the covenant. To eliminate a distinct concern with it is to confine God's relation to the world to God's relationship with Israel. When this is done, as indeed it was done by the kabbalists, one loses any Jewish constitution of nature and natural law because, in effect, there is no constitution of the external world. It is no accident, then, that there is nothing even resembling the idea of natural law in kabbalah.[55]

So, if created nature is not the ground of revelation and is not conflated into revelation, just what is its relation to revelation? I would answer that creation and its order, that is, nature, is the necessary precondition for revelation to occur. Just what does this mean?

When we speak of nature in natural law, we are primarily concerned with human nature, namely, those structures that make authentic human life possible. It is a *conditio sine qua non*. When we speak of revelation, we are primarily concerned with God's address to a historical human community, God's speaking with the community for the sake of their mutual and ongoing relationship, which is the covenant. Only secondarily and derivatively do we intend something essentially nonhuman when we say "nature"; and only secondarily and derivatively do we intend an individual Jew when we say "revelation."[56] Nonhuman nature is minimally the wider physical support for human nature, which we subsequently constitute.[57] The individual Jew is one who is to personally internalize what has been given to the community and to develop its meaning for them. Even Moses' solitariness is for the sake of Israel.[58] Therefore, the juncture of revelation and creation is human community. This is where revelation is to occur in the world. Indeed, since revelation is God's speech to humans in their own language, where else could it possibly occur except within a real human community in history?[59] Wittgenstein was right when he insisted there are no private languages.[60]

Accordingly, natural law or its equivalent is what a number of more rationalistically inclined thinkers within the Jewish tradition have seen as something that had to be in place for Israel to be enough of a human community, with insight into the nature of human sociality, to be able to accept the Torah from God. Only then can their existing polity be elevated and become a holy people, God's portion in the world. Creation is not only for the sake of revelation, which would mean that it is solely for the sake of man—indeed, solely for the sake of Israel. The author of Job dispelled the notion of the anthropocentric character of creation in God's speech to Job out of the whirlwind.

"Where were you when I laid the foundation of the world?" (Job 38:4). And Amos dispelled the notion of the Israelocentric character of history when he spoke God's word to Israel, saying, "Did I not bring Israel up out of Egypt, but also the Philistines from Caphtor and the Arameans from Kir?" (Amos 9:7). Created nature is more than just potential for revelation, which would totally subsume it within a particular revelation. Instead, created nature is the sphere of finite human possibilities, some of which are realized in history by revelation and its content. One can see these finite human possibilities being realized in other historical communities as well as in Israel.[61]

The interest in creation and its structures from the standpoint of Jewish revelation is minimally that creation makes it possible for that revelation to occur within its sphere. Maimonides speaks of the Torah as not natural but "entering into nature."[62] This is what enables Israel to accept God's law, which would be unintelligible if she were not aware of law's initial function as a natural limit on human projection. Natural law, then, is the recognition of the normative significance of the limits of nature. It can only operate in human community; any use of it elsewhere is metaphorical. That is how the normative idea of nature functions. It is not a name for the sum of all phenomena but, rather, it is the name for that which functions as a limit on the chaotic expansion of activity that regards all limits as mere obstacles to be overcome because they all can be overcome. Such frantic activity is fueled by the illusion of invulnerable immortality by essentially fallible, finite creatures, who continually hope to be immortal and invulnerable like the God who made them.[63] Natural law emerges when humans realize that all their historical acts have limits within them, just as their life itself has an outer limit. Only with this recognition can the world be cosmos.[64] Since leaving the Garden of Eden, our mortality and all that it entails is part of our continuing process of the *definition* of ourselves in the world.[65]

Thus, nature is the medium through which we initially yet indirectly encounter the creative will of God. It is the product of God's intelligent making. But only revelation saves creation from being reduced to nature, to being taken as nature's application, as is the case for Plato. In revelation, we encounter the creative will of God immediately, that is, through no medium at all. God speaks directly to us. From that experience, we can appreciate nature as the product of creation rather than being its ground. When one has met the artist in person by hearing what he has to say about his work, one is unlikely to think the artist is in any way subordinate to either the form or the matter of his picture, however much they seem to stand on their own for those who have only seen the picture alone.

Notes

Part of this paper is an adaptation of a section of my book *Natural Law in Judaism* (New York: Cambridge University Press, 1998).

1. See Leo Strauss, *Natural Right and History* (Chicago: University of Chicago Press, 1953), 81ff.; and David Novak, *Suicide and Morality* (New York: Scholars Studies Press, 1975), 25ff.

2. For the origin and subsequent meaning of *ancilla theologiae* in Western philosophy, see Harry A. Wolfson, *Philo* (Cambridge, Mass.: Harvard University Press, 1947), 145ff. Cf. Northrop Frye, *Anatomy of Criticism* (Princeton: Princeton University Press, 1957), 315ff.

3. Helmut Koester, "Nomos Phuseos: The Concept of Natural Law in Greek Thought," in *Religions in Antiquity*, ed. Jacob Neusner (Leiden: E. J. Brill, 1968), 521ff.

4. See, e.g., A. P. d'Entreves, *Natural Law* (New York: Harper and Row, 1965), 17ff. Cf. Leo Strauss, "Natural Law," *International Encyclopedia of the Social Sciences* 11:80.

5. See Benedictus de Spinoza, *Tractatus Theologico-Politicus*, chap. 4.

6. That is why Thomas Aquinas rightly notes that all law, including natural law, requires "promulgation" in order to qualify as law (see *Summa Theologiae*, 2/1, q. 90, a. 4). Natural law being inherent in the created order could be promulgated by no one other than God. And in order to know it as such, one would have to infer that law per se is part of the divine design of the universe.

7. It is only in the covenant that laws are addressed to God by himself, viz., God binds himself to norms resulting from his own irrevocable promises. In this sense, God is autonomous in the strongest sense of autonomy. These norms are seen to be the content of God's covenantal relationship *with* Israel, viz., they *both* practice them *together*. Hence, the theonomy under which Israel lives in the covenant is distinct both from human autonomy, whereby humans give commands *to* themselves, and from "divine command" heteronomy, whereby God merely gives commands *to* Israel in an external, nonreciprocal way (see David Novak, *The Election of Israel* [Cambridge: Cambridge University Press, 1995], 248ff.). But norms cannot be heteronomously addressed to God, because such address would presuppose an authority higher than God himself—hence, God would cease to be absolute. For the notion of divine autonomy, see Y. Rosh Hashanah 1.3/57b re Lev. 22:9; B. Berakhot 32a re Exod. 32:13. For the notion, though, that God submits himself to the interpretation of his autonomous law by the Sages of Israel, see B. Baba Metzi'a 59b re Exod. 23:2; *Shir ha-Shirim Rabbah* 8.13 re Hab. 3:3. For further discussion, see David Novak, *Halakhah in a Theological Dimension* (Chico, Calif.: Scholars Press, 1985), 116ff.; idem, *Jewish Social Ethics* (New York: Oxford University Press, 1992), 45ff.

8. In his critique of the idea of natural law, Hans Kelsen writes: "Nature has no will and therefore cannot enact norms. Norms can be assumed as immanent in nature only if the will of God is assumed to be manifested in nature. . . [That] is a metaphysical assumption, which cannot be accepted by science in general and by legal science in particular. . . ." See Hans Kelsen, *The Pure Theory of Law*, trans. M. Knight (Berkeley: University of California Press, 1967), 221. However, for Kelsen, following Logi-

cal Positivism's view of science, "nature is a system of causally determined elements" (ibid.). Nevertheless, if one assumes that human beings are free enough to be addressed by law, then nature per se cannot be totally determined because human nature is a part thereof, indeed, the part which is able to formulate a concept of the whole. And wouldn't even Kelsen have to admit that human life is inconceivable without law? Hence, isn't law an essential aspect of human nature? As such, one cannot separate law and nature or freedom and reason. Of course, nature itself as structure does not promulgate laws, but in the case of natural/moral law, the designation of *human* nature is the *reason* for the promulgation of the law by one free *person* to another. If one sees human nature as part of a total cosmic nature, then the ultimate promulgator of natural law is the creator God. However, that is an inference abstracted from the experience of lawfulness; it is not its presupposition as Kelsen seems to think. Coming from the wisdom of God, natural law reasons are discernable before one affirms the divine authority who promulgated that rational law ("the will of God" in Kelsen's words).

9. *Iqqarim*, 1.7.

10. See *Summa Theologiae*, 2/1, q. 93, a. 2ff. For the question of Aquinas's influence on Albo, see David Novak, *The Image of the Non-Jew in Judaism* (New York: E. Mellen Press, 1983), 346, n. 4.

11. Although the word "metaphysics" comes from Aristotelian philosophy, the metaphysical impetus is more originally Platonic. See Plato, *Theatetus*, 176A–B.

12. See Novak, *The Election of Israel*, 128ff.

13. The logic of the argument from design has been enunciated no more lucidly than by Etienne Gilson in *God and Philosophy* (London: H. Milford, Oxford University Press, 1941), 140f.: "Being an absolute, such a cause is self-sufficient; if it creates not only being but order, it must be something which at least eminently contains the only principle of order known to us in experience, namely, thought. Now an absolute, self-subsisting, and knowing cause is not an It but a He. In short, the first cause is the One in whom the cause of both nature and history coincide, a philosophical God who can also be the God of a religion. . . ."

14. See Aquinas, *Summa Theologiae*, 1, q. 19, a. 4 and a. 5.

15. *Emunot ve-De'ot*, 4, intro.

16. M. Sanhedrin 4.5. Cf. B. Sanhedrin 38a; Novak, *Jewish Social Ethics*, 145ff.

17. See L. E. Goodman's note on Saadia Gaon, *The Book of Theodicy*, trans. L. E. Goodman (New Haven: Yale University Press, 1988), 99ff.

18. See John Calvin, *Institutes of the Christian Religion*, 1.2.1.

19. *Emunot ve-De'ot*, intro., 6.

20. Ibid., 3.3.

21. Ibid., 3, intro.

22. See Franz Rosenzweig, *The Star of Redemption*, trans. William W. Hallo (New York: Holt, Rinehart, and Winston, 1971), 160f.

23. See *Devarim Rabbah* 1.18 re Exod. 31:17.

24. I have translated *le'olam* as "wordly time" following Martin Buber and Franz Rosenzweig's translation of it as *Weltzeit* throughout their own Bible translation (see Novak, *The Election of Israel*, 262f.). Rosenzweig's influence can be seen in this exegesis of Psalm 73; indeed, he selected this psalm himself to be read at his funeral

and to be inscribed on his headstone. It was read at the funeral (12 December 1929) by Martin Buber: See Franz Rosenzweig, *Franz Rosenzweig: His Life and Thought, Presented by Nahum N. Glatzer*, 2d rev. ed. (New York: Schocken Books, 1961), 175f.

25. Wilhelm Dilthey, *Introduction to the Human Sciences*, trans. Ramon J. Betanzos (Detroit: Wayne State University Press, 1988), 83ff.

26. See Karl Lowith, "M. Heidegger and F. Rosenzweig or Temporality and Eternity," *Philosophy and Phenomenological Research* 3 (1942): 55ff.

27. See Maimonides, *Commentary on the Mishnah*: Avot, intro. (Shemonah Peraqim), chap. 6. Cf. *Emunot ve-De'ot*, 9.2.

28. See Novak, *The Image of the Non-Jew in Judaism*, 278ff. Cf. Marvin Fox, *Interpreting Maimonides* (Chicago and London: University of Chicago Press, 1990), 124ff.

29. See Maimonides, *Guide of the Perplexed*, 1.69.

30. See *Mishneh Torah*: Yesodei ha-Torah, 7.5.

31. See Exod. 34:34–35.

32. Maimonides, *Guide of the Perplexed*, 3.27.

33. See Plato, *Republic*, 484Dff.

34. Maimonides, *Guide of the Perplexed*, 3.27.

35. See Aristotle, *Nicomachean Ethics*, 1177a10ff.

36. See Leo Strauss, *Philosophy and Law*, trans. Eve Adler (Albany: State University of New York Press, 1995), 124ff.; also Novak, *Suicide and Morality*, 22ff.

37. See Maimonides, *Guide of the Perplexed*, 3.49.

38. See Novak, *The Election of Israel*, 225ff.

39. See, e.g., *Shemot Rabbah* 15.5; also Novak, *Halakhah in a Theological Dimension*, 120ff.

40. See Ernst Cassirer, *The Logic of the Humanities*, trans. Clarence Smith Howe (New Haven, 1961), 165ff.; Leo Strauss, *Natural Right and History* (Chicago: University of Chicago Press, 1953), 8; Jurgen Habermas, *Communication and the Evolution of Society*, trans. Thomas McCarthy (Boston: Beacon Press, 1979), 201; Alasdair MacIntyre, *After Virtue* (Notre Dame, Ind.: University of Notre Dame Press, 1981), 152.

41. Thus, Kant sees an ideal as the final cause of an idea of pure reason (*Critique of Pure Reason*, B838). It is thus a projection of the rational will (845B); *Religion within the Limits of Reason Alone*, trans. Theodore M. Greene and Hoyt H. Hudson (New York: Harper, 1960), 54. Following Kant, Hermann Cohen confines ideality to the human sciences. See his *Religion of Reason out of the Sources of Judaism*, trans. Simon Kaplan (New York: F. Ungar, 1972), 353f.

42. See Novak, *Jewish Social Ethics*, 141ff.

43. See Rosenzweig, *The Star of Redemption*, 250.

44. See B. Berakhot 34b re Isaiah 64:3.

45. That is why the investigation of these matters is dangerous to those who are not spiritually prepared for their profundity (see M. Hagigah 2.1 and Maimonides, *Commentary on the Mishnah* thereon).

46. Rosenzweig better than anyone else showed how revelation must be understood as presence/present (*Gegenwart/Heutigkeit*) and not as a historical memory.

See *The Star of Redemption*, 177; also *Sifre*: Devarim, no. 33 re Deut. 6:6; Novak, *The Election of Israel*, 151f.

47. See, e.g., Y. Pesahim 6.1/33a; Temurah 16a.

48. See, e.g., M. Avot 2.12 (the statement of R. Simon) and Maimonides, *Commentary on the Mishnah* thereon. Such reasonable anticipation is the basis of virtually all rabbinic legislation, which is made on the anticipation of what people are likely (*shema*) to do in the imminent future (see, e.g., B. Avodah Zarah 36a–b).

49. See B. Eruvin 13b; M. Sanhedrin 10.1.

50. That is best expressed by the verse that has become in the Jewish liturgy the anticipation of redemption in the *'alenu* prayer that concludes almost every service, viz.: "And the Lord shall be king over all the earth; on that day he shall be unique (*'ehad*) and so shall his name" (Zechariah 14:9). Thus, the historical/political order will be fully ruled by God *then* as the physical/natural order is ruled by God *now* (see *Sifre*: Devarim, no. 31/end). That will be accomplished by God apocalyptically. Conversely, one can see Hegel's notion of the ultimate unity of nature (*Ansichsein*) and history (*Fürsichsein*) effected by the self-development of reason (of which human reason is our only example) as being the major expression of the modern attempt to secularize the ancient eschatological hope: see *Phenomenology of Spirit*, preface, trans. A. V. Miller (Oxford: Clarendon Press, 1977), 11; cf. Novak, *The Election of Israel*, 152ff.

51. See Cohen, *Religion of Reason*, 250.

52. See, e.g., B. Kiddushin 39b; Hullin 142a.

53. See Novak, *Jewish Social Ethics*, 76ff.

54. See Plato, *Crito*, 46B, 48A–D.

55. See Novak, *The Image of the Non-Jew in Judaism*, 268.

56. See, e.g., B. Rosh Hashanah 18a on Deut. 4:7 and Isaiah 55:6.

57. See Gen. 8:22–9:7 and *Bereshit Rabbah* 34.11.

58. See Exod. 32:32 and B. Rosh Hashanah 16b.

59. This point is based on the rabbinic principle "the Torah speaks as does human language" (*dibrah torah ke-lashon benei 'adam*). In its original presentation, it expresses the view of R. Ishmael that Scripture speaks as does ordinary human language, including repetition of words for rhetorical effect (see *Sifre*: Bamidbar, no. 112 re Num. 15:31; Y. Shabbat 19.2/17a; also R. Levi ben Gershom [Ralbag], *Commentary on the Torah*: Exodus–Pequdei [end], ed. Venice, 116a). For the classic study of the theological roots of this view and the opposing one of R. Akiva, see the two-volume work of my late revered teacher Abraham Joshua Heschel, *Torah min ha-Shamayim b'Ispaqlaryah shel ha-Dorot* (London, 1962), esp. 1:3ff. Later, rationalist Jewish theologians like Maimonides invoked this principle to justify Scripture's use of anthropomorphic language for describing the acts of God. Thus, the exoteric language of Scripture is for ordinary believers, who cannot think unimaginatively about anything, even about God, whereas only extraordinary believers can understand the deeper, esoteric meaning of the text (see *Mishneh Torah*: Yesodei ha-Torah, 1.9ff.; *Guide of the Perplexed*, 1.26, 33, 46). But, even for Maimonides, Scripture in general speaks as does human language because the Torah is a created entity (*Guide of the Perplexed*, 1.65), hence, *in the world*, where human language is the only vehicle to intelligibility available. The specific difference is between ordinary and extraordinary

human language, the latter being occasionally used in Scripture and, therefore, to be interpreted literally, unlike the former which is used more often and is to be interpreted figuratively (see, e.g., *Mishneh Torah*: Yesodei ha-Torah, 1.8; Teshuvah, 5.1ff.). Despite my own differences with Maimonides over where exactly to draw the line between literal and figurative meaning in Scripture (see Novak, *The Election of Israel*, 200ff., 225ff., 262f.), I accept the general premise underlying his whole view of language, viz., that the language of revelation must be one already employed in the world.

60. See Ludwig Wittgenstein, *Philosophical Investigations*, 2d ed., trans. G. E. M. Anscombe (New York: Macmillan Press, 1958), 1.242ff.; also R. Rhees, "Can There be a Private Language?" in *Wittgenstein: The Philosophical Investigations*, ed. George Pitcher (Garden City, N.Y.: Anchor Books, 1966), 267ff.

61. See David Novak, *Jewish-Christian Dialogue* (New York: Oxford University Press, 1989), 129ff.

62. Maimonides, *Guide of the Perplexed*, 2.40. I am here using Maimonides' statement in a way he himself probably did not mean it (see Novak, *The Image of the Non-Jew in Judaism*, 290ff.); nevertheless, his phraseology as I have appropriated it here does express with beautiful precision a fundamental doctrine found in rabbinic theology.

63. See Gen. 3:3–5 and *Bereshit Rabbah* 19.4.

64. See Reinhold Niebuhr, *The Nature and Destiny of Man* (1941; reprint, New York: Scribners, 1964), 251ff.

65. See *Bereshit Rabbah* 9.5 re Gen. 1:31 and Ezek. 28:13.

Response.
Natural and Supernatural Justice

JON D. LEVENSON

I

The papers of Stephen Geller, Neil Gillman, and David Novak touch, each in its distinctive way, on a central issue of Jewish theology, the relationship between nature and divine revelation. In the Jewish context, this is the familiar problem of the relationship of two sources for the knowledge of God—observation of his creation, on the one hand, and his verbal revelation in the historical experience of the people of Israel, on the other.

Professor Geller's subtle and highly original paper speaks of a dramatic change within the Wisdom schools of Israel in the seventh and sixth centuries B.C.E., a change brought about, as he sees it, by the increasing prominence of "Torah piety [which] redefined Wisdom as the study of holy texts and the observance of covenantal commandments" and thus located all authority in "sacred canon, not observation of nature and humanity." The earlier form of Wisdom thinking "represent[ed a] type of nature-rooted speculation, which sought to establish the essential unity of natural and moral orders." It constituted "an international tradition, common to all ancient peoples, [and] drew its answers from observation of nature, both cosmic and human, not from the particular religious traditions of any people." In this, as Professor Geller frames the issue, it stood in stark contrast to the "monotheistic Deuteronomic covenant faith," which "demanded total, single-minded submission to One Deity, the national God . . ." and "the radical exclusion of anything foreign."

In response, the Wisdom teachers effected "a subtle melding" of the two ways of thought, "a kind of hybrid, pietistic, Wisdom faith that focused on obedience to covenant law, but still used the universalistic language of the Old Wisdom tradition." In the process, as Geller puts it in one of his more memorable phrasings, "[c]ause and effect were deified, or, better, the reverse: God was discussed as if he were merely the embodiment of the cause-and-effect relationship."

The outstanding exemplars of the new hybrid piety are the friends of Job, who represent "the doctrine of cause-and-effect retribution" ably and, as Geller shows in the case of Eliphaz, also more subtly than has usually been recognized. "The friends of Job talk the language of traditional theism, still speak of 'God' as a person," he writes, "but they really mean by it a Ruling Principle of retribution which also incorporates the underlying order of the cosmos." Though Geller does not find this "mechanistic" position to be "logically satisfactory," he does see it as akin to "the pattern of human spirituality in Stoicism" and thus to "possess a certain stoic nobility in suffering."

As Geller sees it, the unyielding monotheist who wrote the speeches of God in Job 38–41 never answers the innocent sufferer's question, but instead silences and humbles him by filling him with "that emotion that uniquely combines opposites: terror, awareness of one's insignificance, and fear of extinction, on the one hand, and, on the other, feelings of exaltation, forgetfulness of self, and fascination." This is the emotion that Geller, invoking an ancient term that became especially influential in eighteenth-century English literary criticism, terms "awe at the sublime." And so, as the poetic inner section of the Book of Job comes to its end, "[t]he issues remain unresolved intellectually," but something important and even comforting has nonetheless happened: "through awe at the sublime in nature one may forget enough of one's self to neutralize one's pain":

> Intellect must give way to emotion. Revelation and nature cannot be reconciled by human wisdom. Only through transfiguring emotion can even the demand for reconciliation be made sublimely irrelevant.

Or so Geller argues.

II

As is well known, biblical studies is a field plagued by philological and chronological uncertainties, and more than occasionally it is thought to be aptly characterized by its Library of Congress designation, "BS." It is to the credit of Stephen Geller that he has not flinched from addressing some of the literature in the Hebrew Bible that is most difficult to interpret and to date, and he has done so with the intelligence, erudition, sophistication, and elegance characteristic of all his work. To the extent that my own perspectives on the issues he raises are different from his, I offer them in hopes of doing justice to the large issues that he raises and of advancing our collective understanding of their relevance to the subject of this volume, "Judaism and the Natural World."

What Geller calls "Old Wisdom" held that there is a universal moral order that can be intuited through ordinary observation and experience. In order to perceive that order, one should not rely on one's own idiosyncratic observations and experiences, but avail oneself of those of others older and wiser. In that sense, historical testimony is essential, but despite, not because of, its historical and temporal particularity. The moral order that Old Wisdom teaches centers on a nexus of deed and consequence. At times, this nexus can be taught in a totally nontheistic way, without any specification of the agent of the connection:

> He who digs a pit will fall in it,
> And whoever rolls a stone, it will roll back on him.
> (Prov. 26:27; all biblical translations taken from the JPS
> Tanakh)

To the modern ear, this may sound like a variety of naturalism, but ancient Israelite culture did not make the characteristically modern move of polarizing nature and God. It would even be incorrect to think that the ancient sages saw a tension between the ways of Israel's God and the causal nexus that governs life. Thus, in the Book of Proverbs, one often finds the same sort of connection between deed and consequence expressed as the action of the Israelite national God:

> A good man earns the favor of the LORD,
> A man of intrigues, His condemnation. (Prov. 12:2)

The theistic phrasing of this idea that one reaps what one sows was extremely widespread in ancient Israel and by no means limited to Wisdom circles. Here is one of my favorite examples:

> You shall not ill-treat any widow or orphan. If you do mistreat them,
> I will heed their outcry as soon as they cry out to Me, and My
> anger shall blaze forth and I will put you to the sword, and
> your wives shall become widows and your children orphans.
>
> (Exod. 22:21–23)

In this law, the God of Israel acts in accordance with the observations of Old Wisdom, the difference being that the Wisdom teachers were more comfortable with a nontheistic phrasing of the ethic than were those circles who authored and transmitted legal and covenantal materials. Though this difference matters in some ways, I suspect the ancient Israelites would be perplexed by the question of whether the nexus of deed and consequence was of natural or supernatural character. To ask that question, one has to imagine a Godless nature or a totally supernatural God, neither of which seems to have been an item in the conceptual universe of ancient Israel. I suspect, for example, that the author of the Book of Esther would be mystified and perhaps eventually even amused by our question about the fate of his villain Haman, who is hoist with his own petard, dying on the stake he erected for the hero Mordecai: is God responsible for this delicious turn of events, or is the foolish Haman a victim of his own folly and the craftiness of his Jewish antagonists? The author of the Megillah would have trouble even giving the answer I would give, "both of the above," because the very dichotomy would have been foreign to him.

Let me try to make my point clearer. It is not that ancient Israel believed in a self-sufficient natural order but, because of a cultural contingency, the Israelites happened to cast their worldview in God-talk. Nor is it the case that they believed in a supernatural God and thought the world made sense only because of his constant, miraculous intervention. Rather, the relationship of God to the world was more subtle and of a sort that is well-nigh impossible to capture in our modern Western philosophical and theological vocabulary.

To us, the obvious question about this natural and supernatural bond between the deed and the fate of the doer is, what happens when it fails to appear? Why do the righteous suffer, and the wicked prosper? Before assessing Geller's understanding of the response of the Book of Job, it is worthwhile to ask why the question comes up as rarely as it does in the Hebrew Bible. Geller already alludes to one explanation when he discusses a verse in Psalm 37, best known because of its eventual incorporation into the rabbinic grace after meals:

> I have been young and am now old,
> but I have never seen a righteous man abandoned,
> or his children seeking bread. (Ps. 37:25)

This he rightly compares with the words of Job's friend Eliphaz:

> Think now, what innocent man ever perished?
> Where have the upright been destroyed? (Job 4:7)

Geller calls such ideas "amazing," "absurd," and "pious sophistry," though he also sees some "elements of a true faith" in them because he thinks they foreshadow the Stoic notion that "suffering is illusory, a matter of mental opinion, because no one can ever really be harmed, in his inner being, by illness or evildoers." The analogy with Stoicism is, however, misleading.

Geller is closer to the truth when he tells us that these statements "can only reflect, not observable reality, but religious dogma," provided, I would add, that we purge the term "dogma" of the pejorative connotations it has acquired in modern times. What these statements actually do is to articulate an ideal not in the volitive, as we might, but in the indicative mood and present perfect tense. They say, that is, how things ought to be as if this is how things are. To us, this may indeed seem amazing, absurd, and sophistical, even offensive, but that is because our sense of experience is less stylized, more personal and individualistic, and more solid, and we tend to think of "is" and "ought," the real and the ideal, as far apart, whereas the ancient Israelites often seem to have thought of the ideal as all that is, in the long run, real.

Thus, if we pressed the author of Psalm 37 with a counter-example and said, "OK, Mr. Psalmist, here is a righteous man who has been abandoned and his children are seeking bread. Now what?" we need not search for his response. He has already given it earlier in his poem:

> Do not be vexed by evil men;
> do not be incensed by wrongdoers;
> for they soon wither like grass,

like verdure fade away.

. . . .

A little longer and there will be no wicked man;
you will look at where he was—
he will be gone. (Ps. 37:1–2, 10)

This belief in the impermanence of disorder and injustice is rather typical of Wisdom literature, though in other idioms it is also widespread throughout the Hebrew Bible. Another psalmist takes the failure to recognize the time lag as emblematic of the "brutish man" and the "fool," who fail to see that when "all evildoers blossom, / it is only that they may be destroyed forever" (Ps. 92:7). It is interesting that in its current shape, the Book of Job still upholds this theology of the impermanence of injustice. Stricken unjustly and horrifically in the prologue, Job is restored in the epilogue and dies at 140, "old and contented" (Job 42:17). The protests of the innocent sufferer are not the last word, and Job's idiosyncratic experience finally rejoins the more general pattern—or at least what the Wisdom teachers thought was the more general pattern—of human life. The counsel to the innocent sufferer here, as in Proverbs, is not Stoic imperturbability, as Geller would have it, but confidence that the world order that God has ordained will be restored. What is called for is not resignation, but patient faith.

I should add that it might be better to take some of these affirmations of divine justice in the psalms and elsewhere as liturgical in character, as theurgic attempts to bring about that ideal world of justice by a verbal process akin to sympathetic magic. In this, we would do well to be instructed by Professor Gillman's use of Clifford Geertz's thought to the effect that in liturgy, "the transcendent mythical world and the real world of real people fuse and become one."

What I do not see in the Old Wisdom is any tendency to attribute adversity to other deities than the national God of Israel or, for that matter, to malicious witches practicing their amoral craft outside of God's control, or to demons of whatever sort. Therefore, I am doubtful of Geller's claim that the crisis that produced the Book of Job in its current version derives from the triumph of the "monotheistic Deuteronomic faith" and its demand of "total, single-minded submission to One Deity." The Book of Proverbs does not speak of submission, covenantal fealty, or of the singularity of YHWH, but it and other literature that represent what Geller calls "Old Wisdom" are no less monotheistic than Deuteronomy.

Geller is correct, of course, in seeing in God's poetic speech in Job 38–41 a different answer to the problem of the suffering of the innocent from that of the prose framework to the same book. It is even conceivable that this speech originally answered a different Job from the innocent sufferer in protest that we see in the poetic disputations. Perhaps the Job answered out of the whirlwind was a Promethean figure who sought to displace the creator God and, like similar figures in Israelite and other ancient Near Eastern literature, learned his lesson the hard way.

Even if God's answer is directed to the innocent sufferer who is the Job of the disputations, however, I question Geller's claim that the answer to him lies in the evocation of an emotion, namely, "awe at the sublime." Rather, God's tour of the marvels of creation in these chapters makes a thoroughly *cognitive* point, a point about the limited capacity of human cognition itself. "If you know of these [marvels of creation]—tell Me!" God challenges Job (Job 38:18). The point made repeatedly here is that the world is not ordered by any principle that human beings can understand after all; it is incomprehensible. Job is not consoled by the grandness of creation. Instead, he recants his position, because he spoke of things beyond his ken (42:3). Neither overpowered, unconvinced, nor overwhelmed by sublime emotion devoid of cognitive content, Job does, in fact, learn something new— that there are things human beings can never learn, that nature is not set up to human scale, and that creation is not anthropocentric, but radically, bafflingly, terrifyingly theocentric. Though this theology has some affinities with the poem in Job 28, it represents a position radically different from both Job's and his friends' in their disputation and profoundly undercuts their common framework

III

If we may apply Stephen Geller's helpful dichotomy of Old Wisdom and covenantal monotheism to David Novak's paper "The Doctrine of Creation and the Idea of Nature," we see a strong preference there for the latter. Novak, following Rosenzweig's triad of creation, revelation, and redemption, insists on the priority of history over nature.

Without this, if I understand Novak rightly, the crucial idea of covenant will be lost, as the special historical relationship of the people Israel to God sinks back into the generality of nature. Employing a familiar rabbinic dichotomy, Novak thus insists on the priority of the commandments between human beings and God over those between one human being and another. In this, he sees the limitation of any notion of natural law within Judaism. "A theory of natural law, "he writes, "must fit into the context of the covenant." At the same time, to collapse nature into revelation is, in his view, also a mistake, for it is "to confine God's relation to the world to God's relationship with Israel." Nature must be given a proper place in Jewish theology, a place that neither elevates it over covenant and historical revelation nor disregards it.

Novak proposes to do this by Judaizing the classical Greek and Roman idea of natural law so that it now "sees the order of the universe itself as obedience to the commandment of its creator—*ex nihilo*." In this way, he proposes to purge law of its arbitrariness and to give nature the capacity to "mak[e] demands on rational beings." Later in his paper, Novak limits his understanding of natural law. "When we speak of nature in natural law," he writes, "we are primarily concerned with human nature, namely, those structures that make authentic human life possible," and in the Jewish context, this means "something that had to be in place for Israel to be enough of a human community, with insight into the nature of human sociality, to be able to accept the Torah from God." Whereas Geller explores in a historical and literary mode the interactions of Old Wisdom and the covenantal faith, Novak, in a normative, philosophical mode, seeks to subordinate the former firmly to the latter. In fact, he does this so thoroughly that he interprets the divine involvement in nature as only indirect, whereas " [i]n revelation, we encounter the creative will of God immediately, that is, through no medium at all. God speaks directly to us."

It is hard, however, to see how verbal revelation can be immediate and direct, since it occurs through the culturally particular human institution of language. In fact, I can imagine an argument that, reversing Novak's priorities, would see natural law as superior to revealed law precisely because of its universality and its relative independence from historical contingency and ethnic particularity. In any case, Novak's brief discussion leaves it unclear about how we are to derive any specific norms from natural law and what we are to do when these norms and those of the revealed law conflict. If he does not see natural law as a source of specific directives at all, but only, in his words, as "those structures that make authentic human life possible," perhaps he should avoid the confusion by dropping the term "law" altogether. If all he means is that God has created human beings with a capacity to recognize Him and His will when God presents Himself and His will in historical revelation, then I think Novak only muddies the waters by using a term like "natural law."

One last point. Reading David Novak's paper after Stephen Geller's, I found myself bothered by Novak's constant affirmation of the purposefulness and lawfulness of life, which he sees attested both in nature (perceived *sub specie creationis*) and in revelation. After a while, he began to sound to me like Job's friends or like someone who had never absorbed the message of God's answer in Job 38–41 about the terrifying incomprehensibility of the created order, and I found myself longing for a dialectical counterstatement that would acknowledge that disorder, horrific suffering, and death still reign in nature and in history. Novak so stresses creation and revelation that I found myself wanting to hear more about the third term in Rosenzweig's triad, redemption. More specifically: what are the flaws in nature as God has created it, including human nature, that He still needs to rectify if the well-ordered world of lawfulness and purposefulness of which Novak writes is to become a reality? I think, in short, that David Novak needs to climb down a bit from his high philosophical theology and to consider Neil Gillman's interpretation of the breaking of the glass at the Jewish wedding, which he views as

> a return to history, a breaking of the messianic spell . . . it separates the two worlds, the mythic and the real, that had been momentarily fused. For just a moment, redemption was in the air; but we know that the world has not been totally redeemed, that chaos still rules "out there," and that this couple must now return to the unredeemed real world.

As liturgical affirmations, statements about the lawfulness and purposiveness of nature and history under the governance of a just God do indeed have their place, as we saw in the case of Psalm 37. As static philosophical propositions, however, they can give the impression that the world has been redeemed. After reading Novak's learned philosophizing, I much prefer the psalmist's approach, one that conjoins liturgical affirmation of the ideal with the counsel to wait until it appears.

Nature and Revealed Morality

Concepts of Torah and Nature in Jewish Thought

SHALOM ROSENBERG

This essay concerns the relationship between revealed truth and human morality. The question "Is a human being capable of attaining moral consciousness through his or her own autonomy?" has engaged philosophers and scholars over the ages. The goal of this essay is not to articulate yet another answer to this and related questions, but to elucidate the fundamental approaches to nature in Jewish thought. After a preliminary consideration of the uses of the concept of nature in Western thought, I will consider the views of various Jewish texts and thinkers. I arrange the discussion chronologically, presenting an array of biblical, rabbinic, medieval, and modern viewpoints. The various views will be presented as pictures in an exhibition. I will look at each text separately, highlighting its nuances, and relate the text to the others. The survey makes clear that in Judaism we find diverse, and even conflicting, ideas about the relationship between humanity, God, and nature and about human responsibility toward the natural world.

The Meaning of "Nature"

The term "nature" is multifaceted. The following discussion focuses mostly on the notions of "natural law" and "moral autonomy"—terms that raise substantive and functional questions. In the history of ideas, the term "natural law" has had political and social meanings. On the one hand, especially during the modern period, an appeal to "natural law" implied a call for an ethical change and was often enlisted for political purposes. On the other hand, in classical debate, the concept of "natural law" was used in discussion of human autonomy in philosophy, psychology, and education, and the discussion involved the relationship between morality and human understanding in regard to ethics, conscience, and psychology.

The term "natural law" is ambiguous because the term "nature" is used to mean two different things. "Nature" may refer to the totality of the cosmos or to the biological world. It may refer, as well, to "human nature." Some philosophers occasionally have used the term "human nature" to refer to human understanding. At this level, a discussion of "nature" hides the idea of moral philosophy that may be attained through simple intuition. I think that a discussion of "nature" must avoid this latter dimension of the topic. I will limit myself to the problems of morality and the cosmos and, in a certain respect, to human nature.[1]

To clarify the confusion, we may focus the discussion not on the concept of "nature" but on the general *function* that the term plays in various approaches. We should note that in different periods the appeal to "nature" was articulated for different and even contradictory purposes or functions. In the modern period, the appeal to "nature" was used to critique existing ethical and legal situations. However, "nature" was used in contradictory ways by those who called for a radical critique of society, and by those who championed the antinomian approach. Frequently, the function of "nature" is conservative, with an attempt to anchor morality in the existing social order.

In the Enlightenment, "natural law" functioned as a radical critique of the existing order, a tool for social criticism and change. A thinker who appealed to "natural law" claimed that there is a moral order that transcends the laws of the state, which are artificial values, customs, and social conventions of differing societies. The natural, moral law was in conflict with the norms of positive laws, which are the laws used in the state. It is possible that legal practices and procedures are unjust. Positing the existence of natural law enabled Enlightenment thinkers to claim that one could appeal to a higher authority when one was abused by the laws of the state and its rulers. This view implied that there is justice that transcends the laws of the state. Natural law appears, then, as an absolute morality that binds together the various factions of society that are periodically trapped in polarizing positions.

Paradoxically, what began as a radical critique of society, over time was transformed into a "conservative" mold. Since "customs" differ from country to country and from one nation to another, the appeal to natural law served as the basis for the struggle against relativism and historicism. In this context, "nature" refers to the belief in the existence of more basic laws than the laws of the state. These laws constitute "nature" (*physis*), namely, the reality that is not subject to random manipulations of time and place. Natural law in this sense is related to *ius gentium*, an international law that binds everyone. It creates a bond between all people, even those representing divergent legal traditions.

Today, we attest to a new function of natural law—the struggle against historicism. Natural law transcends not only space but also time and allows us to judge different historical cultures,[2] as Leo Strauss explained in his many works. According to Strauss, the central struggle in the modern world is between historicism and the school of thought that believed in the existence of natural, moral law.[3] The vanquished in the Second World War conquered the victors: historicism—the child of German thought—defeated the natural law tradition, the basis of Western, liberal political theory.

Thus far, we have seen that natural law is used as an expression of a radical critique against the existing given, positive law. Additionally, the term "nature" connotes a struggle for antinomistic change. Many passages of Plato's *Republic* illustrate this view. Yet, natural law's most salient exponent is, without doubt, late nineteenth-century Social Darwinism. The Social Darwinists co-opted Charles Darwin's theories of biological evolution—specifically, the idea that in nature there is an ongoing amoral struggle, in which the survivor is the most fit in a specific place and a specific time, or, simply, the most powerful. For the Darwinists this was an indisputable fact. Furthermore, the cruelty of the victory guarantees the development of the species and its advancement. Social Darwinism is the application of a biological principle to the sphere of human affairs: what is perceived as a fact of life in the natural world is deemed applicable to human affairs. The two most obvious examples of Social Darwinist thinking are Nazi ideology, on the one hand, and a certain idealization of capitalist competition with its relentless preoccupation with egoistic self-fulfillment, on the other. In other words, the theoretical laws of the biological world are hereby transformed into normative social doctrines.[4] Natural law came to be understood as amoral.

The antinomistic position makes a conceptual distinction between a system of justice based on natural law and the notion of a social system based on a social contract. This social contract is the unique beginning of human society that separates humans from nature. We now have a rupture between nature and morality. In nature, cruelty persists, while human society is founded on a construct that rejects absolutely these very laws. Again, *nomos* is pitted against *physis*. But here, morality is rooted in *nomos* that now becomes the true alternative to the cruelty of *physis*. (We will see this position articulated in the thought of R. Judah Loew of Prague, known as the Maharal.)

Whereas in the antinomistic view there is a fundamental contradiction between classic morality and nature, an interesting attempt to bring the two together is found in the teaching of the anarchists. Their solution is not based on a moral system that defies nature, but on an alternative description of nature itself, a different world order. Instead of emphasizing the violent and bloody competition between different types, the anarchists emphasized the existential cooperation that is found between animals, cooperation best exemplified in the beehive and the anthill. The anarchists thus tried to return to the classical doctrine of the laws of nature, against the standard view that saw in nature the source for nihilism and moral antinomism. The anarchists attempted to bring us back to the starting point, but this is only a historic accident. The Darwinian notion that struggle is the force that compels the evolutionary process has been accepted, without question, by the modern mind.

Monotheism and Nature: The Bible

The Imperfection of Nature

Having outlined the broad relationship between morality and nature in Western thought, I will now turn to a presentation of the array of attitudes toward nature in Jewish sources, beginning with the Bible.

The ancient world witnessed two anti-mythical revolutions: one inaugurated by the Bible, the other by Greek philosophy. These two revolutions converged in Alexandrian Jewish thought, whose prime example was Philo.

The philosophical revolution created a new scientific and philosophical language that demythologized the world for the first time. This anti-mythical revolution was an attempt to build a theory of the world that was not the product of childhood dreams. It was to be the beginning of an ongoing, endless process of interpretation. However, the new theory—like every new theory—succeeded only when it transformed its predecessors into myths and its own concepts into anthropomorphism. This would happen to the new philosophical revolution. To paraphrase the rabbinic dictum, philosophy, too, would commit the "original sin" when it conveyed its theoretical truths "in human language."

By contrast, the biblical revolution was a religious revolution that brought to the world a new conception of God and a new concept of morality. It too destroyed the basic concepts of the existing world. It terminated slavery to nature. The mythical gods of Greek mythology were found in and were part of nature. The Bible overturned this worldview because the biblical God is outside of nature. In the classical language of the Midrash Rabba, Genesis 68:9, "He is the Place of the cosmos but the cosmos is not His place." The biblical viewpoint thus made possible the concept of miracles and paved the way to a struggle against magic.

The Bible pits the moral order against nature. In nature there are wars, and cruelty rules the day; the wolf devours the lamb. Human society also is part of nature, since it comprises strong and weak people, rich and poor, people who have enough to eat and people who are hungry. The biblical revolution was to distinguish between what is and what should be. The Bible projects an eschatological vision onto the given order of reality: "the wolf will live with the lamb." The conclusion that follows from this vision is that morality is not self-evident in nature, but is found in opposition to and in confrontation with it. The moral order critiques nature from God's perspective, and God is not part of nature. God exists outside and beyond nature and enters a covenantal relationship with humanity against nature. God is posited as the alternative to nature, and the human, who is created in the image of God, is called to emulate God. God stands before humanity as the moral ideal that is in opposition to the natural world. In God's world, humans receive the mandate to transform nature.

This same stance is evident in the attitude toward human society. We generally hold that law regulates social relations. But the Bible contends that law comes to perfect society in order to bring about *tiqqun 'olam*, namely, the repair of the world. Morality is not the product of society, but something that is found in opposition to it as well as in opposition to nature, which the law must transform. This revolution can be projected as the revelation of the possible, something that could be other than it is, as a revelation of ideal categories. Nature, then, is to be evaluated and judged in accordance with God's revealed criteria. The biblical approach to nature and its continuation in rabbinic thought stood in sharp contrast to views of the pagan, classical world.

The biblical outlook framed Jewish thinking, and especially the views of the rabbis, during the Second Temple period. But the biblical-rabbinic perspective stood in conflict with the Greek outlook. The practice of circumcision is a case in point. To the Greeks and the Romans, the rite of circumcision inflicted a permanent blemish on men, whereas to Jews, circumcision was regarded as the symbol of human acts that perfect nature, which is itself imperfect. The rabbis of late antiquity were aware of this disparity in perception and reflected on it in their writings.

The social differences between the Greek and the biblical perspectives are evident in the case of charity. To give charity involves intervention of the divine order in the natural order. If God created rich people and poor people, how do people dare to give charity? For the rabbis, this is indeed humanity's function in God's world. Humanity was created to be God's partner in creation. It is a human duty to correct evil that exists in the world. The practice of charity is an example of the biblical revolution in which the moral stands in conflict with reality, with nature.

The biblical-rabbinic attitude is diametrically opposed to the antinomistic view, where morality is a product of nature, as Darwinism and Nazism held. They express the "fact" that in the world there exists a struggle for survival, and only the mighty and the fit have the right to survive. The struggle is a function of nature. If I fight against war, or interfere with the victory of the mighty in this bloody war, or if I perform acts of charity for the poor, I strike a pose against the ultimate principle, "real nature." To the biblical-rabbinic model this attitude is repugnant. The thrust of the Bible and rabbinic thinking is that the vocation of morality is to correct nature.

The Biblical Conception and Its Philosophic Formulation

The biblical, anti-mythical conception was the basis for the thought of the modern Jewish philosopher Hermann Cohen. Cohen saw in pantheism the conceptual continuation of idolatry. Cohen's views shed light on the conflict between morality and nature in Judaism.

It is widely known that Hermann Cohen saw at the center of biblical thinking the idea of unity. For Cohen, unity is not numerical but conceptual, in that God's oneness is outside the cosmos. Cohen noted that the concept of being expressed in the Divine Name is close to the speculation of the Eleatic school, but with an important difference. Cohen quotes Aristotle, where he describes the position of Xenophon: "When we consider the total cosmos, he said, oneness is God."[5] And Cohen adds: "He [Xenophon] is not satisfied with the fact that the cosmos is considered as a unity, not with that alone, that God is considered as a unity, but that these two unities are essentially one. But the two of them represent being and the two of them comprise being. Thus we come to the doorstep of the pantheism in Greek philosophy." As Cohen sees it, the Bible sings the song of nature, a song that reaches its climax in Psalm 104. In this hymn the simplicity of the song of nature is fused with the sublimity of God who transcends all natural beauty.[6] This fundamental distinction will never be obliterated.

Undoubtedly, Cohen's dualistic approach, which recognizes the difference between the world of pure reason and the world of practical reason, is more biblical than the monism of Spinoza. The distinction between the real and the ideal creates the possibility for biblical monotheism and the normative world that follows from it. In the contradiction of unity we find "not only the saying *deus sive natura* but also the ontological proof."[7] From an ethical point of view, the ideal is not found in nature and not even in the myth of the Golden Age of the ideal past. Cohen reminds us that "the past rolls into the future."[8] Cohen's rationalism does not allow him to grasp the verses that speak of nature in their simple literalness. Following Maimonides, the concept of nature's perfection, that is, the disappearance of sickness and death, is understood allegorically. Cohen emphatically states: "There is no doubt that all these examples are allegories."[9] But there is also no doubt that even were we to accept this view, the critique of nature is not eliminated.

What is the source of nature's imperfection? The Jewish tradition provides two answers to this question, and at times they complement

each other. The first is that nature's imperfection is the result of human, original sin. Nature was violated by that sin and is, therefore,
imperfect. The second is that the imperfection preceded the creation
of humanity. Paradoxically, God could have created a perfect world,
but He did not do so, in order to give humanity the mandate to complete His creation. Rabbi Moshe Hayyim Luzzatto expressed this view
in his kabbalistic writings, and it was further developed in Hasidic
thinking.

The Talmudic World

'Olam Ke-Minhago Noheg (The World Pursues Its Natural Course)

The intersection between the radical and the antinomistic positions
leads us to reconsider the controversy in the classical world between
the Sophists and the natural philosophers, and also to examine the
conflict between the pagan world and the world of the Talmud. As
noted above, the central problem in the world of nature is the existence of evil. In the talmudic worldview, this is expressed in the claim
that nature goes its own way, irrespective of religious or moral consideration. Nature is totally indifferent to human consideration. A passage from the Babylonian Talmud Avodah Zarah 54b illustrates the
point:

> Our rabbis taught: Philosophers asked the elders of Rome, "If your
> God has no desire for idolatry, why does He not abolish it?" They re-
> plied, "If it was something of which the world has no need that was
> worshiped, He would abolish it; but the people worship the sun, the
> moon, the stars, and planets; should He destroy the universe on account
> of fools! The world pursues its natural course and as for the fools who
> act wrongly, they will have to render an account." Another illustration:
> Suppose a man stole a measure of wheat and went and sowed it in the
> ground; it is right it should not grow, but the world pursues its natural
> course and as for the fools who act wrongly, they will be called upon to
> render an account. Another illustration: Suppose a man has intercourse
> with his neighbors' wife; it is right she should not conceive, but the
> world pursues its natural course and as for the fools who act wrongly,
> they will have to render an account.' This is similar to what R. Shimon
> b. Lakish [a Palestinian rabbi of the third century c.e.] said: "The Holy

One, Blessed be He declared, Not enough that the wicked put my coin-
age to vulgar use, but they trouble Me and compel Me to set My seal
thereon."[10]

One of the most important ideas in the Talmud is that the existence
of the natural world is contingent upon the acceptance of the Torah by
the Jewish people. Had they rejected the Torah, the world would have
returned to primeval chaos. Yet, in this text we see a clear awareness
of the existence of two independent orders: the Torah and nature. Nature follows its own laws, irrespective of any moral commitment. This
notion would receive its philosophic embellishment in Hermann
Cohen's exposition on the bond that exists between nature and morality, despite the sharp distinction between them. In the writings of
Cohen, the Torah and nature are two parallel lines that come together
in eternity. The contact point and their union is the idea of God.

Nature as Observant of the Commandments

That nature follows its own laws means that it is independent of moral
concerns. Nevertheless, this very determinism itself reflects a wondrous manifestation: nature should not be taken for granted. It is as if
"nature has its own will." And so we find numerous literary references
dating back as early as the apocryphal writings, which make reference
to nature's following its own will in conformity with the divine plan.
Here is an example from 1 Enoch 2:1ff.:

> Contemplate all the things that are in the heavens. They do not alter
> their ways. The lights that are in the heavens—they come and they
> go—each one in its order. They do not change their positions. . . . Ex-
> amine the earth. . . . Study the summer. . . . Contemplate and see the
> trees all of them. . . . and you [man] were not faithful. You did not
> follow the commandments of the Master, and you have sinned.

The notion that natural phenomena observe the commandments of
God, and "rejoice and delight in fulfilling the will of their master,"
draws its strength in no small measure from the equivocal meaning of
the concept of law and the role of law in divine plan. Eliminated here
is the distinction between descriptive law, which describes nature and
the involuntary way it works, and normative law, which sets standards

for what human conduct should ideally be.[11] Normative law can be violated, but not so descriptive law. The laws of nature, as observing God's laws, are incapable of being violated. Throughout the ages, many of the advocates of natural law identified these two types of law, commiting what we can consider to be a classical version of the naturalistic fallacy. A typical example is Stoic philosophy. The Stoics did not distinguish between moral law and natural law. Interestingly, Jewish religious thought also did not accept this distinction between descriptive law and normative law. In many instances, Jewish religious thinkers drew analogies between the laws of nature and nature's observance of God's law. The cosmos was created by God, and its laws— the laws of nature—are expressions of God's will. So too are the laws of morality; they flow from the same source and we can, or should, learn one from the other.[12]

This is one perspective found in the talmudic teachings. In order to understand it fully in all its manifestations, we need to add another dimension that is biblical in origin. I refer to the recognition that nature experienced a radical change as a result of human original sin. In the future—in the end of days—nature will return to its primeval perfection and morality, when the wolf will live with the lamb. The original natural order was morally perfect, but it was corrupted through Adam's sin. Interestingly, nonhuman reality, or nature, still preserves the primeval purity. In the Babylonian Talmud Kiddushin 82b, we read:

> R. Simon, the son of Elazar said: "In my whole life I have not seen a deer engaged in gathering fruit, a lion carrying burdens, or a fox as a shop keeper, yet they are sustained without trouble, though they were created to serve me whereas I was created to serve my Maker. Now, if these who were created only to serve me are sustained without trouble, how much more so should I be sustained without trouble, I who was created to serve my Maker! But it is because I acted evilly and destroyed my livelihood, as it is said, 'your iniquities have turned away these things'" (Jer. 5:25).[13]

This talmudic passage expresses the notion that nature maintains its purity and its perfection in spite of man's original sin. However, in another variant of this idea, we read that the laws of nature, morality, and religion were all corrupted by man's action. Were man to change his ways, the natural order would change.

The Talmud speaks about the "animals of the righteous" as models for human conduct. They do not sin, because they know intuitively what the law is and what is required of them. They also know how to apply the law to the world in which they live. For example, the "animals of the righteous" would not eat grain that was not "fit" for them to eat. In this case "fit" means grain that was not duly prepared by having had tithes taken from it and transmitted to the priest and the Levite. The animals of the righteous live in perfect harmony with their Creator. Humanity has much to learn from animals—not only the principle of observing God's will, but also specific lessons.[14]

The human need to learn from animals is discussed in another Talmudic passage (Babylonian Talmud Pesahim 53b):

> The scholars asked: "Was Thaddeus, the man of Rome, a great man or a powerful man? Come and hear: This too did Thaddeus of Rome teach: What [reason] did Hananiah, Mishael and Azariah see that they delivered themselves, for the sanctification of the [Divine] name, to the fiery furnace? They argued *a fortiori* themselves: if frogs, which are not commanded concerning the sanctification of the [Divine] Name, yet it is written of them, *and they shall come up and go into thy house . . . and into thine ovens, and into they kneading troughs*; when are the kneading troughs to be found near the oven? When the oven is hot. We, who are commanded concerning the sanctification of the Name, how much the more so."[15]

Derekh 'Eretz

Rabbinic sources are replete with different variations of these ideas, whose common denominator is the fact that nature is subservient to the Torah. To put it differently, the rabbis of the Talmud do not aspire to anchor morality in nature but, conversely, they ask the question: Why is it that nature does not observe the moral law? With this question we return to the biblical notion that morality is anchored in an Archimedean point outside the cosmos, from which we judge the cosmos.

Rabbinic sources clearly admit that humanity is guilty for having perverted nature, but humanity was not the only guilty party. The Bible tells us that before the Flood all flesh corrupted its ways, even the wild beasts, the domesticated animals, and the birds. But we need not go all the way back to the biblical story of the flood to see that the animals are guilty. A similar incident is found in the words of Rabbi Shimon bar Yohai (second century C.E.) when he spoke about the raven of the biblical narrative. In Talmud Yerushalmi Peah, 1:1 we read:

> R. Shimon bar Yohai taught: "as reward is the same [for the command-ment of honoring one's parents and sending away the offspring after taking the mother hen] so is the punishment the same." For what rea-son? [It is written in Proverbs 30:17] *"The eye that mocks at his father, and despises to obey his mother, the ravens of the valley shall pick you out, and the young eagles shall eat it."* Rabbi Shimon interpreted the verse, *"the eye that mocks his father and mother and who wantonly takes the mother and its offspring"* . . . "the ravens of the valley shall pick you out." The raven who is known to be cruel will pick you out [shall punish you]—even though he will not benefit therefrom. *"And the young eagles will eat it"* [he interprets as] "the young eagle who is known to be merciful, he will come and will enjoy it."

Despite the cruel conduct of the raven—according to rabbinic sources—nature fundamentally abides by the laws of morality. Therefore, by observing the examples of the animals in nature, we may learn *derekh 'eretz*. The following passage from Midrash Tanhuma, Genesis 10, illustrates the ability to learn from nature:

> When Cain killed Abel, his body was lying in the field. Cain did not know what to do. God called forth to him two pure birds. One of them killed the other, dug a pit and buried the dead one. From here Cain learned to bury Abel. Because of this the pure birds merited the *mitzvah* of the covering of the blood.

We can generalize and say that not only animals observe the moral laws, but all of nature is perceived as fulfilling the will of God in the performance of their normal functions. With this in mind we can un-derstand the discussion between the River Ginai and Rabbi Pinhas ben Yair, who went to perform the *mitzvah* of redeeming captives. The rabbi asked the river to split its water so that he could pass through. And the river said to him: "You are going to fulfill the will of your Creator [to redeem the captives] and I [by natural flowing] also fulfill the will of the Creator. It is uncertain if you will be successful in your *mitzvah*, perhaps you will be successful, perhaps not! I for sure will fulfill my *mitzvah*." The meaning of this passage was summarized by the nineteenth-century Hasidic Rabbi, Zadok Ha-Cohen of Lublin, who said: "when one is performing a natural deed, one is fulfilling the will of the Creator just as the river when it flows is performing a *mitzvah*. Thus he too is thereby performing a *mitzvah*."[16]

A passage from the Babylonian Talmud Eruvin 100b expresses the same idea:

> Rabbi Hiya said: "Why does the verse say '[God] teaches us from the beasts of the earth and makes us wise from the birds of the heaven' (Job 35:11), this is the donkey . . . this is the chicken. . . ."

> Rabbi Yohanan observed: "If the Torah had not been given [to the Jewish people] we could have learnt modesty from the cat, honesty from the ant, chastity from the dove, and good manners [*derekh 'eretz*] from the cock who first coaxes and then mates."

In the quote attributed to Rabbi Yohanan, the concept *derekh 'eretz* is used in its restrictive sense. However, in its broader meaning, the concept captures the outlook of the talmudic rabbis. Scholars have failed to recognize the point because they did not realize that the Aramaic phrase *orakh ar'aa* is but a translation of the Hebrew *derekh 'eretz*. Both the Aramaic *orakh* and the Hebrew *derekh* are similar to the Chinese term Dao, which means both "nature" and "norm." This is how we should understand Mishnah Bava Metzi'a, which states: "A deer running in his *derekh*." The term *derekh* connotes natural activity. Conversely, we have the expression *shelo ke-darko*, namely, "not according to its nature." Unable to address this concept in full here, let me only point out the various usages of the term *derekh 'eretz* in rabbinic literature. The term denotes 1) natural activity, 2) the instinctive nature of humans, 3) practical wisdom, 4) acceptable social norms of activity, 5) basic social values, and 6) normative moral behavior. These meanings are not sharply delineated, and at times they may be used together in a given statement. For example, we are told in the Babylonian Talmud Berakhot 7a that Rabbi Joshua ben Levi learned morality from God and said: "We conclude from here that it is not *orah ar'aa* to behave in such a manner, for it says (Psalms 145:9), . . . 'for His tender mercies are over all His works,' and it says (Proverbs 17:26), 'To punish also the righteous is not good'."[17]

Sins against Nature

The assumption that nature itself is moral underlies the claims that it is possible to sin against nature. This is how Robert Gordis, the American Conservative theologian, interprets the biblical story of the Tree of Knowledge.[18] He understands "knowledge" to be related to sex.[19] I am not convinced that this interpretation is correct, yet it is important to take note of the novel twist in Gordis's interpretation, when he claims that "good and evil" relate to two different types of sexual relations. The "good" sexual interaction leads to reproduction, and its opposite, the "evil" sexual interaction, consists of homosexuality and rape. Several biblical passages can be cited to support Gordis's reading of "evil" sexual conduct (for example, Gen. 19:7, Judg. 19:23, and Isa. 1:4 and 14:20). The notion of sexual perversity (activities which are *shelo ke-darko*) also have parallels in apocryphal writings. For example, the third chapter of the Testament of Naftali discusses the natural order in contrast with *derekh sedom* ("the way of Sodom"). "Natural" sexual intercourse conforms to "the way of heaven," whereas idolatry and the "ways of Sodom" (mostly likely, homosexuality) are viewed as distortions of the natural order.

The rabbinic discussion of human activities that are in violation of nature brings up an interesting point. The term "natural" assigned to specific acts does not point to an absolute determinism. Rather, "natural" refers to the optimal situation that nature creates. Certainly, we can "cheat" nature and force it to act differently. The biblical story (Judg. 3:15) about the tribesmen of Benjamin who forced themselves to use both their right and left hands is a case in point. This is a very unusual situation, in which human acts go against nature. It can be compared to the case of people born left-handed. The medieval Aristotelian considered left-handedness a mistake of nature. According to Aristotle, these mistakes are attributable to Matter, the metaphysical principle that underlies all concrete and individual activity. Even though there is room for deviation, medieval thinkers upheld the orderliness and stability of the "laws of nature." Maimonides combines violation of nature with sexual conduct when he states in his *Commentary on the Mishnah* (Sanhedrin 7:6) that homosexuality and bestiality are activities of which "Jews were never suspect . . . [they are] ugly things because they are alien to the custom of nature."

Another way to consider the relationship between nature and morality concerns two different moral attitudes: the "intuitionist" and the "naturalist." The "naturalist" view maintains that morality is related to things that exist in the world. The "intuitionist" view holds that morality is founded on the intuition of values or entities that are not obvious in nature; they may not even exist. Plato's philosophy is an example of the "intuitionist" viewpoint, whereas Aristotelian morality is an obvious example of a system built on the nature of humans.

Hermann Cohen attempted to prove that Maimonides held the Platonic view, but I find this reading very problematic. Philo is a much better example of a Jewish moral intuitionist. He developed the conception of Torah as natural law because he accepted the midrashic idea that Abraham observed the Torah. If so, it follows that the Torah must have existed before it was revealed to Moses at Mt. Sinai. According to Philo, Abraham taught himself the unwritten laws of nature that are found in the noetic cosmos, where the Platonic ideas are located. On the other hand, the written Torah is present in the physical cosmos, in which everything that exists must allow for the possibility of its being imperfect. Philo concluded that the laws of Moses are the most perfect imitation of the ideal law.

My presentation of Philo's position is not self-evident, but I can support it by references to Josephus Flavius.[20] Natural phenomena are capable of perversion, and for that reason they must be protected vigilantly. It is possible that there is such a thing as natural justice, but natural justice may succumb and be perverted because of human diversity, passions, interests, and a variety of other reasons. In *Antiquities* 1.60–66, Josephus depicts Cain and his descendants as builders of civilization. Cain ended the primeval simplicity with the creation of measures and tools. He changed the idyllic life that preceded him to one of artifacts and artificiality. He is the first to build a city, to protect it, and to compel his family to live in one place. The final stage in this transformation was the creation of weapons and the destruction of war. These were the products of a technological development.[21] Urban living and the end of free dispersion are examples of the artificiality that appeared after the Flood in the days of Noah.[22] Nimrod is the symbol of a tyrant who rebels against the yoke of heaven, yet he does not thereby gain freedom, because instead of the yoke of heaven, he assumed the yoke of flesh and blood.[23]

The Medieval World

The Return to Nature

The problematic relationship between nature and the Torah is pursued further in medieval Jewish philosophy. The Hasidic thinker Rabbi Zadok Ha-Cohen of Lublin summarizes the problem as follows: "And as I have heard—that God made a book that is the world, and wrote a commentary on that book, that is the Torah."[24] Let me explore the tension in the thought of medieval Jewish philosophers.

It is well known that in the Middle Ages Jewish culture absorbed two different philosophical systems: Aristotelianism and Neoplatonism. (Other philosophical schools also penetrated the Jewish Middle Ages through Islamic Kalam, particularly through the Mu'atazilite version of it.) Neoplatonism emphasizes an alienation from the natural world. The Neoplatonists spoke of the sequential emanation of three hypostases: Intellect, Soul, and Nature. All three are present in the human being, and within the human they struggle for domination. In this anthropological theory there is an internal struggle against nature. Neoplatonic Jewish philosophers anchored morality in physiology, but they also recognized the gap between human nature and morality. A typical example is Ibn Gabirol's *The Improvement of the Moral Qualities*, where he writes: "passion is the sickness of the body that needs to be cured."[25] This treatise articulates the Neoplatonic theme of the confrontation between reason and nature. Ibn Gabirol also states: "When the lower part of him [man] follows after the upper part . . . then the mind rules over nature."[26] We will return to this confrontation in our discussion of the Maharal.

Rooting morality in biology was not a dominant theme in medieval Jewish thought. Morality developed out of a philosophical understanding of man's place in the cosmos. These ancient ideas resurfaced in various ways, and under different terminology, throughout Western history. In Jewish thought these ideas were very influential, but they implied that the discovery of the truth is possible—yet only after a victory over nature. This notion is found again in the twentieth century. For example, Rabbi Abraham Shmuel Finkel, the son of the Sabba (Great Old Man) of Slobodka and one of the leaders of the Grodno Yeshivah, states:

> In truth there is a full-proof way to achieve faith. This source is not really the Torah. Two thousand years before the Torah was revealed at

Sinai, people were punished when they violated the obvious commandments. . . . It is the Torah of faith. This scroll of the Torah is—the Creation. For this reason Creation is the source of faith. . . . Our father
Abraham . . . from where did he learn [faith]? He learned [it all] in
Creation [i.e., from what he observed in the world around him] and that
was his Torah. In this fashion the source of the Torah is not only in
Creation outside of man, but also the Creation which is within him, [as
it is said] *from my flesh I have perceived God* [Job 19:26].[27]

We may deduce from this citation that human nature teaches us that
which is good. Evil has its source in humans passions because it hides
the true knowledge which we may gain from nature.

In medieval Aristotelianism the concept of nature implied an additional element. Medieval Aristotelians developed the idea that there
exists a parallel between morality and the instinctive activities of animals, and neither of these is a learned response. The comparison with
the instinctive activities of animals is interesting and leads us to a related idea. For the Aristotelians, all natural phenomena are characterized by the fact that they contain within themselves their efficient
cause for their activities (Aristotle *Physics* 2.1). Causal relations are
not artificial; they are rooted in the natural order. Defining humans as
political animals, the medieval Aristotelians understood political activity, and specifically the creation of a state, as a function of a natural
proclivity. In this system morality draws its authority from the nature
of humans. Or, to put it differently, natural morality is built upon a
teleological foundation. Nature is thus subordinated to the telos, the
natural end of the human species.

This "naturalist" approach to morality conflicts with moral intu-
itionism, a position that was held by the Jewish Mu'atazilites. The
theme that underlies the several variants of this view is that moral
controversies can be resolved by relying on the intuition of human
reason. Saadia Gaon and Bahya ibn Pakuda are the best exponents of
this viewpoint. Saadia teaches: "I say then, that reason demands that
whoever does something good be compensated either by a means of a
favor shown to him, if he is in need of it, or by means of thanks, if he
does require any reward."[28] Similarly, Saadia taught that "reason compels [man] to accept all good."

Saadia's intuitionist morality was severely criticized by Maimonides,
who followed the Aristotelians. According to Maimonides, Saadia's
line of thought "suffers from the sickness of the Mutakallimun,"

namely, the Muslim scholastic theologians whose speculations were
not rooted in the structure of reality but in their own imagination.
Contrary to Saadia, Maimonides held that to achieve morality it is
necessary to study human nature and the goal of human life as a
whole, namely, to articulate systematic, philosophical anthropology.
For Maimonides, the Torah emanates from human nature and enables
humans to attain perfection appropriate to the human species.[29]

Maimonides' view is characteristic of all medieval Jewish Aristotelians.[30] This approach reaches its climax in the formulation of the Torah as the law of nature in the writing of Rabbi Joseph Albo in the
Sefer ha-Iqqarim (Book of Principles). He was an outstanding thinker
who developed the notion of the Torah as natural law in medieval Jewish thought. An earlier exponent of this view was R. Moses ben Isaac
ibn Waqar, in the book *Matoq La-Nefesh* (Sweet for the Soul).[31]

R. Isaac Arama

The fifteenth-century thinker Isaac Arama will serve as our main example of the notion that the Torah is natural law. Here is his comment
on natural justice:

> Our rabbis in the Talmud commented in Hullin 57b that ants kill those
> who tell lies. And we have already spoken of big birds or storks who
> kill adulterers and [pluck out] the eyes of the wicked when they are
> observed. In the alien books there are animals called elephants who kill
> those who run away from them in war and others.[32]

In contrast to those who speak of a confrontation between nature
and spirit, Isaac Arama finds in nature a paradoxical thing: Animals
"do not follow perversity or stray from their normal behavior. Yet,
man, who is the most devious of all the creatures, seeks what is useful
or pleasurable from that which is close [to him] and that which is far
away."[33] In other words, humans are different from other animals in
that they can distort their natural inclination. We can summarize
Arama's approach by characterizing it as "back to nature," where
morality truly is found.

Arama sees in Aristotle's *Ethics* (5.9) a starting point for his own
discussion on natural law and its relation to the Torah. According to
this text, there are two sources of political justice—justice and *nomos*,

or convention. In his critique of Aristotle, Arama claims that the Torah is natural law. It is natural from a teleological standpoint, that is, the Torah brings one to perfection. Arama says:

> We read in Exodus, "If you will listen to My voice and observe My covenant, then you will be for Me the chosen from all the nations. . . . And you will be a kingdom of priests and a holy nation," which means that through the Torah man may attain the perfection of virtues which is the path to ultimate perfection, namely, happiness.[34]

According to Arama, this is the "general principle of the Torah" and not the "general principle of morality": the laws help lead one to the Torah's goal, namely, the attainment of truth and human perfection. This is how Arama understand Hillel's saying, "that which is despicable to you, do not do to your neighbor" (Shabbat 31b). The natural Torah also does the same, but from a different vantage point. Laws in society lead people to happiness and perfection, which is the ideal of "kingdom of priests and a holy nation." This is the social-utilitarian aspect of morality.

In this manner, Arama explains the words of Rabbi Simeon b. Gamaliel, who said that "the world stands on three pillars, on justice, on truth, and on peace." In its conventional aspects, as far as positive law is concerned, the laws of the Torah constitute justice. As far as the agreement between the "natural truth" and the divine archetype of justice" is concerned, Arama holds that "the laws of God are truth." And, as for the impact on society, the laws of the Torah are the source of peace. This explains, according to Arama, the importance of the section of the Torah that involves legal matters that appear to be repugnant and distasteful. For Arama, these laws, too, are inseparable from divine wisdom, inasmuch as they are holy. The involvement with law and with moral problems between people is only the involvement with the holy archetype of the Torah that is close to God.

Arama writes also about different types of laws. The social code is determined by people, but the effectiveness of statutes and religions in this regard is a function of the social code's approximation to "the truth of the nature of things . . . or its distance from it," because, were "the social norms [to] be far from the natural truth . . . there would develop between people controversies and quarreling that would not allow them to be led, and the leaders would not be received pleasantly. This would develop into great social friction that would be to the detriment of the community."[35] The prophetic vision of Isaiah for the end of days receives here its full explanation. Natural law brings with it total and complete peace. Divine law brings union to its perfection, for God alone is "in counsel and might in work: whose eyes are open upon all the ways of the sons of men, to give to everyone according to his ways and according to the fruits of his doings (Jer. 32:19). Only He could judge each man according to his true nature." That is to say, only the Torah law which is natural and not a matter of social convention can bring humans to perfections.

Arama continues:

> The words of the Divine Torah are identical with natural justice. There is no distinction between them, between [the time prior to the] Revelation at Mt. Sinai and thereafter. Only their exposure changed, as God said, "Truth speak the daughters of Zelofhad." Our rabbis commented on this verse that thus it is inscribed on high. This teaches us that their [Zelofhad's daughters'] eyes saw what the eyes of Moses did not see. This is a profound insight into the Hebrew word *ken*, meaning "truth." Truth" may be used only where the words of truth are in accordance with external reality, found outside the soul. They are inscribed before God in heaven. Everything teaches us that the laws of God are true, [that is to say] true nature. And if they can be seen partially through conventional wisdom . . . here we see that they are the true natural justice known before God on High and hidden from man. . . .[36]

Saadia's claim concerning the difference between revealed commandments and the rational commandments receives here a new meaning. Arama distinguishes between three types of human activities: natural, learned, and social. The natural activities are "the forces that function as they have been ordained from the very beginning." They are not learned. They cannot be forgotten; they are not memorized. They happen even while a person sleeps and are completely outside human cognitive faculties. In modern parlance we might call these "instincts." The social and moral virtues are located in the middle between intellectual activities and natural activities. They begin with a cognitive act, since moral virtues are learned, but eventually they become a habit. From then on they become natural and inseparable from the human personality. Arama attempts to make the same point: there is an inherent identity between Torah and nature. (This view stands in stark opposition to the relationship between Torah and nature in the thought of the Maharal.)

Arama summarizes the philosophic position by saying:

> that man is like a tree whose roots are virtues, whose branches are in-
> tellectual truths and whose fruit is the recognition of God. Ethics is the
> surge for the first end. Because of its importance the early rabbis tried
> diligently to remove the impediments from the path, [they tried] to
> straighten the ways and wrote many books of human conduct. Political
> philosophy was a great challenge for them. They placed it above every
> other type of knowledge so that it will prepare the way for the ultimate
> attainment of human perfection.[37]

Arama concludes that there is a great similarity between Jewish ethical teachings and philosophical ethics. The latter's importance is to be
found in the structure that it provides, so that "When people ask the
questions that are found scattered in the Torah, in the Prophets, and in
the Writings and in the Talmud, such as we are accustomed to search
for them wherever they are. Now we should be grateful to those writers who structure them rationally and debate among themselves to
give rational explanations for that which they write." Arama conveys
the point through an analogy: just as people are accustomed to having
different wardrobes, one set of clothes for weekdays and a different
set of clothes for the Sabbath, so "every Jew should accept two different kinds of ethical actions, which are called in the language of the
Talmud *derekh 'eretz*, that they are the wardrobe for the weekday, and
then there are divine commandments that are the wardrobe one should
wear on the Sabbath."[38]

The World of Kabbalah

The Position of the Shelah

We now enter the fourth gallery in our exhibition: the world of kabbalah. In a previously published essay on prayer,[39] I clarified the distinction between theurgy and mysticism in kabbalistic thought. This is a
distinction relevant as well to the relationship between nature and morality. Kabbalah reversed the relationship between reality and its symbolic representation. Everyday experiences of reality are transformed
into phenomena, which become symbols of a hidden, true reality that
is expressed symbolically in language. In kabbalah, language becomes
reality and reality becomes a language. Nature is transformed into a

symbol of the divine. This is not to say that nature loses its significance. Nature is significant especially in its theurgic sense. We can clarify this point by looking at R. Isaiah Horowitz, who is known as the Shelah, the acronym of his influential work *Sheney Luhot Ha-Berit.*

The rabbis of the Talmud, as we already noted, emphasized that the "world pursues its own course" and juxtaposed the moral indifference of nature to the human world. This notion raises the question of divine providence, and subsequently the question of reward and punishment, both prevalent themes in Jewish religious thought. One position highlights the naturalness of punishment. According to it, there is a natural connection between sin and punishment—namely, the punishment is the necessary response to human misdeeds, just as an electric short circuit or electrocution may be the direct result of improper or careless use of electricity. In terms of punishment for a wrongdoing, this may be called "punishment follows evil."

The early antecedents of this view could be traced to the apocryphal Wisdom of Solomon. The Shelah explained the various alternatives to this "naturalistic explanation" within the context of the kabbalistic worldview.[40] One position, which could be called "anti-natural," is represented by Nahmanides (Ramban). To him, the relationship between a good deed and its reward, or between an evil deed and its punishment, is entirely "miraculous." According to him, a religious or a moral act will not add to the agent "anything, nor will [non-performance] detract anything from him, but the reward and punishment that the whole Torah promises in this world, everything is a miracle and hidden from us. He who sees it may think that this is the way the world runs . . . punishment and reward are true."[41] What Nahmanides is saying is that the miraculous does not express itself in providential determinism. It is a fact that providence exists and that there is a relationship between morality and events, but there is no cause-and-effect relationship between them. Unlike Nahmanides, Rabbi Meir ibn Gabai, the author of *Avodat Ha-Qodesh,* held that reward and punishment do not come as miracles but as natural occurrences.

The Shelah offers a third view, and it too has a long history in Jewish thought. This view is based on the existence of two types of causality: one is "natural, rational causality," and the other one is "nonrational," a karma-type causality, which the Shelah calls *segulit.*[42] This distinction changes the relationship between the Torah and nature by broadening nature to include dimensions that transcend nature. There are two levels to nature: one is the apparent world of phenomena, and the other is the hidden. The Jewish theologians who were influenced by classical Greek philosophy attempted to avoid ascribing to God any change. Therefore, providence (namely, divine response to human deeds) became problematic for them. The Shelah offers a way to solve the problem by transferring providence from God to nature. Yet, the Shelah's understanding of "nature" is not devoid of a theological component, because he also wishes to avoid assigning to God a change of will. Relying on the anonymous *Ma'arekhet Ha-Elohut* and on the *Aqedat Yitzhaq*, the Shelah claims that "change exists only from the perspective of the [human] recipients."[43]

Kabbalistic sources developed the notion of hidden nature. Interestingly, this idea could be found in the works of medieval rationalist philosophers, the most outstanding of whom is Gersonides (Ralbag). He posited the existence of an additional structure of providence alongside the natural cosmic structure that is described by the Aristotelian philosophers. Paradoxically, Gersonides and several strands of kabbalah were quite close to each other, although modern scholars have failed to notice this because they missed the religious pathos of Gersonides' works. It is evident in the lawfulness of the cosmic order that comes at the cost of the existential relationship to a personal God.

If we were to juxtapose the theurgic position with one of the positions described above, we could state that, whereas in talmudic literature the analogy of a father king who rewards and punishes is dominant, in kabbalah an impersonal language that expresses the notion of trans-natural causality is dominant.

Tzimtzum and Nature in Hasidism

The discussion so far indicates that Jewish religious sources recognized both the notion of natural causality and the opposite idea that providence is contrary to nature. The classic view of nature is found in the kabbalah, which posits a close connection between the lower world and the supernal world; the latter serves as the paradigmatic model of the former. The opposite view, which we have labeled "anti-nature" is based on the idea that the Torah's source is in the realm of *Atzilut* and that the Torah emanates in the world as an act of divine grace, or as part of the divine plane; the source of the Torah is not in nature. Moshe Cordovero expresses this view in *Tomer Devorah* (Palm Tree of Deborah), where, in chapter five, he states:

> [a.] that [in doing] acts of loving kindness in this [the lower] world, a person's true intention should be to bring the perfection to the upper world, that he is performing an act of loving kindness to his Creator . . .
> [b.] in visiting the sick and curing them in such a way as to know that the *Shekhinah* is love-sick . . . [c.] in giving alms to the poor, following the example of *Yesod* and *Malkhut* and that charity is worthy of them . . . [d.] [in] welcoming the stranger into his home, he is [in fact] following the example of *Tife'eret* and *Yesod* . . . which is *Malkhut*. . . .
> In brief, a person should perform his action in such a way as to allude to the upper world. In that way he is guaranteed that he is performing in the upper worlds as well. . . .

In this passage the moral act is perceived as expressing the divine reality and not just the mundane reality of the natural world. We can find the same notion in the teachings of Rabbi Hayyim of Volozhin. According to him, the Torah also preceded, as it were, the uppermost *sefirot*. He says: "The supernal source of the holy Torah is in the highest of all worlds that are called the worlds of Ein Sof."[44] The Torah is Holiness, in contrast to the world of nature which is separated from holiness. It is profane.[45] Even after its descent, the Torah "remains in its primordial holiness." The symbolic expression for transcendence of the Torah is the prohibition of meditating on it in inappropriate places.[46]

The teachings of Rabbi Hayyim of Volozhin on this point stand in direct opposition to the position of Hasidism, which holds that "there is no space void of Him." Underlying this conflict is the internal kabbalistic debate about the doctrine of *tzimtzum* ("contraction" or "withdrawal"). Is it real or illusory? "Real *tzimtzum*" means the absolute transcendence of God who withdraws from contact with the natural world. "Illusory *tzimtzum*" means apparent withdrawal, so that a hidden immanence continues even after the act of creation. Thus, God is actually present in the physical world, even though God cannot be perceived by the naked eye. Rabbi Joseph Dov Soloveitchik is purported to have said that this is the theological basis for the controversy on natural morality. Transcendence is expressed even in the impossibility of natural morality. By contrast, "illusory *tzimtzum*" leaves room to find the "fingerprint" of God within natural morality.

Despite the internal debate, it is safe to say that even in Hasidic thought we find that Judaism is considered a victory over nature. This is the view of R. Judah Aryeh Leib, the second rabbi of the Gur dynasty and the author of *Sefat Emet*.[47] He contrasts the Ten Sayings, with which the world was created, and the Ten Commandments. The Sayings are descriptive and the Commandments are normative—they may be willfully rejected. The concept of sin is a function of the normative. The connection between them is apparently found outside them, in the ten plagues that manifest the overpowering of nature to balance the descriptive with the normative.

Let me end this section by saying that Hasidism is not pantheism, even though the views are quite close to each other. More accurately, Hasidism is panentheism: God exists within the created world and also transcends the created world. Additionally, God does not just "participate" in nature. Rather, God is hidden in nature. Nature is thus godly, but to find its godliness one needs to remove the veils of God's hiddenness. This hiddenness is the basis for the existence of evil in the world.

Nature, Wisdom, and Torah: The Maharal of Prague

We now come to the views of the Maharal of Prague, who I have mentioned several times already. The Maharal presents us with a worldview divided into three aspects: nature, reason, and Torah. The distinction emphasizes the chasm between human culture and nature. The concept of *derekh 'eretz*, as explained, relates to reason, that is to human culture, which belongs to the second aspect. That the rabbis chose the term *'eretz* (earth) and not *'olam* (world) indicates, according to the Maharal, that they had in mind human civilization and not the cosmos.[48]

The Maharal uses the following analogy: if the seed performs its task "in its unique way, due to its very nature," man performs his task according to his "soul, which is from above. It is pure and perfect and was put into the body of man in the world below . . . and for that reason God gave the Torah which is not part of nature and through it the man labors to achieve perfection." Reason, according to the Maharal, is the source of all culture, which conflicts with the general forces of nature and especially with human nature.[49] Morality consists in acts of loving kindness that are not justice, but mercy, thereby enabling a human being to rise above nature. The virtue of mercy reaches its fullest expression in imitating God. Nature, by contrast, is egotistical, because the "physical substance does not bestow anything. It only receives." Law is the product of necessity, and "man is required to live according to the law. Yet, there is no specific benefit to be derived from it. But when he acts beyond the call of duty [*lifnim mi-shurat ha-din*], he shows that he voluntarily and mindfully is going in the way of God."[50]

The Maharal claims, then, that the single, autonomous act is *hesed*, loving kindness. It is the one exception in the natural world whereby man "surpasses his nature and elevates himself to follow God. . . . That is the meaning of the verse 'after the Lord your God should you go and to Him should you cling' and then he overcomes his physical nature, thus elevating himself up to God."[51]

The Modern World: Rabbi Samson Raphael Hirsch

The Commandments between Man and Nature

We are now at the close of our conceptual tour through the various galleries of Jewish thought, and we come to the views of Samson Raphael Hirsch who revolutionized Jewish thinking about the relationship between Torah and nature. To understand Hirsch, a preliminary comment is in order, pertaining to the question of autonomy.

It is common to present Hirsch as a thinker who presented a theonomic interpretation of Jewish law. I reject this interpretation. While it is true that there is a theonomous element in Hirsch's method, it does not explain his interpretation of the ethical teachings of the Torah. Fear of heaven is a factor—perhaps the basis and origin of the Torah—but only one factor. The ethical commandments are not related to this area.

We see this clearly in Hirsch's exposition of the Garden of Eden. In direct contrast to the commentary of Maimonides, Hirsch states that the tree is void of any virtues. It becomes the tree of the knowledge of good and evil only later, in the end. The tree is thus called from the beginning by what it will ultimately become. Neither the snake nor the woman refers to the tree as such. And, original sin refers to the relationship between God and man.

The Levels of Morality

It is possible to describe morality, according to Hirsch, as if it were a building consisting of several stories. In his *Nineteen Letters*, Hirsch teaches that human destiny can be discerned from three different books: nature, the human heart, and the Torah. The ground floor is the book of nature. Natural morality presents man the challenge of his integration into the cosmic order, as expressed in the created order. The entire cosmic order can be summarized in a simple sentence, "receive in order to give." This is the general ecological principle. As Hirsch sees it, "the world is one large camp of creatures who are joined together in one great peace effort, each one functioning in his place and time with the gift allotted to him."[52] The first function, the mandate humans received in creation, is "to work it and to preserve it" (Gen. 2:15). The earth is given to humans, but humans have responsibility to the earth and, says Hirsch, "towards each of its creatures as created by God, as brothers to respect it, to love it and advance it through his deeds to the goal of the will of God."

In Hirsch's exposition of the human place in God's creation, the distinction between descriptive law and prescriptive law disappears. The Bible describes the entire cosmos as fulfilling the world of God. A few citations will clarify Hirsch's views:

1. "Everything around serves God. Each created thing has a place assigned to it, for God to work on it, in it and through it according to His laws. Everything serves God! Each thing in its place, in its time with the strength that it has and with the means at his disposal fulfills the words of God, brings his offering in his hand. And he adds it to the entire building, all are servants of God" (*Letters*, 3:12).

2. "The same law, that all the forces serve Him unconsciously, without choice [applies to man]. Before Him you too must bend, but consciously and willingly. Consciously and willingly, this is the exalted mandate of man. All the heavenly powers stand and serve before God's throne, hidden from them is the place where they stand, with their faces covered so that they do not see the substance of their vocation, but they feel the flight of their strength and they function according to their destiny! And you, o man, to you your destiny is exposed partially. . . . We will not ask you to burst out in song amidst the great choir of the servant of God and to declare: We will do and then we will listen." (*Letters*, 4:14–15).

The image of the blind servant is common in talmudic literature. Hirsch uses it in his commentary in two different ways. On the one hand, man needs to decide to follow the law; nothing is autonomic. On the other hand, man is capable of understanding also for whom the law applies. The image of the blind sun fits here with the description of the Seraphim as described by the prophet Isaiah: "Above Him stood the Seraphim; each one has six wings; with two he covers his face, and with two he covers his feet, and with two he flies (Isa. 6:2). The words of Isaiah about the angels describe the works of nature. Here is Hirsch's commentary on the passage from Isaiah:

> 3. "The words of Isaiah about the angels describe the works of nature. All the powers stand and serve before the divine throne, hidden from them is the place where they stand [*'with two he covers his feet'*]. The face is covered so that they do not see the essence of their mission [*'with two he covers his face'*], but emphasizing that with the flight of his strength to function [*'and with two he flies'*], to perform his destiny. (*Letters*, 4:14)

These are the facts that are expressed in the laws of nature, the so-called "descriptive laws." Man, by contrast, must humble himself "consciously and willingly." The positive integration between man and the world around him creates a balance. This is given to him not as a fait accompli but as a desired goal. This is the normative realm.

The full significance of Hirsch's unique way of relating the Torah and nature is seen in his confrontation with the Reform movement, for whom that Torah was a product of history. For the reformers, everything is subject to change according to the whims of history. Hirsch, the founder of Neo-Orthodoxy, held that the Torah and its commandments transcend historical changes. Nature, therefore, has a theological significance. Furthermore, behind this theological dimension hides a more basic element, the specific way morality applies to nature. Nature is not only a model for us in fulfilling its law, but it places on humans its own demands, its own *mitzvot*.

This idea that nature places commandments on humans is elicited from Hirsch's distinction between *mishpatim* (laws) and *huqqim* (statutes). This distinction has a long history in Jewish philosophy. Saadia Gaon was the first to make the distinction between "revealed commandments" (*mitzvot shim'iyot*) and "rational commandments" (*mitzvot sikhliyot*). These parallel the distinction between "laws" and "statutes."

The Torah is the single authority of the former, whereas human reason is the source of the latter. The rational commandments are binding in their own right, and not because they were divinely prescribed. But, did Saadia take this distinction from the Kalam thought, or did he find it already in talmudic sources? The standard answer is to credit Saadia with the distinction, but we can actually find it in the Sifre on Leviticus.[53]

Hirsch presents a new reading of the distinction between *huqqim* and *mishpatim*. While retaining the distinction between "rational" and "revealed" commandments, he explains it through the scope of the possibility of human understanding. *Mishpatim* are the commandments that connect us to human beings. We may understand them, because through them we relate to people like ourselves, people toward whom we can feel deep empathy. Hirsch states: "The requirements to act justly as the *mishpatim* compel us to do, teaches us to feel as brothers" (*Letters*, 11:43). By contrast, the *huqqim* designate responsibilities that we have to various forms of existence and to nonhuman creatures with whom empathy is almost impossible. It is impossible for us to understand them and, therefore, the *huqqim* appear to us irrational. Our rational faculties are limited regarding them. From here, Hirsch deduces the principle that "were we able to know the processes of reciprocity of other types of creatures, as we know our own bodies and minds, then the *huqqim* would be as clear to us as are the *mishpatim*" (ibid.). We may conclude that the difference between *huqqim* and *mishpatim* is not contingent upon the existence of a rational explanation of the commandments, but upon a basic distinction that divides human beings and creatures of other types. The *mishpatim* bind us to human beings that are close to us; the *huqqim* bind us to the world that is alien to and further from us. The former are accessible to our own understanding, whereas the latter can only be perceived as divine precepts. The measure of justice relating to the cosmos in toto "flows here from the concept of being subject to God, who is a shield for all who subject themselves to Him" (ibid.).

According to Hirsch, nature is the source of commitment. Above nature there is another source: the human heart or conscience. This is human morality. Hirsch describes human conscience as an acoustical resonance: "As every living thing extends its image to your spirit, as it enters the human heart, the heart strings respond as they do to the cry of pain which is heard throughout the entire creation, to all the voice of rejoicing that bursts forth from the mouth of a joyous soul" (*Letters*, 4:14). Mercy has its source in the feeling of empathy, and is common also to animals. In *Horeb*, Hirsch says, as we climb up the ladder of living things, "creatures become gifted more and more . . . to feel in themselves the echo of the voices of pain."[54]

Hirsch's exposition of *mishpatim* and *huqqim* could be used as the basis of Jewish ecological thinking. Our responsibilities to nature are expressed in the *huqqim*; our responsibilities to other human beings are the *mishpatim*. While our hearts beat along with all living creatures on earth, there is no doubt that human beings are uniquely attuned to other humans. The love of the neighbor is built on his being like yourself. In Hirsch's language: "in his being a man like yourself. By contrast to the *huqqim* that relate to man's obligations to all the creatures that are below you" (*Letters*, 11:43).

Hirsch teaches the meaning of our obligations toward nature. These are not obligations derived from our obligations to other humans, such as the concern not to destroy the environment because it will be detrimental to humanity in the distant future. Neither is Hirsch concerned with the aesthetics of nature, which for him is prior to ethics, but is still an egotistical concern. The human obligation toward nature is *sui generis*. We have finally reached a Jewish source that derives human obligation toward nature *not* from the function of nature itself.

Concluding Reflections

We can now reflect on the Jewish contribution to ecological thinking. In the 1970s, we witnessed the development of an approach that saw in biblical monotheism the cause for the ecological crisis that threatens human existence.[55] This claim was voiced by Lynn White, Jr., and by Arnold Toynbee. According to their charge, the first chapter of Genesis portrayed the human as a being endowed with a mandate to conquer the earth and control the fish in the sea, the birds in the sky, and the animals and beasts in the field. But, as I have tried to show, this reading of biblical monotheism does not do justice to the balance in nature envisioned by the Bible.

In fact, the reading by White and other environmentalists typifies Western secular culture: it inherited some of the biblical values but lost the biblical balance, precisely because it denied the practical commandments. I maintain that we need to expand Hirsch's emphasis on human obligations toward nature in order to understand that the totality of the commandments—including the prohibitions against: wanton destruction of nature, inflicting necessary pain on animals, hunting, drinking of animal blood, mixing of linen and wool; and the commandments that require us to share our food with the animals during the sabbatical years—articulates a distinctive Jewish ecological ethos. It is an ethos of respect for nature and for God's creation. Conversely, the commandments to observe the Sabbath and the sabbatical year, the prohibition against taking the mother and its offspring on the same day, and other commandments teach us that the earth does not belong to man, but rather the earth belongs to God. God's ownership of the earth means the establishment of limits on human subjugation of nature and the discovery of human duties toward nature that humans do control.

The Garden of Eden is the biblical ideal description of human relations to nature. In the Garden, man was a vegetarian. And the biblical text, at least in my reading, expresses concern not to destroy plant life as well. In the Garden there were trees. The trees provided man with fruit as an act of beneficence that the trees bestowed on man, while they continued to grow after giving their gifts to man. Only after the sin in the Garden did man develop agriculture that destroyed plant life through eating. The prohibition not to eat from the Tree of Knowledge indicates that not everything is permitted to man in the Garden. Human authority itself is limited, and the boundaries are expressed in the commandment to observe the Sabbath. On the Sabbath, authority returns to God.[56]

We should rethink the meaning of human conquest of the earth along the lines proposed by Hirsch. Before man was created, he was guaranteed "dominion" (Gen. 1:26). According to Hirsch the root *k-b-sh* (Gen. 1:28) expresses a relationship of conquest over inanimate objects. The root *r-d-h*, used in this verse in Genesis, has a different meaning, that of "guiding." Hirsch concludes: "it is man's mandate in his relation to the animal world. His function is not to rule over all of them. Perhaps there is a task for the earth and its creatures should be free of his reign. They may have their own goals. . . . [I]f he were to rule over them as Adam, created in the image and likeness of God, in that way the creation would accept his Kingship."[57]

With this final comment we return to the original discussion of nature and monotheism. Let us recall Genesis 2:15: man is placed in the Garden, not as an autocratic ruler, but as one who must preserve it, protect it, worry about it, and as one (like Noah in the subsequent generation) who must save the animals who are faced with the danger of extinction. We are commanded, *le-'ovdah u-leshomrah*, namely, to develop the earth and protect it.

Notes

1. In the extensive literature on the subject see, Ralph Lerner, "Natural Law in Albo's Book of Roots," in *Ancient and Moderns*, ed. Joseph Cropsey (New York: Basic Books, 1964), 132–47; Jose Faur, "La doctrina de la ley natural en le pensamiento judio del medioevo," *Sefarad* 27 (1967); and Marvin Fox, "Maimonides and Aquinas on Natural Law," *Dine Israel* 3 (1972): 5–36. Fox discusses natural law in Jewish thought. His central thesis is related to the understanding of natural, moral law in Christian thought. This doctrine of natural law allowed Christian thinkers to distinguish, according to Fox, between the eternal in the biblical text, which is anchored in natural law, and the transient, which according to them was nullified with the coming of Jesus Christ. I do not accept the second half of Fox's analysis. According to Fox, there is no natural morality in Judaism, and there can be none. Judaism entrenched itself in the concept that the entire Torah—its ethical and ritual aspects—is anchored exclusively in revelation. By contrast, I hold that we must recall the distinction between *mishpatim* and *huqqim*, between the rational and the revealed commandments. The distinction was explored during the Middle Ages in the writings of Saadia Gaon and Judah Halevi. Halevi's analysis of the law employed the notion that the Torah has two functions: the perfection of society and the perfection of the individual. The dual functions fulfilled the purpose of the rational *mitzvot*: to transform the moral human being into a divine being. A similar idea is also found in the writings of the Maharal, who will be discussed later in this paper. See Abraham Melamed, "Natural Law in Jewish Political Thought in the Medieval and Renaissance Periods," *Da'at* 17 (1986): 49–66, for further discussion of this point and relevant bibliography.

2. A similar function is the description of nature in the thought of Rabbi Samson Raphael Hirsch in his dispute with Reformers who used history as the basis for halakhah.

3. See Leo Strauss, *Natural Right and History* (Chicago: University of Chicago Press, 1953).

4. Karl Marx believed that his Socialist doctrine was the continuation, and the next stage, of Darwinian theory. This is obviously absurd. The utter simplicity of Marx's theory could not grasp the totality and the consequences of the Darwinian struggle for survival. There is no doubt that the biological parallel to the Marxist view is found in the development theory of Lamarck, as Lisenko tried to develop it. Lamarck's approach was a positive one, namely, that function creates the tools for survival. In contrast, Darwinism emphasized the negative aspect, namely, the need for selection, since death eliminates the weak and allows the fittest to survive.

5. See Hermann Cohen, *Religion der Vernunft aus den Quellen des Judentums*, First Gate, 10, Hebrew translations by Zevi Wisslevsky (Jerusalem: Mosad Bialik, 1971), 76, where Cohen quotes Aristotle *Metaphysics* 1.5.

6. Ibid., 83.

7. Ibid., 81.

8. The future is also one of the basic elements in the thinking of Rabbi Abraham Isaac Kook. But unlike Cohen, Rav Kook sees the importance of the Golden Age in the guarantee that the past could be realized in the future.

9. See my "The Return to the Garden of Eden: Comments on the History of the

Idea of Jewish Restorative Redemption in the Middle Ages," in *The Messianic Idea in Israel: Papers from a Seminar Honoring the Eightieth Birthday of Gershom Scholem* (Jerusalem: Israel National Academy of Science, 1982), 37–86.

10. For further discussion of this point, see Ephraim E. Urbach, *The Sages: Their Concepts and Beliefs*, trans. Israel Abrahams (Jerusalem: Magnes Press, 1975), 92–94; and Max Kadushin, *The Rabbinic Mind* (New York: Bloch Pub. Co., 1952), 143–52.

11. The discussion of the morality of nature requires that we examine the relationship between value and fact, between normative and descriptive law in systems that discuss natural law. This type of criticism is found in the works of such different modern writers as John Stuart Mill, Thomas Huxley, and Wilfred Pareto.

12. Until now we have considered the normative nature of natural morality, a system of commandments and prohibitions built on nature. Yet, we may also consider the theoretical structure. This can easily be shown with a simple example: egoism. Egoism can be perceived as the ultimate moral norm that engenders a normative system, according to which humans must live life. Or it may be seen as a description of the way people actually live their lives. All of us, including the greatest idealists, are, in fact, egoists. Thus, we may understand the law of nature as a guide of the principle of human behavior.

13. I quote from the Soncino edition of the Babylonian Talmud. The quote originally appeared in Tosefta Kiddushin in a fuller version that expresses the same idea. Were I bold enough, I would say that this follows the tradition of Rabbi Simeon b. Yohai, who said that a man should devote himself to the study of the Torah, and God will provide his physical needs, as God provided for the needs of R. Simeon b. Yohai and his son while they were hiding in the cave. This statement expresses not only the importance of Torah study, but also the opposition to the artificiality of human action and the return to the primordial human condition. This approach is quite different from the notion that people should study the Torah and depend on others to provide for their ordinary needs.

14. Tanumah, ed. Solomon Buber, Ma'asei 8, n. 6. On the raven, see the impressive comment of Rabbi Moshe Avigdor Amiel, who preached a sermon in condemnation of the raven; El Ami, part 1, 10.

15. See Victor Aptowizer, "Rewarding of Animals," *HUCA* 3 (1926): 117.

16. Rabbi Zadok Ha-Cohen of Lublin, *Zidkat Ha-Zadik* (Lublin, 1840; reprint, Bnei Brak, 1973), 173.

17. Max Kadushin analyzed the several components of the concepts *derekh 'eretz*. It is important to mention the words of R. Shmuel ben Meir, the Rashbam, who writes that the prohibition to seethe a kin in its mother's milk is for moral reasons. He comes to enlighten us about *derekh tarbut* (the way of culture) against excessive cruelty. The phrase *derekh tarbut* parallels *derekh 'eretz*. About *derekh 'eretz* as the way of the natural world, see also his commentary on the Pentateuch, on Gen. 24:58, 34:25, and Lev. 11:34. Interestingly, in his commentary on Gen. 41:38, he says: "The wisdom of *deretz 'eretz* is apparently politics!" For further discussion of this point, consult David Rosin, *R. Samuel b. Meir als Schrifterklärer, Jahresbericht des jüdisch theologischen Seminars* (Breslau, 1880), 125.

18. Robert Gordis, *The Word and the Book* (New York: Ktav, 1976), 75–83.

19. This interpretation is found in the commentary of Abraham ibn Ezra, who writes about the "tree of knowledge" (Gen. 3:6): "and one of them, the tree of knowledge, engenders sexual passion." There are parallel passage in the Bible where the word "knowledge" has a sexual connotation. For example, Deut. 1:39, Isaiah 7:15, and 2 Samuel 19:36.

20. The same idea is found in the works of Josephus. See *Antiquities* 1.60–66.

21. While Josephus does not claim this explicitly, we can infer that technology is a transgression of the divine commandment "to fill the earth."

22. Josephus *Antiquities* 1.111.

23. Ibid., 1.113.

24. *Zidkat Ha-Zadik*, 216.

25. The Arabic original, *Islah al-akhlaq*, was published with an English translation by Stephen C. Wise, *The Improvement of the Moral Qualities* (New York, 1902). The Hebrew translation by Yehuda ibn Tibbon, *Tiqqun Middot Ha-Nefesh*, was published in the appendix to *Meqor Hayyim* (Tel Aviv: Machberot le-Sifrut, 1951), 9.

26. Noah Brown, the modern editor of the text, cites different parallels, in which the emphasis is on the mind's rule of the passions. But the citation above specifies that the mind rules over nature.

27. *Nethivot Ha-Musar* (Tel Aviv, 1961), 41–42.

28. Saadia Gaon, *The Book of Beliefs and Opinions*, trans. Samuel Rosenblatt (New Haven: Yale University Press, 1948), treatise 3, chap. 1, p. 39.

29. In Hilkhot Teshuvah 5.1, we read: "That is, what is written in Torah 'that man will become like one of us, to know good and evil' (Gen. 3:22). This means that man is unique in the world, that he, from within himself, by his own mind and thought knows the difference between good and evil. He is capable of doing whatever he chooses and nothing will stop him from doing good or evil. Therefore he might stretch forth his hand." This interpretation follows the translation of Onkelos to that verse: "for man is unique in the world because he knows good and evil." The German Jewish philosopher Moritz Lazarus already noted the significance of Onkelos's translation. See Moritz Lazarus, *Die Ethik des Judenthums* (Frankfurt am Main: J. Kauffmann, 1898), para. 97. Cf. Urbach, *The Sages*, 321ff. Urbach claims that "anyone who is familiar with Onkelos' method of translation knows that he seeks to eliminate anthropomorphic expression in the biblical phrase 'as one of us.'" According to Urbach, Onkelos translated the biblical verse as "to know [by himself] good and evil," rather than "to be wise to distinguish [by himself] the difference between good and evil." However, it seems to me that precisely because Onkelos was struggling against the anthropomorphism of the biblical text, he hinted at the possibility that a human being may know moral values from within himself, as Maimonides explained.

30. The epistemological basis of natural law claims specifically that there exists a natural source from which we draw morality. This epistemological dimension connects with the substantive dimension. Because of the multiplicity of options, one wonders if there exists one absolute natural law that is valid and binding universally for everyone. As Aristotle says in the *Ethics* (and I am using the medieval translations): "the good and proper things that political [wisdom] studies are the various contending views that do not really relate to nature except for religious motivation" (*Ethics* 1.1). The wide variety of views teaches us, apparently, about "religion,"

which means the arbitrariness of the law. Why are there so many differences of opinion among those who accept the authority of nature? Is there no historical development in the perception of its models? Apparently, if we can speak of the development of natural law, then we cannot speak of it as eternal. But we must distinguish between natural law, as it is perceived by people, and eternal natural law, as it exists in and of itself, which is absolutely binding—in other words, between the Torah as it is understood by us and between the Torah as it is in truth before God. Natural law is the law that will be realized in the end of days.

31. See Efraim Kupfer, *Qovetz al-Yad*, Minora Manuscripta Hebraica, vol. 9 (Jerusalem, 1980), 295–331. For further discussion, consult Melamed's essay cited in n. 1 above.

32. *Aqedat Yitzhaq*, section 95.

33. Ibid.

34. Ibid., section 46.

35. Ibid.

36. Ibid.

37. Ibid., section 27.

38. Ibid.

39. Shalom Rosenberg, "Prayer in Jewish Thought: Directions and Problems," in *Jewish Prayer: Continuation and Novelty*, ed. Gabriel C. Cohen (Jerusalem: Kedem Press, 1978), 85–130.

40. Isaiah Horowitz, *Sheney Luhot Ha-Berit* (reprint, Jerusalem, 1975), 9b.

41. Ibid., Beit David, part 1, 20a.

42. Ibid.

43. Ibid.

44. *Nefesh Ha-Hayyim*, gate 4, chap. 10. See Norman Lamm, *Torah Li-shemah* (Jerusalem: Mosad Ha-Rav Kuk, 1972), 81.

45. *Nefesh Ha-Hayyim*, chaps. 27, 28. Cf. Lamm, *Torah Li-shemah*, 83.

46. See Lamm, *Torah Li-shemah*, 71 n. 270.

47. Judah Aryeh Leib, *Sefat Emet on the Torah* (Jerusalem: Nekhdei Sefat Emet, 1979). For an analysis of his thought, consult Yoram Jacobson, "Galut and Geulah in Gur Hassidut," *Da'at* 2-3 (1978-79): 175–215; Yitzhak Alfasi, *Ba'al Hidushei Ha-Rim, Hayav, Mahshavto ve-Torato* (Tel Aviv: Sinai, 1954), and the bibliography cited there; Meir Orian, "The Idea of Shabbat in the Sefat Emet," in *Be-Ma'agalot Ha-Hasidut*, ed. Meir Orian (Jerusalem: Reuven Books, 1977), 83–91.

48. Judah Loew ben Bezalel (Maharal of Prague), *Netivot Olam*, Netiv Derekh Eretz (Warsaw, 1884), chap. 1.

49. This idea is found in the writings of Saadia Gaon: "That which has already been condemned by the eyes of human wisdom, the things that his nature lusts for, such as whoring, robbery, impudence and revenge through murder and the like." This translation is based on the modern Hebrew translation of Joseph Kafih (Jerusalem, 1970) from the Arabic original, section 9, chap. 1. p. 265.

50. Maharal of Prague, *Netivot Olam*, Netiv Gemilut Hasadim, chap. 1, 44a.

51. Ibid., 44b.

52. Samson Raphael Hirsch, *Iggrot Tzafon* (1948; reprint, Jerusalem: Mosad Ha-Rav Kuk, 1976), 14. All citations are to this edition. The translations are my own. For

an English translation, consult *The Nineteen Letters on Judaism*, ed. Jacob Breuer (New York: Feldheim Publishers, 1969).

53. Sifre, Aharey Mot, 13.10, ed. Weiss, p. 66a. Cf. B. T. Yoma 67b. We can conclude that the *mishpatim* transcend the tight theological strictures. Perhaps they are autonomous. This is autonomy that relates not to my conscious side but to my ability to make laws for myself. This is the autonomy of someone who is not committed to fulfilling the commandments because they are prescribed.

54. Samson Raphael Hirsch, *Horeb*, trans. Moshe Zalman Ahronson (Vilna, 1875), 321.

55. See *Ecology and Religion in History*, ed. David Spring and Eileen Spring (New York: Harper and Row, 1974).

56. Hirsch, *Horeb*, The Law of Evidence, 1.

57. Hirsch, Commentary on Genesis 1:26.

Respect for Nature in the Jewish Tradition

LENN E. GOODMAN

The Torah pioneers in developing the ideas of a political contract, and it fosters the notion of the consent of the governed by making God himself a party to covenants with Israel, and with humanity in general. But the Torah does not rest the authority of its Law on the idea of a contract. Many of those who are subject to the requirements of that Law were not literally present when it was accepted and revealed—and besides, a covenant is made with nature as well as with humanity in general and Israel in particular: "While the earth remaineth, seed-time and harvest, cold and heat, summer and winter, day and night shall not cease" (Gen. 8:22).

What God is doing here, clearly, is to assume responsibility for the continuance of nature in its rhythmic patterns and regularities—those which benefit humanity and those which simply sustain the natural continuity. The warrant for that commitment of God's is no reciprocity on nature's part, but rather, divine regard for creatures and creation. Creation is sustained for its own sake and not for any yield or reciprocity it may bring to God. What is recognized, even by God, are the deserts of the beings He has created. And God here is made the model of human concern for nature, a responsibility that is seen to rest on human shoulders in recognition of the objective deserts of beings and the capabilities that humans have for respecting those deserts. The biblical position is admirably summed up in a typical jewel-like midrash: "When the Holy One, blessed be He, created the first man,

He took him and led him 'round all the trees of the Garden of Eden,
and said to him: 'Behold my works, how fair and lovely they are. All
that I have created, I created for your sake. Take heed that you do not
corrupt and destroy my universe. For, if you spoil it, there is no one to
repair it after you'" (Eccl. Rabbah 7.13).

Here, working at the heart of the teleological and anthropocentric
conception of nature, for which the monotheistic tradition is so often
blamed, we find God commending His creation to humanity, not for
its utility or commodiousness but for its beauty. And the rhetoric that
urges a sense of responsibility for nature is not a prudential warning
against fouling one's own nest or polluting one's own well, but an
appeal to the preciousness and irreplaceability of each of God's cre-
ations—whose paradigms are the trees in Eden. The argument parallels the Mishnah's appeal to the uniqueness and, thus, irreplaceability
of each human individual as the mark of the sanctity of human life
(Sanhedrin 4.5). Indeed, the argument in the human case is made a
special case of the argument in behalf of nature at large and the species it contains. For the Mishnah predicated the special sanctity of
each human life on the likeness of each human being to a world or a
natural kind. Note the order of the argument: Not, thou shalt respect
and protect nature because it is the abode of human beings, but rather:
thou shalt respect and protect human lives because they are, in their
own way, miniature worlds and complete natural kinds.

For some twenty years now I have been elaborating and developing
an ontological theory of justice grounded in what I call a general
theory of deserts.[1] Human rights, I have been arguing, are a special
case of a larger class of deserts that pertain to all beings. All deserts, I
argue, arise ontically, from the conative and entitative claims of beings. Deserts belong not just to humans or persons, but to all manner
of beings, including individual animals and plants, species, eco-
niches and habitats, monuments of nature and of art, ideas, and, of
course, the ecosystem and nature at large. This line of thinking is
rooted in the Torah, and my purpose here is to discuss the footings and
paradigm cases of the approach in the classical and canonical Jewish
sources. After briefly sketching the general theory of deserts, I want
to discuss the metaphysical foundations it affords for an ethic of respect for nature and to call out some of the concretely codified applications of that ethic and the ethos that it builds.

Deserts and the General Theory of Justice

Contract theories of justice suffer from what I have called the Sky-hook Problem and the Exclusion Problem. On the one hand, they find no warrant beyond agreement or convention for assigning authority or prescriptivity to the norms and obligations that they seek to legitimate. This leaves no room and affords no basis for assigning authority to agreements or conventions themselves. On the other hand, contract theories exclude from moral concern all parties who are not actual signatories or participants in the putative agreements or conventions that are their moral nerve. In both cases, such theories are highly anthropocentric. Not only do they leave out of account the interests of foreigners, the very ill, the socially inactive or alienated, but they systematically exclude the concerns of future generations and the interests of nonhuman species, their habitats and ecosystems, and the larger, material environment, including the nonorganic environment. In place of the notion that right and wrong are matters of negotiated convention, I have proposed that we seek value in beings themselves. Beings are the loci of value. Indeed, the being of things is their value.

One strength of adopting an ontological approach to values is that it obviates the quest for a "property," of goodness, which we must then deem natural or "non-natural." The being of things is their nature. But that nature is no static and neutral fact. Each being constitutes itself in its own project. For that reason beings vary in kind. They also vary in attainment or achievement. For although we can never judge one being's project by the standards of another, the fact remains that in absolute terms not every project is as significant as every other.

Value here is not dependent on some external evaluator but on the intrinsic merit of the claims each being makes. For all beings make claims, and those claims belong ultimately to the beings that make them and have a legitimacy reflective of the reality of the claimant. The appraisal of claims remains a task for intelligent beings, a task that is more than hinted at in the biblical idea that humankind is created in the image of God: we have the responsibility to understand and care for nature—to master and preserve it, in the biblical language. No other creature can make the necessary judgments or even recognize the pertinent claims. Stewardship is part of the human condition, an inalienable charge. For even neglect is a policy choice, and even wilderness areas (as long as humans exist) require management.

All beings make claims. These I take to be the equivalent of their being. For what I take to be the being of a thing is its project, what Spinoza called its *conatus*. The prima facie deserts of a being are equivalent to its claims. But objective deserts are the resultant of all claims balanced against one another. The deserts of beings rest on their intrinsic value. But such value resides in all things. It is found in persons par excellence. For consciousness renders persons subjects. They conceive themselves as ends, they choose values and plan a life, they are capable of good and evil, and for that reason we must say that finitude finds its most powerful means and most compelling meanings in the lives of persons. But the ends of persons are not the only ends—just the only self-consciously self-constituting ends. All living beings pursue a project. All are at least virtual subjects, whose implicit goals, even if not articulated by a consciousness, still constitute an identity with objective interests of its own. Even inanimate beings make claims, to space, to endurance, to the expression of their natures, which may be simple without thereby becoming inchoate.

Human fallibility and liability to bias in evaluating deserts may seem to argue the subjectivity or conventionality of deserts themselves. But such limitations on our part, I think, prove just the opposite. For the notions of bias and error, long pled as evidence for subjectivism or relativism of some other sort, presuppose a legitimacy that can be strayed from. Where there is corrigibility, there is a truth to be known; and where unfairness can be detected—as it is when bias is uncovered—there are Socratic grounds to hope that fairness can be found as well. Found, not merely imposed. For some standard of fairness was implicit in the knowledge by which bias was exposed. The fact of subjectivity, then, is not the ally but the enemy of subjectivism. Subjectivity has no meaning if there is no truth or objectivity against which it can be disclosed.

Societies do not create justice. Rather, justice creates societies. Justice is the imparting of what beings deserve. Thus, it is not out of place, but indeed morally appropriate and necessary, to speak of justice to other species and to nature at large and in all its parts. All beings have deserts, insofar as they are beings. Deserts reach a plane of sanctity and mutuality in the case of persons. It is here that we rightly talk of rights. For the legitimate claims of all beings are scaled to the stature of their projects; and the claims of persons (and so of human beings) are grounded in their subjecthood. This is an objective matter.

It is not because we humans belong to the same taxon or have affinities to one another that we privilege humanity in our moral schemes, but because the human species is the only species in which we have encountered personhood. Personhood makes society possible. That is, it makes practical a mode of cooperation or collaboration that is grounded in the mutual, conscious, and explicit recognition of subjects by one another. But the pervasiveness of such recognition at the foundation of virtually all our actions should not distract us from the moral basis of our obligations to our fellow persons: it is not because they can aid us or accord us recognition that we owe special recognition to our fellow human beings, but because of what they are. Their subjecthood, like our own, is a thing of beauty and value, to be cherished for its own sake. (For to predicate the preciousness of others on their usefulness to us would dangerously leave open the question why there was any special worth in ourselves that would warrant our making instruments of any things at all, let alone our fellow humans.) Similarly, our obligations to animals are not grounded in their similarities to us. Rather, what we must respect in all beings—to the extent possible—are the claims made by their projects. What makes human claims unable to be compromised, at least in certain crucial areas, are the splendid prospects opened up by the possibility of choice and the fact of consciousness. What imparts value to other beings as well are the projects they pursue, not in the first instance as objects of our potential use but as constituents of a world and loci of intrinsic value.

All beings are dynamic in some measure. All affirm, as it were, a certain character that is their own and that they define in the course of their history. A being, viewed telically just is the agency that stakes out for itself a project, an identity grounded in a system of interests that is constituted in part through its own activity. Any claim or interest is worthy of concern and attention. The interests of a being, prima facie, lie in the furtherance of its project, an open-ended goal. Any dynamic claim is implicitly or potentially infinite in some respect. Yet wisdom demands recognition of the limitations inherent in all claims made by finite beings. Moral wisdom is the ability to adjudicate among rival claims and to discover among them not only the roots of competition but the potentials for complementarity.

My view that beings are constituted by and through their claims is akin to the existentialist identification of a being with its project, and to Spinoza's equation of the essence of each being with its *conatus*, its

striving to preserve and promote its reality. A being is not the mere
sum of its history or amalgam of the facts about its static self-identity.
Still less can it be identified with its apprehension by other subjects or
its impact on other objects. For both impact and apprehension are
aspectual. Perception or conception can apprehend only some abstract
or sampling of a thing; to engulf it would not be to know it but to eat it,
absorb it, and destroy it. By the same token, a thing cannot be its impact on another, or even the sum total of its impacts on all other
things. For what, then, would remain as the cause of all those impacts? I find it striking and amusing that philosophers who, in an epistemological context, stress the aspectual character of all our appre-
hensions turn in pragmatics to an identification of things with those
very surface encounters that they have so carefully shown us cannot
be the whole.

The moral realism of our theory of deserts rests on an ontic realism:
it is because beings are not just aspects of our experience or functions
of their effects that they have deserts of their own. The world contains
a great variety of beings, each actively affirming its identity, setting
out its own project and interests. If there were nothing to contradict
such interests, their affirmation might well warrant their legitimacy.
But in a world of multiple particulars, interests will collide. They may
also harmonize or complement one another. But because interests can
conflict, we cannot simply equate deserts with claims. Interests are
prima facie deserts. To find the legitimate deserts of all beings we
must attend to their specific and particular projects, consult the conflicts and the potentials for complementary results. Ecology and the
economy of the garden are valuable models here—but models, not
oracles. They yield no trivial or automatic resolutions to all conflicts.

To map the hierarchy of deserts in detail is not a necessary part of
the philosophical theory of justice, and efforts to do so might seem
only to appeal, suppositiously, to familiar notions of the relative worth
of beings and their projects. The normative task of regulating our
practical and notional responses to claims of all sorts is a task of cultures in general and of laws and religions in particular. Indeed, it is
among their chief tasks. Philosophy cannot successfully usurp it. But
philosophy can observe and thematize the criteria in use and criticize
intellectually and morally the outcomes of various systematizations
and axiological schemes.

We can say that the interests of a being, its project or *conatus*, are the very essence of that being as it expresses itself in the world. That means they are the being; they are what it is. Sensation, sensibility, considerateness and consideration are strengths, not weaknesses, in *conatus*. For they enable a being to seek, discover, or even devise its own good, and to confront its own limitations without first being brought up short by them. Sentient beings are adept at finding complementarities that will optimize the realization of deserts. Conscious beings, that is, persons, can uncover or create intellectual realms in which even infinite claims are not invidious or self-undermining. And, as self-conscious beings, persons, can expand their individual identities to accept as their own the interests of other beings. But, for all beings, legitimate deserts are grounded in claims. Indeed, deserts and claims are identical if the claims are evaluated contextually and not taken as if in isolation (where they are never found). Justice will be the recognition of each being's deserts, equilibrated against those of all others. For there is no reason why one being's deserts should count more than the equivalent claims of another.

But not all claims are equivalent. For beings vary in ontic worth; their deserts must be scaled to their reality. Claims vary in merit, and their equilibration is not easy. Yet even without a recipe for assaying the relative worth of all rival claims, I can say with confidence that justice cannot be achieved, or understood, if we do not assign deserts to beings; and it will never be complete or universal if we confine deserts to ourselves.

The primary rule of the general theory of deserts is that all beings should be treated in accordance with what they are. We can compare this demand for a proper response to the claims all beings make with the recognition called for by facts: just as facts demand cognitive acknowledgment, deserts claim moral recognition. In both cases we have an obligation to respond to things' being as they are. In neither case have we a tautology. For the according of recognition goes beyond the demand for it, although the demand is implicit in the self-affirmation of a being (or a fact). Otherwise, the recognition sought would not answer the demand made, or the demand would not be needed.

To implement so broad and potentially nebulous a rule as the demand that the reality of things be recognized, two cardinal principles are needed: 1) Deserts are scaled to the reality each being claims. We do not rightly sacrifice a child to a virus, as though their claims were equal—even though the quasi-life of the virus is all it has. 2) The interests of persons take special precedence and make a special claim. Persons need not be human. They do not win their special consideration on the grounds of looking like us or behaving as we do, nor even, in the first instance, by their potential usefulness to us or others, but on the grounds of their subjecthood, a precious achievement in nature. Persons evoke and deserve special recognition because of what they are, not simply because they are capable of returning regard—for a dog can respond to recognition, and a person often cannot, whether in infancy or incapacity, or simply in ignorance or absence. It is the status imparted to persons by their standing in the hierarchy of being, not their affective claim on our sympathies or their effective impact on our interests, that grounds their deserts—their rights and dignity, as subjects, as moral persons, choosers of their life patterns and their destiny.

Persons, then, stand on a moral plateau. Personhood, in whatever form it discovers itself, is never to be·sacrificed to interests of some lesser order; and even the highest subjects may not rightly subordinate or negate the subjecthood of the rest. All subjects deserve a level of consideration that can be called absolute, in the sense that nothing can be traded for it; it has no price or counterpart; it is not measured on a scale commensurate with other interests. Underlying the special regard deserved by subjects is our primary rule, that all beings must be treated in accordance with what they are. Subjects, in self-consciously constructing their own life-projects, call upon one another in a language that is not to be ignored, not only for cooperation but for recognition of the intension of their aims.

The moral consideration that is the due of nonpersons can be treated as an extension of the model we use in assigning deserts to persons. That, in fact, is what is done by those who adopt the language, say, of animal rights. But this political, rhetorical way of stating the case lays claim to the status of subjects in behalf of nonpersons. That is a misappropriation, and when efforts are made to extend the notion still further, the breakdown becomes complete. For plants do not have rights, and it is a category error to speak of habitats or ecosystems in such terms. But animals, plants, even ecosystems have deserts.

In ontic terms, subjects are the special case. The general rule is to respect beings for what they are, not for their approximation to our self-image. Living organisms, species, ecosystems like the riverbank or the canyon, the mountain range or the shore, implicitly claim recognition. Persons claim recognition explicitly. The difference is one not of degree but of kind. It is not simply a matter of language or commerce, any more than it can be reduced to a matter of appearance and sympathy. Persons genuinely are subjects, whereas nonpersons are analogous to subjects in having projects and thus interests. In both cases recognition is deserved by the reality that is each being. But those realities differ crucially because of the role that consciousness plays. The interests of nonpersons deserve consideration, other things being equal. But those of persons are in some sense inviolable, so long as the persons can be treated as such, and not, like the sniper in the tower, as a public menace or a pest.[2]

The ontological theory I have proposed assigns a special status to persons, but it does not confine interests to persons. The relative deserts of animals, plants, species, monuments of nature and of art, institutions and practices, make claims upon our consideration. But the legitimacy of such claims never extends as far as the categorical claims of personhood. To underscore this point, I would urge, for example, that I think it is an error of moral judgment to compromise the nutritional needs of a child to meet the demands of vegetarianism, as I have sometimes seen done. But norms of stewardship can be derived from an ontic account of justice. They cannot be derived from a strictly Kantian view. Kantian ethics, crucially, rejects cruelty to animals on the grounds that humane sensibilities are a virtue to be cultivated. It does not elicit regard for animals as a corollary of the categorical imperative. Still less can a universal ethic be derived from a consistently contractarian account. As for the effort to derive the standards of a universal regard from Utilitarian precepts, such attempts are fraught with paradox and inconsistency. For appeals to sentience like those of Bentham or Tom Regan try to warrant rights by identifying a lowest common denominator of sensibility among the various forms of animal life. By proposing susceptibility to pain as that denominator, they transform an emotive appeal for the "rights" of sentient beings into an undermining of the special place of subjecthood, upon which the idea of rights depends, and still they fail to regard the claims made by trees and other nonsentient life-forms—let alone species and ecosystems, institutions, practices, cultures and ethnicities.

An ontic theory can and should acknowledge a hierarchy of deserts, in which personhood makes singular claims. Some romantic programs deny such hierarchies—engratiatingly, for the element of ritual necessary in implementing any value system can grow so familiar as to become at once transparent to view, and irksome. But to exclude hierarchies of value is to negate deserts. For recognition, like nourishment, must be shaped to the contours of beings' claims. I cannot claim that the life of the mantis or the ant means as much to that creature as your life or mine means to us, since the insect has no plan of life in the sense that you or I have. But, more importantly, I cannot claim that the insect's life matters equally with ours in the universal scheme of things. Only alienation fosters so sardonic a romanticism as that; and such alienation presses for the negation, not the affirmation of universal values. In practice, when such schemes are implemented, lesser claims are honored only expressively and in the breach; human claims are diminished, and a broad passivity takes hold at both levels, symptomatic, perhaps, of alienation and loathing for life. In practice, once the special claims of personhood are made commensurate with those of lesser beings, the principle of ontic recognition is violated, and no sound basis remains for the allocation of recognition. The same is true even if deserts that are lesser only in degree are placed on a par with others that exceed them, as, 'for example, when a whole ecosystem, say, a forest, is placed at risk by the protection in it of some feral species or invading weed.

Efforts to extend the rights of persons to other sorts of beings, then, are not just inappropriate (since animals cannot vote and plants cannot enjoy an art museum) but are misguided. The effect is not an extension of rights (as though plants were now made voters), but the spread of the relativity of deserts into the realm where deserts are properly conceived as rights and are not relative at all. The outcome is not the announced expansion of the moral franchise, but debasement of its meaning. Animals and plants, species and eco-niches deserve protection, for what they are as well as for what they may mean to us, pragmatically or otherwise. But persons have dignity as well as the more graded sort of value that every being attains in its own way. Persons are holy. Genesis expresses this by saying that humans are created in God's image. Rabbi Akiva draws the moral: "Cherished is man, being created in the divine image; but all the more cherished is he, in that this was made known to him, as it is said: 'For in the image of God did He make the man'" (Avot 3.18).

Our ontological account fosters an objectivist idea of justice. And it allows, indeed requires, a general, rather than a restrictive assignment of deserts. Far from confining attention to the interests of some consensual body, it extends consideration to all beings, subjects and non-subjects, animate and inanimate, natural and artificial. It finds deserts in animals and plants as well as in humans; in mountains, rivers, species and ecosystems, as well as in sentient beings; in works of art, institutions, memories, traditions, sciences and ideas, as well as planets and galaxies. Not all value depends on the value of persons or on the values assigned by persons. Claims may deserve recognition even if they are not are own, even if they are not of the type we make. Indeed, our ability to recognize claims other than our own is part of what gives precedence to human claims.

What a general theory of deserts entails is that utility, to ego or to us, is not the sole basis of worth. Recognition of deserts extends to those persons who are not in league with us. Nor need we cloak our impulse to save the rain forest in appeals to the usefulness of its biomass as a source of oxygen. Mere instrumental values, after all, might be secured by alternative means, perhaps technologically; the interests they once protected might then be overridden by the commercial value of the lumber in the Matto Grosso, or the gold in its streams. Discovery of intrinsic worth in persons, and in all beings, obviates embarrassing appeals to Epicurean anxiety fables: even if the Amazon watershed harbors no cure for cancer or AIDS and will never be enjoyed or appreciated as wilderness by the bulk of humanity, its intrinsic value is not the less for that. For the worth of things does not depend exclusively on their use or appreciation. On the contrary, these rest on intrinsic worth.

The theory I have proposed is a form of naturalism. It is not, as some may fear,[3] a form of materialism. For the natures in which it finds value are dynamic seekers of goals, which they themselves help to constitute but which are never reducible (as matter traditionally is) to the mere facticity of the given. That is, part of what is precious in beings, signaled by the open-endedness of their quest, is their linkage to eternity. We see evidence of that linkage clearly in human becoming. But even beings that are not sentient at all show their linkage to the divine, in the transcendent reach of their projects.

The ontology underlying our general theory of deserts avoids the reductionism familiar in most forms of naturalism. The theory equates being with value in the classic way that regards being as a perfection—and, in the case of finite, contingent beings, as a gift. The theory is naturalistic in equating interests with claims and claims with prima facie deserts. "Interest" here is understood objectively rather than subjectively, as in Ralph Barton Perry's famous equation of value with the object of any interest. Interests need not be consciously articulated. Value need not be instrumental, because interest need not be external. It need not belong to someone else. A being can have interests, and so deserts, even if no one cares about it. Its worth is not proportioned to the extent and intensity of the concerns of others for it—let alone, their desires to appreciate, possess, or consume it.

But the naturalism I have proposed avoids the naturalistic fallacy, because it does not equate any mere fact about a thing with its value. Still less does it entail that whatever exists should exist. Rather, the thesis is that the claims of beings deserve recognition, prima facie, simply because they are the claims of beings: beings deserve recognition *insofar as* they are beings. It follows that recognition of claims should be scaled to the magnitude of the claims. Justice, classically understood as giving each his due, here would mean the adequate or optimal recognition of the deserts subtended in the claims of beings. But claims are made (and can only be made good) in a world where there are other claims. They could never be made in isolation; and they can never be fairly recognized unless they are equilibrated, balanced, or reconciled, with one another.

Ultimately, all beings, perforce, obey the laws of nature. But nature's sentence may be delayed, as when the Soviet Union, for example, had not yet fallen under the growing weight of its long battle with history. Such denouements, dark as the fate of the house of Atreus, are not inevitable. For we humans can study nature's imperatives, which the biblical idiom calls the laws of life. We can adapt consciously, not just genetically, grasping and even rethematizing nature's commands, accepting or rejecting or restructuring what presents itself as the given. We may celebrate and enhance or despise and degrade the values we encounter in nature, seeking to ignore them, or struggling to enshrine and enlarge them in individual memory and communal practice. It is because nature lays out the parameters of every creature's project, defining what it is for each being to be and to become, that the laws of nature are prescriptive. Their prescriptivity rests on the worth of each ontic status that nature provides and on the *conatus* of each being to which nature opens a path, or a fork in the road.

The same is true, of course, of the laws of nature's God. Each being has its own worth; each person, his own dignity. This worth or dignity is the substance of God's existential gift and is nothing different from the project imparted by the act of creation. In the riot of nature, such projects may and will encroach on one another. The exuberance of the lightning or the tornado, the easing of the earth in its traces, relaxing the tension along fault lines—the Lisbon earthquake and Job's storm-wind—acknowledge no face. But persons, as persons, have the power and responsibility to give names to one another, to recognize faces and acknowledge individual worth and dignity. We persons, and we alone, can grant one another recognition, not just as objects of use or annexes of ego, but as subjects. That, too, is part of the special worth and dignity of persons—where the worth inherent in all things reaches the pitch of awareness and so is capable of returning or acknowledging but, primarily, of according and receiving consideration and regard.

The special deserts of personhood, like the general deserts of all beings, issue a demand for recognition. Like any demand, it is rightfully curbed only to the extent that it is undermined by incoherence or overreaching. Exploitative demands, like those of a pimp, a thief, a tyrant, or a traitor, are undermined by the incoherence of the notion that one person grows in stature by threatening the being or negating the dignity or trust of another. Pestilent demands, like those of a virus, a spot of mold, or a serial killer, are overruled by the victim's higher standing or more innocent claims, and by the demands and presumptions of civil society, on which the realization of all human claims depends. The serial killer, of course, is not a virus or a spot of mold, but a person. Yet, in negating the deserts of others, he becomes, pragmatically, little more than the threat he represents, and the responsibility devolves upon society of removing that threat while preserving what it can of the killer's residual deserts.

The moral scheme, like being itself, is hierarchical, since deserts arise in the measure of the beings they constitute. But the laws of nature are not the same as the laws of God. For the latitude of natural beings to aggress and the freedom of persons, out of ignorance or willfulness, to withhold recognition allow intrusions, encroachments, neglect, and violation of legitimate deserts. The natural power to withhold recognition is the counterpart of the capacity to recognize deserts, cherish worth, and sanctify dignity. Freedom and naming are counterparts. Both are gifts of God. For God loves freedom as much as He loves the play of nature; and God's explicit law makes room for and presupposes freedom in the same way that His implicit law, the law of nature, leaves room for and gives energy to the play of nature, while allowing freedom to those who claim it. Negligence is the natural concomitant of freedom. Without freedom humans would never rise above the blind justice of nature or attain a dignity beyond the animal claims of the organism, in which subjecthood is given body and thereby comprised as an actor and compromised as an object in the world. Nature allows the wildfire to overwhelm the forest, although man must not; and nature allows man to drain the wetlands, but God (as we now think) commands us to restore them.

Judaism and the Metaphysics of the General Theory of Deserts

All things, even inanimate objects, have a worth and beauty, not merely *for* or *to* anyone else, but in themselves, in virtue of what they are. Thus, the Torah commands us not to make an enemy of the tree in the field (Deut. 20:19–20) and warns us that even the land will be requited for the Sabbaths of fallow years it may be scanted (Lev. 26:34). The world is the better for the existence of Mauna Kea or Diamond Head, the Mona Lisa or Venus de Milo. We would not suffer the destruction of these in equanimity. Yet the first two were not made for us, and none of them is human.

Clearly persons have and deserve a lexical priority to things in our moral calculus, and the fetus is no person. But it is a work of art, or rather a marvel of nature that far outshines Diamond Head. It is the only marvel of nature that will ever become a person. So I find it hard to see the moral grounds for according it less worth than the rain forest or the wetlands. I find it a daunting display of the social power of conformity over conscience that a woman who would not dream of marring a Michelangelo would not hesitate to destroy the fetus within her, or would stridently defend the right of others to do so, for any reason at all, or for none. My point here, however, is a broader one: the anchoring of norms in the being of things. This is what laws must respect. It is by reference to the value of beings that laws can be made, enlarged, applied, revised, and even—insofar as they fail to respect the worth of things and the dignity of persons—rescinded.

I do not possess some algorithm for adjudicating all conflicts among claims. Nor do I have some divining rod for discovering all the complementarities latent among the claims that beings make. The "art of measurement" capable of assaying ontic claims, adjudicating among them and discovering their complementarities will be no mere Benthamite calculus but a broad appreciation of the open potentialities of nature in general and human nature in particular. We can readily understand why Plato would urge that only by access—direct or indirect, clouded or clear—to the pure idea of the Good can we adequately assay the relative worths among which our finitude calls on us to assign priorities. But even without reference to such thoughts, the aspirations visible in the projects of all beings make me confident that the naturalism I am broaching is nonreductive. If being is so variously realizable and is always dynamic and creative, as I have suggested, there is no danger of its being confused with mere facticity.

I find value in all beings and argue that if value does not reside in beings there is nowhere else to find it. The legitimate criticism of the naturalistic fallacy by Hume, Moore, and others, shows that facticity does not entail or amount to legitimacy. But being is more than facticity. To assume that reality is a bare or neutral fact, devoid of value, is to beg that question, and in a direction belied by every natural quest and attainment. For to deny the identity of being and value is to deny that being is an achievement and thus to deny the most manifest fact of our experience, the dynamism of being.

Part of what I am arguing is that existence is better than nonexistence. Certainly there are many things that the world might be better without. But I do not think that any reality is purely evil. For, as evil in a thing increases, so does its incapacity to sustain itself. Evil tends to self-destruct, partly because it saps the strengths (for which read virtues) of those in whom it takes hold, and partly through its destructiveness to the milieu on which any being must depend. Thus, evil disappears long before it can reach totality. Beings are sustained only by the perfections they win. The things we picture as evil are such by their destructiveness to other things; but what preserves even the most destructive is their small measure of good. So a universe could not survive, let alone come to be, if it contained only evil. That is not a truth of logic but a fact of metaphysics; its necessity arises from the nature of being as it is constituted; its universality is the hallmark of God's handiwork and grace. A universe of beings whose perfection is only partial and relative can exist and does sustain itself. That, I believe, is the sort of universe we live in.

What I have claimed is that to make all values subjective and to find none in reality is to deny that anything has any real worth. That position, I believe, is untenable. It is refuted, I argue, by every act we make, including every speech act. For one who speaks, implicitly affirms the value of his speaking. Even in taking a breath one implicitly affirms the value of life—denying it, perhaps, in words, but affirming it again as one inhales. Yet, lecturing around the country about the ontological theory of justice that I have been advocating here, I have often heard professional philosophers deny that there is any value in being at all. Some defenders of the idea that values are only notions are apparently so committed to that view (doubtless because they link the claim with their own moral freedom, taking that in turn to be the same as the power to legislate morals for themselves) that they would rather deny that there are any values at all than admit that there is value in things. This leads me to ask again: What else is there, besides beings in general and persons in particular, that could warrant our acts of valuing? Or is valuing always irrational?

One who actually thought being itself devoid of value would be committed to the view that the universe at large might just as well not exist. I find it very hard to understand such nihilism about being, but moral conventionalists and subjectivists, in earnest conversation, seem not to shrink from it. Against such a rejection of realism about values, I respond that even to affirm a subjective value seems to entail an affirmation that what I choose is good or right objectively, even if only for me. To act at all seems to entail that something in the world— if only my will and the assertion of its desires—is worthwhile. Obliquely, it seems to affirm the worth of the willer. But all such arguments are only dialectical.

I cannot refute the nihilism I reject without appealing to some value. So there might seem to be an impasse between my affirmation and the nay-saying of those who voice disagreement—unless I beg the question in favor of being. For it is the value of anything at all that is in dispute. But the position is not quite so symmetrical as might seem. If I assume what my interlocutor denies, at least I do not assume the contrary of what I hold, as one who denies all value to reality must do, to affirm anything at all.

Dialectically, I can say that one who rejects all value in being would have no grounds for staying the hand of some nuclear or ecological terrorist bent on destroying the universe. If there were a doomsday machine (a possibility far more readily envisioned than a real person who found no value in anything), and if some maniac had his finger on the button, the nihilist would have no reason even to try to prevent the madman from pushing the button. I do not rest my affirmation of the value of beings on such negative and dialectical considerations, but on an open appreciation of being as we know it. In such an appreciation, scientific understanding, aesthetic awe, and religious celebration all respond to the same underlying givens.

The Jewish sources are of help here, for they attest to the value of being and invite our appreciation of it. When God surveys the newly created world and sees that it is good, He might appear to be making a redundant judgment. Was He not the almighty author of it all, who made exactly what He wanted? Who was present, or qualified, to judge His work? Yet, like a craftsman who has made a table or a cabinet, God assays His creation and judges that it meets His expectation and intent. And more, that it is a good thing, good in itself, a thing that should exist, that deserves to exist, for the beauties it now bears, through no prior claim, but for its value now—not to God, who stands in need of nothing, but in itself, as a work of art might be valuable, not because it can be sold or put to some use, but intrinsically. For, although the world holds many utilities, they serve no function beyond it, but are perfections relative to *its* purpose, which is the sustenance and flourishing of all sorts of beings—all the myriad things, as the Chinese philosophers might say. All these things, in their diverse ways and to their diverse degrees, exist for their own sakes and plot their own projects. Maimonides writes:

> According to our doctrine of the creation of the entire world out of nothing, the search for a final cause of all existence might well seem necessary. Thus it might be supposed that the end of all existence is simply that the human species should exist to worship God and that all things are done solely for man's sake, even the heavens turning solely for his benefit and in order to bring his needs into being. . . . If this view is examined critically, however, as intelligent men ought to examine

views, the fallacy in it is exposed. For the advocate of this belief has only to be asked, "This end, the existence of man—is God able to bring this about without all these preliminaries, or is it the case that man cannot be brought into being until all these things have been done?" If he replies that it is possible for God to give being to man without, say, creating the heavens, then it must be asked, "What is the utility to man of all these things which were not themselves the object but which exist 'for the sake of' something that could have existed without any of them?" Even if the universe does exist for man, and man's end, as has been said, is to serve God, the question remains: What is the object of man's serving God? For His perfection would not be augmented by the worship of all things that He created, not even if they all apprehended Him as He truly is. Nor would He lack anything if nothing but Him existed at all. . . .

For this reason, the correct view, in my judgment, in keeping with religious belief and in consonance with the theories of reason, is that all beings should not be believed to exist for the sake of man's existence. Rather all other beings too were intended to exist for their own sakes, not for the sake of something else. . . . We say that all parts of the world were brought into being by God's will, intended either for their own sake or for the sake of something else intended for its own sake. . . . This view too is stated in the prophetic books: "The Lord made each thing *le-ma'anehu*" (Prov. 16:4). The reference might be to the object [each thing for its own sake]; but if the antecedent is the subject [the Lord], the sense is 'for Himself,' i.e., His will, which is His Identity . . . also called His glory. . . . Thus His words, "All that are called by My name and created for My glory, I created, yes and made" (Isa. 43:7). . . .

If you study the book which guides all who seek guidance toward what is true and is therefore called the Torah, this idea will be evident to you from the outset to the end of the account of creation. For it never states in any way that any of the things mentioned was for the sake of something else. Rather, of every single part of the world, it is said that He created it, and its being agreed with His purpose. This is the meaning of its saying, "God saw that it was good" (Gen. 1:4). For you have learned what we have explained on how "Torah speaks according to human language" (B. Bava Metzi'a 31b, cited at *Guide of the Perplexed*, 1.26; cf. 1.46, citing Gen. Rabbah, 27.1). 'Good,' for us, refers to what agrees with our purpose. (*Guide of the Perplexed*, 3.13, citing *Guide*, 1.2)

In saying that God created all things by His own will and intent, then, Scripture is saying that God created them for their own sake, and only secondarily for the uses they may afford one another. If we judge anthropocentrically, we shall inevitably find many things whose "purposes," in terms of utility to us, baffle us; many will seem to have no purpose at all or to be "detrimental."[4] Yet all serve God's purpose, which is their existence. That is what is meant by their existing for God's glory, distinguishing God's purpose from any merely instrumental end. God's glory is found in the creation of all things for their own sakes. Maimonides is aided to this view by the Neoplatonic response to Stoic anthropocentrism.[5] But the thesis, which he aims at the occasionalists and anthropomorphizers of providence in his own day,[6] is clearly biblical. His reading of "God saw that it was good" is borne out in Isaiah's vision (6:3) of the complementarity of God's transcendence ("Holy, Holy, Holy") with his immanence: "The fill of all the earth is His glory."

Genesis envisions God examining His creation and seeing that it is good. What we see here is neither the bending of God's judgment to the world's standards nor the capricious imposition of God's demand—as if we were ordered to call the world good because it is the work of a powerful artisan. Rather, nature, the world, is God's, not only in the sense that He is its Creator and the Author of the values it displays but also in the sense that God has scrutinized His work and found it a fair expression of the values intended. Even here, God's judgment cannot substitute for our own, but it can instruct ours, aid us in seeing God's more universal goodness exemplified in the multiplicity of things. The varieties of goodness in nature make it a text in which we can recognize God through the references to His goodness and wisdom implicit in His handiwork. The finite goodness in things intends the Infinite. It points beyond itself, toward the Ultimate that is its Ground.

The Sufferings of Living Beings

Relatively few biblical passages directly address human regard for and responsibility toward nature. But the nisus of the commands these passages voice is not mistaken when the rabbis set about thematizing the Mosaic law. Consider the biblical response to what was perhaps a pagan frisson of cruelty. We are commanded no less than three times: "Thou shalt not seethe a kid in its mother's milk" (Exod. 23:19, 34:26, Deut. 14:21). Legislatively, this *mitzvah* is made the foundation of an

elaborate system of ritual separations of dietary milk from meat that
are a matter of daily attention for observant Jews to this day. But, if
the Law is to affect our ethos and not just our behavior and is thereby
to contribute to the Torah's declared aim of making Israel "a kingdom
of priests and a holy nation" (Exod. 19:6), it would help to have some
inkling of the connection of the biblical restraint with the idea of the
holy. The sages find the hint they need in the structural relationship
between this prohibition and that against taking a mother bird with
her young. They immediately draw the inference as to the pertinent
theme:

> Just as God shows mercy to man, so too does He show mercy to beasts.
> How do we know? Because it is said, "[Whether it be cow or ewe,] ye
> shall not kill it and its young on the same day" (Lev. 22:28) . . . and in
> the same way God was full of mercy for the birds, as it is said, "If along
> the road thou comest on a bird's nest, in a tree or on the ground, with
> fledglings or eggs and the mother bird sitting on them, thou shalt not
> take the mother with the young. Thou must surely let her go and take
> only the young" (Deut. 22:6–7). (Deuteronomy Rabbah 6.1).

Mercy is the theme, which God himself introduces, since God provides the ordinances here. Human beings are the subject, and God's
creatures are the object. Human needs are not rejected, but their service is restricted. Beasts will be slaughtered and sacrificed or eaten;
birds and eggs will be taken for human use. But excess will be cur-
tailed. The frisson of cruelty is restrained, barred from becoming a
religious, or a secular, value. The grasping and gobbling that would
say, of all of nature, "This is mine, I take the mother with her young,"
is disciplined and gentled.

The context of the prohibition against seething a kid in its mother's
milk seems to matter in the rabbis' recognition of an ethical rather
than merely ritual (e.g., totemic or ascetic) significance in the Law.
For it is nestled among commandments about our responsibility to
restore lost property, assist at the scene of a roadside spill, and avoid
hazardous negligence in construction (Deut. 22:1–8). The ethical
thrust that the ancient rabbis discover here is pursued by the authors
of the codes. Taking up the biblical prohibition against yoking an ass
and an ox together (Deut. 22:10), they derive a prohibition against
setting a bird on eggs of another species. The stated reason is not the
biblical distaste for hybridization but the rabbinic identification of

this practice as a form of cruelty to animals (Code of Jewish Law 191.4).

The ultimate paradigm of cruelty in the Mosaic system, as the rabbis understand it, is a practice once again associated with paganism, namely, *'ever min ha-hai*, tearing or taking a limb or member from a living animal, a practice that rabbinic jurisprudence conceives as forbidden to all mankind—the children of Noah (Gen. 9:4)—by the basic laws of humanity. The Talmud (B. Bava Batra 20a) does not confine the restraint here to the dietary realm, where the human ethos would be most immediately tainted. Cutting off a limb from a living creature, even to feed it to the dogs and even in the case of animals that are not to be eaten at all, because they are unclean, is prohibited. The grounds are clearly stated: they are the demands of humaneness toward animals.

I assign pagan associations to such practices as *'ever min ha-hai*, because I take it that their frissons can be made loci of the pagan *horrendum* when piety has not sundered shock from sanctity. But the direction of the rabbinic reasoning must remain clear: It is not because the act is pagan that it is forbidden as cruel, but because it is cruel that it is forbidden and branded as pagan. The analysis is underscored by the biblical legislation regarding sacrifice and the slaughter of animals for the table. For the nisus of all that ritual legislation is toward the pacific in the choice of animals (the dove, the bullock, the sheep and goat), away from beasts of prey and carrion; and toward the swift and merciful in modes of slaughter (a sharp clean blade, not a jagged, toothed, or notched edge). Again rabbinic authority is not reticent in making the thematic principle explicit: "This is the reason (*ta'am*) for *shehitah* (the ritually restricted practice of animal slaughter): the biblical regard for the suffering of animals" (Nahmanides on Gen. 1:29).

Humaneness is not the sole concern. It is balanced, as the Rambam argues, against the desiderata of nourishment and economy. It matters to the Holy One, blessed be he, as the rabbis say, whether a poor housewife needs to spend a few extra pennies, or waste good food.[7] These, too, are ethical concerns. The Torah is not a romantic document, concerned only with emotive rhetoric. But it is concerned with cruelty, and with the human ethos.

My friend David Shatz argues, on Kantian/Aristotelian lines, that the Torah recognizes the suffering of living beings as a kind of "spring training" for humaneness in our character. Clearly that is true in part. The prohibition against seething a kid in its mother's milk does concern the ethos. The kid is dead, after all, before it is cooked. But the biblical prohibition and all that is strung from it looks beyond the ethos to a way of living and being that would orient the ethos appropriately and that would test that ethos against identifiable, conceptually coherent, and materially appropriable standards.

It is the suffering creature that we are called upon to regard. And the principle invoked is a general one, against causing or countenancing undue suffering. Behind that demand lies the ontic claim that living beings do suffer. They are not, as on some Cartesian model, mere automata. Morally, moreover, these sufferings matter. That is why they are relevant to a humane ethos—and why real sufferings matter more than, say, mere notional or semeiotic sufferings, such as might be inflicted virtually or symbolically in a video game or pictorial representation. The focus on actual sufferings clearly regards not simply the observer or afflictor but the victim. If humaneness is a virtue, it is a virtue that extends toward all potential sufferings and that rejects all wanton causing of pain, that is, all cruelty. It is not just a matter of delicacy about the infliction of pain. It is true, as Hogarth saw, that cruelty to animals is a stepping stone toward greater cruelties. But there are intrinsic as well as instrumental reasons for not countenancing cruelty in any of its forms. Such reasons, after all, are what give moral weight to the orientation of any ethos.

Thematizing the biblical concerns does lead on from negative protections to positive obligations. Vegetarianism is not one of them. This is an option that is repeatedly ruled out, for humanity at large, when Adam's permission to eat freely of every tree but one in the garden (Gen. 2:16) and of the herb of the field (Gen. 3:18) is enlarged to Noah's ration of clean animals (Gen. 2:7) and every moving thing that liveth (Gen. 9:3), and for the Israelites when Moses finds that they require quails as well as manna (Exod. 16:3, 12–13; cf. Num. 11:31; Ps. 105:40). But the Law does require positive acts of kindness toward animals. As we read in the Code (191.1): "It is biblically forbidden to hurt any living creature. On the contrary, it is one's duty to save any living creature from pain, regardless of whether it has an owner or not, and regardless of whether or not its owner is a Jew."

The same complementarity that transforms negative liberties into positive rights can here be seen to be at work in transforming the deserts of animals to be free from sufferings imposed by the hand of man into a positive desert to be freed from unnecessary pain and suffering. We may say, if we like, that the aim of such legislation is the refinement of the human ethos or the evincing of respect for God's creation. But the impact on the animals is the same regardless; and, in fact, the legislation will be empty if the sensibilities of the animals themselves, that is, their liability to sufferings, is not the focus of human concerns.

The principle laid down here, however, is far from empty. One could say that it has numerous concrete applications. But, as so often happens, the concrete applications here are the substance of the Law. The general principle is simply an underlying premise that later jurists derive inductively from thematizing surveys of the laws and their intent—and then use in forming further applications.

Chief among the deserts of animals under biblical law is the Sabbath rest:

> Six days shalt thou labor and perform all thy work. But the seventh day is a Sabbath unto the Lord thy God. Thou shalt do no manner of work—thou, thy son, thy daughter, thy man servant, thy maid servant, thine ox and thine ass, and all thy beasts, and the stranger who liveth within thy gates—so that thy man servant and maid servant may rest as thou dost. And thou shalt remember that thou was a servant in the land of Egypt. (Deut. 5:13–14)

The commandment has multiple tiers of application: to the self and family, to servants of both sexes, but also to the beasts. The ethical regard for servants reflects the experience of slavery in Egypt—as does the inclusion of strangers. For the Israelites in Egypt were strangers as well as slaves. The verse suggests that animals are spared for the sake of sparing the servants. But, regardless of the reason, animals are included in the Sabbath rest, and the Codes devise their inclusion not as an incidental by-product of human rest, but as an independent biblical mandate, implying, *inter alia*, that beasts are not to be laden or made to carry a burden on the Sabbath (Code 87.1).

As usual with the rabbis, the point is carried further. Suppose one has, purposefully or in error, mounted or loaded one's animal on the Sabbath. Is one permitted to dismount or unload? To compound an original infraction would normally be forbidden. But the Law permits one to dismount and requires one to unload the beast. For under no circumstances may one leave a burden on an animal over the Sabbath. The reason, plainly stated, is the alleviation of suffering in a living being (Maimonides, MT, Shabbat 21.9–10, following B. Shabbat 154b).

Similarly, one must alleviate the suffering of an animal that has fallen into a cistern or ditch on the Sabbath, bringing food, or pillows and blankets to help it climb free. The normal restrictions against such labors on the Sabbath are waived. For they are of rabbinic provenance, whereas the duty to alleviate animal suffering is biblical (MT III Shabbat 25.26, following B. Shabbat 128b). Even a measure of casuistry is permitted, so as to prevent the suffering of an animal (Maimonides, MT III Repose on a Festival 2.4, following B. Betzah 26a).

Just as the Sabbath does not take precedence over risks to human life or health, so its restrictions are overridden by the suffering of animals. Cattle must be milked and geese fed, lest the buildup of milk in the one case or hunger in the other cause suffering to a living being (Code 87.9). The fresh wound of an animal must be dressed with oil, to ease its pain (Code 87.23). An animal that has overeaten may be run in the courtyard, to ease its pain (Code 87.24). Even a stray dog must be fed—and in doing so one emulates God, who enabled it to live for as long as three days on what it has been able to find (Code 18.18).

The Sabbath provides a good measure of the seriousness of the provisions against animal suffering, but it is not their sole occasion. The Torah directly mandates that an ox shall not be muzzled when it treadeth out the corn (Deut. 25:4). Once again this ordinance falls in the context of varied ethical commandments, such as the provision that a condemned man not be humiliated when he is punished (Deut. 25:4) and that a widow shall be given an opportunity for offspring by her husband's surviving brother (Deut. 25:5–10). The rabbis generalize the anti-muzzling provision to cover any working animal and any restriction of its free access to food—even by hollering (Code 186.1). If lack of water prevents a beast from eating, one must water it as well (Code 186.3), for one must not frustrate the beast. Suffering, then, is not confined to direct, physical torment.

Accordingly, when a beast is hobbled in a field, one may not tie the fore leg to the hind leg or bend one leg upwards and tie it in place, leaving the animal to walk on three legs, for such hobbles cause suffering to the animal (Code 87.7). Again, regarding the key ethical provision to help even an enemy reload his fallen ass (Exod. 23:5; Deut. 22:4), while the primary obligation is to the enemy—an obligation that Maimonides reads as aiming to help us overcome our irascible tendencies and so improve our character—there is an obligation as well toward the animal that lies sprawled (*rovetz*) beneath its load. For the obligation to unload a fallen beast takes precedence to a similar obligation to help load one for an owner who needs assistance loading up. As Maimonides explains: "If one encounters two animals, one sprawled under its load and the other unburdened because the owner needs help in loading, one is obligated to unload first to relieve the animal's suffering. . . . But if one owner is an enemy and the other a friend, one must load for the enemy first, so as to subdue one's evil inclination (Maimonides, MT XI Laws of Murder and Preservation of Life 13.13; Code 189.1).

The laws regarding the suffering of animals may seem to reach an ethical peak of sorts when we read that when one sees horses drawing a cart uphill or over a rough spot that they cannot manage, one has a religious obligation to help push—lest the owner beat the animals to force them to pull more than their strength permits (Code 191.2). But the laws go further. It is forbidden to eat a thing before having fed one's beasts. The proof text: "I will provide grass in the fields for your cattle, and thou shalt eat and be sated" (Deut. 11:15). God again here is the model, providing first for the cattle in the pattern Israelites are meant to follow: "only then," when the animals have been fed, the Talmud urges, shall we humans "eat and be sated" (B. Berakhot 40a).

Naturally, the ideal is to create a sensibility of love and kindness. The sages, as they read the Torah for its themes, clearly see that such a sensibility reaches far beyond the treatment of animals alone. It is a way of relating to God, of emulating His mercy and thus fulfilling the commandment to pursue His holiness (Lev. 19:2). And it is a way of acquiring the character we need to relate to our fellow human beings and, when the desired virtues are most perfected, to lead them. For leaders need to emulate the divine attributes of mercy above all, as Moses learned when he sought to know God for the sake of learning how to lead (Exod. 33:13, 34:6–7). The rabbis put it simply: the great leaders of Israel were chosen only after showing mercy first to a flock of animals (Exod. Rabbah 2.2). The point is relevant not only with regard to leaders. If compassion is a virtue, then compassion at its most basic and most general is learned and practiced in our comportment toward other living creatures. But the relevance of compassion as a virtue is not confined to the human case. Compassion lies at the

core of our regard for all creatures, in treating them, insofar as in us
lies, as is their due. It is in that sense that compassion is most relevant
to leadership. For in the Judaic conception, compassion is no supplement or antagonist, but the very heart of justice.

"Is a Tree a Man . . . ?"

It is sometimes said that the biblical imperative, "Be fruitful and multiply," pronounced as blessings upon all living things at the creation
(Gen. 1:22), upon humanity in general (Gen. 1:28), and upon the new
founders of animal (Gen. 8:17) and human (Gen. 9:1, 7) life on earth,
represents an ethos of conquest and subjugation. The same ethos, it is
said, was already spoken for in God's original blessing to Adam and
Eve, admonishing them to "fill the earth and master it and exercise
dominion over the fish in the sea and the fowl of the sky" (Gen. 1:28).
These words and others like them are often taken as imparting a license for environmental exploitation, even rapine.[8] Commentators
and glossators may seek to soften the language, just as others have
read a harshness into the words that is redolent more of the issues they
nourish than of the values bespoken in the text. Some understand mastery apologetically, as a reference to acts of understanding; others
take it accusingly, as a mandate for wanton and wasting usage. But the
Jewish tradition has clearly and articulately understood the biblical
theme in terms of stewardship.

De facto, humanity has charge over nature. We do dominate our
environment, and the text of Genesis starts from acknowledgment of
that fact, which it sees as a divinely imparted blessing. Creation at
large, nature, as it will later be called, is good, very good when man
and woman are added to the scene. It is good for nature to be "filled,"
to teem with life—nonhuman as well as human; and when life is diminished, almost to extinction, it is good for it to be replenished, and
not by humans alone (Gen. 9:2). Thus we read in Isaiah, "So saith the
Lord, who created the heavens, God, who formed the earth and fash-
ioned it, who founded it: He did not create it as a waste but made it to
be lived in" (Isa. 45:18). Here, as in Genesis, we do not read, to be
lived in by man, but simply to be lived in. The world is not meant to be
empty. It is better full, and the fullness here, as in Genesis, is not just
the absence of void but the fullness of life, the opposite of desolation.

For the words of Isaiah reflect the vision of Genesis, "the fill of all the earth is His glory" (Isa. 6:3).

Genesis arrays not just the panoply of creation but a hierarchy of values. Indeed, it tables the hierarchy of creation *as* a panoply of values—heaven and earth as the setting, plants as the adornment and the food for animals (Gen. 1:30); animals as a higher good, in virtue of their higher claims; humankind, as the crowning achievement, the creation that makes the whole no longer merely good but very good, in God's eyes and in reality.

Man is the crowning achievement on earth for no arbitrary reason but because of his capabilities. His dominion and his charge rest on those capabilities. For these are what make us responsible for nature and to nature. To repeat our opening midrash: "When the Holy One, blessed be He, created the first man, He took him and led him 'round all the trees of the Garden of Eden, and said to him: 'Behold my works, how fair and lovely they are. All that I have created, I created for your sake. Take heed that you do not corrupt and destroy my universe. For, if you spoil it, there is no one to repair it after you'" (Eccl. Rabbah 7.13).

Fruit trees are the symbolic cynosure of human responsibility for nature at large, just as blood and suffering are the cynosure in the special case of the human responsibility toward animals. For fruit trees are singled out in the biblical account of creation, and again in the biblical law:

> When thou besiegest a city for many days in the course of warfare, in order to capture it, thou shalt not destroy the trees by taking an ax to them. Thou mayest eat of them, but mayest not cut them down. For is a tree of the field a man to retreat before you into a fortified place? Only trees that thou knowest are not food trees mayest thou destroy, cutting them down so as to build siege works against the fortified city that maketh war against thee—until it be reduced. (Deut. 20:19–20)

Warfare here, as in the law of the fair captive or the law sparing newlyweds from conscription, serves as an index of the Torah's priorities. Trees may be cut down for siege works, but only those that are known not to be food trees. The reasoning proffered by the text shows that it is not to preserve their fruit alone that these trees are spared. For the appeal is to what I have called virtual subjecthood,[9] the same that was used when the text gives a voice to Balaam's ass, to remonstrate with him for beating it when Balaam, in his moral blindness, fails to see the obstacle that blocks his path. The trees are assigned interests, and their interests are made vivid, rhetorically, by pleading the trees' defenselessness: they cannot withdraw into the city. Indeed, they have given no offense by locking themselves up in a warlike posture. They are innocent, and it follows that they should be spared. The trees have interests, and because they have interests they have deserts,[10] not absolute deserts like the right of the accused to a trial, but phased deserts, that make them worthy of protection, so that fruit trees, the more valuable prudentially, but also, in the biblical scheme, the more valuable intrinsically, deserve to be spared, even against the demands of military exigency, even (or especially) amid the ravages of war.

As the Midrash makes clear, the Law points up the value of fruit trees, because "man's living comes from the tree"—but Rabbi Ishmael goes further. He says: "Hence we learn that God's mercy extends even to the fruits. For if Scripture cautions you concerning the tree, which merely grows the fruit, how much more so to the fruit itself" (Sifre to Deut., Piska 203). We might say the reverse: If R. Ishmael can find grounds for asserting that God's mercy extends to the fruit, how much more so may we infer that it applies to the tree, which is the fruit's living source. Thus we read: "Whenever they cut down a fruit tree, the cry rings out from one end of the earth to the other" (Yalkut Reuveni to Genesis). The Midrash, indeed, sets forth the instance of a king who kept a special garden of non–fruit bearing trees, so as to spare any fruit trees that might be threatened in an emergency (Exod. Rabbah 7.4). Note the parallel between this bit of homily and the operative command to assist a struggling beast lest its owner beat it.

With jurisprudential diligence, the halakhah extends its protection from cutting with an ax, as biblically specified, to other means of destruction, including diversion of a water channel (Maimonides, MT XIV Laws of Kings and Wars 6.8, Sanhedrin 19.4). And the ethos represented in the laws sparing fruit trees in siege warfare reaches out from the military to the civil sphere, allowing fuller generalization of the biblical theme: the precedence of stewardship over ownership as the model of the human relationship to nature.

Like the canon itself, we start from God's placement of Adam in the Garden of Eden, "to work it and tend it (*le'ovdah u-le-shomrah*)" (Gen. 2:15), or, translating less literally, "to dress it and keep it" (Old JPS), "to till it and tend it" (New JPS). However we render the simple and transparent Hebrew words, the point is clear that Adam was not the owner but the caretaker. *A fortiori* was this so when Adam and Eve went out into the world of the human condition as we know it, which was no Eden and no garden, where Adam had to learn to till the ground that was "cursed" to him, to grow his livelihood from soil that seemed, in irony and spite, to yield only thorns and thistles (Gen. 3:17–18). Even now, the model was one of caring. Only the hardship was new.

Taking God as the paradigm of human responsibility, the Midrash makes God himself the first agriculturalist: "The Holy One, blessed be He, from the very beginning of the creation of the world was, before all else, occupied with planting, as it is said: 'And the Lord God planted a garden at the outset (*mi-qedem*) in Eden' (Gen. 2:8)." The Midrash playfully reads *mi-qedem*, in the East, as though it meant, "at the outset," establishing the primacy of agriculture. It then goes on, pointedly and in earnest, to draw the moral: "So do you also, when you enter into the land: Occupy yourself first with nought else but planting, as it is written: 'And when ye come into the land, ye shall plant' (Lev. 19:23)" (Lev. Rabbah 25.3). Leviticus goes on to reserve fruits of the fourth year for dedication to God (Lev. 19:24), but the homilist's concern is with the primacy of planting, and the reason is the role it assigns to man, as a participant at God's table, but also as a tenant who cares for God's land and tends His crops.

Thus, the transition is easily made from the universal human condition to the role of Israel in particular. God instructs Isaac, even in time of famine: "Go not down into Egypt. Dwell in the land" (Gen. 26:2). The Midrash glosses: "Dwell, that is, cultivate the land. Be a sower and a planter" (Gen. Rabbah 64.3). The homilist wants to assign intrinsic, rather than merely economic, value to this activity. Tenure in the land is a value for Israel, and tenure means cultivation. The rhetoric is pressed in the well-known story of Hadrian's observing an ancient man planting a fig tree whose fruits he will never enjoy (Lev. Rabbah 25.5; Tanhuma, Kedoshim 8). It is pointed up still further in the rabbinic admonition: "If you have a plant in your hand and they tell you that the Messiah is coming, first plant it and then go and welcome the Messiah" (Avot de-R. Nathan 2.31). We can say that these stories celebrate and valorize ordinary life and human hope for the future, since the old man plants for his offspring, as his ancestors planted for him, and since the worldly task of planting is given precedence even to the welcoming of the Messiah. But the fact remains that both the hope and the content of a fulfilling life are expressed in terms of planting. The land exists not to be laid waste but to be used, and planting is emblematic of the intrinsic worth as well as the instrumental worth of the simple tasks of everyday life by which human beings integrate themselves in nature and find themselves—make themselves—at home there.

Is the concern only with use and habitation? Thematizing the values of the Mosaic Torah, the Talmud does not confine its interest to fruit trees or to wartime exigencies but pronounces broadly: "Those who cut down beautiful trees will never see a sign of blessing" (B. Pesahim 50b). Rashi cautiously glosses this in terms of cutting down fruit trees for their wood. But the Talmud itself corrects his caution: "For four reasons are the lights of heaven eclipsed . . . and because of people who cut down good trees" (B. Sukkah 29a). This time, Rashi glosses more in keeping with the biblical thematic: even if the trees cut down are one's own property, there is a wrong in destroying them, "because those who do so are acting destructively and seem to be spurning God's blessing." The blessing spreads beyond utility to mankind, opening up to a notion that even vegetation has deserts. Hence the mishnaic laws regulating trees that impinge on wells hinge not simply on economic value but on precedence: if the tree was there before the well, or if there is doubt as to which was present first, the tree takes precedence (Mishnah Bava Batra 2.11; Y. Bava Batra 7a). Which is to say, the tree has deserts; and, indeed, its deserts can take precedence to human economic interests.

Accordingly, we find the Talmud moving beyond the biblical issue of fruit trees in wartime, to speak of any wanton destruction of plants. It takes green shoots as its exemplar of what need not, and so *should not* be destroyed. The talmudic text reads that "One who cuts off his own shoots, even though he has no right, is exempt from punishment" (B. Bava Kamma). But the force of the statement, made clear by the stress on the fact that the shoots are one's own, is that, even though such destructive actions are exempt from punishment, they are wrong: Even though the cutter is exempt, he has no right.

The theme is biblically grounded in the commandment that one is not to plant one's field with alternating rows of incompatible crops (Deut. 22:9). Lest we doubt that the concern here is for the vitality of the crops, the text itself confirms it, by warning that those who do so place both of their two crops at risk.[11] This issue of the crops' vitality itself has both a pragmatic, utilitarian side and a side that regards the intrinsic worth of the plantings and their flourishing. But in the laws of *shemitah* (Lev. 25:1–7), intrinsic desert comes clearly to the fore. For the fallow, seventh year is called a sabbatical (*shabbaton*) "for the land." The land itself is *entitled* to a rest.

There are still utilities involved: the produce of the land is to be left for the poor, the land itself will regain its fertility if fallow years are kept to preserve it from exhaustion. But alongside these stand the deserts imputed to the land itself, expressed, once again, in terms of virtual subjecthood, when the Torah warns, with bitter irony, that the land will be repaid for the Sabbaths it may be scanted (Lev. 26:34; cf. 2 Chron. 36:21).

"His Mercies Are on All His Works"

Fruit trees, for the rabbis, are a paradigm case of God's blessings, and thus of the act of creation, much as animals are. That, perhaps, is why fruit trees are numbered talmudically among the amenities that must grace a town that would in turn be graced by the presence of a scholar (B. Sanhedrin 17b). Here, fruit trees play a role similar to the one that Aristotle was prone to ascribe to the agora, the palaestra, theater, temples, and other public places: they help to humanize the conditions of human life. But the reason, I have suggested, is not just the pleasantness of the fruit. Rather, it seems to lie in the discovery of a palpable and biblically endorsed instance of the bounty of creation. That bounty surely does benefit humanity and is even said rabbinically to be provided for our sake. Yet the human share in God's bounty does not exhaust its blessings. Animals and even trees and other plants receive that bounty too. And they too have deserts. Part of what the scholar seems to need to ponder is how and why this can be so. The answer, expressed thematically throughout the Law, is that if nature does benefit humanity, it does not exist exclusively for that benefit; nor does humanity exist only to reap the benefits that nature affords. Rather, all creatures exist for their own sake, and man exists, in part, to tend and care for nature.

The ideal is a garden—nature tended and cared for. Man in general and Israel in particular are to be planters. They are to put down roots, to settle and dwell in the land that God provides and not to exhaust or overtax it. They may eat not only of its fruits but of the flesh that those fruits nourish, and they may do so with a clear conscience. But, just as they may not pollute or corrupt or despoil the land or spurn its bounties, so they may not cause, or even allow needless suffering to animals. These basic principles are constitutive in the good life, and they are building blocks for the emergence of character, including the character of those who would wield authority.

The Midrash tells us (Gen. Rabbah 33.3; B. Bava Metzi'a 85a) of R. Judah the Prince, the author of the Mishnah, that while studying the Law, he chanced to hear a calf that cried out on its way to market. "What can I do?" he said, "It was for this that you were created." With an irony characteristic of midrashic narrative—and perhaps of life in some of its phases—R. Judah suffered a toothache for thirteen years, "as a punishment for his heartlessness." According to the Midrash, he learned his lesson, reproving his daughter when she was about to kill some creeping creature that was running across her path.

The point the Midrash draws is not that one should never kill a calf; still less that one should never swat a fly or crush a scorpion—quite the contrary. The themes the Torah teaches run broader and deeper than concern for humankind in ourselves and others. They include regard for the sufferings of living creatures. They include the deserts of trees and other plants. They include even the intrinsic worth of the environment that houses living beings but does not exist solely for their sake. As Judah the Prince put it, in the verse he cited to instruct his daughter but that summed up what his thirteen-year ordeal had taught him about God and nature and the relevance of compassion: "His mercies are on all His works" (Ps. 145:9).

Notes

1. See Lenn E. Goodman, *On Justice: An Essay in Jewish Philosophy* (New Haven: Yale University Press, 1991), and *God of Abraham* (New York: Oxford University Press, 1996). The theory was first elaborated in my Baumgardt Lectures of 1979, published as *Monotheism: A Philosophic Inquiry into the Foundations of Natural Theology and Ethics* (Totowa, N.J.: Allanheld Osmun, 1981).

2. Operatively, the sniper in the tower must be treated as the exigencies of his pragmatic role demand, as long as he represents an immediate danger. Once disarmed, he is a full person once again. He now forfeits many of the civil presumptions that society has accorded him in fleshing out the dignity of personhood. For his actions defeat many of those presumptions. But he does not lose all of them. And never does he lose the basic existential rights of personhood: He may not be tortured to reveal the whereabouts of his accomplices. Even while armed, his deserts as a person are not nugatory. Thus, the moral requirement of phased measures: Deadly force may not be brought against him, even as he fires, if lesser measures would suffice to halt the danger he presents.

3. See Jude Dougherty, review of *On Justice*, by L. E. Goodman, *Review of Metaphysics* 46 (1993): 614–15.

4. The anthropic principle, popular among speculative cosmologists in recent years, is a special case of the anthropocentrism Maimonides criticizes here, an intellectualist version that presses all values in the direction of service to science. The principle is subject to a similar line of attack to the one that Maimonides raises against anthropocentrism in general: If God created the universe so as to make it intelligible to us (or if we "create" it in the fashion that will make it intelligible), then we must ask why so much that is extraneous to that purpose is included—and why there remains so much that is unintelligible.

5. See, e.g., Porphyry, *De Abstinentia*, 3.20; Ikhwan al-Safa', *The Case of the Animals vs. Man before the King of the Jinn*, trans. L. E. Goodman (New York: Twayne, 1978; reissued, Los Angeles: Gee Tee Bee, 1984).

6. Thus, he plays on their views about omnipotence and voluntarism to generate the inference that God created things that would be otiose on their assumptions; see *Guide of the Perplexed*, 3.17.3, 25.

7. Cf. Maimonides, *Guide of the Perplexed*, 3.26, ed. Munk 3.58b: "As necessity occasions the eating of animals, the commandment was intended to bring about the easiest death in an easy manner."

8. The position is critiqued in John Passmore, *Man's Responsibility for Nature: Ecological Problems and Western Traditions* (London: Duckworth, 1974), 3–40.

9. See Ikhwan al-Safa', *Animals vs. Man*, trans. Goodman, 12, 15–17, 20, 22, 29.

10. Cf. the imputation of hope to a tree in Job 14:7, again a projection of the nisus of growth and life as a claim of virtual subjecthood.

11. The particle *pen* clearly introduces a warning here, not the threat of a penalty. Cf. Gen. 3:3, 19:19, 26:7, 31:31; Exod. 23:29; Lev. 10:7; Deut. 6:15, 8:11, 19:6, 20:5–7, etc.

What Are the Ethical Implications of Jewish Theological Conceptions of the Natural World?

MOSHE SOKOL

I

My aim in this paper is programmatic and methodological. In studying the (slowly) growing literature on environmental issues in the Jewish tradition, I found myself asking certain questions about the objectives of many of the papers I read, as well as about the methods used by the authors to achieve their objectives. I would like to raise some of these questions, and, by way of conclusion, make some suggestions for furthering inquiry in this crucial area.

Perhaps the best way to begin is to try to clarify a core tension many perceive to exist within the Jewish tradition, between Judaism and nature. In a by now classic essay (cited mostly for the purposes of quasi-apologetic refutation), Steven Schwarzschild puts this in characteristically pungent terms: "The main line of Jewish philosophy (in the exilic age) has paradigmatically defined Jewishness as alienation from and confrontation with nature."[1] Schwarzschild's argument is (again, characteristically) both rich and elusive, but mostly reduces to what he regards as the theologically normative Jewish conception of a transcendent God, which he believes stands in tension with nature. The main reason for this tension derives from a conception of nature as amoral, coupled with the conviction that Judaism is centrally concerned with imposing a moral order upon nature. This places Judaism in opposition to nature.

Michael Wyschogrod, while far more careful in many ways in his formulation of the tension than Schwarzschild, likewise writes that "the conflict between history and nature is fundamental to the development of Judaism."[2] For Wyschogrod, this conflict originates in the intense biblical polemic against pagan nature religions and extends through the moral perils of affirming a Nietzschian evolutionary morality. Ultimately, Wyschogrod suggests, the nature/history conflict turns on the question of whether the world was created by God.

Placing to one side for the moment the merits of their respective positions, I wish to argue that this putative opposition between Judaism and nature, at least as here formulated, is to my mind incoherent. How can Judaism, or any religious tradition, be in "conflict" with (Wyschogrod's phrase) or in "confrontation" with (Schwarzschild) nature? What, after all, do we mean by the term "nature"? Do we mean the objects and processes which constitute the natural world, that is, trees and grass and their growth, rivers and the speed with which they flow, dogs and people (for they too are objects in the natural world) and their growth, birds and the gravity they overcome while flying, and so on? If this is what we mean, then I fail to understand how Judaism can be in conflict with nature. Does it make sense to say that Judaism disapproves of trees or grass, or the processes which account for their growth and decline? No more than it makes sense to say that Judaism is opposed to the Pythagorean theorem, or to the physical relation captured in the formula $f = ma$. Trees, and all constituents and processes of the natural world, are just there, irrespective of religious beliefs, and to me it makes no sense at all to be in conflict with them. We might try to *control* these objects or processes for our own purposes, by curing disease to prolong life or tilling the soil to grow wheat. But that is not the same as "confronting," or being "in conflict" with them. For the terms "confrontation" or "conflict" suggest a moral or ideological or ideational relationship, as if there were a disagreement or clash of values between the farmer and the soil he tills. But surely that is absent from the farmer and his soil, except in a metaphoric sense, in which the farmer's labors are a kind of "battle" against the unyielding soil. This is not a battle of values or ideas, but a battle of (metaphoric) "will," as if the soil has a will of its own which runs contrary to the will of the laboring farmer.

If there is any lingering sense at all to the idea of a valuational conflict between the soil and the farmer, I think it is borrowed from, and parasitic upon, another usage which does make sense. There is no reason why we can't coherently discuss a possible opposition or tension between Judaism and certain *ways of thinking about* objects or processes in the natural world. For example, many ancient pagans believed that objects in the natural world are sacred and their processes are deities. It surely makes sense to say that biblical religion opposed these conceptions of the natural world. It likewise makes sense to say that Judaism opposes a conception of nature according to which trees are more valuable than God, or than human beings. But it is to these *conceptions* of nature which biblical religion or Judaism objected, and not to nature's *constituents*.

This point leads me to another. Upon further reflection, can one really sustain this very distinction between the constituents of nature and conceptions of nature? For how I apprehend a tree depends upon my conception of the natural world. If I am a romantic, I will apprehend a tree one way; if I am a nineteenth-century Hasidic rabbi ecstatic in the forest, I will apprehend the same tree differently; and if I am a twentieth-century industrialist, I will apprehend it yet another way. Surely there are trees out there, but, as Kant argued long ago, we have no access to them unmediated by our mental structures. It is now widely accepted that our culture, too, mediates between reality and ourselves, and that there really is no culture-independent way of knowing a tree. If this is true for such relatively simple objects as trees, what then should we say of "nature"? To the extent that "nature" is a noun which either denotes or connotes anything other than the aggregate of all constituents of the natural world—which it seems to do—then it is an abstraction. As such its sense is even more dependent upon culture than objects like trees. There simply is no such thing as nature as a kind of *Ding an Sich*. Human beings experience what they do of the world, and out of that experience they construct the category of nature, and indeed have varyingly constructed that category over different periods in history, among different classes of people with different conceptions of the world, and in different geographic locations.[3] The content of discourse about the natural world is itself not "natural," but is rather an artifact of human intervention and culture. This implies that there simply is no "nature" out there to which Judaism can be opposed even if it so desired. Judaism's is one set of possible constructions of nature out of many, and if Judaism is in conflict, it is in conflict with these alternative constructions of nature.

I think we can conclude from this line of argument that Judaism neither dislikes trees nor flowers themselves, nor does it stand in opposition to "nature" as such. To speak simplistically of a "conflict" between Judaism and nature is thus misconceived. Indeed, it seems to me that the popularity of this way of thinking about the relationship between Judaism and nature is rooted more in the sociology of the Jews than in the beliefs they hold. For large periods of their history, Jews were urban creatures. People who live in cities are by the nature of things not always at home in the world of nature. Thus, there arose a kind of cultural alienation from the natural world which in the mind of some came to be perceived not as a relatively recent, socially conditioned sensibility, but as something deeper and more valuational or ideational. It is to this probably unconscious and uncritical transition from sociology to theology which I object.

The real theological questions which should engage us, I believe, are: 1) What are Jewish *constructions* of nature and how do they relate to others? 2) What, if any, are the implications of these varying constructions of nature for developing a useful environmental ethic? It is to this latter question that I wish to devote the remainder of my essay.

II

Two central theological issues shape current Jewish discussions of environmental issues. First, there is the immanentist/transcendentist polarity and, second, the anthropocentric/theocentric/biocentric polarity. While I shall briefly explain, and explore, each separately, it should be noted at the outset that the general structure of the discussions of these polarities runs as follows: "If you take position X on question Y of Jewish theology, then you are well situated to take position Z on environmental ethics." I wish to argue in what follows that the move from X to Z is made in far too facile a fashion. In general, I shall suggest that the relationship between theology and any branch of normative or applied ethics, not only environmental ethics, but biomedical ethics, business ethics, and so on, is more complicated than first meets the eye.

One of the earliest essays on Jewish enviromentalism, Norman Lamm's "Ecology in Jewish Law and Theology," published in 1971,[4] focused attention on the implications of the immanentist/transcendentist controversy in Jewish theology for environmental issues, a perspective which continues to centrally occupy those who write on the subject.[5] Let us call those who apply this controversy to environmental issues the "Where-Is-God?" theologians and briefly trace their position. Ancient pagans had more or less believed that nature and its forces were living powers which required propitiation by humans to ensure the latter's beneficent treatment. While biblical religion subsequently rejected this way of thinking about nature, the question which has long preoccupied religious thinkers is: Rejection in favor of what? The biblical materials themselves are not as clear about the question as one might wish, and the rabbinic sources are multidimensional and nonsystematic. The first systematic, philosophical, and widely available reflections on Judaism (with the major exception of Philo) appeared in the medieval world. Most of the great medieval Jewish (and Christian) philosophers took the view that God was in some sense wholly other than the natural world, a position which came to be known as transcendentalism, or, better, transcendentism. In part under the influence of these philosophers, this conception came to be taken by post-Enlightenment scholars of Judaism as the "orthodox" (lowercase "o") one, although it required downplaying, or figuratively interpreting, certain biblical and especially rabbinic texts. Jewish mysticism, on the other hand, provided a framework for conceiving a more intimate link between God and the natural world. This is because of kabbalah's hierarchical conception of God, according to which only the highest manifestation of God—the *ein sof*—is wholly other and unknowable. The existence of "lower" manifestations of God, however, makes a "closer" link between God and nature possible. This "closer link" has been variously described as pantheistic, panentheistic, or immanentist, depending upon the mystical figure studied and the scholar engaged in the study. Hasidic mysticism is often held to be more frequently immanentist than earlier sources, and, indeed, one prominent scholar argues that immanentism is one of Hasidism's characteristic doctrines.[6]

Surely a careful analysis of each of these terms, and the extent to which each is affirmed by which sources, is a crucial undertaking, but one which need not detain us here. The overall thesis of those who draw environmental conclusions from this discussion, the "Where-Is-God?" theologians, is straightforward enough. The view that God is in some sense immanent in the natural world gives rise to an ethic which shows great reverence and awe toward the natural world, through which God's sacred presence is manifest and can be experienced. In Lamm's widely influential formulation, "For Hasidism, which is immanentistic and panentheistic, man has a kinship with other created beings, a symbiotic relationship with nature, and hence should maintain a sense of respect, if not reverence, for the natural world which is infused with the presence of God."[7]

The transcendentist view, by contrast, is taken to evacuate the natural world of God's presence. Contemporary environmental literature is rife with condemnations of this theological position, attributing the exploitation of the environment to its widely influential desacralization of nature. Lamm identifies Hasidism's opponents, the "Mitnagdim" as classic Jewish proponents of the transcendentist view which, in Lamm's characterization, leaves nature "completely profane."[8] For our purposes in this essay, we can put aside the question of whether this characterization is fair, and whether the Mitnagdim should be singled out as prime expositors of the transcendentist position in Jewish thought. The "Where-Is-God?" theologian proceeds to draw certain environmental conclusions from the transcendentist thesis. In Lamm's words:

> The Mitnagdic view, emphasizing divine transcendence, leaves no place for such feelings [viz., respect and reverence for the natural world—see quotation cited above], and conceives the Man-Nature relation as completely one of subject-to-object, thus allowing for the exploitation of nature by science and technology and—were it not for halakhic restraints which issue from revelation, and not from theology—the ecological abuse of the natural world as well.[9]

Let us assume, for argument's sake, that halakhah does not issue from theology but from revelation. Does this passage then mean that Jewish law which governs the environment is a *gezerat ha-katuv*, a divine decree lacking any rationale? It seems altogether likely that Jewish laws governing the environment do have some explanation—and emerge from, as well as help create—a comprehensible worldview, even for the transcendentist. If so, why couldn't that worldview, one which the transcendentist himself would buy into, justify treating the environment with great respect? Indeed, I can imagine various theological strategies available even to the transcendentist which would yield the same results regarding the natural world which the "Where-Is-God?" theologian attributes to the immanentist. Perhaps the most obvious strategy is to assert that the natural world deserves respect and awe because it was created by God, who Himself is so awesome as to transcend the very world He created by an act of His will.

Maimonides is in many ways the philosophical father of transcendentism within the Jewish tradition. Throughout his voluminous works, Maimonides argues again and again that God is metaphysically other in the most fundamental ways from all other existents. Indeed, for Maimonides, God's metaphysical otherness is so radical that it yields stark epistemological consequences as well: human beings can in principle never fully know God's essence or even assert anything directly of it.[10] Now the "Where-Is-God?" theologian should be bound to conclude from Maimonides' transcendentism that he would not endorse awe and respect for the natural world. In point ot fact, however, just the reverse is true. Maimonides maintains that contemplating the wonder of the created world leads to love and awe of God:

> And what is the means to achieve love and fear of God? When a person contemplates God's actions and His great and wondrous creations, and apprehends through them God's infinite and invaluable wisdom, immediately he loves, praises and exalts God, and desires with a great desire to know His great name.[11]

This passage suggests that the proper attitude toward the "wondrous" natural world is one of contemplative awe, as a vehicle to know and love God, its creator.

This view of the natural world is reinforced by another position Maimonides takes, in the *Guide of the Perplexed*. He argues there against a view widely held among theists, that everything was created for the purpose of human beings:

> It should not be believed that all the beings exist for the sake of the existence of man. On the contrary, all other beings too have been intended for their own sakes and not for the sake of something else. . . . In respect to every being He intended that being itself. . . .[12]

Following each day of creation in Genesis, God calls everything that He had made "good." Maimonides interprets this to mean that each created kind conformed well to its *own* purpose, and not the purposes of some other kind. This view follows from Maimonides' thesis that creation is an act of God's will, which is beyond human reason:

> Thus we are obliged to believe that all that exists was intended by Him, may He be exalted, according to His volition. And we shall seek for it no cause or other final end whatever. Just as we do not seek for the final end of His existence, may He be exalted, so do we not seek for the final end of His volition. . . .[13]

A word of caution: the significance of this perspective should not be overstated, since in the very same chapter Maimonides says that God "stamped" into human nature the role of ruling over the fish of the sea, and that "plants were brought into existence only for the sake of animals, for those of necessity must be nourished."[14] Indeed, this very tension indicates that the chapter is a difficult one, and fully explicating it would involve us in a complex discussion of different levels and kinds of final ends as well as of the impenetrable nature of God's will, an undertaking far beyond the scope of this essay. Nevertheless, Maimonides does provide us with a theological perspective on the natural world which promotes reverence and respect, since all species "exist for their own sake" and were all intended by God's own will.

What I have tried to demonstrate thus far is that the most influential exponent of transcendentism in the Jewish philosophical tradition advocates an attitude toward the natural environment which is no less reverential than the attitude "Where-Is-God?" theologians maintain is the exclusive province of the immanentist. Maimonides represents a counterexample to the "Where-Is-God?" claim which, I would argue, illuminates a fundamental flaw in their whole line of reasoning: reverence and awe for the natural world need not flow only from immanentist considerations.

Consider now the other half of the "Where-Is-God?" claim, that immanentism leads to an attitude of reverence and awe for the natural world. But what does that purported reverence or awe amount to? Hasidism does not advocate vegetarianism, and to my knowledge none of the great Hasidic theoreticians of immanentism were vegetarians. That means that eating part of a cow is consistent with treating it with reverence and awe. I must confess that I'm not sure what "reverance and awe" toward something really amounts to if eating it isn't precluded. Are Hasidim any "greener" than non-Hasidim? Indeed, just calling Hasidism "green" seems odd, if not slightly comical. In short, there seems to be something amiss with this whole way of thinking.

Both immanentists and transcendentists believe that God created the world for His own purposes, and those purposes, according to virtually all major schools of thought, envision a hierarchy of being, according to which some forms of being have greater potential for godliness than others. Since virtually all schools of Judaism hold that plants and animals have less potential for godliness than humans, human well-being is valued above the well-being of plants or animals. This difference between the value of humans and animals is so great that, historically, immanentists and transcendentists alike have agreed almost universally that animals can be killed to satisfy human interests, even such interests as making leather shoes.

What then becomes of the "reverence and awe" to be felt for the natural world? I think that these emotions, and emotion-based attitudes, do have real significance, and that they do indeed flow from affirming immanentism, and certain versions of transcendentism, too. Nevertheless, there is a crucial difference between emotions and emotional attitudes, on the one hand, and moral principles, on the other.[15] It may be morally correct for me to punish my child for swiping the cookies even if I love her and my heart is not in it. Emotions, and emotion-based attitudes, are defeasible by normative rules. There is a certain looseness, a vagueness or abstraction, to feelings of awe and respect which places them a step removed from the world of concrete moral ajudication. When I make a decision about whether I should eat this salad (for lettuce is no less part of the natural world than cows), I may remember my general feelings of awe toward the natural world, and recall that this lettuce was once part of the natural world. But I recall too that God created human beings with a capacity to realize a distinctive form of holiness. In order for human beings to achieve that end they must eat, and God created lettuce (at least in part) so that it can be eaten by human beings. Although I think that I myself maintain at least some of this respect for the natural world, I don't feel myself violating that respect one iota when I eat my salad even while picnicking at the top of a mountain in awe of a particularly sublime sunset. Perhaps this is a failure on my part, but I don't think so. Rather, I think it is a reflection of the distance between general feelings of awe or reverence for the natural world as a whole, on the one hand, and concrete moral decisions emerging from entrenched moral or religious principles, on the other. I don't maintain that all morally sensitive environmentalists feel as I do, but I would venture to suggest that the greatest majority of Jewish immanentist and transcendentists do, and they are the ones who concern us here.

Perhaps another example will make this point even sharper. Even the most sensitive environmentalist is unlikely to insist that the pneumonia which is suffocating her should not be treated by antibiotics. But of course, bacteria are causing the infection, and bacteria are no less a part of the natural world than human beings. Thus, reverence and awe for the natural world do not preclude killing at least some of its constituents for good reason, according to even the most sensitive of environmentalists. The real question is where to draw the line, and general feelings of reverence and awe are less helpful than one might suppose in drawing the line in the real world of environmental policy.

What then leads to the misapplication of these perfectly legitimate, indeed highly important, feelings of reverence and awe toward the natural world implicit in classical theism? I suspect that lurking behind their misuse, at least in part, is what logicians call the "Fallacy of Division." What one asserts of the whole need not apply to individual parts of the whole. For example, you may assert that IBM is an efficient company, but it doesn't follow from your claim that each individual employee of IBM is efficient. Now, the conviction that God created the natural world and cares for it should, I believe, lead to a deep feeling of respect for the natural world. But this feeling of respect need not apply—at least in equal measure—to each individual *constituent* of the natural world. Must I revere or feel in awe of cow dung? Must I feel the same measure of reverence and awe for the snail darter as for the the sun or the Amazon? And if the glisten of the sun through a field of moist spider webs astonishes me on a brisk walk in the morning, and evokes in me an awe for God and his creation, does this mean that I must revere the black widow crawling up my leg? The reverance and awe that the theist justly feels for the natural world as a whole need not transfer to each of its parts. More precisely, the extent to which it transfers, and the practical implications of that transfer, depend upon many factors.

I shall return to this theme once again in the concluding section of this essay to sharpen this discussion and draw some general methodological conclusions. But before doing so, it would be helpful to turn our attention to that other major polarity which engages Jewish theologians of the environment: anthropocentrism, biocentrism, and theocentrism.

III

While theologians who speak of the relevance of Judaism's theocentrism to environmental issues are on far safer ground than the "Where-Is-God?" theologians, several cautionary remarks are nevertheless in order. First, however, we should define our terms. The environmental anthropocentrist, in the words of Paul Taylor, maintains that:

> . . . it is to humans, and only to humans, that all duties are ultimately owed. We may have responsiblities *with regard to* the natural ecosystems, and biotic communities of our planet, but these responsibilities are in every case based on the contingent fact that our treatment of these ecosystems and communities of life can further the realization of human values and/or human rights.[16]

Western monotheistic religions in their classical form could never affirm this view, since they maintain that human beings owe obligations not only to other human beings, but to God as well. The alternative to anthropocentrism which Taylor develops in his influential essay—a view paralleled by other environmental thhinkers, and carried even further by the deep ecologists—is environmental biocentrism, which holds that:

> . . . we have moral obligations that are owed to wild plants and animals themselves as members of the Earth's biotic community. We are morally bound (other things being equal) to protect or promote their good for *their* sake. . . . Such obligations are due those living things out of recognition of their inherent worth. They are entirely additional to and independent of the obligations we owe to our fellow humans.[17]

The question which plagues the environmental biocentrist is *why* plants and trees should be owed obligations. Human beings are usually thought to possess certain distinctive qualities by virtue of which moral obligations are owed them. But what accounts for the existence of obligations to plants and trees? Taylor's answer to this question is instructive. He argues that it emerges from what he calls a "biocentric outlook on nature" according to which humans are members of the earth's ecosystem on terms no different than any other member of the ecosystem; that all members of the ecosystem are interdependent; and that each individual organism is conceived as a "teleological center of life," meaning that the world can be looked at from the perspective of

its own life. The conjunction of these three theses yields a fourth, crucial one: ". . . the claim that humans by their very nature are superior
to other species is a groundless claim and in the light of elements (1),
(2), and (3) above must be rejected as nothing more than an irrational
bias in our own favor."[18]

There is much to be said about the Taylor position, but I shall confine my remarks to the concerns of this essay. It should first be noted
that there is an important gap between a particular ethic, *environmental biocentrism*, and the *biocentric outlook on nature*, a perspective on
nature which Taylor advances to justify it. The former maintains that
obligations are owed to plants and animals independent of their human utility. The second, in seeking to justify the existence of this obligation, denies that humans have any greater worth or merit than
plants or animals. Now one prima facie problem with the biocentric
outlook is that it can lead to according plants and animals an absolute
value at the expense of human life and basic well-being. (Whether or
not this can be solved or, indeed, whether or not it is even a *problem*,
is worthy of separate analysis.) But can the basic claim of environmental biocentrism, that plants and animals are owed obligations independent of their human utility, be justified on less problematic
grounds? One candidate for this task, for the theist, is what has been
called an *environmental theocentrism*. According to this doctrine,
writes Eric Katz, "God Himself, not human life or welfare, is the
source of all religious and moral obligation. . . . Humanity cannot have
unrestricted dominion over the natural world because the world belongs to God. . . ."[19] God can simply mandate obligations owed by
humans to plants and animals, the basic biocentric claim, without resorting to the problematic "biocentric outlook," or to any absolutist
sacralization of nature.

So far so good. But the problem here is that the theocentric environmental theologian typically goes further than I have in making out
the theocentric case, and, I might add, for very good reason. Thus
Katz, later in the essay from which I quoted above, writes:

> On a practical level, the theocentrism of Judaism . . . is functionally
> equivalent to a nonanthropocentric doctrine of the intrinsic value of
> nature without endorsing the sacredness of natural entities themselves.
> Natural objects are valued, and cannot be destroyed, because they be-

long to God. They are sacred, not in themselves, but because of God's creative process.[20]

Katz maintains that environmental theocentrism is the "functional equivalent" of nonanthropocentric views of nature, and that natural objects, according to Judaism, cannot be destroyed. Katz is referring to the Jewish prohibition against wanton destruction, *bal tashhit*. But, as Katz himself points out elsewhere in his essay, the laws of *bal tashhit* prohibit only wanton destruction, not destruction for economic gain, and Jewish legal standards for "wanton destruction" probably permit far more than the typical biocentrist is willing to countenance. Underlying this point is another, deeper one. Theocentrism may indeed provide a basis for holding that humans owe obligations to plants and animals for nonprudential reasons. However, theocentrism does not in itself shed much light on the *scope* of those obligations. And the question of scope is the critical one in constructing a useful environmental ethic. It is perfectly plausible, from a purely theocentric perspective, that God, who owns the world and establishes human obligations to preserve and protect it, would also establish the human obligation to exploit the natural world for reasons of justice. Environmental literature of the theological and nontheological sort is rife with explorations of the tension between ecology and justice. If the poor will benefit from an industry which pollutes the local river, and if that pollution is not so severe as to endanger human health, then considerations of justice might require that pollution controls not endanger the financial well-being of the industry. Now, I am *not* arguing that this is in fact, on balance, the morally correct position. What I am arguing is that theocentrism does not *in itself* yield an environmental ethic which is "functionally equivalent" to a biocentric ethic. Theocentrism in virtually all, or all, forms of Judaism admits of a hierarchy among creatures, and that very hierarchy can under certain construals allow for positions on environmental issues which would be problematic at the very least for many environmentalists, even moderate ones. Theocentrism must be supplemented by other norms or theological considerations to yield that "functional equivalency."

So far I have focused on the implications of justice and the hierarchy of being in demonstrating the limits of environmental theocentrism. There is another perspective as well, which further illuminates the limitations of theocentrism as a sufficient basis for constructing an environmental ethic. Consider the following theological model: God is the perfectly creative, majestic Being. Humankind was created in God's image. This means that humankind must attempt to be creative and majestic, like God. How? To quote from one of the twentieth-century's most important Jewish theologians, Rabbi Joseph B. Solo-veitchik, "through his majestic posture vis-à-vis his environment."[21] R. Soloveitchik, in his highly influential essay "Lonely Man of Faith," articulates a bipartite conception of human nature, according to which human beings must take a dialectical stance toward God and the world. The first stance, which is that of (what R. Soloveitchik calls) Adam I, after the first creation story in Genesis, is "aggressive, bold, victory-minded." Adam I is told "to have dominion over the works of Thy [God's] hands," and is bidden to "harness and dominate the el-emental natural forces and to put them at his disposal."[22] It should be added that for R. Soloveitchik, Adam I is a normative form of life. To be fully "Adamic," and thereby Godly, humans must live out the man-date of Adam I.

Certainly, the Adam I mode of being stands in dialectical tension with the Adam II mode of being, which submits itself, in a sacrificial act of faith, to God and His will. Certainly, too, we have no evidence that R. Soloveitchik is advocating an ethic which *exploits* the natural world. That said, we nevertheless do have a theological model, flow-ing from a well-entrenched theocentrism, which provides a ringing endorsement of technological aggressiveness in manipulating the natural world. In the words of Gerald Blidstein, "R. Soloveitchik enthusiatically endows Western scientific technology with the fullest acknowledgment Judaism could offer."[23] There is very little doubt that R. Soloveitchik's thinking was influenced by the prevailing ethos of the post-Sputnik era, but that is besides the point I wish to make, which is that *theocentrism itself* can yield an ethic which is very far indeed from the ethic of the biocentrist, and indeed the ethic of even many a moderate environmentalist.

I have cited R. Soloveitchik's theological views not only because they themselves provide a counterexample to environmental theo-centrism, but more importantly because they illustrate a general flaw in the whole line of reasoning the environmental theocentrist advocates. Theocentrism alone does not tell us enough about what the deity *wills*, and what the deity wills—for the theocentrist—must be the crucial determinant for constructing an environmental ethic.

IV

Our examination of the two central nodes of Jewish theological discourse about the environment has exposed what I take to be a common flaw: both move too unself-critically from theology to ethics. There simply is no algorithm which links the two. If one thinks of this from the perspective of logic, then one might say that between theological premises, at least of the sort here discussed, and ethical conclusions there are unacknowledged missing premises. But why is this so? What explains the gap here exposed?

Environmental ethics as a discipline, at least as it is usually understood, must achieve two ends. First, it must articulate and justify basic moral laws, *grundnorms*, which govern treatment of the natural world. Second, it must articulate and justify a series of lower-order laws, derivable from the *grundnorms*, which provide moral decision procedures for real-life environmental issues, which often involve conflicts among different obligations, say, between those to plants and animals, on the one hand, and those to humans, on the other. In this respect environmental ethics is no different from any field in applied ethics, such as biomedical ethics or business ethics. Now, theology of the "Where-Is-God?" or theocentric sort operates at a level which is *even prior to* the *grundnorms* themselves. These theological models are not normative but descriptive. That is, they describe a state of affairs, for example, that God is immanent in the world, or that God owns the world and establishes human obligations. But they don't in themselves prescribe any behavior, unlike the Kantian categorical imperative, for example, which is, as its name reveals, an *imperative,* and does indeed function as a *grundnorm*. And as ethicists ever since Hume have pointed out, it is notoriously difficult to derive ought from is, even if that "is" is a description of a state of affairs one of whose components is God.

Now, this is not to say that one can never derive *grundnorms* from theological premises. Suppose, for example, one were to hold the following two premises: 1) God's own treatment of all plants and animals on the earth reflects a maximization of their individual well-being; and 2) humans ought to emulate God. One could make a good case that it would follow from these theological premises that humans ought to maximize the well-being of each plant and animal on Earth. Premise 2, which I would classify as theological, is nonetheless normative, and permits us to derive norms coupled with a premise such as premise 1, which describes some feature of God or His behavior. However, theological positions such as immanentism or theocentrism are very general and abstract and lack normative content, which is ultimately why, as I have argued, they are each consistent with widely divergent norms.

Indeed, the abstraction of immanentism or theocentrism derives from another factor as well. They are not once but twice removed from the concrete moral situation. Environmental ethics as applied ethics must provide moral guidance for complex practical problems such as the preservation of certain species at great economic cost. Even *grundnorms* such as the categorical imperative are too general to do that kind of moral work (even if they can be applied to plants and animals), and they must be supplemented with a series of lower-order principles. Abstract theological principles lacking even a *grundnorm* level of normativity are thus twice removed from the arena of applied environmental ethics.

This observation about the level of specificity required of applied ethics leads to another point. Even if our theological premises did have some normative content there would still be difficulties. Consider an analogy from another field of applied ethics, that relating to medicine. The "sanctity of life" is often trotted out as a principle governing such moral dilemmas as euthanasia. Life is sacred and must always be preserved, so the argument runs, and therefore euthanasia is immoral. But almost everyone, with very few exceptions, maintains that under certain circumstances the sacredness of life does not preclude the taking of it, for example, for self-defense. The question then becomes: under what circumstances may life be taken and under what circumstances may it not be taken? Appealing to a very general principle such as the sacredness of life, then, does not get us as far as we would like. Much the same problem afflicts the use of immanentism or theocentrism as vehicles for constructing an adequate environmental ethic.

V

So far, my aims in this essay have been largely critical ones. I would like to conclude with three programmatic suggestions for future work in this area.

Is there any role for Jewish theology to play in environmental ethics? Well, at one level that depends in part on the theology. Theological premises which have a normative component will obviously fare at least somewhat better than those, such as immanentism and theocentrism, that don't. So one promising avenue of study is to explore the Jewish tradition for precisely such theological premises. I believe that deeper, more sophisticated theological work in this area, which after all is still in its infancy, can overcome the limitations I have outlined in this essay, and it is to be hoped that some of the essays included in this volume will indeed carry this enterprise forward.

One fruitful approach to working up this kind of theology might be to focus on close readings of individual Jewish texts, to get a sense of what their theological underpinnings are, on a microscale, before (or even without) extrapolating to large-scale theological generalizing, always a somewhat hazardous undertaking. Let us call such an approach *textual theology*. Classical texts, with all their subtleties, nuances, tensions, and subversions, carefully and self-consciously chosen for the richness of their environmental/*ethical* implications, can provide methodologically sound and fertile bases for developing a useful Jewish environmental ethic. Indeed, textual theology is likely to yield not one environmental ethic but a plurality of ethical perspectives, reflecting different conceptions of the natural world embedded in different texts. To my mind, this is a desirable result, and is one of the virtues of textual theology.

A second programmatic suggestion turns on an equivocality in the very meaning of the phrase "environmental ethic." Until now I have been using it to refer to the development of a set of well-justified moral laws governing human behavioral interaction with the environment. What obligations do humans owe the natural world, if any? What are the bases of these obligations? And what is the morally correct thing to do when these obligations come into conflict with one another or with other obligations? My argument so far has been that the Jewish theological premises commonly put forth fail to do this particular job adequately.

But that isn't the only job that an environmental ethic can, and even should, do. Indeed, ethical theory prior to the modern era didn't even think in these terms. Prior to the modern era, ethical theory was not about rules for action, but about virtue, about analyzing what constitutes the moral *character*. Aristotle, the most influential ancient moral philosopher, devoted all his moral-theoretic energy to justifying his view of what constitutes the virtuous personality; to analyzing individual virtues, such as continence, humility, and so on, and the virtuous personality as a whole; and to reflection about how to cultivate a virtuous character. The ancient and medieval philosophers believed that guidance for morally correct action flowed not from rules, but from what a person possessing a virtuous character could be expected to do under the circumstances. In recent years "virtue theory," as it is now called, has gained new currency in the philosophical world.

If we adopt virtue ethics as our model, then perhaps we can also think about environmental ethics as an attempt to justify the cultivation, and spell out the contours, of an *"environmentally virtuous"* moral character. Are there specific moral virtues and sensibilities which characterize the individual who shows care and concern for the natural world? What justifies their cultivation? How do they relate to other virtues? What are their implications for engaging the natural world?

My own list of environmental virtues and sensibilities would include a deep sense of humility, not only individually but species-wide; the capacity for gratitude; the capacity to experience awe and sublimity; the virtues of temperance, continence, and respectfulness, among others. Classical Jewish sources contain a vast amount of material on these virtues, and in some instances apply them to human engagement with the natural world. Future scholarship would do well to examine these resources, in order to refine our understanding of these virtues and their application to the natural world, and to develop from them answers to some of the questions enumerated above. This would enable us to draw a portrait of the "environmentally virtuous" personality. One special advantage of this way of thinking is that its impact on humans and human behavior, for those who pay attention, is probably greater than the more traditional way of going about environmental ethics. Most of our day-to-day responses to the world are pretheoretic and emerge from our personality traits and character.

Cultivating virtuous character, as the ancients understood, is a highly effective route to cultivating virtuous behavior.

Judaism and other religious traditions are particularly well situated for this undertaking, more so than nonreligious philosophies, not only because they have so long reflected in this mode, but because they provide a theistic *justification* for developing these virtues in relation to the natural world. As the Psalmist says, "the earth is the Lord's and the fullness thereof" (Psalm 24:1). What better justification can there be for assuming an environmentally virtuous stance toward the natural world? It is here, I believe, that theological reflection about the natural world can provide great ethical benefit. The theological worlds of Abraham Joshua Heschel, Rabbi Avraham I. Kook, Habad mysticism, and Bahya ibn Pakuda's contemplative spirituality—to mention just a few—profoundly deepen, each in its own distinctive way, our thinking about God, ourselves, and the natural world. Each provides a perspective which justifies, as well as promotes, the cultivation of environmental virtues, and each perspective stresses one or another of those virtues, in different ways. My sense, too, is that the different virtues would yield differing ethical sensibilities, with somewhat different results for environmental ethics. Fully exploring these theological worlds, their nuanced implications for developing environmental virtues, and the implications of those virtues for real-world applications, strikes me as a rich and fruitful avenue for future work in Jewish environmental ethics.

Nevertheless, despite the effectiveness and importance of this proposed approach to environmental ethics, taken by itself it is not wholly adequate to the task at hand. In general, one of the problems with a virtue ethic is its lack of specifity. What counts as a proper amount of food for Milo the great athlete, Aristotle noted, would obviously be excessive for a seventy-five-pound child, and ultimately the practically wise person must serve as a role model for the ethical neophyte. Conversely, one of the great strengths of an action-centered ethic is its law-like specificity. Now, I find it very hard to imagine how constructing an environmental virtue ethic can solve complex ecological problems involving, for example, the economic costs of preserving the snail darter. The critical discussion about theology which forms the heart of this essay applies in some measure to an environmental ethic grounded in virtue as well. This observation leads me to my third programmatic suggestion.

Overall, applied Jewish normative ethics is characterized by a strong legal rather than virtue orientation. Discussions of concrete problems in business, biomedical, or legal ethics are typically (although of course not always) found in Judaism's vast legal corpus, which is centrally concerned with moral issues. Indeed, it has recently been argued that in Judaism, where there is a conflict between the norms of virtue and those of action—as in the case of altruistic self-sacrifice—norms of action take precedence over virtue.[24] The historically strong legal orientation of Judaism, and its vast corpus of legal material and case law, positions Judaism for responding in a substantive manner to the complexities of practical environmental ethics with an unusual richness of resources. Time will tell how fruitful this area of research will prove.

But my primary concern in this paper has been the link between theology and environmental ethics. And I think that one way to develop a constructive link is to aim the theoretical arrow not from theology to ethics, as has been the case so far, but (at least at first) from ethics to theology. By that I mean that the theologian would do well to examine what the applied Jewish normative tradition—its body of case law—has to say about environmental issues and, using that as data, attempt to construct a theology which explains or grounds these normative materials. What picture of God, humanity, or the world best accounts for the normative data? How might this picture lead to fresh new thinking and help chart new directions to the challenges posed by evolving threats to the well-being of the planet? The strength of this approach is that its theological reflections are grounded in concrete Jewish normative data, and thereby connect theology to how the Jewish tradition—at least in its legal manifestation—practically responds to the natural world.[25]

These three suggestions are no more than programmatic, but they may be helpful in thinking about how to think about Judaism and the natural world, in the theological mode. It need hardly be added that such an undertaking is of the greatest possible moment.

Notes

1. Steven Schwarzschild, "The Unnatural Jew," *Environmental Ethics* 6 (winter 1984): 349.

2. Michael Wyschogrod, "Judaism and the Sanctification of Nature," *The Melton Journal* (spring 1992): 5–7. Wyschogrod is considerably more careful than Schwarzschild in the way he formulates the tension, and for him the problem may be more linguistic than conceptual.

3. In Neil Evernden, *The Social Creation of Nature* (Baltimore: Johns Hopkins University Press, 1992). Neil Evernden traces the changing constructions of nature from the classical world through the medieval, renaissance, and modern periods. See R. G. Collingwood, *The Idea of Nature* (New York: Oxford University Press, 1960); and C. S. Lewis, *Studies in Words*, 2d ed. (Cambridge: Cambridge University Press, 1967).

4. In Norman Lamm, *Faith and Doubt: Studies in Traditional Jewish Thought* (New York: Ktav Publishing House, 1971), 162–85.

5. For a recent survey of this and other theological discussions on Judaism and the environment, see Eilon Schwartz, "Judaism and Nature: Theological and Moral Issues to Consider While Renegotiating a Jewish Relationship to the Natural World," *Judaism* 44, no. 4 (winter 1995): 437–47.

6. Rachel Elior, "The Affinity between Kabbalah and Hasidism: Continuity or Change?" in *Ninth World Congress of Jewish Studies, Division C* (Jerusalem, 1986), 107–14. See, too, Rivkah Shatz, *Hasidism as Mysticism* (Princeton, N.J.: Princeton University Press, 1993). This entire question has been the subject of considerable scholarly discussion. See, for example, Gershom Scholem, *Kabbalah* (New York: Quadrangle, 1974), 144–52; Moshe Idel, *Kabbalah: New Perspectives* (New Haven: Yale University Press, 1988), 144–46, 153–54, and idem, *Hasidism: Between Magic and Ecstasy* (Albany: State University of New York Press, 1995), 17–18 and references cited there.

7. Lamm, *Faith and Doubt*, 177.

8. Ibid., 176.

9. Ibid., 177.

10. This is so recurrent a motif in the Maimonidean oeuvre that almost any list of references falls short. But see, for example, *Mishneh Torah, Yesodei Ha-Torah* chap. 1; *Guide of the Perplexed*, book 1, chap. 50–60, and book 3, chap. 8–9.

11. *Mishneh Torah, Yesodei Ha-Torah* 2:2.

12. *Guide of the Perplexed*, 4:13, page 453 in Shlomo Pines's translation (Chicago: University of Chicago Press, 1963).

13. Ibid., 455.

14. Ibid., 454.

15. Unless, of course one is an Emotivist, a school of ethics popular in the wake of logical positivism, but long since out of fashion, and surely inconsistent with the religious tradition under discussion here.

16. Paul Taylor, "The Ethics of Respect for Nature," *Environmental Ethics* 3 (fall 1981): 197–218; reprinted in *People, Penguins and Plastic Trees*, ed. Donald Vande-

veer and Christine Pierce (Belmont, Calif.: Wadsworth, 1986), 169–84, quotation from p. 169.

17. Ibid.

18. Ibid., 175.

19. Eric Katz, "Judaism and the Ecological Crisis," *Worldviews and Ecology*, ed. John Grim and Mary Evelyn Tucker (Lewisburg, Pa.: Bucknell University Press), 58. Katz is summarizing the view of many writers on the subject, e.g., Jonathan Helfand, "The Earth Is the Lord's: Judaism and Environmental Ethics," in *Religion and Environmental Crisis*, ed. Eugene Hargrove (Athens, Ga.: University of Georgia Press, 1986); and David Ehrenfeld and Philip Bentley, "Judaism and the Practice of Stewardship," *Judaism* 34 (1985).

20. Katz, "Judaism and the Ecological Crisis," 67.

21. Joseph B. Soloveitchik, "Lonely Man of Faith," *Tradition* 7, no. 2 (1965): 13.

22. Quotations are from ibid., 13–15.

23. Gerald Blidstein, "On the Jewish People in the Writings of Rabbi Joseph B. Soloveitchik," *Tradition* 24, no. 3 (spring 1989): 24.

24. See David Shatz, "'As Thyself': The Limits of Altruism in Jewish Ethics," in *Reverence, Righteousness, and Rahmanut*, ed. Jacob J. Schacter (Northvale, N.J.: J. Aronson, 1992), 251–75. There is a considerable literature on supererogation and virtue ethics in Judaism. See some of sources cited in the Shatz article and the recent volume by Walter Wurzburger, *The Ethics of Responsibility: Pluralistic Approaches to Covenantal Ethics* (Philadelphia: Jewish Publication Society, 1994). For a brief overview see Moshe Sokol, "Jewish Ethics," *Encyclopedia of Ethics*, ed. Lawrence C. Becker and Charlotte B. Becker (New York: Garland, 1992), 647–53. For a survey of the history of the revival of interest in virtue ethics in moral philosophy and some of its strengths and weaknesses (alluded to in my brief discussion in the main text of the present essay), see *The Virtues: Contemporary Essays on Moral Character*, ed. Robert B. Kruschowitz and Robert C. Roberts (Belmont, Calif.: Wadsworth, 1987).

25. For discussions about this as a method for Jewish ethics, see Moshe Sokol, "Some Tension in the Jewish Attitude toward the Taking of Human Life," *Jewish Law Annual* 7 (1988); idem, "The Allocation of Scarce Medical Resources: A Philosophical Analysis of the Halakhic Sources," *Association for Jewish Studies Review* 15, no. 1 (spring 1990); and idem, "Jewish Ethics."

Response.
Construction, Discovery, and Critique in Jewish Ecological Ethics

BARRY S. KOGAN

If philosophy expresses itself distinctively in the analysis, system-atization, and critique of our descriptive and normative claims, then Professors Goodman, Rosenberg, and Sokol have jointly made a very substantive philosophical contribution to the task of clarifying what Jewish ecological ethics is and what it entails. All of their discussions are philosophically well-informed and theologically rich, although each one also has a different programmatic emphasis. In what fol-lows, I shall try to identify the most important and interesting claims that they make and discuss some of the strengths and weaknesses of those claims. Inevitably, there will be points of disagreement; but even where this is the case, the fact that I disagree in no way dimin-ishes my deep appreciation for the erudition, ingenuity, and philo-sophical seriousness that our authors have brought to this discussion.

Lenn Goodman presents a characteristically erudite and often movingly beautiful exposition of what is meant by respect for nature in Jewish tradition. In its attempt to integrate philosophical and reli-gious considerations, it is essentially a constructive work of philo-sophical theology. As such, it builds upon 1) a general theory of deserts, which holds that all things are loci of value because of what they are and because of the projects through which they constitute themselves, 2) the idea of a divine covenant with the natural world, in which 3) God recognizes the deserts of all created beings, while

4) God also serves as a model to human beings of what constitutes proper concern for nature by what is expressed in both legislation and divine action. These are all important claims. But each one raises important questions and, in certain cases, serious difficulties as well.

First, we should ask whether Goodman's general theory of deserts is clear, coherent, and consistent in its own right, and whether the line of thinking it articulates is clearly rooted in the Torah, as he suggests. Despite the appealing universality of his account and his desire to avoid anthropocentrism in grounding values, I am not convinced that the theory as currently formulated is successful. For example, we are told in quick succession that the being of things is their value, that all beings make claims, that these claims are the equivalent of their being, that the being of each thing is its project, and that the prima facie deserts of a being are equivalent to its claims. The cumulative effect of these assertions of identity or equivalence between a thing's being (which is surely identical with the thing itself) and its value, its claims, its project, and its deserts is to imply that all of these predicates are somehow identical with or equivalent to one another. But, on the face of it, that could hardly be the case. Each one is surely distinguishable from the others both in name and definition. Moreover, we hardly speak of them as identical or equivalent in ordinary discourse as well as in religious discourse. We ascribe deserts to beings because of what they do, not because of what they are. Even in the Bible, notably in the story of the Flood, all flesh is punished because they have corrupted their ways, not because they are what they are. Moreover, in both the biblical and midrashic contexts, "all flesh" includes both human beings and the animals.[1] By contrast, if one argues that values, claims, projects, and deserts are really distinct properties or characteristics of the beings that have them, this new claim runs counter to one of the key advantages that Goodman ascribes to his ontological approach to values, namely, that "it obviates the quest for a 'property' of goodness, which we must then deem natural or 'non-natural.'" Accordingly, if we wish to retain that advantage, we would have to suppose that a thing's value must at least *pertain to* the thing as a whole, and presumably the same would hold true for its project or projects as well. But this relation would apparently not rise to the level of strict identity, nor would it be reducible to having a property. What follows from this analysis, I think, is that the basic logical claims that are meant to ground the theory are either implausible as such or they have not yet been stated with sufficient clarity to show just how they do not entail the difficulties mentioned. In either case, the account needs to be reworked.

Other difficulties attend the notion of a thing's project. While the concept is first introduced in abstract terms, so that a thing's being is said to be its project, it is soon made clear that living beings are the paradigm cases of things that pursue "*a* project" (italics mine). Insofar as living things possess at least virtual subjecthood by having ends or goals and, in their most developed forms, can articulate them in words, we understand what it is for a being to pursue a project or, as Goodman later speaks of it, a quest. But do all beings, whether as unique individuals or as members of a given species, ultimately have only one project? Goodman's language suggests that they do, but one could maintain equally well that they have many projects, both successive and simultaneous, and that these are not easily subsumed under a single project, if indeed a single, overarching project can be identified at all. The issue here is not merely numerical, and it is certainly not trivial, even when we are speaking of only one kind of being. It is rather that beings express what they are in many diverse and often ambiguous ways. Bernard Williams illustrates the point nicely when he comments on Aristotle's selection of intellect as the distinguishing mark of human beings. He observes that rationality and intellect are no more distinctive of man than artistic creativity, making fire and cooking, having sexual intercourse without regard to season, despoiling the environment and upsetting the balance of nature, or killing things for fun. "If we offer as the supreme moral imperative that old cry, 'Be a man!' it is terrible to think of many of the ways in which it could be taken literally." [2] Projects, in sum, like essences, are notoriously difficult to characterize, much less to define adequately. Yet that appears to be just what an ontological theory of deserts requires us to do in order to apply the theory justly. So, we are immediately left with the question of whether an ontic theory of deserts such as this can actually help us "to adjudicate among rival claims and to discover among them not only the roots of competition but the potentials for complementary claims." We know far too little about the being of things and their ultimate projects to fulfill the task of adjudication. Here, a philosophical analysis of contemporary paradigm cases could make a real difference by showing precisely whether and how the theory can work successfully.

Short of clear evidence that the theory can perform its basic task, the practical ecological result is likely to be that most discussions will focus on the putative claims and interests of creatures, species, eco-niches, and the like, as well as their value to various interested parties on a more or less ad hoc basis. This seems plainly plausible, if only because these kinds of variables allow for more concrete formulation and description than either their being, their project, or their intrinsic value. I agree with Goodman in this connection that mapping the hier-archy of their deserts in detail is not necessarily part of philosophy's task, but I would also want to add that what he calls "the normative task of regulating our practical *and notional responses* to claims of all sorts" (italics mine) is as much the task of philosophy—specifically, normative ethics and political philosophy—as it is the task of laws and religions. Certainly, philosophy has an equal, if not superior claim to be an expression of *human* culture as those of religion and law, especially when traditional, revealed religions trace their origin to a divine Source beyond culture. In that and many other respects, it is surely hard to see how philosophy could ever usurp the tasks of religion and law. Still, as long as philosophy represents an autono-mous human effort to understand and appraise claims about matters of truth and falsehood, good and evil and what they entail, I also do not see how it could altogether avoid clashing with the claims of religion, at least insofar as the latter are presented as factual and normative claims.

Having mentioned the notion of a hierarchy of deserts, we should also take note of the hierarchy of beings that corresponds to it. For to all intents and purposes, Goodman's account presupposes the contin-ued validity of the Great Chain of Being in either its traditional form or a variation of it. On reflection, it seems to be rather close to the traditional Platonic and Neoplatonic conceptions, especially insofar as they invoke the ancient idea of degrees of reality. In this case, it is because beings vary in their ontic worth, that "their deserts must be scaled to their reality." Those with the highest ontic worth turn out to be constituted by the properties of personhood, such as conscious-ness, mutual recognition, sociality, and cooperation, among others, from which they derive their rights and dignity. Those with lesser worth lack one or more of these properties on a descending scale. One might be inclined to charge Goodman here with the very anthropo-centrism he seeks to avoid, were it not for the fact that he clearly states that "persons need not be human." While he does not furnish specific examples of nonhuman persons, we can easily infer that they might include legal persons, such as corporations and governments, or "spiritual machines" such as robots and computers, or divine beings, such as God or the angels. But whatever persons are, it is their deserts alone that actually reach the level of sanctity. Thus far, the theory.

Now, even though the notion of a natural hierarchy has important common sense and metaphysical underpinnings, it remains problematic even in this formulation. The problem does not lie in the extraordinary worth we ascribe to persons and personhood, but rather in the incompatibility of affirming the supreme ontic worth of persons while at the same time maintaining that "we can never judge one being's project by the standards of another." For if a thing's being and its project are identical, then it would appear that we, as human beings carrying out our projects, cannot ultimately avoid judging other beings and other projects by our own standards. Indeed, we repeatedly try to make sense of them by reference to models, metaphors, processes, *and values* that reflect distinctively human experiences and projects. Even if we allow for the possibility of some degree of self-transcendence and imaginative identification, we do not thereby leave behind our human perspective or our own standards of value. If anything, we extend them further. The result is that beings that are said to possess greater ontic value and reality necessarily trump the claims of beings that are said to possess less, whenever there is a serious conflict between them. For the hierarchy itself always makes clear that their respective claims are by the nature of things unequal. That is why there is really no contest between the interests of the virus and those of the child as far as the ontic theory of deserts is concerned, and the same is usually true for conflicts between the interests of development companies and rain forests, and those of toxic waste disposal companies and water tables. Even when the rights of persons are sometimes curbed because of what Goodman calls incoherence or overreaching, this is typically not the result of recognizing the ontic worth of an eco-niche or an endangered species, but of recognizing instead the interests of a significant or powerful group of persons who are quite capable of speaking for themselves. All of these, I think, are inevitable consequences of regarding persons and personhood as ontically sacred and supreme.

Given the catastrophic consequences of failing to respect the sanctity of human life during the past century, one would hardly wish to

see the value of such life weakened further by denying it sanctity. Still, it
is worth noting that even the Bible does not actually pronounce human life to be sacred as such. It states only that humanity is created in
the image of God—without telling us just what that image consists in.
It does not even pronounce the creation of human beings "good," as it
does for virtually all other creatures. It tells us only that after surveying everything God had created and made, the totality was found to be
"very good." Human beings would appear to be good only insofar as
they are part of the whole and fit into it as God has designed. Clearly,
too, humanity has a special status and even relationship to the divine,
but *holiness* is apparently not intrinsic to what human beings are. It
characterizes only God by nature, as the angelic chorus in Isaiah's
Temple vision makes clear: "Holy, holy, holy! The Lord of Hosts!"
(Isa. 6:3a). Moreover, if that holiness extends to other beings beyond
God, it is clearly not limited to persons. For the second half of the
verse proclaims, "His presence / glory fills all the earth!" or, more
literally, "The fullness of the whole earth is His glory" (Isa. 6:3b). To
be sure, this does not clearly say that all creatures on earth are holy,
much less intrinsically so, but it implicitly allows all creatures a relationship to holiness through the divine presence that fills all the earth.
And the relationship is made real by "keeping the way of the Lord."[3]
In effect, then, if the difficulties involved in associating sanctity and,
at least, earthly supremacy with persons can be resolved at all, they
should be resolved not by diminishing the value of persons, but by
raising that of all other creatures. That would entail, at the very least,
showing how they are objects of divine concern and thus in a relationship to God. It would also recognize that what creates a relationship to
the divine, which is a hallmark of sanctity, is not so much what we are
or what we seek as it is what we do, no matter who or what *we* are.

   This brief exegetical exercise brings us to the larger question of
whether the line of thinking represented by Goodman's ontic theory
of deserts is indeed rooted in the Torah. Recognizing that a line of
thinking is not necessarily the same as a full-fledged theory, there is
probably no simple answer to this question. Much depends on the selection and analysis of sources, such as those presented in the second
half of the essay, to which we shall turn shortly. But careful attention
to what is argued in the first half—the theory itself—provides sufficient grounds for raising at least several serious doubts. What distinguishes the line of thinking in question is the emphasis it places on

beings themselves as the locus of their value, where "value is not dependent on some external valuer but on the intrinsic merit of the claims each being makes." While there are hints of such a view in certain rabbinic and medieval philosophic sources, the Torah itself and much else in the Bible, not to mention the preponderance of rabbinic literature, suggests that a thing's value lies in its conformity to a divine norm, that is, in relation to an external standard willed and articulated in some way by God. Thus, the various creatures called into being in Genesis 1, for example, are pronounced "good" by God, the "external Valuer" par excellence, once they come into being in conformity with each divine fiat. Again, the Patriarchs and their descendants, despite palpable human flaws, prove their value not through their intrinsic personhood, nor their innate intelligence, nor even their superior skill at adjudicating the conflicting claims of other creatures, which is in fact exercised rather unevenly, but through their faithfulness to "the way of the Lord," as it is progressively defined over time by a source they recognize as external to themselves.

Another major divergence between the line of thinking in question and the tendency of both the Bible and rabbinic theology lies in the latter's sober and sobering estimate of the powers of the human mind (or rather, heart, as they were inclined to put it) to attain practical moral wisdom on its own and to act upon it properly. Thus, at the very moment after the Flood when God establishes (or, perhaps, reestablishes) his covenant with nature, we are told ". . . the Lord said to Himself: 'Never again will I doom the earth because of man, since the devisings of man's mind are evil from his youth; nor will I ever again destroy every living being as I have done'" (Gen. 8:21). Even as human centrality in the scheme of creation is once again acknowledged, the text links it with the profoundest possible misgiving about human motivation and what we actually contemplate. Moreover, the cautionary note expressed here is not merely about human subjectivity, bias, fallibility, or overreaching, all of which allow that there are purely commendable motives that somehow go awry. Rather, it calls into question the unalloyed goodness of human motivation to begin with, quite literally. At best, it would appear, our motivations are mixed and always in need of divine guidance in the form of commandments and prohibitions as well as incentives to adhere to them. Hence, the covenant. Such grounds as we have for hoping that fairness can be achieved, according to the biblical author, begin with accepting and obeying the Law and ultimately culminate in fully internalizing its norms.[4] But, as far as I can see, this is not the same as the Socratic hope that fairness can be found and ultimately achieved by *elenchus* and *noesis* alone, which is not to say, of course, that they have no role at all in realizing justice. The upshot of these reflections is that the sanctity and supremacy ascribed by Goodman to human personhood vis-à-vis the natural world is neither unambiguous nor unqualified.

   Lest these exegetical observations appear too limited and too selective to support my point, let us consider also what follows in these texts. The subsequent adventures and misadventures of the Patriarchs and their descendants are a virtual demonstration *ad oculos* of the need for divine instruction in human affairs. Even Job, who is certifiably the most blameless and upright of men and easily one of the most critical and independent-minded, learns midway through his tribulations that only God knows the way to wisdom, and that wisdom is nothing else but the fear of the Lord, while shunning evil is the real meaning of understanding (Job 28:23–28). By the end of the story, it still takes a theophany to make sure that the lesson sinks in (Job 42:2–6). The point here is not that our capacity to attain the knowledge and acquire the proper motivation needed to till and tend the garden representing the natural world is utterly compromised and worthless. That need not be so, if the guidance embodied in the tradition is taken seriously. But neither may we proceed autonomously to give all things their due with the best of intentions, the latest of methods, and the promise of objectivity, without fear of going astray. It may be that "sentient beings are adept at finding complementarities that will optimize the realization of deserts," but we are equally, if not more, adept at overlooking incoherences, underestimating our tendency to overreach, and complacently aggrandizing ourselves until deserts are eventually distributed in the form of unanticipated and truly frightful poetic justice. It seems to me that the project of a universal assignment of deserts to other beings on a single scale of reality and value offers a plausible example of overreaching, and the confidence it assumes regarding our ability to understand the whole is not well founded. If anything, Alexander Pope (1688–1744) seems to come closer to the truth in his "Essay on Man," when he describes the ambiguity of the human condition implied by our position at the midpoint of the Great Chain of Being:

Plac'd in this isthmus of a middle state,
A being darkly wise and rudely great,
With too much knowledge for the sceptic side,
With too much weakness for the stoic pride,
He hangs between; in doubt to act or rest;
In doubt to deem himself a god or beast;
In doubt his Mind or Body to prefer;
Born but to die, and reasoning but to err;
Chaos of Thought and Passion all confus'd,
Still by himself abus'd, or disabus'd;
Created half to rise, and half to fall,
Great lord of all things, yet a prey to all;
Sole judge of Truth, in endless error hurled;
The glory, jest, and riddle of the world.
("Essay on Man," Epistle 2:3–18)

One other feature of Goodman's ontic outlook deserves mention. While there are references to "the divine" and "nature's God" late in the exposition of the theory, and God is credited with offering beings the gift of existence, it does not appear that God is really essential to the theory. As Goodman acknowledges, the theory is a form of naturalism. As such, its essential elements are natural entities, taken together with their intrinsic values, projects, claims, interests, deserts, and, finally, rational persons able to articulate and adjudicate between them. *Given this fact and the way in which the theory is formulated*, God is in no way *necessary* to perform these tasks, although the claim that God established the existing order, models what is meant by giving each being its due, and mandates our doing likewise, and so on, is certainly compatible with it. With respect to its essentials, in fact, the ontic theory of deserts resembles nothing so much as natural law theory, which is currently receiving renewed attention and a variety of new formulations.[5] Even in this well-known philosophical theory, the question of God's role is conspicuously peripheral to its main concerns. (As Hugo Grotius famously observed regarding the foundations of natural law, "What we have been saying would have a degree of validity even if we should concede what cannot be conceded without the utmost wickedness, that there is no God, or that the affairs of men are of no concern to Him.")[6] But however great the appeal of natural law theory to a rationalistic way of looking at things, it is not at all clear that nature in all its variety expresses commensurable values that can be ranked on a single hierarchy or "prescribes" laws of conduct in anything more than a figurative sense. Moreover, natural law theory has historically had its greatest appeal either when there was no divinely revealed Law in authority or where such a Law was thought to have been either superseded or in serious need of supplementation. For all of the aforementioned reasons, it is hard to think of this "line of thinking"—excepting, of course, the value it places upon all creatures and its commitment to justice—as clearly rooted in the Torah. At most, the theory can be made compatible with it.

Nevertheless, Goodman identifies the Torah as a source for the notions comprising his theory because it also allows us to assign deserts to all manner of beings from plants and animals, to eco-niches, to monuments of nature and art. At best, it would seem that Scripture might serve as an indirect source for assigning deserts insofar as it states human obligations explicitly. We might ask, then, aren't entitative and conative claims ultimately reducible to divine commands? If so, it makes sense to ask whether we really have enough commands, and the kinds of commands, needed to address the kinds of questions environmentalists are raising today. More importantly, do the textual sources give us real guidance on what to do and what not to do, or are we guiding the sources through our selection and interpretation of them to say what we want them to say? If we are guiding the sources in this way, in what way do *they* make a claim upon *us*? Goodman succeeds in identifying many rich and illuminating sources to serve as the elements of a Jewish ecological ethic. But he also seems to recognize the problem we face when he observes that, "Nature allows the wildfire to overwhelm the forest, although man must not; and nature allows man to drain the wetlands, but God (*as we now think*) commands us to restore them" (italics mine). Which is it? That God commands us to restore them or that we now think it mandatory? There is surely still a difference, indeed, a very important difference.

But now consider a commandment like "Thou shalt not seethe a kid in its mother's milk" (Exod. 23:19; 34:26; and Deut. 14:21). Admittedly, this is an enigmatic verse. Does its significance lie in an alleged protest against a pagan zest for cruelty? Or is it a concern for the possible suffering of the mother goat in seeing her kid boiled in her milk? We are not told, and I am not sure. If, as is traditional, it is associated with the commandment to release the mother bird while taking her chicks and also with the commandment not to slaughter a cow or ewe and its young on the same day, the commandment may imply that one must not slaughter both mother and offspring, lest one end the familial line and threaten the species which God created. Using the mother's milk to boil the kid would add insult to injury by perverting divine teleology, for what was meant to give life to the kid becomes an occasion, indeed, an incentive, for consuming it. If so, one might say that the commandment challenges people not to allow their desires for food to contravene God's promise to human beings never again to destroy whole lines of living things, nor to pervert God's teleology in the process. Much the same would be entailed by forbidding the destruction of *a line of birds*, for "the chicks may be taken but the dam must be released (to hatch others). Here, the symbolism [is] made explicit by the rubric so pregnant with meaning: 'That it may go well with you and you long endure,'" as my teacher Herbert Chanan Brichto cogently argued.[7] In sum, much more than mercy may be involved in the rationale for these laws, namely, maintenance of the family line and continuity of the species. If that is so, it may contribute a much broader grounding to the project of constructing a Jewish environmental ethic of species-preservation for all species than a prohibition against cruelty to animals alone. Here, Lenn Goodman is surely right: "Human needs are recognized but wantonness is restricted." The ideal is one of balancing needs in order to let all species survive and actively enabling the lines of life to continue. By doing so, one maintains the original balance God which established "from the beginning."

In his erudite presentation on the functionality of nature in relation to Torah, Shalom Rosenberg offers a remarkably broad overview of the different roles nature has played from the biblical period to the twentieth century. His interest is the interplay between a revealed ethic and a natural law ethic, and his stated focus is on ethical obligation in relation to nature. In essence, he aims at uncovering the recurrent themes and innovative contributions that should inform any Jewish ecological ethic. Thus, he argues that in the history of Jewish thought nature functions variously as an amoral setting which ethics must redeem, a higher standard of ethics by which to judge the norms and practices of states and societies, and as a foundation for combating relativism and historicism. Depending on its function, certain aspects of nature are highlighted over others, as, for example, conflict over cooperation and symbiosis, or morality over amorality, and teleology over dysteleology.

Thus, in the context of depicting the intellectual and social revolution inaugurated by the Bible, he presents the world of nature in largely Darwinian terms. It is filled with strife, violence, and cruelty that are characteristically visited by the strong upon the weak. Ethics are not a reflection of nature but a set of constraints established to oppose it. While this view of what came to be called "nature" is certainly defensible, it is also overstated. It does not accord well with Genesis 1 and 2, or Psalm 8, 19, 104, and 145, or Job 38–42, or with many comparable passages in the prophetic writings. If we can even speak of *the* biblical view, given the fact that the Bible is an anthology of books and traditions, must we not ask: Is it nature that is out of kilter, or human beings? Is God attempting to be a covenant-partner with man against nature or a covenant-partner with people *and* nature against chaos? I would incline to the latter view in both cases.[8] Again, is God simply the archetype of morality as the Neo-Kantians contend, or a far deeper, more complex and conflicted figure, as the literary historians and biographers of God maintain? Here, too, I would incline to the latter view, although, admittedly, it makes the formulation of a Jewish environmental ethic more difficult, since God's behavior toward the natural world is neither uniformly benevolent nor practically consistent. We need only consider, for example, God's role in the story of Noah, God's actions against the people of Sodom and Gomorrah and the region in which these cities were located, and the fate of the natural environment depicted in the covenant curses of Deuteronomy 28–29.

Shalom Rosenberg's discussion of the Sages' views on the natural world is more nuanced and richer. Nature is variously depicted as 1) a morally indifferent set of processes (*'olam ke-minhago noheig*), *or* 2) a repository of ethical exempla in which the heavens fulfill God's law and we learn morality and *derekh 'eretz* from the animals, *or* 3) a virtuous person who has suffered harm and disruption because of human sin and who will return to perfection in the future by having preserved more of its integrity intact than humankind. Here, nature signifies what ought to be, the optimum condition of things. However, the discussion of this last category is limited for the most part to forbidden sexual relations. Accordingly, we should ask 1) whether this notion is a classic rabbinic rubric or a modern construction, and (regardless of the answer), 2) whether "offense against nature" can be invoked and expanded into at least the *proscriptive* component of an environmental ethic. Such questions are not raised here, but they need to be raised and addressed. Beyond that, we are equally in need of a broader *prescriptive* component, which would consist mainly in the identification of what can only be called *mitzvot bein 'adam laberiyot*, "commandments between man and [other] creatures."

If we turn to the medieval philosophers, Shalom Rosenberg rightly notes the importance of a "back to nature" orientation. But while there is indeed a greater concern with the natural world, understood as God's "attributes of action," the focus easily shifts from the natural world and our possible relation to it to a preoccupation with returning to human nature at its best, that is, to human nature in its most rational form. But this only scratches the surface. What we need to examine is how specific traditions in the philosophic literature—such as Kalam, Neoplatonism, Aristotelianism, and their philosophically informed critics—address the question of how we are to relate to the creatures and ways of living that can be found in the sublunar world. Saadia's concluding chapter of *Emunot Ve-De'ot* would be a relevant source. So would Bahya's *Sha'ar Ha-Behinah*, Abraham ibn Ezra's *Yesod Mora*, the various commentaries on the *Sefer Yetzirah*, and Maimonides' discussions of cosmology and its relation to ethics in the *Guide of the Perplexed* and elsewhere, not to mention generations of later thinkers who elaborate on and refine these themes.

Rosenberg concludes by taking special note of Samson Raphael Hirsch's views on nature and the natural world and, more specifically, his identification of Torah law with natural law. He especially commends Hirsch for emphasizing the limited nature of man's right to rule over other creatures, for the earth belongs to God. This is unquestionably a fundamental religious postulate in Judaism and a potential cornerstone for a Jewish ecological ethic, insofar as it brings the natural world into the sphere of the sacred without at the same time pronouncing it "divine." But regardless of whether this postulate is derived from the Bible's creation narratives or legal texts, it is at most a preliminary step in developing a religious conception of the natural world and a full-fledged environmental ethic adequate to what we know about it. Even so, we need much more than postulates. We need to spell out ecological meanings, implications, and imperatives. But even as a postulate, it is problematic. For, with all due respect, it is too

easily seen as merely asserting God's property rights over the world
and everything in it. Apparently, the intended moral effect of doing so
is to call to mind the principle that we must not damage or destroy
someone else's property. In this particular case, the obligation is
meant to apply absolutely. But in a culture that is drowning in the
assertion of competing claims about property rights of all kinds, this
has the unfortunate and, I assume, unintended effect of making God
one more claimant. Also, we should note that the implied content of
the principle is only to do no harm. It says nothing about protecting,
preserving, and caring for what belongs to God. Accordingly, something that is both more positive and more personally compelling is
needed, even by religious people, perhaps especially by religious
people. Hence, the impetus to search for new paradigms or novel interpretations of old ones in order to awaken a sense of personal obligation toward the environment.

   In this connection, Hirsch's novel reading of the distinction between *mishpatim* and *huqqim,* that is, between laws for which the justification is immediately intelligible to us because they define our obligations toward other human beings, who are essentially like
ourselves, and statutes for which the justification is largely unintelligible to us because they define our obligations toward nonhuman
creatures, who are essentially unlike ourselves, carries us a long way
toward defining the new category of commandments that I ventured
above to call *mitzvot bein 'adam la-beriyot,* obligations between human beings and other creatures. What is particularly attractive about
his interpretation is the fact that such commandments and the creatures to which they refer need not be altogether opaque to our minds.
If we knew the "processes of reciprocity" or mutual influence obtaining between these creatures and ourselves, the *huqqim* could become
as clear in their justification as the *mishpatim.* In principle, nothing
precludes our learning about these creatures and the "processes of
reciprocity" that exist between us *as a matter of religious obligation.*
In other words, the study of ecology, the policy implications that follow from its findings, and the practical intent of the *huqqim,* as explained by Hirsch, would all be religiously mandated. What remains
to be seen is how much guidance the *huqqim* themselves can give toward the formulation of a concrete and practical environmental ethic.
Here, careful investigation of classic compendia on the 613 *mitzvot,*
such as Maimonides' *Sefer Ha-Mitzvot,* the *Sefer Ha-Hinnukh* as-

cribed to Aaron Halevi of Barcelona, and Joseph Babad's commentary on it, the *Minhat Hinnukh*, not to mention classical commentators and Hirsch's own observations on these passages would all be very welcome. Rosenberg himself offers a brief list of relevant *huqqim* with a concluding comment on the lesson they teach at the end of his essay; but the list is only partial, and the lesson—about God's ownership of the earth—is in need of a much fuller discussion, as noted above.

Hirsch is surely correct that the notion of humanity's being created to have dominion over fish, fowl, and cattle (as tokens for all aquatic, aerial, and terrestrial animals) does not mean that we are to conquer them. It is less clear, however, that the Hebrew root RDH in Genesis 1:28 means "guiding" rather than "ruling." Brown, Driver, and Briggs render it in general as "have dominion, rule, dominate" (p. 921). However, they note H. Graetz's reading of Psalm 72:8 as *yoru*, "let them teach," as preferable to the standard reading, "Let him rule from sea to sea" (p. 922). This is consistent with Hirsch's understanding of the meaning of the root, but does not support his applying it to Genesis 1:26. Similarly, Koehler and Baumgartner's lexicon of biblical Hebrew records a considerable number of variant meanings derived from studies of ancient Near Eastern languages, but lists only two basic meanings for the simple active verb, "–1. To tread the wine-press Jl 4:13. –2. To rule (with the associated meaning of oppression . . .)." Intriguingly, however, they note the following just before the aforementioned entry: "E. Zanger *Gottes Bogen in dem Wolken* 91: Jl 4:13 text uncertain; the basic meaning of the verb is not to rule; the word actually denotes the travelling around of the shepherd with his flock." This comes quite close to Hirsch's suggestion, and it is not restricted to any particular biblical verse. Still, as an illustration of the meaning ". . . to rule (with the associated meaning of oppression)" linked with the preposition B', Koehler and Baumgartner list Genesis 1:26 and 28. The two most recent scholarly translations of the passage in use among Jews render it respectively as 1) "They shall rule. . . ." (NJPS), and 2) "Let them have dominion. . . ." (Schocken/Everett Fox). It appears that we are still not in a position to write a Q.E.D. after either proposed or prevailing translations of this biblical text.

It may very well be that the two creation narratives in Genesis 1 and 2 reflect divergent attitudes toward our intended relationship to the natural world, just as they reflect divergent perspectives on much else.[9] Of the two, however, both Rosenberg and Goodman rightly prefer the mandate given to Adam in Genesis 2:15: "The Lord God took the man and placed him in the garden of Eden, to till it and tend it." Both stress that it identifies the human role vis-à-vis the Garden as being not one of ownership or autocratic rule, but rather of caring for the environment in order to preserve it and protect it. This is surely correct; but I would add that the exegesis ought to be part of a comprehensive theology of creation, lest it be disregarded or marginalized as no more than a detail in a story. What is needed is a theology of creation that coheres with what we know about the natural world, one that does justice to both the subtlety and fragility that characterizes the world of creatures and highlights the concomitant need for human beings to care for and maintain that world. Minimally, such a theology would articulate and explain the principles underlying the commandments already identified within the tradition that call for and define the character of such care. Beyond the minimum, however, such a theology might also identify other commandments that have not yet been recognized as relevant to this task. Further, it might undertake to explain how care for the natural world, so understood, also expresses the intelligence and imitates the moral attributes of its Creator. Indeed, it might even attempt to show why the account it has developed represents an indispensable paradigm of how care is exercised.

Finally, we have Moshe Sokol's treatment of the ethical implications of our theological conceptions of nature. It is essentially methodological and critical, and, for the most part, I find myself in sympathy with his desire to identify incoherences and overstated claims and to suggest fruitful avenues of approach for constructing a contemporary environmental ethic. His care for the natural world starts, as it should, with the effort to think carefully about it and about how we think about it. We should do likewise.

Still, misunderstandings can arise even in an attempt to clear them up, and sometimes one overstatement replaces another. For example, the confrontation with nature to which Schwarzschild refers does not signify disapproval of trees or grass or the processes that account for their growth and decline. It signifies instead all that is immoral and amoral about *what is the case* over against what ought to be. That would include both natural evils as a real category and our mistreatment of creatures in nature. Disapproval, therefore, is reserved for behavior, ideologies, conditions, and states of affairs, not natural objects per se. In Wyschogrod's case, it is even clearer that pagan ideologies of nature and the natural are the real object of his disapproval. Sokol is right that we cannot get through to nature as it really is (assuming, of course, that nature is identical with the noumenon of things) and must deal instead with alternative constructions of nature, but his point is hardly ignored by the figures he criticizes.

Again, I would agree that theologies that stress divine transcendence do not necessarily culminate in desacralizing the world or exploiting nature, as he shows with Maimonides. Nor do theologies stressing immanence culminate in *unqualified* reverence for and awe toward all things natural, as he argues regarding early Hasidism. But merely citing counterexamples does little, if anything, to account for them. Maimonides is not simply a "transcendentist" theologian. He has a theology of immanence as well, expressed in his account of the attributes of action, in which the nurturing behavior of the various species of animals figures prominently. And, as a thinker who regards contemplative understanding of God's creation and governance of creatures as the fourth and highest perfection (*Guide of the Perplexed* 3.54), it is no wonder that he endorses awe and respect for the natural world. Conversely, Hasidic "immanentists" were not vegetarians, not because they had less awe for nature, but because they were shaped by the prevailing understanding of what is and is not possible and what the Torah permits. The same applies to Maimonides, who was also not a vegetarian. But he knew that beliefs and practices could change over time, just as he knew that sacrifices could be superseded by prayer and prayer superseded by contemplation. We know it too, which is why we are here.

Finally, Sokol argues that a theocentric outlook can yield a stance toward nature that is very far from biocentrism, such as that of Soloveitchik's majestic man (which I readily concede), but he also contends that a theocentric outlook does not in and of itself yield a functional equivalent to a biocentric outlook (which I want to dispute). Consider, for example, Judah Halevi (ca. 1075–1141). Surely, he is no defender of the equality of the species. Yet in his comments on the *Sefer Yetzirah*, traditionally regarded as a work of philosophical speculation by Abraham, he argues that the world is like a book, a *sefer*, and articulates a story, a *sippur*. As such, it represents God's speech and writing. He further explains that God's writing is identical with God's creatures—all of them. God's speech, in turn, is identical with the divine writing, and God's determinate measure (*sefar*) for both is identical with his speech. Thus, the three expressions signify one and the same thing in relation to God, but three separate things in relation to us (*Kuzari* 4.25). What does this imply? Essentially this: If God's speech, writing, and determinate measure for things are identified with the creatures of the natural world—ourselves included—then all are to be treated with the kind of awe and reverence we reserve for a *sefer Torah*. And here, of course, there exists a well-defined praxis. What God wills would be that the divine speech be preserved and nurtured, not destroyed, that it be studied and learned from, not exploited or abused, that it be maintained and replicated generation after generation, not diminished and left to wear out. Significantly, tradition claims that *after* Abraham reached this level of understanding, he was deemed worthy of receiving divine revelation so that he might be guided further. It is not clear from this sequel whether the revelation came to him because of his speculative preparation or in order to supersede and replace it. What is clear is that Halevi's reference to the story, together with his comments on the true nature of both creatures and the world, was meant to be instructive, not merely charming. If so, then the old maxim of the rabbis, *ma'asei 'avot siman la-banim* ("The acts of the ancestors are a sign to their descendents"), still applies, not only to the text of Scripture, but also to the World-Text of which we and all other creatures are part.[10] The acts and insights of our ancestors are indeed a sign to their children—not necessarily as a portent of what will inexorably happen, but rather as a model of what we ought to do and what we ought to become.

Notes

1. See Gen. 6:12–13, 17, 19; 7:21; Genesis Rabbah 28:8; and Rashi on Gen. 6:12.

2. Bernard Williams, *Morality: An Introduction to Ethics* (New York: Harper and Row, 1972), 64.

3. Cf. Gen. 6:11–13; Prov. 30:18–20; Gen. 17:1; Isa. 55:9.

4. Cf. Isa. 55:1–3; Jer. 31:31–34.

5. See, for example, Robert P. George, *Natural Law Theory: Contemporary Essays* (Oxford: Clarendon Press, 1992); and David Novak, *Natural Law in Judaism* (Cambridge: Cambridge University Press, 1998).

6. Hugo Grotius, *De Jure Belli ac Pacis Libri Tres*, vol. 2; translation of book 1 by Francis W. Kelsey et al. (Oxford: Clarendon Press, 1925), Prolegomena, p. 13, sec. 11.

7. Herbert Chanan Brichto, "Kin, Cult, Land, and Afterlife: A Biblical Complex," *Hebrew Union College Annual* 63 (1973): 33.

8. See Gen. 8:21–22; 9:1–17; Jer. 31:35–36; 33:20–22.

9. See Joseph B. Soloveitchik, "The Lonely Man of Faith," *Tradition* 7, no. 2 (summer 1965): 5–67.

10. See Barry S. Kogan, "Judaism and Scientific Cosmology: Redesigning the Design Argument," in *Creation and the End of Days: Judaism and Scientific Cosmology*, ed. David Novak and Norbert Samuelson (Lanham, Md.: University Press of America, 1986), 97–155.

Nature in Jewish Mysticism

Mirror of Nature Reflected in the Symbolism of Medieval Kabbalah

ELLIOT R. WOLFSON

> One cannot drive a nail into empty space.
> —Rinzai Gigen

Mirror as Epistemological Veil

The poetic symbol of the mirror of nature, a well-attested literary motif that can be traced back to ancient Greek philosophical sources,[1] reflects the idea that nature is a mirror, an idea that implicates the mind, which itself has often been compared to a mirror, in the overly determined representationalism underlying much of Western epistemology.[2] In the positing of a reflection that reflects the reflection, a process that seemingly would lead to an infinite regress of reflexivity, the mind is caught in a game of mirrors, a play of invisible surface against another invisible surface.[3] Whatever we see, we see as double.

The image of nature as a mirror assumed prominent significance in the High Middle Ages, particularly in the twelfth century, for at that time this motif was one of the most important ways in which philosophers and theologians expressed the principle of divine immanence. That nature is a mirror of God signifies the symbolic participation of the immaterial spirit in the body of the universe.[4] In the history of Christianity, with its well-attested emphasis on incarnational theology, this philosophic turn simply expanded the possibility of finding God in an embodied state, although with the important difference that the incarnate presence was not limited to one historical figure but presumed to be manifest equally in all things. This omnipresence entailed an ontological transformation as things in the world were no longer viewed as merely reflecting the glory of God in a passive manner, but were perceived as symbolic representations portrayed by the human imagination in iconic and linguistic forms. For Jews and Muslims, the matter had to be cast in a distinct way insofar as the notion of incarnation or embodiment of the divine expressed itself somewhat differently in their respective theological beliefs. But Jewish and Muslim thinkers of this period were equally influenced by the strand of philosophical thinking that viewed nature as the symbolic manifestation of God.

In line with this tendency, the kabbalists looked upon nature as a mirror of the divine. As a number of scholars have noted, the symbolic propensity of the *ba'alei sefirot*, to use the terminology current in the late thirteenth century, led them to view all things of the corporeal world as a reflection of an inner process within the divine reality.[5] Building upon an idea expressed in rabbinic texts (although it is in fact much older than these sources), regarding the symmetry between the earthly and the celestial realms, the kabbalists maintained that the ten resplendent emanations (*sefirot*), which make up the divine pleroma, are the archetypal spiritual beings that function as the formal causes for all that exists in the physical universe.[6] According to the formulation of some kabbalists, however, the *sefirot* are not only the cause but the very substance of that which is real. The issue, then, is not merely the structural parallelism between the divine and the mundane, but their ontological conjunction, which facilitates divine omnipresence in both realms. As we read in one zoharic passage, "The blessed holy One made everything so that this world would be found in the pattern of that which is above, and the one would be conjoined to the other, and His glory would be above and below."[7]

Indeed, in an ontological sense there is only one ultimate reality, the divine light, which manifests itself in the garb of the twenty-two letters of the Hebrew alphabet that derive, in turn, from the four-letter name, YHWH, the root word of all language, the mystical secret of the Torah. Basic to the theosophic orientation of the kabbalists is the notion that the infinite energy of the divine is expressed in the pleroma of ten *sefirot*, which are related to the twenty-two Hebrew letters. The sundry attempts of the kabbalists to work out the complex relationship of the *sefirot* and the letters is based in great measure on the tradition of the thirty-two paths of mysterious wisdom that was first articulated in the preamble of the older esoteric work on cosmology, *Sefer Yetzirah*, a book whose provenance is still a matter of scholarly debate.[8] I cannot enter here into all of the details of the discussion in medieval kabbalistic sources regarding the precise relationship of the twenty-two "foundational letters" (*'otiyyot yesod*) and the ten "intangible emanations" (*sefirot belimah*).[9] Suffice it to say that even those kabbalists who accorded ontic priority to the *sefirot* maintained that the underlying reality to which the *sefirot* point is the ineffable name, YHWH, for the latter is the only legitimate signifier of that which cannot be signified and the only appropriate image of that which cannot be portrayed in images.[10] In the final analysis, the letters constitute the spiritual being of the sefirotic gradations for the medieval kabbalists.

The linguistic nature of the spiritual force of the divine is articulated, for instance, in a relatively early kabbalistic source, the commentary on the account of creation attributed to the Provençal kabbalist, Isaac the Blind. Commenting on the biblical reference to the "spirit of God, *ruah 'elohim* (Gen. 1:2), he writes:

> The spirit itself when it enters together with the drop enters in its letters, for in accord with the subtlety of the spirit (*daqut ha-ruah*) is the subtlety of the letters (*daqut ha-'otiyyot*), and a force is formed within the spirit until the infinite. The spirit is called form (*tzurah*) in the locution of the philosophers, for the sensible body (*guf murgash*) is called matter (*golem*), and the spirit that establishes the matter is called the form.[11]

The standard hylomorphism of the medieval philosophical tradition, which has its roots in ancient Greek thought, is here employed to describe the two levels of being, the divine and the mundane, the world of unity and the world of separation. The form, which is surely the higher expression of what is real, is identified with the letters, which are comprised in the Tetragrammaton, the underlying essence of the Torah. The ontological mystery, one might say, consists of the paradox that the luminous letters shine forth through the veil of the physical entities of this world. It is in this sense that kabbalists would speak of nature as a mirror, for the corporeal world reflects the spiritual forms in the manner that a mirror reflects images. Just as the image is not what is real but only its appearance, so nature is naught but the representation of that which is real. Yet, in the mirror of nature, the dichotomy between image and reality collapses, for here appearance is truth and truth appearance.

The matter is expressed in the following zoharic interpretation of the verse "Their voice carries throughout the earth" (Ps. 19:5): "Even though the supernal beings are hidden and never known, their over-flow and emanation pours out and issues forth below . . . and all the members of this world contemplate the mystery of faith of the blessed holy One through those gradations of which it is as if they are re-vealed and are not hidden and concealed."[12] The sefirotic potencies overflow to the world through the agency of the last of the divine gra-dations, the *Shekhinah*, which is alluded to in the verse in the word "earth," a term that concurrently denotes the physical universe and the spiritual potency that corresponds to the principle of materiality. On the one hand, the author of the zoharic passage adamantly affirms that it is only through the emanation of the *sefirot* in this world that one can apprehend the divine potencies; on the other hand, he is appropri-ately ambivalent regarding this epistemic possibility, for he states that people of this world contemplate the mystery of faith only through the presumption that it is "as if" the concealed gradations are revealed. The phenomena of nature are the garments by means of which the hidden light is disclosed, but it is disclosed only insofar as it is con-cealed. Moses de León makes a similar point in his *Mishkan ha-'Edut*:

> Understand the secret of the matter that when the inner lights (*ha-me'orot ha-penimiyyim*) come to the end of Thought (*sof ha-mahsha-vah*) they are garbed in her and she is a garment for them. Thus the soul (*neshamah*), which is above, is garbed in the secret of the spirit (*ruah*), which is from the end of Thought, and similarly the inner matters (*ha-devarim ha-penimiyyim*) are garbed within the matters that are not in-ternal like them. And this is the dictum of R. Eliezer the Great[13] that the blessed holy One was garbed in the light and He created the heavens, as it says, "You were wrapped in a robe of light, and You spread the heav-ens like a tent cloth" (Ps. 104:2), and it is written "You are clothed in glory and majesty" (ibid., 1).[14]

Just as the higher and immaterial aspect of the soul (*neshamah*) is attired in the lower aspect of the spirit (*ruah*), so the upper sefirotic potencies, which are "inner lights," are arrayed within the last of the *sefirot*, the *Shekhinah*, which is appropriately designated as the "end of Thought."[15] Although the process of investiture is described in the above passage, closely following the locution of the older aggadic source, as the creation of the heavens, it is questionable whether an actual act of creation is involved at all. That is, it is more likely that what is intended, already implicit in the earlier rabbinic tradition, is the emanation of the heavenly body from an attribute of the divine.[16] In the theosophic perspective adopted by Moses de León, the heavens are produced as a consequence of the luminous sefirotic gradations being garbed in the garment of the *Shekhinah*, a process that results in the overflow of light from this gradation and the consequent extension and condensation of the spirit into the material universe. In the continuation of the passage, de León emphasizes that the heaven is never separated from the garden whence it derives its sustenance and vitality. The point of this statement is surely to underscore that there are no gaps in the ontological chain even at the point of transition from the inner spirit of the divine to the material nature of the mundane, a theme that is repeated elsewhere by this kabbalist in language that is overtly pantheistic in tone. Consider, for example, a second passage from the same treatise:

> God, blessed be He, brought forth His existence and His being above and below, and He brought it forth from within the supernal Thought, and from there all the entities emanated in the secret of the supernal beasts, which are the secret of the supernal chariot in the supernal world, and the drawing forth of the inner, spiritual matters (*ha-devarim ha-penimiyyim ha-ruhaniyyim*), the form of sapphire (*gizrat sappirim*),[17] and their secret and their character is to draw forth from there the entities below. Know and contemplate that all the matters that are from the side of the Creator, blessed be He, above are all in the secret of the inner spirit (*ruah penimi*) and they are removed from all the corporeal matters (*ha-devarim gufaniyyim*).[18]

The *sefirot* in the supernal realm are of an inner spiritual nature and thus they stand in marked contrast to the physical beings below.[19] Nevertheless, the latter emanate from the former, the somatic from the spiritual. According to the kabbalistic orientation vividly portrayed by de León, the line separating theosophy and cosmology cannot be easily drawn. Indeed, in kabbalistic accounts of creation, the cosmogonic and the theogonic elements are not separable; the unbroken chain of being effaces any unambiguous distinction between creation and emanation.[20]

An examination of the commentaries on the account of creation written by kabbalists already from the formative period of the literary evolution of the kabbalah (e.g., the texts attributed to Isaac the Blind, referred to by the honorific title "the pious one," *he-hasid*, Asher ben David, Ezra ben Solomon, and Joseph bar Samuel, to name a few of the better known authors)[21] demonstrates conclusively that for these thinkers, as for Maimonides,[22] there is an intrinsic connection between the two esoteric disciplines delineated by the rabbis, the account of the chariot (*ma'aseh merkavah*) and the account of creation (*ma'aseh bereshit*). For the kabbalists, however, the link between the two is not simply the intersectedness of the physical and the metaphysical, the cosmic and the theosophic, but the inversion of the two so that the one becomes the other as the other becomes the one.[23] That is, from the kabbalistic perspective, it is not merely that natural science borders on divine science; in a very real sense, the two are identical. The study of nature involves philosophically decoding phenomena as signs that reveal the invisible unity of God, and contemplation of the divine involves poetically encoding the ineffable form with a plurality of imagined symbols. When this aspect of kabbalistic thought is pushed to a limit, as Gershom Scholem correctly noted,[24] the theistic perspective gives way to, or at least competes vigorously with, a pantheistic tendency. As I have already noted, Moses de León provides a good example of this tension between theism (related to the traditional notion of creation) and pantheism (which flows more naturally out of the philosophical doctrine of emanation). Let me cite a passage from another one of his compositions, *Sefer ha-Rimmon*: "God created the worlds in accordance with His will, and He established each and every one in accordance with its measure so that He, may He be blessed, will unify His glory in them so that they will be prepared to stand in His unity, and He will be discerned in all of them, above and below."[25] De León maintains the theistic language of creation, but the pantheistic element is so strong that it renders very dubious the possibility of preserving it in any meaningful sense. If all the worlds are viewed as links in a continuous ontological chain that not only leads back to the Infinite but guarantees that the spirit/breath/light of the Infinite permeates through every aspect of the universe, how is it possible to affirm the theistic conception of creation, which is predicated on the notion of a created world that is ontically distinct from the Creator? The glory of God is discernible equally in the supernal and the terrestrial worlds. Indeed, even though the medieval kabbalist continues to speak of an upper and a lower realm, the vertical orientation is precisely what is undermined by the mystical experience of God's omnipresence, an experience that is best expressed in the terms of pantheistic cosmology.

To apply the matter exegetically, the esoteric reading of the creation narrative yields secrets about the sefirotic potencies.[26] Numerous examples could be drawn from kabbalistic texts to illustrate the point that the words ostensibly describing the creation of the cosmos are understood as referring symbolically to the *sefirot*. Nahmanides, one of the towering rabbinic figures of the thirteenth century, concisely expressed the operative hermeneutical principle underlying this approach: The scriptural text speaks explicitly about the physical world of creation, but it alludes to the spiritual world of emanation.[27] What provides the connection between the two realms, the bridge between the visible and the imaginal, is the symbolic understanding of biblical language, the word of revelation. For example, the terms "heaven" and "earth" can concurrently signify the physical bodies to which these terms generally refer and the sefirotic potencies to which they are correlated. From an ontological perspective, however, the primary meaning of the terms relates only to the latter since the *sefirot* are what is most real, the luminous emanations that express the ontological name, the *shem hawayah*, that is, the name that imparts being upon all the beings that radiate from its pulsating power.

Many kabbalistic sources would confirm the view that the "*sefirot* are the divine master-copy of nondivine existence," and thus "contemplation of the created world leads to the revelation of the divine model that is reflected there, and the locked gates of the world of emanation are opened for man to pass through."[28] Yet, it seems to me that closer scrutiny of the relevant sources would justify reversing the order here, for once one is enlightened with mystical insight, it becomes clear that revelation of the divine model leads to a correct apprehension of the created world. To comprehend natural phenomena properly requires one to understand their symbolic meaning, which relates to the divine hypostases. When the matter is judged from that perspective it is accurate to say that nature is naught but a mirror in which the imageless form of God is seen.

Scholem astutely expressed the matter: "nature, Kabbalistically seen, is nothing but a shadow of the divine name."[29] The name, YHWH, is the one reality, which is configured in the human imagination in the form of an anthropos, the primordial Adam in whose image the lower Adam was created;[30] nature, the corporeal world, is but a shadow of this shadow, a reflection of this reflection. In the crucible of kabbalistic symbolism, the motif of nature as a mirror assumes a new form. Not only is it the case that nature reflects the glory of God, but in the most elemental sense nature is that glory, for only the latter is real, although by necessity it is invested by the garment of the former.[31] It must also be borne in mind that kabbalists posited that the divine nature is reflected in the ideal human soul, which is embodied from their standpoint in the Jewish male.[32] Indeed, kabbalists repeatedly emphasize that the soul of the Jew emanates from the divine glory in such a manner that there is no ontic separation between the two. Of the many texts that I could have cited in support of this claim, I note the expression of this motif in the poem that introduces Asher ben David's *Sefer ha-Yihud*: *we-'at nafshi 'atzulah mi-kevodo / be-rukhah 'at be-khol rega we-'onah*, "You, my soul, emanate from His glory / blessed are you in every moment and time."[33] In simple but poignant terms, this Provençal kabbalist of the thirteenth century expressed a rudimentary principle of the kabbalistic orientation: The soul of the Jew emanates from the light of God, and it is thus isomorphic with the divine. Scholarly attempts to distinguish the theosophical and anthropological concerns of the kabbalists, a distinction that has even been employed to explain typological shifts in the history of Jewish mysticism, are feeble and misguided. Basic to the symbolic orientation of medieval kabbalists is the belief that the divine spark is reflected in the soul of Israel, which itself may be viewed as a microcosm and hence as a mirror of the mirror of nature.[34] Consider, for example, the following passage from the zoharic anthology:

> R. Simeon said we have learned that when the blessed holy One created the world He engraved in the engravings of the mystery of faith within the lights of the supernal mysteries, and He engraved above and below, and everything was in one mystery. He made the lower world in the pattern of the supernal world; the one stands parallel to the other so that everything will be one in a single unity. Thus the blessed holy One engraved the engravings of the letters above and below, and He created the world through them. Come and see: In the manner that the blessed holy One made the world, thus He also created the primal Adam.[35]

The same idea is formulated in the words of Moses de León, which can be considered a typical expression of the idea that by turning inward one can attain knowledge of God and of the world:[36]

> In the beginning of my words and at the outset of my treatise, I have come to acknowledge and to praise the Lord of everything, for He is the origin of everything and He is prior to everything, the beginning of all beginnings and the end of every limit. He created man in His pattern, in the image of the likeness of His form. In miniature He comprises the form of the world, which is in the image of all the [sefirotic] entities. And He placed in him power from the totality of the gradations in the mystery of the One who is "awesome in splendor" (Exod. 15:11). That which goes out of the general principle does not go out in order to teach about itself, but to teach about the general principle in its entirety,[37] so that one may discern the Lord of everything who suspends His world like a cluster.[38]

The human being (in its idealized form as the embodied male Jew)[39] and the universe are depicted in the above citation as two parallel beings that are both in the pattern of the divine form, which is manifest in the luminous emanations configured as an anthropos in human imagination. The convergence of these three nodal points in the kabbalistic onto-theology, God, Israel, and world, can be traced back to a symbolic structure operative in the second part of *Sefer Yetzirah*. The letters of the Hebrew alphabet are manifest on three planes of being, *'olam* (spatiality), *shanah* (temporality), and *nefesh* (vitality/breath). If we substitute God for *shanah*, a substitution that I think is justified by the assumption that time in its interminable surging forward and turning backward best captures the present absence of the absent presence, we can establish the parallelism: That which is may be viewed from three vantage points, divine, human, and cosmic. The correlative nature of these three points entails the possibility of one being the surface through which the other is seen, a doubling of vision in the hermeneutical circle of reflection: The world is a mirror of God, for God is a mirror of the world; the soul is a mirror of the world, for the world is a mirror of the soul; God is the mirror of the soul, for the soul is a mirror of God.

To be sure, as I have already remarked, for the kabbalist, what is ultimately real is the name of four letters, YHWH, which comprises the twenty-two letters of the holy language, Hebrew. This name, moreover, is the hidden meaning of Torah, the light of the invisible and formless God concealed in the shapes and forms of each of the letters. It would seem, therefore, that there is no possibility to get behind the mirrors, for the ultimate being is fathomable only through the investiture of the name, which is itself a surface that reflects the rays of infinite light, a delimitation that deflects the utterance of the voice that has no limit.[40] Inasmuch as reality in its most elemental being is apprehended as the unfolding of the letters of the name, the luminous secret that shines in and through the letters and scribal ornamentation of the Torah, human experience of the world is viewed as inherently symbolic, a poetic thinking that transforms external reality into a mirror through which the internal image of the invisible God can be seen in its invisibility. While medieval kabbalists undoubtedly assumed that the corporeal world was independent of the human mind, and they further presumed the existence of the divine being beyond the physical universe, their ontological realism is significantly qualified by the fact that they allowed for only a symbolic approach to both of these realms. It is precisely this reciprocal reflection that occasions the semiotic transmutation of the corporeal, the textualization of reality. Further on I shall have the opportunity to expand on this process of linguistic expiation by means of which physical nature is redeemed in the mindset of the kabbalists.

Perhaps it is not anachronistic to say that kabbalists were well aware of the inevitable plight of human consciousness that has been so well documented by modern philosophers who ponder nature from a post-Kantian constructivist perspective: The immediacy of the world as it is in itself cannot be apprehended by human beings since all knowledge is mediated. Even more relevant for understanding the kabbalistic orientation is the application of the Kantian epistemology by Ernst Cassirer to the realm of symbols. According to Cassirer, every form of existence can become visible only through the prism of the symbol. The tangled web of human experience is such that one cannot confront reality in an immediate sense; the universe is symbolic in its nature. "Instead of dealing with the things themselves," writes Cassirer, "man is in a sense constantly conversing with himself. He has so enveloped himself in linguistic forms, in artistic images, in mythical symbols or religious rites that he cannot see or know anything except by interposition of this artificial medium."[41] Elsewhere Cassirer expresses the matter as follows: "For all mental processes fail to grasp reality itself, and in order to represent it, to hold it at all, they are driven to the use of symbols. But all symbolism harbors the curse of mediacy: it is bound to obscure what it seeks to reveal."[42]

The basic mode of human apprehension is the symbol, but the symbol is not merely a figure that reflects a given reality; it is rather the form that produces and posits that reality. To be sure, if we begin from this standpoint, then the question regarding a "reality" independent of these symbolic forms becomes irrelevant. However, the price of solving one problem is leaving another unattended. That is, the "curse of mediacy" to which Cassirer referred is in no way alleviated; on the contrary, it is intensified, for every form of existence can become visible or comprehensible only through the prism of the symbol. If this is the case, however, that which is imaged is itself best captured in the image of the image, which leads to Cassirer's insight that the symbol inevitably obscures what it seeks to reveal. To get beyond the ostensible contradiction, we can posit a logic of paradox predicated on the assumption that the concealment is itself the disclosure. To apply the hermeneutic of secrecy to the specific theme of this analysis, the only thing that is real is the infinite light of God that shines upon the surface—as if through a veil—of the natural world. The divine reality is accessible through the reflection of nature, which is real as that which is not real, but that is all we can hope to attain in the hopelessly endless series of semiotic refractions and ocular displacements.

The inevitable consequence of the symbolic orientation of medieval kabbalah can be expressed precisely in terms of the doubling of vision to which I have alluded, for that which is seen is always an image of an image. There is no way to extricate oneself from this entanglement of symbolic reflection. To speak of nature as the mirror of God means that God is symbolically reflected in the events of this world, but such a claim problematizes the possibility of gaining direct access to either the world or to God. The mirror is like a garment inasmuch as it facilitates the representation of that which is beyond representation, but in so doing it presupposes distance and otherness, the space that makes reflection possible and necessary.[43] Language itself is the ultimate veil through which the nature of being is unveiled, a theme that has reverberated especially in the contemporary notion of poeisis (which can be traced to the Romantic conception of language) as the most authentic path of thought, an idea particularly prominent in the "thinking poetics" of Martin Heidegger's later work,[44] but affirmed by other prominent philosophers of this century, including in the new thinking of Franz Rosenzweig[45] and in the critical hermeneutics of Hans Gadamer.[46] If, however, language is the veil through which that which is veiled is unveiled, then the manner in which it is unveiled is itself a form of veiling. In a separate study, I have argued that the hermeneutical position adopted in zoharic literature (and this may be extended to theosophic kabbalists more generally) is such that there can be no unveiling of naked truth, for truth that is stark naked—divested of all appearance—is mere simulation. Truth that is apparent is disclosed in and through the garment of its enclosure.[47]

Few kabbalists actually discuss in an explicit manner the nature of the symbol. One exception, however, is Joseph Gikatilla, who has a brief, but very poignant, discussion on the symbol in the introduction to *Sha'arei 'Orah*.[48] While we must certainly allow for diversity of opinion on this seminal issue, as we do with respect to all of the issues that engaged the imagination of the kabbalists, Gikatilla's remarks can nevertheless be taken as representative of a hermeneutical perspective adopted by a wide range of kabbalists. In an effort to explain the use of anthropomorphic expressions to characterize the divine, Gikatilla begins with the axiomatic statement, which was a central tenet of medieval religious philosophy, that God is not a body and thus there is no exact resemblance between human corporeality and the divine being. Whatever positive meaning is assigned to the biblical notion of Adam having been created in God's image, the latter cannot refer to the human body. "Do not think," writes Gikatilla, "that the eye [of God] is in the form of the actual eye or the hand in the form of an actual hand, but these are the innermost of the internal matters with respect to the truth of the existence of the Lord, blessed be He. . . . The intention of the forms of the limbs, which are in us, is that they are made in the image of signs (*be-dimyon simmanim*), the hidden, supernal matters that the mind cannot know except in the manner of signification (*ke-dimyon zikkaron*)."[49]

In line with the hermeneutical stance adopted by a number of philosophically oriented exegetes, including, most prominently, Maimonides, Gikatilla rejects the possibility of interpreting biblical anthropomorphisms in a literal sense since God does not have a physical body. Yet, he differs from the philosophical approach insofar as he maintains that the ontological reality of the divine is not merely conveyed in anthropomorphic terms, but it must be experienced in that very manner.[50] For Gikatilla, therefore, the use of anthropomorphisms in theological discourse is not to be explained as a concession to the limitations of human reason; on the contrary, anthropomorphic representation of the divine is indicative of an ultimate truth about the nature of embodiment, including the corporeal nature of the world and that of the human being. From the kabbalistic perspective, well articulated by Gikatilla, the presumption that the limbs of the physical body signify the limbs of the spiritual body entails as well the presumption that the reality of the former, much like that of the latter, is constituted by letters. The ontological conclusion that Gikatilla draws from the fact that God is incorporeal is thus opposite from what is adopted by Maimonides, that is, the nature of human and cosmic corporeality as such is called into question. The anthropomorphic images, when viewed under the lens of the kabbalistic symbolism, indicate that the semiotic nature of the body is what is real. The concreteness of carnality is determined by linguistic measurement, what we may call the tonality of the textual body. Although in this context Gikatilla himself focuses on the human body in relation to the divine, it is feasible to extend his orientation to the nature of the body of the universe more generally since he would have surely assented (in line with other kabbalists of his time and place)[51] to the view that the human body is a microcosm of the world at large, which can be depicted as a macro-anthropos.[52]

Engendered Body-Image in Reflection of Nature's Mirror

In the kabbalistic worldview, the understanding of nature as a symbol for the divine relates as well (as we might expect) to the centrality of gender as a hermeneutical category. It lies beyond the scope of this study to enter into a lengthy discussion related to this topic, but suffice it to say that the prevalent orientation toward gender in kabbalistic sources rests on two axes. First, a distinctive feature of the kabbalistic symbolism is the rendering of ontology in embodied terms; there is no body devoid of gender, even a sexless body. Second, the model of gender that the kabbalists adopted is phallomorphic in orientation, which is to say they viewed the construction of gender identity, both male and female, from the perspective of the phallus. The first point is obvious enough and thus demands no elaboration.

With respect to the second point, the evidence regarding the phallo-centric orientation of the kabbalists is clear and beyond doubt. The presumed adoration of the feminine on the part of kabbalists, which I supposedly have eclipsed by my incessant and obsessive phallo-morphism, has no textual grounding.[53] In studies published in the last six years, and others to come out in the course of the next few years, I have provided dozens of textual samples, which are culled from authors living in disparate places and times, to support my interpretative stance. The protests notwithstanding, the evidence that I have marshaled in support of my thesis has hardly been touched, although some have cleverly presented their claims in the semblance of credible arguments. The case stands, as far as I can tell, that the construction of gender ensues from a decidedly phallocentric perspective. This is not to deny the utilization of imaginative representations of the feminine. The question at the end of the day is: what is the hermeneutical standpoint regarding the respective values that are assigned by medieval kabbalists (and their modern lineage) to the feminine and the masculine? I readily acknowledge a fair degree of fluidity, of crossing gender boundaries, but this movement occurs within a well-demarcated framework marked by the ascription of the power to overflow to the male and of the power to receive to the female. The female can overflow, but in doing so she is masculinized; a male can receive, but in doing so he is feminized.

The rationale for mentioning this matter here lies in the fact that the perspective on gender is obviously relevant to a reflection on the theme of nature as a mirror in medieval kabbalah. Both the image of the mirror and that of nature as a reference to the corporeal world are related specifically to the female. Nature is, first and foremost, the signature of body, which is assigned by the kabbalists, following the conventional wisdom of the Middle Ages, to the feminine. In the hierarchical polarity widespread in medieval culture, spirit or soul corresponds to the male and body to the female. To avoid potential misunderstanding, I state clearly that my use of the term "body" in discussing kabbalistic thought is conditioned by the kabbalists' own understanding of embodiment. Accordingly, "body" does not denote the physical mass that is quantifiable and measurable, but the phenomenological sense of the corporeal as lived presence. Moreover, as I have already intimated, the kabbalists adhered to the claim that the nature of body so understood is constituted by the Hebrew letters, the language of creation. That is to say, the experience of embodiment for the kabbalists entails the visual discernment of the linguistic nature of body. I have noted above, and I shall expand the discussion below, that the transformation of the material into the semiotic serves as the means by which nature is redeemed from its corporeality, not by divesting the sheath of the body but by investing it with the garment of the name.

It is precisely the correlation of nature and the feminine that underlies the widespread association in kabbalistic sources of *Shekhinah* and the account of creation (*ma'aseh bereshit*). The logic of this symbolic alliance is transparent enough: As I have already observed, there is an ontic intersection between the mundane and divine spheres such that the act of creation overlaps with the process of emanation. For most of the kabbalists this occurs with the emanation of the last of the *sefirot*, the point of transition from the realm of unity to the realm of particularity. All the divine potencies overflow to *Shekhinah* and out of the matrix of the latter the heavens and earth come to be. It is certainly for this reason, for instance, that Ezra of Gerona interpolates his *sodot ma'aseh bereshit*, the "secrets of creation," after his comment on the words, "hedged about with lilies," *sugah ba-shoshanim* (Song of Songs 7:3), which is applied to *Shekhinah* who is "comprised of the six extremities and sealed in everything."[54] At this juncture (both textually and ontologically) it is appropriate to speak of the account of creation, since *Shekhinah* is the end of the realm of unity and the beginning of the world of multiplicity. To be sure, in his description of creation, exegetically linked to Psalm 104, Ezra weaves back and forth from the sefirotic realm to the physical universe. The exegetical crisscrossing reflects the fluidity of ontological boundaries well attested in kabbalistic literature. The dual meaning of the creation narrative mirrors the two spheres of being that intersect in the imagination of the visionary's soul.[55]

Creation of the world is thus linked to the last of the emanations, for (in an obviously Neoplatonic fashion) the light is successively more condensed as it emanates from the source. But there is another reason for this symbolic connection: Just as nature is a mirror of the divine, so *Shekhinah* is portrayed as a speculum (*mar'ah* or *heizu* are the terms most frequently employed in zoharic literature) in and through which the upper image appears. The association of these terms with *Shekhinah* also underscores that this divine attribute corresponds to the element of the soul that makes the visual contemplation of the image of the imageless God possible. Hence, *Shekhinah* is the mirror (*mar'ah*) through which the vision (*mar'eh*) is beheld. The specularizing role of *Shekhinah* suggests that it corresponds to the imagination, the agency of the soul that facilitates the seeing of the imaginal form of that which has no form. Alternatively expressed, when the kabbalist visualizes the image of God as the sacred name that assumes an anthropomorphic form, *Shekhinah* becomes a tangible and concrete presence within the soul. The theosophical attribute of *Shekhinah*, which is manifest in the psychological plane as the faculty of imagination, is the (feminine) mirror that reflects the (masculine) image that contains within itself all the images.[56]

To cite one example here: Commenting on the expression *ba-mar'eh*, "in a vision" (Num. 12:6), the zoharic authorship writes: "For this appearance is like a mirror (*mar'ah*) in which the images (*diyoq-nin*) are seen. Therefore, it says, 'And I saw' (Gen. 31:10), I perceived His image in El Shaddai, which is the mirror in which is seen the other image, and all the supernal images are seen within it."[57] One might contend that, according to this text, the feminine *Shekhinah* is the object of vision, but such an interpretation fails to comprehend the symbolism properly. The feminine is the mirror and the mirror is not an object of vision per se, but the medium for visualization. The real object of vision is the image reflected within the speculum that does not shine, the invisible surface that allows the concealed image to be seen. And to what may that image refer? Let us heed the continuation of the passage:

> Therefore in that moment regarding Jacob it is written, "He dreamt and behold there was a ladder that was standing on the ground" (Gen. 28:12). What is the ladder? The gradation in which the other gradations are dependent and it is the foundation of the world. "And its head reached heavenward." . . . What is the head? The head of the ladder. And what is it? The one of whom it is written "the head of the bed" (ibid. 47:31), for it is the head of that bed and from it she is illuminated.[58]

The image that is beheld in the speculum is identified as the head of the ladder, which is also encoded symbolically as the head of the bed. It is obvious that both of these expressions refer to the gradation of the divine that corresponds to the phallus.[59] For my purposes what is significant is the implicit gender reversal that is associated with the double mirroring: The feminine is the mirror that reflects the image that is itself a mirror in which is contained all the other images. Previously, I have had the opportunity to discuss the gender implications of the motif of *Shekhinah* as the archetypal image through which the (phallic) image is visualized.[60] In this study, I should like to deal directly with the philosophic implications of this symbolism for the kabbalistic orientation toward nature, and the larger consequences this might have for the effort to elicit an ecological sympathy on the basis of traditional kabbalistic material.

Those who would draw upon the sources of medieval kabbalah for a more positive view of nature, related especially to the adoration of nature as the creative feminine principle, have misread the symbolism of the classical sources, a misreading that I readily endorse as a human being but regrettably reject as a historical scholar. Scholem already recognized that when the creative element is attributed to *Shekhinah* in kabbalistic sources, the feminine potency is depicted in male symbols.[61] I have gone further than Scholem, however, for both psychoanalytic and feminist criticism have provided me with a mode of discourse to describe the subtle gender shifts by means of which we can speak intelligibly of the masculine transvaluation of motherhood and the phallic womb.[62]

Running the risk of beating a dead horse, I would stress that the textual evidence is as clear as daylight to one with eyes to see. When the female is portrayed in positive terms, she is consistently transposed into part of the male. To provide a litany of symbols for the feminine as a criticism of my paradigm is insufficient because it fails to take note of my central contention regarding the ontological transformation of these symbols. The female appears to be ontologically distinct, but in truth she is no more than the looking glass that reflects what is genuinely real, the masculine image, which is attributed more specifically to the phallic gradation. This very transposition applies to the image of nature as mirror, for from one perspective the mirror assumes the character of something independently real, but from another perspective the mirror is constituted by the image reflected therein. Simply put, if there is no face facing the mirror, then how does the mirror appear? The mirror best performs its function as a reflecting medium to the extent that its surface is invisible: to see a thing in a mirror requires that one does not see anything on the mirror.[63] This visual duplicity is the import of assigning the symbol of the mirror to *Shekhinah*: she is what she is because she is what she is not, and only in not being who she is not, is she what she is. *Shekhinah* is an invisible surface that allows the images from above to be seen because she has no image of her own. To appreciate the kabbalistic understanding of the mirror of nature, one must understand the nature of dissimulation associated with the mirror along the lines that I have suggested.

A feminist ecology that purports to be rooted in traditional kabbalistic sources is based on a misreading, albeit a form of midrashic eisegesis that is morally demanded by the times in which we live. In spite of my own personal predilection, as a historian of medieval texts, I must say that the pervasive attitude of the kabbalists toward the body of nature is quite typically androcentric in its orientation. Nature is not adored as a goddess; it is treated as that which must be conquered and subdued, not in the sense of abusing nature but in the sense of transforming the corporeality of nature and elevating it to the higher, spiritual level. According to some passages, the earth (or nature) is depicted as the locus of the demonic power (related exegetically to Gen. 1:2).[64] The basis for this symbolic association is that the earth is the feminine, and the feminine is correlated with the attribute of judgment, which is the source of the demonic potency within the economy of the Godhead. Moreover, in kabbalistic sources, the creative potency is consistently located in the phallus.[65] The phallomorphic attitude is exemplified in the following passage that describes the four images of the beasts that bore the throne according to Ezekiel's vision of the chariot, which correspond to the divine emanations of *Hesed, Gevurah, Rahamim,* and *Malkhut*:

> When these four images, which are formed in their form, come forth, they shine, sparkle, and glow, and they sow the seed upon the world. Then [the earth] is called the "seed-bearing plant" (Gen. 1:12), the plant of those seeds that are sowed upon the world. The image of Adam, which comprises all the images, comes forth, and then it is written, "and trees of every kind bearing fruit with the seed in it upon the earth" (ibid.). The seed is discharged only for a purpose. Upon the earth "with the seed in it," precisely. From here [we learn] that the Jewish male[66] does not have permission to discharge semen in vain.[67]

The world, which signifies both the principle of corporeality in the divine realm and physical nature, is the feminine, but the feminine is transformed into a creative force (in the scriptural language, a "seed-bearing plant") only by virtue of the seminal fluid that she receives from the male. While one might wax romantic about the equally important role accorded the feminine in kabbalistic symbolism, this passage, and countless others that could have been cited, indicate that the female is accorded significance only in virtue of being the receptacle that receives the male seed. This is precisely the notion of nature implied in this text. We can look upon nature in positive terms if we appreciate this phallomorphic perspective.

On balance, kabbalists adopt a rather negative view toward the material universe as that which must be overcome. To be sure, kabbalists follow standard rabbinic thinking to the degree that there is recognition that fulfillment of ritual requires the physical world. From that perspective, nature serves as a vehicle for divine worship. But true spiritual piety, which is cultivated by the mystical fraternity, demands an abrogation of the sensual pleasures of the body, which goes beyond the strict letter of the law. When this is translated into the standard categories of gender, then we are justified in speaking of the transmutation of the feminine (body) into the masculine (spirit), the restoration of the female into the male. In this respect, the kabbalists reflect the typical medieval attitude toward the body as that which must be surmounted. Naturally, I do not deny that it is a salient characteristic of kabbalistic symbolism that the anthropomorphic representation of God is augmented and intensified (and not merely interpreted as we find in the case of Maimonides). However, the use of anthropomorphism to depict God does not betoken a more positive approach toward corporeality. The contrary is the case: The imaginal construction of the divine configuration is predicated on a nullification of the physical body. As I put the matter in an earlier study, the ultimate goal of mystical contemplation is the separation of the intellect from the body, but the consciousness fostered by proper intention in prayer is predicated on the iconic visualization of the divine Presence in bodily terms. The ascetic negation of the physical body, therefore, allows for the ocular apprehension of God's imaginal body.[68] A more specific application of this dialectic is that the eroticism of kabbalistic symbolism is based on sexual abstinence. In medieval kabbalistic symbolism, there is no celebration of the body, nature, or the feminine. To presume that there is such a veneration of nature is to fail to grasp the intellectual world that fostered the creation of this material. If one wishes to appreciate the tonality and texture of the kabbalistic worldview, it is necessary to accord the proper place to the ascetic predilection of the mystical tradition[69] and the consequent annulment of nature, or at the very least, the ontological transmutation of corporeal nature into the image that she reflects as the mirror of that which is invisible.

Notes

1. Herbert Grabes, *Speculum, Mirror, und Looking-Glass: Kontinuität und Originalität der Spiegelmetapher in den Buchtiteln des Mittelalters und der englischen Literatur des 13. bis 17. Jahrhunderts* (Tübingen: M. Niemeyer, 1973), 76–78.

2. See Richard Rorty, *Philosophy and the Mirror of Nature* (Princeton: Princeton University Press, 1980), 131–311.

3. For a superb study of Derridean philosophy in the context of a study on the philosophical criticism of reflexivity, see Rodolphe Gasché, *The Tain of the Mirror: Derrida and the Philosophy of Reflection* (Cambridge, Mass.: Harvard University Press, 1986). To understand my reflections in this study, it behooves one to become acquainted with the history of this discussion in philosophical (especially post-Cartesian) thought. Gasché's book is an excellent place to begin.

4. Amos Funkenstein, *Theology and the Scientific Imagination from the Middle Ages to the Seventeenth Century* (Princeton: Princeton University Press, 1986), 49–50.

5. Isaiah Tishby, *The Wisdom of the Zohar: An Anthology of Texts*, trans. David Goldstein, 3 vols. (Oxford: Oxford University Press, 1989), 1:272–73.

6. *Zohar* 1.145b, 156b, 158b; 2.15b; 3.20a.

7. *Zohar* 1.129a.

8. For three relatively recent attempts to assess the date and provenance of *Sefer Yetzirah*, see Yehuda Liebes, "The Seven Double Letters BGD KFRT: On the Double Reish and the Background of Sefer Yezira" (in Hebrew), *Tarbiz* 61 (1992): 237–47; Joseph Dan, "The Religious Meaning of Sefer Yezira" (in Hebrew), *Jerusalem Studies in Jewish Thought* 11 (1993): 1–35; Steven M. Wasserstrom, "Sefer Yesira and Early Islam: A Reappraisal," *Journal of Jewish Thought and Philosophy* 3 (1993): 1–30.

9. See Gershom Scholem, "The Name of God and the Linguistic Theory of the Kabbalah," *Diogenes* 79 (1972): 72–76.

10. In this matter, I do not see any reason to contrast the so-called two major trends of kabbalah, the theosophic and ecstatic, which has become fashionable in contemporary scholarship. For preliminary discussion and citation of some relevant kabbalistic texts, see Elliot R. Wolfson, "The Doctrine of Sefirot in the Prophetic Kabbalah of Abraham Abulafia," *Jewish Studies Quarterly* 2 (1995): 347 n. 35.

11. I translate from the text included in Daniel Abrams, *R. Asher ben David: His Complete Works and Studies in His Kabbalistic Thought* (in Hebrew) (Los Angeles: Keruv, 1996), 310. For an alternative version with some important textual variations, see ibid., 314.

12. *Zohar* 2.137a.

13. *Pirqei Rabbi Eli'ezer* (Warsaw, 1852), chap. 3, 7b–8a.

14. MS Berlin, Staatsbibliothek Or. Quat. 833, fol. 69a.

15. In Moses de León's works, "thought" (*mahshavah*) is one of the terms assigned to *Hokhmah*, the second of the ten *sefirot*. Insofar as the entire pleroma can be viewed as a manifestation of divine wisdom, often expressed exegetically in terms of the verse "You have made them all with wisdom" (Ps. 104:24), it makes perfectly good sense to refer to the last of the emanations as the "end of thought." This expres-

sion conveys another idea as well: There is a homology between the upper Wisdom and *Shekhinah*, which is called the lower Wisdom, a relationship that is conveyed as well in terms of the special connection between father and daughter.

16. See Alexander Altmann, *Studies in Religious Philosophy and Mysticism* (Ithaca: Cornell University Press, 1969), 128–39.

17. Based on Lam. 4:7.

18. MS Berlin, Staatsbibliothek Or. Quat. 833, fol. 15a. See the discussion on pantheism, with particular reference to the passages from de León, in Gershom Scholem, *Major Trends in Jewish Mysticism* (New York: Schocken Books, 1954), 221–23.

19. For an explicit denial of the attribution of corporeal images to the divine, in language that is strongly reminiscent of Maimonides, see *R. Moses de Leon's Sefer Sheqel ha-Qodesh* (in Hebrew), ed. Charles Mopsik (Los Angeles: Cherub Press, 1996), 2.

20. See Scholem, *Major Trends*, 213–15, 224–25; idem, *Kabbalah* (Jerusalem: Keter, 1974), 147–52; Ephraim Gottlieb, *Studies in Kabbala Literature* (in Hebrew), ed. J. Hacker (Tel-Aviv: Tel-Aviv University Press, 1976), 23–26; Tishby, *Wisdom of the Zohar*, 1:273–83, 2:549–55.

21. For discussion of some of the early kabbalistic approaches to cosmology (*ma'aseh bereshit*), see Gottlieb, *Studies in Kabbala Literature*, 18–28, 59–87. Many of the relevant texts are conveniently described and partially transcribed in Abrams, *R. Asher ben David*, 301–53.

22. See *The Guide of the Perplexed*, trans. S. Pines (Chicago: University of Chicago Press, 1963), introduction, 9.

23. With regard to this issue, kabbalists should not be isolated from a more general phenomenon attested in the Middle Ages. Consider, for example, the following description given by Edward Grant, "Cosmology," in *Science in the Middle Ages*, ed. David C. Lindberg (Chicago: University of Chicago Press, 1978), 266: "In the Middle Ages, the structure of the world was never conceived solely in physical and metaphysical terms, but had to be made compatible with a variety of theological concepts which, in the end, transformed the Aristotelian cosmos into a Christian universe." This sober observation could certainly be applied to the case of Judaism and to Islam if we substitute the adjective "religious" for "Christian." With respect to the medieval kabbalists it is especially the theosophical concepts that transformed the Aristotelian (or, if you like, the Aristotelian-Neoplatonic) cosmos into a Jewish universe. On the dependence of medieval kabbalists on philosophical cosmology, see Scholem, *Kabbalah*, 87–88, 117.

24. See above, n. 18.

25. *The Book of the Pomegranate: Moses de León's Sefer ha-Rimmon*, ed. Elliot R. Wolfson, Brown Judaic Studies, no. 144 (Atlanta, Ga.: Scholars Press, 1988), 102 (Hebrew section).

26. This is a particular example of the more general hermeneutical perspective regarding the fact that scriptural verses describe concurrently events in nature or history and stages in the divine process. See Scholem, *Major Trends*, 209–10.

27. See Elliot R. Wolfson, "By Way of Truth: Aspects of Nahmanides' Kabbalistic Hermeneutics," *Association for Jewish Studies Review* 14 (1989): 110–11.

28. Tishby, *Wisdom of the Zohar*, 1:273.

29. David Biale, "Gershom Scholem's Ten Unhistorical Aphorisms on Kabbalah," in *Gershom Scholem*, ed. Harold Bloom (New York: Chelsea House Publishers, 1987), 113.

30. Tishby, *Wisdom of the Zohar*, 1:295–98.

31. The idea that nature is the divine reality was reinforced by the numerical equivalence of the Hebrew word for nature, *ha-teva*, and the name of God, *'elohim*, i.e., both words equal 86. On the history of the exegetical applications and resonances of this numerology, see Moshe Idel, *Maïmonide et la mystique juive*, trans. Charles Mopsik (Paris: Les Editions du Cerf, 1991), 105–34.

32. The divine nature of the human soul is duly noted by Scholem, *Major Trends*, 239–43, but it is not always clear that he appreciated the necessary limitation of this anthropological conception to the Jews. Thus, he speaks of the "Kabbalistic view of the nature of man" (p. 239) or the soul as "a spark of the divine life" without specifying that the reference is to the soul of Israel. He does, however, remark that the *neshamah*, or the "holy soul," according to the zoharic literature is "identical with the Kabbalist" who acquires it "only by penetrating into the mysteries of the Torah" (p. 241). For a more comprehensive discussion of the divine nature of the Jewish soul in zoharic kabbalah, see Tishby, *Wisdom of the Zohar*, 2:677–98. It is lamentable that contemporary scholars of medieval kabbalah, especially scholars writing in English in North America, have rendered terms such as *ben 'adam*, or its Aramaic equivalent, *bar nash*, generically as human, a rendering that effectively conceals the ethnocentric and androcentric tendency of the kabbalistic anthropology. I have explored the matter briefly in "Remembering the Covenant: Memory, Forgetfulness, and the Construction of History in the *Zohar*," in *Jewish History and Jewish Memory: Essays in Honor of Yosef Hayim Yerushalmi*, ed. Elisheva Carlebach, John M. Efron, and David N. Myers (Waltham, Mass.: Brandeis University Press; Hanover, N.H.: University Press of New England, 1998), 240–41 n. 74, and again, in much more detail, in "Ontology, Alterity, and Ethics in Kabbalistic Anthropology," *Exemplaria* 12 (2000): 129–55. I note, in passing, that the ethnocentric attitude of the kabbalists has been properly recognized by David Novak, *The Election of Israel: The Idea of the Chosen People* (Cambridge: Cambridge University Press, 1995), 16–17, 218 n. 68. Many of the criticisms of my gender paradigm are easily removed when one attends properly to the meaning of such key expressions as *bar nash*. Critics may insist that my phallocentric interpretation is skewed and has led me to offer a distorted picture of the kabbalah, but such remarks are rendered meaningless in light of the overwhelming textual evidence that medieval kabbalists understood the notion of humanity in the fullest sense as embodied in the male Jew. Naturally, the individual male Jew needs to be completed by the female, for the unity of the person requires the engendered other, but that hardly justifies the claim that kabbalistic symbolism celebrates the female as much as the male.

33. Abrams, *R. Asher ben David*, 49.

34. To some extent, the medieval kabbalistic motif evolves out of earlier rabbinic statements. Consider *Avot de-Rabbi Natan*, ed. Solomon Schechter (Vienna, 1887), chap. 31, 46a–b. In a lengthy tradition attributed to Yose the Galilean, the position that is affirmed is that whatever God created in the universe He created in man.

35. *Zohar* 1.38a.

36. Regarding this theme in Moses de León, see Adolph Jellinek, *Moses ben*

Schem-Tob de Leon und sein Verhältnis zum Sohar (Leipzig: Heinrich Hunger, 1851), 10; Altmann, *Studies in Religious Philosophy and Mysticism*, 16–18.

37. Based on one of the thirteen hermeneutical principles attributed to R. Ishmael in the beginning of *Sifra on Leviticus*, ed. L. Finkelstein (New York: Jewish Theological Seminary of America, 1983), 2:4 (in Hebrew).

38. *Book of the Pomegranate*, ed. Wolfson, 4–5 (Hebrew section).

39. The tension between the more rationalist approach according to which the divine image is linked to the invisible soul that is hidden in the body, on the one hand, and the more imaginative approach that links the image to the body of man, especially the Jewish man since the circumcised phallus plays such a key role in the visual contemplation, is evident in the following remark of de León in *Sheqel ha-Qodesh*, 2–3: "None of the inhabitants of the world or any of the sages 'who perform the holy labor' (Exod. 36:4) can compare the soul (*nefesh*) to any image or form in the world. And if it is the case that no one can compare this soul, which dwells constantly with men, to any image or form, how much more so is it the case for the blessed One who made this soul that is separate from any image or form. The rabbis, may their memory be for a blessing, already said in the [tractate of the] gemara, Berakhot [10a] with respect to the verse, 'Bless the Lord, O my soul' (Ps. 103:1), that the virtues of the soul are compared to its Creator. And I have seen in the midrash on the secret of what the sages, pillars of the world, said . . . 'From my flesh I will see God' (Job 19:26). 'From my flesh,' from the matter that is hidden in my flesh I must know and discern the matter of the stature and the glory of the blessed One. Therefore, you can comprehend from the way of this soul that is within you the matter of the greatness of His stature, may He be blessed, for He is separated from all the corporeal events and entities of this world. Thus I alert you in order to set you straight to know that no one can comprehend the splendor of His stature and the greatness of His strength and power. And thus [from the] content of the structure of the human body one can comprehend in accordance with His thought." As Mopsik pointed out (*R. Moses de León's Sefer Sheqel ha-Qodesh*, p. 2 n. 19), the citation of the midrashic source by de León probably refers to a zoharic passage like the one that he mentioned, viz., *Zohar* 1.94a. But, as Mopsik also notes, the "flesh" mentioned in Job 19:26 is interpreted therein as a reference to the embodied phallus and not to the formless soul. Regarding the former interpretation, see Elliot R. Wolfson, *Through a Speculum That Shines: Vision and Imagination in Medieval Jewish Mysticism* (Princeton, N.J.: Princeton University Press, 1994), 342.

40. On the mirror as a metaphor for limit, see Pierre Legendre, *Dieu au miroir: Etude sur l'institution des images* (Paris: Fayard, 1994), 82–84.

41. Ernest Cassirer, *An Essay on Man: An Introduction to a Philosophy of Human Culture* (New Haven: Yale University Press, 1944), 25.

42. Ernest Cassirer, *Language and Myth*, trans. Susanne K. Langer (New York: Harper and Brothers, 1946), 7.

43. On the narcissistic element underlying the depiction of the mirror as the means that occasions the differentiation of the other, see Legendre, *Dieu au miroir*, 55–58, 73–82.

44. See Marc Froment-Meurice, *That Is To Say: Heidegger's Poetics*, trans. Jan Plug (Stanford: Stanford University Press, 1998).

45. For a discussion of language in the new thinking of Rosenzweig with particu-

lar sensitivity to the poetic, see Barbara E. Galli, *Franz Rosenzweig and Jehuda Halevi: Translating, Translations, and Translators* (Montreal: McGill-Queen's University Press, 1995), 360–98. See also Yudit Kornberg Greenberg, *Better Than Wine: Love, Poetry, and Prayer in the Thought of Franz Rosenzweig* (Atlanta, Ga.: Scholars Press, 1996).

46. Four recent studies that explore the intricate relationship of philosophical reflection and poetry include *Philosophers' Poets*, ed. David Wood (London and New York: Routledge, 1990); *Beyond Representation: Philosophy and Poetic Imagination*, ed. R. Eldridge (Cambridge: Cambridge University Press, 1996); Paul Colilli, *The Idea of a Living Spirit: Poetic Logic as a Contemporary Theory* (Toronto: University of Toronto Press, 1997); Philippe Lacoue-Labarthe, *Poetry as Experience*, trans. Andrea Tarnowski (Stanford: Stanford University Press, 1999).

47. Elliot R. Wolfson, "Occultation of the Feminine and the Body of Secrecy in Medieval Kabbalah," in *Rending the Veil: Concealment and Secrecy in the History of Religions*, ed. Elliot R. Wolfson (New York: Seven Bridges Press, 1999), 113–54.

48. To date, the most comprehensive discussion of this subject is found in B. Huss, "R. Joseph Gikatilla's Definition of Symbolism and Its Versions in Kabbalistic Literature" (in Hebrew), *Jerusalem Studies in Jewish Thought* 12 (1996): 157–76.

49. *Sha'arei Orah*, ed. Yosef Ben-Shlomo (Jerusalem: Mosad Bialik, 1981), 1:49. For an extended analysis of this passage, see Huss, "Gikatilla's Definition of Symbolism," 160–64.

50. With respect to the recognition that the anthropomorphic representation of God relates to experience (and thus ultimately embraces the ontological) and not merely to literary depiction, there is an interesting similarity between the thought of Rosenzweig and kabbalists. The understanding of Rosenzweig's interpretation of anthropomorphism and the trust in the theological experience is developed further by Michael Oppenheim, *Speaking/Writing of God: Jewish Reflections on the Life with Others* (Albany: State University of New York Press, 1997), 28–41; and idem, "Foreword," in Franz Rosenzweig, *God, Man, and the World: Lectures and Essays*, ed. and trans. Barbara E. Galli (Syracuse, N.Y.: Syracuse University Press, 1998), xxiii–xxxii. A similar approach can be found in Elliot R. Wolfson, "Facing the Effaced: Mystical Eschatology and the Idealistic Orientation in the Thought of Franz Rosenzweig," *Journal for the History of Modern Theology* 4 (1997): 74–80. On the question of anthropomorphisms in the thought of Rosenzweig, see also Barbara E. Galli, "Rosenzweig Speaking of Meetings and Monotheism in Biblical Anthropomorphisms," *Journal of Jewish Thought and Philosophy* 2 (1993): 219–43; and Michael Oppenheim, *Mutual Upholding: Fashioning Jewish Philosophy through Letters* (New York: Peter Lang 1992), 83–116 (a discussion based on an exchange of letters between the author and N. Joseph).

51. See Altmann, *Studies in Religious Philosophy and Mysticism*, 19–28.

52. On the adoption of the microcosmic motif by Gikatilla, see *Ginnat 'Egoz* (Jerusalem, 1989), 200; on the theme of the stature of the world, *shi'ur qomat ha-olam*, see op. cit., 138–43, 162–63. In the latter instance, however, the dominant issue is not the anthropomorphic application of these measurements, but the mathematical dimension, the decade representing the perfect number in reference to which a variety of classifications is organized. Inasmuch as the first ten letters of the Hebrew alphabet graphically represent the numbers, there is no conceptual way to separate the math-

ematical and the linguistic. I would contend that this is a base principle of kabbalistic semiotics, a matter to be explored in detail elsewhere.

53. See Arthur Green, "Kabbalistic Re-Vision: A Review Article of Elliot Wolfson's *Through a Speculum That Shines*," *History of Religions* 36 (1997): 265–74, esp. 270–72; idem, *Keter: The Crown of God in Early Jewish Mysticism* (Princeton: Princeton University Press, 1997), 143 n. 30, 152 n. 3, 161–62 n. 35 (I am not mentioned explicitly in that note, but it is evident that the allusion is to my work). A similar criticism has been expressed by others, including Yehudah Liebes, "Judaism and Myth" (in Hebrew), *Dimmuy* 14 (1997): 15 n. 10. The notion that I ignore the heterosexual aspect of the erotic symbolism of the *Zohar* (not to mention other kabbalistic sources) is ludicrous. The issue is contextualizing that dimension of eros within the larger framework of the kabbalists' assumption regarding the ontological nature of gender—that is, what they would have considered to be a matter of ontology. See Elliot R. Wolfson, *Circle in the Square: Studies in the Use of Gender in Kabbalistic Symbolism* (Albany: State University of New York Press, 1995), 92–98; idem, "*Tiqqun ha-Shekhinah*: Redemption and the Overcoming of Gender Dimorphism in the Messianic Kabbalah of Moses Hayyim Luzzatto," *History of Religions* 36 (1997): 289–332; idem, "Coronation of the Sabbath Bride: Kabbalistic Myth and the Ritual of Androgynisation," *Journal of Jewish Thought and Philosophy* 6 (1997): 301–44; idem, "Eunuchs Who Keep the Sabbath: Becoming Male and the Ascetic Ideal in Thirteenth-Century Jewish Mysticism," in *Becoming Male in the Middle Ages*, ed. Jeffrey Jerome Cohen and Bonnie Wheeler (New York: Garland, 1997), 151–85; idem, "Constructions of the Feminine in the Sabbatian Theology of Abraham Cardoso, with a Critical Edition of *Derush ha-Shekhinah*," *Kabbalah: A Journal for the Study of Jewish Mystical Texts* 3 (1998): 11–143; idem, "Asceticism and Eroticism in Medieval Jewish Philosophical and Mystical Exegesis of the Song of Songs" (to be published in the proceedings of the conference "With Reverence for the Word: Medieval Scriptural Exegesis in Judaism, Christianity, and Islam," University of Toronto, 11–14 May 1997).

54. *Kitvei Ramban*, ed. Hayim Dov Chavel (Jerusalem: Mosad Harav Kook, 1967), 2:504. On the intrinsic connection between the act of creation and the last of the *sefirot*, cf. the statement from Shem Tov ibn Gaon's *Keter Shem Tov*, in *Ma'or wa-Shemesh* (Livorno, 1839), 25b: "Know that the act of creation (*ma'aseh bereshit*) emanates from the final *Hokhmah*." It is of interest to note that in the *Book of the Pomegranate*, ed. Wolfson, 191–206 (Hebrew section), the author includes a lengthy commentary on the account of creation, in part copying the text of Ezra of Gerona without attribution, in the context of explicating the mystical significance of the blessing of the moon. The thematic justification for this interpolation is clear enough: the moon symbolizes the *Shekhinah*, which is viewed as the locus of divine creativity.

55. The term that I am rendering "visionary" is the Hebrew *maskil*, one of the honorific expressions used by kabbalists to refer to themselves. I assume it carries the connotation of visual contemplation. See Wolfson, *Through a Speculum That Shines*, 276–77, 285–86, 383–84.

56. On the nexus between *Shekhinah*, prophetic vision, and human imagination, see Joseph ben Shalom Ashkenazi, *A Kabbalistic Commentary on Genesis Rabbah* (in Hebrew), ed. Mosheh Hallamish (Jerusalem: Magnes Press, 1984), 222–23.

57. *Zohar* 1.149b. See *Zohar* 1.183a; 2.82a.

58. *Zohar* 1.149b. I have previously discussed this passage in *Through a Speculum That Shines*, 307.

59. On the symbol "head of the bed" (based on Gen. 47:31) applied to *Yesod* in relation to *Shekhinah*, which is the "bed," see *Zohar* 1.225b, 226b; 2.54b.

60. For further discussion of this process, and citation of additional texts to support my interpretation, see *Through a Speculum That Shines*, 306–17.

61. Gershom Scholem, *On the Mystical Shape of the Godhead: Basic Concepts in the Kabbalah*, trans. Joachim Neugroschel and rev. Jonathan Chipman (New York: Schocken Books, 1991), 186.

62. Wolfson, *Circle in the Square*, 98–106.

63. My formulation is indebted to Jonathan Miller, *On Reflection* (London and New Haven: Routledge, 1998), 79.

64. See, for example, *Zohar* 1.16a.

65. Countless examples to support this claim could be cited, but for these purposes consider *Zohar* 1.3b, wherein the phallic potency in the Godhead is described as the "pillar that produces offspring, the limb that is the holy foundation upon which the world is sustained." In this context, the "world" refers to the feminine potency of *Shekhinah*, the ontological reality of which derives entirely from the phallic potency of *Yesod*.

66. The original text reads here *bar nash*, which literally means human being, but I have rendered the expression in accord with the anthropological position adopted by the zoharic authorship. See above, n. 32.

67. *Zohar* 1.19a.

68. Elliot R. Wolfson, "Sacred Space and Mental Iconography: *Imago Templi* and Contemplation in Rhineland Jewish Pietism," in *Ki Baruch Hu: Ancient Near Eastern, Biblical, and Judaic Studies in Honor of Baruch A. Levine*, ed. Robert Chazan, William W. Hallo, and Lawrence H. Schiffman (Winona Lake, Ind.: Eisenbrauns, 1999), 599–600.

69. See Wolfson, "Eunuchs Who Keep the Sabbath," and idem, "Asceticism and Eroticism." On sexual asceticism and erotic spirituality in theosophic kabbalistic literature, see also Scholem, *Major Trends*, 235; Georges Vajda, "Continence, mariage et vie mystique selon la doctrine du Judaism," *Mystique et continence: Travaux scientifiques du VIIe Congrès International d'Avon* (Bruges, 1952), 82–92; R. J. Zwi Werblowsky, *Joseph Karo: Lawyer and Mystic* (Philadelphia: Jewish Publication Society of America, 1977), 38–83, 113–18, 133–39, 149–52, 161–65; Mordecai Pachter, "The Concept of Devekut in the Homiletical Ethical Writings of Sixteenth-Century Safed," *Studies in Medieval Jewish History and Literature*, ed. Isadore Twersky, vol. 2 (Cambridge, Mass.: Harvard University Press, 1984), 200–210; Lawrence Fine, "Purifying the Body in the Name of the Soul: The Problem of the Body in Sixteenth-Century Kabbalah," in *People of the Body: Jews and Judaism from an Embodied Perspective*, ed. Howard Eilberg-Schwartz (Albany: State University of New York Press, 1993), 117–42; David Biale, *Eros and the Jews: From Biblical Israel to Contemporary America* (New York: Basic Books, 1992), 113–18. Regarding asceticism in the ecstatic kabbalah, see Moshe Idel, *The Mystical Experience in Abraham Abulafia* (Albany: State University of New York Press, 1988), 143–44.

Nature, Exile, and Disability in R. Nahman of Bratslav's "The Seven Beggars"

SHAUL MAGID

Hasidism can be described as a Jewish revivalist movement begin-ning in the latter third of the eighteenth century in the provinces of Podolia and Volhynia of Eastern Europe (what is now largely known as Ukraine). Its enigmatic and mysterious founder, Rabbi Israel ben Eliezer, known as the Baal Shem Tov (Master of the Good Name, 1700–1760), used earlier Jewish traditions of kabbalah and medieval pietism as a foundation for what can be called a Jewish renewal of devotion and praxis based on joy and ecstasy.[1] The Baal Shem Tov's charismatic personality and his reputation as a faith healer and miracle worker attracted other Jewish mystics and pietists and even some prominent rabbinic figures to his circle of disciples. Many of these disciples became the inner circle of the Baal Shem Tov's admir-ers.[2] After his passing in 1760, some of these figures began to develop circles of their own, migrating into Poland, Lithuania, White Russia, Hungary, and other parts of Eastern Europe, spreading the Baal Shem Tov's popular pietistic message of serving God with joy and challeng-ing the asceticism of earlier pietistic movements and the hierarchical rabbinical societies that had come to dominate the Eastern European Jewish landscape.[3]

While Hasidism after the Baal Shem Tov largely grew out of two of his most prominent disciples, Rabbi Dov Baer of Mezhirech (Mied-zyrzecz) and R. Ya'akov Yoseph of Polonnoye, the Baal Shem Tov's family also produced some masters who gained prominence outside the circles of these leading figures. The two most prominent members of the Baal Shem Tov's family were his grandsons Rabbi Barukh of Medzhibozh (1750–1812) and Rabbi Moshe Hayim Ephraim of Sudilkov (1737–1800), both of whom were sons of the Baal Shem Tov's daughter 'Odel. In the next generation, 'Odel's daughter Feige (the sister of Barukh and Moshe Hayim) gave birth to a son, Nahman, who would become the celebrated Hasidic master R. Nahman of Bratslav.[4]

At the century's close, Hasidic dynasties were beginning to emerge in many parts of Eastern Europe, mostly in Poland, Hungary, and Galicia. The Baal Shem Tov's family, however, stayed close to their birthplace in Ukraine. While not attracting large numbers of Jews like the disciples of the Mezhirech circle, these Hasidic masters, most notably R. Nahman of Bratslav, had a tremendous impact on early Hasidism. Independent, rebellious, and sometimes audacious, R. Nahman rose to become one of the most celebrated Hasidic masters of any period. This essay is dedicated to an analysis of one aspect of his thinking—his relationship to the natural world, exile, and his use of the mythic fable as an alternative mode of communicating his complex ideas, complimenting his homilies and the more informal advice he offered his students, much of which was posthumously published.

As great-grandson of the Baal Shem Tov (known as the Besht), R. Nahman was reared in the shadow of the first generations of Eastern European Hasidic masters. However, as opposed to most other Hasidic masters who emerged as leaders through discipleship, R. Nahman claimed to be a self-made zaddik, never attributing his stature to any master other then his great-grandfather, who died in 1760, a decade before he was born. The audacity of R. Nahman's claim to be a self-made zaddik caused a mixture of admiration and animosity among his peers, culminating in a controversy that nearly ripped apart the nascent Hasidic movement in Poland and Ukraine.[5]

R. Nahman's collected teachings, *Liqqutei MoHaRan* (1808) and *Liqqutei MoHaRan Tinyana* (1811), serve as the backbone of his thought. Various hagiographic and aphoristic works published posthumously supplement these two volumes.[6] In addition, R. Nahman is renowned for a series of thirteen tales he told near the end of his short life (he died of tuberculosis at the age of thirty-nine), which are viewed as the culmination of his entire intellectual oeuvre. While much scholarship has been done on these tales, the relationship between the tales and his homiletic writings is still in question. In this essay I will explore that relationship, arguing, against earlier readings, that the tales do not always reflect his earlier work but often change his earlier thinking, specifically on the binary way he presents many of his ideas in *Liqqutei MoHaRan*. The tales offer a more dialectical rendering of those ideas, using the genre of fable as a tool to nuance the texture of his religious anthropology.

This essay will focus on R. Nahman's view of nature and the natural world, both as it is presented in *Liqqutei MoHaRan* and again in his final tale "The Seven Beggars." In his homilies, nature (and natural law) is viewed as exilic because it represents false security, logic, and a vision of the world severed from the constant influx of divine effluence. It is presented as the binary opposite of miracle. In the tale, nature is viewed in a more dialectical fashion. Through a close reading of a portion of the tale, I will argue that nature is re-presented in the tale as human disability (all seven beggars are inflicted with a specific disability) and, while rectifying the false view of nature as independent of God, nature/disability is not viewed in stark opposition to miracle as perfection. Rather, the disability and thus imperfection of each beggar becomes the source of his very perfection. The nullification of one (nature) does not bring about an understanding of the other (miracle), as is implied in his homilies. Rather, a deep understanding of nature (presented as the reason for the beggars' disability) enables one to see how the natural world, as exilic, already contains within it the elements of redemption.

Nature, reconstrued and reconstructed, becomes the vehicle *for* and not the impediment *to* redemption. However, unlike his great-grandfather's quasi-pantheistic appropriation of nature, R. Nahman maintains the Neoplatonic dualism common in medieval kabbalah and pietism suggesting that one can, through prayer and joy, understand how nature and miracle are dependent upon, and not in opposition to, one another. The dialectic of deformity and perfection in the tale is a revision of this dualism that does not simply collapse into a mystical monism.

The Tales as the Final Failed Attempt for the End

In the summer of 1806, immediately preceding and then following the tragic death of his infant son Shlomo Ephraim that spring,[7] Rabbi Nahman of Bratslav announced to his disciples, *"ikh vel shoyn onheybn mayses dersteyen*" (the time has come for me to begin to tell stories).[8] In the years following that proclamation, R. Nahman told thirteen stories, which were transcribed and published as *Sippurei Ma'asiyot* in Ostrog in 1816[9] (five years after R. Nahman's death on 15 October 1810) by his scribe and most cherished disciple R. Nathan Sternhartz of Bratslav.[10] Most scholars agree that these tales constitute the culmination of R. Nahman's creative thinking,[11] deepening many of the essential themes presented in his Torah discourses, published in two volumes as *Liqqutei MoHaRan*.[12]

In this essay I will focus on various sections of the final tale in *Sippurei Ma'asiyot*, "The Tale of the Seven Beggars." Told over the period of a few weeks, and culminating a few months before R. Nahman's death, it is unanimously viewed by scholars and disciples as the most obscure and difficult of the thirteen tales.[13] In many ways, this final tale is R. Nahman's last will and testament, incorporating recurring themes in the other tales, all contributing to form R. Nahman's overarching "theology of exile" and his prescription for redemption. It is an unfinished tale, as were numerous other tales, its finale intentionally concealed for the messianic future.[14]

"The Seven Beggars" illustrates R. Nahman's tortured relationship to nature and the natural world. From his homilies one can easily see how he is simultaneously enraptured and repelled by nature, viewing it as a place of solitude and peace yet also seductive and theologically precarious. Reared in the early period of Hasidism and profoundly influenced by the Besht's exaltation of nature as a forum and vehicle for divine worship, R. Nahman struggled with the mystical monism of his great-grandfather and the pietistic dualism that attracted him in the traditional literature he read. As a result, R. Nahman's assessment of nature is far more complex then that of his great-grandfather. In his collected homilies, he returns to a model of assessing nature more in concert with classical kabbalah and medieval pietism, viewing nature as exilic because it represents order and fate in opposition to miracle (the suspension of order) and freewill (prayer or the human ability to override natural law).[15]

The tension of nature being both beautiful and demonic emerges again and again in this final tale, resonating with the themes in his homiletic discourses. However, in the tale the polarities of good and evil begin to collapse. The seven beggars, all of whom are deformed, appear twice in the tale, first to bless the children to "be like them" (with no explanation), and then again at the end of the tale to give martial gifts to the children (in the form of a story), explaining why their deformity is an illustration of their perfection. My reading of the tale will incorporate various comments from the homilies in an attempt to see the ways in which R. Nahman's mythic turn to fantasy transforms his dualistic view of nature and miracle to a dialectic of the human struggle for God, who is ontologically *beyond* nature but experientially *in* nature.[16] This realization does not result in the nullification of nature nor does it yield a view, closer to the Besht, that one can experience God *through* nature. Rather, it is the foundation of an exile of sadness, an ability to retain joy even in the depths of exile because one holds a primordial memory of a pre-exilic past. Joy never effaces or erases sadness—it lives deeply within it.

A Structural Introduction

The difficulty of this tale lies not only in its highly symbolic/mythic character (which is true of all of the tales) but more specifically in its complex structure, comprising a dizzying network of stories within stories, each internal story serving simultaneously as an independent unit and part of the larger mosaic of the tale as a whole. It has been a long-standing belief among close readers of the tales that their esoteric nature can be divided into four distinct categories, the first two biographical, the third literary, and the fourth theological.[17] While the fourth approach has usually been the theater of traditional commentaries, my reading is closest to this approach as it seeks to navigate a two-way path between the homilies and the tales. Traditional commentaries usually read the tales through the homilies. I will argue that we can also reverse this equation. That is, since the tales change what is written in the homilies, the homilies should also be (re)read through the tales.

The underlying assumption of most traditional commentaries is that the tales are mythological representations of kabbalistic symbols deeply couched in folklorist themes, told (and then written) specifically for the purposes of "waking up those who are asleep."[18] The tales thus serve as a literary embodiment of "descent for the sake of ascent," a concept with roots in Lurianic kabbalah and Sabbatianism and popularized in early Hasidism's notion of Zaddikism.[19] Accord-

ing to this, the tale was the way of the zaddik lowering himself to the
language of the people in order to arouse and elevate the remaining
sparks embedded in their souls as a precursor to the messianic era.
This does not mean that the tales were bereft of all the complexity and
nuance of classical kabbalistic theosophy. They always function on
various levels simultaneously.

To decipher the tales one must be intimately acquainted with the
Zohar and Lurianic kabbalah, both of which serve as the urtext of
R. Nahman's own imagination, mystical ideology, as well as his
homiletic discourses.[20] Scholars and disciples agree that R. Nahman's
imagination was fed by zoharic symbolism and Lurianic myth and
that his tales represent his unique "remythologization" of kabbalistic
literature that could not be accessed by the non-initiate.[21] In this
sense, the zaddik, who is the teller of the tale, serves as a translator of
mystical lore to the simple Jew in order to arouse him or her to divine
worship. In doing so, the hidden sparks embedded in their souls are
uplifted and reunited with their divine source. Coming at the end of
his life (when he knew his death was near), and perhaps drawn from
Shabbatai Zevi's failed messianic descent into the netherworld (i.e.,
his conversion to Islam), coupled with his infatuation with fantasy,
these tales serve as R. Nahman's final contribution to the messianic
project that was a central part of his identify as a self-made zaddik.
More strikingly, it is, perhaps, the reluctant acknowledgment of his
failure to achieve his messianic goal.

The Symbiosis of Nature and Disability

"The Tale of the Seven Beggars" revolves around various themes,
each becoming manifest in different ways.[22] One of the central themes
in the story is the apparent deformity of each beggar and the way each
beggar explains to the two children in the story (representations of
Israel) that his deformity is not a deformity at all but an illustration of
his perfection. My claim is that the theme of physical deformity in the
tale alludes to R. Nahman's attitude toward nature in *Liqqutei MoHa-
Ran*. In his homiletic discourses, the term *teva* (conventionally translated as nature) is almost exclusively pejorative, suggesting a view of
the natural world independent of any higher source. Nature appears
perfect, R. Nahman argues, in its stability and predictability. Yet, this

appearance of perfection, which is illusory, is actually the source of
its imperfection. Alternatively, *'olam* (world) is a term that refers to
the natural world in a constant state of renewal. It implies that nature
is unstable, dynamic, and unpredictable—in short, miraculous. In
Liqqutei MoHaRan, nature (*teva*) is the imperfect and exilic perception of the world (*'olam*). In "The Tale of the Seven Beggars" the
(apparent) deformity of each beggar is viewed as the result of an inability to see the world as *'olam*. That is, it is the result of the world
seeing them only in relation to nature (*teva*). This can be illustrated
through his notion of higher wisdom and lower wisdom in *Liqqutei
MoHaRan*.

> There are two kinds of wisdom, higher wisdom and lower wisdom.
> Lower wisdom draws from higher wisdom. The Torah is the embodi-
> ment of higher wisdom. Worldly wisdom, which is lower wisdom,
> draws from this higher wisdom. When worldly wisdom is severed from
> higher wisdom (Torah) the result is the diminishing of the moon, which
> is the exile of the *Shekhinah*. . . .[23]

According to R. Nahman, exile is the state when wisdom becomes
severed from that which sustains it. This also applies to nature (*teva*),
which is the exilic state of the world (*'olam*). It should be emphasized
that nature is not identical with the natural world—it is only a false
perception of it. Finally, R Nahman implies that exile is false security
while redemption is perpetual insecurity.[24] The "security of exile"
rests on the fact that we are seduced into believing the ultimate truth
of our rational, scientific vision of the world. This security is not rejected because it is ontologically false as much as it sublimates the
longing for redemption. The maintenance or revival of longing requires destabilizing the security that lies at the heart of reason. The
unfolding of the tale is R. Nahman's way of destabilizing these conventional notions, problematizing our system of values in an attempt
to take his reader from the exilic state of false security to the instability of renewal.[25] "To arouse those from sleep," the expressed intention
given for telling stories, can now be understood as awakening the
longing for redemption by destabilizing the human inclination to believe in security, which, by definition, is false. As I will suggest later,
"sleep" is not only a state of the disciples of reason but can also describe those who succumb to the false security of faith.

This is the foundation of my reading of "The Tale of the Seven

Beggars." Unlike most of the classical commentators, who stick more closely to the explicit themes in the tale, I think R. Nahman's relationship to nature and the natural world in his homiletic discourses underlies much of the tale, even as the tale never overtly mentions nature per se. However, the tale reveals a more dialectical understanding of nature then we find in *Liqqutei MoHaRan*. In his homilies nature (*teva*) must be overcome as a prelude to redemption, as nature represents coincidence and fate, the very opposite of prayer and miracle. In the tale, this dualism is changed, or at least diminished. At the end of the tale, the children once again experience joy when they understand that the apparent unnaturalness of the beggars, i.e., their deformity, is really their perfection: that is, that exile and suffering does not stand in contradiction to divine election but holds the key to redemption because exile creates the longing to pray and prayer holds the potential to change nature and thus to redeem the world.

The Prelude of the Tale as the Universal Stage of Jewish Redemption

Before moving to the analysis of the tale, a few brief remarks are in order on the literary structure of the tale, playing close attention to the way the structure impacts my reading. "The Tale of the Seven Beggars" can be divided into three major sections, the final section including six subsections, each subsection itself comprised of numerous super-subsections. The first section of the tale is an unfinished prelude about a king and his son. There are three characters in the prelude: the king, the son, and the wise men in the king's country. The setting of the prelude is a grand ball celebrating an anonymous king handing over his kingdom to his son. The king interrupts the joyous occasion to tell his son two things. First, that his son's tenure as king is solely dependent upon his remaining in a state of constant joy (*simha*). Second, as a stargazer, the king predicts that in the future his son will lose his kingdom because he is not worthy, that is, he could not maintain the perpetual state of joy required for his kingship. However, the king warns his son that he should still be joyous, even in losing his kingdom, implying that true joy should never be contingent upon anything other than divine Will. If God wills that he should lose his kingdom, that too should be cause for joy.[26]

The second part of the unfinished prelude draws an important connection between joy and wisdom, or, alternatively, between sadness and false wisdom—a recurring theme in R. Nahman's writings—by telling us some details about the son's tenure as king.

> The prince (the son) was a wise man, he loved wisdom dearly, and gathered around him many wise men. Whosoever came to him with some sort of wisdom was highly esteemed by him. . . . Since wisdom was so esteemed, everyone adopted wisdom and the whole kingdom engaged in the practice of wisdom. . . . Because of this wisdom, the wise men of the land fell into heresy and drew the prince into their heresy. . . . Only the wise men and the prince became heretics. And since the prince had goodness in him because he had been born with goodness . . . he always remembered, "Where am I in the world and what am I doing?" And he would groan deeply and remember, "What is this? . . . What's happening to me? Where am I in the world?" Yet, no sooner had he begun to use his reason than the heretical ideas were strengthened within him. . . .

As a lover of wisdom (*hokhmah*), the son mistakenly allowed wisdom to become exclusively equated with the good.[27] The consequence of this absolute love of wisdom was that the educated classes in the kingdom fell into heresy (*apikorsis*).[28] R. Nahman uses the term *hokhmah* as a distortion of true wisdom infused with faith, similar to his use of the term *teva* (nature) in *Liqqutei MoHaRan*. The severing of wisdom (higher wisdom, Torah) from what sustains it (lower wisdom, science) is the beginning or at least the condition of heresy. The son, however, never became a heretic like the other wise men. Because he was "of good character," a concept R. Nahman never explains but which seems to reflect the notion of the innate goodness of the simple Jew so common in Hasidism, he never stopped asking the essential questions of human existence, even in light of the answers wisdom provided. Yet, even as he was never completely seduced by wisdom into believing that it provided adequate answers to these questions, as soon as he began to reflect rationally on these questions, he again fell into heresy.[29] This is R. Nahman's narrative description of a particular kind of exile of the Jewish people. Israel is caught in a circle that it cannot transcend. The only thing that will save them is the advice of the king, i.e., to remain in a perpetual state of joy. However, for some unknown reason, the son could not absorb his father's advice. As long as he lived in the world of false wisdom, joy always eluded him.

For R. Nahman, misunderstanding and misappropriating the limits of reason is the struggle that produces exile and alienation. Everyone in the tale is in exile—the king's son, the wise men, the beggars, and the children (who serve as the main characters in the body of the tale). All exiles, however, are not the same. There are three distinct types of exile in the tale, each one carrying its own unique qualities and challenges.[30]

The first type of exile is the exile of the wise men in the prelude. It is an unredeemable exile, one that does not contain longing and therefore can never bring about redemption. For R. Nahman it is the exile of the Nations, particularly in the modern world. Because it holds the promise of logic and reason as the answers to all questions, it is an exile that does not contain suffering or sadness, both of which result from a feeling of incompleteness. For R. Nahman, sadness is the underside of longing. This is the most dangerous kind of exile, likened to the "black hole" of existence (*hallel ha-paneui*) in *Liqqutei MoHaRan* 1.64, the place where God is absent.[31] This exile is terrifying to R. Nahman, yet plays no part in redemptive history. Therefore, it disappears from the narrative after the prelude. There is no correlate to the wise men in the body of the tale.

The second type of exile is the exile of the son in the prelude, replicated in the children in the tale. It is an exile of longing for that which is unknown; it is an exile of sadness.[32] This exile can be overcome through prayer, which R. Nahman maintains changes nature (*teva*) into world (*'olam*) by recognizing the instability of reason, enabling the reconciliation between higher and lower wisdom to emerge. This is the exile of Israel, embodied in the king's son, who is "of good character" and the children, who wander aimlessly in search of happiness, always in danger yet always protected. The place of wandering is the forest; a part of the natural world that simultaneously holds the potential for all kinds of sustenance and untold dangers. In this sense, the prelude is the universal model of exile that becomes particularized in Israel in the children in the forest. Note that the son in the prelude is never redeemed, as are the children in the tale. He appears forever caught in the cycle of reason and longing, unable to pray and thus unable to achieve the necessary tools to transcend his situation.

The third type of exile is the exile of the beggars. This is also the exile of the zaddik. This is an exile that is more deeply felt than the other two because the zaddik has a memory of the world before exile. The exilic experience of the zaddik is that he has to live in the world *before* redemption with the memory *of* redemption. The role of the zaddik (the beggars) is that he can teach those stuck in the second exile how to overcome it. The king in the prelude introduces the exile of the zaddik. He warns his son that joy, and joy alone, can achieve a return to the kingdom. The beggars are more developed embodiments of the zaddik in the prelude, revealing the true nature of this third exile, the exile of redemption. Perhaps the king in the prelude represents all the zaddikim before R. Nahman. While he holds the answer to his son's dilemma, he can do no more than programmatically tell him how to survive. Finally, his advice is not enough to save his son. The beggars, however, do much more. They sustain the children in the forest and then teach them the key to the third exile under the wedding canopy by telling them stories. As tellers of stories, the beggars represent R. Nahman as the zaddik who is a storyteller.

The second important trope of the tale, after exile, is the notion of heresy, which is understood in unique ways in R. Nahman's overall discourse.[33] The difference between the wise men in the prelude (who are unredeemable heretics) and the king's son (who is a redeemable heretic), can be understood in light of the discussion of the "two types of heretics" in *Liqqutei MoHaRan* 1.64. In this lesson the first type of heretic (the king's son in the tale) is one who falls into a redeemable heresy. "Even though he should have fled it [heresy], he may find a way to be saved from there. God can be found there, if one looks for him and seeks him out." The second type of heretic (the wise men in the tale) is far more dangerous. "It seems that his opinion is a most profound one, even though it is all based on a wrong interpretation. . . . There is no answer to this heresy: it comes from the void, from which God, as it were, has withdrawn himself." The first type of exile discussed above embodies the second type of unredeemable heresy. The second type of exile, the exile of sadness, embodies the first type of heretic, the son in the prelude and the two children who are lost and alienated, yet always respond to the question, "where are you from?" with "we don't know." They never stop longing, even in the midst of the joy of their wedding at the conclusion of the tale.[34] The second type of heretic (who is in the first type of exile) is unredeemable because, convinced of his own logic, he stops asking questions. This heretic is presented in the prelude (the wise men) and then disap-

pears from the narrative, as it plays no role in the redemptive message
of the tale.

There may be another reason why the second type of heretic disappears in the body of the tale. The frame of the tale, presented in this
prelude, is that of temporal exile.[35] The body of the tale intends to
overcome the dilemma of the king's son (temporal exile) via the bride
and groom's confrontation with the deformed (and unnatural) beggars, all of whom show the children how to achieve the absolute value
of joy (*simha*) even, or precisely, in exile.

For R. Nahman, the act that brings one from exile to redemption,
from sadness to joy, is prayer. Exile is temporal by definition, as its
existence is contingent on the possibility of redemption. Prayer actu-
alizes the "possibility of redemption" by facilitating a dramatic
change in the worshiper's perspective of nature, resulting in the transformation of sadness to joy. The second unredeemable heretic in
Liqqutei MoHaRan 1.64 has no part in this process. His exile is permanent, holding no possibility of redemption because he does not feel
the longing for things to be other then they are. Therefore, he does not
experience exile, as he views his state as permanent and complete.
Seduced by the certainty of his own rational view of the world,
R. Nahman considers him lost. The depth of his so-called exile is exhibited by the fact that he does not feel sadness, as sadness is a response to the experience of imperfection. The second type of heretic
in *Liqqutei MoHaRan* 1.64 and the wise men in the prelude have no
need for prayer, the condition of prayer being brokenheartedness
(*shevirat ha-lev*) and longing.[36]

For our purposes, the most significant point in the prelude is the
connection R. Nahman draws between reason and sadness, which is
never developed in the body of the tale but serves as its subtext.
Through the king's warning to his son that joy be the sole criteria for
kingship, i.e., redemption, R. Nahman suggests that redemption is
only possible when the sadness indicative of the second type of exile
is confronted and overcome. Sadness is rectified, although not nullified, through prayer and overcome through joy.[37] Joy for its own sake,
resulting from humanity's recognition of the divine source of human
and natural life, overshadows the second type of exile, diminishing
the first type of heresy. When the beggars bless the children to "be like
them" in the forest and then explain the blessing under the wedding
canopy as a marital gift, they are blessing them to embody the third
kind of exile, the exile of the zaddik.

This kind of exile is unique in that it does not contain sadness, as we know it, but does contain longing, because it contains the memory of the world before exile and the recognition that this is the place to which the world will ultimately return. The eclipse of sadness in the zaddik is not because he doesn't feel longing. It is because he mimetically knows that his experience of longing will bear fruit. The disability of the beggars is not about their personal deficiency; it is that, as zaddikim, they are estranged from the exilic world, even as they are an integral part of it. The zaddik laments the fallen state of the world by carrying it on his shoulders as he walks through the world deformed. He participates in the redemptive process by helping others overcome the seduction of reason by giving them the gift of joy—the joy the king told his son about in the prelude. The gift they give is the memory of a world before exile—even before creation—a world that will be the culmination of their suffering. But, the beggars add, one can experience that world here, in exile, through joy. The first type of heresy becomes the third type of exile when reason becomes subsidiary to prayer and false security (fate) yields to redemptive instability (miracle).[38]

"Be Like Me": The Blessing of Primordiality

The body of the tale opens with a description of two children lost in a forest. Hungry for food, the children scream for help. They are approached by seven beggars, one at a time, all of whom have a physical disability; one is blind, one deaf, one stutters, one has a twisted neck, one is hunchbacked, one has no hands, and one has no feet. Each beggar gives the children bread to eat, temporarily alleviating their suffering, and then departs saying, "be like me" without ever explaining what that means. The children continue to wander, ultimately becoming beggars themselves. Finally, they end up at a fair celebrating the birthday of an anonymous king (a reference taking us back to the prelude). All the beggars of the land (not only the seven beggars) are gathered at this fair. Seeing the children, who are now also beggars, they decide that it would be fit for them to marry since they are orphaned and have no other family. The beggars at the fair raise a wedding canopy and designate the children as bride and groom. Under the wedding canopy the children joyously recall all the favors that God bestowed upon them during their wanderings in the forest. Their joy is immediately interrupted, however, by the memory of the beggars who gave them food and helped them survive. They cry out longingly (a reference to prayer), "How do we find the first beggar, the blind beggar, who brought us bread in the forest?" At that moment, the blind beggar emerges from the crowd and blesses the children by telling them a story, illustrating that his blindness is not a deformity but a state of perfection. Then he blesses the children to "be like him" and disappears.

The wedding continues in this manner for seven days. Each day the children begin joyous and then become sad, longing for another beggar, who arrives to bless them, telling them an elaborate story to illustrate why his deformity is really not a deformity at all. The children are joyous at the arrival of each beggar yet their joy disappears the next morning as they long for the next beggar. The tales that each beggar tells are intricate and elaborate, all of which explain their deformity as the result of some vision, hearing, or memory of the primordial past or a time before exile. Before departing they give this memory as a gift of joy to the couple. While this gift works in that it brings the children joy, the gift never lasts because the children mix that memory with the memory of another beggar, who is deformed, thus bringing their joy to an abrupt and crashing halt.

The body of the tale contains two main parts: 1) the second type of exile exhibited in the king's son in the prelude is revisited in the lost children who are alienated in the forest, crying (i.e., praying) for sustenance; and 2) the appearance of the beggars in the forest and then again under the wedding canopy. The beggars (the zaddik) teach the children the way to the third type of exile (the exile of the zaddik that the king alludes to in the prelude but can never quite communicate to his son) through the renewal of joy contained in their blessings. The body of the tale draws the reader more deeply into R. Nahman's exilic anthropology by reading his prescription for redemption. This redemptive process emerges in three significant points in the body of the tale: 1) the lost children in the forest, exiled but longing; 2) the disabled seven beggars who reveal the nature of their disability; and 3) the joy of the wedding that is still unfulfilled because the seventh beggar, the beggar without feet, never arrives. In this unfinished tale the expression of joy remains temporal in that the final beggar (the Messiah) tarries.[39]

However, the notion that longing is the vehicle for joy becomes the prescription for surviving the exile. Each day the wedding ends in joy, but each morning that joy disappears as the bride and groom lament the absence of the next beggar. The king's warning to his son in the prelude that perpetual joy is the sole criteria for kingship, i.e., redemption, looms over the entire narrative as it loomed over R. Nahman's tortured life. The dependence on the zaddik is paramount. Without the zaddik (the beggars) reminding the children of the world before exile, the children could never get beyond the son in the prelude. Only the zaddik keeps messianism alive. Only the zaddik prevents redeemable heresy from the fate of unredeemable heresy. Only the zaddik prevents the son's exile from becoming the wise men's exile. Only the zaddik can teach the children the redemptive way of suffering.

The overarching theme of the tale, which appears in many different guises, is that wisdom (*hokhmah*) and nature (*teva*) are the sources of human imperfection and the perpetuation of exile.[40] This imperfection initially emerges in the description of the deformity of each beggar in his or her first encounter with the children in the forest, and is resolved in their subsequent meetings with the children under the wedding canopy. At that auspicious moment each beggar reveals that his deformity is really his perfection, implying that perfection appears imperfect in a world that it is imperfect.[41] The correlation between wisdom and nature serves as the two poles of exile; but this correlation lies beneath the surface of the tale, never fully disclosed.

Before attempting to disclose the implicit connection between wisdom and nature in the tale, I will briefly review R. Nahman's views about "nature (*teva*) as exile" explained in *Liqqutei MoHaRan*. Perhaps the most succinct statement on this issue appears in *Liqqutei MoHaRan* 1.150:

> The pain of Israel in exile is the result of the absence of the consciousness of God (*da'at*) and the belief that everything is dependent upon nature (*teva*), coincidence (*miqrim*) and fate (*mazal*). This is the cause of Israel's pain. If they knew that everything was the result of providence (*hashgakhah*) [and not nature—ed.] they would not suffer any pain at all. In truth, Israel is rooted above nature. It is only when they sin, God forbid, that they become subject to the laws of nature.

Nature (*teva*) for R. Nahman is a view of the world that is unchanging and necessary (*mehuyav*). *Liqqutei MoHaRan* 1.7 speaks about

exile as a deficiency of faith, true faith being the belief in the temporality of nature which is constantly destabilized via miracle, providence, and prayer. The possibility for miracle requires the acknowledgment that the world, even as it appears ordered, is unstable. This is
nothing new. What R. Nahman contributes is that prayer is the devotional act that creates this possibility in the human psyche for such a
posture. To pray properly, R. Nahman suggests, requires two things:
1) a suspension of reason; and 2) an act of protest against reason.
"Miracles are above nature, prayer is above nature. This is because
nature is necessity and prayer changes nature." The children scream in
the forest in protest against their fate of starvation.

> Prayer encapsulates miracle, which is not the way of nature (*derekh ha-
> teva*). Sometimes nature necessitates that something will occur and
> prayer reverses that occurrence . . . those people who deny miracles,
> and say that everything flows according to the laws of nature, in effect
> they destroy prayer, for prayer is miraculous in that it changes nature.
> They also impair faith, because they deny divine providence [which is
> also miraculous]. They also impair the Land of Israel as this land is the
> land of miracles. . . .[42]

World (*'olam*) as opposed to nature (*teva*) represents a perspective
of the natural world infused with divine Will in a constant state of
renewal and transformation. Both nature (*mada*, science) and logic
(*higayon*, philosophy), two dimensions of false wisdom, or *hokhmot
hitzoniyot* (extraneous wisdom), are embedded in the realm of necessity (*mehuyavut*), which R. Nahman believed denies the transcendent
character of the creation. There is a correlation here between the false
wisdom or logic (depicted as reason) of the wise men in the prelude of
the tale and nature in the body of the tale in the appearance of the
seven beggars. As deformed, each beggar seems imperfect, yet the
beggars' stories all teach how their deformity reflects the very attainment of perfection.

For R. Nahman, both wisdom (*hokhmah*) and nature (*teva*) hold the
illusion of truth precisely because they *claim* to resolve the essential
questions of human existence, either by observation (empiricism) or
human intellection (logic). The danger of both is the susceptibility of
imperfect beings to see them as paths toward perfection by incorporating them as absolute values. Both are exilic in his eyes not because
they are false in any objective sense but because they diminish joy

resulting in either sadness (*'atzvut*) or hopelessness (*ye'ush*).[43] The connection between reason (*hokhmah*) and sadness (*'atzvut*) is often alluded to but never made explicitly in the tale, but it does play a prominent role in R. Nahman's homilies and the hagiographic stories about him. It appears that the correlation is built on his assumption that wisdom can never achieve that which it claims, always failing to realize expectations, leaving one disillusioned and subsequently hopeless. Wisdom itself is not exilic. It is only exilic when it is holds the expectation of resolving the essential questions of human existence.[44] The mistake of the son in the prelude was not to love wisdom per se but to elevate it to an absolute value. This is because the son did not pray—as prayer (as a protest against reason) will always prevent the overextension of reason that is so seductive in the natural world. However, being "of good character," the son was able to avoid the fate of the wise men, perhaps a surreptitious reference to the Jewish Enlightenment R. Nahman became so familiar with at the end of his life.[45]

Another example of wisdom and nature as the cause of sadness can be seen in R. Nahman's understanding of divine election. He argues that from a logical and empirical standpoint the election of Israel can be easily and convincingly construed as a fallacy, because "the Gentiles are successful and Israel is in a constant state of subjugation and humiliation." Therefore, it is both to the advantage of the Gentile and logically defensible to claim that Israel is no longer God's chosen people. In a sense, R. Nahman is advocating, from the perspective of reason, a kind of Hegelian supersessionism whereby Judaism and the Jewish people are negated through history. From a logical and empirical (i.e., historical) perspective, the Gentile's (i.e., Christian) argument against God's covenant with Israel in exile is valid. If Israel would submit to this logical evaluation of its fate, however, its covenant would indeed be nullified and its exilic consciousness would move from the first heretic to the second, ending the quest *for* redemption and thereby erasing the possibility *of* redemption. The son would become one of the wise men. Whereas wisdom in the prelude to our tale yields personal sadness and exile, the empirical observation of the natural world potentially yields submission to the collective subjugation of exile, destroying the possibility of turning sadness into joy and exile into redemption.[46] At that point, the children in the forest (Israel) would no longer hear the exile of the zaddik (the beggars' blessing "be like me") because they would no longer have the requisite longing necessary to hear him. If the children did not scream in the forest, they would have never met the beggars and would have collapsed into nature (fate) and disappeared forever.

The Gift of Primordial Memory

The lost children in the forest embody the second type of exile, expressed in human anguish and prayer. Each time they get hungry, they "scream and cry" (*geshreien un gevent*). Even though it is not given significant attention in the tale, the screams of the children play an important role in the narrative. The screams represent authentic (primal) prayer, introducing the most important theme in the body of the tale that is absent in the prelude.[47] The forest introduces us to the natural world, simultaneously a place of beauty and seduction. The potential tragedy of the natural world is that observing it through the lens of natural law can seduce one away from recognizing God as its source, resulting in a belief in the independence and absolute status of nature (*teva*). Lost in the forest, the children exist outside of civilization. Being children, they cannot survive independently, as they are not trained in foraging food for themselves. The natural consequence (i.e., nature without miracle) should be that these two children starve and die in the forest. In protest of nature and fate, however, they scream for sustenance. This scream is their prayer that "change(s) nature (*meshaneh ha-teva*)," breaking through the illusory boundaries of necessity and fate, resulting in the appearance of the beggars who save them.[48]

In *Liqqutei MoHaRan* 1.55, para. 4, R. Nahman states, "prayer is founded upon the faith that everything is in God's hand, even altering nature." Drawing on kabbalistic teaching, he further argues that prayer (*mayyim nuqvin*, feminine arousal) activates the creative power of God (*mayyim dekhurin*, masculine arousal), renewing divine creativity and nullifying the perceived necessity of natural law (*'olam keminhago noheg*). R. Nahman's message is strikingly straightforward. Prayer changes fate by activating a renewal of creation (*hidush ha-'olam*), nullifying the perception of natural order upon which fate is founded. It is not that nature is nullified in this equation. Moreover, we are not dealing with a concept of transcending nature or even nullifying the physical (*hitpashtut ha-gashmiut*), so common in early

Hasidism.[49] R. Nahman's interests are existential and not ontological. The beggars are trying to teach the children about living and surviving *in* the world, perceiving and evaluating their external environment by understanding that exile and redemption are existential states as much or more than states of reality.[50] This point stands at the center of the story and serves to nuance R. Nahman's more blatantly negative appraisal of nature in *Liqqutei MoHaRan*. In his homiletic lessons we are taught that nature stands diametrically opposed to miracle, that science stands in opposition to prayer, that exile is the result of being seduced by reason. Although all of these assumptions are, in principle, maintained in the tale, the tale explains the ways in which this exilic stance can be rectified by changing one's orientation toward the natural world while living in it. The tale creates a solution to exile and heresy while remaining a part of the exilic world. Prayer (the screams of the children in the forest and their longing at the wedding) opens up the possibility of witnessing miracle. Miracle is not something different from nature—it is a new way of understanding it. The juxtaposition of the themes (reason, exile, sadness, nature, deformity) with the tale's characters (the king's son, the children, the beggars) yields a more dialectical rendering of R. Nahman's dualistic thinking.

The wedding of the children in the final scene of the tale begins by bringing the reader back to the first scene of the children lost in the forest. Just as their longing for food and prayer in the forest resulted in the appearance of the blind beggar, the blind beggar immediately appears when they long for him under the wedding canopy. The blind beggar enters, stating that "[previously, i.e., in the forest] I offered you my blessing but today I bestow this upon you outright as a gift. You should be as old as I am." Instead of simply vanishing, as he does in the forest, he remains and reveals the true nature of his deformity. "You think I am blind? Not at all. It is just that the entire world does not amount to the wink of an eye (*heref eyin*) to me." Then he embellishes his paradoxical claim with a story, which is replicated in different ways by all of the six subsequent beggars who appear at the wedding. The blind beggar says that "he is very old yet hasn't begun to live," which is the "outright gift" he gives to the children.[51] The proof of his claim unfolds in a story he tells which describes the beggar's memory as remembering "nothingness" (*'ayin*), i.e., a memory of the world before creation.

Once people set sail upon the seas in many ships. A tempest arose and destroyed the ships but the people were saved. The people came to a tower. . . . They called upon each other to recite an old tale, one that he has remembered from his earliest recollection, that is, what he remembered from the inception of his memory. . . . And I (the blind beggar) . . . declared, "I remember all those tales and I remember nothingness." They all declared, "That is a very old tale, older than all the others." . . . [then a great eagle came and addressed all those shipwrecked.] And to me (the blind beggar) the great eagle said, "You come with me because you are just like me in that you are extremely old and yet very young. And you have not yet begun to live, though you are very old. . . .

The blind beggar is the oldest of the group. However, because of the exile he also "hasn't yet begun to live" because the element of *'ayin* (no-thingness), the root of creation, remains concealed for the future redemption. He is blind because his vision, or more precisely his memory of perfection (*'ayin*) makes it impossible for him to envision imperfection (the natural world). By seeing the end in the primordial beginning, he cannot bear to witness the imperfect process toward that completion. His blindness is thus his unwillingness, and not his inability, to see.

The blind beggar's story rests on the relationship between perception and memory. How does one live with memory and not be thrown into despair? As discussed, for R. Nahman the deepest exile is the exile of the zaddik (the third type of exile). This exile is a feeling of alienation from the exilic world resulting from an experience, memory, or vision of the world before exile (i.e., perfection). Only the truly righteous experience this exile that serves as the necessary bridge to redemption. The one who feels in exile in the exilic world (and appears to others as abnormal, i.e., deformed or disabled) is more capable than others to direct the world toward completion because only he has a memory of the end in the beginning. His deformity is an externalization of his memory of perfection (the world before creation/exile).

The important lesson of this third exile is that it is an exile of joy— not in place *of* sadness, but a joy *in* sadness. It brings us back to the king's warning to his son in the prelude that he should maintain joy even though he loses the kingdom, because joy is the only way to retrieve the kingdom. The children are like the son in that they long to be redeemed, and thereby experience sadness, but cannot maintain joy long enough to live joyously in the sadness. In some sense, they are stuck in the dualistic cycle that joy and sadness are binary opposites. The beggars, as the zaddik, come to teach them otherwise. The opaque message of the king to his son in the prelude is now disclosed. One must be joyous in exile by remembering his tenure as king. This memory of his stature before exile will enable him to retain joy in sadness, eliminating his continual fall into heresy, thus securing the renewal of the kingdom. It is only the tale (both R. Nahman's tale and the specific tales of the beggars) that makes this possible.

For R. Nahman, the zaddik (always a reference to himself) is the most tragic figure of all because he must live joyously in an exilic world while maintaining a memory of redemption (the primordial world before exile).[52] It is this anxiety that makes the zaddik always occupy the margin of insanity, a psychological abnormality that R. Nahman transfers into the physical disability of each beggar. When the blind beggar says, "be like me," he is attempting to move the children from the second type of exile (longing for redemption) to the third and final type of exile, the exile of joy in sadness, the bridge to redemption achieved by realizing the memory of no-thingness, the world before exile.

For the sake of brevity I will skip the next beggar, the beggar who cannot hear, and move directly to the beggar who stutters. The beggar who stutters appears at the wedding to bless the couple. He tells them that he stutters because he cannot speak words that are not praises of God, or more precisely, "[he cannot speak] words that contain no perfection." He is the master of "words of perfection," he claims, which he illustrates in his ability to clearly recite complex riddles and divine praises with no impediment. His mastery of riddles and divine praises is proven with a story about a heart and a spring.[53]

A heart existed at one end of the world. At the other end of the world was a mountain. On top of that mountain there was a spring. The heart longed for the spring, yet could never ascend the mountain, for when it did it lost sight of the spring. Hence, it had to be content gazing upon the spring from afar while longing to unite with it. The spring also longed for the heart. This mutual yearning of the heart for the spring and the spring for the heart sustained the world. The problem was that the spring didn't really exist in time (i.e., it was either above or before time—an illusion to its primordial status). Therefore, each day the heart gave the gift of one day's time to the spring so that it could exist in time and be the object of its longing, which in turn sustained the world.

This ambiguous gift of time is now explained as consisting of a collection of songs and poems of kindness that an unidentified Man of Kindness delivered to the spring each day. These songs, an illusion to the prayer of the zaddik, are rooted in the place before created time (the no-thingness ['*ayin*] of the blind beggar) and thus constitute the gift of time, a time that must be renewed daily. The spring on the mountain, or the effluence of divinity into the world, is the source of life that is in a constant state of renewal. It is renewed by prayer, more precisely by the prayer of the zaddik, or the stuttering beggar, which is facilitated by the longing of the heart. The stuttering beggar says that he travels the world and collects all kinds of songs of praise and gives them to the Man of Kindness, who creates praises from them and gives them to the spring each day so that it can remain in time and continue to be the object of the heart's longing which, in turn, sustains the world. Therefore, he is the source of the gift of time, the state of constant renewal that sustains the world.

The story of the stuttering beggar, retold here in abbreviated form, takes place amidst a larger debate among "men of science" each of whom take credit for their inventive discoveries, utilizing natural resources for human consumption (iron, silver, and other metals). The stuttering beggar intervenes in the debate of the scientists and claims superiority over all the scientists because he is the master of time, as opposed to each scientist who is only the master of "an hour of time," or one small component of nature. The stuttering beggar then turns to the couple and blesses them to be like him, that is, to utilize prayer to access the power which sustains the longing between the heart (the yearning for divine presence) and the spring (the source of divine wisdom).

As discussed above, for R. Nahman prayer is that which activates the creative power of world ('*olam*) over nature (*teva*). To pray is to hold the gift of time (the master of the day—the one who prays), as opposed to utilizing a component of time (the master of the hour—the scientist). Like the blind beggar, the stuttering beggar has access to that which is above nature, the unity of which is the source of joy and redemption. By collecting these "songs of praise," the stuttering beggar can appreciate the natural world by seeing the extent to which nature is sustained by longing: the heart for the spring, the human being for God. Prayer, the human response to longing, should not yield sadness, as it does in its exilic form (the second exile), but joy in sadness (the third exile/the beggars/the zaddik), as it maintains existence. The stuttering beggar blesses the children that they should recognize their longing as redemptive, taking them from the second to the third exile.

The stuttering beggar, like his predecessors, is perfect (and thus appears deformed) because he has access to that which is beyond the created world ("the songs of praise" before time). Therefore, he is, unlike the wise men, never satisfied but, unlike the son, never hopeless. All the beggars have access to the source of creation, the memory of nothingness, or its sustaining power, the gift of renewal that is rooted in the primordial nothingness (*'ayin*) before creation. The deformity of each beggar is the result of being confined to the natural world which each has already transcended by means of perfecting a particular virtue. Thus, from the perspective of the imperfect world, perfection appears deformed. The zaddik is always a deformed creature as he refuses to submit to nature. More precisely, he is deformed because he carries the burden of transforming the children to see the world "otherwise."

It is clear that the inner frame of the body of the tale, as opposed to the outer frame of the prelude, is based on prayer. The fact that the prelude contains no reference to prayer is significant. The prelude is the presentation of the second exile, the exile of sadness, the inability of the son to overcome the sadness that resulted from his loss of the kingdom. The son and the wise men represent two foci of humanity. Israel, while potentially embodied in the son, is only fully disclosed in the children in the body of the tale, where the story moves from the universal to the particular. The Gentile world, represented in the wise men or the son in the prelude, lives either in the false security of reason or is caught in the endless cycle of longing and heresy.

As discussed above, the construct of prayer for R. Nahman is that prayer opposes both reason (logic) and nature (fate). In the following text from *Liqqutei MoHaRan* 1.217, the juxtaposition of prayer and nature is made explicit in a way that deepens our understanding of the stuttering beggar, connecting his story back to the unfinished prelude:

> The philosophers call nature (*teva*) the "mother of all existence" (*'em kol hay*). However, through prayer we nullify nature. Nature is neces-

sity, prayer changes nature. Thus the eighteen benedictions (of prayer) exclude the blessing to wipe out the heretics [the nineteenth benediction inserted at a later time]. By means of the eighteen [benedictions, the letter representation of eighteen as *het, yod,* i.e., life] we nullify nature as necessity and simultaneously debunk the heretic [the subject of the nineteenth blessing].

In the prelude and the tale itself we have three villains; the philosopher or lover of wisdom, the heretic, and the scientist. Each, to varying degrees, bases their knowledge on reason (logic) or nature (science). Each beggar represents another way of debunking one or all of those villains, either by the memory of origins (the blind beggar), the songs of praise (the stuttering beggar) or, as we will presently see, the one who lives on the edge of space (the hunchback). The songs of praise, which the stuttering beggar hears and collects, are simultaneously the prayers that sustain the world (*mehadesh ha-'olam*) and the prayers that "change" the world (*meshaneh teva*).

The identification of maintenance and change is significant here. If the world would be void of prayer, that is, if Israel, or perhaps more accurately the zaddik, would disappear, nature (as necessity) would collapse. The illusion of nature as necessity only exists because there are those who pray and, in doing so, create the condition for the illusion. The illusion, as exile, exists because of the longing for redemption. While prayer makes the illusion possible, the beggars are telling the children that the more one sees that the illusion is dependant on prayer, the more one is able to live joyously in nature manifesting the third exile, the exile of the joy in sadness. As this posture becomes more prominent, the notion of nature (as necessity) collapses in the mind of the worshiper. The power of renewal (*hidush*) inherent in prayer results in breaking the illusion of necessity (*mehuyavut*). To pray requires a bracketing of the necessity of nature. The heart and the spring in the stuttering beggar's tale is a metaphor for the dialectic of human prayer, simultaneously creating the condition for nature and dissolving it.

The final beggar I will discuss is the hunchback who appears on the fifth day of the wedding. The hunchback claims that he appears deformed because he carries so much weight on his shoulders. In a brilliant interpretation of the midrashic image of "the little-that-holds-much" (*ha-mu'at hehezik 'et ha-merubeh*),[54] R. Nahman presents this beggar as the one who carries the entirety of space, only appearing to be a hunchback. In truth, the hunchback claims, he carries the world on his back. The hunchback illustrates this with a story.

The story is about a group of people who want to travel to a special tree whose branches hold all the birds of the world and whose shade provides a resting place for all the world's animals.[55] The tree is rooted in three virtues: faith, reverence, and humility. The root of the tree is truth (*'emet*, EMT).[56] Only those who achieve these three virtues can reach the tree. The hunchback is included in the group of journeymen who finally merit seeing this tree in the distance. The journeymen soon realize, however, that even as they see the tree they cannot reach it because the tree doesn't really exist in space; it exists on the edge of space, between space and nothingness.

> And I (the hunchback) was also there with them. So I declared to them: "I can lead you to the tree. For this particular tree has no space; it is entirely above (superior to) the earth's space. And yet, the trait of "the little that holds much" still involves some space. . . . And my "little that holds much" is at the very edge of space, and beyond it there is no space at all. . . . That is why I can lead all of you to this tree which is totally above the space it stands on.

The tree is the place of true virtue that encompasses and nurtures the disparate elements of creation. It embodies a transformed view of nature, reminiscent of Isaiah's redemptive vision of Israel because all the birds of the world can rest there peacefully and the entire animal kingdom can enjoy its shade without conflict. True virtue does not exist in the center of space (in nature) but only on the very margins where space comes into being, the meeting place of the infinite and the finite.[57] While a certain element of virtue can be achieved in nature, thus resulting in the journeymen seeing the tree from a distance, the longing for righteousness, which is beyond virtue, can only be achieved in the place where the world meets its infinite source. According to R. Nahman, a moral order, reflecting natural law, may perhaps create a moral society, but it can never fulfill the longing for true virtue and thus cannot be the harbinger of redemption. This is because the view of nature as *teva* (natural law) is the epitome of imperfection. It is the center and not the margin of space.

Moving back to the central motif in the tale, that sadness is the perpetuation of the second type of exile: as long as the aspiration for virtue is sought solely in the center of space (i.e., in nature), it will always yield sadness. Perhaps this is another allusion to R. Nahman's distinction between world (*'olam*) and nature (*teva*) discussed earlier. World (*'olam*) is the intermediary between the infinite (God) and the finite (nature). The recognition of the constancy of divine effluence into nature, embodied in the concept of *'olam*, enables one to maintain the connection between nature and God. To carry space, as the hunchback does, is to retain the consciousness of the world's constant state of renewal. To see the world as *'olam* is to inhabit that edge of space where the tree of virtue, and true joy, reside.

The virtues of faith, reverence, and humility stand at the center of classical Jewish conceptions of righteousness. R. Nahman was living at a time (late eighteenth–early nineteenth century) when philosophical debates were underway concerning the relationship between natural law and morality/ethics.[58] Although it is unlikely that he has first-hand knowledge of these debates, it is likely that he at least knew of their existence.[59] His notion here that virtue dwells on the edge of space and not in its center may reflect a surreptitious response to some of the Enlightenment ideas he may have heard during his residence in Uman, which was a Maskilic center in the early nineteenth century. In conventional kabbalistic thinking, the more material the world becomes, the more God becomes concealed. Materiality is often defined as a condition for *deus absconditus*. The upper levels of space—in kabbalistic nomenclature, the world of the *sefirot*—are the realms where God's presence is most profoundly felt. The message of the hunchback is that true virtue (faith, reverence, humility) is founded upon the consciousness of divine effluence, which is only evident as one approaches the boundaries of space itself. It is at the edge of space when nature becomes most unstable, where natural law succumbs to miracle. The attainment of true virtue is not achieved solely through the practice of the law, which exists in the center of space, but only by approaching the margins of space where nature dissolves into miracle. At best, the law serves as a vehicle for that virtue.

In conclusion, I have offered a reading of part of this complex tale as a window into R. Nahman's exilic anthropology, arguing that the tale reworks his dualistic notion of nature and miracle in his homilies. I used various examples from his homiletic writings, not as proof texts for the tale, but rather to illustrate the extent to which the tale problematizes some of his apparently more straightforward opinions in these writings. I argued that it is not nature that is exilic but the human being who, for numerous reasons, cannot see how order is conditioned on miracle—that is, how nature is redemptive.

R. Nahman relates that he began to tell stories to "wake people up from their slumber." I assume this statement was also directed to his disciples, men of deep faith who were intimately familiar with his ideas. Perhaps those sleeping were not only those lost in the cyclical nightmare of reason but also believers who had become overly secure in their belief? That is, perhaps R. Nahman was trying to communicate that the dichotomy between security and perpetual instability is not identical with those who live by reason or faith. Even, or perhaps precisely, the faithful are vulnerable to the compelling tendency for false security. Even believers can be the son and not the children in the tale.

As he faced his own death and confronted the limited influence of his message, by both skeptics and disciples alike, perhaps he became concerned, even agitated, that his listeners did not fully grasp the complexity of his discourses. Perhaps he felt this was because the genre of homily was not the best vehicle for communicating his ideas. The tale, his final attempt at being understood, became his last word, representing all he had previously taught in the form of fantasy, whose allusive images would forever spark the imagination and make readers believe they have not fully understood what lies beneath. Perhaps the tale serves to awaken its readers by evoking the longing to fully comprehend the narrative that always alludes full disclosure.

Nature, characterized in almost demonic language in *Liqqutei MoHaRan*, is presented in our tale in a much more textured light. The beggars are redeeming the world by changing the way the children see the natural world. Revealing to them the source of their disability does this. The beggars never negate the world, or the reality of their deformity, only an exilic perception of it. This is illustrated in my suggestion that the tale presents three realms of exile, the exile of the unredeemable heretic, the exile of the redeemable heretic, and the exile of the zaddik. The second exile of sadness (the king's son in the prelude, the children in the tale, and the redeemable heretic in *Liqqutei MoHaRan*) and the exile of joy (the beggars/the zaddik) serve as the two relevant poles of R. Nahman's vision of the world and the vocation of Israel. The blessings each beggar bestows on the children are directed toward overcoming the false view of nature and the absolute status of reason, both of which are indicative of the second realm of exile.[60]

Each beggar holds only one piece of the redemptive puzzle. False wisdom, which resulted in the exile of the king's son in the prelude, is coupled with a false view of nature as necessity (*mehuyavut*) in the body of the tale. The beggars seek to heal the imperfections of civilization by drawing it back to the source of life, the root of true wisdom, and the true appreciation of nature in a perpetual state of renewal. The vehicle toward this end is prayer, the devotional act that is conditioned on the bracketing of nature as necessity.[61]

The blessings of the beggars are blessings of perfected virtue that manifest as deformity in exile. As opposed to what the children may have thought each beggar's statement, "be like me," meant in their first encounter in the forest, under the wedding canopy the blessings become clear when they become gifts. The gift is that each beggar reveals the source of his particular virtue, which appears as his deformity. As a result, each beggar revalues the couple's conception of normalcy and well-being, resulting in joy. Each day of the wedding the couple's sense of reality is turned upside down as the apparent disability of each beggar becomes the reflection of his perfection. The joy that ensues indicates the slow retrieval of the joy lost by the king's son in the prelude to the tale.

This process of retrieval is never complete and the tale remains unfinished. This is because the seventh beggar, the beggar without feet, never arrives.[62] The couple remains in exile, living a life in tension between joy and longing. The king's son remains in exile, struggling between his legitimate questions and his heretical answers. Israel remains in exile, never fully overcoming the deception of nature as fate and necessity, still lost in the seductive world of rationality. Finally, R. Nahman remains in exile, a messianic figure who lived out his last debilitating days without ever achieving overwhelming acceptance outside his closed circle of followers.[63] A few months after finishing this unfinished tale, R. Nahman left the world of nature he struggled so passionately to transform. As to the legitimacy of his messianic claim, we will have to wait for the seventh beggar to arrive.

Notes

This article was completed before the publication of Ora Wiskind-Alpert's *Tradition and Fantasy in the Tales of Rabbi Nahman of Bratslav* (Albany: State University of New York Press, 1998). Therefore, I was regrettably unable to incorporate her insightful analysis of this tale.

1. For a discussion on Hasidism in light of earlier models of Jewish mysticism, see Gershom Scholem, *Major Trends in Jewish Mysticism* (New York: Schocken Press, 1941), 325–50; and Moshe Idel, *Hasidism: Between Ecstasy and Magic* (Albany: State University of New York Press, 1995), 45–102.

2. See Moshe Rosman, *Founder of Hasidism: A Quest for the Historical Ba'al Shem Tov* (Berkeley, Los Angeles, and London: University of California Press, 1996), 1–94; Immanuel Etkes, *The Besht: Magic, Mysticism, Leadership* (in Hebrew) (Jerusalem: Zalman Shazar Institute, 2000), 54–87 and 122–62; and Simon Dubnow, "The Beginnings: The Baal Shem Tov (Besht) and the Center in Podolia," reprinted in *Essential Papers in Hasidism,* ed. Gershon Hundert (New York: New York University Press, 1991), 25–57.

3. See Ada Rapoport-Albert, "Hasidism After 1772: Structural Continuity and Change," in *Hasidism Reappraised,* ed. Ada Rapoport-Albert (London and Portland, Ore.: The Littman Library of Jewish Civilization, 1997), 76–140; and Simon Dubnow "The Maggid of Miedzyrzecz, His Associates, and the Center in Volhynia," reprinted in Hundert, *Essential Papers in Hasidism,* 58–85.

4. For a history of the birth and childhood of the young Nahman, see Arthur Green, *Tormented Master: A Life of Rabbi Nahman of Bratslav* (1979; Woodstock, Vt.: Jewish Lights, 1992), 23–62.

5. On this, see Joseph Weiss, "R. Nahman on the Controversy about Him" (in Hebrew), in Joseph Weiss, *Studies in Bratslav Hasidism* (Jerusalem: Mosad Bialik, 1974), 42–57; and Green, *Tormented Master,* 94–134.

6. On the publication of these texts and other Bratslav texts, see Weiss, *Studies in Bratslav Hasidism,* 251–77; Gershom Scholem, *"Kuntrus 'Eleh Shemot*: The Books of MoHaRan of Bratslav and the Works of His Disciples" (in Hebrew) (Jerusalem, 1928). Compare the recent bibliographical study of traditional and scholarly literature of Bratslav Hasidism: David Asaf, *Bratslav: An Annotated Bibliography* (in Hebrew) (Jerusalem: Zalman Shazar Institute, 2000). Asaf's study is the most comprehensive bibliographical study to date on Bratslav literature and an indispensable tool for anyone working in Bratslav Hasidism.

7. On the death of his son from tuberculosis and its effect on his life, see R. Avraham Hazan, *Avnekha Barzel* (Jerusalem, 1961), 30 n. 32, and *Hayye MoHaRan* (Jerusalem, 1991), 199, 200 n. 151. Cf. Mendel Piekarz, *Studies in Bratslav Hasidism* (Jerusalem: Mosad Bialik, 1972), 78–81.

8. This statement is considered a paradigm shift in R. Nahman's life and his teaching by both disciples and scholars alike. The most comprehensive studies of the stories can be found in Yaakov Elstein's "Structuralism in Literary Criticism: A Method and Application in Two Representative Hasidic Tales" (Ph.D. diss., University of California, Los Angeles, 1974); Martin Irving Mantel, "R. Nahman of Bratslav's Tales: A Critical Translation from the Yiddish with Annotations and Commentary"

(Ph.D diss., Princeton University, 1977); Joseph Dan, *Sippur Ha-Hasidi* (Jerusalem: Keter, 1975), 132–87; Henie G. Haidenberg and Mikhal Oron, *From the Mystical World of R. Nahman of Bratslav* (in Hebrew) (Tel Aviv: Papirus, 1986); Piekarz, *Studies in Bratslav Hasidism*, 132–50; Green, *Tormented Master*, 337–71; Abraham Berger, "Approaches to R. Nahman and His Tales," *Studies in Jewish Bibliography, History, and Literature in Honor of I. E. Kiev* (New York: Ktav Press, 1971), 11–19; and, most recently, David Roskies, *A Bridge of Longing: The Lost Art of Yiddish Storytelling* (Cambridge, Mass.: Harvard University Press, 1995), 20–58. The stories have been translated into many languages. The most well-known translations are by Martin Buber into German, in 1909, and by Adin Steinsaltz, Aryeh Kaplan, and Arnold Band into English. For more references, both scholarly and popular, see Green, *Tormented Master*, 367–68 n. 1. For a historical overview on these and other translations, see "The Text and the Translation," in Arnold Band, *Nahman of Bratslav: The Tales* (New York: Paulist Press, 1978), 43–48.

9. The text was originally published with *Shivhei ve-Sihot Ha-Ran*; additional material by and about R. Nahman was later published separately. Also included in this first printing were numerous lessons from *Liqqutei MoHaRan* that were not included in the first printing. See R. Avraham Hazan, *Avnekha Barzel*, 74 n. 62; and Chaim Kramer, *Between Fire and Water* (Jerusalem and New York: Breslov Research Institute, 1992), 255.

10. R. Nathan Sternhertz is usually known in scholarly literature as R. Nathan of Nemerov because he was a leading rabbinic figure in that city before becoming a disciple of R. Nahman. However, after becoming a disciple of R. Nahman, he explicitly stated that he wanted to be known as R. Nathan of Bratslav (Breslov), and he is referred to as such by adherents to the Bratslav tradition. He is buried in Bratslav, a short distance from R. Nahman's grave in Uman, and his grave remains a shrine for Bratslaver Hasidim.

11. It is not only scholars who took this view. R. Nathan was recorded as saying, "In the eulogies [for me] they will say, 'Here is the man who printed *Sippurei Ma'asiot*.' This will be my great honor." See *Siah Sarfei Kodesh* (Jerusalem, 1991), 3:155

12. This is true in the Bratslav tradition as well. Most of the traditional commentaries on the tales explain them according to *Liqqutei MoHaRan*, *Liqqutei Etzot*, *Liqqutei Halakhot*, and subsequent Bratslav literature. See, for example R. Nahman of Cheryn's *Rimzei Ma'asiot*, perhaps the most widely read commentary on the tales, and R. Avraham Hazan's *Hokhmot u Tevunot*. The former is published at the end of standard bilingual editions of the tales. For discussions of these commentaries, see Piekarz, *Studies in Bratslav Hasidism*, 147–50.

13. See Dan, *Sippur Ha-Hasidi*, 145ff.; Green, *Tormented Master*, 360–67; Mantel, "R. Nahman of Bratslav's Tales," 223–39. On the importance of the story, see *Sihot Ha-Ran*, 149–51, and *Hayye MoHaRan*, "Conversations Relating to His Stories," 189–90. "The Tale of the Seven Beggars" was told over a period of a few weeks. The first part was told on Friday evening, 10 March 1810, when R. Nahman's lung ailment was worsening. The story of the third day, the story of the heart and the spring discussed later in this essay, was told a few days before the death of his young son Shlomo Ephraim. The story of the sixth day was told on 10 April 1810. The story of

the seventh day was never told. R. Nahman died on the intermediate days of the festival of Sukkot that year, 15 October 1810. See *Yemey MoHaRan* (The Life of R. Nathan of Bratslav), 1.42; and Kramer, *Between Fire and Water*, 172–74. For an elaborate description of his final days and hours, see *Yemey MoHaRan*, 1.62–66.

14. See Elisheva Schoenfeld, "The Story of the Seven Beggars of R. Nahman of Bratslav," in *Fourth International Congress for Folk-Narrative Research in Athens: Lectures and Reports* (Athens, 1965), 459–65; Michal Oron, "Exile and Redemption: An Analysis of the Tale of the Seven Beggars of R. Nahman of Bratslav" (in Hebrew), *Davar, Literary Supplement* 9 (September 1979): 14–15; and Aviad Lipsker, "The Bride and the Seven Beggars: On the Question of the Sources of the Story 'The Seven Beggars'" (in Hebrew) *Jerusalem Studies in Jewish Folklore* 13–14 (1992): 229–48.

15. Another important early Hasidic example of the relationship between nature and miracle can be found in R. Levi Isaac of Berdichev's *Qedushat Levi*, "Second Sanctification on Purim" (Jerusalem, 1966), 6b–9d. The original publication of *Qedushat Levi* (Slovita, 1818) only included his comments on Purim and Hanukkah, both of which speak about the nature of miracle. The later editions, beginning with the 1836 Berdichev edition, include his more extensive commentary on the Torah. Subsequent editions include his comments on Purim and Hanukkah at the end of the book, with new page numbers.

16. See, for example, in *Liqqutei MoHaRan* 1.7,1; 1.8,7; 1.250; 2.10,7.

17. This approach has been documented most thoroughly by Joseph Dan and Yaakov Elstein. Mantel notes that Dan is largely following R. Nahman of Cheryn's *Rimzei Ma'asiot* by fleshing out the literary structure and substance according to kabbalistic literature. Mantel prefers a more comparative analysis, showing the ways in which the literary framework of the story resembles folk tales of Ukraine and Eastern Europe (*marchen*). Cf. Mantel, "R. Nahman of Bratslav's Tales," 223–39.

18. *Liqqutei MoHaRan* 1.60, para. 6: "You wake a person up through tales, tales which take place in the midst of years, representing one of the seventy faces [of the Torah]. Some people have fallen so low that they can only be aroused and awakened by means of tales of 'ancient days,' the place where all seventy faces derive their sustenance." Cf. Green, *Tormented Master*, 345–46. This lesson was given on Rosh Hashanah 1807, after R. Nahman had already begun his storytelling. See R. Nahman of Cheryn, *Pearparot l'Hokhma* (Brooklyn, 1976), 31a–33a.

19. The descent of the zaddik is paradigmatic in early Hasidism. See Arthur Green, "Typologies and Leadership and the Hasidic Zaddik," in *Jewish Spirituality II: From the Sixteenth-Century Revival to the Present*, ed. Arthur Green (New York: Crossroads Press, 1989), 127–56; and Joseph Weiss, "The Beginning of the Way of Hasidism" (in Hebrew), *Zion* 16 (1951): 89–103. Cf. Mark Verman, "Aliyah and Yeridah: The Journeys of the Besht and R. Nahman to Israel," in *Approaches to Judaism in Medieval Times*, ed David Blumenthal (Atlanta, Ga.: Scholars Press, 1988), 3:159–71.

20. Scholars, of course, acknowledge this as well. See, for example, Joseph Dan, preface to *Nahman of Bratslav: The Tales*, trans. Arnold J. Band (New York: Paulist Press, 1978), xiii–xix; Green, *Tormented Master*, 340–44.

21. On this, see Roskies, *Bridge of Longing*, 29; Dan, preface to *Nahman of Bratslav: The Tales*, xvii: "Still, we do find major Kabbalistic elements, especially

the Lurianic concepts of mythological history and mystical redemption, serving as major motifs within the tales. But there is a basic difference between 'using' Kabbalistic ideas and 'expressing' them in the tales: those elements which are present in the tales ceased to be building blocks of a mystical theology and became chapters in the mystical biography of Nahman's soul. . . . This process of identification in a deep spiritual way with cosmic developments is rare, but not impossible, in both mystical and literary creative work."

22. The tale embodies the same methodology as R. Nahman's homiletic writings. Terms are expressed and then tied into other terms via association (*behinot*), creating a complex terminological labyrinth used to create a frame for his lesson. On this, see R. Nahman of Cheryn, *Pearparot le-Hokhmah*, 2a–2d; and Green, *Tormented Master*, 285–87. Cf. my "Associative Midrash: Reflections on a Hermeneutic Theory in R. Nahman of Bratslav's *Liqqutei MoHaRan*," in *God's Voice from the Void: Old and New Studies in Bratslav Hasidism*, ed. Shaul Magid (Albany: State University of New York Press, 2001), 15–66.

23. *Liqqutei MoHaRan* 2.101.

24. Exile is a complex term in R. Nahman's thinking, especially in the tales. For a more textured definition, see my discussion earlier in this essay. Here I only mean that exile, as alienation, requires longing as the vehicle for reconciliation. The security of exile threatens the continuation of this longing.

25. What I mean by this is that the turn toward redemption in R. Nahman's eyes is a revolutionary move, turning the world on its head to reveal the illusions of exile. The "security of exile" rests on the fact that we are convinced that what we think is true is in fact true. This security is the most dangerous dimension of exile because it diminishes the longing for redemption. This is, for R. Nahman, the fundamental malaise of modernity.

26. See *Rimzei Ma'asiot*, 17a: "One who is unable to maintain the state of joy at the time of great despair (losing the kingdom), it is fitting that he should be dethroned because fitness for kingship necessitates maintaining joy even in the time of despair" (my translation). R. Nahman of Cheryn's comment implies that authentic joy cannot be contingent upon an external event or circumstance but needs to be an orientation toward all possible circumstances. For R. Nahman of Cheryn, it is joy and not wisdom that is an absolute value.

27. See *Liqqutei Etzot*, "*Haqirot*," 4: "Sometimes individuals involve themselves in 'wisdom' for frivolous purposes. For example, for honor, money, etc. . . ." Cf. *Rimzei Ma'asiot*," 18. R. Nahman's description of wisdom here, as in many other places, is sarcastic. This sarcastic thread filters through all of the tales and plays the most prominent role in the tale "The Wise Man and the Simpleton." *Liqqutei MoHaRan* 1.64. This also seems to be a comment about the Jewish infatuation with the Enlightenment. That is, the Jew is easily drawn to the security of reason but, as a result of his/her innate goodness, is never fully convinced by it. Thus, while the Jew may think he/she is being accepted by the Gentile world, like the son, he/she is forever estranged from their surroundings (the wise men).

28. For the connection between heresy and nature, see *Liqqutei MoHaRan* 1.52: "There are heretics who say that the world is necessary (*mehuyav*). According to their

mistaken opinion they imagine that they have wondrous proofs. . . . In truth it is just empty breath because only God is a necessary Existent. All the worlds are only contingent existents. . . ." Cf. ibid., 2.7, para. 9; and Maimonides, *Mishneh Torah* Laws on the Foundation of the Torah 1.1, para. 2.

29. The son represents the redeemable heretic spoken about in *Liqqutei MoHaRan* 1.64. For a translation and discussion of the two types of heretic in R. Nahman, see Green, *Tormented Master*, 312–22. Mantel understands the son's response, "where am I in the world," as "the first niggling of penitential regret," thereby introducing repentance into the narrative. See Mantel, "R. Nahman of Braslav's Tales," 226. While this may be true, prayer, as depicted in the screams of the children in the forest, does not appear in the prelude.

30. The notion of three distinct types of exile is not new in R. Nahman. This idea exists, in a very different form in early Hasidism. See, for example, R. Ya'akov Yoseph of Polonnoye, *Toledot Ya'akov Yoseph*, "*parshat ve-ethanan*," 178d, and *Sefer Ba'al Shem Tov*, vol. 2, "*parshat balak*," 474–75.

31. See *Liqqutei MoHaRan* 1.64. Cf. my "Through the Void: The Absence of God in R. Nahman of Bratslav's *Liqqutei MoHaRan*," *Harvard Theological Review* 88, no. 4 (1995): 495–519; Green, *Tormented Master*, 285–336; Weiss, *Studies in Bratslav Hasidism*, 109–49; and, most recently, Mordecai Pachter, "Studies in Faith and Heresy in the Teachings of R. Nahman of Bratslav" (in Hebrew), *Da'at* 45 (2000): 105–34.

32. The correlation between sadness and exile goes back to rabbinic literature and takes center stage in early Hasidism. See, for example, the Besht's rebuke to his disciple R. Ya'akov Yoseph about his excessive fasting. "This [fasting] is the way of depression and sadness. The *Shekhinah* does not inspire one through sadness but only via the joy [*simha*] of performing *mitzvot*"; *Shivhei Ha-Besht*, 49. Even though *Shivhei Ha-Besht* was first published in 1815, more than five years after R. Nahman's passing, many of its traditions were widely known before that time. See Rosman, *Founder of Hasidism*, esp. 187–211.

33. On this, see Green, *Tormented Master*, 285–336; Piekarz, *Studies in Bratslav Hasidism*, 21–55; Weiss, *Studies in Bratslav Hasidism*, 109–50; Joseph Weiss, "Sense and Non-Sense in Defining Judaism: The Strange Case of Nahman of Bratslav," in *Studies in East European Jewish Mysticism*, ed. David Goldstein (Oxford: Oxford University Press, 1985), 249–69; and my "Through the Void."

34. See *Rimzei Ma'asiot*, 18: "Meriting the gifts from each beggar is the result of the greatness of the children. However, all that the children merit is the result of their longing and yearning" (my translation). In this comment, R. Nahman of Cheryn makes the important connection between the son in the prelude and the children in the body of the tale.

35. R. Nahman's notion of the redeemable and unredeemable heretic plays an important role in his assessment of secularism and modernity. See Mendel Piekarz, "The Episode of Uman in the Life of R. Nahman of *Bratslav*," in Piekarz, *Studies in Bratslav Hasidism*, 21–55.

36. On brokenheartedness as the foundation for prayer, see *Sihot Ha-Ran*, 31, and *Liqqutei MoHaRan* 2.25 and 47. On the connection between prayer and redemption, see *Liqqutei MoHaRan* 2.71.

37. See the discussion in Azriel Shochet, "On *Simha* in Hasidism" (in Hebrew), *Zion* 16 (1951): 30–43.

38. See Adin Steinsaltz, *The Tales of Rabbi Nahman of Bratslav* (Northvale, N.J.: Jason Aronson, 1993), 254. Steinsaltz reads the prelude in a similar manner but misses, in my opinion, the complexity of the interplay between sadness and exile. His depiction is that the prelude replays another tale, "The Wise Man and the Simpleton," where R. Nahman develops the notion that the pursuit of wisdom as an end in itself (i.e., as an absolute value) leads to heresy. The focus here, however, is less about the distortion of wisdom and more about the failure of such wisdom to produce joy (*simha*). For R. Nahman, redemption is an emotional state and not a correct opinion. Sadness is exilic because it reverses the redemptive process of human perfection.

39. The significance of the beggar without feet as the Messiah relates to R. Nahman's emphasis on dance as a redemptive act, one that can elicit joy like no other act. On this, see Michael Fishbane, "To Jump for Joy: the Rites of Dance According to R. Nahman of Bratslav," *The Journal of Jewish Thought and Philosophy* 6 (1997): 371–87.

40. R. Nahman uses "wisdom" in a pejorative sense. It is like the Yiddish *hokhmas*, which implies deception, the appellation *hokham* almost meaning "wise guy." See Weiss, *Studies in Bratslav Hasidism*, 25; and Green, *Tormented Master*, 331 n. 12.

41. On this, see Elisheva Shoenfeld, "The Seven Beggars of R. Nahman of Bratslav" (in Hebrew), *Yeda Am* 11, no. 30 (1965): 65–78.

42. *Liqqutei MoHaRan* 1.9,5.

43. *Azvut*, perhaps best translated as depression or the demonic (*sitra ahra*). For its connection to hopelessness see, *Sihot Ha-Ran*, 41, and *Liqqutei MoHaRan* 2.25.

44. In this sense, R. Nahman is echoing Pascal (contra Descartes), who he most probably did not know, that skepticism can teach us about the things reason cannot achieve, such as answering the basic questions of human existence, i.e., "Who am I?" See Blaise Pascal, *Pensées* (New York: E. P. Dutton and Company, 1996).

45. See Piekarz, *Studies in Bratslav Hasidism*, 21–55.

46. See *Liqqutei MoHaRan* 1.17,1, where R. Nahman gives us a description of '*am segulah*, the biblical depiction of Israel as chosen. "This is like the '*segulah*' of healing. Even though naturally a particular medicine will not necessarily work [lit., nature cannot determine the efficacy of healing] healing (*segulah*) is higher than nature, which the human intellect cannot comprehend."

47. On the importance of the scream and song in Bratslav Hasidism, see Pachter, "Studies in Faith and Heresy in the Teaching of R. Nahman of Bratslav."

48. See especially *Liqqutei MoHaRan* 1.8, para. 7, where R. Nahman presents three distinct but interrelated categories: 1) nature—order; 2) world—renewal; and 3) prayer—creativity. Prayer contains the potential to activate the renewing power of "world," which then overcomes the order of "nature."

49. See, most recently, Miles Krassen, *Uniter of Heaven and Earth* (Albany: State University of New York Press, 1998), esp. 106–21.

50. For a detailed analysis of this in early Hasidism, see Rivka Schatz-Uffenheimer, "Self-Redemption in Hasidic Thought," in *Types of Redemption*, ed. R. J. Z. Werblowsky and C. J. Bleeker (Leiden: Brill, 1970), 207–12.

51. Each beggar begins to tell his tale by making a logically incongruous statement, thus challenging logic as a way of seeing the world and enabling the children to comprehend the ways in which imperfection in this world is often a sign of perfection.

52. On the concept of suffering in R. Nahman, particularly the fate of suffering of the zaddik, see Martin Mantel, "The Meaning of Suffering According to R. Nathan of Nemerov" (in Hebrew). *Da'at* 7 (1981): 109–18.

53. For a fascinating literary reading of "the heart and the spring," see Dov Sadan, "The Heart of the World," in *Bein She'elat le-Qinyan* (Tel Aviv: University of Tel Aviv Press, 1968), 137–57.

54. See *Bereshit Rabbah* 5.7, in *Midrash Bereshit Rabbah*, ed. J. Theodor and C. H. Albeck (Jerusalem, 1965), 36–37.

55. See *Liqqutei MoHaRan* 1.15, para. 5, where R. Nahman interprets the talmudic Rabba bar bar Hanna story about the tree that contains all virtues and that dwells at the edge of space. Cf. Mantel, "R. Nahman of Bratslav's Tales," 236–37. The connection between R. Nahman's interpretations of the Rabba bar bar Hanna fantasy stories in Talmud Bava Batra and *Sippurei Ma'asiot* is a desideratum. Green alludes to this in *Tormented Master*, 342–44.

56. The importance of the tree being EMT is that *'emet* is composed of three letters of the Hebrew alphabet, the first, middle, and last letter. Based on the kabbalistic notion, rooted in Midrash, that God created the world with the Hebrew letters, *'emet* is a linguistic sign of the entirety of existence. See, for example, in Elliot R. Wolfson, "The Tree that Is All: Jewish-Christian Roots of a Kabbalistic Symbol in *Sefer Ha-Bahir*," *Journal of Jewish Thought and Philosophy* 3 (1993): 31–76. The tree is a central motif in both the Talmud and the Zohar; see, for example, Babylonian Talmud Ta'anit 7a, and the tree as the *Shekhinah* in *Sabba de-Mishpatim*, Zohar 2.105a–108b. Cf. the exegesis of R. Pinhas ben Yair in Zohar 3.200b–202b; Yehuda Liebes, "Sections of the Zohar Lexicon" (Ph.D diss., Hebrew University, Jerusalem, 1976), 107–31; idem, "Zohar and Eros" (in Hebrew), *Alpayyim* 9 (1994): 27 n. 46; and Pinchas Giller, *Reading the Zohar: The Sacred Text of the Kabbala* (Oxford and New York: Oxford University Press, 2001), 58–60. These and other examples are brought and discussed in Pinchas Giller, "The World Trees in the Zohar," in *Trees, Earth, and Torah: A Tu B'shvat Anthology*, ed. Ari Elon, Naomi Mara Hyman, and Arthur Waskow (Philadelphia Pa.: Jewish Publication Society, 1999), 128–34; and Michael Fishbane, "The Book of Zohar and Exegetical Spirituality," in *Mysticism and Sacred Scripture*, ed. Steven T. Katz (Oxford and New York: Oxford University Press, 2000), 103–5.

57. This is in contrast to earlier kabbalistic views that understand holiness as the center rather than on the margin. See, for example, Rabbenu Bahya ben Asher, *Kad va-Qemah*, "Shabbat," in *Kitvei Rabbenu Bahya*, ed. Hayim Dov Chavel (Jerusalem, 1970), 12a. Cf. a relevant summary of Bahya's position in Reuven Kimmelman, "Introduction to Lekha Dodi and to Kabbalat Shabbat" (in Hebrew), *Jerusalem Studies in Jewish Thought* 14 (1998): 433: "Jerusalem is the center of the world, Shabbat is the center of the week. Everything that is in the center is holy. Everything on the margin is profane. The desecration of the Sabbath is a desecration of the center by making it marginal." For R. Nahman, the center is the materiality of nature, the place

of God's deepest concealment. The margin is the place where the finite and the infinite meet.

58. This was true in Jewish Enlightenment circles as well. After his move to Uman, R. Nahman had sustained dialogue with some of the leading Enlightenment figures in Uman. It is therefore likely that he had some exposure to some of these ideas. See Piekarz, "The Episode of Uman in the Life of R. Nahman of Bratslav," esp. 49–55.

59. See Piekarz, *Studies in Bratslav Hasidism*, esp. 27–32. Piekarz traces R. Nahman's relationship to the Uman heretics (*maskilim*) during this final period of his life. While traditional literature cites the existence of a cemetery of Jewish martyrs as the reason for R. Nahman's choice to move to Uman, the city was also a center of Enlightenment activity. For an alternative view, see Yakov Travis, "Adoring the Souls of the Dead: Rabbi Nahman of Bratslav," in *God's Voice from the Void: Old and New Studies in Bratslav Hasidism*, ed. Shaul Magid (Albany: State University of New York Press, 2001), 155–92.

60. This also is the foundation of the first exile, the exile of the unredeemable heretic.

61. R. Nahman often speaks of prayer as a weapon, using the terms bows and arrows. See, for example, *Liqqutei MoHaRan* 1.2,1, and 2.83. Interestingly, the bow in both lessons represents the phallus (Joseph as the *sefirah* of *yesod*, in 1.2, and *tiqqun ha-berit*, or sexual purity, in 2.83), while the arrows represent prayer. The power of prayer as the battle against sadness and exile also plays a role in various interpretations of the prelude of our story. In an attempt to connect the prelude to the body of the tale, R. Nahman of Cheryn states: "Since the people of the country [in the prelude] were solely involved in wisdom (*hokhmot*), they completely forgot the art of war. That is, how to wage the great war in this world which is the battle against the evil inclination." *Rimzei Ma'asiot*, 18. Cf. Steinsaltz, *Tales of Rabbi Nahman of Bratslav*, 255, where he comments that there is no textual basis for this reading. However, given that the prelude contains no mention of prayer (the tools of the great war in R. Nahman), and the body of the tale is founded upon prayer as the antidote for sadness, heresy, and exile, R. Nahman of Cheryn's insertion is well founded.

62. On this see Fishbane, "To Jump for Joy," cited in n. 39 above.

63. Although R. Nahman and Bratslav Hasidism had a profound impact on Hasidism in general, R. Nahman achieved only moderate success during his short life. Most of his teachings were published posthumously and his audacious and extreme personality led to controversy inside and outside the circles of early Hasidism. His creative mind and unique perspective attracted many from the neo–Hasidic movement in the late nineteenth and early twentieth centuries, including Martin Buber, Samuel Abba Horodetzky, Hillel Zeitlin, Yehudah Leib Peretz, Adin Steinsaltz, and Areyh Kaplan, among others. The Breslov Research Institute in Jerusalem has done a remarkable job translating, reprinting, and interpreting his teachings to the larger popular audience. My deep thanks to Moshe Mykoff of the Breslov Research Institute, my friend and perennial *havruta*, for his ear, his heart, and his love of "Rabbenu's" teaching.

Early Hasidism and the Natural World

JEROME (YEHUDAH) GELLMAN

The Hasidic movement started in the latter part of the eighteenth century in the Podolia section of Ukraine, under Israel Baal-Shem Tov (1698–1760).[1] By the middle of the nineteenth century, Hasidism came to dominate the religious sensibilities of Eastern European Jewry. Hasidim remains an important movement within contemporary traditional Judaism. Hasidism's focus on joy and immediacy, its valuing of the uneducated peasant, and its penchant for stories about the common and the everyday would seem to go together quite naturally with an openness to and engagement with nature. My purpose here is to investigate whether a positive attitude toward the natural world might emerge from early Hasidic thought.

By far the most important presentation of early Hasidism is that of Martin Buber. In Buber's eyes, early Hasidism had a positive attitude toward the world and nature unprecedented in Jewish history. In Buber's words, the Hasidim were "open to the world, pious toward the world, in love with the world."[2] Buber's way of looking at Hasidism has been extraordinarily influential. It was Buber more than anyone else who introduced Hasidism to Western culture. For close to five decades, in works including collections of Hasidic stories, collections of sayings, essays, and a historical novel, Buber brought the riches of Hasidism to the world.

Buber's interpretation of Hasidism was subject to criticism by both Gershom Scholem and Rivkah Schatz-Uffenheimer.[3] Buber responded to each with rigorous defenses. These exchanges are particularly helpful for elucidating the attitude of early Hasidism to the natural world.

I begin with a brief sketch of Buber's picture of Hasidism. Then I will take up the exchanges between Buber and Scholem and Buber and Schatz-Uffenheimer, respectively.

In his introduction to the Hebrew edition of *The Origin and Meaning of Hasidism,* Buber wrote: "I don't know a better description of what Hasidism taught me to believe [than this]: that the Divine Being is hidden in things and in objects, and that I am not permitted to feel this Being save through a true encounter with them, through an encounter of I-and-Thou." To understand Buber on Hasidism, then, we must begin with his conception of "I and Thou."

In an I-Thou encounter, one person relates to another with her "whole being," in what Buber calls "presence" and "concentration." One relates with one's whole being to the whole of the being of another. The encounter has no purpose other than the meeting. In an "I-It" relationship, one meets another for some purpose, with an interest beyond the meeting. As such, in "I-It" one attends to only a presently relevant part, a fragment, of the other, not to her whole being. The "I" of the I-and-Thou is thus different from the ego of the I-It relationship. In the former, the "I" and the "Thou" form a unitary nexus. The "I" is relational. In the I-It relationship, on the other hand, one does not speak with one's whole being. And the "I" is atomistic.

Buber proclaims the possibility of having a relationship of I-Thou not only with another person, but also with nature, with an animal, or with a tree. In his work *Between Man and Man,* Buber describes an I-Thou encounter between himself and a horse, when he was a boy:

> I must say that what I experienced in touch with the animal was the Other, the immense otherness of the Other, which, however, did not remain strange . . . but rather let me draw near and touch it. When I stroked the mighty mane, sometimes marvelously smooth-combed, at other times just as astonishingly wild, and felt the life beneath my hand, it was as though the element of vitality itself bordered on my skin, something that was not I . . . and yet it let me approach, confided itself to me, placed itself elementally in the relation of *Thou* and *Thou* with me. The horse . . . very gently raised his massive head, ears flicking, then snorted quietly, as a conspirator gives a signal meant to be recognizable only by his fellow-conspirator; and I was approved.[4]

In *I and Thou,* Buber writes of the possibility of having such a relation with a tree:

I contemplate a tree. . . . I can assign it to a species and observe it as an instance, with an eye to its construction and its way of life. . . . I can dissolve it into a number, into a pure relation between numbers, and eternalize this. Throughout all of this, the tree remains my object and has its place and its time span, its kind and condition.

But it can also happen, if will and grace are joined, that as I contemplate the tree I am drawn into a relation, and the tree ceases to be an It. . . . Whatever belongs to the tree is included . . . all this in its entirety. . . . What I encounter is neither the soul of a tree nor a dryad, but the tree itself.[5]

In encountering the "tree itself," one enters into an I-Thou relationship with one's whole being to the whole being of the tree.

Crucial to the I-and-Thou relationship is what Buber calls "reciprocity," or "mutuality": You cannot be a Thou for me unless I am also a Thou for you. This raises the question of how there could be a relationship of I-Thou with non-animal nature. To this Buber replies:

It is altogether different with those realms of nature where the spontaneity we share with the animals is lacking. It is part of our concept of a plant that it cannot react to our actions upon it; it cannot "reply." Yet, this does not mean that we meet with no reciprocity at all in this sphere. The deed or attitude of an individual being is certainly not to be found here, but there is reciprocity of the being itself, a reciprocity that is nothing but being in its course. That living wholeness and unity of the tree, which denies itself to the sharpest glance of the mere investigator and discloses itself to the glance of one who says *Thou*, is there when he, the sayer of *Thou*, is there. . . . Our habits of thought make it difficult for us to see that here . . . something lights up and approaches us from the course of being.[6]

Being reciprocates, says Buber. When we allow it to, the Being of a tree leaps out to us. Reciprocity with nature is possible, then, because nature knows no hiding. Nature stands openly before us, with no masks and no restraints.[7] Nature is a *waiting* Thou, waiting to be addressed by the wholeness of our own being.

The lines of our I-Thou encounter with nature, says Buber, can extend from us, through nature, beyond, to God, the "Eternal Thou." For Buber, we can apprehend God *only* as a Thou, never as an It. We can encounter the Eternal Thou *only* through meeting another, a person, a horse, a tree, as a Thou. The world engages us with God. The world is not a rupture between God and us.

When Buber turns to Hasidism, he ascribes to it a vigorous engagement with "the world-as-Thou." It is specifically in his relationship with the world, says Buber, that the Hasid realizes his relationship to God as the "Eternal Thou." By relating to each event and object in the world with his "whole being" and with complete "concentration," according to Buber, the Hasid "hallows" the world. It is in *hallowing* the world, in this way, and in this alone, that the Hassid meets God. Therefore, a Hasid can meet God in the "hallowing" of a tree or of a horse.

Informed as it was by Buber's dialogical philosophy of I and Thou, Buber's Hasidism seemed to many to be a historical, real-life embodiment of that very philosophy.

Accordingly, in Buber's interpretation of Hasidism, the Hasidim are portrayed as anti-ascetic, because they affirm and "hallow" the world. The Hasidim are: "open to the world, pious toward the world, in love with the world."[8] The Hasidim, neither condemning nor elitist, laud the simple, unlettered person, to whose entire being they could relate in an ongoing I-Thou relationship. The simple could hallow the world with their whole being no less than could the wise talmudic rabbi or the learned kabbalist. Moreover, Buber's Hasidim are anti-mystical, insofar as mysticism denotes a detachment from the world.

In keeping with this way of seeing Hasidism, Buber claimed that the early Hasidim made a major departure from the traditional kabbalistic doctrine of the "holy sparks." Rabbi Isaac Luria, the "Ari," taught that sparks of holiness were scattered into the lowest world of '*asiah*, including the world of matter, at creation. These sparks are encased by the *kelippot*, or "shells," which hide the presence of the sparks and get their life from them. Luria taught that the sparks wished to be released from their captivity in the world, and that it was the obligation of the Jew to release them and enable their ascent to the upper worlds where holiness reigned. The lifting up of the sparks was to be accomplished by the performance of the commandments. Buber sees the original doctrine of the *nitzotzot*, or holy sparks, as anti-worldly. It teaches that the phenomenal world is ontologically empty, its appearance of reality due only to the hidden sparks whose home is in the otherworld. On this doctrine, the mystic's concern is with the release of the hidden sparks from their nethermost captivity. The phenomenal world falls to the side in the mystic's theurgic exercise.

In Hasidism, Buber ventured, the doctrine of the sparks is not a metaphysical teaching, but a metaphor for the hallowing of the world. The "sparks" are the potential of the world to be hallowed by humans. They are "concealed" when the world is not yet hallowed and become "redeemed" when one relates to the world as a Thou: "In all are hidden sparks that are anxious for redemption, and if you have to do with the things and beings with carefulness, with good will, and faithfulness, you redeem them."[9]

No longer are the *nitzotzot* (sparks) removed from the world and the world left behind in the holy act of raising the sparks. Instead, says Buber, when one engages the world with one's whole being, in concentration, as an I to a Thou, then one meets God, the Eternal Thou, in the world. "Everything wants to be hallowed," writes Buber, "to be brought into the holy, everything worldly *in its wordliness; it does not want to be stripped of its worldliness . . .* everything wants to come to God through us" (my emphasis).[10] "The raising of the sparks" means a hallowing of the world, in all its worldliness. And there is nothing in the world that cannot be hallowed: "The not-holy . . . does not exist; there exists only the not yet hallowed, that which has not yet been liberated to its holiness, that which he shall hallow."[11]

Buber stresses in the strongest possible terms the difference between the old Lurianic idea of the sparks and the new Hasidic, metaphorical understanding. Of Hasidic literature as a whole, Buber writes this:

> *Nowhere . . . is it intimated* that the indwelling principle would draw itself out of the world; rather the unification of the separated means just the unification of God with the world, which continues to exist as world, only that it is now, just as world, redeemed. (my emphasis)[12]

As I have already noted, both Gershom Scholem and Rivkah Schatz-Uffenheimer subjected Buber's "dialogical interpretation" of Hasidism to severe criticism. Each of them rejected Buber's dialogical treatment as not true to the historical facts. Their major criticism was that Buber misrepresents the doctrine of the "raising of the sparks," when he sees it metaphorically as hallowing of the world and as an encounter with God in and through the world. In truth it is, for the Hasidim, still a metaphysical doctrine realized in proper mystical awareness of the metaphysical spark within everything that is. In Hasidism, the world is not "hallowed," but passed through, not engaged in as is, but neutralized, as in the kabbalah of Isaac Luria. The

Hasid, they asserted, goes "through" the world of appearances to the inner "sparks" of holiness imprisoned in the world, and frees the sparks to ascend back to their source. The world itself falls to the side, unattended.

Furthermore, they charged, Buber completely ignored the doctrine of the shedding of corporeality in Hasidism according to which there is a higher meeting with the Divine beyond the physical world. While it is true that to Hasidism service of God can be found in the commonplace and mundane, in *'avodah be-gashmiut* ("service within the corporeal"), they argued against Buber that in such service the physical world is nothing more than a screen that hides God and is to be overcome for the sake of a higher meeting with God, in the world of "thought."[13] Buber claims that for the Hasidim, God was to be met with *only* in our world. This, they argued, was simply not true.[14]

In his replies to Scholem and Schatz-Uffenheimer, respectively, Buber conceded what was in fact a major concession. After decades of writing about "Hasidism" per se, Buber now contended that his treatment of Hasidism was not meant to be historically encompassing. He had not intended to write a history of the movement as a whole, he says. Rather, he meant to interpret a *part* of the movement, at the inception of Hasidism, which to him was its most important manifestation. In his reply, Buber restricts his claims about Hasidim mainly to the founder, the Baal Shem Tov (the Besht), and to what he calls the "Polonnoyer tradition." Buber claims that "spiritualization," or otherworldliness, was first introduced into Hasidism only by R. Dov Ber, the Maggid of Mezhirech (Miedzyrzecz), the famed disciple of the Baal Shem, and the central figure of the second generation of Hasidism. Spiritualization, Buber insists, was not present in the thought of the Besht or in the "Polonnoyer tradition."

In his replies, therefore, Buber no longer claims to have been interpreting "Hasidism" as such, but only a small part of the Hasidic phenomenon—what he calls the "event," the life of the Baal Shem Tov, the founder of the movement, as well as some of his immediate disciples. Buber claims that these were the living spirit of the Hasidic movement before it was intellectualized and spiritualized by the Maggid of Mezhirech and many of the Maggid's followers. In saying this, Buber is once again depending on his notion of "I and Thou." "In the beginning is the relation," wrote Buber in *I and Thou*.[15] Only after came the word. The Baal Shem Tov manifested relation, in an elemental, pre-intellectual "event." With the Maggid, so says Buber, came the transformation of the event into thought—the "word."

Buber conceded implicitly that the doctrine of the sparks was indeed a metaphysical teaching in the writings of the Maggid and that there was in these teachings an element of turning away from the physical world toward higher levels of existence "above time," in the Maggid's words. Buber now claimed the historical correctness of his interpretation insofar as it was meant to apply *only* to the Besht and to some other of his disciples other than the Maggid.

I quote extensively from Buber's reply to Scholem about the Besht and the "Polonnoyer tradition":

> The way of spiritualization comes into Hasidism with its great thinker, the Maggid of Mezritch; the second way, the hallowing of life, was introduced by his teacher, the Baal-Shem-Tov . . . the teaching of hallowing the everyday provides the original thesis, and . . . the doctrine of spiritualization comes later . . . again and again, in sayings, parables, and tales, the Baal-Shem and *many of his disciples* praise the simple, ignorant man whose life-forces are combined in an original unity and who serves God with this unity . . . man, according to other sayings of the Baal-Shem, shall "have mercy on his tools and all his possessions," and each action shall be directed "to heaven." We know from the first-person sayings of the Baal-Shem that he excluded nothing corporeal from this intention. Thus in the Polnaer tradition, *which is undoubtedly true to the teaching of the master*, the relation between body and soul is compared to the relation of a husband to a wife: each is only half a being and needs the other half *to attain the fulfillment of life. . . . Nor can one find any "nullification" of the concrete whatsoever in this line of Hasidism*—which begins with the beginning of Hasidism itself. The beings and things that we hallow *continue to exist undiminished; the "holy sparks" that are "raised" are not thereby withdrawn* from the forms of man's earthly life . . . it is clear that *no form of annihilation is involved* but rather a dedication, a hallowing that transforms without loss of concreteness. (all emphases mine)[16]

Following the exchange between Scholem and Buber, there were attempts to defend Buber against their objections. I can relate only some of them here and then in only a most general way.[17] Steven Kepnes argued that Buber had an I-Thou relationship with the Hasidic texts, and so his interpretation differed from those of historians, like Scholem, who do not approach texts in that way.[18] "The development of the philosophy of I-Thou," Kepnes informs us, "led to a hermeneutical approach to Hasidic texts which . . . attended to the meaning which resulted from a 'dialogue' between Buber and the texts."[19] Scholem was interested in the historical phenomenon of Hasidism. Buber was interested in "questions of meaning and modern relevance," Kepnes tell us. Laurence Silberstein, in a somewhat similar way, attempted to argue that the parties to the debate were involved in two quite different kinds of valid, legitimate enterprises.[20] Buber was not concerned with historical scholarship, he says, but with an entirely different enterprise, that of "edification." It makes no sense, says Silberstein, to speak of the "true meaning" or "real meaning" of a text. What "meaning" a text has depends on your interests and purposes. "To recover the sources of authentic life," Silberstein says, "we must abandon objectivist scholarship in favor of imaginative, artistic creativity."[21] Hence, since Buber's purposes were not that of the historian, we cannot fault the way he interpreted the Hasidic texts. Silberstein charged that the approach of Buber's critics to Hasidism was no less an interpretation than was Buber's approach. The question of the "validity" of Buber's interpretation, therefore, should not arise.

Jon Levenson has shown conclusively that these defenses fail.[22] They deny that in writing about the Hasidim, Buber meant to be faithfully recording any historical phenomenon. However, as Levenson clearly shows, this is not what Buber says in his own defense. True, Buber does state that he did not mean to be presenting a historical account of Hasidism. He says this, however, *only with respect to the fact* that he was not trying to encompass Hasidism as a movement. With regard to that part of Hasidism that did come under his purview, the Besht and the "Polonnoyer tradition," Buber insists he had a historical basis for what he wrote. Levenson notes "the amount of effort Buber devoted to vindicating his historical analyses" in his reply to Scholem.[23] Therefore, we cannot understand Buber as Silberstein and Kepnes attempt to present him. Buber was making a historical claim about the Baal Shem Tov and the "Polonnoyer tradition."

By the "Polonnoyer tradition," Buber means the writings of R. Ya'akov Yoseph, who authored the first published Hasidic work, *Toledot Ya'akov Yoseph*, in 1780, as well as other major Hasidic works.[24] Unfortunately, R. Ya'akov Yoseph's writings fail to support Buber. R. Ya'akov Yoseph has no new understanding of the doctrine of the *nitzotzot*. His understanding of the world is no different from the earlier kabbalistic doctrine.

There is a cluster of ideas showing that R. Ya'akov Yoseph thought we had to *remove* the sparks from the world. When all of the sparks in an object "are raised," he writes, they empty out the object, leaving it in a state of real, or metaphysical, "death."[25] And he writes that the physical cover, or "shells," over the sparks "die" when the sparks are raised.[26] R. Ya'akov Yoseph bases the biblical commandment not to return to Egypt, as did the Ari, on the fact that all of the holy sparks were already extracted from Egypt when the Jewish people were slaves unto Pharaoh. There simply are no more sparks to be removed from Egypt.[27] In addition, he writes that a zaddik may bring about the death of his enemy by *removing* the sparks from him.[28] In addition, the Jewish people could overcome the seven nations dwelling in the Land of Israel by removing the sparks from them and thereby leaving them dead.[29] Buber's hallowing of the world, on the other hand, is never exhausted, and one cannot kill one's enemies by hallowing them à la Buber. When Buber's sparks are raised, they do not leave the world dead. They ennoble the world with life.

I conclude that there is little backing for Buber's reply to Scholem, that in the Polonnoyer tradition: "The beings and things that we hallow *continue to exist undiminished; the "holy sparks" that are "raised" are not thereby withdrawn* (my emphasis) from the forms of man's earthly life. . . . it is clear that *no form of annihilation is involved* but rather a dedication, a hallowing that transforms without loss of concreteness."

There are a number of passages where R. Ya'akov Yoseph clearly endorses a negative assessment of the world as the place where the sparks are captured. He writes that the sparks fell into the world because of Adam's sin, and continue to fall into the world because of sins.[30] The sparks are in *exile* in the world, for R. Ya'akov Yoseph. The world is their "fecal clothing."[31] The physical covering of the sparks is *hametz*, the forbidden "fermented bread" of the Passover holiday, the holiday of redemption.[32]

A cluster of ideas shows that R. Ya'akov Yoseph places limits on the scope of the raising of the sparks. For example, he says that a person has to redeem exactly one spark each day. It also appears that one raises sparks only from, or at least mainly from, one's personal possessions. So, for example, R. Ya'akov Yoseph says that a person is poor in this world because he has few sparks to raise at this point of the reincarnation of his soul. Thus, he is given few possessions. The rich person, on the other hand, has a high quota of sparks to raise.[33] Also, there is no raising of sparks on the Sabbath, the holiest day of the week.[34]

On Buber's ascription of a metaphorical meaning of the doctrine of the sparks, one is simply "in love with the world." There can be no in-principle restrictions on the scope of the activity of raising the sparks. It cannot be limited to one's own possessions. Certainly, the "hallowing" of the world should not be suspended on the holiest day of the week! Furthermore, the reason for the limitation of raising of sparks from one's personal possessions is itself anti-Buberian. The reason is that only one's possessions have sparks from the "root of one's soul" and that one attaches the sparks to one's soul when releasing them. Thus, the raising of the sparks has nothing to do with the relationship between the person and the object enclosing the sparks, but with an interest in removing the sparks for the sake of completing one's own soul. Raising of the sparks, then, focuses on the individual and his personal fate, not on the hallowing of the object.

R. Ya'akov Yoseph, in an endorsement of the Talmud, says that an *am ha'aretz* ("unlettered person") should not eat meat. The reason he gives is that such a person does not know how to release the sparks from the meat. It is significant that it is the lack of learning that disqualifies, not a lack of Buberian "seriousness." This suggests that one raises the sparks, not by one's eating with one's entire being, as Buber would have it, but by eating with a proper implementation of kabbalistic intentions. If there were any "hallowing" of meat involved here, it would be nothing more than perhaps zealously guarding meat from finding its way to the mouths of the untutored.

Particularly damaging to Buber are passages in which R. Ya'akov Yoseph states that if one only *merits* it, he will be granted the ability to raise sparks from a distance. He will not have to be present to an object to raise its sparks to Heaven. Biblical Noah was granted such grace.[35] Buber's I-Thou encounter cannot take place from a distance. I-Thou relations require proximity between the I and the Thou, for what Buber calls the mutual making of oneself "present" to the other. It is in the face-to-face encounter that an ontological nexus of I and Thou is possible for Buber.

According to R. Ya'akov Yoseph, the Patriarch Jacob was blessed with "dwelling in the tent," from where he could redeem the sparks of the world solely with the study of Torah. He did not have to move from his tent. This was a blessing reserved for the "greatest" of the Patriarchs. R. Ya'akov Yoseph also says that God folded all of the Land of Israel under the tent so that Jacob would not have to go out to remove the sparks. A staunch Buberian defender might want to see this as a super-Buberian attitude to the world: Jacob was in such intimate relation with the world that the entire world was as though present right before him. However, this will not do, for three reasons: 1) the "world" here is only the Land of Israel; the rest of the world is omitted; 2) the land is placed *under* Jacob's tent, not in his face-to-face presence, as we would expect in an I-Thou encounter; and 3) he redeems the sparks by studying Torah, not by relating to the land.

Altogether, I conclude there is little to Buber's assertion that in the "Polonnoyer tradition" we can find the historical basis of Buber's interpretation of Hasidism.

I turn now to the Baal Shem Tov. There are serious historical problems in determining just what the Besht did and taught. The problems include distinguishing between what the Besht really said and what others attribute to him that may not be his actual teachings. The adjudication of these problems is beyond my professional competence.[36] However, insofar as there are problems here, Buber himself is prevented from claiming a clear distinction between, for example, the Besht and the Maggid. I propose to proceed on the basis of what has been attributed to the Besht, which is what Buber himself had to go on.

Before turning to the Besht himself, however, I want to make a comment about the other disciples of the Besht.

Buber saw correctly that the greatest disciple of the Besht, the Maggid, was not a Buberian. However, neither were any of the Besht's other major disciples. I have already discussed R. Ya'akov Yoseph of Polonnoye. He was not a Buberian. Neither was Yehiel Michel of Zlotchov, who became a follower of the Maggid after the death of the Besht. Yehiel Michel taught the old doctrine of the sparks. He was also reported to have taught that when walking outdoors one should make sure not to look up outside of one's immediate bodily location.[37]

Another follower of the Besht, Nahman of Kosov, left no writings but reportedly endorsed the distinction between people of material and people of form, and is quoted by R. Ya'akov Yoseph in connection with these ideas. Pinhas of Koretz is often counted as a disciple, but apparently was not. He met the Besht only a few times. He left no writings. In any event, he was said to have lavished praise on the author of the *Toledot Ya'akov Yoseph*. Moshe Shoham of Delino was a disciple of the Besht and a great fan of R. Ya'akov Yoseph. In his work *Divrei Mosheh* he takes a clearly non-Buberian position on the sparks. For example, he says that: 1) the people of *Amaleq* are destroyed by taking the holy sparks out of them;[38] 2) Adam was forbidden to eat meat because he had already removed the sparks from the animals when he gave them their names;[39] 3) there are appointed times and places for removing sparks;[40] and 4) an *'am ha-'aretz* may not eat meat, because he does not know how to remove the sparks from it.[41] None of these can be made consistent with Buber.

Given this list of Beshtian disciples, all of whom were decidedly non-Buberian in their teachings or who supported the non-Buberian teachings of R. Ya'akov Yoseph, it would be highly surprising were the Besht to have been as Buber portrays him. We would have to believe then that, although the Besht was a true exemplar of a Buberian relationship to the world, all of his well-known students were anti-Buberians.

When we look at the sayings his disciples attributed to the Besht, we find that the anti-Buberian themes of the disciples are ascribed to the Besht himself. For example, R. Ya'akov Yoseph's teaching on the merit of being able to free the sparks from a distance is attributed to the Besht. He also attributes to the Besht the teaching that one who thinks he is close to God, thinking of God as *'atah*, "Thou," is in reality far from God. The person who believes he is far, and does not say "Thou" to God, is really quite close to God![42] This furnishes us with a religious phenomenology at odds with Buber's conception of encountering God as the "Eternal Thou," through an encounter with the world. I would not go so far as to claim that the Besht means that one *never* encounters God as "Thou." However, the Besht is far more attuned to the difficulties and dangers of self-deception in meeting the Eternal Thou than is Buber. One must always be on guard for false pride in thinking one had met up with God.

In the *Toledot Ya'akov Yoseph,* it says that the author heard from "my teacher," the Besht, that the soul was given physical tasks to do, such as eating and drinking, to ensure its separate existence from God.

If not for the material tasks, the soul might return to God from the ecstasy of spiritual attainments. The soul was conjoined to a body to ensure its separate identity from God; otherwise, in moments of great ecstasy it would become extinct.[43] This is quite far from an attitude of hallowing the world.

In the collection *Keter Shem Tov*, the Baal Shem Tov is quoted as saying that when a person eats and drinks and engages in commerce, the soul desires to return to a "higher" cleaving to God.[44] In addition, the idea is presented there, in his name, that a person has a body only in order not to be extinguished in his higher mystical states.[45] And he is quoted as saying that one should pray for one's enemies, thereby removing the good that is in them, so that what remains perishes.[46] These are all quite distant from Buber's presentation of the Besht.

Buber at times seems to have misunderstood some of the Besht's alleged sayings, in ways that accord with Buber's conception of Hasidism. Here are two examples:

In *Hasidism and Modern Man*, Buber included a chapter entitled "The Baal Shem Tov's Instruction," which he says consists of the "words" of the Besht. (At best, the work consists of the words of followers, *attributing* something to the Besht.) In that chapter, we find this entry:

> When you talk with people, do not examine whether their thoughts constantly cleave to God. The examining soul suffers injury.[47]

Buber wishes to convey to the reader the Besht's openness to everyone and, ultimately, to everything in the world. The original of this passage appears in the anonymous *Tzava'at Ha-Rivash,* and elsewhere, and reads quite differently from Buber's rendition of it. In *Tzava'at Ha-Rivash* we read this:

> One should not look at the faces of people when talking with them, if their thoughts are not always connected with God, for one will suffer injury by looking. However, one should look at fitting people, whose thoughts are always connected to God, and thereby gain holiness for one's soul.[48]

Buber's rendition of this passage is thus in opposition to its original meaning.

In the same chapter of *Hasidism and Modern Man*, we find the following entry attributed to the Besht:

> Man eats them, man drinks them, man uses them; these are the sparks
> that dwell in the things. Therefore one should have mercy on his tools
> and all his possessions for the sake of the sparks that are in them; one
> should have mercy on the holy sparks.[49]

The reader gets the impression that here the Besht is teaching an engagement with the world expressed through the metaphorical language of the doctrine of the sparks. We are to have "mercy" on things
that come to hand, because of the sparks within them. Again, Buber
no doubt wishes the reader to appreciate the Besht's openness to everything and everyone in the world. The original passage appears in
Tzava'at Ha-Rivash, in *Liqqutei Yeqarim,* and in *Hanhagot Yesharot*
(ascribed to R. Ya'akov Yoseph) and reads quite differently. In *Tzava'at
Ha-Rivash* the first sentence reads as follows:

> One eats people, sits with people, and uses people, that is the sparks in
> those things. Therefore a person should have mercy on his tools and all
> his possessions.

This formulation, I suggest, is corrupted. (I conclude this from the
lack of parallel construction between "one eats people," on the one
hand, and "sits with people, and uses people," on the other.)[50] The
uncorrupted version seems to be in the work *Liqqutei Yeqarim,* and
goes like this:

> And Israel Baal Shem Tov said: one eats people, one sits on people, and
> one uses people, that is the sparks in those things.[51]

The meaning is clear: the passage is referring to people who are *in* the
food one eats, who are *in* the chair upon which one sits, and *in* the
objects one uses. This refers not to the doctrine of the sparks per se,
but to the teaching of *nitzotzot ha-neshamot,* that human soul-sparks
are scattered about in material objects, and it is up to us to redeem
them from their captivity. Our mercy, then, should go out to the sparks
of the human *souls,* not to the objects themselves that hold them.

Now, of course there are places where the Besht clearly speaks of
sparks per se, and not of soul-sparks. I submit, though, that the passage before us represents the attitude of the Besht to the entire topic,
namely, that the focus is not on the world but on concern for the
sparks waiting to be released from the world.

I humbly submit, therefore, that Buber's interpretation of early Hasidism as "in love with the world" is ill founded.

What we have learned is that early Hasidism retained the kabbalistic conception of the raising of the sparks, which implies an instrumental attitude toward the world as the place where the sparks are found, and therefore the place we have to turn to if we are going to raise the sparks up to their divine origin. The early Hasidism did not teach an immediate I-Thou engagement with the world, as Buber contended. Therefore, when seeing a tree, wetlands, or a chestnut horse running freely through the grass, in accordance with their teaching, the early Hasidism would not have thought of them as needing to be preserved. As the outer shells of inner divine sparks, these natural objects would have struck them as needing to be emptied out of their holiness, and then left aside for the next task of redeeming the sparks.

Even though historical early Hasidism cannot be recruited directly to provide an ecological ethic, could it be the basis for some creative thinking toward a Jewish-based ecological ethic? I conclude with a suggestion in just that direction.

We saw that early Hasidism sometimes, at least, restricted the raising of the sparks to the sparks captured inside one's personal possessions. One way to relate the sparks doctrine, then, to the natural world would be to widen the concept of "possession." We could widen it beyond personal possessions to the possessions of "humankind" as a collective, and then relate to the world and nature as humankind's "possession." It would then be incumbent on humankind to raise the sparks of nature, just as it is to raise the sparks of one's legal possessions.

I realize that this contravenes the usual ecological ethic which forcefully rejects the idea of the world as humankind's possession, because this attitude, it is claimed, has brought about humankind's indiscriminate destruction of nature for its own selfish desires. However, in this critique the conception of what it means to "possess" something is diametrically opposed to the Hasidic teaching on the subject. As we saw above, according to early Hasidism, objects come into one's possession in the first place because their sparks belong to the "root" of one's soul. The sparks of one's soul and the sparks in objects are thus mutually attracted to one another, resulting in the objects becoming one's possessions. Seeing nature as our "possession," then, would be predicated on seeing nature as one with the roots of our very souls.

We could give a traditional explanation of how it is that nature's sparks match the "roots" of our souls in terms of the biblical story of Adam being formed from the dust of the earth. A midrash relates that when God said, "Let us make Adam," God was addressing the created order of nature, which was called upon to cooperate in the creation of Adam. Thus does the natural order hold the roots of our souls.

In a more contemporary idiom, we might refer to our evolutionary history instead. In the kabbalistic tradition, which Hasidism shares, reality is a chain of being, with each successive level receiving from the core the power and vitality of the preceding level. There is also a teaching, prominent in the works of R. Schneur Zalman, founder of the Hasidic sect of Habad, that the apparent ladder of reality—human, animal, vegetative, and inanimate—is not the true scaffolding of reality.[52] In truth, the inanimate stands at the apex of spiritual power and activity, followed in turn by the vegetative, animal, and, last, human.

R. Schneur Zalman explains the disparity between the manifest spiritual power and the real, objective spiritual power through the need for restraining the more potent spiritual reality lest it be too powerful for the world to endure. Thus, while the inanimate enjoys the highest level of spiritual reality, its spiritual potency must be severely muted to allow its appearance in this world. Thus the inanimate appears to be the lowest on the scale, though it is the highest in reality. Conversely, the human, possessed of a lesser spiritual charge, may be given a fuller expression in this world, without "exploding" beyond what the world can endure. Thus, while the human seems to be at the pinnacle of the ladder, in reality it is at the bottom.

On this upside-down look at reality, the evolutionary development of humankind indeed becomes a "descent" of the human being from higher spiritual sources—the inanimate, vegetative, and animal. Thus, evolution becomes a process of the roots of our souls becoming manifest in us in a way they could not possibly manifest in the higher world of nature, of mountains, orchids, and fawns.

However, the doctrine of nature holding the deepest sources of the roots of our souls will not yet yield an ecological ethic from early Hasidic thought. As long as the raising of the sparks means emptying nature of its divinity and leaving it aside, we will have gained nothing. To complete our picture, we would have to adopt only half of the

Hasidic picture of the raising of the sparks, that half in which the raising of the sparks is not for our own sake, but for the sake of returning the sparks to their divine source. We would have to forsake the other half of the Hasidic notion, however, that when so doing we leave nature "empty" or "dead." Perhaps the best way to do so would be, alas, to take the doctrine of the sparks metaphorically, as Buber wished. To return the sparks to their divine source would mean to celebrate the mutual attraction between the sparks of our own souls and the sparks of our soul-roots in all of nature.

Notes

1. Recent scholarship has questioned whether the Baal Shem Tov was the *founder* of Hasidism, as opposed to its inspiration. See Moshe Rosman, *Founder of Hasidism: A Quest for the Historical Ba'al Shem Tov* (Berkeley: University of California Press, 1996).

2. Martin Buber, *The Origin and Meaning of Hasidism*, ed. and trans. Maurice Friedman, with introduction by David B. Burrell, C.S.C. (Atlantic Highlands, N.J.: Humanities Press, 1988), 174.

3. See Gershom Scholem, "Martin Buber's Interpretation of Hasidism," *Commentary* 32 (1961): 305–16; and Gershom Scholem, *The Messianic Idea in Judaism* (New York: Schocken, 1971), 227–50; Rivkah Schatz-Uffenheimer, "Man's Relation to God and World in Buber's Rendering of the Hasidic Teaching," in *The Philosophy of Martin Buber*, ed. Paul Schilpp and Maurice Friedman (La Salle: Open Court, 1967), 403–34; and Rivkah Schatz-Uffenheimer, *Hasidism as Mysticism: Quietistic Elements in Eighteenth-Century Hasidic Thought* (Princeton: Princeton University, 1993), introduction.

4. Martin Buber, "Dialogue," in *Between Man and Man*, trans. Ronald Gregor Smith (New York: Macmillan, 1965), 11.

5. Martin Buber, *I and Thou*, trans. Walter Kaufmann (New York: Scribner's, 1970), 57–59.

6. *The Philosophy of Martin Buber*, ed. Paul Arthur Schilpp and Maurice Friedman (La Salle, Ill.: Open Court, 1967), 708.

7. In a later essay, *Between Man and Man*, Buber refined his position and wrote that our relationship with nature differs somewhat from our overall relationship between people. That is because, contrary to Sartre, Buber held that a person could never be reduced to an It in the eyes of another. One always retained a residue of one's Thouness toward another person. Thus, there could never be a purely I-It relationship between persons. There could be between a person and nature, though. However, this was not Buber's view while he was writing his works on Hasidism.

8. Buber, *The Origin and Meaning of Hasidism*, 174.

9. Ibid., 84.

10. Ibid., 181.

11. Ibid., 171.

12. Ibid., 85.

13. For more on their anti-Buberian interpretation of *'avodah be-gashmiut*, see especially Schatz-Uffenheimer, *Hasidism as Mysticism*, introduction.

14. Schatz-Uffenheimer quotes from a saying in the name of R. Dov Ber of Mezritch: ". . . one who travels to the fair . . . cannot travel without a horse, but should he therefore love the horse? Is there a greater foolishness than that?" ("Man's Relation to God," 425). I invite the reader to compare R. Dov Ber's attitude to a horse with Buber's.

15. Buber, *I and Thou*, 69.

16. In Maurice Friedman, "Interpreting Hasidism: The Buber-Scholem Controversy," *Yearbook of the Leo Baeck Institute* 33 (1988): 223.

17. I omit entirely the defense of Buber made by Friedman in "Interpreting Hasidism: The Buber-Scholem Controversy," 449–67. The reader should also see the

discussion of Moshe Idel, "Martin and Gershom Scholem on Hasidism: A Critical Appraisal," in *Hasidism Reappraised*, ed. Ada Rapoport-Albert, The Littman Library of Jewish Civilization (London and Portland, Ore.: Vallentine Mitchell, 1996), 389–403.

18. Steven D. Kepnes, "A Hermeneutic Approach to the Buber-Scholem Controversy," *Journal of Jewish Studies* (1987): 81–98.

19. Ibid., 87.

20. Laurence J. Silberstein, "Modes of Discourse in Modern Judaism: The Buber-Scholem Debate Reconsidered," *Soundings* 71 (1988): 657–81.

21. Ibid., 662.

22. Jon D. Levenson, "The Hermeneutical Defense of Buber's Hasidism: A Critique and Counterstatement, *Modern Judaism* 11 (1991): 299–320.

23. Ibid., 307.

24. These are: *Ben Porat Yoseph* (1781), *Tzafenat Pa'aneah* (1782), and *Ketonet Passim* (1866).

25. *Ketonet Passim*, critical edition with introduction and notes by Gedalyah Nigal (Jerusalem: Peri Ha-Aretz, 1985), 261; See also, *Toledot Ya'akov Yoseph*, 2.570.

26. *Toledot Ya'akov Yoseph*, 2.320, 570.

27. Ibid., 1.62, 150; 2.549. See also *Tzafnat Pa'aneah*, 39–40.

28. *Toledot Ya'akov Yoseph*, 1.324.

29. *Ketonet Passim*, 261.

30. *Toledot Ya'akov Yoseph*, 2.534.

31. *Tzafnat Pa'aneah*, 157.

32. *Toledot Ya'akov Yoseph*, 2.576.

33. Ibid., 1.150–51.

34. Ibid., 1.36.

35. *Ben Porat Yoseph* (Pietrekov, 1884), 39.

36. A recent study of the Baal Shem Tov that attempts to separate fact from legend is Rosman, *Founder of Hasidism*.

37. Attributed to Yehiel Michel in *Sefer Mayim Rabim* (Jerusalem), 37. See also another collection of sayings attributed to him, *Yeshu'ot Malko* (Jerusalem: Harim Levin Institute, 1974), 140, where he is said to have taught that one should not look at a Gentile, an angry person, a crazy person, an evil person, a fool, or a sad person. One should look only at a person who cleaves to God.

38. Moshe Shoham, *Divrei Mosheh* (Bnei-Brak: Nahalat Zvi Institute, 1988), 10.

39. Ibid., 4.

40. Ibid., 21.

41. Ibid., 4.

42. *Toledot Ya'akov Yoseph*, 1.50.

43. Ibid., 1.312.

44. *Keter Shem Tov* (Brooklyn, N.Y.: Kehot, 1987), 11, section 34.

45. Ibid., 31, section 121.

46. Ibid., 7, section 18. There are many more sayings in *Keter Shem Tov* that are inconsistent with Buber's portrayal of the Besht. See sections 44, 107, 116, 144, 178, 179, 199, 200, 267, 277, and more. Tradition attributes *Keter Shem Tov* as a whole to the Baal Shem Tov. However, the work is really a collection of early Hasidic sayings

of various authorship, including those of the Maggid. In the text I have referred only to (but not to all) sections cited in the text in the name of the Besht that are anti-Buberian. *Tzava'at Ha-Rivash* also contains many non-Buberian citations explicitly in the name of the Baal Shem Tov.

47. Martin Buber, *Hasidism and Modern Man* (New York: Harper and Row, 1984), 209.

48. *Tzava'at Ha-Rivash* (Brooklyn, N.Y.: Kehot, 1991), 9.

49. Buber, *Hasidism and Modern Man*, 188.

50. Ze'ev Gries, an expert on Hasidic printings and variants in Hasidic texts, has graciously devoted his precious time to try to uncover the most reliable version of this text on historical grounds. Alas, he concluded it was not possible to determine this based on the historical data.

51. *Liqqutim Yeqarim* (Jerusalem, 1974), 56b. The name of the work is variously referred to as *Liqqutei Yeqarim* (meaning, "Collections of Dear Ones") and *Liqqutim Yeqarim* (meaning, "Dear Collections").

52. For an exposition of this view, see my "Zion and Jerusalem: The Jewish State in the Thought of Rabbi Abraham Isaac Kook," in *Rabbi Abraham Isaac Kook and Jewish Spirituality*, ed. David Shatz and Lawrence J. Kaplan (New York: New York University Press, 1995), 276–89.

Response. The Textualization of Nature in Jewish Mysticism

HAVA TIROSH-SAMUELSON

The attitude of the Jewish mystical tradition toward nature is marked by ambivalence. The root of the ambivalence, I believe, can be traced to the tension between the two foundational beliefs of Judaism: the doctrine of creation and the doctrine of revelation. Whereas the former leads to a certain openness toward the natural world as manifested through expressions of awe, wonder, praise, gratitude, or curiosity about nature, the belief in revelation entailed a Torah-centered piety in which there is a certain alienation from the natural world. The tension between the two core beliefs of Judaism is best exemplified in the Jewish mystical tradition.

The papers by Elliot R. Wolfson, Jerome (Yehudah) Gellman, and Shaul Magid establish that the Jewish mystical tradition had a negative attitude toward the natural world. According to Wolfson, kabbalah was spiritual piety cultivated by a mystical fraternity of kabbalists who demanded "an abrogation of the sensual pleasures of the body." In other words, to worship God, the body must be overcome. Wolfson brilliantly exposes the linguistic foundation of the kabbalists' conception of creation according to which "what is ultimately real is the name of four letters, YHWH, which comprises the twenty-two letters of the holy language, Hebrew." Given the "textualization of reality," argues Wolfson, the kabbalists did not venerate nature and body but rather treated it symbolically, resulting in the "nullification of the physical body."

Corporeal nature did not fare any better in Hasidism. According to

Gellman's reading of early Hasidic sources, the doctrine of uplifting divine sparks—if properly understood, contrary to Buber's reading—entails a "negative assessment of the world as the place where the sparks are captured." If the natural world is exile par excellence, redemption entails not the celebratory embrace of the natural world, but rather its subjugation and transcendence. And, in Magid's reading of R. Nahman of Bratslav's last tale, "The Seven Beggars," "nature" is a negative construct that denotes static, necessary, unchanging laws known to us through "false wisdom," namely, the empirical sciences. For R. Nahman, the physical world is diametrically opposed to the realm of genuine creativity within which the devotee can communicate with the transcendent source of reality, the origin of life which is "above nature," through the ritual act of prayer.

My response attempts to clarify some of the inherent difficulties in the attitude of kabbalah and Hasidism toward the natural world and to take issue with certain interpretations proposed by the three presenters.

I

Wolfson correctly notes that the key to the kabbalistic attitude toward the natural world lies in the link between theosophy and psychological anthropology, between what is known, how it is known, and by whom it is known. Wolfson also appropriately spells out the ethnocentric nature of kabbalistic worldview: the soul of Israel is the ideal human soul, a particle of the divine essence that functions as a dual mirror, reflecting the essence of God, on the one hand, and nature, on the other hand. This two-fold reflection, Wolfson insightfully suggests, allows for what Wolfson calls "the symbolic approach to both of these realms," which, in turn, "affects the semiotic transmutation of the corporeal." In continuity with his published works, Wolfson uncovers the androcentric posture of kabbalah, showing that the mirroring capacity of the human soul pertains only to men and not to women and that kabbalistic theosophy is gender specific: the female is but an extension of the male. Therefore, Wolfson argues that the kabbalists did not "adore nature as a goddess," but rather treated nature as "that which must be conquered and subdued."

I wish to focus on Wolfson's exposition of kabbalistic ontology and its ramification for kabbalistic attitude toward nature. Medieval kabbalists, I maintain, conflated two ontological schemas that are in tension with each other. Wolfson actually alludes to both schemas in the opening of his paper where he makes two important observations. He says 1) that the kabbalists viewed "all things of the corporeal world as a *reflection* of the inner process within the divine reality"; and 2) that, according to the kabbalists, "there is only one ultimate reality, the divine light, which manifests itself in the garb of the twenty-two letters of the Hebrew alphabet that derive, in turn, from the four letter name, YHWH, the root-word of all language, the mystical secret of the Torah." I suggest that these two sentences presuppose distinct ontologies, each with a corresponding epistemology, and that they yield different attitudes toward the natural world. While Wolfson is fully aware of the tension between the two schemas, I don't think that the kabbalists themselves were.

Wolfson's first sentence presupposes an ontology that views the physical world as both different from God as well as similar to God in some sense. To say that nature is a *mirror* of God entails that God and nature are *not* the same; each retains a distinct identity, much as the object reflected in the mirror is ontologically distinct from its mirrored image. But neither are God and the physical world totally dissimilar. Indeed, the mirror motif states that nature *resembles* God in some way, much as the reflected image in the mirror is similar, but not identical, to the object reflected in the mirror. The same can be said when the mirror motif is applied to the human soul: the ideal human soul mirrors both God and nature and as such it is similar but not identical with both God and nature.

The mirror imagery operates within a spatial model of transcendence that is consonant with the emanationist ontology that the kabbalists adopted from medieval Neoplatonic Jewish philosophy.[1] From these sources, kabbalah also inherited the motif of the human as a microcosm as well as the analysis of human knowledge as analogous to sight. Within the ontology of mirroring and its corresponding epistemology, kabbalistic symbolism is *iconic*: the symbols constitute what Wolfson calls, following Henri Corbin, "the imaginal world," in which the divine is both present and absent at the same time. Kabbalistic theosophy thus displays the imaginal world through a dizzying array of images, in which the soul of the mystic passively reflects the fullness of the *Shekhinah*, who itself acts as a mirror that reflects the *sefirot* above her.

Within emanationist ontology, noncorporeal entities were arranged spatially and hierarchically, as each rank was given a value. In the Great Chain of Being, the corporeal world known to us through the senses is but the lowest rank, and corporeality is considered an obstacle to mirroring the divine. For the soul to function successfully as a mirror, the body had to be controlled and subdued so as to be transcended. This was the primary purpose of kabbalistic ritual, which could easily be given an ascetic interpretation, as was done in the kabbalistic practices of sixteenth-century Safed. Kabbalistic ritual and its corresponding ethical directives constituted the praxis of polishing the mirror of the soul so that divine reality could shine in it.[2]

This model, however, is not the only one operative in kabbalistic texts. Alongside it the kabbalists employed a different model which, following Wolfson, I will call the *semiotic* model. This model is consonant with a *creationist* ontology and it views the physical world to be the corporeal manifestation of an underlying noncorporeal, linguistic structure whose elemental units are the letters of the divine language, Hebrew. In this schema, knowledge is not analogous to sight, as the kabbalists said in accord with Western philosophy, but to the productive activity of combining and manipulating discrete units. These are the letters of the divine language, the building blocks of the created universe as well as of the primordial Torah, the ideal paradigm of the universe.[3]

I suggest that kabbalistic symbolism, the key to our understanding of kabbalistic attitudes toward the natural world, operates differently in these two schemas. In the *mirroring-emanationist* scheme, the symbol functions iconically, namely, it serves as the prism that either refracts or reflects divine reality. The poetic language of the kabbalists did not distinguish between these two, and hence kabbalistic iconism, which Wolfson discusses especially in his magisterial work, *Through the Speculum That Shines: Vision and Imagination in Medieval Jewish Mysticism*,[4] is necessarily opaque and imprecise. As we shall soon see, they each yield a different attitude toward nature.

The story is further complicated by the fact that in the *semiotic-creationist* model, the symbol signifies, not because it reflects or refracts existing reality, but because the symbol gives us a privileged information on the way words signify the essences of things. In this model, the knowledge of the divine and the knowledge of nature are not predicated on the visualization of symbolic icons, but on a theoretical knowledge of the linguistic formulas that constitute what the thing is. In the semiotic model, nature is a text whose interpretation brings forth the esoteric meaning, making the posture of the kabbalist vis-à-vis the natural world hermeneutics par excellence.

Unlike his original sources, Wolfson is aware of the conflation of the two models and admits that whereas the emanationist model is pantheistic, the creationist model is theistic. Wolfson, however, believes that the tension can be resolved and that the visionary and the semiotic models can be conflated. Wolfson can do so because he turns to the language of phenomenology derived from Husserl and his disciple Heidegger. This is why Wolfson can say that the term 'body' "does not denote the physical mass that is quantifiable and measurable, but the phenomenological sense of the corporeal as lived presence." When kabbalistic doctrines are turned into phenomenology, in which what is studied is subjective experience rather than objective reality, language changes its lexical meaning. When 'body' becomes 'lived presence,' the lexical meaning of 'corporeality, 'matter,' or 'physical nature' no longer conforms to ordinary usage. In Wolfson's phenomenological interpretation of kabbalah, it is possible to bridge the reflected image with the linguistic entity.

Whether one accepts this phenomenological understanding of kabbalah or not, it is clear that the kabbalists are totally alienated from the natural world. Their lived experience takes place strictly in the world of imagination that is conjured through linguistic symbols. For the kabbalists there is no reality outside the sacred text; the "imaginal world" is Ultimate Reality. The mirroring of nature and the symbolic function of language become one and the same on the phenomenological level. This is what Wolfson means when he states that "the phenomena of nature are the garments by means of which the hidden light is disclosed, but it is disclosed only insofar as it is concealed." In kabbalah nature is textualized.

With this clarification in mind we can briefly comment on the gendered language of kabbalah, without entering the debate about Wolfson's theories. The kabbalists claimed to possess, or aspired to possess, the knowledge of the secret code for the created universe. The kabbalists sought to discover the mystery of life, a life that begins with God's first act of self-revelation and will end with the re-pairing of the masculine and feminine aspects of the deity in redemption. Since life means reproduction of species, and since humans are created in the image of God, it is not surprising that the kabbalists attempted to delve into the rhythm and processes of human sexuality. Kabbalistic interpretation of Torah are thus dominated by the dynamics of penetration and withdrawal, of attraction and recoiling, of expansion and contraction, the same dynamics that operates in the reproduction of all life, especially human life.

The kabbalists, as Wolfson stated in his many writings, adopted a one-sex biological theory prevalent in their day.[5] Life originates from and is initiated by the male, whereas the female is but the passive receptacle of the seeds of life. From this theory they abstracted a general principle: the giver is always masculine, the receiver is always feminine.[6] And since these are relational categories, the kabbalists analyzed all reality in terms of masculinity and femininity even when it did not pertain to the act of reproduction. But Wolfson is right to insist that the female is not recognized as a separate principle; she is but the extension of the male. Ideally, the female will be contained in the male.

As a gloss on Wolfson's analysis, I would suggest, however, that sex and gender operate somewhat differently in the two schemas that I delineated above. In the *semiotic-creationist* model, the feminine is an extension of the male whenever she acts as a life-giving force, as a power that nourishes and sustains life. But the female becomes a negative, threatening, and dangerous force whenever she is not open to receive the divine overflow (*shefa*) or whenever she acts alone without the overflow of life from the male. In the *emanationist* model the focus is not sex or the reproduction of life, but iconic envisioning of the divine. In this context, gender and not sex is important: whatever protrudes and/or penetrates is a phallic representation of masculinity; whatever functions passively or receptively constitutes the feminine. The connection between phallic representation and mirroring was proposed in psychoanalytic theories of Lacan, which French feminists, who inspired Wolfson's works, adopted in their critique of allegedly masculinist Western philosophy.[7]

With this in mind we can suggest a more nuanced understanding of the kabbalistic approach to nature. Each of the models can yield both positive and negative postures.

1.a) In the *mirroring-emanationist* model the corporeal functions differently whether the mirror reflects or *refracts*. If the mirror is understood as a reflecting medium, then the physical universe in general and the human body in particular are considered the cause for the distancing of the kabbalist from God. To achieve the desired clinging to God (*devequt*), one must practice the ritual life of kabbalah with its proper intention (*kavanah*) so as to bring about the polishing of the soul's mirror. From this perspective, kabbalah neither adores nature nor considers nature to be a vehicle for spiritual energy. The corporeal world is understood as an obstacle for the spiritual and must be spiritualized so as to become transparent. This understanding of the mirror motif expresses the ascetic tendencies of kabbalah, reflecting older tendencies in rabbinic Judaism.

1.b) However, if the mirror *refracts* rather than reflects, then the physical world is viewed positively. It is the medium that makes it possible for the Ein Sof to be accessible to the finite, precisely because it is mediated and indirect. The physical world in general and the human body in particular can be viewed as a necessary and a positive vehicle for communication with the divine. When the rays of the divine light are refracted in the prism, the rich beauty of the divine overflow produces awe and reverence in the observer, as well as humility and the desire to serve God.

In the *semiotic-creationist* model we find two other different postures toward the physical world.

2.a) According to the first, the kabbalist is primarily an interpreter of nature, but his focus lies not on the physical world accessible through the senses, but on the Torah, i.e., the coded blueprint of the created world. Like contemporary biologists who decipher the structure of DNA as the blueprint for all life processes, so does the kabbalist decipher the code of elemental bits of information, the Hebrew letters, and with it the grammar of nature's language.[8] This hermeneutical focus leads the kabbalists to ignore the sensual world, precisely because they are so focused on the semiotic of nature, namely, on the theory of nature's linguistic signatures. Put differently, in kabbalah the degree to which the myth of Torah replaces the experience of the natural world becomes most pronounced. It is most evident in Lurianic kabbalah, where the secrets of the divine life, which spell the processes of God's inner life, are made exoteric. Accordingly, the Lurianic kabbalist experiences not nature but the pulse of divine energy which vitalizes the physical world.

2.b) The *semiotic-creationist* model, however, can also yield an activist attitude toward nature. The interest in the nature of language could have led some kabbalists to gather information about natural phenomena and to try to impact the observable world by manipulation of linguistic formulas. This activism toward nature, in which kabbalah interfaces with magic, began with Yohanan Alemanno in the late fifteenth century and flourished in the sixteenth century, especially in Italy.[9] In this context, the kabbalist attempts to manipulate and control nature through the use of linguistic formulas either to ease human suffering, or to prognosticate future natural events, or even to create a homunculus. It is important to note, nonetheless, that in both versions (2.a) and (2.b) the kabbalist acts as a creative artist because he possesses the secret code of creation. In version (2.a) the creative ability is limited to the realm of language as manipulated by the imagination of the kabbalist; in version (2.b) the product of kabbalistic creativity is itself an event in the natural world.

In sum, to understand kabbalah's attitude toward nature we need to take into consideration the ambiguity of its poetic language that obscures divergent ontological schemas and epistemological assumptions. Wolfson's phenomenological interpretation of kabbalah indicates that for the kabbalists the created universe is ultimately a linguistic reality and that, by definition, God's linguistic creation can never be fathomed: language necessarily conceals and reveals at the same time. Human attempts to break through the veils of language are thus misguided and doomed to failure; all the human can do is a hermeneutics of a linguistically based nature.

II

Hasidism, as it is well known, inherited the conceptual framework of Lurianic kabbalah and gave it a new understanding, though modern scholars hotly debate what that meaning is.[10]

While Hasidism shared a certain mindset and a general approach to Jewish religious life, it did not speak in one voice on theoretical matters. It is, therefore, difficult to generalize about the Hasidic approach to the natural world given the theoretical difference between the founder of Hasidism, Israel Baal Shem Tov (the Besht) and his main disciple Dov Ber, the Maggid of Mezhirech, the Habad school of R. Schneur Zalman of Liadi, R. Nahman of Bratslav, and the masters of Polish Hasidism.[11] But within the limits of generalizations, we can say that the Hasidic approach to nature has to be understood in the context of the attempt to fathom the paradox of existence: how can that which is no-thing (*'ayin*) become some-thing (*yesh*).[12] This is, of course, not a new paradox but the core of the kabbalistic worldview. Classical kabbalah (of the Zohar, Moses Cordovero, or Isaac Luria), however, addressed the paradox more scholastically, since the kabbalists absorbed the philosophic discourse of medieval Jewish Neoplatonized Aristotelianism. In Hasidism the interface between that which is—i.e., external, sensory appearance—and that which is not—i.e., true, Ultimate Reality—was negotiated through the framework of human, subjective experience.

To attain *devequt* and thereby fulfill the task of redemption (as Lurianic kabbalah already taught), Hasidic masters delved into the depth of one's own mystical experience. With profound subtlety they explained how one must annihilate the self (*bittul ha-'ani*) in order to dissolve the veils of corporeal reality (*bittul ha-yesh*) and release the divine sparks (*nitzotzot*), divine energy that is concealed in corporeal reality. Unlike the Lurianic kabbalists who attempted to account for the existence of the divine sparks, the Hasidic teachers were interested in the dynamics of religious life that culminate in the redemption of imperfect reality, that is in messianic activity. Given the focus on the personal experience, it is no wonder that Hasidic masters preferred the fable, the analogy, and the sermon to convey their teaching. These literary modes, which Hasidic masters creatively constructed,[13] were more suitable to express the subtle nuances of personal, religious experiences than were the systematic, theoretical analysis of medieval kabbalah or the elaborate, "technical" fantasies of Lurianic kabbalah. But, regardless of the style of discourse, Hasidism taught that physical nature is not only experienced through the mediation of language, but also that to live a holy life within the parameters of halakhic Judaism, the Hasid must dissolve the veils of corporeality through concentrated intention, culminating in ecstasy. Briefly put, the alienation from nature, present in rabbinic Judaism, is further exacerbated in Hasidism even though the founder of Hasidism, the Besht, was reported to meditate in and commune with nature.

Shaul Magid's sensitive reading of R. Nahman's tale illustrates the tension between the emanationist and the creationist ontology of the kabbalistic heritage. Writing in the early nineteenth century, R. Nahman had to contend with the rise of modern, positivist science and its corresponding epistemology: the radical separation of observed object and observing subject. While still using the inherited schema of medieval philosophy, R. Nahman juxtaposes "nature" to "world." The first is inert, passive, and static, governed by unchanging natural laws which human reason claims to know. But that claim is false and misleading; human reason of the "philosophers" (namely, the Jewish *maskilim* of his generation) fails to grasp the real, living energy that pulsates in the world due to ever-renewing divine creation. The realm of "nature" is governed by necessity, whereas the "world" breathes of freedom and creativity. The realm of necessity belongs to the imperfection of nature, a realm occupied by the non-Jews, whereas the perfect world belongs to Israel. Nature is a category of exile; it stands against the world of redemption.

R. Nahman is no less ethnocentric than the medieval kabbalists and, like them, no less androcentric. The juxtaposition of "nature" (*teva*) and "creation" (*beri'ah*) is not R. Nahman's invention; it can be traced to writings of sixteenth-century philosophers, especially R. Judah Loew of Prague. According to this approach, Israel belongs to the realm of free will and authentic, creative energy, which is captured by the ritual act of prayer. The world of creation, or better still, the realm of creativity, is not dominated by the fixed natural laws that govern the physical world known to us through the senses. In fact, the two worlds are diametrically opposed, as Magid explains: what appears deformed in the level of nature is in fact perfection; and what appears as perfect is in fact deformed. R. Nahman betrays the medieval spatial categories of the emanationist scheme when he posits the world of prayer "above nature"; that too is to be traced to sixteenth-century texts.[14]

What I find problematic in the teachings of R. Nahman, as Magid presents them, is the role of wisdom. For sixteenth-century Jewish thinkers such as the Maharal, the realm of choice (*behirah*), which was ethically superior to nature, was the Torah, and the study of Torah yielded all the important secrets about how nature behaves. Thus, the Maharal refers to nature as "wise" because it reflects the Wisdom of God. Therefore, he sees no tension between the empirical study of nature and the devotion to the realm of prayer and Torah.

Three centuries later, R. Nahman lived in a world where the belief that the Torah is a sacred blueprint of creation was challenged by the forces antagonistic to Hasidism, namely, the Jewish Enlightenment.

In defense of traditional Judaism, R. Nahman produced an antiphilosophical approach to nature, one that is hostile to the attempt to fathom the stable laws of the universe, as medieval Jewish philosophers were trying to do. As far as R. Nahman is concerned, natural philosophy is a form of exile, an alienation from the divine source. The creative energies of the divine world could be captured only by the teller of tales, the artist who can use kabbalistic symbols in a creative way. He is no longer the kabbalist that manipulates the combination of letters, but his imagination enables him to operate with large symbolic units in a narrative style, inspired by literary conventions of European folk tales.

It seems reasonable to suggest that R. Nahman's alienation from nature and total escape into the world of myth could have been related to his messianic self-understanding.[15] The creative capacity of the mystic-messiah lies in his own psyche, the roots of which go to the origin of creation. The mystery of the soul is the real focus of R. Nahman's doctrine of redemption, and it depends not on visualization but on genealogy of the origin of the soul. The prescribed *tiqqunim* of his own soul are to bring about the "final *tiqqun*" of nature, of Israel, and of God. In this creative, artistic environment we can capture the gist of kabbalistic and Hasidic attitude toward language. Language is not a curse, as Wolfson has suggested, following Cassirer, but a blessing, and creative manipulation of language is a divine act of *poeisis*: a redemptive act.

III

With R. Nahman's tales we come to the modern predicament and the travails of kabbalah in modern Judaic scholarship. Jerome (Yehudah) Gellman discusses two approaches to early Hasidism, siding with Gershom Scholem and Rivkah Schatz-Uffenheimer against Buber and his defenders, among them Steven Kepnes and Laurence Silberstein. I agree with Gellman that Scholem was a better historian of ideas than Buber, and that Scholem's rendering of Hasidic sources was factually more accurate then Buber's. There is no doubt that Buber interpreted the Hasidic sources in the image of his own philosophy of dialogue and that, as such, Buber produced a very strong reading of Hasidic tales. Yet to understand Buber's views properly, we need to take into consideration not only his Zionist proclivities but also his political anarchism, his early interest in Eastern mysticism, and his philosophical anthropology.[16] Hasidism resonated for Buber in a manner that neither Orthodoxy nor its early twentieth-century alternatives could provide. As a constructive theologian rather than a historian of ideas, Buber used his sources creatively in order to pave for his readers a Jewishly informed philosophy of life. Buber's immense influence on twentieth-century Jewish and non-Jewish culture need not be recited here; it requires no *apologia*. The question is whether Jews in the twenty-first century could use Buber's reading (or misreading) of Hasidic sources, as a basis for Jewish *biophilia*.[17] The answer to this question requires a more systematic engagement with Buber's philosophy than could be undertaken in this response.

Gellman accuses Buber of imposing on the Hasidic sources and the "I-Thou" paradigm and thereby missing their original intent. I would venture to say that Gellman oversimplifies Buber's philosophy. The I-Thou does not simply mean exuberance, joyful posture, or ecstatic behavior, as Gellman thinks, and hence fails to find in the original sources. The I-Thou relationship is Buber's phenomenological re-working of creation theology, which is embedded in the kabbalistic *semiotic* model and in R. Nahman's realm of creative artistry. Buber's philosophy truly employs a semiotic model in which the act of reading is not one temporal activity (like cutting a tree), but rather an ongoing, creative activity in which reader and text are open to each other and continually influence each other. This semiotic model, as I attempted to show, was presupposed by kabbalah and facilitated an activist attitude toward nature, though one mediated through language.

According to Buber, it is indeed possible to enter an I-Thou relationship with natural creatures, be they a human being, a tree, or a horse, if one is truly and genuinely open to the pulsing of creative energy of God's creation. The problem is that in an unredeemed world, the I-Thou relationship cannot be sustained in the temporal, created order and that it necessarily turns into the objectifying scheme of the I-It of domination, exploitation, and denigration.[18] (Parenthetically I would add that this is precisely what we as scholars are doing to texts, sacred or not, when we treat them as objects of self-gratification, advancement, or academic politics.) Buber's anarchistic spirit and his genuinely mystical sensibility rejected this objectification as much as he realistically understood how unable we are to live without it. Buber's interpretation of the Hasidic sources is thus intended to suggest a path toward Jewish renewal that transcends the boundaries of the secular academy, as exemplified by Scholem and his many admirers and followers.

As a creative Jewish theologian, Buber challenges us to treat nature as a Thou, that is, with respect, concern, care, and responsibility, because this determines our collective "I." To be in an I-It relationship with texts or with nature means to corrupt them, to ignore their divine source, to deny their authenticity, and ultimately to doom texts and nature to death. If this volume is to formulate a Jewish response to the contemporary ecological crisis, Buber's dialogical philosophy, regardless of his misreading of Hasidic sources can serve as an insightful inspiration.

In sum, I maintain that the Jewish mystical tradition experienced most acutely the tension between creation and revelation posited by rabbinic Judaism. For the Jewish mystics, the physical world created by God and known through the senses is but a veil that conceals Ultimate Reality. The mystic can communicate with Ultimate Reality through the linguistic act of symbolic interpretation that is quite removed from the physical reality. Since Jewish mysticism is the elaboration of rabbinic theology and not a departure from it, the Jewish mystics continued to view their performance of *mitzvot* as vehicles for the sanctification of nature, hallowing the corporeal through intentional acts. In mystical ritual life the physical world (especially the mystic's own body) was believed to be spiritualized, transcending the order of the merely natural. By focusing on the spiritualization of nature and placing textual reality over and against nature, the Jewish mystics exacerbated the Jewish alienation from nature.

If this is correct, we can understand why until most recently the Jewish voice has been absent from the environmental movement. Precisely because rabbinic Judaism insists on the primacy of Torah, the natural world has been relegated to a secondary status. Historical conditions, of course, further made Jewish alienation from the natural world inevitable. The loss of Jewish control over the Land of Israel, the transformation of Jewish life from rural to urban, and the eventual prohibition on Jewish ownership of land would place serious obstacles to Jewish interaction with nature. Modern Zionism attempted to reverse this alienation both practically and theoretically, and was able to do so in large part because it rejected the rabbinic myth of

Torah. The secularist ideology of Zionism, especially in A. D. Gordon's version, is suffused with the desire to affect a Jewish return to nature. But it is doubtful whether Zionist thought could serve contemporary Jews who are seeking to ground a Jewish attitude toward the nature in religious sources. If kabbalah is to serve as an inspiration for a Jewish theology of nature, as some seem to suggest, then the doctrines and practices of kabbalah will have to undergo a comprehensive reinterpretation. A Jewish religious perspective on nature and the environment will require a theology in which the revealed Word of God does not substitute for the created world of God, but rather serves as a vehicle for protection and respect toward God's nature. This volume is but the first step toward this necessary and lofty goal.

Notes

1. This point is indebted to Steven Schwarzchild. See *The Pursuit of the Ideal: Jewish Writings of Steven Schwarzchild*, ed. M. Kellner (Albany: State University of New York Press, 1990), 63.

2. Viewing ethics as a practice of polishing the mirror of the soul was not limited to kabbalists. In the sixteenth century it was widely shared by Jewish philosophers who were also conversant with kabbalah. See Hava Tirosh-Samuelson, "The Theology of Nature in Sixteenth-Century Italian Jewish Philosophy," *Science in Context* 10, no. 4 (1997): 529–70, esp. n. 69.

3. This is the foundation of the long Jewish involvement in magic and the speculations about the creation of a Golem through manipulations of the Hebrew letters. See Moshe Idel, *Golem: Jewish Magical and Mystical Tradition on the Artificial Anthropoid* (Albany: State University of New York Press, 1990).

4. Elliot R. Wolfson, *Through the Speculum That Shines: Vision and Imagination in Medieval Jewish Mysticism* (Princeton: University of Princeton Press, 1994).

5. See Joan Cadden, *Meaning of Sex Difference in the Middle Ages: Medicine, Science and Culture* (Cambridge: Cambridge University Press, 1993).

6. This general principle can be traced to the writings of Aristotle. See Aristotle *Generation of Animals* 1.18.729a. All aspects of Aristotle's philosophy, including his biological theories and their ramifications, have been subject to extensive feminist critique. Consult *Feminist Interpretations of Aristotle*, ed. Cynthia A. Freeland (University Park, Pa.: Pennsylvania State University Press, 1998).

7. See my review of *Through the Speculum That Shines*, by Elliot R. Wolfson, *The Journal of Religion* 76, no. 3 (1996): 506–9.

8. It is important to note that the analogy between the kabbalist and the modern scientist is only structural. Even though there is some similarity between the two endeavors, we must be very clear about the difference between them. The letters of the genetic code are a shorthand representation of specific molecular structures that actually exist in nature. However, the letters that the kabbalist manipulates have no objective referent (even if such reference is claimed for them), but only derive from the language of Torah and its elaboration by rabbinic imagination. Therefore, contemporary scientists can begin to clone life, whereas the kabbalist can only fabricate stories about the possibility of making a Golem. Kabbalah, in short, is not science in the modern sense of that term.

9. See David Ruderman, *Kabbalah, Magic, and Science: The Cultural Universe of a Sixteenth-Century Jewish Physician* (Cambridge, Mass.: Harvard University Press, 1988), esp., 102–21.

10. For a recent evaluation of Hasidism and a critique of previous approaches, see Moshe Idel, *Hasidism: Between Ecstasy and Magic* (Albany: State University of New York Press, 1995). Idel's reading of Hasidism is most relevant to this discussion, and I believe that it fits into the schemas I have attempted to outline in this response.

11. For an overview of modern scholarship on Hasidism, consult *Hasidism Reappraised*, ed. Ada Rapoport-Albert (London and Portland, Ore.: The Littman Library of Jewish Civilization, 1997).

12. See Rachel Elior, "The Paradigms of Yesh and Eyin in Hasidic Thought," in ibid., 168–79.

13. See Ze'ev Gries, *The Book in Early Hasidism* (in Hebrew) (Ha-Kibbutz Ha-Meuhad, 1992); and Joav Elstein, *The Ecstatic Story in Hasidim Literature* (in Hebrew) (Ramat Gan: Bar Ilan University, 1998).

14. See Hava Tirosh-Rothschild, "On the Eve of Modernity," in *History of Jewish Philosophy*, ed. Oliver Leaman and Daniel H. Frank (London: Routlege, 1997), 532–35.

15. For a brilliant analysis of R. Nahman's messianism, consult Yehudah Liebes, "Ha-Tikkun Ha-Kelali of R. Nahman of Bratzlav and its Sabbatean Links," in his *Studies in Jewish Myth and Jewish Messianism* (Albany: State University of New York Press, 1993), 115–50, notes, 184–210.

16. Consult Paul Mendes-Flohr, *From Mysticism to Dialogue: Martin Buber's Transformation of German Social Thought* (Detroit: Wayne State University Press, 1988).

17. I cannot substantiate this claim in the context of this article and intend to do so in future work.

18. Scholem's arguments against Buber reflected the stance of the professional scholar of Jewish mysticism who was annoyed with Buber's creative approach to the Hasidic sources. But Buber's initial attempt was to *interact* with his Hasidic sources as an I-Thou paradigm in order to find a creative solution to the predicament of the modern Jew.

From Speculation to Action

Reverence and Responsibility:
Abraham Joshua Heschel on Nature
and the Self

EDWARD K. KAPLAN

At first glance, the problem of nature plays a subordinate role in Abraham Joshua Heschel's philosophy of religion. His two foundational books—*Man Is Not Alone* (1951) and *God in Search of Man* (1955)—both feature a modern mind discovering its divine foundation. Readers are impressed by the writer's ability to evoke the nuances of faith and piety in passages of great poetic beauty, while he elucidates his confidence in a caring God.

Heschel's goal is also ethically pragmatic. There is a prophetic urgency, even an undercurrent of dread, in his efforts to bring contemporaries into God's presence. Reflecting on the recent catastrophes of Auschwitz and Hiroshima as early as 1951, he alerts us:

> Horrified by the discovery of man's power to bring about the annihilation of organic life on this planet, we are today beginning to comprehend that the sense for the sacred is as vital to us as the light of the sun; that the enjoyment of beauty, possessions and safety in civilized society depends upon man's sense for the sacredness of life, upon his reverence for this spark of light in the darkness of selfishness; that once we perceive this spark to be quenched, the darkness falls upon us like a thunder.[1]

Heschel does not respond to this potential devastation by emphasizing traditional Jewish law.[2] Instead, while maintaining a (mostly implicit) halakhic frame of reference, he appeals primarily to inner spiritual discernment as it precedes theology, ideology, and formulations of belief. His books develop what he calls "depth theology,"[3] a cognitive process, analogous to depth psychology, which conveys knowledge through insight. Comprehension of the world through awe and wonder can lead to "radical admiration," preparing the mind and heart for intuitions of the divine presence.

Heschel's theology of nature derives from his epistemology of religious insight. As a religious philosopher, he seeks to effect nothing less than a religious Copernican revolution. Extending Kant's transfer of cognitive authority from external sense data to the categories of the mind, Heschel recenters his frame of reference from human to divine subjectivity. He leads readers from an ego-centered perception of the individual and the world to a theocentric discernment of unity encompassing animate nature, the cosmos, and human history. God, according to Heschel, cares about the world and calls for human beings actively to redeem it.

This essay explores the vision shared by environmentalism and Heschel's prophetic charge of saving the world from destruction. Heschel's principal task is to train readers to perceive themselves as objects of God's concern so that we may cooperate with God in eliminating suffering, injustice, and cruelty. Correspondingly, according to Mitchell Thomashow, my representative environmental thinker, a mature "ecological identity" allows "people [to] perceive themselves in reference to nature, as living and breathing beings connected to the rhythms of the earth, the biochemical cycles, the grand complex diversity of ecological systems."[4] How do we reach this connection with the whole? Perhaps Heschel's answer to this question will provide a language common to both secular environmentalism and Jewish thinking.

Biblical Identity Work

God, for Heschel, is the primary reality, and the key to religious thinking is a *recentering of subjectivity from the person to God*. We would read the Bible, for example, not to learn about Israel's search for the divine, but rather to gain insight into God's active pursuit of the errant people; the Bible is not human theology, but God's anthropology.[5] For people of today, Heschel's model is authentic prayer, as he explains in *Man's Quest for God*:

> We do not step out of the world when we pray; we merely see the world in a different setting. The self is not the hub, but the spoke of the revolving wheel. In prayer we shift the center of living from self-consciousness to self-surrender. God is the center toward which all forces tend. . . .
>
> Prayer takes the mind out of the narrowness of self-interest, and enables us to see the world in the mirror of the holy. For when we betake ourselves to the extreme opposite of the ego, we can behold a situation from the aspect of God.[6]

Heschel's epistemological journey prepares us to receive insight from God, and our response to that divine revelation (for that is what he considers "insight" to be) is commitment. The culmination is not mystical absorption in the Godhead, but prophetic sensitivity, courage, and action.

While keeping in mind Thomashow's environmentalist pedagogy, we explore how Heschel systematically inculcates the divine preciousness of natural and human existence in *Man Is Not Alone*, his general work of religious philosophy.[7] Briefly stated, Heschel revises common rational categories in which the mind seeks to adapt the ineffable mystery to its limited preconceptions. His method seeks to reconcile concepts with intuitive certainties: "What is subtle speculation worth without the pristine insight into the sacredness of life, an insight which we try to translate into philosophy's rational terms, into religion's ways of living, into art's forms and visions?"[8] The sanctity of life is the irreducible given, from which an ethics and a theology can be deduced.

Heschel systematically transforms anthropocentric thinking into theocentric (or biblical) categories, first, by interpreting the world through wonder or "radical amazement." Radical amazement, "the state of maladjustment to words and notions," is the beginning of religious understanding, since it throws into question all habitual ways of thinking about the world.[9] As the mind begins to perceive the world as "an allusion" to God, as an object of divine concern, we develop "reverence" for creation. He has effected a conceptual leap from intimations of God's involvement with the world to our reverence for God.

Religious and ethical commitments, in Heschel's ideal scheme, are products of what I call "radical reverence."

The mortal mind is his proving ground. To confirm the divine foundation common to the human personality and the natural world, quite early in *Man Is Not Alone*, he analyzes the subtle modalities of religious consciousness, targeting the basic phenomenological notion of a split between subject and object. Using a polemic method, his metaphors draw, literally, a sharp antithesis between two manners of thinking:

> Our self-assured mind specializes in producing knives, as if it were a cutlery, and in all its thoughts it flings a blade, cutting the world in two: in a thing and in a self; in an object and in a subject that conceives the object as distinct from itself. A mercenary of our will to power, the mind is trained to assail in order to plunder rather than to commune in order to love.[10]

Heschel considers pride to be humankind's greatest barrier to appreciating the reality beyond the mind, beyond the self. Injecting value judgments into the analysis, vivid images dramatize the banal epistemological fact of a thinking subject who requires an object of consciousness. The process of concept formation appears here as a sadistic butcher whose rational preconceptions betray their imperialistic attacks to gratify the will to power.

Heschel's complex rhetoric dramatizes religious thinking by joining poetry and analytic investigation. The exaggeration of this otherwise logical demonstration serves to feature communion as a higher form of knowledge. While he inspects the dynamics of consciousness quite rigorously, his imagery kindles an emotional tone that both undermines the ego and flatters our yearning for spirituality.

Religious thinking, in other words, is a form of ecological vision. Depth theology views the self, not as an antagonist seeking knowledge of God, but as a member of the cosmic community. Displacing its focus from *objects* to a *state of being* in which an individual feels in harmony with the universe, the humble mind can overcome the subject/object split. Heschel's recentering of the reader's consciousness has begun, reinforced by the flowing, rhythmical sentences:

> Where man meets the world, not with the tools he has made but with the soul with which he was born; not like a hunter who seeks his prey but like a lover to reciprocate love; where man and matter meet as

equals before the mystery, both made, maintained and destined to pass away, it is not an object, a thing that is given to his sense, but a state of fellowship that embraces him and all things. . . .[11]

This new perspective firmly distinguishes the hunter pursuing prey from the lover yearning to yield and to bestow affection: "where man and matter meet as equals before the mystery, both made, maintained and destined to pass away, it is not an object, a thing that is given to his sense, but a state of fellowship that embraces him and all things."

Ecological ethics, building upon specialized knowledge and assurances of natural harmony, emerges at this crucial intermediate stage of religious insight. Now, the person changes his or her conception of personal identity. Heschel's theocentric epistemology thus joins Thomashow's environmental perspective: "Intrinsic to an ecological worldview is the ability to see an ecosystem as part of oneself. This knowledge is gained both through an understanding of scientific ecology and through the ability to observe and internalize the interconnections and interdependence of all living things."[12] Heschel thus corrects the common misunderstanding of the biblical injunction to "subdue" or dominate nature by insisting upon equality before the divine Mystery.

Religious self-awareness, humility, and recentering of subjectivity to God places the individual self both beyond and more deeply within the system of nature. Repeating the idea of "fellowship" in the same paragraph, Heschel reconceives the structure of the human condition in religious terms. When the self leaves the center of the spiritual quest, when subject and object are reversed in favor of God as Subject, epistemology can lead to prophetic ethics:

> *To* our knowledge the world and the "I" are two, an object and a subject; but *within* our wonder the world and the "I" are one in being, in eternity. We become alive to our living in the great fellowship of all beings, we cease to regard things as opportunities to exploit. Conformity to the ego is no longer our exclusive concern, and our right to harness reality in the service of so-called practical ends becomes a problem.[13]

Communion is the penultimate stage of pre-theological awareness; we sense our kinship with the visible cosmos, feel its spiritual unity, and, as a consequence, relinquish our self-centered motives of expedi-

ency. But Heschel, instead of jumping directly to the ethical consequences of this insight, continues to dislodge our secular certainties.
An unheard-of significance begins to penetrate our consciousness:
"Things surrounding us emerge from the triteness with which we have
endowed them, and their strangeness opens like a void between them
and our mind, a void that no words can fill."

Remaining focused on the reality of God, Heschel, at this delicate
stage, continues to reexamine the dynamics of thinking itself. He interprets as a religious insight our awareness of the "void"—the breach
between consciousness and its contents—described by this scrupulous introspection (or phenomenology). This gap within consciousness can arouse an uncanny feeling for the true incommensurability
between mind and reality. (Kant might speak of the discrepancy between representations and the "thing-in-itself.") Feelings of "strangeness" advance our estrangement from ordinary, "realistic" perception.

The next stage passes from this intuition of *impersonal* transcendence, beyond our ken, to a *personal God* who relates to humankind.
Heschel injects a specific interpretation—a divine message—into our
sense of the ineffable. As we delve even more deeply into consciousness, the "personal" aspect of Deity appears as a metaphor of what we
begin to perceive about ourselves: "The self is more than we dream of;
it stands, as it were, with its back to the mind. Indeed, to the mind
even the mind itself is more enigmatic than a star."[14] Within the
knowledge conveyed by radical amazement, the mystery of consciousness joins with distant stars in evoking the sacred meaning underlying both.

At this decisive point in his demonstration, Heschel makes another
conceptual leap by claiming to perceive the human self's divine foundation. From *feelings* of "fellowship" with creation the person *perceives* a higher will, of which our intelligence is but an echo. What is
mystery to us *alludes* to superior truth. The self's enigma echoes
God's own consciousness, the source of human self-awareness:

> Once we discover that *the self in itself* [my emphasis] is a monstrous
> deceit, that the self is something transcendent in disguise, we begin to
> feel the pressure that keeps us down to a mere self. We begin to realize
> that our normal consciousness is in a state of trance, that what is higher
> in us is usually suspended. We begin to feel like strangers within our
> normal consciousness, as if our own will were imposed upon us.[15]

That is how Heschel, as "edifying philosopher" (in Richard Rorty's terms),[16] places a theological insight within the chasm he has opened within self-reflection. He magnifies the self's imponderability by polarizing two views: that the human ego ("the self in itself") is either a "monstrous deceit" or "something transcendent in disguise." Having defined his antithesis, he then surpasses the polemic.

The transition from a mode of thinking centered *on* self to one centered on and emanating *from* God is complete. To convince readers of its validity, Heschel advances his almost microsurgical removal of the outer layers of self-awareness:

> Upon the level of normal consciousness I find myself wrapt in self-consciousness and claim that my acts and states originate in and belong to myself. But in penetrating and exposing the self, I realize that the self did not originate in itself, that the essence of the self is in its being a non-self, that ultimately man is not a subject but an *object*.[17]

Until chapter 5 of *Man Is Not Alone*, the philosopher anatomizes the finite mind that asks questions about God; he does this in order to undermine our intellectual pride, deconstruct our ego-centered epistemology, and make plausible the idea that God is the origin of human thought—as of Being itself. We can now think about God, and our world of experience, from a biblical perspective.[18]

Nature and Creation

Heschel's theology of nature elaborates the view of divine unity.[19] His version of "ecological identity" is strengthened by the "revelation" or mystical insight described in chapter 9, "In the Presence of God," of *Man Is Not Alone*, in which the divine Subject becomes even more concrete.[20] We strive further to imagine the world as an object of God's concern or "love":

> Over and against the split between man and nature, self and thought, time and timelessness, the pious man is able to sense the interweaving of all, the holding together of what is a part, the love that hovers over acts of kindness, mountains, flowers, which shine in their splendor as if looked at by God.[21]

This insight reinforces "ecological identity" in a theological idiom, as Heschel's vision of interrelatedness justifies a simultaneous perception of immanence and transcendence: "God means: No one is ever alone; the essence of the temporal is the eternal; the moment is an image of eternity in an infinite mosaic. God means: *Togetherness of all beings in holy otherness*."[22]

Here, it is crucial to clarify a theological technicality: we must not overstate Heschel's panentheism, his celebration of God's presence within the world.[23] Heschel insists that the divine essence is not one with nature; at the same time, he insists equally that the *Shekhinah*, God's exiled Presence, remains within the world. The notion of God's simultaneous transcendence and immanence is merely a frozen thought that should give way to a dynamic "depth theology":

> *The whole earth is full of His glory.* The outwardness of the world communicates something of the indwelling greatness of God, which is radiant and conveys itself without words. *"There is no speech, there are no words, neither is their voice heard."* And yet, *"their radiation goes out through all the earth and their words to the end of the world"* (Psalms 19:4–5).
>
> The glory is neither an esthetic nor a physical category. It is sensed in grandeur, but it is more than grandeur. It is, as we said, a living presence or *the effulgence of a living presence*.[24]

Heschel submits binary categories to the ineffable, for words and concepts are not adequate to reality. Although he prefers the notion of polarity, I consider "amalgam" or "mixture" of transcendence and immanence to be a more accurate descriptive term—and that is probably what Heschel means by "the effulgence of a living presence" within nature. In any case, his refinement of often inchoate *feelings* of communion with nature is certainly not pantheistic.

God's glory pervades nature; that is the conclusion of radical amazement and wonder. But Heschel considers God's transcendence to be as crucial as humankind's responsibility to God, who is both within and beyond nature and civilization. Nature is not in itself sacred. In *God in Search of Man*, evoking the Hebrew Bible's denunciation of paganism, Heschel reaffirms the similar status of human beings and nature:

> [The prophets] tried to teach us that neither nature's beauty nor grandeur, neither power nor the state, neither money nor things of space are

worthy of our supreme adoration, love, sacrifice, or self-dedication. Yet the *desanctification of nature* did not in any way bring about an alienation of nature. It brought man together with all things in a fellowship of praise. The Biblical man could say that he was "in league with the stones of the field" (Job 5:23).[25]

Nature stands, in Heschel's suggestive phrase, "with its back to the mind" and participates, with humankind, in a process of sanctification. After transcending ego-centered thought, our task is not only to perceive and to experience the world as an "allusion to God" but more so, in practical terms, to join nature in its act of prayer: "To think of God man must hear the world. Man is not alone in celebrating God. To praise Him is to join all things in their song to Him. Our kinship with nature is a kinship of praise. All beings praise God. We live in a community of praise."[26] "The heavens are not God, they are His witnesses; they declare His glory."[27]

Ecological and Prophetic Responsibility

Heschel insists upon the ethical consequences of monotheism. Although he focuses primarily on the human world, the implications for preserving and saving natural ecosystems are strong and clear:

> In paganism the deity was a part of nature, and worship was an element in man's relation to nature. Man and his deities were both subjects of nature. Monotheism in teaching that God is the Creator, that nature and man are both fellow-creatures of God, redeemed man from exclusive allegiance to nature. The earth is our sister, not our mother.[28]

In becoming responsive to, and responsible for, nature, we serve the Creator. The interrelation of all realms of being, natural and spiritual, is the keynote of both communities, religious and environmental.

Heschel's theology of nature thus requires practical action, as do the revealed laws of ritual and ethical *mitzvot*. He helps us enter that faith, characteristically, not through injunctions, external rules, but by means of original spiritual insight. Personal participation in divine unity energizes the moral imperative:

> When God becomes our form of thinking we begin to sense all men in one man, the whole world in a grain of sand, eternity in a moment.

To worldly ethics one human being is less than two human beings, to the religious mind if a man has caused a single soul to perish, it is as though he had caused a whole world to perish, and if he has saved a single soul, it is as though he had saved a whole world (Mishnah Sanhedrin, 4, 5).[29]

This poetic notion (recalling William Blake's "eternity in a grain of sand"), which reinforces Heschel's biblical perspective, has been effectively secularized by liberal thinkers—both leading to vigorous social commitment. Again, the events of World War II make the emergency inescapable: "In our own age we have been forced into the realization that, in terms of human relations, there will be either one world or no world. But political and moral unity as a goal presupposes unity as a source; the brotherhood of men would be an empty dream without the fatherhood of God."[30]

Although Heschel's focus remains upon civilization and its divisions, he explicitly includes nature in his understanding of divine concern. The animate world is precious to God. Heschel's scrupulous disavowal of pantheism again highlights God's priority and humankind's responsibility:

> The world is *not* one with God, and this is why His power does not surge unhampered throughout all stages of being. Creature is detached from the Creator, and the universe is in a state of spiritual disorder. Yet God has not withdrawn entirely from this world. The spirit of this unity hovers over the face of all plurality, and the major trend of all our thinking and striving is its mighty intimation. The goal of all efforts is to bring about the restitution of the unity of God and world. The restoration of that unity is a constant process and its accomplishment will be the essence of Messianic redemption.[31]

Efforts to restore and augment ecological harmony are necessary for civilization, truly, to join nature in enhancing divine values. Theocentric thinking strives to judge, and to alleviate, discord, thus fulfilling the divine vision of unity and peace.

Sabbath as Jewish Ecology

To complete theory with practice, we examine Heschel's nuanced repudiation of sacred space in *The Sabbath* (1951) and its relation to his dythrambic celebration of the Holy Land in his 1969 book, *Israel: An Echo of Eternity*.[32] Without emulating the detail of Heschel's phenomenology of religious thinking, we can rapidly erase the shallow rumor that Heschel dismisses space and technology and civilization. As he asserts at the beginning of *The Sabbath* and reiterates in the epilogue: "This . . . is the answer to the problem of civilization: not to flee from the realm of space; to work with things of space but be in love with eternity. Things are our tools; eternity, the Sabbath, is our mate."[33]

Human ownership assumes an identification with space, self-centered to a significant degree, possibly excluding the ecological view. For Heschel, however, all land and human property is subordinate to God's sovereignty—"the earth is the Lord's," as the title of his early essay proclaims. Thomashow also analyzes the meaning of property, "a convenient illusion," in terms of space, self, and temporality: "It represents a distinction, a differentiation, an ego boundary that allows us to separate what is mine from what belongs to others. Yet I know that 'my' property is the essence of impermanence. My land and belongings are projections of my personal identity, cultural configurations that bring a sense of order to my life."[34] Nature's durability far surpasses that of civilization.

For Heschel, Sabbath observance helps transform our awareness in such a way that, at least during the holy Seventh Day, we celebrate time over space and cease striving to exploit or dominate the world. The notion of the Sabbath as eternity within human time, as a vehicle of divine presence, has been applied by Susan Power Bratton to ecological thinking that respects the slowness of nature, its seasonal cycles, and the necessity for replenishing threatened resources.[35] A grossly pragmatic, androcentric view imposes upon natural cycles of rest and renewal a homogenous technological time, based on the twenty-four-hour day and market competition. Sabbath observance, on the contrary, by honoring time over space, can advance the interrelatedness of God and the world: "Time . . . is *otherness*, a mystery that hovers above all categories. . . . Yet, it is only within time that there is fellowship and *togetherness* of all beings."[36]

Heschel seeks to reconcile space and time under the aegis of eternal values. Human acts are necessary for space to achieve spiritual status: "To be sacred, a thing had to be consecrated by a conscious act of man. The quality of holiness is not in the grain of matter. It is a preciousness bestowed upon things by an act of consecration and persisting in relation to God."[37] And yet, Heschel insists, it is perilous to associate God's presence with a specific place, as he continues: "If God is everywhere, He cannot be just somewhere. If God has made all things, how can man make a thing for Him?" And finally: "In the Bible, no thing, no place on earth, is holy by itself. Even the site on which the only sanctuary was to be built in the Promised Land is never called holy in the Pentateuch, nor was it determined or specified in the time of Moses."

Heschel's real point, however, is more inclusive. Space—civilization and nature—can become holy if God's sovereignty remains absolute. Religious history defines a hierarchy of values that safeguards space from idolatry:

> The holiness of the Sabbath preceded the holiness of Israel. The holiness of the Land of Israel is derived from the holiness of the people of Israel. The land was not holy at the time of Terah or even at the time of the Patriarchs. It was sanctified by the people when they entered the land under the leadership of Joshua. The land was sanctified by the people, and the Sabbath was sanctified by God.[38]

Heschel alters these passages slightly in his celebratory essay *Israel: An Echo of Eternity*, composed after the June 1967 war to explain to Christians the preciousness of the Holy Land. There, he stresses the importance of space in Jewish self-definition and its connection to the Land of Israel. Jews have always attributed sanctity to the Holy Land through prayers and aspirations: "Even those who believe that God is everywhere set aside a place for a sanctuary. For the sacred to be sensed at all moments everywhere, it must also at this moment be somewhere."[39]

It is beyond the scope of this paper to unravel the complexities of *Israel: An Echo of Eternity* and Heschel's relationship to Zionism. As Bratton has suggested, its very title suggests that the author values time—or eternity—over space. Yet, while Heschel does not spiritualize the Land as deftly as some Christians, he emphasizes the geographical territory's unworldly dimension:

> We will never be able to sense the meaning of heaven unless our lives on earth include the cultivation of a foretaste of heaven on earth. This may also explain why the promise of the land is a central motif in biblical history. God has not given the land away—He remains the

Lord and ultimate owner: "For Mine is the land" (Leviticus 25:23). Living in the Holy Land is itself a witness to the almost forgotten truth that God is the Lord and owner of all lands.

We must cultivate the earth as well as reflect on heaven. The Hebrew Bible is a book dealing with all of man, and redemption involves spiritual purification as well as moral integrity and political security.[40]

At that excruciating historical moment, when Heschel wrote the book, time and space, spiritual and political survival, were equally menaced. Within this mixture of perspectives, he asserts both the necessity of national (and military) security for the State while demanding that Israel, and the non-Jewish world, cultivate justice and holiness. "Jerusalem is not divine, her life depends on our presence. Alone she is desolate and silent, with Israel she is a witness, a proclamation."[41]

A Modern Temperament

Heschel and Thomashow (who quotes Heschel in his final chapter) similarly acknowledge the internal tensions shared by environmentalists and prophetic activists: "how can they at once convey a sense of wonder and appreciation about the natural world, and also be the harbingers of impending doom, warning the world about ecological catastrophes?"[42] Anguish and faith are inseparable when facing, realistically, today's world. Secularists and religious people conjoin opposing but equally authentic perspectives: dismay at the pervasiveness of human selfishness, greed, self-deception, and evil—versus basic trust in the persistence of natural balance and the efficacy of human compassion.

Heschel revealed his own internal battle only in his final book, *A Passion for Truth* (1973), delivered to the publisher weeks before his death. Two Hasidic extremists, "two teachers," as he called them—the uncompromising Rabbi Menahem Mendl of Kotzk and the compassionate Baal Shem Tov—compose his dynamic sensibility:

> In a very strange way, I found my soul at home with the Baal Shem Tov but driven by the Kotzker. Was it good to live with one's heart torn between the joy of Mezbizh [the town of the Baal Shem] and the anxiety of Kotzk? To live both in awe and consternation, in fervor and hor-

ror, with my conscience on mercy and my eyes on Auschwitz, wavering between exaltation and dismay? I had no choice: my heart was in Mezbizh, my mind in Kotzk.[43]

Mitchell Thomashow's solution is to recognize that environmental activists need healing: "there is an emotional detritus, sifting through the cracks and settling on the bottom of a task-driven professional life—feelings of anxiety, despair, and grief juxtaposed with reverence, compassion, and wonder."[44] He calls for environmentalists to develop a "radical confidence" which can reconcile frustrations and anguish with optimism and basic trust in nature and humankind. Even secularists can find the Sabbath.

In the end, all concerned people meet at the gates of "radical reverence" for humankind and the animate world. The Bible, as Heschel applies it, requires us to "revere our father and mother," calling us to experience each and every human being as, literally, body and spirit, an image of God. Nature, too, commands our reverence in light of God's ultimate sovereignty and concern. "Environmental identity work," in Thomashow's terms, "is a way of saying grace," grounded on four basic questions: "Where do things come from? What do I know about the place where I live? How am I connected to the Earth? What is my purpose and responsibility as a human being?"[45]

Our future depends upon such reciprocity. Heschel asserts, "There is no reverence for God without reverence for man. Love of man is the way to the love of God."[46] The environmentalist would add, "If ecological identity enables people to love the earth, then to love the earth is to love oneself."[47] If love cannot give us the courage to learn and then to act, fear of catastrophe must rouse us. We are now called upon to find the productive blend.

Notes

1. *Man Is Not Alone* (New York: Farrar, Straus and Young, 1951), 146. See the important book of John C. Merkle, *The Genesis of Faith: The Depth Theology of Abraham Joshua Heschel* (New York: Macmillan, 1985), esp. chap. 6, pp. 153–72.

2. See the lucid summary of Norman Lamm, "Ecology in Jewish Law and Theology," in his *Faith and Doubt: Studies in Traditional Jewish Thought* (New York: Ktav, 1971): 161–85. For a general survey of the literature, see Jeanne Kay, "Human Dominion over Nature in the Hebrew Bible," *Annals of the Association of American Geography* 79, no. 2 (1989): 214–32.

3. See Abraham Joshua Heschel, *God In Search of Man* (New York: Farrar, Straus and Cudahy, 1955), chap. 1, sections entitled "Philosophy and Theology," "Situational Thinking," and "Depth Theology," 4–8; see "Depth Theology," in his *The Insecurity of Freedom* (New York: Farrar, Straus and Giroux, 1966), 115–26, and his *Who Is Man?* (Stanford, Calif.: Stanford University Press, 1965).

4. Mitchell Thomashow, *Ecological Identity: Becoming a Reflective Environmentalist* (Cambridge, Mass.: MIT Press, 1995), xiii.

5. Heschel, *Man Is Not Alone*, 129. See, especially, Heschel, *God in Search of Man*, chap. 13, 136–44.

6. Abraham Joshua Heschel, *Man's Quest for God: Studies in Prayer and Symbolism* (New York: Charles Scribner's Sons, 1954), 7.

7. The following analysis has been developed in Edward K. Kaplan, *Holiness in Words: Abraham Joshua Heschel's Poetics of Piety* (Albany: State University of New York Press, 1996), chaps. 2, 3.

8. Heschel, *Man Is Not Alone*, 15.

9. Ibid., 11–17; Heschel, *God in Search of Man*, 45–53.

10. Heschel, *Man Is Not Alone*, 38. See also chap. 5, "Knowledge by Appreciation," 35–41.

11. Ibid., 38.

12. Thomashow, *Ecological Identity*, 12–13.

13. This and the next quotation are from Heschel, *Man Is Not Alone*, 39.

14. Ibid., 45.

15. Ibid., 47.

16. See Kaplan, *Holiness in Words*, 19, 171 n. 2.

17. Heschel, *Man Is Not Alone*, 48; and chap. 14, "God Is the Subject," 125–33.

18. Thomashow, *Ecological Identity*, 44. He cites these two perspectives in describing the famous 1903 camping trip in Yosemite National Park of the pragmatic President Theodore Roosevelt, who was "anthropocentrally oriented," and the "ecocentric" John Muir, who saw "humans as one of many species in a broad, cosmic context—believing in preserving wild lands for the sake of *their* wilderness, without any ulterior human motives."

19. Heschel, *Man Is Not Alone*, chap. 12, pp. 97–109, 111–23. See also his *God in Search of Man*, 88–113.

20. See Heschel, *Man Is Not Alone*, the end of chap. 6, "A Question beyond Words," 47–49. The next quotation is from p. 48. The footnote refers to Heschel, *Man Is Not Alone*, 128. The divine revelation occurs in chap. 9, pp. 67–79. For a complete

analysis of this passage, see Kaplan, *Holiness in Words*, chap. 5. Heschel evokes a similar moment of illumination in *God in Search of Man*, chap. 13, esp. pp. 140–41, which holds an equally decisive place in the narrative.

21. Heschel, *Man Is Not Alone*, 108–9.

22. Ibid., 109; cf. p. 78, the conclusion of mystical insight: "Refraction of that penetrating ray brings about a turning in our mind: We are penetrated by His insight. We cannot think any more as if He were there and we here. He is both there and here. He is not *a being*, but *being in and beyond all beings*."

23. See Abraham Joshua Heschel, *Between God and Man*, ed. Fritz A. Rothschild (New York: Harper, 1959), introduction, 16–18; Merkle, *The Genesis of Faith*, chap. 4, pp. 78–103.

24. Heschel, *God in Search of Man*, 83.

25. Ibid., 91.

26. Ibid., 95. The two sections of chap. 9, "The World," which explore this relation are entitled "Nature in Adoration of God" and "A Thing through God."

27. Heschel, *Man Is Not Alone*, 116.

28. Ibid., 115; cf. *God in Search of Man*, 92.

29. Heschel, *Man Is Not Alone*, 109.

30. Ibid., chap. 13, "One God," 112.

31. Ibid., 112.

32. Much of the following discussion has been inspired by Susan Power Bratton's paper, "Abraham J. Heschel's Theology of Sacred Time and the Value of Environmental Temporality" (originally prepared for a Jewish-Christian dialogue held at Brite Seminary, Texas Christian University, Fort Worth, mimeograph).

33. Abraham Joshua Heschel, *The Sabbath* (New York: Farrar, Straus and Young, 1951), 48; also, Heschel, *The Sabbath*, 6, 116–17.

34. Thomashow, *Ecological Identity*, 76.

35. Bratton, "Abraham J. Heschel's Theology of Sacred Time," 3, 5–10.

36. Heschel, *The Sabbath*, 99.

37. This and the following quotations are from ibid., 79–81.

38. Ibid., 82.

39. Abraham Joshua Heschel, *Israel: An Echo of Eternity* (New York: Farrar, Straus and Giroux, 1969), 11. For a fuller account of Heschel's relationship to Israel and Zionism, see Arnold Eisen, *Galut: Modern Jewish Reflection on Homelessness and Homecoming* (Bloomington: Indiana University Press, 1986).

40. Heschel, *Israel*, 146–47.

41. Ibid., 14. Thanks to Jacob Teshima for this quotation.

42. Thomashow, *Ecological Identity*, xvii.

43. Abraham Joshua Heschel, *A Passion for Truth* (New York: Farrar, Straus and Giroux, 1973), xiv.

44. Thomashow, *Ecological Identity*, 142.

45. Ibid., 205; see the entire epilogue, introduced by a quotation from Heschel, 201–5.

46. Heschel, *God in Search of Man*, 375.

47. Thomashow, *Ecological Identity*, 168.

Can Judaism Make Environmental Policy? Sacred and Secular Language in Jewish Ecological Discourse

TSVI BLANCHARD

This volume is not a typical academic exercise. Instead, it reflects Jewish attempts to respond to the present ecological crisis of global proportions.[1] Our production and consumption patterns are dangerously disordering the natural processes needed to sustain human life.[2] International governmental conferences are now held regularly for the purpose of formulating and implementing the environmental policies that will constructively address these issues. Do Jews and Judaism have a role to play in these policy discussions?

Unfortunately, the answer is not immediately obvious.[3] To be effective, environmental discussion must lead to policy proposals capable of implementation. Minimally, this requires a degree of mutual understanding and perceived common interests sufficient for participants to formulate and commit to a shared plan of action.[4] To succeed, we must speak enough of a common language to understand, evaluate, and discuss both the proposals and the arguments offered for them. Discussions in which the participants do not actually understand each other's arguments do not generally lead to commitments to common action.[5]

Perhaps, then, there are real barriers to effective Jewish participation. The language of contemporary environmental policy discussion is highly secular.[6] In contrast, the inherited languages of our many Judaisms are all significantly religious. In addition, many of the most significant images and arguments found in Jewish texts are particular to the Jewish tradition. Hence, they are not presently part of the more universal language of environmental debate. The principal question underlying my paper is then: Given the primarily non-Jewish and secular international language in which policy debates take place, is there an interpretative understanding of Jewish tradition that might afford Jews and Judaism a role in these critical environmental discussions?

For Jews and Judaism to find a place in general environmental discussion, three difficulties must be addressed. First, although traditional Jewish texts provide important conceptions of the natural world and of the human relationship to it, they were never meant as a response to the world-threatening ecological problems we face today. We simply do not find a sense of ecological crisis in traditional Jewish texts. As a result, rabbinic environmental policy dealt primarily with more local issues, such as fairness and risk management. If we are to use traditional Jewish texts to advance our discussion of present ecological challenges, we must be ready to do some exegetical and philosophical reconsideration and reconstruction.

Second, in premodern society Jews lived as a relatively segregated subgroup. We should not be surprised, then, that the scope of Jewish environmental policy discussion was limited. Where policy making was concerned, Jews talked primarily to, for, and about Jewish society.[7] Hence, the language and methods of Jewish texts do not neatly transfer to policy debates with a wider range of participants. Once again, some thoughtful reconstruction will be needed if classical Jewish sources are to play a helpful role in present debates over our ecological practices.

Finally, in contemporary discussion, the impact and worth of religious and theological language are still being critically examined. For example, in the Hebrew Bible, God creates both nature and the human species. He then commands a relationship between them that, it has been alleged, can only be construed as one of human domination over nature. This alleged dominating, rule-over-it biblical attitude toward nature has recently been suggested as the root of our environmentally destructive policies.[8] This would seem to make the Jewish tradition part of the problem, not the solution. Ironically, the biblical understanding of creation as sacred has also been offered as an antidote to what are seen as the destructive aspects of instrumental reason and its dominating relationship to nature. This latter reading of the Hebrew Bible complements a call for a change in ecological consciousness as part of a solution to the present environmental crisis.

This view and similar nonbiblical views call for the reintroduction of theological and/or spiritual concepts and attitudes into discussion of the environment. There is talk of the re-sacralizing—even re-enchantment—of nature in order to remedy the alleged destructive blindness of the secularizing, scientific, disenchanting consciousness that is presented as essential to the Enlightenment.[9]

In all of its diverse forms, contemporary Judaism tends to refract the Bible through the lens of rabbinic literature. Hence, while the wider debates over ecological consciousness have focused on the Hebrew Bible, contemporary Jews will need to be equally concerned with ecological issues in rabbinic literature. Of course, introducing rabbinic literature does not eliminate the need to further clarify what role, if any, will be played by Jewish religious and theological language in more general discussions of environmental policy.

In this paper, I respond to the three difficulties discussed above by using classical Jewish texts to explore the role of religious and secular discourse[10] in environmental policy making.[11] My focus, therefore, is ecological policy formulation. Hence, I offer neither an environmental theology nor a phenomenology of the Jewish religious experience of nature. Instead, I suggest a model for environmental policy discussion that is responsive to both the limits and the potentials of Jewish texts. In order to accomplish this goal, I will argue for a model of policy discourse that: 1) examines Jewish texts attending to the demands of the present ecological situation rather than to the historical circumstances in which these texts were created, written, collected, or arranged; 2) limits the particularizing role played by the religious origins of the texts in order to enhance the ability of Jews and Judaism to find an influential voice in the general debates over environmental policy; and 3) provides a meaningful place for the religious/sacred dimension of Judaism without compromising the contemporary, more universal quality of ecological discussion.

For heuristic reasons, I employ three preliminary—and admittedly only briefly sketched—models of environmental discourse. First, there is the secular model. I have in mind the kind of discourse we find in most contemporary environmental discussion in the United States and throughout Europe.[12] This kind of language, as well as the theory and policy formulated in it, is almost exclusively secular, scientific, moral, ethical, and political.[13]

The second model of discourse is a discourse that nearly completely mixes language that today we would term secular with language now typically understood to be theological, religious, and spiritual.[14] Hence, within the discourse, there is no way to avoid the limits set by the particular theological and religious traditions of which the discourse is a part. As a result, meaningful participation in discussion usually requires sharing to some extent the religious identities of other participants. Those who do not share the group's particular traditions and identities will have serious trouble finding an effective voice in the group discussion.

Finally, there is a third model in which both secular and religious languages are employed, sometimes together, sometimes separately. The relationship between the two types of discourse, however, is made explicit and is relatively well regulated. Hence, with minimal attention to the rules of usage and translation, participants from alternative religious traditions, as well as those with an entirely nonreligious approach, can find their places within the debates.

I argue that, given the three difficulties I described above, it is this third model that serves us best. This model alone, however, does not compel or even urge us to use Jewish materials either within or in preparation for general ecological policy discussions. It only shows the possibility of such an approach. We may actually elect to use Jewish materials for two reasons. First, because we are independently committed to Jewish materials and equally strongly committed to playing a part in the formulations of environmental policy. In this sense, we feel we must understand inherited Jewish texts in ways that allow us to find our voice within wider policy debate. Second, we have fruitfully and constructively employed Jewish texts either within or in preparation for discussions of concrete environmental policy issues and believe it helpful if we share these texts with other participants.[15]

I develop my presentation as follows. First, I consider a biblical passage, used in the daily Jewish liturgy, that serves as an example of discourse in which secular and sacred/religious languages are blended. As a further example of this model, I offer a rabbinic text. Having done this, I introduce a second rabbinic text to illustrate how rabbinic literature moves beyond the blended language. In this talmudic text, we find a secularizing shift.[16] Having moved beyond blended discourse,

I then present a third rabbinic text on the regulation of urban environments that exemplifies a primarily secular discourse.

Finally, I consider two apparent intrusions of religious/theological language into this otherwise secular rabbinic text. These intrusions[17] allow me to explore the third model of discourse in which secular and religious/spiritual languages may both be employed and even sometimes linked, so long as they are not merged. I argue that this third model is the best model for bringing Judaism into wider environmental policy discussions. The third mode of discourse, I argue, allows us to effectively address the issues of both the benefits and the limits of the secularization or disenchantment of environmental language.[18]

The Shema

One central component of Jewish liturgy is a twice-daily repetition of three biblical passages[19] known as the Shema. The second paragraph of the Shema, Deuteronomy 11:13–21 (see appendix 1), is an example of discourse about the environment that inseparably blends secular and theological language. Equally important, the Shema text is not only biblical and rabbinic, but it has also found an important place in the various Judaisms of history, including those of the present day.

In the Shema, natural processes are described, understood, and explained in a nearly seamless weave of secular and theological terms and reasoning. The opening of the passage tells us that obedience to God, here specifically displayed by wholehearted love and service, will result in God's sending the proper kinds of rain (lighter and heavier) in their proper times (earlier and later). As a result, we humans will harvest an abundance of grain, wine, and oil. The harvest is explained by reference to rain, but the rain is explained by reference to God's actions.

Divine action, in its turn, is a response to the appropriate human actions and attitudes, the correctness of which, in turn, is understood as obedience to God's commands. Plant growth is not simply the natural result of a good rainfall. Immediately, the reader is told that it is God who directly provides the grass for grazing domestic animals. In sum, proper human action, defined in theological (here covenantal) terms, leads to the satisfactions brought by an abundance that is interchangeably attributed both to natural growth processes and to divine intervention.

As the passage continues, we learn that it is idolatry, the love (or desire for) and service of other gods, that leads to divine wrath. Divine anger results in God's direct intervention to restrain the heavens—no rainfall—and, as a second result of divine wrath, no produce will be harvested from the land. Note that just as right action and attitude and their consequences were defined in both theological and natural terms, so wrong action and attitude and their consequences are also defined in both theological and natural terms.

We should note that the semantic value of certain individual terms also mixes the secular and the sacred. For example, the meaning of the term for "land" used in this passage fuses the meaning of geographical Canaan (i.e., secular) with the meaning of covenantal Canaan (i.e., sacred). Banishment from, or loss of, the good land that provides abundant harvest is at the same time banishment from, or loss of, the land that God gives to you—as well as of the covenantal intimacy and protection that this implies. The logic and flow of the passage presents the same picture. For example, agricultural produce can be understood as coming directly from God and also as coming indirectly through God's withholding of the appropriate rains in their appropriate seasons.

While it would be misleading to characterize the Shema as presenting us with an enchanted world, it is fair to say that the world of the Shema is a world described at once as sacred and secular, theological and scientific. The religious power of this language to direct attention to environmental concerns is clear. But there would be clear drawbacks to using it to re-sacralize the language of policy discussion. For example, were the language of the Shema used to conduct a discussion of environmental policy in modern-day Israel, failure to practice biblical and rabbinic rituals could then be fairly offered as a potential cause of environmental problems. A governmental policy enforcing conformity to traditional ritual norms might then be offered as prevention or remedy. Such an approach is not likely to create much of a place for Jews and Judaism in general environmental discussion.[20]

A Rabbinic Example of the Blended Language Model

The Mishnah, the founding document of rabbinic Judaism,[21] also contains texts with much the same interconnecting sacred–secular language we saw in the Shema. Examples are found throughout the Tractate Ta'anit. Consider the discussion of rainfall, the same topic found in the Shema. At the opening of the tractate, the text discusses the seasonal insertion into the daily prayers of the words "who makes the wind to blow and causes the rain to come down" as a phrase describing God.[22] On the same folio page in the Gemara, rainfall is treated as deriving solely from God:

> Rabbi Johanan said: Three keys the Holy One blessed be He retained in His own hands and not entrusted to the hand of any messenger. . . . Why does not Rabbi Johanan include this key [i.e., the key of sustenance]? Because [in his opinion] sustenance [*parnasah*] is included in [the key for] rain. (Babylonian Talmud Ta'anit 2a)

As in the Shema, rain is sent directly by God and is also the intermediate source of human sustenance. As before, rainfall depends, in large part, on the religious merit gained or lost through right or wrong religious action or attitude.[23] After this passage, the Gemara's discussion of rain widens to include snow, wind, and clouds, as well as various types of rainfall. The language of the text has both a religious and a secular dimension. Although scripture is often cited, it is clear that the rabbis have in mind the kind of knowledge about the weather that would constitute a part of their general, scientific agricultural knowledge. Consider the following text, for example:

> Rab Judah further said: Wind after rain is as beneficial as rain, clouds after rain are as beneficial as rain, sunshine after rain is as beneficial as twofold rain. . . . Raba further said: Snow is beneficial to the mountains, heavy rain to the trees, gentle rain to the fruits of the field, drizzling rain even to the seeds under a hard clod. . . . (Babylonian Talmud Ta'anit 3b–4a)

Prayer, however, remains the main practice in the technology of rain. The rabbis are so convinced of the power of praying for rain that, in one opinion, such prayer should "begin fifteen days after the feast [Sukkot, the fall pilgrimage festival] so that the last Israelite [who traveled to the festival] may reach the river Euphrates" (Mishnah Ta'anit 1.2).

And what if there is not the required seasonal rainfall? At first, those with some special spiritual identity (*yehidim*) fast. Then, if no rain falls, the general populace fasts. Of course, the fasts are of increasing severity (Mishnah Ta'anit 1.3, 4).[24] The details of the observance of these fasts and their liturgy reflect the central place of theological language in formulating rabbinic understanding of the weather.

We should note, however, that the sacred does not entirely crowd out the secular. Prayer is fully integrated into an awareness of seasonal rainfall patterns. For example, as the season passes without rainfall, the fasts become increasingly severe. I assume that this is because the rabbis understood that, as time passed, the lack of rainfall was increasingly less likely to be the mere result of the expected variance in weather patterns. Hence, in their worldview, as more of the rainy season passed without rainfall, it was increasingly more likely that God was actively withholding the rain.

As in the Shema, theological discourse and scientific discourse are fully blended. Once again, we note the positive value of this language to insiders, that is, believers. What else should believers do in cases where they cannot rely on direct human control of crucial features of the environment? Should they act as if God is powerless or simply doesn't care?

I am not merely referring here to the somewhat less than exalted psychological value in such cases of relying on prayer, or on other theological/religious beliefs and practices. I am referring primarily to the way in which such language and practice express a commitment to an ultimate connection between religious/moral goodness and good fortune. This connection is a necessary postulate of any religious discourse that preserves the morality of God and of God's commandments.[25] Therefore, for traditionally religious Jews, praying for rain is one part of an appropriate, logical social policy.

Yet, this rabbinic text makes equally clear that the blended language model of environmental discourse fails to bring traditionally religious Jews into any policy discussion in which others participate. We need only ask: How would this discourse sound in a contemporary Israeli discussion of the crucial issues raised in formulating policy on water use? Any traditional believer who wants to participate in this public policy discussion must make very sure not to propose the government funding of a Jewish prayer group. I can't imagine Israel's secular citizens opting for this way of re-enchanting their environment.

The Rabbinic Shift: First Steps toward a Secular Discourse

In rabbinic Judaism, as in most religious systems grounded in divine revelation, God participates in policy-making discussions. But how?

In the texts from Tractate Ta'anit, God weighed in by withholding rainfall and, in this way, triggering individual and communal reflection on the religious propriety of personal or communal behavior.

In this theory, if God thought that social choices were wicked, God could choose to delay the rain or withhold it altogether until people altered their behavior. Since people find it hard to infer specific mistakes in their behavior from the mere lack of rainfall, their only option would be to repent of *everything* they imagine might be responsible for the lack of rainfall. God could, of course, become more specific by revealing His Will directly through charismatic, wonder-working individuals. In general, rabbinic Judaism did not make this move.

In a much cited text from the Babylonian Talmud (Bava Metzi'a 59a–b; see appendix 2), we find a concern with methods of policy discussion that reflects a move away from religiously particular methods of decision making—that is, away from the discourse found in the biblical and talmudic texts discussed above. In this next text, the initial topic under discussion is the ritual purity of an oven.[26] Quickly, however, the talmudic dispute between R. Eliezer and the sages becomes one concerned with charisma and religious expertise.

R. Eliezer attempts to influence the final policy outcome by demonstrating superior control first over nature and then over material culture. His opponents, the sages, decline to make policy by recourse to special powers. In his final attempt to convince them, R. Eliezer calls on a confirming heavenly voice (*bat kol*). Despite their belief that Heaven is the original source of their system, the rabbis again refuse to accept R. Eliezer's position, saying "It [the Torah] is not in heaven." Discussion is now limited to the human sphere.

In this text, God no longer has the right to exert direct influence on policy. He has had His say on Sinai and must now rely on a community of scholars who employ both their own reason and the reasonable interpretation of precedent texts and present experience. To be sure, as far as this specific text is concerned, neither the vocabulary nor the participants have been significantly secularized. The vocabulary of the text and the persons qualified to participate in discussion are mostly religious and highly particular to Judaism. Yet, the rules of interpretation, argument, inference, and decision making have moved away from earlier religious methods toward more generally employable, less particular methods, and the notion of exegesis at work here is not limited to Jewish religious traditions.[27]

In this text, decisions are made by majority rule and not by appeal to the special spiritual practices of adepts. The sage with his wisdom has clearly replaced the wonder worker or charismatic figure, implying that claims must be validated by shared argument, even if the inherited language of the arguments is, if not exactly sacred in quality, certainly religious and particular. Here we have only a partial shift away from highly particularistic methods rooted in specific revelations toward a more open, more rational, and, in this sense, more secular style of policy consideration.[28]

A Secular Language Emerges for Environmental Policy Debate

Texts from the second chapter of Tractate Bava Batra (see appendix 3) reveal the use of an essentially secular language of environmental policy debate. Underlying their discussion of potential and/or actual environmental damage is a fundamental dispute concerning the assigning of responsibility for taking preventive action. Is the one likely to suffer the damage (the *nizak*) required to take preventive action and, if so, in what circumstances? Or, is the likely source of damage (the *mazik*) required to take preventive action and, if so, when?[29]

Of course, these talmudic discussions are not concerned with damages to something called "the environment."[30] Their concern is solely with damages to the property and well-being of persons. In this sense, their inheritors in the ecology movement are the social ecologists whose primary concern is with persons.[31]

Nonetheless, veterans of environmental policy discussions will easily recognize the relevance of the specific sources of damage cited in the text. These sources are: 1) intentional modification of the environment: planting a tree; or constructing material infrastructure, e.g., digging a fuller's pool that may impact negatively on agricultural land; or building ground and material infrastructure, e.g., a wall; 2) harmful side effects of improper positioning of certain substances: e.g., olive refuse (whose existence and proximity is the result of human activity) on agricultural land; crumbling soil; and material infrastructure, e.g., a wall.

The terms, the syntax, and the reasoning we find in these texts are secular in the sense that they refer to substances and their observable properties, to natural processes and their anticipated effects, to the intentions of the parties in the situation, as well as to the expected protective effects of actions taken to prevent damage. As with all jurisprudentially framed discussions of policy, there is a reliance on precedent texts, their interpretation, and their harmonization. However, only the particular language, the literary style, and the specific precedent texts cited identify these texts as particularly Jewish.

These texts do not read like theology. Their author(s) may very well have believed that damaging the property of others was a religious error *(het)*, a sin *('averah)*, a violation of the Divine Image *(tzelem 'elokim)* in every human being, or a breach of the covenant *(berit)* instituted by God. But these theological concepts are not explicit in the text, nor is it necessary for us to introduce them in order to explain the passages cited.

Of course, serious modification of language would still be necessary in order to participate in a discussion with those for whom the precedent texts of rabbinic Judaism are not convincing. Other kinds of additional support—evidential, for example—would have to be offered for the various positions reported. Nonetheless, analysis of the Jewish materials might help in drafting possible policy strategies as well as in framing the key questions to be asked and answered. Given appropriate interpretation, Jews committed to traditional texts could find a place and a voice in secular environmental policy discussion.[32]

Two Not-So-Secular Intrusions

The language of the extended talmudic discussion found in Bava Batra, chapter 2, is not uniformly secular. There are two interpretations (Bava Batra 19b–20b; see appendix 4).

The discussion concerns materials that, if they were placed in a hole in a wall, might impede the flow of *tum'ah* (ritual impurity). Clearly, the discussion is not conducted in secular language. What, we may wonder, is it doing in the middle of a discussion of the damaging effects of urine on walls?[33] Although such questions are always somewhat speculative, let me offer a suggestion.

Assume that the introduction of the *tum'ah* theme is triggered by the topic under discussion in the text: urinating on walls. We should first remind ourselves that both the degree of human control over a bodily process and the boundary-loosening effects of that process (namely, leaking) figure prominently in the system that regulates *tum'ah*.[34] When the specific bodily conditions that create a state of *tum'ah* are being considered, lack of control and loosening of boundaries (as in leaking) bring about a state of *tum'ah*.[35] Taken as a whole, however, the system of *ritual* purity and impurity (*tum'ah/tahara*) has a kind of technology that allows for partial control in avoiding becoming *tame*[36] and in correcting its effects through ritual action.[37]

Understood in these terms, urination is, like the system of ritual impurity taken as a whole, partly under our control and partly not. There is something we can do about it by controlling the timing of urination. Its ritual consequences are also partially in our control (that is to say, they are correctable).[38] But, in the end, we cannot entirely avoid urination or its consequences.

Perhaps a somewhat less than fully conscious concern or anxiety about bodily control and boundaries is at work here. After all, these same concerns surround urination. And, with respect to these concerns, the system of ritual purity and impurity is similar to urination. What if this concern or anxiety about control and boundaries lies behind the unexpected introduction of a discussion about rebuilding effective blockages or boundaries against the flow of *tum'ah*?

To be sure, it is hard to explain this priestly language with its quasi-spiritual qualities in any but a functional way. After all, the rabbis, and we as well, do not actually perceive *tum'ah* as a substance in the way we perceive, for example, clouds or pudding. Nor do we or the rabbis experience being *tame* as a property of objects, as we perceive the property of being red. But this problematic intrusion does forcefully put us in mind of the perplexing forces, fears, anxieties, and distresses that trouble us and sometimes disturb the reasoned course of even our most scientific environmental policy debates.

A second intrusion into the otherwise secular, scientific, and jurisprudential language of Bava Batra (see appendix 5) allows us to draw some general conclusions about the value of preserving languages specific to individual religious traditions. The Mishnah's concerns are with distancing carrion, graves, and tanyards from towns. In the case of keeping a tanyard some distance from a town, the text is concerned with protecting townspeople from noxious odors.

In its commentary on the Mishnah, the Talmud understands Rabbi Akiva as prohibiting any tanyard on the west side of a town. His reason for doing so is not clear. The original, *mipnei she-hee tadira*, might be rendered "because it [the west] is constant/regular/frequent." The Talmud offers the possibility that the phrase refers to the west wind and means "blows frequently" (or, following Rashi, more frequently than the other winds). Using a precedent text that contradicts this interpretation, the Talmud offers as an alternative interpretation: "it [the west] is [the regular location of] the *Shekhinah* [the Divine Presence]."

The shift from "the west wind blows frequently" to "the west is the regular place of the Divine Presence" is a shift from quasi-scientific cosmology to a sacred cosmology that is in the main specific to Judaism.[39] The text then continues this theological discussion of the location of the Divine Presence. At this point, the text shifts to a less overtly sacred mode, first by using more general cosmological doctrines about the winds to interpret a biblical verse, and then by presenting two alternative scientific cosmologies. The text will continue shuttling back and forth between primarily religious concerns and language and more general, scientific language, finally returning to the more typical, secular topics and language of the chapter as a whole.[40]

While the first intrusion showed us the nether side of the sacred universe (the world of impurity, *tum'ah*), these passages show us the more transcendent, exalted side, the *Shekhinah*. Although we can still hear anxiety over the uncontrollable powers of the universe, the primary attitude is one of awe in the presence of the sacred. If the earlier text presented an intrusion from below, this text offers an intrusion from above.

Both texts, it seems to me, are examples of two types of concerns that defy easy rendering into more secular, more easily shared language. The first type expresses our deepest conscious, and more often unconscious, fears and anxieties. The second expresses our most profound conscious, and often superconscious, sense of the sacred. Both naturally call for principally symbolic language and/or artistic expression. Both tend toward languages and other forms of symbolic expression that derive from relatively particular traditions.

But more needs to be said. The phenomenology of religion, as well as techniques of depth analysis, have shown us that texts from differing sacred traditions can in fact be made generally accessible. There are two ways in which parts of such texts might find their way into global environmental discussions. First, these texts remind us that

important and real features of human experience operate outside the
control of secular, scientific reasoning and discourse. This is as true
for texts that reach up as it is for those that reach down.

Discussions of environmental policy run significant risks if they
ignore our deep, hidden, and not-so-hidden, fears and anxieties about
nature and our place in it. Especially in the implementation stage, we
should expect that environmental policies that have not allowed for
irrational concerns might, at the very least, be ineffective and, at
worst, wreak more havoc than the problems they were formulated to
remedy. But ecology also runs a serious risk if it ignores the kind of
imaginative utopian language that might uncover a sense of the environment too profound at present to find adequate expression in the
language of scientific policy debate. In formulating and implementing
environmental policy, we need to leave room for the unexpected
blessings and opportunities that as yet only our most compelling
dreams can convey.[41]

Second, using appropriate interpretive methods, these texts may reveal more shared and even more secular meanings than we have expected to find. If we do find such meanings, this would provide traditional Jewish texts with a point of entry into wider discussion. Of
course, we need to be very careful not to reduce the language of Jewish texts to the more scientific shared discourse used to interpret them.
There may still remain a sacred dimension of experience available
only to those for whom these symbolic languages and images constitute "natural languages." As I see it, experiences of the sacred are
more likely to be expressed in the languages of particular religious
traditions. And, as I noted, we need to allow for these experiences and
symbols even when we can find no interpretive language as yet suited
to bringing them into general policy discussion.

I have indicated that I strongly value the existence of culturally particular and sacred religious languages. But, in arguing for a version of
the third model, I have not argued that religious, sacred, and spiritual
language should be used to justify environmental policy. What I have
suggested instead is that the essentially secular discourse of policy
discussion should pay careful attention to the heuristic functions of
such language, as well as to its role in implementing policy.[42]

Religious or spiritual language and experience can indeed help
shape forms of ecological consciousness. But, in the end, it is the job
of a more secular, shared discourse to decide which forms of ecologi-

cal consciousness should be encouraged and which discouraged. Similarly, the sheer transcending quality of religious experience can reveal policy options that would otherwise have gone unnoticed. Nonetheless, the acceptability of these options should only be argued in the shared, secular discourse. That is why materials brought from particular traditions must be appropriately translated into a language with global scope and suitable for participants who are not a part of that particular religious tradition.

By Way of a Summary

I have argued that, given the global scope of environmental problems, the environmental policy discussion itself must have global scope. Such a global discussion of environmental policy will surely have to draw on differing traditions, both religious and secular. It seems reasonable to assume that, in addition to allowing for global discussion, our inclusion of a variety of particular traditions, discourses, and languages would also expand policy and implementation options.

If we attach importance to Judaism's participation in contemporary ecological policy discussion, then the Jewish tradition will have a place within this global discussion. I have given two reasons for believing that Judaism can find its place in discussions of environmental policy. First, rabbinic literature[43] contains texts about environmental issues that speak in what is the essentially secular language of contemporary environmental policy discussion. This was important because I also suggested that the language of contemporary environmental policy decision making should be essentially as secular and universal as possible.[44]

Second, I believe that Judaism can find a place in global discussions because there is good reason to believe that Jewish texts can be creatively interpreted in ways that render them pertinent to contemporary environmental issues. Indeed, until relatively recently, this was a given in educated circles comfortable in the world of Jewish texts. In sum, I have argued that those of us concerned with Judaism and its impact on environmental policy can and should seek to interpret and reconstruct Jewish texts in ways that bring them into global ecological policy formulation, implementation, and decision making.

Notes

1. Mary Evelyn Tucker made this clear to me by at a meeting held to discuss the possibility of the conference from which this volume grew.

2. It seems that we have moved past the point of being able to manage many of these risks. A discussion of this theme, as well as of the implications for politics and society, can be found in Ulrich Beck, *Risk Society: Towards a New Modernity*, trans. Mark Ritter (London: Sage Publications, 1992); Ulrich Beck, *Ecological Enlightenment: Essays on the Politics of the Risk Society*, trans. Mark A. Ritter (Atlantic Highlands, N.J.: Humanities Press International, 1995).

3. Note the difficulties that the Roman Catholic Church has encountered in its attempts to participate in political policy discussions. Despite efforts to articulate its position in theologically neutral language, its opponents inevitably insist on treating its views as a priori unwelcome, because their origin is particular to one religious tradition.

4. If we understand goals to differ from perceived interests, then joint action need not imply shared goals. If "objectives" describe the specific actions taken to achieve goals, we are more likely to share objectives, since we can pursue the same objectives for very different reasons, i.e., in the hope of realizing differing goals.

5. Extensive philosophical discussion surrounds the issues raised by my necessarily brief remarks about mutual understanding, reason, pluralism, particular identities, and common rational discussion. My argument in this paper is based on the practical necessity for a common language for environmental policy formation in a situation requiring the cooperation of persons from otherwise different life-worlds. Note, however, that this rests on the regulative principle (moral principle) that we ought to construct common languages to formulate policy and resolve differences rather than resorting to the use of force. Arguments for these regulative principles are clearly beyond the scope of this paper. See *The Communicative Ethics Controversy*, ed. Seyla Benhabib and Fred Dallmayr (Cambridge, Mass.: MIT Press, 1990); Selya Benhabib, "The Generalized and Concrete Other," in her *Situating the Self: Gender, Community, and Postmodernism in Contemporary Ethics* (New York: Routledge, 1992), 148–77; Onora O'Neill, *Bounds of Justice* (Cambridge: Cambridge University Press, 2000). Specifically on the environment, see John S. Dryzek, "Green Reason: Communicative Ethics for the Biosphere," in *Postmodern Environmental Ethics*, ed. Max Oelschlaeger (Albany: State University of New York Press, 1995), 101–18; John Gray, *Isaiah Berlin* (Princeton, N.J.: Princeton University Press, 1996); Thomas Nagel, *The View from Nowhere* (New York: Oxford University Press, 1986).

6. A typical example of such secular policy discussion would be Arjun Makhijani and Kevin R. Gurney, *Mending the Ozone Hole: Science, Technology, and Policy* (Cambridge, Mass.: MIT Press, 1995).

7. I am not suggesting that we stop these discussions. It does seem to me, however, that a religious tradition committed to the concept of *tiqqun 'olam* (mending the world), must of necessity move beyond its own discussion of its traditions and find some way to seriously engage those who live in the world that needs mending.

8. Lynn White, Jr., "The Historic Roots of Our Ecologic Crisis," *Science* 155 (1967): 1203–7. On the theme of domination independent of biblical roots, cf. Eric

Katz, "The Call of the Wild: The Struggle against Domination and the Technological Fix of Nature," in *Postmodern Environmental Ethics*, ed. Max Oelschlaeger (Albany: State University of New York Press, 1995), 163–72; and Thomas H. Birch, "The Incarceration of Wildness: Wilderness Areas as Prisons," op. cit., 137–61. For a summary of approaches to the domination issue, see *Ecology*, ed. Carolyn Merchant (Atlantic Highlands, N.J.: Humanities Press, 1994), 1–25.

9. See the section entitled "New Sensibilities," in *Liberating Life: Contemporary Approaches to Ecological Theology*, ed. Charles Birch, William Eakin, and Jay B. McDaniel (Maryknoll, N.Y.: Orbis Books, 1991), 151–258. For a classic statement of the need for a new consciousness, including the insight that "secular" approaches may themselves have a built-in mythic dimension, see Thomas Berry, *The Dream of the Earth* (San Francisco, Calif.: Sierra Club Books, 1988), esp. 70–88. For a sympathetic presentation of the concept of "animist nature," see Christopher Manes, "Nature and Silence," in *Postmodern Environmental Ethics*, ed. Max Oelschlaeger (Albany: State University of New York Press, 1995), 43–56. On these themes see also Theodore Roszak, *The Voice of the Earth* (New York: Simon and Schuster, 1992); and Max Horkheimer and Theodor W. Adorno, *Dialectic of Enlightenment*, trans. John Cumming (New York: Herder and Herder, 1972).

10. By "discourse," I include the following: 1) the vocabulary and syntax of the language of environmental and ecological policy discussion; and 2) the rules of providing acceptable descriptions, making justified inferences, formulating argument, offering supporting evidence, and constructing compelling narratives and explanations.

Discourses are, then, roughly "coherent, self-referential bodies of statements that produce an account of reality by generating 'knowledge' about particular objects or concepts, and also by shaping the rules of what can be known and said about these entities"; Foucault's view as presented in *Columbia Dictionary of Modern Literary Cultural Criticism*, ed. Joseph Childers and Gary Hentzi (New York: Columbia University Press, 1995), s.v. Discourse.

11. Of course, all contemporary policy debates will involve Jews in ways that differ significantly from premodern, pre-emancipation involvement. We should not expect that there could be a general argument to the effect that Jewish sources will *always* find a point of entry into wider policy debates.

12. While remnants of earlier "sacred languages" are part of this secular talk, their effect is so minimal that nearly anyone, whatever their religious beliefs or lack of them, can easily join in the considerations; see above, n. 5.

13. While exact definition of these terms eludes us, it seems to me that their meaning is clear enough for our present purposes.

14. Historically, native speakers of this language do distinguish between the secular and the religious or sacred. For example, even in biblical texts, slaughtering a domestic animal at home is treated as significantly different from the sacrificial slaughtering of domestic animals as part of the Temple or Tabernacle service. As my own discussion will make clear, however, the discourse as a whole blends the two sorts of language.

15. The success of the program I am suggesting, as well as Judaism's ability to participate in addressing global environmental issues, rests with the production of

text-based studies that, at the very least, help bring important basic values or principles to ecological discussion and decision making.

16. Although not primarily a text concerned with ecological issues, the text's discussion clearly rejects "supernatural" modes of setting policy. Included in those "supernatural" modes are significant references to both natural and constructed environments. For our purposes, this is surely quite enough.

17. I grant that terming them "intrusions" reveals my own theoretical assumptions about text interpretation.

18. The requisite next step would be a detailed discussion of these limits and benefits.

19. The three sections of the Shema are, in the following order: Deuteronomy 6:4–9; Deuteronomy 11:13–21; and Numbers 15:37–41. Here I use the term to refer only to the second paragraph.

20. To stay within the rules of secular, scientific discourse, we may not appeal to inherited religious norms or text as sufficient justification for policy. This is not to say, however, that we should dispense with a belief in the connection between the practice of traditional Jewish ecological principles and the positive consequences attributed to such behavior. We need to note, however, that it is the ecological theory that is primary. It is the meaning and value of the Shema that is being interpreted, justified, and thus preserved by our belief in ecological theory, and not vice versa.

21. Jacob Neusner, *The Classics of Judaism* (Louisville, Ky.: Westminster John Knox Press, 1995).

22. The Hebrew words *"mashiv ha-ruah u-morid ha-geshem"* are inserted into the main prayer known as the Eighteen Benedictions.

23. R. Johanan further said: "Rain may fall even for the sake of an individual but sustenance [is granted] only for the sake of the many. . ." (Ta'anit 9b).

24. They cease only after the entire rainy season has passed without rainfall when, as we might have expected, rainfall is "a sign of divine anger."

25. I make no apology for adapting this profoundly insightful Kantian position to religious and sacred discourse. Although we ought not to equate sanctity and saintliness, we must nevertheless refuse to countenance as religiously obligatory policies that are morally wrong. While ethical acceptability is not a sufficient condition for an adequate religious or theological conception of the sacred, it certainly is a necessary one. For two, very different, interpretations of Kant that bear on the important relationships between goodness, fortune, religion, and social policy, see Allen W. Wood, *Kant's Moral Religion* (Ithaca, N.Y.: Cornell University Press, 1970); and Susan Neiman, *The Unity of Reason: Rereading Kant* (New York: Oxford University Press, 1994).

26. This is of a piece with the rabbinic style of deliberating about philosophical topics via the details of material culture. Here, the issue is the classic problem of the one and the many, or how to conceptualize the unity and plurality of beings or Being.

29. One example of exegetical rules—Alexandrian in origin—is found at the beginning of the Sifra and forms a part of the traditional daily morning service.

30. Although there is plenty of room for discussion of the historical record, I am prepared to grant that pre-rabbinic, essentially secular language may have existed. From the later rabbinic point of view, however, such secularized government lan-

guage was, in general, illegitimate. Since the language of the late rabbinic period eventually came to represent what we call Judaism, I think it is acceptable for our purposes here to speak of a rabbinic shift toward secularization.

31. Later authorities decide in favor of the rabbis, requiring primarily the *mazik* to take the precautions.

32. Even the rabbinic texts discussing the prohibition against cutting down fruit trees, *bal tashhit*, are primarily concerned with the impact this will have on human beings and not simply with preserving the environment. See B. Bava Kama 91b–92a as well as the medieval codification of these laws found in Maimonides, *Mishneh Torah*, Book of Judges, Laws of Kings, 6.8–6.10.

33. In contrast to rabbinic literature, social ecology pays direct attention to the ways that human socioeconomic structures influence how the environment is treated. Re-reading rabbinic texts with an eye to the questions of social ecology should, I believe, be both exciting and worthwhile. See Murray Bookchin, *Toward an Ecological Society* (Montreal: Black Rose Books, 1980). For a more politically oriented version, see Dimitrios I. Roussopoulos, *Political Ecology: Beyond Environmentalism* (Montreal: Black Rose Books, 1993).

34. Those to whom religious authenticity is of concern should note that, in operating in a secular environmental discourse, we would be doing no more than what the rabbis themselves are now seen to have done.

35. The Tosafot understand the seeming intrusion of this topic as connected to the Mishnah's reference to "seeds" from which one of the proposed "hole-blockers" grows. The text of the Gemara, however, says nothing about this subject when commenting on the Mishnah's "seeds" and instead waits to introduce it in the middle of the passage commenting on the word "urine." As a result, I must admit that I do not find their explanation particularly compelling.

36. One example of such an approach is the now classic work of Mary Douglas, *Purity and Danger: An Analysis of Concepts of Pollution and Taboo* (London: Routledge and Kegan Paul, 1966).

37. Death, certain venereal diseases, and menstruation are paradigmatic bodily conditions that create the state of being ritually impure (*tame*). In the case of discharges due to menstruation and venereal disease, the body "leaks" (loosens its boundaries) in a way that is beyond human control.

38. We can often avoid contact with conditions that communicate *tum'ah*. The control is only partial in the sense that, if only because of the ubiquity of death, we cannot avoid *tum'ah* entirely.

39. Although, again, this control is only partial. If the discharge does not stop, no ritual action will void the condition of being *tame*.

40. Although urinating does not make one *tame*, one must "clean up" after urination in order to pray or recite the Shema.

41. The continuation of the debate connecting cosmology to Jewish prayer practice only makes the textual move more particular to Judaism.

42. Within this talmudic chapter, then, we have an example of a discourse that seems to manage the use of both secular and religious language without merging them.

43. It is important to remember that imaginative utopian theorizing may play an

important role in policy discussion simply by allowing for possibilities not yet within the realm of "the practical." See Ernst Bloch, *The Principle of Hope,* trans. Neville Plaice, Stephen Plaice, and Paul Knight (Oxford: Blackwell, 1986); and Vincent Geoghegan, *Ernst Bloch* (London: Routledge, 1996). A version of this point may be made based on the openness in the meaning of general terms. See Saul A. Kripke, *Wittgenstein on Rules and Private Language* (Cambridge, Mass.: Harvard University Press, 1982).

44. Given the extended philosophical discussion on these matters, I grant that no hard and fast distinction can or should be made between the contexts of discovery, justification, and implementation. In my view, however, this need not imply that distinguishing between them is always a mistake. We simply need to be careful how we use the results of any such distinction.

45. This is enough, I believe, to justify a construal of Judaism that allows for the presence of an essentially secular discourse as part of a wider Jewish discourse that includes blended as well as almost exclusively sacred language. Of course, this is acceptable only if the relationship between the languages is appropriately explicit and fairly well regimented.

46. Note that I am not suggesting granting modern or rabbinic secular discourse a *logically* privileged position.

Appendix 1

If you will only heed His every commandment that I am commanding you today—loving the Lord your God, and serving Him with all your heart and with all your soul—then He will give the rain for your land in its season, the early rain and the later rain, and you will gather in your grain, your wine, and your oil; and He will give grass in your fields for your livestock, and you will eat your fill. Take care, or you will be seduced into turning away, serving other gods and worshiping them, for then the anger of the Lord will be kindled against you and He will shut up the heavens, so that there will be no rain and the land will yield no fruit; then you will perish quickly off the good land that the Lord is giving you. You shall put these words of mine in your heart and soul, and you shall bind them as a sign on your hand, and fix them as an emblem on your forehead. Teach them to your children, talking about them when you are at home and when you are away, when you lie down and when you rise. Write them on the doorposts of your house and on your gates, so that your days and the days of your children may be multiplied in the land that the Lord swore to your ancestors to give them, as long as the heavens are above the earth.

—NRS Deuteronomy 11:13–21

Appendix 2

We learnt elsewhere: If he cut it into separate tiles, placing sand between each tile: R. Eliezer declared it clean, and the Sages declared it unclean; and this was the oven of *Akhnai*.

It has been taught: On that day R. Eliezer brought forward every imaginable argument, but they did not accept them. Said he to them: "*If* the halakhah agrees with me, let this carob-tree prove it!" Thereupon the carob-tree was torn a hundred cubits out of its place, others affirm, four hundred cubits. "No proof can be brought from a carob-tree," they retorted. Again he said to them: "If the halakhah agrees with me, let the stream of water prove it!" Whereupon the stream of water flowed backwards. "No proof can be brought from a stream of water," they rejoined. Again he urged: "*If* the halakhah agrees with me, let the walls of the schoolhouse prove it," whereupon the walls inclined to fall. But R. Joshua rebuked them, saying: "When scholars are engaged in a halakhic dispute, what have ye to interfere?" Hence they did not fall, in honor of R. Joshua, nor did they resume the upright, in honor of R. Eliezer; and they are still standing thus inclined. Again he said to them: "*If* the halakhah agrees with me, let it be proved from Heaven!" Whereupon a Heavenly Voice cried out: "*Why* do ye dispute with R. Eliezer, seeing that in all matters the halakhah agrees with him!" But R. Joshua arose and exclaimed: "*It* is not in heaven."

What did he mean by this? Said R. Jeremiah: That the Torah had already been given at Mount Sinai; we pay no attention to a Heavenly Voice, because Thou hast long since written in the Torah at Mount Sinai, After the majority must one incline.

R. Nathan met Elijah and asked him: What did the Holy One, Blessed be He, do in which hour? He laughed [with joy], he replied, saying, "*My* sons have defeated Me, My sons have defeated Me." It was said: On that day all objects that R. Eliezer had declared clean were brought and burnt in fire.

—B. T. Bava Metzi'a 59a–b

Appendix 3

Mishnah—A man should not dig a pit [in his own field] close to the pit of his neighbor, nor a ditch nor a cave nor a water-channel nor a fuller's pool, unless he keeps them at least three handbreadths from his neighbor's wall and plasters [the sides].

A man should keep olive refuse, dung, salt, lime, and flint stones at least three handbreadths from his neighbor's wall or plaster it over. Seeds, plough furrows, and urine should be kept three handbreadths from the wall.

Mill stones should be kept three handbreadths away reckoning from the upper stone, that means four from the lower stone. An oven should be kept three handbreadths reckoning from the foot of the base, that means four from the top of the base.

Gemara—It has been stated: If a man desires to dig a pit close up to the boundary [between his field and his neighbor's]. Abaye says he may do so and Raba says he may not do so.

Now in a field where pits would naturally be dug, both agree that he may not dig close up. Where they differ is in the case of a field where pits would not naturally be dug; Abaye says he may dig, because it is not naturally a field for digging pits [and therefore his neighbor is not likely to want to dig one on the other side], while Raba says he may not dig; because his neighbor can say to him, "Just as you have altered your mind and want to dig, so I may alter my mind and want to dig."

Others report [this argument as follows]: In the case of a field where pits would not naturally be dug, both [Abaye and Raba] agree that he may dig close up to the boundary. Where they differ is in the case of a field where pits would naturally be dug.

Abaye says that in such a field the owner may dig, and would be allowed to dig even by the Rabbis who lay down that a tree must not be planted within twenty-five cubits of a pit; for they only rule this because at the time of planting the pit already exists, but here when the man comes to dig the pit there is no pit on the other side.

Raba on the other hand says that he may not dig, and would not be allowed to dig even by R. Jose, who laid down that [in all circumstances] the one owner can plant within his property and the other dig within his; for he only rules thus because at the time when the former plants, there are as yet no roots that could damage the pit, but in this case the owner of the other field can say to the man who wants to dig the pit, "Every stroke with the spade that you make injures my ground."

Seeds, plough furrows, and urine should be kept three handbreadths from the wall. The reason is that there is a wall, but if there is no wall he may bring these things close up to the boundary?—No; even if there is no wall he may not bring them close up. What then does the mention of the wall here tell us?—It tells us that moist things are bad for a wall.

And plaster the sides. The question was raised: Is the proper reading of the Mishnah "and plaster" or "or plaster"?—Obviously "and plaster" is the proper reading, for if the Mishnah meant to say "or," then the first two clauses could have been run into one. But possibly ["or" is after all the right reading, and the reason why the two clauses are not combined is because] they are not in the same category. The damage in one case arising from moisture and in the other from steam?

Come and hear: R. Judah says. If there is crumbling rock between the two properties, each owner can dig a pit on his own side and each must keep away from the boundary three handbreadths and plaster his pit. The reason is [is it not,] that the soil between is crumbling, but otherwise there is no need to plaster?—No. This is the rule even if the soil is not crumbling; he still has to plaster. The case of crumbling soil, however, is specified, because otherwise I might have thought that with crumbling soil a greater distance still was required. Now he teaches us [that this is not so].

—Selected from Bava Batra 17a–17b1;18a; 19a.
The Mishnah text is in italics.

Appendix 4

And urine must be removed three handbreadths, etc. Rabbah b. Bar Hana said: It is permissible for a man to make water on the side of another man's wall, as it is written, And I will cut off from Ahab one that pisseth against the wall and him that is shut up and him that is left at large in Israel.

But did we not learn, *urine must be kept three handbreadths from the wall?*—This refers to slop water.

Come and hear: A man should not make water on the side of another man's wall, but should keep three handbreadths away. This is the rule for a wall of brick, but if the wall is of stone, he need keep away only so far as not to do any damage. How much is this? A handbreadth. If the wall is of hard stone, it is permitted. Does not this refute the dictum of Rabbah b. Bar Hana?—It does. But Rabba b. Bar Hana based himself on the Scripture?—The meaning of the verse is this: "Even a creature whose way is to piss against a wall I will not leave him." And what is this? A dog.

R. Tobi b. Kisna said in the name of Samuel: A thin wafer does not narrow a window space. [Note from the Soncino translation: If a dead body is in a room between that and an adjoining room there is an opening of a handbreadth square or more, the uncleanness spreads to the adjoining room unless the opening is reduced to the dimension of less than a handbreadth square by means of something that is not useful for any other purpose.]

Why a thin one? The same can be said even of a thick one?—The Rabbi gave an extreme instance. It goes without saying in the case of a thick cake that since it is fit for food the owner does not mentally ignore its existence, [and therefore it does not narrow the window space]; but with a thin one, since it soon becomes uneatable, I might think that he does ignore its existence. Therefore R. Tobi tells us [that even a thin cake does not narrow the window space. . . .

—Excerpted from a longer discussion found in Bava Batra 19b–20b. The Mishnah text is in italics.

Appendix 5

Mishnah—Carrion, graves, and tanyards must be kept fifty cubits from a town, a tanyard must only be placed on the east side of the town. R. Akiba, however, says it may be placed on any side except the west, providing it is kept fifty cubits away.

Flaxwater must be kept away from vegetables and leeks from onions and mustard plants from a beehive. R. Jose, however, declares it permissible [to come nearer] in the case of mustard.

Gemara—The question was asked: How are we to understand R. Akiba's ruling? [Does he mean to say that] *It* [a tanyard] *may be placed on any side*, namely, be set close to the city, *except on the west*, where also it may be set, but only at a distance of fifty cubits? Or [to say that] *it may be placed on any side . . . providing it is kept fifty cubits away, except on the west,* where it must not be placed at all?

Come and hear: R. Akiba says: [A tanyard] may be set on any side at a distance of fifty cubits, save on the west side, where it must not be placed at all, because it is a constant abode.

Said Raba to R. Nahman: A constant abode of what? Shall I say of winds? How can this be, seeing that R. Hana b. Abba has said in the name of Rab: Four winds blow every day and the north wind with all of them, for without this the world could not endure a moment. The south wind is the most violent, and were it not that the Son of the Hawk stays it with his wings it would destroy the world, as it says, Doth the hawk soar by the wisdom, and stretch her wings towards the south?

No; what it means is that it is the constant abode of the *Shekhinah.* For so said Joshua b. Levi: Let us be grateful to our ancestors for showing us the place of prayer, as it is written, And the host of heaven worshipeth thee.

R. Aha bar Jacob strongly demurred to this [interpretation]. Perhaps, he said, [the sun and moon bow down to the east], like a servant who has received a gratuity from his master and retires backwards, bowing as he goes. This [indeed] is a difficulty.

R. Oshaia expressed the opinion that the *Shekhinah* is in every place. For R. Oshaia said: What is the meaning of the verse, Thou art the Lord, even thou alone; thou hast made heaven, the heaven of heavens, etc.? Thy messengers are not like the messengers of flesh and blood. Messengers of flesh and blood report themselves [after performing their office] to the place from that they have been sent, but thy messengers report themselves to the place to which they are sent, as it says. Canst thou send forth lightnings that they may go and say to thee, "here we are." It does not say, "that they may come and say," but "that they may go and say," that shows that the *Shekhinah* is in all places. R. Ishmael also held that the *Shekhinah* is in all places,

R. Judah said: What is the meaning of the verse, My doctrine shall drop [*ya'arof*] as the rain? This refers to the west wind that comes from the back ['*oref*] of the world. My speech shall distill [*tizzal*] as the dew' this is the north wind that makes gold flow and so it says: Who lavish [*ha-zalim*] gold from the purse. As the small rain [*se'irim*] upon the tender grass: this is the east wind that rages through the world like a demon [*sa'ir*]. And as showers upon the herb: this is the south wind that brings up showers and causes the grass to grow.

It has been taught: R. Eliezer says that the world is like an exedra and the north side is not enclosed, and so when the sun reaches the northwest corner, it bends back and returns [to the east] above the firmament.

R. Joshua, however, says that the world is like a tent, and the north side is enclosed, and when the sun reaches the northwest corner it goes round at the back of the tent [till it reaches the east], as it says. It goeth toward the south and turneth again toward the north, etc. "it goes toward the south"—by day, and "turneth again toward the north"—by night. It turneth about continually in its course and the wind returneth again to its circuits: this refers to the eastern and western sides of the heaven, that the sun sometimes traverses and sometimes goes round.

He [R. Joshua] used to say: We have come round to the view of R. Eliezer, [since we have learnt]: "Out of the chamber cometh the storm: this is the south wind; and from the scatterers cold: this is the north wind. By the breath of God ice is given: this is the west wind: and the abundance of waters in the down pouring: this is the east wind."

But it has just been stated by a Master that it is the south wind that brings showers and makes the grass grow?—There is no contradiction; when the rain falls gently [it is from the south], and when it falls heavily [it is from the east.] R. Hisda said: What is meant by the verse, Out of the north cometh gold? This refers to the north wind that makes gold flow; and so it says: Who lavish [*ha-zalim*] gold from the purse.

R. Isaac said: He who desires to become wise should turn to the south [when praying], and he who desires to become rich should turn to the north. The symbol [by which to remember this] is that the table [in the Tabenacle] was to the north of the altar and the candlestick to the south. R. Joshua b. Levi, however, said that he should always turn to the south, because through obtaining wisdom he will obtain wealth, as it says. Length of days is in her [wisdom's] right hand, in her left hand are riches and honor. But was it not R. Joshuah b. Levi who said that the *Shekhinah* is in the west?—[He means that] one should turn partly to the south.

—Excerpted from Bava Batra 25a–25b.

The Mishnah text is in italics.

Jewish Environmentalism:
Past Accomplishments and Future Challenges

MARK X. JACOBS

W hat role do Jewish conceptions of nature, the spiritual and legal obligations required by Judaism, or Jewish understandings of the place and purpose of the human being play in the emergence of "Jewish environmentalism"?[1] Does "Jewish environmentalism" contribute to addressing the global ecological crisis? And, if it does, what is the role of Jewish concepts in shaping and propelling that contribution?

The answers to these questions are emerging as self-conscious Jewish engagements with environmental challenges develop and mature. In this essay, I will attempt to describe the motivations and activities of the increasing number of Jewish individuals and institutions working to address local, national, and even global environmental problems through efforts that are rooted self-consciously in a Jewish approach to ecology and/or take place in a Jewish setting and context. I also will share some thoughts on what I believe Jewish environmentalism has accomplished and will reflect on its future.

I offer the following report and reflections as a participant-observer in the "Jewish environmental movement." For the past eight years, I have served as executive director of the Coalition on the Environment and Jewish Life, a national organization embracing twenty-nine national Jewish organizations and thirteen regional affiliates and dedicated to engaging Jewish individuals and institutions in environmental education, action, and advocacy rooted in a Jewish vision of ecological responsibility. Outside of a brief description of Jewish environmental activities in Israel and England, the description and analysis presented should be considered as applying only to North American Jewish environmentalism.

A Brief History of Jewish Environmentalism

Contemporary Jewish environmentalism can be seen as having four "stages," though the major project of each stage remains unfinished and actively continues. Beginning as a discovery and defense of Judaism's environmental credentials in the late 1960s, Jewish environmentalism has emerged in the past decade as a significant development in American Jewish life that engages thousands of grassroots activists, hundreds of congregations, and the most senior American Jewish leaders.

Defense and Inquiry

The first signs of a Jewish response to environmental issues were articles written in the late 1960s defending Judaism against accusations that the Judeo-Christian tradition is responsible for Western society's destruction of nature. The most discussed source of this accusation was the now famous article by Lynn White, Jr., "The Historical Roots of Our Ecologic Crisis."[2] In response, scholars from across the denominational spectrum sought to establish Judaism's environmental credentials by citing various texts that called for or alluded to the need for human action to preserve the environment.[3]

In the early 1970s, the defensive presentation of traditional Judaism's conception of and relationship to the environment evolved into a wide-ranging inquiry into how Jewish sources conceive of the relationship between humankind and nonhuman nature as well as the implications of Jewish law for contemporary environmental issues.[4] During this time, the biblical and talmudic moorings for the articulation of a Jewish environmental ethic were uncovered, as were theological and philosophical writings by Martin Buber, Abraham Joshua Heschel, Nahman of Bratslav, and others that dealt explicitly with the spiritual relationship between humankind and nature. Through the publication of articles in Jewish studies journals, environmental studies journals, anthologies, and popular publications, a rich array of Jewish perspectives on the environment and nature became available to the broader Jewish public.

Some writers focused exclusively on the environmental benefits of various biblical practices, halakhot (laws), and talmudic principles. Others wrote imaginatively about the application of various Jewish ideas and practices to contemporary ecological and economic circumstances. Among the most imaginative has been Rabbi Arthur Waskow, who published articles suggesting the adaptation of the Sabbath, sabbatical year (*shmitah*), and jubilee *(yovel)* to contemporary society as a way to enforce cessation of economic activity and promote reflection concerning the effects of our work and economy on the earth and each other.[5] Waskow's writings on the environment captured the imagination of many who have since become involved in Jewish environmentalism as an effort to effect broad social and environmental change. The most widespread popularization of Waskow's ideas has been through *Seasons of Our Joy: A Modern Guide to the Jewish Holidays,* in which he integrated environmental awareness into Jewish observances.[6]

Grassroots Awakening and Foundation Building

Beginning in the late 1960s, in the context of an emerging environmental movement in the United States, a small number of Jewish individuals and institutions across North America began to think about and act on the connections they saw among the Jewish tradition, contemporary Jewish life, and environmental problems. While some of this thinking and action was inspired by articles on Judaism and the environment, much, perhaps even most, of it emerged independently and simultaneously. As American society began to grapple with the environmental crisis, Jews did so self-consciously in the context of their religious beliefs and practices.

Two efforts organized in the early 1970s linked nature and Judaism. "Trees for Vietnam" was organized by Washington, D.C., area Jewish activist Mike Tabor to raise money from Jews to refoliate areas of both North and South Vietnam that had been defoliated by U.S. government use of Agent Orange. This effort gained the support of prominent rabbis who opposed the war, including Abraham Joshua

Heschel and Shlomo Carlebach. In 1972, Tabor and several friends created on the outskirts of Washington, D.C., an intentional rural Jewish community, which they referred to as a "Diaspora kibbutz." Though environment was not an explicit concern, exploration of the connections between nature, Judaism, and spirituality was a strong feature of the community's culture. Other Jews active in exploring the connection between nature and Judaism at this time included Rabbi Everett Gendler, who integrated farming and gardening into the observances of Jewish festivals at his rural Massachusetts congregation.

It was not until 1988 that the first Jewish environmental organization, Shomrei Adamah—Keepers of the Earth, was founded by Ellen Bernstein. A former river rafting guide in Colorado, Bernstein reconnected with Judaism while in a graduate program in environmental studies at the University of California, Berkeley. She described her experiences and motivations in the introduction to *Ecology and the Jewish Spirit: Where Nature and the Sacred Meet*:

> . . . I was convinced that the spiritual and ecological dimension that I discovered for myself had the potential to enrich Judaism and provide meaning for my generation and those to come. . . . In 1998 . . . I founded *Shomrei Adamah*—Keepers of the Earth, the first organization dedicated to cultivating the ecological thinking and practices that are integral to Jewish life. With the input of many Jewish scholars, teachers, and rabbis around the country, *Shomrei Adamah* developed programs, publications, and curricula to illuminate Jewish ecological values and enhance Jewish spirituality.[7]

Bernstein succeeded in interesting a number of Jewish and environmental foundations in creating a Jewish environmental organization through which a new idea in Jewish life—Jewish environmentalism— could be introduced to American Jews and Jewish institutions. Shomrei Adamah's publications[8] brought Jewish environmental ideas into many synagogues and Jewish classrooms for the first time.

Bernstein and her colleagues popularized the idea of Jewish environmentalism through speaking engagements at both Jewish and environmental conferences and institutions, as well as through stories in the Anglo-Jewish and secular media, including National Public Radio. Bernstein focused considerable effort on the revival and elaboration of a *seder* (ritual meal) for the minor Jewish holiday of Tu B'Shvat, the New Year of the Trees. Shomrei Adamah succeeded in popularizing this holiday and the celebration of it with a focus on environmentalism. Shomrei Adamah also organized wilderness trips with a strong Jewish component. Through its publications and programs, approximately three thousand people became supporters of Shomrei Adamah.

In over a dozen communities, interested individuals formed local chapters of Shomrei Adamah to promote Jewish environmentalism. In 1989, Tabor, then an organic farmer on the land that had once been the Diaspora Kibbutz, heard Bernstein speak at the P'nai Ohr Kallah (a Jewish renewal conference) and was inspired to create a local effort. Tabor worked with De Herman, Rabbi Barry Schwartz, and Rabbi Warren Stone to establish Shomrei Adamah of Greater Washington, a community-based education and organizing effort. Though grassroots interest was growing, national Shomrei Adamah did not have the staff to support chapters effectively and instead focused its efforts on publications and outreach to rabbis and Jewish educators, rather than on grassroots action-oriented organizing. All of the chapters soon ceased functioning, with the exception of Shomrei Adamah of Greater Washington, which still continues as an independent organization.

In 1995, Bernstein, who was the central driving force of Shomrei Adamah, decided to move on to other projects. Without someone prepared to step into her role, Shomrei Adamah could not continue to operate. The name of the organization was franchised to Surprise Lake Camp, which was creating Jewish environmental education programs based in part on the Shomrei Adamah curricula. Surprise Lake Camp is the host of the Teva Learning Center, which began in 1994 as a pilot project funded by the UJA Federation of New York to create a residential Jewish environmental education program for Jewish day school students. By 2001, this program was providing multiday Jewish environmental outdoor education programs to approximately fifteen hundred students a year.

At the same time Bernstein was creating Shomrei Adamah, Arthur Waskow began to promote Jewish environmental activism through the Shalom Center, an organization that until that time had been focused primarily on building Jewish support for a nuclear weapons freeze. Waskow's environmental organizing focused attention on fossil fuel consumption and the notion of "eco-kashrut," evaluating the appropriateness of products for Jewish consumption based on their environmental and social costs.[9]

By 1992, through independent local initiative and the pioneering work of Shomrei Adamah and the Shalom Center, a Jewish approach to environmental education and issues in North America had grown from a rather obscure topic addressed in Jewish studies and environmental studies journals into a varied landscape of grassroots interest and initiative.

Substantial Jewish responses to environmental issues also have taken form in England and in Israel, where there is acute air, water, and land pollution and increasingly severe water scarcity. Israeli environmental organizations have been secular in orientation, connecting environmental preservation to knowledge and love of the land of Israel and its history but not generally making a connection between environmentalism and Jewish religious tradition. Though there is slowly increasing attention to the environment in a range of religious communities in Israel, the only sustained effort (to my knowledge) to stimulate consideration of environmental issues from the perspective of Jewish tradition and history is the Heschel Center for Environmental Learning and Leadership, founded in 1998 by American émigré Eilon Schwartz.[10] The Heschel Center has established *"Le'ovda U'Leshomra": The Israeli Forum on the Environment in Judaism,* through which leaders of Israeli religious movements, particularly those associated with the National Religious Party, engage in both discussion and project planning. The forum organized a conference in 2001 in collaboration with Bar Ilan University's Center for Jewish Identity, the Ministry of Education, and Jerusalem's Mila Institute and held under the auspices of the then Minister of the Environment Dalia Itzik and Chief Rabbi Eliyahu Bakshi Doron. The forum is currently focusing efforts on teacher training and the development of new models for integrating Jewish environmental perspectives into the national religious school system. In addition, the Heschel Center has worked to create a critical discourse about Zionism's view of land and development, critiquing the traditional focus on industrial development that remains present in some Zionist thought.

Jewish environmentalism has taken root in the United Kingdom as well. The United Kingdom Reform synagogue began addressing environmental issues in 1998, and British Jewish leaders were among seven religious groups that testified to the All-Party Committee of Lords and Commons on Conservation that same year.[11] A volume entitled *Judaism and Ecology* was published in England in 1992.[12] In the late 1990s, activists founded The Noah Project, an organization dedicated to integrating Jewish environmental education and action into British Jewish life.

Engaging Leadership

The earliest engagement of national Jewish leadership on environmental issues emerged from concerns about the implications of Arab oil embargoes for the U.S.—Israel relationship. Once a policy favoring increasing U.S. energy independence was adopted, a debate began about how best to achieve it. Major Conservative Jewish organizations, including United Synagogue, the Rabbinical Assembly, and the Women's League for Conservative Judaism, began adopting resolutions in the mid-1970s calling for energy conservation, followed by resolutions calling for recycling. Yet it was not until 1991 that these and other major Jewish organizations articulated broad concern about the environment. In the Reform movement, the Union of American Hebrew Congregations (UAHC) and its large Washington operation, the Religious Action Center of Reform Judaism (RAC), first called for the conservation of natural resources in 1965, followed by resolutions on environmental pollution in 1969 and environmentally sound energy policy in 1979. In 1991, the UAHC adopted a comprehensive resolution statement calling for protection of endangered species and wilderness areas and the protection of air, land, water, and people from pollution; the resolution also focused attention on the disproportionate impact of pollution on poor and minority communities. In a similar pattern, beginning in the mid-1980s, the consensus-building body for national and local Jewish public affairs agencies, the National Jewish Community Relations Advisory Council (NJCRAC), adopted positions on energy policy favoring increased conservation and increased production of both fossil fuel sources and environmentally safe alternatives. Again, it was not until 1991 that the NJCRAC considered a wide range of environmental issues and adopted positions both to set environmental standards for increased oil production and nuclear plants and to support protection of the environment more broadly.

The broad consideration of environmental issues in national Jewish organizations coincided with the participation of senior American

Jewish leaders in a series of interfaith meetings on religion and the environment that began in 1990. These meetings were organized by Paul Gorman (the director of advocacy at the Cathedral of St. John the Divine in New York City) in collaboration with cosmologist Carl Sagan and then-Senator Al Gore, Jr. In 1990, Sagan organized an open letter to the religious leaders, signed by thirty-two Nobel laureates expressing doubts about the sufficiency of the response to the earth's environmental crisis up to that time and calling for engagement by religious communities:

> Many of us have had profound experiences of awe and reverence before the universe. We recognize that what is regarded as sacred is most likely to be treated with respect. Efforts to safeguard the planetary environment need to be infused with a vision of the sacred and [considered] as a universal moral priority.

This letter was presented at the January 1990 meeting of the Global Forum of Spiritual and Parliamentary Leaders in Moscow. Two hundred and seventy-one well-known spiritual leaders from eighty-three countries signed their names to an urgent appeal based on the letter, "Preserving and Cherishing the Earth: An Appeal for Joint Commitment in Science and Religion."

Consultations with scientists, economists, and public policy experts enabled senior Catholic, Jewish, mainline Protestant, and evangelical Christian leaders to learn about the environmental challenge and to begin to present public reflections on environmental protection from the perspective of their particular faith tradition. Through these meetings, a consensus emerged that the crisis in relationship between humankind and creation is intrinsically related to religious obligations and spiritual life and that it requires a response both theological and practical from faith communities. In addition to Gorman, the major organizers of this effort in the Jewish community were: Rabbi Steven Shaw, then director of community education of the Jewish Theological Seminary of America (JTS); Dr. John Ruskay, then vice chancellor of JTS; Rabbi David Saperstein, director of the Religious Action Center of Reform Judaism (RAC); and Jerome Chanes, then director of domestic concerns of the NJCRAC.

On 11–12 March 1992, senior Catholic, Jewish, mainline Protestant, and evangelical Christian leaders met in Washington, D.C., to establish a framework for a collaborative environmental initiative across the major faith communities in the United States. Present were the leadership of the major organizations of American Jewish life, eminent rabbis, denominational presidents, and Jewish U.S. senators.[13] Non-Jewish participants included: The Most Reverend Edmond Browning, Presiding Bishop of the Episcopal Church of America; Bishop James Malone, Chair of the Domestic Policy Committee of the U.S. Catholic Conference; Dr. Roberta Hestenes, President of Eastern College and World Vision International; and His Eminence Archbishop Iakovos, Primate, Greek Orthodox Church. At that event, the Jewish leaders issued a statement "to inaugurate a unified Jewish response to the environmental crisis":

> We, American Jews of every denomination, from diverse organizations and differing political perspectives, are united in deep concern that the quality of human life and the earth we inhabit are in danger, afflicted by rapidly increasing ecological threats. . . .
>
> For Jews, the environmental crisis is a religious challenge. As heirs to a tradition of stewardship that goes back to Genesis and that teaches us to be partners in the ongoing work of Creation, we cannot accept the escalating destruction of our environment and its effect on human health and livelihood. Where we are despoiling our air, land, and water, it is our sacred duty as Jews to acknowledge our God-given responsibility and take action to alleviate environmental degradation and the pain and suffering that it causes. . . .
>
> . . . We pledge to carry to our homes, communities, congregations, and workplaces the urgent message that air, land, water and living creatures are endangered. We will draw our people's attention to the timeless texts that speak to us of God's gifts and expectations. . . .
>
> Our agenda is already overflowing. . . . But the ecological crisis hovers over all Jewish concerns, for the threat is global, advancing, and ultimately jeopardizes ecological balance and the quality of life. It is imperative, then, that environmental issues also become an immediate, ongoing and pressing concern for our community.

At that gathering, the National Religious Partnership for the Environment was established and charged with creating environmental initiatives within each of the four faith communities. The Jewish initiative was named the Coalition on the Environment and Jewish Life (COEJL). Environmental offices were created within the National Council of Churches, representing thirty-seven mainline Protestant, African American, and Orthodox denominations, and the U.S. Catholic Conference, representing the Catholic Bishops. The evangelical Christian initiative, created by evangelical social action and development organizations, was named the Evangelical Environmental Network.

Soon after its establishment, COEJL recruited twenty-two national Jewish organizations from across the spectrum of Jewish religious and communal life to join the coalition. COEJL's office was established at the American Jewish community's consensus-building and coordination body for public affairs, the National Jewish Community Relations Advisory Council, which has since changed its name to the Jewish Council for Public Affairs (JCPA). As director of COEJL, I have staffed the environmental committee of the JCPA, which since 1994 has adopted a wide range of consensus positions on environmental health and justice, climate change, and biodiversity. Through this process, hundreds of Jewish leaders and institutions have been exposed to and have engaged in discussion of environmental policy. Since 1993, COEJL also has maintained a Washington, D.C., office based at the Religious Action Center, enabling COEJL to participate actively in environmental advocacy coalitions.

During the 1990s, numerous scholars of Judaism were engaged in thinking about the environment by attending conferences and meetings on Judaism and ecology organized on behalf of COEJL by Rabbi Steven Shaw of JTS. The most comprehensive of these was the "Consultation on the Development of a Jewish Philosophy of the Natural World," held in upstate New York in May 1994. Shaw was the primary source of energy and imagination for bringing together Jewish philosophers, ethicists, theologians, and historians with environmental philosophers, ecologists, and writers.

Despite the involvement and imprimatur of senior leaders and the establishment of COEJL, many leaders within the Jewish community continued to question whether environment was a "Jewish issue"—an issue that required a distinctively Jewish response. This debate took place in the context of long-standing differences of opinion among Jewish leaders, movements, and institutions concerning the nature of "Jewish issues." For some, only issues that distinctly affect Jews—such as antisemitism, U.S. support of the State of Israel, separation of church and state, and federal funding programs that affect Jewish human service organizations—ought be considered "Jewish issues." It appears that this position is more widely held among organizational leaders than the general Jewish public. Others have long considered economic justice, labor issues, public education, social welfare, and other "social justice" and equity issues "Jewish issues." Indeed, American Jews and their institutions have a long and distinguished history of leadership in the labor and civil rights movements; this is so much the case that a recent survey reported that 75 percent of Jews agree with the statement that "social justice commitment is at the heart of Judaism," and 47 percent of Jews consider commitment to social equality "most important" to their "Jewish identity (24 percent identified religious observance and 13 percent identified support for Israel as most important).[14]

In most quarters, the environment is now considered an appropriate issue for Jewish concern. As a result, support for Jewish environmental education and action programs is increasingly widespread. There remains very limited, but influential, opposition to public Jewish action to address environmental challenges, particularly among two groups: community lay leadership, who often have business interests that conflict with an environmental agenda; and leaders who believe that the Jewish community should expend its resources and political capital on parochial issues of paramount concern to the Jewish community. Much of the growing support among Jewish leaders for a Jewish environmental program is a result of the capacity of environmental programs to involve Jews who might otherwise not be involved in Jewish communal life. This motivation, and others for supporting Jewish environmentalism, will be discussed in the next section.

Movement Building

COEJL, which began operating in late 1993, was the first organization established to integrate broadly environmental education, action, and policy advocacy into the fabric of Jewish organizational life. Building upon the foundation prepared by Shomrei Adamah, the Shalom Center, the many spontaneous grassroots Jewish environmental efforts, and the support of senior Jewish leaders and major institutions, COEJL began in 1995 to systematically organize a grassroots national Jewish environmental movement. Through leadership development, small program grants, print and electronic communications, national conferences, and regional affiliates, COEJL dramatically expanded

the number of individuals and institutions interested and active in
Jewish environmentalism. Furthermore, COEJL helped grassroots activists define themselves as "Jewish environmental leaders" and provided them training and support to organize environmental programs
and action within their communities. Importantly, COEJL provided
legitimacy to Jewish environmentalists who could demonstrate to local leaders that national leadership and institutions supported COEJL
and the mission of Jewish environmentalism.

COEJL's distribution of Jewish environmental education and action materials to virtually every grassroots Jewish organization in
North America[15] and its presentations at national Jewish conferences
created a general awareness of Jewish environmentalism among rabbis, educators, and other Jewish professionals. National issue campaigns built a sense of collective Jewish effort to accomplish specific
environmental protection objectives. The first, in 1995, linked Tu
B'Shvat to the protection of forests by way of reducing the consumption of forest products, recycling, and public policy advocacy to protect national forests in the United States. By writing letters with a
Jewish rationale for forest protection to members of Congress, Jewish
activists participated self-consciously and publicly as Jews in a na-
tionwide effort to oppose a congressional attempt to increase access
of timber interests to national forests. Launched in 1996, the second
campaign, *Operation Noah: Defending God's Endangered Species
and Habitats*, engaged schools, synagogues, other institutions, and individuals in learning about biodiversity, through hands-on actions to
protect biodiversity by restoring habitats and defending the federal
Endangered Species Act (ESA) through letter writing.[16] COEJL's effort played a complementary role to the successful work of the Evangelical Environmental Network in defining protection of endangered
species as a religious issue and defeating a move in Congress to gut
the ESA. This was the first time that religious involvement in a particular environmental issue was both widely broadcast through the
media and credited with a concrete legislative outcome.

In addition to organizing national campaigns, COEJL sought out
and assembled individuals who were providing leadership to Jewish
environmental efforts through national networking and training conferences. The first gathering of this kind, a "Leadership Retreat for
Jewish Environmental Educators and Activists," brought together sev-
enty-five individuals at a camp in Pennsylvania in May 1995. Many of

these individuals—Jewish educators, rabbis, and activists from around North America and from across the spectrum of Jewish observance—had heard of each other but had never met. For many, this event broke a painful and long-standing isolation. Through various networking programs, most importantly the annual Mark and Sharon Bloome Jewish Environmental Leadership Training Institute (beginning in 1997), COEJL has created a network of over three hundred self-identified Jewish environmental activists in thirty states. In thirteen communities, activists have worked with COEJL to establish COEJL regional affiliates to implement grassroots education and action programs which have involved thousands, perhaps tens of thousands, of individuals.

There are three primary arenas of activity that have emerged within Jewish environmentalism: education, community building, and activism. In the arena of education, a number of independent Jewish environmental education organizations have been established since 1996 to provide programs for day-school, religious-school, and college students, as well as for families. Prominent among these are the Teva Learning Center in New York; the Shalom Nature Center in Malibu, California, the project of a Jewish Community Center camp; and the Jewish Nature Center, a project organized by Dr. Gabriel Goldman—a leading Jewish environmental innovator—through the New Jersey YMHA. These organizations focus on integrating Jewish study with experiences of the natural world, and there is much overlap in staff and curricula among them. They were created and are led by highly dedicated individuals who have been trained in outdoor and environmental education—many of them in their twenties and early thirties. In addition to direct programming, these organizations, along with COEJL and its regional affiliates, conduct in-service training programs for Jewish educators and publish curricula. This has enabled many other institutions to incorporate elements of Jewish environmental and outdoor education into their existing programs.

Community building is the primary goal of many of the programs organized by COEJL regional affiliates, numerous grassroots institutions, and chapters of Mosaic Outdoor Clubs of America—a Jewish outdoor club with twenty-one chapters. Such programs provide opportunities for Jews with an interest in the environment to meet each other and have common experiences—including hikes, Tu B'Shvat seders and other holiday celebrations with an environmental theme, retreats, "eco-Shabbat" dinners, lecture series, and Shabbat programs in the backcountry. Such programs have been organized in collaboration with hundreds of synagogues, Jewish community centers, federations, campus Hillel foundations, youth groups, camps, and Jewish public affairs organizations. Many of the individuals who organize and attend such programs have previously felt a separation between their "environmentalism" and their "Jewish lives" that is bridged through Jewish environmentalism. Many of these individuals find a "Jewish home" through Jewish environmental associations and groups.[17]

Jewish environmental action and advocacy efforts have been organized by COEJL and its regional affiliates, the Shalom Center, and a handful of grassroots groups. Such efforts include mobilizing Jewish leaders, individuals, and institutions to speak out concerning various environmental policy issues. COEJL has built a network of activists and a communications infrastructure through which it educates and mobilizes thousands of individuals on such issues as forest protection, biodiversity, global climate change, and energy policy. This work is supported by a small national staff that monitors public policy, works with national Jewish organizations (primarily the Jewish Council for Public Affairs, Union of American Hebrew Congregations, Rabbinical Assembly, United Synagogue for Conservative Judaism, and Central Conference of American Rabbis) to develop positions on those issues, and mobilizes both national institutions and a grassroots network to respond to those issues. In the area of global climate change, COEJL has collaborated with the National Council of Churches since 1998 to establish Interfaith Global Climate Change Campaigns in twenty-one states. In its public policy work, COEJL complements grassroots mobilization with national leadership statements, meetings with policy makers in Washington, D.C., and outreach to print and broadcast media.

Though most Jewish environmental activists pursue their efforts through COEJL, there have been action campaigns organized independently, often with the support of Arthur Waskow and the Shalom Center. Most prominent among these was an effort to protect the Headwaters redwood forest by appealing to the CEO of the company that held the forest, Charles Hurwitz, on the basis of his Jewish affiliation and Jewish values. The campaign, led by student-rabbi Naomi Steinberg—who, along with two other local rabbis, became known as a "Redwood Rabbi"—organized a Tu B'Shvat seder in 1997 that drew over 250 people to the remote forest on the California coast. Some participants trespassed onto the forest and planted redwood seedlings on an eroding bank stream to symbolize hope for the ecological restoration of already degraded land. The following summer, a hike in the forest was organized on Tisha B'Av, a traditional day of fasting and mourning for the destruction of the Temples in Jerusalem. These two observances represent a form of "ritual protest" pioneered and advocated by Arthur Waskow. These kinds of events are deeply moving and compelling for some Jewish environmentalists and alienating—even offensive—to others. More traditional forms of protest, such as letters from rabbis and presentations at stockholder meetings, were also used as tactics. Though the campaign garnered much attention—even Vice President Al Gore mentioned the "Redwood Rabbis" in a speech—it did not succeed in moving the CEO Charles Hurwitz.[18]

The issue that has most galvanized grassroots Jewish support has been forest protection. If one considers the role of trees in Jewish life—the symbolism of trees in the Bible and Jewish mystical texts; the celebration of Tu B'Shvat, the new year of the trees; and the century-long effort of the Jewish National Fund to raise money to plant trees in Israel—the resonance of forest protection is not a surprise.

In addition to action on public issues, Jewish environmentalists have mobilized Jewish participation in local ecological restoration and habitat protection efforts, worked to make synagogues and other Jewish facilities more environmentally sound, and promoted home-based environmental action in the form of recycling and conservation. In some institutions and communities, such efforts have become a regular part of Jewish life and institutional management. In most, however, environmental action and responsibility is not yet integrated into Jewish life.

It is the goal of the Jewish environmental movement to engage all Jewish institutions and their members both in becoming environmentally responsible in their own practices and in using their political and financial power to further the cause of environmental protection.

The Character of Jewish Environmentalism

Jewish environmentalists come from the full spectrum of religious observance, from secular to strictly orthodox. A survey of the COEJL mailing list in 1999 indicates that most activists are affiliated with the

more religiously liberal movements in Jewish life, with the majority
affiliated with the Conservative and Reform movements.[19] Active
Jewish environmentalists include children and seniors alike, though
an unusually large (for the Jewish community) number of leaders of
grassroots groups and organizations are in their twenties. Jewish environmental activists live in every region of North America, but are disproportionately from the Pacific Coast.

In order to understand what has taken and is taking place in the
field of Jewish environmentalism, it is helpful to understand what mo-
tivates people to be involved. I have observed a broad array of ideas
that lead American Jews to organize within their religio-ethnic community on environmental issues. They can be grouped into five categories: fulfilling Jewish obligation; fulfilling universal obligation;
effecting broad cultural/political change; strengthening the Jewish
community; and personal fulfillment.

All of the following motivations influence the variety of Jewish environmental efforts. I believe, however, that the character of particular
Jewish environmental programs and organizations tends to be driven
primarily by the dominant Jewish culture and the motivations and
strategic analyses of the people who lead them and in which they take
place. With rare exception, particular theological conceptions,
halakhic (legal) obligations, and ethical analyses do not seem to be
driving forces for the organizing of specific activities or programs.

Following are among the most salient beliefs, analyses, and circumstances in each of the five categories and an indication of which
types of individuals are motivated by them and/or employ them to
justify their work. Most individuals involved in Jewish environmental
efforts are motivated by more than one of these beliefs. For some, it is
the very convergence of such diverse convictions that compels active
involvement with Jewish environmentalism.

Fulfilling Jewish Obligation

- God commands us to protect creation. Jews must address the ecological crisis in order to be faithful to God.
- God commands us to pursue justice. Jews must act to prevent
  harm to all whose health and well-being are threatened by pollution and/or environmental deterioration.

- Judaism teaches that we are responsible for improving the world (*tiqqun 'olam*). Jews must therefore act to prevent environmental destruction.
- Judaism (kabbalah, Hasidism, theologies of immanence, teleological theologies) teaches that the fulfillment of Divine intention/respect for the Divine will requires that human beings protect the environment.
- Faithfulness to God requires caring for God's creation.

Among the types of individuals for whom these beliefs are a primary source of motivation are rabbis, long-time Jewish social action activists, and halakhically observant individuals. In my experience, most of those individuals who are moved by a sense of Jewish obligation find such inspiration in broad theological and ethical concepts, rather than specific laws—though they may try to act in accordance with such laws as *Bal Tashhit* (do not destroy) and others concerning conservation of resources, preservation of species, and protection of human health from pollution.

Fulfilling Universal Obligation

- All people, communities, and institutions are part of the environmental problem, and they all must become part of the solution. Therefore, Jewish institutions and individuals are responsible for learning about environmental issues and making environmentally responsible choices with respect to their facilities, homes, and businesses.
- Individuals concerned about the environment should engage their own families and communities in environmental education and responsibility. People involved in the life of a synagogue, school, or other religious institution should work to make those institutions environmentally responsible.
- The fulfillment of Divine intention/respect for the Divine will requires that human beings protect the environment.[20]

Among the types of individuals for whom these beliefs are a primary source of motivation are environmental professionals and activists who have an affiliation with the Jewish community but do not necessarily view environmental protection as a religious mandate; nor

are they necessarily motivated by religious mandates, though some
are. Also in this category are individuals who subscribe to a universalistic spirituality and/or theology who choose to root those beliefs in
Judaism.

Effecting Broad Cultural/Political Change

- Environmental issues are, at their core, moral issues concerning
  our basic obligations to other people, future generations, and
  other species. Religion is the source of most Americans' values;
  therefore, it is in religious communities that peoples' values can
  be most effectively changed.
- Judaism has ideas within it that offer ways of thinking or behaving that can help address environmental issues.
- Spirituality/religious vision is a source of commitment to protecting the environment. Rooting environmental commitment in
  Judaism is an effective way to motivate people and to maintain
  that motivation.
- Judaism is the source of comprehensive environmental vision that
  can motivate Jews to be environmentally responsible and active.
- Religious communities have a uniquely powerful voice in political debate in the United States. Presenting a strong and united
  religious voice on environmental issues can be politically effective.
- Because they are a common place where people congregate and
  have a history of engagement in social justice issues, Jewish institutions are effective places to organize for social change.
  Though a small percentage of the American population, Jews are
  disproportionately engaged in organizing and funding social
  change efforts in the United States.

Among the types of individuals for whom these beliefs are a primary source of motivation are: environmentalists who are Jewish who
get involved in the Jewish community because they perceive an opportunity to effect change; environmentalists who are involved in the
Jewish community and see Jewish environmentalism as an effective
way to fulfill their environmental objectives; and rabbis who view effecting cultural and political change part of their calling and/or role as
a rabbi.

Strengthening the Jewish Community

- Environmentalism is becoming a central component of American culture. If Judaism is not seen as an environmentally responsible and/or active tradition, our children will not be interested in it.
- The Jewish approach to nature and environmental issues is a largely unexplored area of Judaism and Jewish scholarship. Research and writing in this area is a contribution to Judaism.
- Providing a "Jewish mission" to Jewish children is necessary for their continuing participation in Jewish communities. Protecting the environment can be for young people a compelling personal and communal mission with roots in Jewish tradition and community. Jewish environmentalism therefore can be useful for engaging young people in Jewish life.

Among the types of individuals for whom these beliefs are a primary source of motivation are: Jewish professionals (rabbis, educators, camp directors, campus Hillel directors, and others) seeking ways to make Judaism relevant to younger Jews and engage them in Jewish life; lay leaders for whom Jewish "continuity" is a driving motivation; and lay leaders whose children and/or grandchildren have become more involved in environmentalism than in Judaism.

Personal Fulfillment

- Both Judaism and environmental protection are important components of my life. It is very satisfying to link two otherwise distinct parts of life, making me feel more whole.
- Jewish environmentalism connects to spirituality, history, and tradition. It has been for me a more deeply satisfying way to be involved in environmentalism than secular environmental organizations.
- Being with other Jews is more comfortable. Jewish environmentalism is a comfortable way for me to be involved in environmentalism.
- Jewish environmental programs are a fun way to meet other Jews and build a sense of community.

Among the types of individuals for whom these beliefs are a primary source of motivation are serious environmental activists and professionals who have felt alienated from Judaism because of a lack of awareness and/or concern about environmental issues, as well as Jewish young adults (twenties and thirties) who care about the environment and/or enjoy nature and are searching for community.

The Accomplishments of Jewish Environmentalism

Presenting the accomplishments of Jewish environmentalism is clearly dependent upon what one considers its goals and objectives. Following are near-term objectives I hold for Jewish environmentalism and a brief description of progress made toward accomplishing each objective.

Establish environmental protection and sustainability as a Jewish concern (and then a Jewish priority) for Jewish leaders, institutions, and individuals

Jewish environmentalists have successfully defined the environment as a Jewish issue and have generated much goodwill within the Jewish community. This is evidenced by such things as the selection by the *New York Jewish Week* annual magazine for the year 2000 (devoted to the future of Jewish life) of "The Greening of Jewish America" as "the next big issue" for the Jewish community.[21] I believe this success emerges from three streams of activity. First, Jewish scholars and writers have articulated distinctive Jewish perspectives on ecological issues. Second, individuals are raising environmental issues within their Jewish communities and organizing Jewish environmental education and action at the grassroots. Third, COEJL has successfully conveyed to Jewish leaders and opinion-leaders both the distinctive messages of Jewish environmentalism and evidence of widespread grassroots engagement.

One example of how these three streams—Jewish scholarship, grassroots activity, and national communications—have worked together is the redefinition of Tu B'Shvat, the New Year of Trees. Jewish congregations and schools around the Diaspora now celebrate Tu B'Shvat as a "Jewish Earth Day." Jewish newspapers now regularly report on environmental issues, programs, and themes in connection with Tu B'Shvat. In 2000, the Jewish Publication Society published its first festival anthology in seventeen years, *Trees, Earth, and Torah: A Tu B'Shvat Anthology*, edited by Arthur Waskow, Ari Elon and Naomi Hyman.[22]

Engage Jewish scholars, rabbis, and educators in an examination of Judaism's perspectives on a range of environmental issues and broadly integrate such examination into curricula

Two major events have been organized to accomplish this objective: the "Consultation on the Development of a Jewish Philosophy of the Natural World," organized by Steven Shaw in May 1994; and the February 1998 "Judaism and the Natural World" conference out of which this volume grows. In addition, several smaller initiatives, seminars, and retreats have been organized. Since 1990, popular articles and books on Judaism and the environment—particularly anthologies—have been published with increasing frequency.[23] However, few of the ideas in them have been systematically elaborated into curricula. In addition, many of the curricula that have been developed do not undertake a sophisticated examination of a Jewish approach to specific environmental issues. Instead, they tend to mobilize specific texts to support environmentally positive conclusions. There is a great need to develop Jewish environmental curricula for a range of ages and denominations.

Integrate moral and ethical concern into the debate about environmental protection in American public life

Along with other religious environmental efforts, Jewish environmentalists have begun to offer consideration of the moral, spiritual, and ethical dimensions of the ecological circumstances we face into public awareness and discussion. Leading environmental magazines have published feature stories on religious environmentalism. Broad anthologies on environmental topics have chapters on religious environmental perspectives. Numerous books and anthologies on faith and environment have been published in recent years, and they are being used in university courses on the environment. Religious environmentalism has been broadly covered in newspapers, including feature stories on the front page of the *Los Angeles Times*[24] and the *Washington Post*[25] and coverage in hundreds of dailies around the United States.

Convey to policy makers the support of the American Jewish commu-
nity and broad religious community for strong environmental protec-
tion laws

In a brief time, members of Congress, the Clinton and Bush adminis-
trations, and virtually all senior environmental organization leaders
have learned of the Jewish community's concern about a range of environmental policy issues. This has resulted primarily from COEJL's
participation in the National Religious Partnership for the Environment (NRPE) and numerous environmental coalitions in Washington,
D.C. Letters to members of Congress have been cited on the floor of
the House of Representatives, COEJL leaders have offered testimony
at House of Representative hearings,[26] and Jewish activists have met
with over two hundred congressional offices to discuss environmental
policy.

The relationship of Vice President Gore to the NRPE created a high
level of interest in religious environmentalism during the Clinton administration, and administration officials took very seriously the concerns of the Jewish community on the environment. The three top environmental officials in the U.S. government—Vice President Gore,
Interior Secretary Bruce Babbitt, and Environmental Protection Agency
Administrator Carol Browner—all addressed COEJL's February 1999
Leadership Institute (held alongside the Jewish Council for Public
Affairs' annual policy conference in Washington, D.C.).

Recently, COEJL has taken a leadership role in organizing interfaith efforts to address global climate change. This effort has a field
presence in twenty-two states and is among the largest organizing efforts on global climate change in the United States. Forty-two senior
religious leaders—including the leaders of every denominational
body and rabbinical organization in the American Jewish community—and more than five hundred rabbis signed an "Open Letter to
President Bush, the Congress, and the American People" titled "Let
There Be Light: Energy Conservation and God's Creation."[27] The letter received attention from congressional leaders in both parties and
from leading American news outlets.[28] Such efforts have made clear
the concern of American religious communities about global climate
change.

Reduce Jewish institutions' and households' negative impact on the environment

Though very difficult to measure, Jewish environmentalists have succeeded in reducing the ecological footprint of some Jewish institutions through recycling and purchase of recycled goods, energy efficiency and water conservation measures, and reduced use of toxic chemicals. Some actions have had significant environmental consequence; others have been symbolic, such as the installation of a solar *ner tamid* (eternal light) in synagogue sanctuaries. Though the majority of Jewish institutions have still not been engaged in these actions, models have been developed for bringing Jewish institutional practice into alignment with Jewish environmental values.

Challenges to Jewish Environmentalism

Given the scope of the ecological crisis and the time frame we have for action on many pressing issues, the accomplishments of Jewish environmentalism seem exceedingly modest. What has prevented the Jewish community from seeing environmental destruction as an immanent threat and taking up environmental protection as a central mission? Why are so few Jewish communal resources allocated to environmental education and action?

There are a variety of challenges to the Jewish environmental movement that have resulted in a rate of growth and development that falls short of the aspirations of many within the movement. I divide these challenges into two distinct, but not mutually exclusive, categories. By "external challenges" I refer to circumstances that are not particular to the Jewish environmental movement; they are broad societal circumstances that create a challenging social context for Jewish environmentalism, as they do for other movements for change. By "internal challenges" I refer to circumstances and dynamics that, while not necessarily unique to Jewish environmentalism, exist and operate in a distinctive manner within the Jewish environmental movement.

External Challenges

Jewish environmentalism faces the same daunting challenges that environmentalism in general faces in American society: citizen apathy, the culture of consumption, opposition from moneyed interests, ignorance, greed, lack of political leadership. (I'm afraid there is not the space to elaborate upon or to defend these assertions.) There are a few challenges on which I can elaborate that are particular to the Jewish community and affect numerous movements for change within the community:

- The relatively weak role of Judaism in the lives of American Jews severely limits the fecundity of arguments rooted in Jewish obligation.
- The private nature of religious life in contemporary Western civilization limits and inhibits the integration of public concerns into religious life for many American Jews. American Jewish life has an increasing emphasis on personal spirituality and a diminishing emphasis on communal responsibility and public life.
- The increasing political conservatism of the leadership of major Jewish organizations prevents consideration of what is incorrectly perceived as a liberal issue.
- The already very full agenda of most Jewish organizations involved in public affairs is coupled with a lack of either professional or volunteer capacity to learn about and address new issues.

There are also challenges particular to Jewish environmentalism presented by exterior circumstances:

- There is a lack of passionate, gut-level commitment to environmental protection among existing Jewish leadership.
- Jewish institutions are governed by a generation for whom environmental protection is not a primary concern.

Internal Challenges

The internal challenges of Jewish environmentalism—circumstances and dynamics that operate distinctively within the Jewish environmental movement—have not been debilitating (as internal conflicts within movements can easily become), though they do exist and do drain resources away from action and organizing.

- Both a strength and challenge, Jewish environmentalists have an exceptionally diverse range of motivations, as outlined earlier. Few programs can address all goals. This can impede establishment of focused goals, objectives, and programs and ultimately lead to a lack of discipline in the movement, undermining what would likely be greater success on particular issues or projects.
- A diversity of views concerning the most effective strategies can lead to fragmentation of an already small movement. One particularly strong difference exists concerning how to address environmentally destructive corporate behavior. There are those who favor working through governmental action and those who favor confronting environmentally irresponsible corporations directly. For example, those who favor direct action—who tend to be younger and hold more radical political views—have felt alienated from COEJL, which only works through governmental channels. Another strong difference exists between those who favor an emphasis on broad education and those who favor mobilizing potentially influential individuals to participate in political activity.
- There are differences in opinion about what constitutes legitimate Jewish environmental action. For some, the action must have a distinctively Jewish motivation and be executed in a manner that is self-consciously and evidently Jewish. For others, organizing Jews to take the same actions all others in society might take (from recycling to advocating) is legitimate Jewish environmental action.
- A diversity of religious cultures and a wide range of levels of religious and cultural knowledge create a challenge for organizing meetings and conferences at which all participants feel equally comfortable and empowered. Fortunately, most of the people who have been attracted to Jewish environmentalism have been eager to work through these challenges.
- The integration of Jewish spirituality and practice with environmental awareness and action presents the possibility that Jewish environmentalists and the organizations and programs they create will focus on providing experiences and building community rather than undertaking action and organizing advocacy.
- Some Jewish environmentalists advocate that Jews should give primary attention to addressing environmental challenges in Is-

rael and the Middle East, while others are motivated to address
the problems they face in their home cities, states, and countries.
Among Jewish environmentalists in North America, there is
much less activity concerning Israel's environment than local,
state, and national environmental issues; leaders within federations, however, are more inclined to focus on Israel's environmental challenges than on domestic or global issues.

Looking Ahead

Without doubt, the human community will struggle with environmental challenges for many generations to come. Creating a human civilization in harmony with the habitats of the earth is a historic challenge
that is increasingly at the center of public debate. Collective and individual choices must continually be made which affect the fate of
whole ecosystems and other species, the nature of the world that one
generation will bequeath to another, the viability of entire cultures
dependent upon particular ecosystems, the food security of nations,
the habitability of entire regions, and the prevalence of environmentally induced illness in various communities.

Such choices have profound moral significance. Yet, the physical
consequences of our choices are obscured by the distance that exists
between investors and the sites of production, between the sites of
production and consumers, and between consumers and waste disposal. Without knowledge of the consequences of our actions, we operate in a moral vacuum. A broad cultural avoidance of considering
the moral implications of the choices we make in either the legislature
or the marketplace compounds the lack of moral attention to economic and environmental decisions.

Jewish environmentalism, alongside other forms of religious environmentalism, will make increasingly possible a broad societal discussion about the morality of our environmental and economic policies and choices. For many people, moral concerns grow out of
religious education and experiences. Furthermore, moral discussion
requires a vocabulary of values and morals, which again comes to
most from religious education and experiences. I believe that when
the majority of people are educated about the consequences of their
choices and government policy and are asked to consider the moral

implications of such choices and policies within familiar values frameworks, they will choose to protect the environment for the sake of other species, other people, and future generations.

Neither Judaism nor other religious traditions offer solutions to contemporary environmental problems. What they do offer is a framework for defining problems and evaluating potential solutions. Most basic human conflicts are addressed in Jewish tradition and law, including conflicts between: competing human needs; the needs of the current generation and the likely needs of future generations; and human needs and the needs of animals. Furthermore, the purpose of human life is a central concern of Judaism and other religions, providing a foundation and context for the evaluation of various choices and behaviors. Judaism provides a rich framework for considering environmental challenges.

Through Jewish environmentalism, those already committed to living a Jewish life can engage the challenges of environmental protection in a Jewish way. Those not already committed to living a Jewish life but who care about the environment can consider complex contemporary issues in the context of a thirty-five-hundred-year-old tradition rich with morals and values, legal frameworks, and ethical guidance. Both committed and noncommitted Jews can create a culture of environmental concern that is shared by a community of people.

Jewish environmentalism has the potential to mobilize a small, though disproportionately influential, constituency in the public and private sectors of American life. Furthermore, given the prominent role of religious communities in American political life, a unified religious voice—which in the United States requires a Jewish presence—in favor of environmental protection can have considerable effect on policy discussions. As the historic source of Christianity, Judaism has considerable moral authority in the American imagination, providing recognizable Jewish leaders an opportunity to make a moral case for environmental protection before the nation at large.

Finally, let us consider the contribution of Jewish environmentalism to Judaism, among the most ancient living traditions on earth. Judaism has survived millennia and the fall of numerous civilizations by adapting itself to changing circumstances in a manner consistent with its fundamental beliefs and values. Indeed, Jewish survival remains a prime concern among Jewish leaders and organizations. It may well be that in order for Judaism to survive the changes in human civilization that will take place over the next century and the presumed continuing emergence of a highly environmentally conscious culture, Judaism must also embody a conscious relationship with the environment and effectively pursue environmental sustainability. And, if we consider the worst-case environmental predictions, we can also deduce that survival for all peoples and cultures requires making environmentalism a central focus of concern and action.

As environmental issues gain increasing prominence, and as generational change brings into leadership individuals with environmental knowledge and commitment, Jewish environmentalism is likely to move from the fringes to the center of Jewish life. If current trends continue, this will take place first in the education and community-building arenas. Full integration of environmental protection into the public policy agenda of the Jewish community is not likely to happen for some time, though individuals for whom this is a priority will likely find opportunities for action through COEJL and other single issue organizations. In the Reconstructionist and Renewal communities, the concept of "eco-kosher" is already becoming popular and I expect it will increasingly provide a framework through which committed non-Orthodox Jews consider their purchases. In traditionally observant communities, I believe we can expect an extension of halakhah (Jewish law) to contemporary environmental issues.

If the Jewish environmental movement continues to grow and achieve its aspirations, Jewish organizational and personal consumption decisions will increasingly be made according to explicit Jewish values. Rabbis and educators will integrate experiences of nature into worship and education and the emerging generation of Jewish scholars will explore Jewish approaches to particular environmental issues. Diaspora Jews concerned for the well-being of Israel will give increasing attention to her severely deteriorating environment. In all Jewish communities, the integration of environmental themes into Shabbat and holiday celebrations—particularly Tu B'Shvat, Sukkot, and Passover—will become increasingly popular and regular. As American Jewish leaders increasingly recognize the severity of national and global environmental challenges and their implications for human well-being, geopolitical stability, and ecological sustainability, they will allocate increased political, financial, and institutional resources to advocating environmental protection. Jewish youth will understand protecting the environment as core to their vocation as Jews, human beings, and citizens, and will make professional and other major life choices informed by their environmental commitments.

I believe Jewish environmentalism has a promising future. Yet, though progress has been made, and we can expect it to continue, neither the intellectual foundation nor the organizational infrastructure has yet been sufficiently established to sustain Jewish environmentalism over the long term. The Jewish community faces a challenge and an opportunity—perhaps a necessity—to organize a Jewish environmental movement that reflects the intellectual and social resources of the world Jewish community and that makes a substantial and enduring contribution to global environmental sustainability.

Notes

1. I use the term "Jewish environmentalism" to describe beliefs or behaviors intended to address environmental issues that are intentionally and self-consciously
motivated by Judaism, Jewish identity, or take place in a Jewish context.

2. Lynn White, Jr., "The Historical Roots of Our Ecologic Crisis," *Science* 155 (10
March 1967): 1203–7.

3. Rather than suggest specific articles, I refer readers to a recent anthology that
provides a balanced selection of such articles: *Judaism and Environmental Ethics: A
Reader*, ed. Martin D. Yaffe (New York: Lexington Books, 2001).

4. Ibid.

5. For example: Arthur Waskow, "What Is Eco-Kosher?" in *This Sacred Earth:
Religion, Nature, Environment*, ed. Roger S. Gottlieb (New York: Routledge, 1996),
297–300; idem, "Is the Earth a Jewish Issue?" *Tikkun* 7, no. 5 (1992): 35–37; idem,
"From Compassion to Jubilee," *Tikkun* 5, no. 2 (1990): 78–81.

6. Arthur Waskow, *Seasons of Our Joy: A Modern Guide to the Jewish Holidays*
(Boston: Beacon Press, 1982).

7. *Ecology and the Jewish Spirit: Where Nature and the Sacred Meet*, ed. Ellen
Bernstein (Woodstock, Vt.: Jewish Lights Publishing, 2000), 12.

8. *Let the Earth Teach You Torah*, ed. Ellen Bernstein and Dan Fink (Wyncote, Pa.:
Shomrei Adamah, 1992); Hadassah, *Judaism and Ecology: A Hadassah Study Guide
in Cooperation with Shomrei Adamah, Keepers of the Earth* (New York: Hadassah
Department of Education, 1993); David E. Stein, *A Garden of Choice Fruits: 200
Classic Jewish Quotes on Human Beings and the Environment* (Wyncote, Pa.:
Shomrei Adamah, 1991); "Judaism and Ecology, 1970–1986: A Sourcebook of Read-
ings," ed. Mark Swetlitz (1990, photocopied compilation produced and distributed by
Shomrei Adamah).

9. See Arthur Waskow, *Down-to-Earth Judaism: Food, Money, Sex, and the Rest of
Life* (New York: William Morrow, 1995).

10. Many of the most prominent environmental leaders in Israel were born outside
of Israel, including Americans such as Jeremy Benstein (Heschel Center), Eilon
Schwartz, Alon Tal (founder of the Israel Union for Environmental Defense and the
Arava Institute for Environmental Studies), and Philip Warburg (the executive direc-
tor of the Israel Union for Environmental Defense), and the Australian Gidon
Bromberg (founding director of EcoPeace: Friends of the Earth Middle East).

11. Manfred Gerstenfeld, *Judaism, Environmentalism and the Environment: Mapping and Analysis* (Jerusalem: Rubin Mass Ltd., 1998).

12. *Judaism and Ecology*, ed. Aubrey Rose (London: Cassell, 1992).

13. "On the Urgency of a Jewish Response to the Environmental Crisis" was
signed by Rabbi Marc D. Angel, President, Rabbinical Council of America; Shoshana
S. Cardin, Chairperson, Conference of Presidents of Major American Jewish Organi-
zations; Rabbi Jerome K. Davidson, President, Synagogue Council of America; Dr.
Alfred Gottschalk, President, Hebrew Union College–Jewish Institute of Religion;
Dr. Arthur Green, President, The Reconstructionist Rabbinical College; Rabbi Irwin
Groner, President, The Rabbinical Assembly; Rabbi Walter Jacob, President, Central
Conference of American Rabbis; Frank R. Lautenberg, United States Senator from

New Jersey; Marvin Lender, President, United Jewish Appeal; Joseph I. Lieberman, United States Senator from Connecticut; Sheldon Rudoff, President, Union of Orthodox Jewish Congregations of America; Rabbi Alexander M. Schindler, President, Union of American Hebrew Congregations; Dr. Ismar Schorsch, Chancellor, The Jewish Theological Seminary of America; Arden Shenker, Chairman, National Jewish Community Relations Advisory Council; Arlen Specter, United States Senator from Pennsylvania; Alan J. Tichnor, President, United Synagogue of America.

14. "The National Survey on Social Justice and American Jews," sponsored by Amos: The National Jewish Partnership for Social Justice; the principal investigator was Steven M. Cohen of Hebrew University, 1991.

15. The most substantial of these has been *To Till and To Tend: A Guide to Jewish Environmental Study and Action*, published by COEJL in 1994.

16. *Operation Noah: A Jewish Program and Action Guide to Defending God's Endangered Creatures and Habitats*, ed. Mark Jacobs (New York: COEJL, 1996).

17. The following quotation from a participant in a COEJL conference provides a vivid example: "This movement makes Judaism alive for me. I thank COEJL for providing me a Jewish home. Before, it was just a bunch of strange words, rituals, and buildings. Now it's something so deep I can't even describe it. It moves me right to the core of my being. The more I get involved with this part of Judaism, the more I think that this is going to save both Judaism and the environment at the same time. What could be better than that." The individual was in his mid-thirties and worked as an environmental engineer for the federal government.

18. Mr. Hurwitz did discuss the issue with Rabbi Lester Scharnberg of Eureka, California, in 1996. Scharnberg raised the morality of Maxxam Corporation's forest management practices at a 1998 shareholder meeting in Houston, Texas. Though the company did respond to the charges (dismissing them), this activity does not seem to have made much impact. The majority of the old-growth redwoods in Headwaters Forest were purchased from Maxxam Corporation by the United States government and the State of California in 1998 for $480 million. The acquired property is now public land being managed to preserve habitat for threatened and endangered species.

19. COEJL distributed a survey in 1999 to its own mailing list of over six thousand people. Two hundred and ninety individuals responded. Their identification with movements was as follows: Reform, 41 percent; Conservative, 30 percent; Orthodox, 5 percent; Reconstructionist, 4 percent; Renewal, 3 percent; other, 16 percent.

20. For some, this conviction is "discovered" through personal experiences in nature, and for others it is learned from one or more contemporary theologies and philosophies.

21. James Besser, "The Next Big Issue: The Greening of Jewish America," *Directions 2000: New York Jewish Week*, 1999.

22. *Trees, Earth, and Torah: A Tu B'Shvat Anthology*, ed. Ari Elon, Naomi Mara Hyman, and Arthur Waskow (Philadelphia: Jewish Publication Society, 1999).

23. Among the most notable: *Ecology and the Jewish Spirit*, ed. Bernstein; Matt Biers-Ariel, Deborah Newbrun, and Michal Fox Smart, *Spirit in Nature: Teaching Judaism and Ecology on the Trail* (New York: Behrman House, 2000); Central Conference of American Rabbis, "A Symposium on Judaism and the Environment," *CCAR Journal: A Reform Jewish Quarterly*, winter 2001; Evan Eisenberg, *The Ecol-*

ogy of Eden (New York: Alfred A. Knopf, 1998); Gerstenfeld, *Judaism, Environmentalism and the Environment*; Ronald Isaacs, *The Jewish Sourcebook on the Environment and Ecology* (Northvale, N.J.: Jason Aronson, 1998); Richard H. Schwartz, *Judaism and Global Survival*, rev. ed. (New York: Lantern Books, 2001); *Torah of the Earth: Exploring 4,000 Years of Ecology in Jewish Thought*, ed. Arthur Waskow (Burlington, Vt.: Jewish Lights, 2000); Waskow, *Down-to-Earth Judaism*; *Trees, Earth, and Torah*, ed. Elon, Hyman, and Waskow.

24. Teresa Watanabe, "The Green Movement Is Getting Religion," *Los Angeles Times*, 25 December 1998, p. A1.

25. Caryle Murphy, "A Spiritual Lens on the Environment: Increasingly, Caring for Creation Is Viewed as a Religious Mandate," *Washington Post*, 3 February 1998, p. A1.

26. For example, see "Statement of Mark X. Jacobs on Behalf of the Coalition on the Environment and Jewish Life," Fiscal Year 2001 Hearing, Subcommittee on Transportation and Related Agencies, Committee on Appropriations, United States House of Representatives, 10 February 2000. This testimony can be found at http://www.coejl.org/action/20000210cafetest.shtml.

27. The letter can be found at http://www.coejl.org/news/20010521_openletter_a.shtml#ENERGY CONSERVATION AND GOD'S CREATION.

28. For example: Associated Press wire story, "Energy Policies Faulted," *Washington Post*, 26 May 2001, p. B9; PBS, Religion and Ethics Newsweekly, 25 May 2001, transcript #439; Michael Paulson, "Bishops Say Fighting Global Warming Is a Moral Duty," *Boston Globe*, 16 June 2001, p. A10; "God's Green Earth: Religious Leaders Take up Environmental Cause," ABCNews.com, 13 August 2001.

Select Bibliography

Allen, E. L. "The Hebrew View of Nature." *The Journal of Jewish Studies* 2 (1951): 100–104. Reprinted in *Judaism and Environmental Ethics: A Reader*, edited by Martin D. Yaffe, 80–85 (Lanham, Md.: Lexington Books, 2001).

Artson, Bradley Shavit. *It's a Mitzvah! Step-by-Step to Jewish Living.* New York: Behrman House, 1995.

———. "Our Covenant with Stones: A Jewish Ecology of Earth." *Conservative Judaism* 44 (1991): 25–35. Reprinted in *Judaism and Environmental Ethics: A Reader*, edited by Martin D. Yaffe, 161–71 (Lanham, Md.: Lexington Books, 2001).

Bak, Benjamin. "The Sabbatical Year in Modern Israel." *Tradition* 1 (1959): 193–99.

Belkin, Samuel. "Man as Temporary Tenant." In *Judaism and Human Rights*, edited by Milton R. Konvitz, 251–63. New York: W. W. Norton and Company, 1972.

Berman, Louis A. *Vegetarianism and the Jewish Tradition.* New York: Ktav, 1982.

Berman, Phyllis, and Arthur Waskow. *Tales of Tikkun: New Jewish Stories to Heal the Wounded World.* Northvale, N.J.: Jason Aronson, 1996.

Bernstein Ellen, ed. *Ecology and the Jewish Spirit: Where Nature and the Sacred Meet.* Woodstock, Vt.: Jewish Lights Publishing, 1998.

Bernstein, Ellen, and Dan Fink. "Blessings and Praise," and "Bal Tashchit." In *This Sacred Earth: Religion, Nature, Environment*, edited by Roger S. Gottlieb, 451–68. New York: Routledge, 1996.

Biers-Ariel, Matt, Deborah Newbrun, and Michael Fox Smart. *Spirit in Nature: Teaching Judaism and Ecology on the Trail.* New York: Behrman House, 2000.

482   *Judaism and Ecology*

Bleich, David J. "Judaism and Animal Experimentation." *Tradition* 2, no. 1,
1–36. Reprinted in *Animal Sacrifices: Religious Perspectives on the
Use of Animals in Science*, edited by Toma Regan, 61–114 (Philadel-
phia: Temple University Press, 1986); J. David Bleich, *Contemporary
Halakhic Problems, Volume III* (New York: Ktav Publishing House and
Yeshivah University Press, 1989), 194–236; and *Judaism and Environ-
mental Ethics: A Reader*, edited by Martin D. Yaffe, 333–70 (Lanham,
Md.: Lexington Books, 2001).

———. "Vegetarianism and Judaism. *Tradition* 23, no. 1 (1987): 82–90. Reprinted in *Contemporary Halakhic Problems*, vol. 3 (New York: Ktav,
1989).

Blidstein, Gerald. "Man and Nature in the Sabbatical Year." *Tradition: A
Journal of Orthodox Thought* 8, no. 4 (1966): 48–55. Reprinted in *Judaism and Environmental Ethics: A Reader*, edited by Martin D. Yaffe,
136–42 (Lanham, Md.: Lexington Books, 2001).

———. "Nature in Psalms." *Judaism* 13 (1964): 29–36.

Bloch, Abraham P. "Respect for Nature." In *A Book of Jewish Ethical Concepts*. New York: Ktav, 1984.

Brooks, David B. "Israel and the Environment: Signs of Progress." *Reconstructionist* 55, no. 4 (1990): 17–19.

Carmell, Aryeh. "Judaism and the Quality of the Environment." In *Challenge: Torah Views on Science and Its Problems*, edited by Aryeh Carmell and Cyril Domb, 500–525. New York: Feldheim, 1976.

Cohen, Alfred S. "Vegetarianism from a Jewish Perspective." In *Halacha and
Contemporary Society*, edited by Alfred S. Cohen, 292–317. New
York: Ktav, 1983.

Cohen, Jeremy, *"Be Fertile and Increase, Fill the Earth and Master It"*: *The
Ancient and Medieval Career of a Biblical Text*. Ithaca, N.Y.: Cornell
University Press, 1989.

———. "On Classical Judaism and Environmental Crisis." *Tikkun* 5, no. 2
(1990): 74–77. Reprinted in *Judaism and Environmental Ethics: A
Reader*, edited by Martin D. Yaffe, 73–79 (Lanham, Md.: Lexington
Books, 2001).

Cohen, Noah J., *Tsa'ar Ba'ale Hayim: The Prevention of Cruelty to Animals,
Its Bases, Development and Legislation in Hebrew Literature*. 2d ed.
Jerusalem and New York: Feldheim Publishers, 1976.

Conservative Judaism 44, no. 1 (1991).

De-Shalit, Avner. "From the Political to the Objective: The Dialectics of Zionism and the Environment. *Environmental Politics* 4, no. 1 (1995):
70–87.

Dresner, Samuel, and Byron L. Sherwin. "To Take Care of God's World: Judaism and Ecology." In *Judaism: The Way of Sanctification*, 131–44.
New York: United Synagogue of America, 1978.

Ehrenfeld, David, and Philip J. Bentley. "Judaism and the Practice of Stewardship. *Judaism: A Quarterly Journal* 34 (1985): 301–11. Reprinted in *Judaism and Environmental Ethics: A Reader*, edited by Martin D. Yaffe, 125–35 (Lanham, Md.: Lexington Books, 2001).

Eisenberg, Evan. *The Ecology of Eden*. New York: Alfred A. Knopf, 1998.

Elon, Ari, Naomi Mara Hyman, and Arthur Waskow, eds. *Trees, Earth, and Torah: A Tu B'Shvat Anthology*. Philadelphia: Jewish Publication Society, 1999.

Felix, Yehuda. *Nature and Man in the Bible: Chapters in Biblical Ecology*. New York: The Soncino Press, 1981.

Freudenstein, Eric. C. "Ecology and the Jewish Tradition." In *Judaism and Human Rights*, edited by Milton R. Konvitz, 265–74. New York: W. W. Norton and Company, 1972.

Freundel, Barry. "The Earth Is the Lord's." *Jewish Action* 50 (summer 1990): 22–26.

Gendler, Everett, "The Earth's Covenant." *Reconstructionist* (1989): 28–31.

———. "On the Judaism of Nature." In *The New Jew*, edited by James A. Sleeper and Alan L. Mintz, 233–43. New York: Vintage Books, 1971. Reprinted in *Torah of the Earth: Exploring 4,000 Years of Ecology in Jewish Thought*, edited by Arthur Waskow, vol. 2, 174–84 (Woodstock, Vt.: Jewish Lights Publishing, 2000).

Gerstenfeld, Manfred. *Judaism, Environmentalism and the Environment: Mapping and Analysis*. Jerusalem: Jerusalem Institute for Israel Studies and Rubin Mass, 1998.

Goldstein, Morris. "Man's Place in Nature." *Tradition: A Journal of Orthodox Thought* 10 (1968): 100–115.

Gordis, Robert. "Ecology and the Judaic Tradition." In *Judaic Ethics for a Lawless World*, 113–22. New York: Jewish Theological Seminary, 1971.

———. "Job and Ecology (and the Significance of Job 40:15)." *Hebrew Annual Review* 9 (1985): 189–202.

Gottlieb, Roger S., ed. *This Sacred Earth: Religion, Nature, Environment*. New York: Routledge, 1996.

Grossman, Karl. "How Green Are the Jews?" *The Jewish Monthly*, January 1991, 7–13.

Hareuveni, Nogah. *Desert and Shepherd in Our Biblical Heritage*. Kiryat Ono, Israel: Neot Kedumim, 1991.

———. *Ecology in the Bible*. Kiryat Ono, Israel: Neot Kedumim, 1974.

———. *Nature in Our Biblical Heritage*. Kiryat Ono, Israel: Neot Kedumim, 1980.

———. *Tree and Shrub in Our Biblical Heritage*. Kiryat Ono, Israel: Neot Kedumim, 1984.

Harris, Monford. "Ecology: A Covenantal Approach. *CCAR [Central Conference of American Rabbis] Journal* 2 (1976): 101–8.

Helfand, Jonathan. "'Consider the Work of G-d': Jewish Sources for Conservation Ethics." In *Liturgical Foundations of Social Policy in the Catholic and Jewish Traditions*, edited by Daniel F. Polish and Eugene J. Fisher, 134–48. Notre Dame, Ind.: University of Notre Dame Press, 1983.

———. "The Earth Is the Lord's: Judaism and Environmental Ethics." In *Religion and Environmental Crisis*, edited by Eugene C. Hargrove, 38–52. Athens, Ga., and London: University of Georgia Press, 1986.

———. "Ecology and the Jewish Tradition." *Judaism: A Quarterly Journal* 20 (1971): 330–35.

Heschel, Abraham Joshua. *God in Search of Man: A Philosophy of Judaism.* 1955. Reprint, New York: Octagon Books, 1976.

———. *The Sabbath: Its Meaning for Modern Man.* New York: Farrar, Strauss and Young, 1951.

Jegen, Mary Evelyn, and Brunno Manno, eds. *The Earth Is the Lord's: Essays on Stewardship.* New York: Paulist Press, 1978.

Isaacs, Ronald H. *The Jewish Sourcebook on the Environment and Ecology.* Northvale, N.J., and Jerusalem: Jason Aronson, 1998.

Katz, Eric. "Are We the World's Keepers? Toward an Ecological Ethics for Our Home Planet." *The Melton Journal* 24 (spring 1991): 3.

———. "Environmental Ethics: A Select Annotated Bibliography, 1983–1987." *Research in Philosophy and Technology* 9 (1989): 251–85.

———. "Judaism and the Ecological Crisis." In *Worldviews and Ecology*, edited by Mary Evelyn Tucker and John A. Grim, 55–70. Lewisburg, Pa.: Bucknell University Press; London and Toronto: Associated University Presses, 1993.

———. "Nature's Healing Power, the Holocaust, and the Environmental Crisis." *Judaism: A Quarterly Journal* 46 (1997): 79–89. Reprinted in *Judaism and Environmental Ethics: A Reader*, edited by Martin D. Yaffe, 309–20 (Lanham, Md.: Lexington Books, 2001).

Kay, Jeanne. "Comments on the Unnatural Jew." *Environmental Ethics* 7 (1985): 189–91; Reprinted in *Judaism and Environmental Ethics: A Reader*, edited by Martin D. Yaffe, 286–88 (Lanham, Md.: Lexington Books, 2001).

———. "Concepts of Nature in the Hebrew Bible." *Environmental Ethics* 10 (1988): 309–27. Reprinted in *Judaism and Environmental Ethics: A Reader*, edited by Martin D. Yaffe, 86–104 (Lanham, Md.: Lexington Books, 2001).

Lamm, Norman. "Ecology in Jewish Law and Theology." In *Faith and Doubt: Studies in Traditional Jewish Thought.* New York: Ktav, 1972.

Levy, Ze'ev. "Ethical Issues of Animal Welfare in Jewish Thought." *Judaism: A Quarterly Journal* 45 (1996): 47–57. Reprinted in *Judaism and Environmental Ethics: A Reader*, edited by Martin D. Yaffe, 321–32 (Lanham, Md.: Lexington Books, 2001).

Novak, David. *Natural Law in Judaism.* Cambridge: Cambridge University Press, 1998.

———. "Technology and Its Ultimate Threat: A Jewish Mediation." *Research in Philosophy and Technology* 10 (1990): 43–70.

Ravitzky, Aviezer. *The Shemittah Year: A Collection of Sources and Articles.* Translated by Mordell Klein. Jerusalem: World Zionist Organization, 1979.

Rose, Aubrey, ed. *Judaism and Ecology.* London: Cassell Publishers, 1992.

Schorsch, Ismar. "Learning to Live with Less." *Spirit and Nature: Why the Environment Is a Religious Issue*, edited by Steven C. Rockefeller and John C. Elder, 27–38. Boston: Beacon Press, 1992.

———. "Trees for Life." *The Melton Journal* 25 (spring 1992): 3.

Schwartz, Eilon. "*Bal Tashchit*: A Jewish Environmental Precept." *Environmental Ethics* 19 (1997): 355–74. Reprinted in *Judaism and Environmental Ethics: A Reader*, edited by Martin D. Yaffe, 230–49 (Lanham, Md.: Lexington Books, 2001).

———. "Judaism and Nature: Theological and Moral Issues to Consider while Renegotiating a Jewish Relationship to the Natural World." *Judaism: A Quarterly Journal* 44, no. 4 (1995): 437–47. Reprinted in *Judaism and Environmental Ethics: A Reader*, edited by Martin D. Yaffe, 297–308 (Lanham, Md.: Lexington Books, 2001).

Schwartz, Richard H. *Judaism and Global Survival.* New York: Atara Publishing, 1987.

Schwarzschild, Steven S. "The Unnatural Jew." *Environmental Ethics* 6 (1984): 347–62. Reprinted in *Judaism and Environmental Ethics: A Reader*, edited by Martin D. Yaffe, 267–82 (Lanham, Md.: Lexington Books, 2001).

Swetlitz, Mark, ed. "Judaism and Ecology, 1970–1986: A Sourcebook of Readings." Mimeograph. Wyncote, Pa.: Shomrei Adamah, 1990.

Tal, Alon. "An Imperiled Promised Land." In *Torah of the Earth: Exploring 4,000 Years of Ecology in Jewish Thought*, edited by Arthur Waskow, vol. 2, 42–71 (Woodstock, Vt.: Jewish Lights Publishing, 2000).

Tamari, Meir. *With All Your Possessions: Jewish Ethics and Economic Life.* New York: Free Press; and London: Collier Macmillan, 1987.

Toperov, Shlomo Pesach. *The Animal Kingdom in Jewish Thought.* Northvale, N.J.: Jason Aronson, 1995.

Vorspan, Albert. "The Crisis of Ecology: Judaism and the Environment." In *Jewish Values and Social Crisis*, 362–81. New York: Union of American Hebrew Congregations, 1970.

Vorspan, Albert, and David Saperstein. *Tough Choices: Jewish Perspectives on Social Justice*. New York: UAHC Press, 1992.

Waskow, Arthur. *Down-to-Earth Judaism: Food, Money, Sex, and the Rest of Life*. New York: William Morrow, 1995.

———. "The Greening of Judaism." *Moment* 17, no. 3 (1992): 45–47, 52, 62.

———. "Is the Earth a Jewish Issue?" *Tikkun* 7, no. 5 (1992): 35–37.

———. "What Is Eco-Kosher?" In *This Sacred Earth: Religion, Nature, Environment*, edited by Roger S. Gottlieb, 297–300. New York: Routledge, 1996.

———, ed. *Torah of the Earth: Exploring 4,000 Years of Ecology in Jewish Thought*. 2 vols. Burlington, Vt.: Jewish Lights, 2000.

Weiss, David. "The Forces of Nature, The Forces of Spirit: A Perspective on Judaism." *Judaism* 32 (1983): 477–87.

Wyschogrod, Michael. "Judaism and the Sanctification of Nature." *The Melton Journal* 24 (spring 1991): 5–7. Reprinted in *Judaism and Environmental Ethics: A Reader*, edited by Martin D. Yaffe, 289–96 (Lanham, Md.: Lexington Books, 2001).

Yaffe, Martin D., ed. *Judaism and Environmental Ethics: A Reader* (Lanham, Md.: Lexington Books, 2001).

Notes on Contributors

Tsvi Blanchard is the director of organizational development and a faculty member at the National Jewish Center for Learning and Leadership (CLAL). He holds doctorate degrees in philosophy (1973) and psychology (1983) and was on the faculty of Washington University in St. Louis. His other teaching posts included Northwestern University, Loyola University, Hebrew Union College–Jewish Institute of Religion, the Jewish Theological Seminary, Drisha, and the Wexner Heritage Program. Rabbi Blanchard has published essays on leadership, social theory, cultural criticism, and health as well as widely anthologized stories and parables. In addition to teaching and writing, Rabbi Blanchard has a private practice as a clinical and organizational psychologist.

Eliezer Diamond is the Rabbi Judah A. Nadich Associate Professor of Talmud and Rabbinics at the Jewish Theological Seminary of America. He has written and taught on the relationship between Jewish law and the environment. He is the author of *Holy Men and Hunger Artists: Fasting and Asceticism in Rabbinic Culture*, to be published by Oxford University Press.

Evan Eisenberg is the author of *The Recording Angel* (1987) and *The Ecology of Eden* (1998). His essays on nature, culture, and technology have appeared in magazines such as *The Atlantic*, *The New Republic*, and *Natural History*, and in the *New York Times*. Eisenberg holds a B.A. from Harvard University in classics and philosophy and studied biology at the University of Massachusetts at Amherst. He has worked as a music critic for *The Nation*, a synagogue cantor, and a gardener for the New York City parks department.

Michael Fishbane is Nathan Cummings Professor of Jewish Studies and chair of the Committee on Jewish Studies at the University of Chicago.

Among his books are: *Biblical Interpretation in Ancient Israel* (1985); *The Kiss of God: Spiritual and Mystical Death in Judaism* (1994); and *The Exegetical Imagination: Studies in Jewish Thought and Theology* (1999).

Stephen A. Geller is Professor of Bible at the Jewish Theological Seminary of America. He has published numerous articles on biblical literature, especially poetry, and religion. His most recent book is *Sacred Enigmas: Literary Religion in the Hebrew Bible* (1996), and he is currently working on a commentary on the Book of Psalms from a literary viewpoint.

Jerome (Yehuda) Gellman is Professor of Philosophy at Ben Gurion University of the Negev in Beer Sheba, Israel. His publications include: *The Fear, the Trembling, and the Fire: Kierkegaard and Hasidic Masters on the Binding of Isaac* (1994); *Experience of God and the Rationality of Theistic Belief* (1997); *Mystical Experience of God: A Philosophical Enquiry* (2001); and a forthcoming book, *"Abraham! Abraham!": Hasidism on the Binding of Isaac.*

Neil Gillman is the Aaron Rabinowitz and Simon H. Rifkind Professor of Jewish Philosophy at the Jewish Theological Seminary of America. His books include: *Sacred Fragments: Recovering Theology for the Modern Jew* (1990), which won the 1991 National Jewish Book Award in Jewish Thought; *Conservative Judaism: The New Century* (1993); *The Death of Death: Resurrection and Immortality in Jewish Thought* (1997); and *The Way into Encountering God in Judaism* (2000). Gillman is a regular contributor to the Anglo-Jewish newspaper *Jewish Week* and is chair of the Advisory Committee of the periodical *Sh'ma.*

Lenn E. Goodman is Professor of Philosophy at Vanderbilt University. His books include: *In Defense of Truth: A Pluralistic Approach* (2001); *Jewish and Islamic Philosophy: Crosspollinations in the Classical Age* (1999); *Judaism, Human Rights, and Human Values* (1998); *God of Abraham* (1996); *Avicenna* (1992); and *On Justice: An Essay in Jewish Philosophy* (1991). A winner of the Baumgardt Prize of the American Philosophical Association and the Gratz Centennial Prize, Goodman has also translated and commented on the writings of Maimonides, Saadia Gaon, Ibn Tufayl, and the tenth-century ecological fable *The Case of the Animals vs. Man before the King of the Jinn,* by the Sincere Brethren of Basra.

Arthur Green is the Philip W. Lown Professor of Jewish Thought at Brandeis University. He is a student of Jewish mysticism and Hasidism as well as a theologian. His books include *Tormented Master: A Life of Rabbi Nahman of*

Bratslav (1979) and *Seek My Face, Speak My Name: A Contemporary Jewish Theology* (1997). Among his most recent works are an essay entitled "Shekhinah, the Virgin Mary and the Song of Songs," published in *AJS Review*, and a forthcoming book entitled *EHYEH: A Kabbalah for Tomorrow*.

Mark X. Jacobs has served as executive director of the Coalition on the Environment and Jewish Life (COEJL) since 1995. COEJL embraces twenty-nine national Jewish organizations and thirteen regional affiliates. As the Jewish member of the National Religious Partnership for the Environment, COEJL works closely with the U.S. Catholic Conference, the National Council of Churches, and the Evangelical Environmental Network on environmental policy and programs. Jacobs holds a B.A. in sociology from the University of California, Santa Cruz, and has done graduate course work in Jewish studies, anthropology, environmental studies, and social work at the University of Michigan.

Edward K. Kaplan is Professor of French and Comparative Literature, a research associate of the Tauber Institute for the Study of European Jewry, and chair of the Program in Religious Studies at Brandeis University. He has written books on Abraham Heschel, the French historian Jules Michelet, the poet Charles Baudelaire, and essays on Martin Buber, Thomas Merton, and Howard Thurman. Volume one of his biography of Heschel, *Abraham Heschel: Prophetic Witness*, co-authored with Samuel Dresner, was finalist in Jewish Scholarship in the National Jewish Books Awards. Kaplan's foundational book *Holiness in Words: Abraham Joshua Heschel's Poetics of Piety* (1996) was published in a French translation by Les Editions du Cerf in 1999.

Barry S. Kogan is the Clarence and Robert Efroymson Professor of Philosophy and Jewish Religious Thought and Philosophy at Hebrew Union College–Jewish Institute of Religion in Cincinnati. He is the author of *Averroes and the Metaphysics of Causation* (1985) and "Judah Halevi: Reflections on the Argument and Action of *Kuzari* I" (forthcoming); the editor of *Spinoza: A Tercentenary Perspective* (1979) and *A Time to Be Born and a Time to Die: The Ethics of Choice* (1991); and cotranslator of Judah Halevi's *Kuzari* (forthcoming).

David Kraemer is Professor of Talmud and Rabbinics at the Jewish Theological Seminary of America. His books include: *The Mind of the Talmud* (1990); *Responses to Suffering in Classical Rabbinic Literature* (1995); *Reading the Rabbis: The Talmud as Literature* (1996); and, most recently, *The Meanings of Death in Rabbinic Judaism* (2000).

Jon D. Levenson is the Albert A. List Professor of Jewish Studies at the Harvard Divinity School, Harvard University. Among his books are: *Sinai and Zion: An Entry into the Jewish Bible* (1985); *Creation and the Persistence of Evil: The Jewish Drama of Divine Omnipotence* (1994); *The Old Testament, the Hebrew Bible and Historical Criticism: Jews and Christians in Biblical Studies* (1993); *The Death and Resurrection of the Beloved Son: The Transformation of Child Sacrifice in Judaism and Christianity* (1993); and *Esther: A Commentary* (1997).

Shaul Magid is Associate Professor of Jewish Philosophy and chair of the Department of Jewish Philosophy at the Jewish Theological Seminary of America. He is the editor of *God's Voice from the Void: Old and New Studies in Bratzlav Hasidism* (2001) and the author of the forthcoming *Hasidism on the Margin: Reconciliation, Antinomianism, and Messianism in Izbica/Radzin Hasidism.*

David Novak is the J. Richard and Dorothy Shiff Professor of Jewish Studies at the University of Toronto. He was formerly the Edgar M. Bronfman Professor of Modern Judaic Studies at the University of Virginia. He is vice-president of the Union for Traditional Judaism, and secretary-treasurer of the Institute on Religion and Public Life. His most recent books include: *The Election of Israel: The Idea of the Chosen People* (1995); *Natural Law in Judaism* (1998); and *Covenantal Rights: A Study in Jewish Political Theory* (2000).

Shalom Rosenberg is Professor of Jewish Thought at the Hebrew University in Jerusalem. He has published numerous articles about medieval Jewish philosophy and theology. He is the author of *Good and Evil in Jewish Thought* (1989), *Torah and Science* (1987), *The World of Rav Kook's Thought* (1987), *In the Footsteps of the Cuzari* (1992), and, most recently, *Not in Heaven* (1996).

Eilon Schwartz is the director of the Heschel Center for Environmental Learning and Leadership, which promotes a sustainable society in Israel through education, leadership fellowships, workshops with local and national government, and publications on the state of the environment. He is also a lecturer at the Melton Centre for Jewish Education at Hebrew University, teaching courses on Judaism, Zionism, the environment, and education. He is currently completing his doctorate on Darwinism and educational philosophy.

Moshe Sokol is Professor of Philosophy and Jewish Studies at Touro College and Dean of its Lander College for Men. He is editor of *Engaging Modernity*

(1997), *Rabbinic Authority and Personal Autonomy* (1992), and *Tolerance, Dissent, and Democracy: Philosophical, Historical and Halachic Perspectives* (2002). He has published numerous essays and monographs on Jewish philosophy and ethics.

Hava Tirosh-Samuelson is Associate Professor of History at Arizona State University. She is the author of *Between Worlds: The Life and Thought of David ben Judah Messer Leon* (1991), which received the Vizhnitzer Award of the Hebrew University, and *Happiness in Premodern Judaism: Virtue, Knowledge, and Well-Being in Premodern Judaism* (Hebrew Union College Press, forthcoming). In addition to editing this volume, she is also the editor of *On Being Human: Women in Jewish Philosophy* (forthcoming).

Elliot R. Wolfson is the Abraham Lieberman Professor of Hebrew and Judaic Studies at New York University. He is the author of *Through a Speculum That Shines: Vision and Imagination in Medieval Jewish Mysticism* (1994), which won the American Academy of Religion and National Jewish Book Awards in 1995. His other books include *Along the Path: Studies in Kabbalistic Hermeneutics, Myth, and Symbolism* and *Circle in the Square: Studies in the Use of Gender in Kabbalistic Symbolism*, both published in 1995, and *Abraham Abulafia—Kabbalist and Prophet: Hermeneutics, Theosophy, and Theurgy*, published in 2000. He is currently working on three monographs: *Language, Eros, and Being: Kabbalistic Hermeneutics and the Poetic Imagination*; *Venturing Beyond: Laws of Limits and Limits of Law in Kabbalistic Piety*; and *Time, Truth, and Narrativity: Kabbalistic Ontology and the Grammar of Becoming*.

Index

Ya'akov Yoseph (Jacob Joseph) of
Polonnoye
Baal Shem Tov on fasting of, 365n.32
and Buber's Hasidism, liv, 376–80
in Hasidism's development, 333
Yam, 7
Yanomami, 94
Yehiel Michel of Zlotchov, 379,
387n.37
Yggdrasil, 28
YHWH, liii, 6, 8, 195, 306, 312, 313–
14, 389, 391
Yohanan, Rabbi, 201, 440n.23
Yotzer benediction, 140–45, 146, 149,
150, 153n.20

Zaddikism, 337–38
Zadok Ha-Cohen of Lublin, 201, 204
Zaphon, Mount, 30, 57n.37

Zeno, 131n.7
Zerubavel, Yael, 94
ziggurats, 28, 35–36, 55n.22
Zilberg, Moshe, 73–74
Zionism
and "holy sparks" model of nature,
xlv, 102
and return to nature, xxxvi, lixn.8,
lxn.10, 102, 401–2
Zohar
and ancient Near Eastern creation
myths, 7
and Nahman of Bratslav's "The
Seven Beggars," 338
and nature as mirror image, 306, 308,
312, 316, 320, 327n.32, 330n.53
and paradox of existence, 397
zoning laws, 64
Zoroastrianism, 83–85